NETWORKS
OF
INTERDEPENDENCE

NETWORKS
OF
INTERDEPENDENCE

International Organizations and the
Global Political System

Second Edition

Harold K. Jacobson

The University of Michigan

Alfred A. Knopf New York

THIS IS A BORZOI BOOK
PUBLISHED BY ALFRED A. KNOPF, INC.

Second Edition
987654321
Copyright © 1979, 1984 by Alfred A. Knopf, Inc.

Library of Congress Cataloging in Publication Data

Jacobson, Harold Karan.
  Networks of interdependence.

  Includes bibliographies and index.
  1. International agencies. 2. International
relations. I. Title.
JX1995. J28   1984   341.2   83–24825
ISBN 0–394–33164–8

Copyediting, proofreading, and art preparation by White River Press, Inc.
Text design by Dana Kasarsky
Cover design by Mary Chris Welch

Manufactured in the United States of America

To the memory of
Walter R. Sharp,
who introduced me to
international organizations.

PREFACE TO
THE SECOND EDITION

Preparing this second edition has been a sobering experience. Several of the encouraging trends relating to security and economic issues that had seemed firmly established in the later 1970s have subsequently suffered interruptions or setbacks. I remain optimistic, and I continue to be convinced that humankind can solve its problems using among other instrumentalities international organizations. I am more sharply aware, though, than I was five years ago of how complex and difficult the problems are. Their solution will require deep understanding, to which I hope this book will contribute, and humankind's best efforts.

I am indebted to students, and to Chadwick Alger, Inis Claude, and Lawrence Finkelstein who pointed out ways in which the book could be improved. William Reisinger and Todd Mathers helped prepare the statistical material in the book, and Barbara Sweier, now Barbara Opal, again efficiently and skillfully transformed bits and scraps into a typescript, then oversaw the transformation of that into a book. I am grateful to each of them. Finally, I appreciate the wise suggestions and patient prodding of Knopf's senior editor, Bertrand Lummus.

Ann Arbor, Michigan   HAROLD K. JACOBSON
October 1983

PREFACE

This is an optimistic book, though I hope not an unrealistic one. It argues that humankind is crafting new political institutions that have already contributed significantly to greater global security, to better material welfare through a larger gross world product, and to higher standards of social welfare. It further argues that human beings can use these new political institutions to cope with the problems posed by cascading scientific and technological developments and to help improve conditions of life throughout the world still more. The argument is not that the activities of the new political institutions have brought unmitigated good, nor that all of the world's problems are in the process of being solved. It is simply that new institutions adequate to the tasks at hand have been created, that they have been put to good use, and that considerable progress has been made.

I am convinced that the empirical evidence provides strong support for the thesis, and a purpose of the book is to publicize this evidence. The book emphasizes a comparative and a dynamic perspective, partly because I believe that pessimism often stems from too narrow a view and too short a time perspective. Since the argument is that things are better, wherever possible quantitative evidence is introduced to permit accurate comparative judgments. Trends and changes in trends are emphasized over rigorous attempts to establish causality, which under the best of circumstances are difficult when dealing with political phenomena.

International organizations—both governmental and nongovernmental—are the new political institutions heralded by the book. In one sense, they are hardly new, since the first modern international governmental organization was created in 1815, and the first modern international nongovernmental organization dates from the seventeenth century. But international organizations are new in the sense that it is only in the second half of the twentieth century that they have become so numerous and so important as to be a prominent feature of the global political system. Part I of the book analyzes this historical development.

Because of the growth in the numbers and the importance of international organizations, since the middle of the twentieth century the global political system has been in the throes of a potentially revolutionary change. From roughly the seventeenth century until the mid-twentieth century, political authority increasingly became concentrated in territorially defined units, nation-states. National governments were the instruments of political authority, and although in several respects the governments of nation-states had novel features, as political institutions their characteristics were those that had preoccupied political philosophers since Plato and Aristotle. International organizations, in contrast, are new types of political institutions. However much they may resemble governments, they are not governments, and they only partly share the characteristics of governments.

The main purpose of this book is to contribute to an understanding of these new political institutions and their potentialities and limitations. Part II analyzes what international organizations can do and develops a comprehensive typology of the possible actions of international organizations. This typology is then employed in Parts III, IV, and V to examine the activities of international organizations with respect to increasing international security, the growth and distribution of the world product, and the attainment of human dignity and justice. Attempts are made in each of the three parts to assess the consequences of these activities. Finally, Part VI analyzes the role of international organizations in the evolution of the global political system.

Like all political institutions, international organizations can be put to bad as well as good purposes. They are merely instruments for human beings to use. They can be used for good only if their characteristics are properly understood by those who have such aims. My hope is that this book will be helpful to those who try to improve human life.

The book is the product of several years of study and teaching. It first took form in Geneva, Switzerland, during 1970–1971, when I was privileged to be the Visiting Research Scholar of the European Center of the Carnegie Endowment for International Peace, and it was finished in the felicitous environment of the Center for Political Studies of the Institute for Social Research at the University of Michigan. I am especially grateful to Joseph E. Johnson and John Goormaghtigh, who during my time in Geneva were respectively President of the Carnegie Endowment and Director of the European Center, and to Warren E. Miller and Raburn Howland, Director and Assistant Director of the Center for Political Studies, for their confidence, advice, and support. My work at the Center for Political Studies was supported by funds from the Ford Foundation and the Earhart Foundation. I gratefully acknowledge this assistance. The basic structure for Parts III, IV, and V of the book was worked out during a month I spent in the fall of 1972 as a Resident Scholar at the Rockefeller Foundation's Bellagio Study and Conference Center, and early drafts of some of the chapters in these parts were also prepared then. I appreciate the opportunity and help given to me by William C. Olson, Director of the Bellagio Center.

Although I bear full responsibility for the book, several people must share credit for it. My thinking about international organizations has been deeply influenced by my close association with four individuals. Walter R. Sharp introduced me to international organizations and continued a challenging dialogue with me about them long after his responsibilities for my graduate education were completed. Inis L. Claude was a delightful and stimulating colleague and friend at the University of Michigan for a decade, and we have continued to exchange ideas since he moved to the University of Virginia. Through our many pleasant associations at the University of Michigan Eric Stein has given me a fresh appreciation of the relevance of international law for international organization and has constantly reminded me of the importance and unique qualities of the European communities. Robert W. Cox and I shared the administrative burdens and intellectual rewards of directing a team research project over several years, and the discussions about international organizations that we started then continue, to my great benefit.

Catherine Ghebali, Susan Lawrence, Nancy Levitt, Katherine Ward, Angelique Matney, Carolyn Somerville, and Peter Scherer all helped in the preparation of the book through their service as research assistants. William Domke provided indispensible aid in preparing the statistical analyses and figures. Georges Abi-Saab, Robert C. Angell, Barbara Crane, Francis W. Hoole, David A. Kay, Louis G. Ortmayer, Jean Siotis, Donald A. Sylvan, Anne Winslow, and William Zimmerman read the manuscript and graciously gave me suggestions for improving it. Barbara Sweier prepared the manuscript, typing and retyping the various drafts, and doing the several other tasks that had to be done to bring order out of the chaotic jumble I gave her. Her diligence and cheerful and outstanding performance of her work were crucial to the completion of the project. The final essential elements in finishing the book were Jane Cullen's sympathetic but firm direction as Knopf's political science editor, Carolyn Eggleston's sensitive and skillful copyediting, and manuscript editor Leslie Strand's superb supervision of the process of producing the book.

I am deeply grateful to all of these individuals, and I also greatly appreciate the kindness of the many national and international officials who took time from their busy schedules to talk with me and to help me know more about international organizations. Whatever wisdom the book has is derived from many sources. Working for a better future will also inevitably be a collective enterprise, which I hope readers of the book will share.

Ann Arbor, Michigan   HAROLD K. JACOBSON
July 1978

CONTENTS

LIST OF TABLES

LIST OF FIGURES

LIST OF ABBREVIATIONS

AAPSO	Afro-Asian People's Solidarity Organization
ABM	anti-ballistic missile
ACA	Agency for the Control of Armaments, Western European Union
AfDB	African Development Bank
AFESD	Arab Fund for Economic and Social Development
AFL-CIO	American Federation of Labor–Congress of Industrial Organizations
AsDB	Asian Development Bank
BIS	Bank for International Settlements
CAP	Common Agricultural Policy, European Economic Community
CarDB	Caribbean Development Bank
CARE	Cooperative for American Relief Everywhere
CCD	Conference of the Committee on Disarmament, United Nations
CD	Committee on Disarmament, United Nations
CE	Council of Europe
CESLC	*Confédération Européene des Syndicats Libres dans la Communauté* (European Confederation of Free Trade Unions in the Community)
CIEC	Conference on International Economic Cooperation
CIO	Congress of Industrial Organizations
CMEA	Council for Mutual Economic Assistance
CMT	*Confédération Mondial du Travail* (World Confederation of Labor)
COMECON	See CMEA
Cominform	Communist Information Bureau
Comintern	Communist International
COMSAT	Communications Satellite Corporation
COPA	*Comité des Organisations Professionelles Agricoles de la CEE* (Committee of Agricultural Organizations in the EEC)

DAC	Development Assistance Committee, Organization for Economic Cooperation and Development
EAEC	European Atomic Energy Community
ECOSOC	Economic and Social Council, United Nations
ECSC	European Coal and Steel Community
ECU	European Currency Unit, European Communities
EEC	European Economic Community
EIB	European Investment Bank
EMCF	European Monetary Cooperation Fund, European Communities
EMF	European Monetary Fund, European Communities
EMS	European Monetary System, European Communities
EPU	European Payments Union
GATT	General Agreement on Tariffs and Trade
GDR	Democratic Republic of Germany
GNP	gross national product
IAEA	International Atomic Energy Agency
IAPF	Inter-American Peace Force
IATA	International Air Transport Association
IBEC	International Bank for Economic Cooperation
IBRD	International Bank for Reconstruction and Development
ICAO	International Civil Aviation Organization
ICC	International Chamber of Commerce
ICFTU	International Confederation of Free Trade Unions
ICJ	International Court of Justice
ICRC	International Committee of the Red Cross
IDA	International Development Association
IDB	Inter-American Development Bank
IFC	International Finance Corporation
IFCTU	International Federation of Christian Trade Unions (World Confederation of Labor since 1968)
IFRB	International Frequency Registration Board, International Telecommunication Union
IGO	international governmental organization
IGY	International Geophysical Year
IIA	International Institute of Agriculture
IIB	International Investment Bank
ILO	International Labor Organization
IMO	International Maritime Organization
IMF	International Monetary Fund
INGO	international nongovernmental organization
INTELSAT	International Telecommunications Satellite Organization
IRO	International Refugee Organization

ISS	Institute of Strategic Studies
ITU	International Telecommunication Union (formerly the International Telegraph Union)
LDCs	less developed countries
NATO	North Atlantic Treaty Organization
NGO	nongovernmental organization
NIEO	New International Economic Order
NWICO	New World Information and Communication Order
OAPEC	Organization of Arab Petroleum Exporting Countries
OAS	Organization of American States
OAU	Organization of African Unity
ODA	official development assistance
OECD	Organization for Economic Cooperation and Development
OEEC	Organization for European Economic Cooperation
OMA	Orderly Marketing Agreement
ONUC	*Opération des Nations Unies au Congo* (United Nations Operation in the Congo)
OPEC	Organization of Petroleum Exporting Countries
OXFAM	Oxford Committee for Famine Relief
PNE	peaceful nuclear explosion
RCD	Regional Cooperation for Development
SAFA	Special Arab Fund for Africa
SALT	Strategic Arms Limitation Talks
SDRs	special drawing rights
SIPRI	Stockholm International Peace Research Institute
STABEX	stabilization system for export receipts, ACP-EEC Convention of Lomé
START	Strategic Arms Reduction Talks
TNCs	transnational corporations
UDEAC	*Union Douanière et Economique de l'Afrique Centrale* (Central African Customs and Economic Union)
UNCI	United Nations Commission for Indonesia
UNCTAD	United Nations Conference on Trade and Development
UNDOF	United Nations Disengagement Observer Force
UNDP	United Nations Development Program
UNDRO	Office of The United Nations Disaster Relief Coordinator
UNEF	United Nations Emergency Force
UNESCO	United Nations Educational, Scientific and Cultural Organization
UNFICYP	United Nations Force in Cyprus
UNFPA	United Nations Fund for Population Activities
UNHCR	United Nations High Commissioner for Refugees
UNICE	*Union des Industries de la Communauté* (Union of the Industries of the European Community)

UNICEF	United Nations Children's Fund (originally known as United Nations International Children's Emergency Fund)
UNIDO	United Nations Industrial Development Organization
UNIFIL	United Nations Interim Force in Lebanon
UNMOGIP	United Nations Military Observer in India and Pakistan
UNOGIL	United Nations Observer Group in Lebanon
UNRRA	United Nations Relief and Rehabilitation Administration
UNRWA	United Nations Relief and Works Agency for Palestine Refugees in the Near East
UNSCOB	United Nations Special Committee on the Balkans
UNTSO	United Nations Truce Supervisory Organization
UNYOM	United Nations Observation Mission in Yemen
UPU	Universal Postal Union
USACDA	United States Arms Control and Disarmament Agency
VER	Voluntary Export Restraint
VRA	Voluntary Restraint Agreement
WCL	World Confederation of Labor
WEU	Western European Union
WFTU	World Federation of Trade Unions
WHO	World Health Organization
WTO	Warsaw Treaty Organization

NETWORKS
OF
INTERDEPENDENCE

1
INTRODUCTION: THE NATURE OF INTERNATIONAL ORGANIZATIONS

NEW PROMINENCE OF INTERNATIONAL ORGANIZATIONS

Even the most casual observer of world politics cannot escape noticing that international organizations have become a prominent feature of the modern global political system. Their physical headquarters are landmarks in major cities throughout the world. The United Nations buildings on the bank of the East River in Manhattan are part of the itinerary of virtually all tours of New York, and visitors in Addis Ababa will inevitably be shown Africa Hall, where meetings of the Organization of African Unity and of the U.N.'s Economic Commission for Africa are held. In Brussels the tourist will have pointed out the buildings that house the Commission of the European Economic Community and its staff, and if one ventures to the outskirts of the city, those for the North Atlantic Treaty Organization. Visitors to Moscow will see the buildings in which the Secretariat of the Council for Mutual Economic Assistance works. Geneva is graced with the *Palais des Nations,* once home of the League of Nations and now of the European Office of the United Nations, as well as the headquarters buildings of seven major U.N. related agencies. This list could be expanded to considerable length, and while other international organizations—such as the European Broadcasting Union, the International Confederation of Free Trade Unions, and the International Cooperative Alliance—cannot claim such imposing architectural monuments, their offices clearly establish their physical presence.

Beyond buildings and offices there are many other indications of the existence and indeed the importance of international organizations. In countries in the southern hemisphere, representatives of the United Nations rank with the accredited chiefs of mission of major states. Meetings and conferences of international organizations are legion. In 1981 almost 5,000 were convened, and one state, the United States, participated in almost 1,000 of these sessions. Many of the meetings of international organizations make headlines, and some occupy the attention of important officials. Rarely can an account of an episode in world politics avoid utilizing one or more of the acronyms by which international organizations are commonly known, for the number of contemporary international political issues that do not involve international organizations in at least some way is small indeed. There can be no doubt that international organizations are a vital component of the modern global political system. Their role in this system is the subject of this book.

IGOS AND INGOS: AN INITIAL DISTINCTION

All international organizations are alike in having participants from more than one state, but beyond this, differences abound. One distinction that needs to be made at the outset is that between international governmental organizations (IGOs) and international nongovernmental organizations (INGOs). This distinction appears self-evident, and in most instances it is. The United Nations and the European Economic Community are clearly international governmental organizations, and the International Alliance of Women and the International Confederation of Free Trade Unions, international nongovernmental organizations. But what about the European Broadcasting Union, most members of which are state-owned broadcasting services, the International Air Transport Association, most members of which are state-owned airlines, and other similar organizations? The issue is not simple. Communication and transport services are subject to varying amounts of governmental control in all countries, and the fact of state ownership may or may not be crucial in determining the amount of control. The British Broadcasting Corporation, for example, has a long tradition of independence and is subject to fewer governmental controls than some privately owned broadcasting services. Governments also have varying degrees of influence in such institutions as labor unions and youth groups. What if an international organization is composed of groups in several states and some of these groups are controlled by their governments while others are not? Another complication of this classification is that the International Labor Organization, the International Telecommunication Union, and certain other international organizations, although composed predominantly of governments, also allow the participation of such private associations as labor unions, employers' groups, operators of telecommunications services, and manufacturers of telecommunications equipment.

To avoid having to make numerous inevitably subjective judgments, the conventional practice is to follow an early decision of the United Nations and base the distinction on whether or not the international organization was established by an agreement among governments: those that were created by such an agreement are described as international governmental organizations; those that were not, as international nongovernmental organizations.[1] This criterion is clear and easy to apply, and it is generally useful, but in a few instances it hides substantial similarities.

Although in the years since World War II there have been six or more times as many international nongovernmental organizations as there have been international governmental organizations, this book will mainly deal with the latter. The reason for this is simple: IGOs are generally much more important in the global political system than are INGOs.

IGOS AND INGOS IN THE GLOBAL POLITICAL SYSTEM

To explore this point briefly, it is necessary to specify the meaning attached to the term "global political system." Politics, according to one widely accepted definition, has to do with the making and execution of authoritative policies for the allocation of values for a society. Hence a political system is one in which such functions are performed. Policies are "a web of decisions and actions"[2]—for example, a law or decree and all of the steps involved in carrying it out. However, the mechanisms need not be as formal as the terms "law" and "decree" imply; they may be much more elementary than a legislature or an elaborate administrative or judicial structure. Consensus achieved within an informal group may suffice. The values that are to be allocated include everything that is important to human beings. One commonly accepted scheme for classifying values, originally elaborated by Harold D. Lasswell and Abraham Kaplan, employs eight categories—power, enlightenment, wealth, well-being (in the sense of health), skill, affection, rectitude, and deference.[3] However one classifies them, though, it is important to recognize that there are many values that people hold to be important and that the relative importance attached to each value differs substantially among individuals. There are many ways of allocating values that would not be considered political (for example, the impersonal mechanism of supply and demand), but political processes are being employed more and more. Increasingly, decisions and actions that vitally affect the kinds of lives that people lead are being taken through political processes.

In the modern world, states—and governmental institutions within them—have become the primary focal points for political activity. When individuals seek to alter the conditions of their life, more and more they turn to political activity directed at the governmental institutions of their state. Governments provide for physical security, as they have for centuries, but their role has become far more extensive than this. Governments now maintain educational facilities, provide health services and care for the aged, and determine standards for working conditions and minimum wages. Throughout the world governments in varying degrees try to steer and manage the economies of their countries. In all countries governments employ a substantial proportion of the work force.

Interdependence of States

As technology has developed, the fate of peoples in different states has become ever more closely linked: states have become interdependent. Nuclear weapons provide the extreme case. Both the United States and the Soviet Union now have arsenals of nuclear weapons capable of destroying a large part, if not all, of humanity. Should a major nuclear exchange occur between these two countries, the effects would surely not be confined to their territories. There are also many other links among states.

Modern technology has provided the communication and transportation capacity required to support a high level of trade among states. This has allowed specialization in production, and consequently a greater total world product, but it has also meant that the economies of states are closely linked with those of their trading partners. In the 1930s the economic recession spread rapidly among both rich and poor states, and in the 1960s economic growth in some states appears to have stimulated growth in others. Plentiful and rapid means of communication and transportation have also contributed to the speedy diffusion of many things beyond material goods—for instance, ideas and disease. Because of the development of television and communications satellites, sporting events, political rallies, and wars can now be witnessed instantaneously and seemingly at close hand by a global audience. An outbreak of cholera in a city in Africa immediately threatens all other cities with which it is even indirectly connected by airline routes.

These many links among states significantly shape the way in which the government of any one state can respond to the demands of its people. Developments abroad can threaten the values that are important to the people of a state, and the external world forms a constraining context for the policies that a government can pursue. Of course some states are more vulnerable to events in the outside world than others: everything else being equal, vulnerability tends to vary roughly inversely with size. And the extent to which various states are linked differs; some are tied closely together while others have hardly any connections. But today no state can completely isolate itself from the outside world. All are sensitive to events in other states. It is because of the interconnections among states that it is possible to speak of a global system. The term simply indicates that developments in one state are likely to affect developments in other states and possibly even in all of them.

It is also possible to speak of a global political system. This is not to assert that all political activity within it always encompasses the entire world. Obviously this is not the case. Very often the participants are confined to a small number of states, and the policies they formulate may be intended for application solely within that group. Yet such activity qualifies as being part of the global political system because it may well have immediate or longer run implications for other states. To cite a case in point, when states in Western Europe eliminate obstacles to trade among themselves, this is bound to have an impact on their trading relationships with other areas, such as Eastern Europe and North America. It is the interconnections among states that gives the political system global dimensions.

In comparison with the political systems that have evolved within many states, the global political system appears primitive because it is diffuse and loosely structured and authority patterns in it are only vaguely and informally defined. Much political activity within the global system is carried on by means of diplomacy, ad hoc negotiations conducted by representatives of states. In these negotiations requests and warnings are frequently backed by implicit and explicit offers of reward and by threats to employ coercion, and decisions to take such action can be made unilaterally. The capacity of states to benefit or injure others differs sharply, and the outcomes of diplomacy usually reflect these differences. Even so, humanitarian concerns have often been protected by diplomacy; for example, the slave trade was abolished through diplomatic actions. Despite the lack of structure in traditional diplomacy, customs have developed which are generally followed, and many rules have been codified in conventions and treaties.

The Roles of IGOs and INGOs

For several reasons which we shall consider later, however, there has been a growing quest for greater structure, and increasingly political activity in the global system has been channeled into international organizations. International organizations have come to play a growing role in formulating international policy. IGOs provide frameworks within which governments can achieve agreement about the elements of international public policy. INGOs play a role in the achievement and maintenance of these agreements. The consequences of this development will be explored throughout this book.

The relatively greater importance in the global political system of IGOs compared with INGOs stems first from the definition of politics. Authoritative policies are more frequently made in and applied by governmental than by nongovernmental institutions; consequently in most political systems the former are more important than the latter. But the global system accords even greater importance to governmental institutions than is usually the case. States are the primary focal points of political activity in the modern world, and IGOs presently derive their importance from their character as associations of states.

Nongovernmental institutions interested in affecting policy are most likely to concentrate their efforts at persuasion on the governments of states, since this is where the most crucial decisions are now taken. Were IGOs to gain greater authority in their own right, this would undoubtedly force nongovernmental institutions to pay greater attention to them, and this shift in attention would contribute to strengthening INGOs and making them more important. To a certain extent, this is happening already. In addition, for various reasons that we will explore, INGOs can be more effective in performing certain tasks than IGOs.

THE DEVELOPMENT OF INTERNATIONAL ORGANIZATIONS

International organizations as they presently exist seem to be particularly products of the nineteenth and twentieth centuries. Although prototypes and forerunners existed in earlier eras, few of them had all of the characteristics of either modern IGOs or modern INGOs, and those that did remained isolated phenomena rather than becoming part of a broad historical movement.

An international governmental organization is an institutional structure created by agreement among two or more sovereign states for the conduct of regular political interactions. IGOs are distinguished from the facilities of traditional diplomacy by their structure and permanence. International governmental organizations have meetings of representatives of the member states at relatively regular intervals, specified procedures for making decisions, and a permanent secretariat or headquarters staff. In some ways IGOs resemble governments, but they are not governments, for the capacity for action continues to rest predominantly with the constituent units, the member states. IGOs can be viewed as permanent networks linking states. Conceivably some international governmental organizations could become governments, but for the moment they must be regarded as voluntary associations of states, largely dependent on the voluntary actions of these states for the implementation of their decisions.

Historical Prototypes of IGOs

The closest historical prototypes of modern international governmental organizations are the Delian League and the Hanseatic League. The former was an association of Greek city states in which Athens played a predominant role and which was created primarily to facilitate military cooperation against common enemies. The Delian League had a relatively long life. It was founded in 478 B.C. and was not disbanded until 404 B.C. Then it was recreated in 378–377 B.C. and remained in being until 338 B.C. At times during its existence the Delian League became more an instrument for Athenian domination than a mechanism for collaboration among autonomous allies. On both occasions of its demise, military defeats were responsible.

The Hanseatic League was an association of North German towns which lasted from the eleventh century through the seventeenth. The primary impetus for its creation was economic, and its main functions concerned trade. Its authority gradually declined under the impact of new trade routes and when it proved ineffective in competition with England and France. At times during their histories both the Delian League and the Hanseatic League closely resembled modern international governmental organizations, but they remained isolated phenomena in the political systems of their times, and their creation was not followed by the formation of other similar institutions.

Large conferences of states such as those that resulted in the Peace of Westphalia in 1648 and the Treaty of Utrecht in 1713–1714 are more recent forerunners of modern international governmental organizations. They provided a structured framework for the conduct of multilateral diplomacy, but this framework was abandoned as soon as the conferences had concluded their tasks.

Modern IGOs

The first modern international governmental organization, the Central Commission for the Navigation of the Rhine, was created at the Congress of Vienna in 1815. Its purpose was to insure free navigation and equality of treatment for the vessels of all countries on the Rhine. Its structure consisted of a commission, which met periodically and on which member governments were represented, and a small secretariat. This was a modest beginning, but it was the first step in the creation of what is now a dense and extensive web of IGO networks.

In the next half-century only two more international governmental organizations were created, but starting in 1865 their number began to grow steadily, with the pace accelerating sharply after each major outbreak of violence—the Franco-Prussian War, World War I, and World War II. The pattern of their growth can be seen through a few selected figures. According to Michael D. Wallace and J. David Singer, in 1914, on the eve of World War I, there were about fifty international governmental organizations; in 1939, on the eve of World War II, about eighty; and in 1980, more than 600.[4] The IGOs in existence in 1980 are listed in Appendix A. This list includes 621 IGOs. The number is larger than that used by some authorities primarily because it includes IGOs that were created by other IGOs, a phenomenon that has occurred particularly in the years since World War II. Although these IGOs are often not completely autonomous from their parent IGOs, they are included because in numbers of member states and in size of budget and staff many of them rank among the more substantial international governmental organizations.

Whether this growth rate for IGOs will continue into the future is moot. Even if it does not, barring unforeseeable catastrophies, such as nuclear war, that might radically change political structures throughout the world, the absolute number of IGOs in the global political system seems unlikely to decline, for since 1815 only about a quarter of the international governmental organizations that have been established have been terminated. For some time now, even with the explosion in the number of states, there have been more IGOs in the global system than there are states.

INGOs

International nongovernmental organizations share with IGOs the three characteristics of having regularly scheduled meetings of representatives of the membership, specified procedures for decision making, and a permanent secretariat. However, their members are individuals or private associations, or perhaps even a combination of both, from two or more countries, rather than the states themselves, and INGOs must have been created by some means other than agreement among governments. INGOs too are networks. Like nongovernmental organizations within states—such as the American Federation of Labor–Congress of Industrial Organizations, the Farm Bureau, and the American Medical Association—INGOs have many purposes and serve many functions, only some of which have immediate political consequences.

The political importance of nongovernmental organizations, however, needs to be measured in broader terms. The social groups of which nongovernmental organizations are formal expressions constitute the infrastructure of a political system; they give it form and cohesiveness. Though they may not engage in political activities, the possibility always exists that they might; therefore if the nongovernmental organizations are of relatively substantial size, political decision makers are likely to take their anticipated reactions into account in making decisions. Thus their very existence can have political effects.

The first modern international nongovernmental organization appears to have been the Rosicrucian Order, an educational fraternal order dating at least from the seventeenth century. Although a few other INGOs were established before 1815, the real growth in their number, as is the case with IGOs, occurs after that date.[5] In 1850 there were five INGOs. By 1914 this number had risen to about 330, and by 1939 to about 730. In 1980 there were almost 6,000 INGOs. Slightly less than one-sixth of these were sufficiently active politically to have sought and been granted consultative status with the United Nations, which gives them the right to submit their views in various ways depending on the particular category of privileges they enjoy. Another roughly 12 percent were closely associated with the European Economic Community and the European Free Trade Association. The INGOs with the most extensive consultative relationships in 1980 are listed in Appendix B.

INGOs with consultative status are in a relationship to IGOs much like that of interest groups to governments within states; their representatives are in effect registered lobbyists. But as those familiar with governments well know, lobbying activities are not confined to those who are registered. Thus the fact that only a fraction of the total number of INGOs have consultative relationships with IGOs does not mean that the number of INGOs that engage in activities having immediate political consequences is this limited, nor does it mean that representatives of INGOs are IGOs' only lobbyists.

TRANSNATIONAL ORGANIZATIONS

Although they are not usually formally classified as international nongovernmental organizations, two other types of institutions are important elements of the infrastructure of the global political system and often perform functions similar to those of INGOs. These are religious bodies and business enterprises that conduct their operations in more than one country. The Roman Catholic Church has seen itself as a universal force since its creation, and this is also true of other religious bodies. Some business enterprises, such as Royal Dutch Shell, have always operated in more than one country, and during the second half of the twentieth century, more and more businesses have ventured abroad. Religious bodies and business enterprises are the two most salient categories of what have come to be called transnational organizations. Transnational organizations are hierarchically organized, centrally directed nongovernmental bureaucracies that perform their relatively specialized functions in more than one state.[6]

Transnational organizations differ from international nongovernmental organizations in that they are hierarchically organized and centrally directed. They do not have the representative features that are characteristic of INGOs. The bureaucracies of transnational organizations may or may not include individuals from more than one state; it is the fact that these bureaucracies operate in more than one state that justifies the adjective "transnational." Since many transnational corporations started off as national corporations, often for a long time after their operations begin to cross international boundaries, their employees are predominantly from the country in which the corporations originated. Few transnational organizations are truly "geocentric."[7] A truly geocentric organization would demonstrate by the composition of its leadership and by its behavior that it had lost all ties to a particular state or states. Even the Roman Catholic Church has a disproportionate number of Italians among its hierarchy.

Although this book is primarily about international organizations, it must also deal with transnational organizations. In the domestic political systems of states, churches and business enterprises are often important political forces, and governments frequently adopt policies that affect churches and businesses. Similar interactions carry over to international politics. The views of the Roman Catholic Church have affected the actions of IGOs with respect to population problems. Actions of IGOs in the years since World War II have facilitated the phenomenal growth in the number of transnational business corporations that has occurred, and IGOs have increasingly become concerned with attempting to regulate the activities of these corporations. Thus transnational organizations must be considered both as political forces relevant to international organizations and as objects of policies adopted by IGOs.

A TYPOLOGY FOR CATEGORIZING INTERNATIONAL ORGANIZATIONS

International governmental organizations and international nongovernmental organizations can each be categorized in a variety of ways. The typology that will be employed throughout this book can be applied to both types of organizations and utilizes two dimensions.

The first dimension concerns the manifest or stated purposes of the organization. A simple distinction can be made between organizations with mandates in specific fields and those with general mandates. Some organizations have been created to function in fields such as education, health, security, social welfare, or trade; others have been authorized to deal with issues in virtually all fields. Among IGOs the World Health Organization is an example of the former type, and the United Nations is an example of the latter. Examples of the two types among INGOs are the International Broadcasters Society and the World Federation of United Nations Associations.

The second dimension involves the membership of the organization. Again a simple distinction can be made between organizations in which membership is limited to a particular group of states, or to individuals or associations from these states, and organizations in which membership is open to all states, or to individuals or associations from all states.

Some organizations limit their membership to certain geographical areas and others to particular cultural groups. Still others limit their memberships on the basis of economic or political criteria. Sometimes the exclusion is written into the organization's constitution, but it can be just as real when it is merely a matter of practice. The World Health Organization, the United Nations, the International Broadcasters Society, and the World Federation of United Nations Associations (mentioned above) should be classified as potentially having universal membership. Comparable limited membership organizations are the Pan American Health Organization, the Organization of African Unity, the Asian Broadcasting Union, and the European Movement.

Using these two dimensions we can place both IGOs and INGOs in four categories according to their manifest purposes and membership. The eight organizations used as examples are classified according to this typology in Figure 1.1. This typology, like most, is not completely without ambiguities. Placing any given organization in one of the cells of the matrix inevitably involves judgement, and some of the several thousand international organizations are more difficult to classify than others. The typology cannot completely avoid debatable classifications, but it is simple and relatively easy to apply, and it will provide a useful instrument for examining the role of international organizations in the global political system. (The IGOs listed in Appendix A are classified according to this scheme.)

Further differentiations are also possible within the framework of the typology. It has already been mentioned that some organizations limit their membership on the basis of geographic, cultural, economic, or political criteria, and this can provide a basis for classification of limited membership organizations. Similarly, organizations with specific manifest purposes or mandates can be grouped by the nature of their mandates into three broad categories: economic, social and

FIGURE 1.1.
A Typology of International Organizations

Membership	Manifest Purposes	
	Specific	General
Limited	1 Pan American Health Organization Asian Broadcasting Union	2 Organization of African Unity European Movement
Universal	3 World Health Organization International Broadcasters Society	4 United Nations World Federation of United Nations Associations

cultural, and security. As used here, economic means relating to the production, distribution, and consumption of goods and services. Social and cultural means relating to human society and interactions and to human intellectual and moral facilities. And security means relating to freedom from danger, especially violence. Thus the organizations in cells 1, 2, and 3 of the matrix in Figure 1.1 can be subdivided respectively into twelve, four, and three subcategories. Applying these subcategories, the organizations in cells 1 (Pan American Health Organization and Asian Broadcasting Union) and 3 (World Health Organization and International Broadcasters Society) would be classified as being in the social field. The organizations in cells 1 and 2 (Organization of African Unity and European Movement) limit their membership on the basis of geographic criteria.

THE WEB OF INTERNATIONAL ORGANIZATION NETWORKS: EXPLANATIONS AND IMPLICATIONS

That a web of international organization networks should come to be established only in the last century and a half is to be explained first in light of broader patterns of political authority. By definition international organizations can exist only within the framework of a political system composed initially of several sovereign states. Such a system existed in antiquity in Greece, but there was nothing comparable until the European state system began to emerge roughly at the time of the Peace of Westphalia in 1648, and the state system only attained global dimensions with decolonization and the ending of European empires in the middle of the twentieth century. In earlier periods there were various large political units in different parts of the world, but they had so few interconnections that they did not constitute a system. Medieval Europe had many political units and there was considerable interaction among them, but authority patterns were arranged in a series of overlapping layers. Both the pope and the emperor claimed universal authority in certain spheres; and local princes and feudel lords exercised authority in their own domains; and some towns gained virtual autonomy. The Peace of Westphalia was decisive in affirming and consolidating the authority of territorial states and in ending pretensions toward universality. It marked the beginning of the modern state system.

A second explanation for the growth of international organizations in the last century and a half is that such institutions seem worth creating only when states appear to be inadequate frameworks for achieving values that are actively sought or when the fates of peoples in various states are closely linked through many interconnections. Such close links among widely separated states came only with the development of communications and transport facilities in the nineteenth and twentieth centuries, and until fairly recently states were an adequate framework for doing most things that people considered important. Technological and economic development had to attain fairly high levels before felt needs outgrew the bounds of most states. In short, before 1815 the need for international organizations was not great because contacts among states were minimal and because states provided adequate framework for almost all activities that were feasible and deemed important.

The existence of a system of sovereign states, the development of extensive interconnections among them, and the outgrowing of their boundaries provided the necessary conditions for the growth of international organizations, but these factors do not constitute a complete explanation of this phenomenon. To explain the growth of international organizations adequately, and its exact sequence and manner, requires a deeper analysis. Before broaching this task, however, the quest needs to be set in a broader field. We are interested not only in why and how international organizations were created, but also in what their role is in the contemporary global political system and in the significance of this role. We want to know what they do, to consider how well they perform their tasks, to ask what values they promote and for whose benefit. We want to know, too, what the record of the past and the present portends for the future.

One perspective on this range of issues is vividly, if simplistically, portrayed in the tapestries hung in the *Palais des Nations* in Geneva. They picture international organizations as a stage in the process of humanity combining into ever larger and more stable units for the purpose of governance—first the family, then the tribe, then the city-state, and then the nation—a process which presumably would eventually culminate in the entire world being combined in one political unit. Few if any serious observers would be willing to accept this view so baldly stated as a comprehensive explanation and forecast except in the broadest historical sense and for the most remote future. However, it is not easy to state a coherent alternative perspective. If international organizations are not way stations on the route toward the creation of ever larger territorial sovereignties, what then are they?

One factor that limits our ability to formulate alternative perspectives with regard to the role of international organizations in the global system is that a principal theme of the history of the last four centuries has been the creation of territorial states in Western Europe and then the extension of the state system to the entire world. It is easiest to see the present and the future as a projection of the past. The unification of Germany was a salient feature of the history of the nineteenth century, and a customs union among the German states, the Zollverein, played a role in this process. Why should not the European Economic Community contribute in a similar way to the creation of a unified European state? In a broader sense, is this not the eventual role of all IGOs? And are not INGOs merely a nascent form of domestic interest groups writ large? What all of these questions really involve is whether or not the territorial state is the ultimate form of political organization. Since the state has been at the center of attention for the last four centuries, it is natural that there should be a widespread predisposition toward an affirmative answer.

Projections of past developments into the future can only be made with confidence, however, when one is certain that the factors that combined to produce the developments in the past will continue to be operative. Consequently we need to probe more deeply what was involved in the development of territorial states.

TERRITORIAL STATES, SOVEREIGNTY, AND POLITICAL AUTHORITY AND LEGITMACY

States have gained and now possess sovereignty. In legal theory this means that states are free from external control and that the policies established and the decisions taken by their governmental institutions are supreme within their own territories. This is also a fairly apt description of reality. Of course all states are subject to some external influences, and small states are particularly vulnerable. The ability of the governments of states to count on their policies being implemented throughout their realm also varies. In some instances local authorities are able to establish considerable autonomy. Nevertheless, the legal meaning of sovereignty roughly accords with reality; this is why the governments of states are the focal point of political activity in the contemporary world.

The processes through which states have gained sovereignty have been complex, but several crucial ingredients can be identified. First, governmental institutions were established which sought to exercise authority and occasionally, or sometimes frequently, backed their decisions with coercive means. A second ingredient was increased interactions or transactions among the population. The interactions were of several types, but in all cases boundaries developed where the rate of interaction dropped sharply, establishing a threshold at the boundaries of the state. Third, the population of the state developed a feeling of commonality, or of belonging together. As Karl W. Deutsch has put it, they developed "shared meanings" or "interlocking habits of communication."[8] They came to understand one another in the deeper sense of being able to use words as a shorthand for commonly understood concepts, concepts that involved not only cognitive issues but also commonly shared values. "Nationalism" is the term most frequently given to this feeling of commonality. Fourth, the population developed the habit of compliance with policies set by governmental institutions: they accorded these institutions legitimacy.

This listing of the elements involved in the development of states is not meant to imply that they always occurred in a particular sequence. From the little that is known about the process of the formation of states, it is clear that while there is usually considerable simultaneity in the development of the ingredients, different ingredients received emphasis in varying order in different states. In England and France governmental institutions were developed before there was a significant degree of nationalism, but many Jews felt that they constituted a political community long before modern Israel was created. The formation of interaction thresholds apparently can precede or follow the establishment of governmental institutions and the growth of nationalism. Whatever the order of emphasis on different ingredients, though, the creation and a state always involves a delicate interplay between the growth of institutions and the development of favorable attitudes on the part of the people subject to these institutions. No government has ever had sufficient coercive means to force indefinitely an unwilling population to comply with its policies; the bulk of the population must comply voluntarily. Governments cannot function long unless they are regarded as legitimate by their populations.

History also demonstrates that the equilibrium between institutional demands and a population's attitudes can change, at times quite rapidly. A population or segments of it may come to regard as oppressive a governmental institution held to be legitimate only a short time earlier. A large part of the story of the creation of states during the last four centuries has involved the dissolution of empires. The record has not been one solely of the creation of larger and larger territorial units. On the contrary, it provides ample evidence that human beings have strong tendencies toward differentiation and secession as well as toward unity.

To accommodate tendencies toward differentiation, states with large territories and populations (e.g., the United States) or with heterogeneous populations (e.g., Switzerland) have usually had to adopt federal or confederal governments, in which authority is divided between central and local institutions, rather than unitary governments. There is no commonly accepted distinction between the two terms "federal" and "confederal." Systems that have made one term part of their formal name frequently have characteristics that are often associated with the other term. Usually a confederation will allow greater local autonomy than a federation, but this has not always been the case. Like unitary states, both states that are federations and those that are confederations possess sovereignty in the modern world.

The locus of sovereignty is the crucial difference between international governmental organizations and states. Unitary states, federations, and confederations all have sovereignty, but in the case of IGOs sovereignty rests with the member states. Because of the many ingredients involved in the formation of a state, the differences between an international governmental organization and even the most loosely connected state are substantial. For an international governmental organization to supersede its member states, many institutional, interactional, and attitudinal changes would be required.

The locus of sovereignty is also crucial in explaining the significant differences between the role of nongovernmental organizations within states and at the international level. The members of a nongovernmental organization within a state share a sense of nationalism, but nationalism divides the members of INGOs. On hardly any occasions have large groups of populations displayed a greater commitment to an international cause symbolized by an INGO than to their individual states. The two world wars powerfully documented the primacy of loyalties to states. The fact that states have great power over people's lives may well be the principal explanation for the strong commitments that they evoke, but whatever the explanation, in the contemporary world states attract greater loyalty from more persons than any other political grouping. INGOs, however, could be a long-run force for changing this situation. Transnational organizations could also bring about a change.

Exploring the role of international organizations in the global political system is thus a task with many facets. Part I of this book examines in greater detail the creation and growth of international organizations. Part II considers how they function as political systems: how decisions are taken within the frameworks that they provide. Parts III, IV, and V analyze the role that international organizations play in formulating and implementing policies for the authoritative allocation of values and attempt to assess the consequences of actions of international organizations. Part III focuses on security issues, Part IV on economic issues, and Part V on social issues, including those involving human rights. Finally, Part VI speculates about the future evolution of international organizations within the global political system, paying particular attention to underlying phenomena, especially those that were so important in the formation of states. The next step in this broad inquiry, however, is to look more deeply into the creation and growth of international organizations.

NOTES

1. Interstatal organizations and international nonstatal organizations might be more accurate descriptions, and several French writers use the term *organisations interétatiques*. However, since conventional English usage employs the adjective "governmental" and since governmental is slightly more euphonic, I use it rather than statal. Those who write in English frequently use the terms "intergovernmental organizations" and "international nongovernmental organizations." I prefer the terms "international governmental organizations" and "international nongovernmental organizations" because of their symmetry and because the term "intergovernmental organizations" is often used within the United States federal system to refer to bodies comprising elements of the national and one or more state governments. In the context in which I am using the word "governmental," it does not mean the cabinet in a parliamentary system, or the executive branch more broadly, but rather the ensemble of institutions that constitute the machinery for making the authoritative value allocations within a state.

2. David Easton, *The Political System: An Inquiry into the State of Political Science* (New York: Knopf, 1964), p. 130.

3. Harold D. Lasswell and Abraham Kaplan, *Power and Society: A Framework for Political Inquiry* (New Haven: Yale University Press, 1950), pp. 55–57 and passim.

4. These rough figures are adequate for present purposes. For more precise figures and a view of the complexities involved in ascertaining them, see Michael D. Wallace and J. David Singer, "Intergovernmental Organization in the Global System, 1815–1964: A Quantitative Description," *International Organization*, 24 (Spring 1970), 239–287. Lists of existing IGOs and INGOs that include a brief statement about each organization are published by the Union of International Associations in the periodic editions of the Union's *Yearbook of International Organizations*. The list in Appendix A of IGOs in existence in 1980 was compiled from material contained in volume 19 (1981) of the *Yearbook*.

5. Again achieving a precise count is complicated. For careful efforts see G. P. Speeckaert, *The 1,978 International Organizations Founded Since the Congress of Vienna: A Chronological List* (Brussels: Union of International Associations, 1957), and Kjell Skjelsbaek, "The Growth of International Non-governmental Organization in the Twentieth Century," *International Organization*, 25 (Summer 1971), 420–442.

6. This definition is based on that contained in Samuel P. Huntington, "Transnational

Organizations in World Politics,; *World Politics,* 25 (April 1973), 333–368. Unlike Huntington's definition, this one, by introducing the adjective "nongovernmental," would exclude departments of the governments of states.

7. Howard V. Perlmutter originally coined the term. See his article "The Tortuous Evolution of the Multinational Corporation," *Columbia Journal of World Business,* 4 (January-February 1969), 9–18. The usage of the term here is drawn from the adaptation in Joseph S. Nye, Jr., and Robert O. Keohane, "Transnational Relations and World Politics: An Introduction," *International Organization,* 25 (Summer 1971), 329–349, 336.

8. Karl W. Deutsch, *Nationalism and Its Alternatives* (New York: Knopf, 1969), p. 14.

FOR FURTHER READING

Dahl, Robert A. *Modern Political Analysis.* Englewood Cliffs, N.J.: Prentice-Hall, 1965.

Deutsch, Karl W. *Nationalism and Social Communication: An Inquiry into the Foundations of Nationality.* New York: Wiley, 1953.

Easton, David. *The Political System: An Inquiry into the State of Political Science.* New York: Knopf, 1964.

Keohane, Robert O., and Joseph S. Nye, Jr. (eds.). *Transnational Relations and World Politics.* Cambridge, Mass.: Harvard University Press, 1972.

Lasswell, Harold D., and Abraham Kaplan. *Power and Society: A Framework for Political Inquiry.* New Haven: Yale University Press, 1950.

Morgenthau, Hans J. *Politics Among Nations: The Struggle for Power and Peace.* New York: Knopf, 5th rev. ed. 1978.

Organski, A. F. K. *World Politics.* New York: Knopf, 2nd, ed. 1968.

Ray, James L. *Global Politics.* Boston: Houghton, Mifflin, 2nd. ed. 1983.

Russett, Bruce M. and Harvey Starr. *World Politics: The Menu for Choice.* San Francisco: W. F. Freeman, 1981.

Waltz, Kenneth N. *Theory of International Politics.* Reading, Mass.: Addison-Wesley, 1979.

I

THE CREATION AND GROWTH OF INTERNATIONAL ORGANIZATIONS

2

EARLY PROPOSALS FOR INTERNATIONAL ORGANIZATIONS

The contemporary webs of international organization networks began in the early years of the nineteenth century, developed steadily in the latter half of that century and the first half of the twentieth century, and mushroomed to their present extensive dimensions in the period since the end of World War II. There is more to the story, though, than this. Long before the first modern IGO was created, plans for such institutions were plentiful. They were published and debated, but they were fruitless. What motivated these plans? Why were they not realized? Do these plans bear any relationship to subsequent developments? Do they offer insights into contemporary problems? We need to explore all of these questions, and to ask why the creation of IGOs became possible in the nineteenth century and why their number has multiplied so greatly in the twentieth. In considering these questions we will want to examine both empirical data and theoretical interpretations. And since our ultimate interest is to assess the role of international organizations in the global political system, we will need to examine this system as it existed in the early nineteenth century and as it has changed.

SIX AUTHORS AND THEIR PLANS

Even before the European state system was fully established in the seventeenth and eighteenth centuries, some writers foresaw that its principal feature would be multiple sovereignties. Each state would be free to develop according to its own individual pattern. Religion was the crucial matter of choice then, but as time went on, the range of domestic issues susceptible to different patterns broadened. With respect to external affairs, the significance of multiple sovereignties was that each state, indeed at that time each sovereign, would be free to decide to employ or not to employ violence; therefore, free to make independent decisions about war and peace.

It is this latter feature that, starting in the medieval period, has most concerned political leaders and writers about international affairs. From the very beginning of the state system, the desire to limit the freedom of sovereignties to make war has been strongly expressed. A minority of writers has persistently argued that the possibility of war can be eliminated only by the establishment of a universal government, and numerous plans for establishing world government have been published. Treasuring the diversity that a system of multiple sovereignties allows, many more writers and virtually all political leaders have sought solutions that did not involve the creation of world government. In a tradition that dates at least from Hugo Grotius' *De jure belli ac pacis*, first published in 1625, several writers have seen the development of international law as a principal means of limiting the freedom of states to employ violence. Grotius sought to minimize war by limiting the circumstances in which resort to violence could be regarded as just.

Other writers and political leaders focused on the creation of international political institutions. Individuals in this tradition advanced a series of proposals to limit war through the establishment of what would now be called international governmental organizations. They accepted the principal feature of the state system as given, but attempted to introduce institutions that would ameliorate its disagreeable aspects. Thus they focused on immediate institutional issues, rather than on the longer run issues of legitimacy and allegiance that are the ultimate basis for political authority. The writers and political leaders with whom we shall be concerned aspired to establish peace in Europe, for it was clear to them that whatever benefits might be derived from the state system in allowing diversity, the system also had the potential for great violence through warfare among states, and the march of history provided all too frequent evidence that this potential would be realized.

We will consider these "peace plans" (as they have been called) generally, but we will particularly concentrate on and use for illustrative purposes those put forward by six individuals during the period of the formation of the European state system: Pierre Dubois (1255–1312c), George Poděbrad (1420–1471), Maximilien de Béthune, Duc de Sully (1559–1641), Emeric Crucé (1590–1648), William Penn (1644–1718), and Charles Irénée Castel, Abbé de Saint-Pierre (1658–1743).[1] Four of these six—Dubois, the Duc de Sully, Crucé, and the Abbé de Saint-Pierre—were French, Poděbrad was king of Bohemia, and Penn was an English Quaker who became proprietor and supreme governor of Pennsylvania.

Starting in the second half of the seventeenth century with the writings of Jean Jacques Rousseau, Jeremy Bentham, Immanuel Kant, and others, more and more persons advanced proposals for the creation of international organizations. The proposals of the six men who have been mentioned, however, merit special attention precisely because they were written either before or early in the development of the state system. Their plans are also noteworthy either because of their comprehensive character or because of the distinctive nature of their approaches. In addition, these six proposals are broadly representative of all of those that have been advanced over the years.

BASIC STRUCTURAL ISSUES

All of the "peace plans" had to deal with two types of issues. The first category concerned the structures that were to be created; the second, the functions that were to be assigned to these structures.

Membership

Perhaps the most basic structural issue was that of membership. The nature of the choice was previewed in Chapter 1 by the dichotomy established there between limited and universal membership organizations. Not surprisingly only a few of these early plans envisaged the possibility of a truly universal organization; Cruce alone among the six authors that we have singled out advocated this. The others, like the vast majority of writers on this subject then, limited their projects to Europe. Some of them, such as the Duc de Sully, included Russia within their concept of Europe, and others, such as Penn, also included the Ottoman empire, but most had a more restricted view of Europe.

That most of the early proposals for IGOs should basically be plans for European organizations was natural since these proposals were essentially responses to the emergence in Europe of the state system. However, there are also explanations for the limitation on membership beyond this historical one. Dubois saw his organization as a vehicle for undertaking a crusade; consequently it was limited to Christian sovereigns. Podĕbrad's organization also was limited to Christian princes, and it had among its purposes the protection of their sovereignties against the Turks. The organization advanced by the Duc de Sully would have had the capability of undertaking the conquest of large parts of Africa and Asia.

These proposals implicitly raised and dealt with the linkage between the functions of an international governmental organization and the characteristics of its member states. They assumed that the best vehicle for advancing Christianity would be an association of Christian sovereigns and that the best vehicle for the defense or aggrandizement of Europe would be a European organization. Different assumptions could have been made. For instance, one strategy for the advance of Christianity might have been to include infidel sovereigns within an organization dominated by Christians, banking on the possibility of conversion through association. Similarly, it could be argued that potentially threatening sovereignties should be included within an organization in the hope of blunting their hostility or ambition. However, the predominant tendency was to accept the notion that, for certain functions at least, a basic homogeneity among the membership of an international governmental organization would be essential.

In the late medieval and early modern periods, when the projects under consideration were drafted, there were few differences among sovereignties other than those involving religion and, of course, power and size. Later, when there were more differences among states, the criteria for restricting membership could be more varied. Even in these early "peace plans," though, there was a tentative groping for other criteria beyond religion. Poděbrad wanted the central institution in his proposal to be organized on the basis of nationalities, which would have forced all the princes of any one nationality to base their participation in this institution on agreement achieved among themselves, because to the extent that nationalities existed then, they spread over several states. Such a procedure would have placed a lower limit on the size of the units that could be accorded membership, and it made nationality the principle for determining legitimacy. The Duc de Sully wanted to redo the political divisions of Europe so that the members of his proposed organization would be relatively equal and hence would neither envy nor fear one another. He also felt that each sovereignty should have a single religion and that the Roman Catholic, Protestant, and Reformed Calvinist churches should be so securely established that none of them could be destroyed.

Thus far we have treated membership issues merely in relation to the definition of eligibility. Another aspect is whether or not membership should be voluntary. Some authors felt that it should be compulsory for European sovereigns, and the Abbé de Saint-Pierre's proposal envisaged the possibility of those sovereigns who had joined his association making war against any who were recalcitrant. Penn also would have allowed the members of his organization to compel other sovereignties to join. These proposals raise the fundamental question of whether or not international organizations require particular members for the pursuit of at least some objectives. Some plans obviously assumed that their organizations did, and none of the plans contained provisions allowing members to withdraw.

Institutions

A second category of structural issues of basic importance concerns the type, nature, and procedures of the institutions to be created. In all of the early proposals, although the precise name assigned to the body varied, the central institution would have been an assembly. Most writers suggested that their proposed assemblies should meet periodically; for instance, Penn recommended meetings annually or at least every two or three years. Crucé and the Abbé de Saint-Pierre wanted their proposed assemblies to be in session permanently. Most of the writers envisaged that the participants in these assemblies would merely be representatives or agents of their sovereigns. Penn, however, foresaw that participants would have some independence and argued that they should be chosen for their wisdom. Generally, the "peace plans" assigned each sovereignty one vote in the proposed assembly, and this is the common practice today. In the Duc de Sully's plan voting strength was varied on the basis of the size of the sovereignty, and in Penn's it was determined on the basis of wealth. The Duc de Sully's ideas find contemporary expression in the European communities, and Penn's ideas foreshadowed the structural arrangements of contemporary international financial institutions. Most of the plans provided for decisions on the basis of some form of majority rule.

Only a few of the early proposals for international governmental organizations provided for other organs beyond an assembly. That of the Duc de Sully envisaged the possibility of regional councils, but it did not develop the notion. Some other plans provided for permanent or ad hoc bodies to which disputes could be referred for judicial settlement or arbitration. Such judicial bodies have been established relatively rarely and late. Beyond this, though, the plans did not provide for special organs to perform particular functional tasks.

These suggestions concerning the type, nature, and procedures of the institutions that were to be created implicitly dealt with two much broader issues—the extent to which the new structures would restrict the sovereignty of their members and the functions that the structures would be capable of performing. On the simplest level, a system that would achieve binding decisions on any basis other than unanimity would possibly force some members to take action against their will and consequently would seriously restrict their sovereignty. As another simple example, one could not have judicial settlement without a court. In general, other things being equal, the more the features of the proposed institution resembled those of governments, the more the organization would restrict sovereignty and the more functions it would be able to perform.

MANIFEST PURPOSES

Turning now to the functions that would be assigned to the structures proposed in the six "peace plans," we began by asserting that the basic purpose of these early plans was to limit the ability of sovereignties to make independent decisions about war and peace. They all sought to maintain peace in Europe. For all of the authors peace in Europe was an end valued in itself; some authors in addition valued European peace because it was instrumental for undertaking external military operations, for maintaining a flourishing commerce, or for still other ultimate objectives.

Although the several plans differed in many details, they all would have forbidden organization members to use military force, at least in Europe, except when authorized by the common institution. The authors of the plans did not completely rule out war because, as we have just recalled, the objective of some of the plans was to facilitate external military operations. Dubois' organization, for example, was to undertake a crusade, and those of others were to serve as instruments for the defense of Europe against the Turks. All of the plans required that military force should be employed to ensure compliance with at least some common decisions, particularly those relating to disputes, and as we have already seen, some of them even provided for the use of force to compel reluctant sovereignties to join the organization. Thus the "peace plans" were schemes for

controlling the use of violence, not for completely eliminating it. One explanation for this is that the authors felt they could not assume that everyone would
voluntarily comply with all decisions of the organization; hence the possibility
of coercive sanctions was seen as essential to insuring the organization's authority. In addition, it was generally held that the use of violence could be justified in
particular circumstances. Defense was the most obvious case, but in an era when
the concept of the "just war" was current, there were many others as well.

To minimize the possibility of war, the plans generally provided that disputes
among organization members should be submitted to the organization for consideration and settlement. Some of the plans provided for settlement by adjudication (by an established court) or arbitration (by an individual or panel
appointed on an ad hoc basis), but most would have had the disputes heard in an
assembly, implying a preference for less rigid procedures. In Penn's plan the assembly would formulate rules of justice to govern conduct among sovereignties
and presumably determine the settlement of disputes. Other plans erected some
general principle, such as maintenance of the status quo, as the standard according to which the positions of the parties to a dispute should be judged. Some
plans, such as that of Podĕbrad, even gave the proposed organization a mandate
to settle disputes among nonmembers.

All of the plans provided that decisions on disputes would be enforced by coercion. Dubois, foreshadowing notions that were to become much more popular
after the Industrial Revolution, proposed that a boycott might be an initial sanction. The ultimate sanction, though, was always military force. Most of the
plans relied on military units under the control of organization members, but
some, such as that of the Duc de Sully, provided that the organization would
have military units assigned to it.

Whether the military units were to remain under the control of the member
sovereigns or be transferred to the control of the organization, the issue arose as
to whether members should make equal contributions of men and material, as
the Abbé de Saint-Pierre suggested, or contribute in proportion to their abilities,
as the Duc de Sully proposed. The rationale for the former course was that it
would avoid rivalries; for the latter, that it was more efficient and might allow a
larger force. These same arguments were to be repeated in the early days of the
United Nations. Penn and the Abbé de Saint-Pierre both wanted the members of
their organizations to undertake disarmament, thus increasing the relative importance of the military forces at the disposal of their organizations. The Abbé
would have limited all sovereignties to military forces of identical size, a suggestion parallel to his idea that all military contributions to the organization should
be equal, and similarly designed to avoid rivalries.

In the classificatory scheme presented in Chapter 1, the organizations projected in most of the plans would have fitted the category of specific purpose organizations, and most of them would also have had limited membership. To put
it more specifically, they would have been European security organizations.
Clearly the dominant initial impulse for the creation of international governmental organizations was a desire to maintain peace in Europe.

LATENT PURPOSES

The adjective "manifest" in the rubric "manifest purposes" carries with it the implication that international organizations could have latent purposes as well, and they certainly do, most broadly in relation to the international order. All of the plans that we have been considering were designed to preserve the European territorial status quo, either that already in existence or one that would be established simultaneously with the creation of the international organization. Not surprisingly, the proponents of the plans were usually identified with sovereignties favored under the existing territorial division, or if they proposed new boundaries, as the Duc de Sully did, their sovereignties would have benefited from the new division. Moreover, as we have seen, many of the plans were oriented toward preserving or aggrandizing Europe's position in the world, and similar motives have been responsible for the creation of many IGOs.

International organizations can also affect the distribution of values within sovereignties; they can serve to preserve the status quo or to promote change. Of the plans that we have been considering, only that of the Abbé de Saint-Pierre explicitly dealt with this. One of the advantages of his proposed organization, he maintained, was that the military forces at its disposal could be used to put down domestic revolts and settle civil wars. His scheme had as a latent purpose the protection of both the international and the domestic status quo.

The latent purposes of international organizations are not always obvious from their constitutional documents or the arguments publicly advanced on behalf of their establishment. Frequently the latent purposes of international organizations can only be inferred or derived by analyzing the objective consequences of their actions. Latent purposes are nonetheless real, and they may be of primary importance for some of the participants in international organizations. No analysis should ignore them.

LEGACY OF THE "PEACE PLANS"

The importance of these early plans for international governmental organization is not in their specific details, but rather in their broad intellectual contribution to attempts to conceive ways of giving greater structure to a political system made up of numerous autonomous units. They had to deal with the practical question of how much existing sovereignties would allow their freedom of action to be restricted. They also had to deal with the value choices involved in estimating the proper balance between the costs and gains of restricting autonomy. The more that autonomy was limited, the greater the risk of stifling diversity, but at the same time it was clear even then that total autonomy carried with it risks of substantial violence. All of the aspects of the plans that we have discussed dealt in one way or another with these issues. The plans raised fundamental questions that had to be faced in the creation of international organizations, particularly IGOs. They suggested various solutions, different ways of handling problems, and they outlined many of the major choices. In fact, as we will see, the repertoire of possible solutions to problems involved in the creation of international governmental organizations owes a substantial debt to the early "peace plans."

INGOS AND INTERNATIONAL SOCIETY

There is no literature comparable to the early "peace plans" containing outlines for international nongovernmental organizations. One reason for this is that there were several significant ties cutting across various sovereignties that existed throughout the medieval period and that already had organizational structures. Religion was the most prominent of these, and transnational organizations in the form of churches and religious orders date to antiquity. Medieval universities too acted as transnational forces, keeping alive the sense of Europe as an entity that might someday become a federation.

The existence of these and other transnational ties and organizations facilitated the creation of international nongovernmental organizations. Contacts among individuals in different countries supported international attitudes and in some cases provided a base for the creation of INGOs. Transnational organizations served as examples and to a certain extent as precedents for the creation of voluntary international associations. When the first modern INGO, the Rosicrucian Order, took its contemporary form toward the end of the seventeenth century, it built on a traditional organization that dated to 1500 B.C. The four other INGOs that were established in the eighteenth century evolved or were created naturally and without obstacles. In short, a literature proposing the creation of INGOs was not produced because those who felt INGOs were needed could simply move to establish them.

Another explanation for the absence of an early literature proposing the creation of INGOs is that the need for INGOs did not appear as pressing as the need for IGOs. While it was obvious as the state system emerged that in the realm of intergovernmental relations war was a considerable possibility, the deleterious consequences of the state system for nongovernmental affairs were not as immediately apparent. It was not until the nineteenth century that the development of nationalism began to significantly sharpen the differences among peoples in different countries, and only in the twentieth century did governments begin to have the desire and the means to substantially control the private contacts of their subjects with those of other countries. INGOs could be and were established to counter both trends, but this function could not be foreseen in the seventeenth century or earlier.

This then is the background for the establishment of the first IGOs in the nineteenth century, and for the evolution of IGO and INGO networks in the nineteenth and twentieth centuries. Now we may consider those developments.

NOTES

1. For a convenient summary of their ideas and other proposals, see Sylvester John Hemleben, *Plans for World Peace Through Six Centuries* (Chicago: University of Chicago Press, 1943).

FOR FURTHER READING

Clark, Grenville, and Louis B. Sohn. *World Peace Through World Law.* Cambridge, Mass.: Harvard University Press, 1958.

Friedrich, Carl J. *Inevitable Peace.* Cambridge, Mass.: Harvard University Press, 1948.

Hemleben, Sylvester John. *Plans for World Peace Through Six Centuries.* Chicago: University of Chicago Press, 1943.

Herz, John. *Political Realism and Political Idealism.* Chicago: University of Chicago Press, 1951.

Kant, Immanuel. *Eternal Peace and Other International Essays.* Translated by W. Hastie. Boston: The World Peace Foundation, 1914.

Parkinson, F. *The Philosophy of International Relations: A Study in the History of Thought.* Beverly Hills, Calif.: Sage, 1977.

Rousseau, Jean Jacques. *A Lasting Peace Through the Federation of Europe and the State of War.* Translated by C. E. Vaughan. London: Constable, 1917.

Souleyman, Elizabeth V. *The Vision of World Peace in Seventeenth and Eighteenth Century France.* New York: Putnam, 1941.

Waltz, Kenneth N. *Man, the State and War: A Theoretical Analysis.* New York: Columbia University Press, 1959.

Wolfers, Arnold, and Laurence W. Martin. *The Anglo-American Tradition in Foreign Affairs: Readings from Thomas More to Woodrow Wilson.* New Haven: Yale University Press, 1956.

3

THE EVOLUTION OF THE WEBS OF INTERNATIONAL ORGANIZATION NETWORKS

THE CONGRESS OF VIENNA

Although plans for international governmental organizations had been mooted for centuries, it was only in the aftermath and as part of the final settlement of the French Revolutionary and Napoleonic wars—the cause of the greatest violence the world had yet known—that the first such body was actually created. And this organization, the Central Commission for the Navigation of the Rhine, created at the Congress of Vienna, was not a broadly based IGO with a mandate of preserving the peace, but rather a limited, technical agency with a highly specific task. The original members of the Central Commission for the Navigation of the Rhine were France, the Netherlands, and five German states, Baden, Bavaria, Hesse, Nassau, and Prussia. The organization's purpose was to guarantee free navigation on the Rhine and to ensure that traffic would be treated uniformly, equally, and as favorably as possible—in other words, to maximize the potential of the river for commerce.

The Central Commission was, however, not totally unrelated to the settlement of the wars. Control of various parts of the Rhine had shifted back and forth among sovereignties during the course of the wars, and the territorial settlement finally adopted at Vienna meant that the river would continue to be subject to several sovereignties. There had long been a desire to insure the free navigation of rivers, and this desire had been heightened by the creation of the first practical steamship in 1802 and by the progress of industrialization, which increased both the opportunities and the demand for commerce. The Congress of Vienna reasserted the general principle of the free navigation of rivers and created an IGO to insure its implementation with respect to the Rhine.

The contribution of the Congress of Vienna to the development of modern international governmental organizations, however, went beyond the establishment of the Central Commission in that the first steps were taken toward the creation of an IGO with a broad mandate including the preservation of peace. The victory of the Allies over Napoleon marked the defeat of his attempt to establish hegemony over Europe, yet his conquests and the wars had destroyed many of the political arrangements that had existed previously in Europe. Since a peace treaty had been signed before the congress opened, its business was primarily that of recreating a political order, an order that clearly would provide for multiple sovereignties. The congress itself could be regarded as a nascent IGO. It lasted for ten months, was attended by some 216 different delegations, and developed a rudimentary committee structure. The principal decisions were made by the Committee of Five, which consisted of representatives from Austria, France, Great Britain, Prussia, and Russia, though the formal directing committee consisted of representatives of the eight states that had signed the Treaty of Paris ending the war—the Five plus Portugal, Spain, and Sweden.

The main preoccupation of the congress was the nature of boundaries and regimes throughout Europe and the disposition of colonies overseas. In addition, the congress drafted the statute for the Central Commission for the Navigation of the Rhine, as has already been mentioned, and prepared a constitution for the Germanic Confederation which among other things required the Diet—the central organ for all the thirty-eight German states, which was composed of representatives of the rulers of these states and operated under the presidency of Austria—to consider means for ameliorating the civil status of Jews in Germany. The congress also drafted a constitution for Switzerland and provided for that state's neutrality, adopted a declaration looking forward to the abolition of the slave trade, and agreed on rules for diplomatic procedure.

The victorious Allies at Vienna were most interested in insuring that any attempt by Napoleon or France to reassert French hegemony over Europe would be forestalled or blocked. Under the Treaty of Chaumont, signed in March 1814, Austria, Great Britain, Prussia, and Russia agreed to combine their forces for the defeat of Napoleon and to concert together for twenty years beyond the end of the war to maintain the peace terms against any future violation by France. According to this treaty, the goal of their cooperation was to be the maintenance of a balance of power in Europe. This commitment to consultations and to joint defensive action to maintain a commonly accepted international order was an important step toward the creation of a broad international governmental organization.

In a sense the Congress of Vienna was a fulfillment of this commitment, as was the joint action undertaken by the four states and others against Napoleon when he returned to France from Elba on March 1, 1815. After the second defeat of Napoleon, Austria, Great Britain, Prussia, and Russia pledged again, in the Quadruple Alliance, to cooperate against possible future violations of the peace terms by France, and they agreed to renew their meetings and to consult about such matters at fixed periods. This last provision and the similar provision of the Treaty of Chaumont provides the conceptual—although not always the legal—basis for the consultations that subsequently were held in the nineteenth century.

Actually only four conferences were legally related to the Quadruple Alliance, those of Aix-la-Chapelle (1818), Troppau (1820), Laibach (1821), and Verona (1822). At the first meeting the joint military occupation of France was ended, and France was admitted to the consultative system. But after the threat of French hegemony had receded, the system foundered and ultimately collapsed at the Verona meeting. The issue on which it failed was the nature of the order that it was designed to protect. As early as the Aix-la-Chapelle conference, Russia's Tsar Alexander I, echoing the Abbé de Saint-Pierre, argued that members of the alliance should guarantee to one another their existing governments and territories. Others wanted to extend this doctrine even further, and at subsequent meetings Austria argued that the alliance should sponsor a collective intervention to suppress revolution in Italy. France favored a similar course with respect to Spain. Britain opposed all of these suggestions. Later when Alexander I wanted collective approval for intervention in Greece, Austria, France, and Great Britain all opposed this suggestion. Because of these divisions, the system of consultation under the Treaty of Chaumont and the Quadruple Alliance collapsed.

Nevertheless, consultations among the major states continued throughout the nineteenth century, even though the legal basis for the meetings changed. These consultations were the major instrumentality for collectively treating security issues and many other issues as well. Although not an international governmental organization by any commonly accepted definition, the consultations came to be regarded as natural, and they occurred frequently, even though there was no legal provision requiring that they be held periodically. Conference secretariats, which began to be composed internationally starting with the Congress of Berlin in 1878, were the forerunners of permanent secretariats. Structural devices such as the use of committees were also refined.

EVOLUTION OF THE WEB OF IGO NETWORKS BEFORE WORLD WAR I

The Growing Number of IGOs

Like the Congress of Vienna, the subsequent consultations also spawned international governmental organizations. The European Commission for the Control of the Danube was created at the Congress of Paris in 1856 as a part of the final settlement of the Crimean War. Its purpose was to assure free and safe navigation on the Danube, and its membership included Britain and France as well as the riparian states. As in the case of the Rhine, the creation of an international governmental organization was necessary because more than one sovereignty exercised control over parts of the Danube, and it was possible to create an IGO only as part of a broader settlement of the territorial problems of the area. The inclusion of the nonriparian states in the commission reflected their interests in the use of the river and also their capacity for influencing events in the area.

The only other international governmental organization to be created before 1865 was the *Conseil superieur de santé* (Superior Council of Health) of Constantinople. This body, composed of delegates of the Ottoman empire and the chief maritime states, was established in 1838, and its function was to supervise the sanitary regulation of the Turkish port. The purpose was to prevent the exportation of cholera from Asia to Europe, a problem which had increased in severity with the increasing rapidity and frequency of communications by sea between various countries, and at the same time to preserve maximum freedom for communications and commerce. Cholera first came to Europe in 1830, and from then until the germ that carried cholera was discovered in 1884 and an effective means for countering the germ was found somewhat later, the principal means of dealing with the problem was quarantine. To be effective, a quarantine required joint action, and if a quarantine were not to stifle communications completely, it had to be applied carefully and selectively. The problem posed by cholera was technical. How it was dealt with had commercial implications. That a sovereign state would allow an international administration to control these matters on its territory can only be explained by the existing political relations. The Ottoman empire was weak, and very much dependent upon the principal maritime states. It had little choice other than to accede to their wishes. So while the *Conseil superieur de santé* was not created as part of a broader political settlement, it was certainly related to existing political relationships.

Two more international governmental organizations were established in 1865: the International Telegraph Union (ITU)—which exists today as a specialized agency of the United Nations with the name International Telecommunication Union—and the International Commission for the Cape Spartel Light in Tangier. Both had as their purpose the facilitation of commerce. The latter, which was the first IGO to have the United States as a member, had an extremely limited mandate and again involved international administration on the territory of a weaker state, Morocco. The International Telegraph Union, on the other hand, was an organization created among states of more equal stature, and although all the founding members were European states, the constitutional provisions were such that the ITU qualifies as the first potentially universal IGO. The first practical electrical telegraph was developed in 1832. Messages transmitted by this means could travel at a velocity of 300,000 kilometers per second. They could travel across Europe in less than a second, but only if political boundaries did not constitute insuperable obstacles. There would have to be means of insuring that the equipment and operating and administrative procedures in different countries were compatible. ITU was created as a forum in which agreement on such issues could be obtained.

By the end of 1865, then, there were five IGOs in existence. All had specific mandates, and only the ITU had the potential of having universal membership. All were closely linked with the expansion of communications and commerce. The system of periodic consultations among the principal states also constituted a prototype IGO in the security field. Although these were modest steps, they were nonetheless the beginning of the web of IGOs that presently exists.

During the last third of the nineteenth century, the pace of IGO creation quickened, and another eighteen were established before 1900. By the eve of World War I in 1914, the total had more than doubled, and there were forty-nine IGOs in existence.

Characteristics of Early IGOs

As in the case of the first IGOs, European states took the initiative in the establishment of most of the IGOs created between 1865 and 1914, and these states comprised the bulk of the membership of the agencies. Non-European countries, particularly the United States, Mexico, China, Japan, and Siam, were increasingly included in the organizations, but they were always a small minority. The principal exceptions to these generalizations were the half-dozen IGOs created among various combinations of American states. Although suggestions for the creation of inter-American IGOs dated from the early nineteenth century, it was not until 1890 that the first such agency with broad membership among the American states, the Pan American Union, was established.

Only three organizations, the International Telegraph Union, the Universal Postal Union (UPU), and the International Institute of Agriculture (IIA), had member states from the four major geographic regions of the world that contained independent states (Europe, the Americas, Asia, and Africa) and thereby qualified for inclusion in the universal membership category. Applying this test to IGOs in the period 1815–1914 is to erect a fairly rigorous standard, for during the nineteenth century most of Africa fell under European colonial control, and those African states that retained their sovereignty had low levels of economic development and hence little need for contact with other states. An additional fifteen organizations had member states from all major geographic regions except Africa and could be regarded as potentially universal. (There were no independent states in Oceania at that time.)

With respect to the other dimension of the scheme established in Chapter 1 for classifying international organizations, 96 percent of the IGOs in existence before World War I had specific mandates. The only two that did not were the Pan American Union and the International Central American Office. The former had both broad membership and a broad mandate, but its powers were limited. The latter stemmed from a conference of Central American states held in Washington in 1907 as a consequence of the mediation of Mexico and the United States, and it was designed as a concrete step toward the political integration of El Salvador, Honduras, and Nicaragua. These two organizations were unusual in that rather than being limited to the performance of clearly delineated tasks, they were given wide-ranging mandates.

Among the specific purposes assigned to IGOs, those relating to economic matters predominated. Thirty-three, or 70 percent, of the specific purpose organizations were in the economic category; eleven, or 23 percent, were in the social and cultural category; and only three, or 6 percent, were in the security category. The predominant impetus for the creation of IGOs was a desire to facilitate commerce. Frequently technological developments, such as the steamship and electrical telegraphy, provided important spurs, for the potential of many inventions could be fully realized only if there were collaboration among states, but this potential was commercial in nature. Economic motivations were even important in the creation of organizations with mandates in other fields. As in the case of the *Conseil superieur de santé*, a principal motive for the creation of IGOs in the field of health was to protect the relatively rich western states against the pestilences, such as cholera and the plague, prevalent in southern and eastern countries while at the same time minimizing the obstacles to commerce. Some IGOs, of course, were unrelated to commercial motivations—for instance, the International Penitentiary Commission, the International Maritime Bureau against the Slave Trade, and the International Bureau for Information and Enquiries regarding Relief to Foreigners—but their number was small.

The three specific purpose organizations with mandates in the field of security were the International Boundary Commission, the International Joint Commission, and the Permanent Court of Arbitration. The first two were bilateral institutions, having as members respectively the United States and Mexico and the United States and Canada. They were established only after broader disputes between the participants had been resolved; their function was to settle detailed issues within the framework of an overall agreement, not to provide the overall agreement.

The Permanent Court of Arbitration truly stood alone. Created by twenty-six states (two from the Americas, four from Asia, and the remainder from Europe) whose representatives assembled at The Hague in 1899 to discuss limitations or armaments, the rules of war, and arbitration, it was an attempt to establish permanent machinery and procedures for the peaceful resolution of disputes. In fact the Permanent Court (which still exists) is not a court in the common understanding of this term, but a panel or list of persons nominated by the signatories from which judges can be selected to arbitrate a dispute should the contending parties choose to submit to arbitration. The only permanent staff is a secretary-general and a small secretariat. The Permanent Court itself was seen as but one in a panoply of techniques for the peaceful settlement of disputes. It was based on the assumption that in the end states would prefer to allow the outcome of a dispute to be determined by a group of judges rather than attempt to gain their own goals through the use of violence.

Here as in other cases a technological development provided the impetus for the creation of an IGO. SInce the technological development in this case was the perfection of the machine gun, the motivating force was not a desire to exploit the potential of the development, but rather a search for means to guard against its being exploited. Even at the time of its creation, the Permanent Court was regarded by some as an excessively narrow and somewhat naive approach to the problem of world order. Its significance lies in the fact of its creation rather than in its subsequent accomplishments. It is an important landmark in the development of international governmental organizations because its mandate was not directed primarily toward matters of commercial interest but entered the realm of security affairs and because it included states from Asia and the Americas as well as from Europe. It was the first putting into practice on a substantial scale of any of the elements of the "peace plans."

Several generalizations are possible about the international governmental organizations that were created in the century from 1815 through 1914. Their general orientation toward commerce and the intimate relationship between their creation and the growth of technology have already been stressed. Probing the history of individual organizations more deeply, one finds that in each instance it was with considerable reluctance that governments agreed to the creation of international institutions. Many times several years elapsed between the introduction of a proposal to create a permanent bureau and its acceptance and implementation. The ITU was created in 1865, but it was three years before the member states decided to create a permanent bureau or secretariat. Governments were also reluctant to give authority either to the secretariats or to the conference machinery of the organizations. Governments generally preferred to limit IGOs to being forums where they could exchange information and coordinate their policies, rather than allowing the organizations to become instruments of action. The few exceptions were more often than not organizations that had as members both rich and powerful states and poor and weak states and that could only take action in the territory of the latter—for example the *Conseil superieur de santé*, The Suez Canal Administration, and the International Finance Commission for International Financial Control in Macedonia.

DEVELOPMENTS SINCE WORLD WAR I

Following the end of World War I, the number of IGOs grew even more rapidly than it had in the preceding half-century. The overall pattern of the growth of IGOs from 1815 to 1964, as traced by Wallace and Singer, is illustrated in Figure 3.1. Only in the period immediately preceding the two world wars did the absolute number of international governmental organizations decline. IGOs grew at an unprecedented rate in the immediate aftermath of each of the world wars: thirty-two were created in the five years starting in 1919, and forty-four in the five years starting in 1945. In each case, in no preceding period had so many IGOs been established.

Clearly, the large-scale violence of the two world wars provided powerful stimuli to the creation of international governmental organizations. The wars provoked new thinking about how security and other problems should be handled and about what institutional arrangements would be appropriate. The political climate at the end of the wars, particularly the resolve widely felt in both the victorious and the vanquished states to create a better world, made govern-

FIGURE 3.1

The Growth of International Governmental Organizations in the Global Political System, 1815–1964

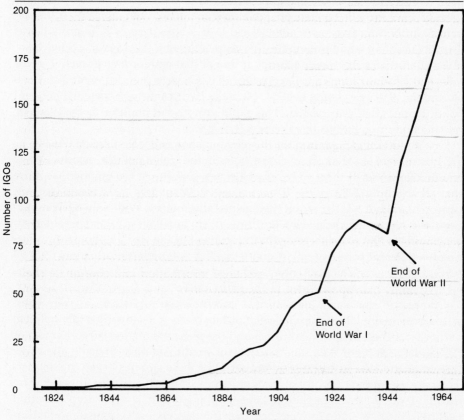

Source: Michael Wallace and J. David Singer, "Intergovernmental Organization in the Global System, 1815–1964," *International Organization,* 24 (Spring 1970), 239–287.

ments more willing to cede aspects of sovereignty than they usually have been.

Changed power relationships among the major states also necessitated new structural arrangements. The constitutional provisions of the IGOs created in the wakes of the two world wars strongly reflected the power relationships generally understood to prevail in each instance. In addition, each war brought new actors into the global political system—the states of the "Old Commonwealth" and the successor states of the Hapsburg and Romanov empires in Eastern Europe at the conclusion of World War I and several states in the Middle East and Asia at the conclusion of World War II. International governmental organizations provided a convenient means of attempting to integrate these new states into the global system.

Although both world wars led to a spurt in the creation of IGOs, there is a sharp contrast (apparent in Figure 3.1) between what eventually happened to the growth of IGOs in the interwar period and what has happened in the period since World War II. In the interwar period, after the initial postwar years, the pace of IGO growth tapered off, and then the absolute number of IGOs declined. In the first five years after World War II, the pace of IGO growth was even greater than it had been in the five years following World War I. Since then, although the pace of growth was not at first at that extraordinary level, it seems to be accelerating rather than decreasing: 28 IGOs were founded in the five years starting in 1950 and ending in 1954, 30 in the five years that ended in 1959, and 33 in the next five-year period. This rapid growth has continued. By 1980, by one method of counting, there were 621 IGOs.

One important explanation for this phenomenon is decolonization. As late as 1914 there were less than 50 sovereign states in the global political system. At the end of World War II there were only 64 states. Since then the number has more than doubled. By 1980, of the 204 countries and territories in the world (see Appendix C), all but 37 (18 percent) had gained sovereignty. With only a few exceptions the remaining dependent territories were small in size and population, accounting for just over three-tenths of a percent of the world's population. Putting it a different way, by the last quarter of the twentieth century, more than 99 percent of the world's population lived in sovereign states. The system of sovereignty had truly been extended to the entire globe.

One reason that early international governmental organizations were composed principally, or even exclusively, of European states was that the political authority of these states extended beyond the metropolitan territories to most of Africa, large parts of Asia, and portions of South America. Starting about the time of World War I, the political authority of these empires began to contract. The pace of contraction quickened considerably after World War II, so that by the mid-1960s world empires were largely a thing of the past. As decolonization occurred, the new states formed their own international governmental organizations. Various motives were involved. Some organizations reflected a desire to protect newly won sovereignty; others, a wish to preserve a cooperative framework that had existed among several territories when they had been under a common colonial regime. The hope that bargaining positions could be improved through association with similarly situated states and a rhetorical commitment to enlarge territorial units through political integration were also important factors.

Decolonization also contributed to the creation of international organizations in other ways. In some instances IGOs were created among rich and poor states to handle matters that had previously been managed through the imperial relationship. Regular collaboration among sovereign states requires an institutional framework, and international governmental organizations assumed some of the functions that had been performed within the administrative framework of empires. For instance, before their independence, France could simply put educational policies into effect in its African colonies. After independence, if France desired to affect the educational policies of francophone African states, agreement could be sought within the framework of an international governmental organization.

In addition, the characters of existing IGOs were transformed as new states swelled their memberships. The tremendous shift in the composition of the United Nations' membership, which will be analyzed later, illustrates the process. As African and Asian states gained a voting majority, they wanted the agenda of these bodies to emphasize their concerns. In some instances this led the governments of Western states, or the advanced industrial states of both East and West, who now were a definite minority in universal membership IGOs, to create new limited membership organizations, or to enhance the importance of existing ones, where they could conduct business concerning matters that they considered to be primarily their own province.

Decolonization, however, has not been the only factor contributing to the growth of international governmental organizations in the years since the end of World War II. Technology has advanced even more rapidly in this period than it had previously, and as in the past, technological developments have continued to provide an impetus for the creation of IGOs. The desire to facilitate commerce, or, more broadly, economic growth and development, has also continued to be important.

A new phenomenon, IGOs begetting IGOs, gained momentum in the 1960s, and this technique for creating new international governmental organizations has been employed with great frequency since then. Examples of the technique are the UN's creation in 1964 of the United Nations Conference on Trade and Development (UNCTAD) and the African Development Bank's creation in 1972 of the African Development Fund. This phenomenon accounts for much of the growth of IGOs since 1960, as can be seen in Figure 3.2. Figure 3.2 portrays the growth of IGOs during the 1960s and 1970s according to two different compilations. The more inclusive compilation—indicated by the broken line—includes IGOs limited to two member states and also IGOs that emanate from other IGOs. The less inclusive compilation includes only IGOs that have three or more member states and does not include IGOs that emanate from other IGOs. (Since Singer and Wallace included IGOs with two members but not those created by other IGOs, neither compilation is directly comparable with theirs.) Although the difference between the two compilations was minor in 1960, it widened considerably during the following two decades.

One reason that IGOs have resorted to creating other IGOs has been to avoid having to request national governments to ratify new treaties. We will examine the consequences of this later. Another reason is to control and structure the proliferation of IGOs; having IGOs nestled within the structures of other IGOs may simplify the tasks of national governments in relating to them. Underlying these two reasons are, again, the consequences of decolonization and of increasing technological development and interdependence. New majorities in organizations with potentially universal membership have sought to undertake tasks that were outside the mandate of the organizations. New technologies and growing interdependence have necessitated new structures for cooperation in a variety of fields. The quickest, simplest, and perhaps most orderly solution in either case has been to have an existing organization create another, rather than to convene a special conference for the purpose.

Optimists might claim that the steady growth of IGOs in the years since World War II reflects a new development in history. They could argue that humankind is learning to cope with its problems through the creation of new institutions that are in the process of substantially altering the global political system.

THE LEAGUE OF NATIONS AND THE UNITED NATIONS

Many of the IGOs that have been established since World War I have closely resembled those created in earlier periods, having limited membership and specific tasks. At the end of each world war, however, an organization was established that was substantially different from the others. Both the League of Nations and the United Nations had broad multipurpose mandates (The U.N. Charter is printed in full in Appendix D), and membership in each was in principle open to all sovereign states.

Mandates

Jarred twice by wars that resulted in more deaths and physical damage than the world had ever known, governments were willing to go considerably beyond the

FIGURE 3.2

The Growth of International Governmental Organizations in the 1960s and 1970s

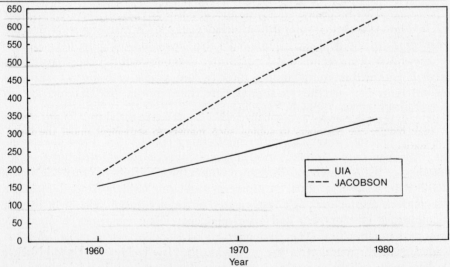

Source: Based on data from Union of International Associations, *Yearbook of International Organizations*, 1981, Vol. 19 (Brussels: UIA, 1981).

step they had taken in 1899 with the creation of the Permanent Court of Arbitration. Both the League and the U.N. had as their primary task the maintenance of peace, but both were also given broad mandates in the economic and social spheres. Both could discuss any dispute, and in certain circumstances both could take military enforcement actions, although the U.N. charter is considerably more explicit in this regard than the League covenant. Between discussion and the imposition of military sanctions, the two organizations could employ a variety of peaceful settlement techniques. They could also use economic coercion. With respect to economic and social matters, both organizations were to collect and disseminate information and to serve as forums where governments could discuss issues, coordinate their policies, and negotiate agreements. Each organization was also empowered to undertake operational activities in certain spheres.

The U.N.'s mandate with respect to economic and social matters was considerably more extensive than that of the League. In addition, several autonomous specialized agencies with mandates in specific functional fields were created after World War II, and others were planned. These agencies, covering a vast range of human concerns, were to be brought into relationship with the U.N., which would perform a coordinating role. The ensemble of institutions would constitute the U.N. system.

One reason for the heightened concern in 1945 with economic and social matters was that the League, especially in latter years, had been considerably more successful in these areas than in that of security, and there was a general desire to capitalize on the League's record of achievement. More importantly, during the years since World War I the conviction had grown that there were important linkages between economic and social issues, including human rights, on the one hand, and security issues on the other. The belief that the amelioration of security problems was at least partially dependent upon progress in the economic and social spheres became widely accepted. Also, governments increasingly accorded importance to economic and social issues in their own right, and within their own territories increasingly adopted policies concerning such issues.

Nevertheless, the U.N.'s greater authority in economic and social matters was hedged with the caveat contained in Article 2, paragraph 7, of its charter:

> Nothing contained in the present Charter shall authorize the United Nations to intervene in matters which are essentially within the domestic jurisdiction of any state or shall require the Members to submit such matters to settlement under the present Charter...

While governments were willing to go farther in 1945 than they had been in 1919, they still were most reluctant to relinquish the right to arrange their domestic affairs as they saw fit. Sovereignty, at least in the sense of right to be different domestically, continued to be highly valued by political leaders. But the U.N.'s broad mandate to deal with economic and social matters and the flexibility provided by the decentralized U.N. system has thus far enabled the United Nations to keep pace with the growing importance of economic and social issues.

Both the League of Nations and the United Nations were clearly full-blown attempts to put into practice the essential elements of the early "peace plans." In their work of creation, the founders of the League and of the U.N. drew on the "peace plans" and on the experience of the nineteenth century with both the system of consultations that had followed the Congress of Vienna and the international governmental organizations that had been established. Despite their novelty, therefore, both the League and the U.N. were firmly part of a broad historical movement that dated at least from the establishment of the state system.

Like all elements of this historical movement, the League and the United Nations were each inescapably linked with broad political relationships. The League covenant was part of the Treaty of Versailles, which embodied the basic settlement of the allied and associated powers with Germany. In Article 10 of the covenant the members of the League undertook:

> . . . to respect and preserve as against external aggression the territorial integrity and existing political independence of all Members of the League.

The League was basically designed to maintain the international order that was created at the conclusion of World War I.

The United Nations was somewhat less clearly connected to the international order resulting from World War II. The U.N. charter is a separate treaty, partly because of the general understanding, developed during the interwar period, that making the League covenant part of the Versailles Treaty had weakened the League's moral authority. The commitment to the territorial status quo embodied in the U.N. charter also differs slightly from that contained in Article 10 of the League covenant. The charter binds member states to "settle their international disputes by peaceful means," and to "refrain in their international relations from the threat or use of force against the territorial integrity or political independence of any state."[1] Later in the charter the General Assembly is empowered to "recommend measures for the peaceful adjustment of any situation, regardless of origin, which it deems likely to impair the general welfare or friendly relations among nations."[2] While the differences are subtle, and both constitutional documents were obviously oriented toward preservation of the territorial status quo, the U.N. charter in contrast to the League covenant allowed a certain flexibility. And in the long run, for several reasons beyond these constitutional differences, the U.N. was to prove far more adaptable than the League to changing circumstances in the global system.

Putting the niceties of constitutional interpretation aside, however, both the League and the U.N. were in the larger historical sense, like the consultative system that followed the Napoleonic wars, attempts to preserve victorious coalitions of allies. Symbolizing this and giving structural reality to it, the principal victorious powers were constitutionally given permanent membership on the Council of the League and the Security Council of the United Nations. And in the case of the U.N., these states were given veto power over all important actions by the Security Council. Such special status was not part of the League covenant only because that document gave all member states veto power in important matters in both the assembly and the council.

Membership and Orientation

Although both the League of Nations and the United Nations qualify as universal membership organizations, from the outset the latter had a more global orientation. One evidence of this is the contrast between the initial memberships of the two IGOs. Table 3.1 gives the original memberships of the League of Nations and the United Nations according to five broad geographical regions. As can be seen, although both organizations had members from all five geographical regions, European and American countries constituted the bulk of the original membership of both organizations. However, these two groups made up 78 percent of the League's original members and only 72 percent of the U.N.'s Or, to put it another way, there were five more African and Asian states among the original members of the U.N.

The initial United Nations membership also had a more global character in a sense not indicated by these figures. Both the United States and the Soviet Union were original members of the U.N. Although Woodrow Wilson and his aides had played a principal role in drafting the League covenant, the United States never joined the League, and the Soviet Union became a member only in 1934.

Because of these differences between the two organizations, and other factors as well, European states played a much more substantial role in the early days of the League than they did in the early days of the U.N. European states provided the leadership for the League, and their concerns dominated the organization's agenda.

Table 3.1
*Original Memberships of the League of Nations and the United Nations**

	LEAGUE OF NATIONS		UNITED NATIONS	
REGION	Number	Percentage	Number	Percentage
Africa	2	5	4	8
Asia	5	12	8	16
Oceania	2	5	2	4
Americas	17	40	22	43
Europe	16	38	15	29
Total	42	100	51	100

*The original memberships of the two organizations were:
League of Nations: Africa (Liberia, Union of South Africa); Asia (China, India, Japan, Persia, Siam); Oceania (Australia, New Zealand); Americas (Argentina, Bolivia, Brazil, Canada, Chile, Columbia, Cuba, Guatemala, Haiti, Honduras, Nicaragua, Panama, Paraguay, Peru, Salvador, Uruguay, Venezuela); Europe (Belgium, Czechoslovakia, Denmark, France, Greece, Italy, Netherlands, Norway, Poland, Roumania, Spain, Sweden, Switzerland, United Kingdom, Yugoslavia).
United Nations: Africa (Egypt, Ethiopia, Liberia, South Africa); Asia (China, India, Iran, Iraq, Lebanon, Philippines, Saudia Arabia, Syria); Oceania (Australia, New Zealand); Americas (Argentina, Bolivia, Brazil, Canada, Chile, Colombia, Costa Rica, Cuba, Dominican Republic, Ecuador, El Salvador, Guatemala, Haiti, Honduras, Mexico, Nicaragua, Panama, Paraguay, Peru, United States, Uruguay, Venezuela); Europe (Belgium, Byelorussian S.S.R., Czechoslovakia, Denmark, France, Greece, Luxembourg, Netherlands, Norway, Poland, Turkey, United Kingdom, Ukrainian S.S.R., U.S.S.R., Yugoslavia).

Of course the membership of both organizations changed over time, and these changes accentuated the differences that existed at the outset. Eventually, 63 states joined the League of Nations, but as some joined, others withdrew. In the late fall of 1934, when the League's membership was at its peak, there were 58 members, only 7 more than the U.N. had at its beginning. By the fall of 1982 the U.N.'s membership had grown to 157. Table 3.2 compares the memberships of the two IGOs in 1934 and 1982. As can be seen from Tables 3.1 and 3.2, Europe's relative share in the membership of the League increased from 38 percent in 1919 to 48 percent in 1934, while the relative shares of Asia, Oceania, and the Americas fell. The effect of these changes was to make Europe and European concerns even more predominant in the League in the 1930s than they had been in 1919.

The pattern of growth in the U.N. has been quite different. The most striking change has been the increase in the number of African and Asian states—from twelve to eighty-five, or from 24 percent of the organization's membership in 1945 to 54 percent in 1982. The relative share in U.N. membership of all other groups has declined, and that of the Americas most substantially, falling from 43 percent in 1945 to 22 percent in 1982. The phenomenon responsible for this change in U.N. membership has been decolonization. The important point here is that while the United Nations had a more global membership than the League from the outset, U.N. membership became even more global as time went on, contributing substantially to its greater adaptability.

NATO, WTO, AND THE EUROPEAN COMMUNITIES

The period since World War II has also brought other institutional innovations. One innovation was the creation of international governmental organizations to manage the affairs of peacetime military alliances. In 1949 Canada and the United States and Belgium, Denmark, France, Iceland, Italy, Luxembourg, the Netherlands, Norway, Portugal, and the United Kingdom signed the North Atlantic Treaty. These states sought to create a deterrent to contain communist expansionism, and after signing the treaty they moved quickly to establish both civilian and military institutional structures. Although such structures had been a feature of wartime collaboration, the North Atlantic Treaty Organization (NATO) was the first modern IGO created to manage the affairs of a peacetime military alliance. Other similar organizations were established subsequently. The most prominent of these is the Warsaw Treaty Organization (WTO), which was created by Albania, Bulgaria, Czechoslovakia, the Democratic Republic of Germany, Hungary, Poland, Romania, and the U.S.S.R. in 1955 after the Federal Republic of Germany became a member of NATO.

A second innovation was the creation of IGOs with unprecedented political authority. In 1952 the governments of Belgium, the Federal Republic of Germany, France, Italy, Luxembourg, and the Netherlands formed the European Coal and Steel Community (ECSC). The purpose of the ECSC was to create a common market for coal and steel. The ECSC was different from other IGOs in that it had substantially greater authority. IGOs have traditionally been unable to act directly on individuals or enterprises. They have been able neither to tax nor to regulate individuals or firms, but instead have had to rely on governments of states to take such actions. In contrast the ECSC could promulgate regulations that would have binding effect on individuals and firms, and it could levy taxes directly. These powers have led some scholars to label the ECSC and other simi- lar institutions that were established subsequently "supranational organizations."

Supranational organizations have the authority to take actions that have direct application to individuals and such legal entities as corporations. Within their spheres of competence, supranational organizations do not need to rely on states to promulgate their decisions; indeed, in these areas their decisions have prece-

Table 3.2
Membership in the League of Nations in 1934 and in the United Nations in 1982*

	LEAGUE OF NATIONS		UNITED NATIONS	
REGION	Number	Percentage	Number	Percentage
Africa	3	5	51	32
Asia	6	10	34	22
Oceania	2	4	7	4
Americas	19	33	34	22
Europe	28	48	31	20
Total	58	100	157	100

*The membership of the League of Nations in 1934 and of the United Nations at the end of 1982 was:

League of Nations: Africa (Ethiopia, Liberia, Union of South Africa); Asia (Afghanistan, China, India, Iraq, Persia, Siam); Oceania (Australia, New Zealand); Americas (Argentina, Bolivia, Can- ada, Columbia, Chile, Cuba, Dominican Republic, Ecuador, Guatemala, Haiti, Honduras, Mex- ico, Nicaragua, Panama, Paraguay, Peru, Salvador, Uruguay, Venezuela); Europe (Austria, Albania, Belgium, Bulgaria, Czechoslovakia, Denmark, Estonia, Finland, France, Greece, Hun- gary, Ireland, Italy, Latvia, Lithuania, Luxembourg, Netherlands, Norway, Poland, Portugal, Rou- mania, Spain, Sweden, Switzerland, Turkey, U.S.S.R., United Kingdom, Yugoslavia).

United Nations: Africa (Algeria, Angola, Benin, Botswana, Burundi, Cameroon, Cape Verde, Central African Republic, Chad, Comoros, Congo, Djibouti, Egypt, Equatorial Guinea, Ethiopia, Gabon, Gambia, Ghana, Guinea, Guinea-Bissau, Ivory Coast, Kenya, Lesotho, Liberia, Libya, Madagascar, Malawi, Mali, Mauritania, Mauritius, Morocco, Mozambique, Niger, Nigeria, Rwanda, São Tomé and Príncipe, Senegal, Seychelles, Sierra Leone, Somalia, South Africa, Su- dan, Swaziland, Tanzania, Togo, Tunisia, Uganda, Upper Volta, Zaire, Zambia, Zimbabwe); Asia (Afghanistan, Bahrain, Bangladesh, Bhutan, Burma, Cambodia, China, Democratic Yemen, India, Indonesia, Iran, Iraq, Israel, Japan, Jordan, Kuwait, Laos, Lebanon, Malaysia, Maldives, Mongo- lia, Nepal, Oman, Pakistan, Philippines, Qatar, Saudia Arabia, Singapore, Sri Lanka, Syria, Thai- land, United Arab Emirates, Vietnam, Yemen); Oceania (Australia, Fiji, New Zealand, Papua-New Guinea, Samoa, Solomons, Vanuata); Americas (Antigua, Argentina, Bahamas, Barbados, Belize, Bolivia, Brazil, Canada, Chile, Colombia, Costa Rica, Cuba, Dominican Republic, Ecuador, El Salvador, Grenada, Guatemala, Guyana, Haiti, Honduras, Jamaica, Mexico, Nicaragua, Panama, Paraguay, Peru, Saint Lucia, Saint Vincent, Surinam, Trinidad and Tobago, United States, Uru- guay, Venezuela); Europe (Albania, Austria, Belgium, Bulgaria, Byelorussian S.S.R., Cyprus, Czechoslovakia, Denmark, Finland, France, Germany-Federal Republic, Germany-Democratic Re- public, Greece, Hungary, Iceland, Ireland, Italy, Luxembourg, Malta, Netherlands, Norway, Po- land, Portugal, Romania, Spain, Sweden, Turkey, Ukrainian S.S.R., U.S.S.R., United Kingdom, Yugoslavia).

dence over those of national governments. Supranational organizations have some of the attributes of governments of federations or confederations, but they fall short of a complete merger of sovereignties. Their jurisdiction is limited, and they lack independent coercive means to enforce their decisions. In a broad sense they continue to rely on the voluntary cooperation of the governments of their member states. Supranational organizations are consequently a species of international governmental organization, albeit a species that is highly evolved and as yet relatively rare. Whether this species will become more numerous and whether supranational organizations will evolve further until they become governments are important questions that provoke considerable speculation, but only the future can answer them.

Six years after the birth of the ECSC, the same six states created the European Atomic Energy Community (EAEC or Euratom) and the European Economic Community (EEC). The first agency was to establish a common market for nuclear energy; the second, a broad common market covering the total economies of the six countries. Although in a strict legal sense the mandates of these two agencies were not as supranational as that of the ECSC, the scope of the EEC was much broader. The creation of the three agencies clearly seemed to point toward the merger of the six economies, and many political leaders and observers in Europe and elsewhere expected economic merger to be a step toward political merger and integration. In 1973 three additional states, Denmark, Ireland, and the United Kingdom, joined the three European communities. Greece became the tenth member of the communities in 1981, and it appeared that Portugal and Spain would also join during the 1980s. The possibility of the European communities leading to the formation of some type of United States of Europe is an issue that must be examined later. What is significant for present purposes is that the governments of these states should have been willing to create and join organizations with such unprecedented authority.

There is no single or simple explanation of why they were willing to take such far-reaching steps. Clearly, economic motives were a factor. The distribution in Europe of natural resources relating to steel production made the creation of the European Coal and Steel Community an economically rational move. Yet a common market in coal and steel would have been rational ever since large-scale steel production began. In a broader sense, of course, the dynamics of technological progress pushed in the direction of increasing the size of political jurisdictions to facilitate large-scale production, and competition from the United States gave added impetus to this.

What triggered acceptance of the proposal to create the ECSC, however, seems to have been concern for security rather than economic motives. In May 1950, when French Foreign Minister Robert Schuman launched the proposal to place the production of coal and steel in France and Germany under a common authority, he said, "The solidarity in production thus established will make it plain that any war between France and Germany becomes not merely unthinkable, but materially impossible."[3] Until that time the Western Allies had maintained controls over the production of steel in West Germany. But the controls would soon have to be abandoned, and with their abandonment France would lose an element of leverage over Germany's war potential. In effect, Schuman proposed to give up control of French coal and steel industries in return for international control over these industries in West Germany. On the other side, the West German government preferred international control to Allied control. More importantly, the European Coal and Steel Community would provide a useful vehicle for bringing West Germany back into a legitimate position in the global political system. Both governments saw the Schuman plan as a way of easing the troublesome Saar question by eliminating the need for concern about which state controlled that territory. In short, like the U.N., the ECSC was closely linked with the outcome of World War II.

The European Atomic Energy Community and the European Economic Community were to a substantial extent the result of dynamics set in motion by the ECSC. Consequently, for present purposes we need analyze in detail only the initial impulse, not later developments. It is important to note, however, that IGOs tend to stimulate the creation of other IGOs. The process has worked in various ways. In the case of the European Coal and Steel Community, an organization created among several states generated pressures toward the creation of further international governmental organizations among the same states—Euratom and the European Economic Community. In other instances the creation of an IGO among some states has led other states to create another IGO. For example, the European Free Trade Association was definitely created by Austria, Denmark, Norway, Portugal, Sweden, Switzerland, and the United Kingdom in response to the establishment of the European Economic Community.

By the 1980s, then, many different types of international governmental organizations had been established, and many different factors had played a role in their creation. In 1980, according to the pragmatic criteria employed here (rather than the more stringent criteria of Wallace and Singer), there were 621 IGOs, more than the number of states in the global political system. IGOs constituted an intricate web that extended throughout the political system. All sovereign states were members of at least some of them, and IGO mandates covered all topics from agriculture (Food and Agriculture Organization) through zinc (International Lead and Zinc Study Group). One could hardly conceive any issue of world politics that would not in some way involve an international governmental organization.

THE WEB OF IGO NETWORKS

Table 3.3 shows how the 621 IGOs in existence in 1980 were distributed among the four basic categories established in Chapter 1 and compares this distribution with the distribution that existed in 1865 and the periods immediately before each of the world wars. (The 621 IGOs in existence in 1980 are listed according to the four categories in Appendix A.)

Universal membership, general purpose organizations were the last to be es-

Table 3.3
*Distribution of IGOs in the Global Political System, 1865–1980**

CATEGORY	1865		1910–1914		1935–1939		1980	
	Number	Percentage	Number	Percentage	Number	Percentage	Number	Percentage
Limited Membership—Specific Purpose	4	80	44	90	46	55	506	81
Universal Membership—Specific Purpose	1	20	3	6	36	43	97	16
Limited Membership—General Purpose	0	0	2	4	1	1	17	3
Universal Membership—General Purpose	0	0	0	0	1	1	1	0
Total	5	100	49	100	84	100	621	100

*Since the phenomenon of IGOs creating other IGOs occurred after World War II, it is appropriate in this instance to compare the list of 621 IGOs in existence in 1980 with the lists that Wallace and Singer used for earlier years. Distortion would occur only if the list of 621 used here were compared with those used by Wallace and Singer for the years after World War II.

tablished and almost by definition are limited to one in each historical era. General purpose organizations with limited membership form the next smallest category, yet by 1980 there were seventeen of these, a substantial number. Specific purpose organizations have dominated the picture from the outset, and IGOs with limited memberships have always constituted the largest number. There has, however, been an interesting fluctuation in the twentieth century: the relative number of universal membership, specific purpose organizations was substantially greater in the interwar period than it was in the years before World War I or after World War II. The interwar period was clearly the high tide of universalism. A plausible explanation for this includes the following: (1) there were fewer states in the interwar system than in the post–World War II system because large-scale decolonization had not yet occurred; (2) the states that were part of the global system in the interwar period had more characteristics in common than has been the case since then; (3) before World War I the pressures toward universalism from technology and commerce were not nearly as great as they have been since then. The relative increase in limited membership organizations since World War II reflects the greater heterogeneity among states that are presently in the global political system.

Subdividing the limited membership, specific purpose organizations further, IGOs with economic functions and geographically determined membership form the largest category. They constituted 36 percent of the total number of IGOs in 1935 and 36 percent in 1980. The constancy of the proportion is interesting, for the relative number of all types of limited membership, specific purpose organizations was substantially greater in 1980 than it had been forty-five years earlier. IGOs with economic functions and geographically determined membership constituted 65 percent of limited membership, specific purpose organizations in 1935 and 38 percent in 1980. The two subcategories that grew most substantially between 1935 and 1980 were IGOs with economic functions and membership determined on the basis of economic criteria and IGOs with social and cultural functions and geographically determined membership. In 1980 the former constituted 12 percent of the limited membership, specific purpose category, while the latter had reached 30 percent.

It also should be noted that although IGOs with economic functions were predominant among universal membership, specific purpose organizations, forming 83 percent of this category in 1935, by 1980 they constituted only 48 percent. Universal organizations with social functions increased both absolutely and relatively between 1935 and 1980, rising from 11 percent of the category to 48 percent. Adding all of the IGOs with economic functions regardless of membership, they were 80 percent of the total number of IGOs in 1935 and 54 percent of the total in 1980.

Although virtually all states were involved in this web of IGO networks, involvement varied considerably—from France, which was a member of more than a hundred IGOs in 1980, to several small states that were members of only one IGO. Table 3.4 lists the twenty-three states that held membership in 60 or more of the 291 principal IGOs included in the UIA's 1977 compilation. Fourteen of the twenty-three are European states; two, Canada and the United States, are from North America; two, Brazil and Mexico, are from South America; two, Japan and India, are from Asia; two, Egypt and Tunisia, are from Africa; and one, Australia, is from Oceania. No state with a communist government is included in the top twenty-three.

EVOLUTION OF THE WEB OF INGO NETWORKS

Just as a web of IGO networks evolved, so did a web of INGO networks.[4] Figure 3.3 illustrates the growth of INGOs from 1860 through 1980. There are, however, several differences between the ways in which the two webs developed. One difference is that INGOs were established earlier than IGOs. The Rosicrucian Order met the criteria for being an INGO in the seventeenth century, but it was 1815 before the first IGO was created. Also, INGOs have always been more numerous than IGOs. By the middle of the nineteenth century there were three

Table 3.4
States Belonging to the Greatest Number of IGOs in 1977

State	Number of IGO Memberships	Rank Order
France	104	1
United Kingdom	91	2
Germany, Federal Republic of	87	3
Netherlands	84	4
Belgium	83	5
United States	78	6
Denmark	76	7.5
Italy	76	7.5
Canada	75	9
Spain	74	10
Japan	71	11
Australia	70	12.5
Sweden	70	12.5
Norway	68	14
India	65	15
Brazil	64	16
Egypt	62	17.5
Tunisia	62	17.5
Austria	61	20.5
Mexico	61	20.5
Portugal	61	20.5
Switzerland	61	20.5
Mexico	60	23

Source: Based on data from Union of International Associations, *Yearbook of International Organizations,* 1981, Vol. 19 (Brussels: UIA, 1981), Table 4.

times as many INGOs as IGOs, and until 1940 INGOs were created at a more rapid pace than IGOs. On the eve of World War II there were thirteen times as many INGOs as IGOs. Although this ratio declined somewhat immediately after World War II because of the more rapid creation of IGOs, by 1980 it had attained about the same level. In 1980, using UIA's restrictive criteria, which exclude organizations that emanate from other organizations, there were 4,265 INGOs and 337 IGOs. If these restrictive criteria are dropped, UIA's counts jump to 9,398 INGOs and 1,039 IGOs. INGOs like IGOs have begun to procreate, though not at the same pace as IGOs. For more comparison, Figure 3.3 also portrays the growth of IGOs counted according to UIA's restrictive criteria during the period 1920 through 1980. The growth curves in the recent period would be different if the less restrictive criteria were used.

It is clear from the record that INGOs have been easier to create than IGOs. Mobilizing individuals or associations of individuals is easier than mobilizing states; it is not necessary to overcome either the legal doctrine of sovereignty or bureaucratic inertia. INGOs also tend to be less substantial than IGOs. They usually have significantly smaller budgets and fewer paid staff members.

FIGURE 3.3
The Growth of International Nongovernmental Organizations in the Global Political System, 1860–1980.

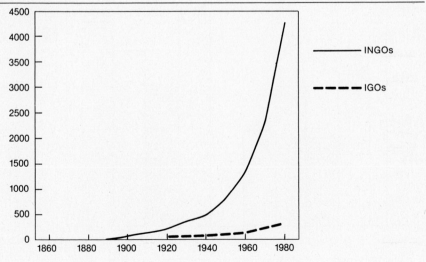

Source: Werner J. Feld, *Nongovernmental Forces in World Politics* (New York: Praeger, 1972); and Union of International Associations, *Yearbook of International Organizations,* 1981, Vol. 19 (Brussels: UIA, 1981).

In Figure 3.4 the average growth rates per decade of IGOs and INGOs are compared. The first two bars in each case represent average rates of growth per decade during the periods 1860 through 1920 and 1920 through 1960 respectively. The third and fourth bars represent actual rates of growth during the 1960s and 1970s. International organizations created by other international organizations have been excluded from all of the counts.

As was the case with IGOs, INGOs with specific purposes were the first to be established, and they continue to outnumber those with general purposes by a substantial margin. Compared to IGOs, a significantly higher proportion of INGOs do not limit their membership in any way. Many such organizations fall short of attaining truly universal membership, but they have that potential. Another difference between IGOs and INGOs is that there have been relatively more INGOs with mandates having to do with social and cultural affairs. This has been the case from the very beginning: the Anti-Slavery Society, the Society of Saint Vincent de Paul, and the International Committee of the Red Cross were among the first INGOs. Two factors help explain why relatively more INGOs than IGOs have dealt with social issues. First, governments have historically been less active with respect to social welfare than with respect to security and economic issues. Second, governments themselves often violate human rights, and they are reluctant to criticize one another in this sphere; nongovernmental organizations are less inhibited.

FIGURE 3.4
Comparison of Growth Rates of IGOs and INGOs

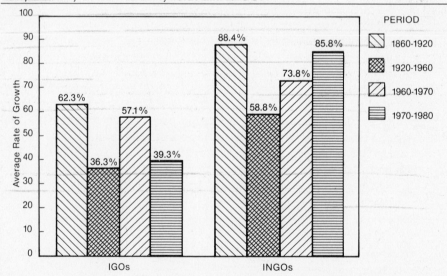

Source: Werner J. Feld, *Nongovernmental Forces in World Politics* New York: Praeger, 1972); Union of International Associations, *Yearbook of International Organizations, 1981*, Vol. 19 (Brussels: UIA, 1981); and Michael Wallace and J. David Singer, "Intergovernmental Organization in the Global System, 1815–1964," *International Organization*, 24 (Spring 1970), 239–287.

The propensity of states to join international organizations, both IGOs and INGOs, varies greatly. It is significantly affected by population and territorial size, level of economic development, and age measured in years since gaining independence. Table 3.5 shows how states' participation in international organizations differs according to geographic region. European states held the greatest number of international organization memberships, and states from the Americas had the second highest number. The web of international organization networks is densest in Europe, where the state system was first established, and sparcest in Africa, Asia, and Oceania, where it was most recently installed. Europe also contains a large proportion of relatively rich states, and the propensity of states to join international organizations seems to vary directly with their level of economic development. Although Table 3.5 does not show it because it aggregates IGO and INGO memberships, national participation in INGOs is more skewed in favor of highly developed states than is participation in IGOs. This is so because open political systems, ones in which there is societal pluralism, are more likely to allow their citizens to participate in nongovernmental organizations, and such systems are highly correlated with relatively high levels of economic development. Thus both factors contribute to the propensity to participate in INGOS.

TRANSNATIONAL ORGANIZATIONS AND CONTACTS

The number of transnational organizations has also increased since 1815, but describing this increase quantitatively is not easy. By far the most spectacular change has been the growth of transnational corporations. By the late twentieth century processes of production, which initially had been local, had become internationalized. National corporations had become transnational corporations. One global register of transnational corporations compiled in the late 1970s listed more than 9,000 firms having operations outside their home countries.[5] Together these firms had more than 34,000 subsidiaries and associates throughout the world. The internationalization of production had been a continuous process but the most dramatic growth in the number of subsidiaries and associates of parent companies occurred after World War II.

Simultaneously, as a consequence of increased contacts among peoples stemming from improved communications and greater trade, the number of transnational interactions zoomed upward.

OTHER CHANGES IN THE GLOBAL POLITICAL SYSTEM

To this point our focus has been primarily on the establishment and growth of the networks of international organizations. Changes in other elements of the global political system have been touched only tangentially. Now it is time to broaden our view and consider other elements of the system in greater

Table 3.5
National Participation in International Organizations, 1980

Region	Territorial Units		Total International Organization Memberships		Average Number of International Organization Memberships per Territorial Unit
	Number	Percentage	Number	Percentage	
Africa	54	26.2	12,328	15.2	228.3
Americas	52	25.2	16,936	20.8	325.7
Asia	44	21.4	12,909	15.9	293.4
Oceania	17	8.3	2,853	3.5	167.8
Europe	39	18.9	36,291	44.6	930.5
Total	206	100	81,317	100	394.7 (Mean)

Source: Based on data from Union of International Associations, *Yearbook of International Organizations, 1981, Vol. 19* (Brussels: UIA, 1981), Table 3.

detail, in order to understand the interaction between them and international organizations.

In 1815, when the Central Commission for the Navigation of the Rhine was created, as now, states—and governmental institutions within them—were the central points of political activity. States possessed sovereignty, and world politics consisted of interactions among states. The number of states then in existence, however, was much smaller than it is now. In the early years of the nineteenth century, there were some thirty units that could be characterized as states. All but a few of these—the United States, Persia, Ethiopia, Siam, China, and Japan—were European. Moreover England, France, Holland, Spain, Portugal, and Denmark had empires, and consequently their authority extended far beyond their European metropolitan territories.

As a consequence of decolonization—beginning in South America—and other changes, there were some forty states in the global system by the middle of the nineteenth century. Although several of the units changed, the number of states remained roughly at this level until the eve of World War I. During the same time, however, the power of England, France, Belgium, and Germany was extended to areas where there had not previously been modern government.

World War I saw the dissolution of the Hapsburg, Romanov, and Ottoman empires, bringing several new states into the global political system. By 1939, the eve of World War II, there were almost 70 states in the system. By 1980 this number had more than doubled, mainly as a consequence of decolonization in Asia and Africa. There were then 168 sovereign states in the global system. (All of the territorial units in the global political system in 1980 are listed in Appendix C, which indicates whether or not each unit is independent and in cases of dependent territories indicates which state is the administering authority. Appendix C also gives the population, gross national product, and per capita gross national product for each unit.) By 1970 more than 99 percent of the world's population lived within the borders of independent sovereign states. Although there were still numerous colonies and other dependent territories, almost all of these were small in size and had limited populations. In 1970 world empires were a thing of the past, and the modern state system, which had its origins in the seventeenth century in Western Europe, had been extended to the entire globe.

As the number of states in the system grew, so did the world's population. Unfortunately, good statistical services are just now being developed throughout the world, and in some areas they are still weak. Figures for earlier periods are extrapolations backward and reconstructions contrived from fragmentary information. Even allowing for vast inaccuracies because of these limitations, however, the growth in the world's population since 1815 is startlingly impressive. At the beginning of the nineteenth century the world's population is estimated to have been somewhat less than 1 billion.[6] By 1900 the total had reached only 1.6 billion, and in 1950 it was 2.5 billion. By 1980 the total was 4.4 billion. In other words, after centuries of stability or relatively slow growth, the world's population increased substantially in the mid-twentieth century.

As population grew, it also became increasingly urban. In 1920 only 20 percent of the world's population lived in "urban areas" (i.e., towns and cities having 20,000 inhabitants or more). By 1960 this total had jumped to 33 percent, and by the 1970s it was 40 percent.

Equally striking has been the change in levels of economic development. In 1815 the per capita gross national product (GNP) of what now would be termed the advanced industrial countries was about $250.[7] It had taken approximately six centuries to grow to this level from about $50. After 1815 the pace of growth quickened: by 1960 these countries had a per capita GNP of over $1,000, and by the end of the next two decades their per capita GNP exceeded $10,000. Some countries, however, did not grow economically, and those that were at a subsistence level at the beginning of the nineteenth century made only marginal progress. In other words, during the time that international organizations proliferated, international stratification increased; the gap between rich and poor countries widened considerably.

The extent to which states in the global political system are stratified can be seen by two simple measures, share of the world's population and share of the world product. In 1980, more than 70 percent of the world's population lived in sixteen states, each of which had a population of more than 50 million: Nigeria, Bangladesh, India, Indonesia, Japan, Pakistan, the People's Republic of China, Vietnam, Brazil, Mexico, the United States, France, the Federal Republic of Germany, Italy, the Union of Soviet Socialist Republics, and the United Kingdom.[8] A total of 73 percent of the world product accrued to these states. However, 60 percent of the world product accrued to seven of them—Japan, the United States, France, the Federal Republic of Germany, Italy, the U.S.S.R., and the United Kingdom—which contained only 19 percent of the world's population, while only 13 percent of the world product accrued to the remaining nine large countries in which more than 51 percent of the world's population lived.

The seven states that produced 60 percent of the world product in 1980 have been the principal powers—either with their present names or with earlier names—for at least a century. However, the relative position of these states has shifted substantially over time. This can be seen most easily by comparing their gross national products, since GNP contributes so much to a state's ability to exercise influence in world politics.

In the early nineteenth century Great Britain's gross national product was larger than that of any of the other six. By the 1870s the GNPs of the United States, Russia, France, and Germany about equaled that of Great Britain. As early as the turn of the century, however, the United States' GNP had grown to be roughly twice as large as those of Great Britain and Russia, and ever since then the United States' GNP has been larger than that of any other state. At the turn of the century Germany's GNP had fallen behind those of Britain and Russia, and that of France lagged even further. At the end of World War I the United States' GNP was roughly three times those of Britain and Germany. Russia's GNP dropped after the Revolution, and not until the mid-1950s was it once more half as large as that of the United States. Japan's GNP, which was the smallest of the seven until the end of World War I, grew consistently over the years and surpassed that of Britain in the early 1960s. As of the early 1970s and continuing into the 1980s, the rank order of the seven states according to the size of their gross national products was: the United States, the U.S.S.R., Japan, the Federal Republic of Germany, France, the United Kingdom, and Italy. Italy's GNP had been the lowest of the seven states since the end of World War I. According to some calculations, in the early 1970s the GNP of the People's Republic of China surpassed that of the United Kingdom and of course that of Italy. China clearly had joined the ranks of the major powers.

Another important development in the global political system is that over the long historical period, trade among states increased substantially with their economic development, and states have consequently become more interdependent. The seven states that have contributed the largest share to the gross world product have also regularly accounted for almost half of world trade.

The nature of governments has also changed during the years since 1815. Of the states in existence then, most were monarchies, although some of these had limited popular participation. The United States was the major exception; it was a republic and had most of the features that one associates with modern democracies—competition for office through open elections, broad suffrage, and free speech. During the nineteenth century these features spread to more and more countries. In the twentieth century three developments occurred. First, although several states that were initially formed from the collapse of empires adopted democratic types of rule, new states increasingly adopted authoritarian regimes. There were various types of authoritarian regimes—neomercantilist oligarchies, military autocracies, and traditional monarchies—but in common they barred or severely limited popular participation in political activities. Second, the Russian Revolution created a new type of regime. Such regimes have come to be called mobilizing regimes. Their principal characteristic is that the elite adheres to an ideology that is used as a basis for mobilizing popular support and for transforming the state. Finally, all governments assumed a more active role in the economic affairs of their states. This came about particularly as a consequence of the widespread economic depression of the 1930s.

The global political system of the late twentieth century, then, differed considerably from that of the early nineteenth century, when international organizations were first established. The number of international organizations had grown, but so had the number of states and the world's population. The world was wealthier too, but the differences between rich states and poor states were much sharper than they had ever been. Governments were more varied, but all of them took a much more active role in economic affairs than had been the case at the beginning of the nineteenth century. In sum, by the time there were really large numbers of international organizations, the global political system was infinitely more complex than the system that had existed when the first international organizations were created. We will want to examine how international organizations function in this more complex system, but first we need a more philosophical analysis of their creation and evolution.

NOTES

1. U.N. Charter, Article 2, paragraphs 2 and 3.

2. Ibid., Article 14.

3. M. Schuman actually said, "La solidarité de production qui sera ainsi nouée manifestera que toute guerre entre la France et l'Allemagne devient non seulement impensable mais matériellement impossible." The text of his speech may be found in Royal Institute of International Affairs, *Documents on International Affairs, 1949–1950*, selected and edited by Margaret Carlyle (London: Oxford University Press, 1953), pp. 315–317. The sentence cited is on p. 316.

4. The account of the development of INGOs given here is based on several sources: Werner Feld, "Nongovernmental Entities and the International System: A Preliminary Quantitative Overview," *Orbis*, 15 (Fall 1971), 879–922; Kjell Skjelsbaek, "The Growth of International Non-governmental Organization in the Twentieth Century," *International Organization*, 25 (Summer 1971), 420–442; G. P. Speeckaert, *The 1,978 International Organizations Founded since the Congress of Vienna: A Chronological List* (Brussels: Union of International Associations, 1957); Lyman Cromwell White, *International Organizations: Their Purposes, Methods, and Accomplishments* (New Brunswick, N.J.: Rutgers University Press, 1951); and Union of International Associations, *Yearbook of International Organizations*, 1974, Vol. 15 (Brussels: UIA, 1974).

5. UN, Commission on Transnational Corporations, *Transnational Corporations in World Development: A Re-examination* (New York: UN, 1978. Sales No. E. 78 II. A. 5, E/C. 10/38), p. 211.

6. Bernard Berelson, "World Population: Status Report 1974," *Reports on Population/ Family Planning*, 15 (January 1974), 3.

7. See Simon Kuznets, *Modern Economic Growth: Rate, Structure, and Spread* (New Haven: Yale University Press, 1966).

8. These figures are drawn from the data in Appendix C.

FOR FURTHER READING

Goodrich, Leland M. "From League of Nations to United Nations," *International Organization*, 1 (February 1947), 3–21.

———, Edward Hambro, and Anne Patricia Simons. *The Charter of the United Nations: Commentary and Documents*. New York: Columbia University Press, 1969.

Haas, Ernst B. *The Uniting of Europe*. Stanford: Stanford University Press, 1958.

Kissinger, Henry A. *A World Restored: Metternich, Castlereagh and the Problems of Peace, 1812–1822*. Boston: Houghton Mifflin, 1957.

Mangone, Gerard J. *A Short History of International Organization*. New York: McGraw-Hill, 1954.

Miller, David H. *The Drafting of the Covenant*. 2 vols. London and New York: Putnam, 1928.

Skjelsbaek, Kjell. "The Growth of International Non-governmental Organization in the Twentieth Century," *International Organization*, 25 (Summer 1971), 420–442.

Wallace, Michael D., and J. David Singer. "Intergovernmental Organization in the Global System, 1815–1964: A Quantitative Description," *International Organization*, 24 (Spring 1970), 239–287.

Walters, F. P. *A History of the League of Nations*. 2 vols. London: Oxford University Press, 1952.

White, Lyman Cromwell. *International Non-governmental Organizations: Their Purposes, Methods, and Accomplishments*. New Brunswick, N.J.: Rutgers University Press, 1951.

Zimmern, Alfred E. *The League of Nations and the Rule of Law*. London: Macmillan, 1936.

4

PHILOSOPHICAL PERSPECTIVES ON THE EVOLUTION OF INTERNATIONAL ORGANIZATIONS

Having surveyed the evolution of international organizations chronologically, we now need to view the process analytically. Several motives were explicitly or implicitly ascribed to those who created international organizations. These can be conveniently summarized in three major categories. First, the desire to exploit the potential of technological developments for greater commerce led to the creation of the first international governmental organization, and this desire has continued to be an important force. Second, international organizations have also been created, as the "peace plans" proposed that they should be, in attempts to gain security or to maintain particular political orders. Third, some IGOs and a larger number of INGOs have been established to advance humanitarian goals, to promote social welfare and human rights.

All of these motives were reformist rather than revolutionary. Virtually all international organizations have been created to make the nation-state system work better, not to overthrow it. This is not to say that some individuals who supported the creation of a particular international organization did not do so with the openly expressed or covert hope that this step would sooner or later contribute to the demise of the state system. Some citizens, publicists, and political leaders have clearly entertained such hopes, but most supporters of international organizations have had much more modest ambitions, usually attainment of some particular immediate goal.

The motives of their founders provide an important starting point for analyzing the creation and growth of international organizations. They provide the proximate causes.

It is also important to recall that historically interstate violence, particularly that of the two world wars, has provided powerful stimuli for the creation of all types of international organizations, not only those with manifest purposes in the field of security. Interstate violence has often created a need to reestablish instruments of order, including institutional frameworks. In addition, organizations in other fields have increasingly been seen as contributing indirectly to the solution of security problems. Decolonization has also provided stimuli for the creation of international institutions.

We need, however, to look beyond the proximate causes and the immediate occasions for the establishment of international organizations. We need to understand the evolution of the webs of international organizations in relation to general social processes and broad historical developments with respect to these processes. Especially because we are dealing with both IGOs and INGOs, no single theory provides an adequate comprehensive explanation, but several theories offer important partial explanations. Some of the theories are equally applicable to both IGOs and INGOs, but others are more pertinent for one or the other category.

FEDERALISM

Theories about federalism are relevant even though they deal with the formation of governments rather than of international organizations. Federalism can be concerned with the expansion of the territorial domain of political authority, which is also the purpose of international governmental organizations. The difference is that federalism can deal with enlarging the domain of political authority through expanding the territorial size of states, while international governmental organizations merely involve cooperation among states without the transfer of formal sovereignty. Although this difference is crucially important, it should not obscure an important similarity in purpose.

The domain of political authority can be expanded through military conquest, and throughout history countless unitary states have been established in this way. Federations, in contrast, come about as the result of voluntary actions. One author, William H. Riker, has defined federalism as "a bargain between prospective national leaders and officials of constituent governments for the purpose of aggregating territory, the better to lay taxes and raise armies."[1] The word "bargain" is important in his definition, for it signifies the voluntary nature of the act of federating. As in all bargains, those who create a federation must be willing to accept the agreement. Riker has postulated that two circumstances must exist for this to occur.[2] First, the political leaders who seek to expand their territorial control are unable to do so by conquest either because they lack the military capacity or because there are compelling ideological inhibitions against the use of military force for such a purpose. Second, the political leaders of constituent governments are willing to form a federation and give up independence in certain spheres because of some external military or diplomatic threat or opportunity.

They seek unity to obtain protection from an external threat or to participate in the spoils of military or diplomatic action against some third party. On the basis of an examination of the successful and abortive attempts to create federations throughout the world, Riker believes that these two circumstances are the necessary and sufficient conditions for the creation of federations.

Like federations, international organizations are created by voluntary actions. The word "bargain" provides an equally apt description of what must occur for an international organization to be established. In forming an international organization, the constituent units, be they individuals, national associations, or governments, agree to give up some of their autonomy to achieve some purpose that can only be gained by aggregating their authority. These conditions are not as restrictive as those that Riker has postulated for the formation of federations; if they were, presumably federations would be formed rather than international organizations. Nevertheless, there is a similarity. For an international organization to be created, those involved must perceive that in the relatively near term the benefits to be gained from membership will outweigh the costs. This is a generalized and less restrictive statement of the conditions for a federation.

That those who would form an international organization must expect that the benefits of doing so will exceed the costs may seem like a trivial point, but it is not. Plans for an international governmental organization with broad membership that would seek to promote security and preserve peace had been mooted since the thirteenth century, but it was 1919 before the first full-fledged such institution, the League of Nations, was created. Then, the United States, one of the League's sponsors, decided not to join, ultimately because the perceived benefits were not sufficiently compelling to overcome the opposition generated in large part by personal antagonisms between President Woodrow Wilson and Senator Henry Cabot Lodge and others. Governments have traditionally been very reluctant to create IGOs, and they have been even more reluctant to grant them broad authority. Sovereignty is highly prized, and even though joining an international governmental organization could mean only a modest limitation on sovereignty, governments have seen this as a real cost, which they have not been eager to accept.

Forming an international nongovernmental organization raises the same questions. At a minimum, members almost always must pay dues, and the money spent for this could be put to alternative uses. But much larger issues are frequently involved. The International Air Transport Association (IATA), for instance, decides the fares to be charged on international routes, and airlines that are members of IATA cannot autonomously determine the fares that they will charge but instead must follow IATA decisions. When IATA was created in 1945, the airline companies preferred renouncing their rate-setting autonomy to a system of unrestricted price competition. This is not the usual pattern prevailing in industries other than transport; at least some form of price competition is the more general rule. INGOs that have as their principal activity the exchange of information, such as the World Veterinary Association, also involve costs in that the diffusion of innovations reduces the advantages held by the innovators.

The literature of federalism thus gives an insight into the nature of the bargain that must be struck for the creation of an international organization. If in fact the two circumstances that Riker listed have been the necessary and sufficient conditions for the establishment of federations, it is clear why so few IGOs have been transformed into federal governments. But even to create international organizations, the participants must feel that on balance they will benefit.

FUNCTIONALISM

The body of theoretical literature that deals most directly with the creation and growth of international governmental organizations is that of functionalism. This literature is a mixture of attempts to describe and analyze historical developments, to predict what is likely to happen, and to prescribe what should happen. No concise, single theory has emerged, yet there are several common themes which together constitute a persuasion if not a theory. David Mitrany is the most prominent example of a writer of this persuasion.

Functionalism argues that two basic and observable trends in modern history are crucially important in shaping the domain and scope of political authority; they are the growth of technology and the spread and intensification of the desire for higher standards of material welfare. Technological developments both bring peoples closer together and make possible higher standards of material welfare. They consequently provide a two-pronged thrust toward broadening aspects of political authority. Railways are a frequently cited example. By providing inexpensive transport, railways made possible greater economic specialization and through this a greater total product. But this result would be achieved only if there were cooperation among states to assure, at a minimum, a standard width for tracks; and to realize the full potential of railways, much more extensive collaboration would be needed covering a variety of technical and administrative details.

Functionalists feel that governments will be pressured by their citizens to engage in international cooperation to take advantage of technological developments. They maintain that people everywhere desire better material conditions, and they postulate that increasingly literate and urbanized populations will more and more be able to make governments respond to this desire. Improving conditions of life will be essential for governments to remain in power.

Development of Functionalist Theory

Early functionalists saw the creation in the nineteenth century of institutions to facilitate such cooperation and collaboration as a hopeful trend. They were impressed with the multiplicity of specific purpose institutions created in the late nineteenth and early twentieth centuries. They contrasted the willingness of governments to establish these institutions with their reluctance to allow more comprehensive limitations upon their sovereignty. From this understanding of what had happened, they began to erect general propositions. They argued that in specific functional fields almost irresistible pressures toward cooperation would develop, and they felt that "technical self-determination" would govern the collaboration. The nature of the problem would determine the institutions that would have to be created and the powers they would have to possess, as well as the states that would have to be included. Following this principle they argued that activities should be "selected specifically and organized separately—each according to its nature, to the conditions under which it had to operate, and to the needs of the moment."[3] Some activities, they felt, could best be organized continentally, others on a broader but still regional basis, while some would require universal participation. Whether or not a particular state would participate in an institution created for a specific activity, and if it were to participate, what share of power it would have in decision making, would be based on the state's capacity for performance in the particular field.

Functionalists applauded the fact that the specific purpose institutions that had been created were staffed by specialists in substantive fields rather than diplomats. They hypothesized that substantive specialists would be more likely to be guided by "technical self-determination," while diplomats would stress issues of sovereignty and prestige, issues which could only be roadblocks to cooperation. Substantive specialists would develop a "professional pride" and would have "a vested interest in good performance."[4] The functionalist strategy was based on the assumption that governments were not unitary actors but rather organizations of departments and individuals that often had different, and sometimes conflicting, interests. When it came to staffing the secretariats of international organizations, functionalists wanted career officials, and they postulated the creation of "a detached international civil service." Not only did functionalists regard regional or global federations as unfeasible, they also considered them undesirable because they distrusted centralized power.

Functionalists felt that the same pressures that would compel governments to form IGOs would also lead to the creation of international nongovernmental organizations. Functionalists favored the creation of INGOs and saw them as essential supports for the IGOs that they wanted to see created. In the functionalist view, specific purpose INGOs and IGOs could collaborate in the solution of problems. There is almost a preference for technocracy in functionalist thought.

Although their approach does not constitute a frontal attack on problems of war and security, functionalists have nevertheless argued that their prescription was a practical way of working toward peace. Functional organizations would gradually enmesh states and lessen their capacity and taste for war. David Mitrany stated the thesis clearly:

> Every activity organized in that way would be a layer of peaceful life, and a sufficient addition of them would create increasingly wide strata of peace—not the forbidding peace of an alliance, but one that would suffuse the world with a fertile mingling of common endeavor and achievement.[5]

Functionalists approached the problem of peace circuitously. In this respect they differed from the authors of the early "peace plans." In part the functionalist approach grew up as a consequence of disappointment with the failure of governments to adopt these plans, and, after the experience of the League of Nations, disappointment with the results achieved when governments did try to apply them. Functionalism was posited as an alternative to unrealizable schemes for regional and global federations. The functional approach also reflected the broadened domestic concerns and activities of governments.

Throughout the functionalist argument there is a dichotomy between "technical" and "political", and a strong bias toward the former. "Technical" is often used as synonymous with "functional." In general it connotes economic and social, as opposed to security, matters, but at other times it seems to mean noncontroversial. On still other occasions the distinction between "technical" and "political" appears to be that between "objective" and "arbitrary."

An explanation related to functionalism, but with a somewhat different emphasis, contributes further insights. This theory, developed by Volker Rittberger, argues that international organizations are a consequence of the development within states of a new social class, the intelligentsia, defined for these purposes as those with university training.[6] The argument is that, as the national state was the creation of the bourgeois class, international organizations have been the creation of the intelligentsia.

Rittberger maintains that intellectual work has a fundamentally international orientation because standards of judgment are universal, not national. Mathematics and the natural sciences provide the best examples; uniform measurements are used and the canons of proof are the same wherever an experiment is conducted. There may be greater room for variance in less precise disciplines, but even in literature and other humanities there are universally accepted criteria of evaluation. International organizations facilitate the work of the intelligentsia by broadening agreement on definitions and standards and speeding the transmission of information. Rittberger and others also maintain that the occupational role of the intelligentsia implies the sublimation of aggressiveness. The intelligentsia support the efforts of international organizations to lessen interstate violence because of their dislike of violence. Finally, the intelligentsia often find themselves in open or latent conflict with their national political authorities; international organizations provide a different political arena in which the intelligentsia can work to achieve their goals.

Rittberger documents his arguments by showing that increases in the number of IGOs have followed, with a certain time lag, increases in the intelligentsia. There would be the same correlation with the growth pattern of INGOs, for the shape of the two curves is similar. He sees the intellectual class as an intervening variable between industrial growth on the one hand and international organizations on the other. So understood, his theory can be seen as a supplement to functionalism.

Limitations of Functionalist Theory

Set against the record of the creation and growth of international organizations in the nineteenth and twentieth centuries, the functionalist explanation is plausible, and this plausibility enhances the attractiveness of functionalism as strategy. The facts that the first international governmental organization to be created had a limited membership and a specific purpose and that organizations of this type form the largest category of IGOs fit functionalist theory well. Yet functionalism falls short of being a comprehensive explanation in a variety of ways, and if taken too literally, it can be quite misleading.

To take up the latter point first, given the definition of "political" used in this book, it is impossible to maintain a clear distinction between "political" and "technical." There are authoritative allocations in the economic and social spheres just as there are in the sphere of security, and debate about economic and social policies can be as acrimonious as debate over security policies. To argue that economic and social issues have been settled in a technical, nonpolitical manner risks failing to examine the value premises that were implicitly involved in the decisions. The benefits of an organized activity can seldom be equally shared among all participants, nor is there often only one way of dividing them. Technical properties may well set certain parameters, but they hardly ever eliminate the necessity for choice. Thus the argument of "technical self-determination" can well mask a refusal to examine how values are allocated. And the preference for settling economic and social matters in a technical, administrative way could remove them from popular control. Debate about what should be done may be noisy and unsettling, but it is an inevitable concomitant of the determination of policy by democratic means.

Turning to the other point, although functionalism seems to explain adequately the creation of many international organizations, it does not explain the creation of all of them. Nor does it explain why particular organizations have been established in some fields and not in others and at certain times rather than others. In reviewing the development of international organizations, one cannot ignore the fundamental quest for security that motivated the "peace plans" and was an important factor in the creation of the League of Nations and the United Nations and also several other agencies. Functionalism does not treat this.

Neo-Functionalism

Before turning to other explanatory theories, however, we need to note how functionalist theories were employed and modified by individuals who were prominently connected with the creation and functioning of the European communities. Jean Monnet in particular deserves mention. As head of the French *Commissariat du plan*, he played a vital role in the initiative that Robert Schuman launched for the creation of the European Coal and Steel Community. Monnet became the first president of the High Authority of the ECSC. Subsequently, as president of the Action Committee for the United States of Europe, he was a leader in the movement to create the European Economic Community. The doctrine that he and others developed has been termed "neo-functionalism."

Like traditional functionalism, neo-functionalism emphasizes initiating inter-state cooperation in limited spheres of activity, but the similarity between func-tionalism and neo-functionalism ends here. Instead of seeking out relatively uncontroversial activities, neo-functionalism stresses organizing cooperation on activities that are politically important—and therefore likely to be relatively controversial—but that also allow considerable scope for planning by techno-crats. Neo-functionalism holds that political institutions and policies should be crafted so that they lead to further integration through the process of *l'engrenage*, or "the expansive logic of sector integration." For example, as president of the ECSC, Monnet sought to use the integration of the coal and steel markets of the six member countries as a lever to promote the integration of their social security and transport policies, arguing that such action was essential to eliminate distor-tions in coal and steel prices. Finally, the neo-functionalism of Monnet and oth-ers has as its ultimate goal, as the full title of the Action Committee proclaims, the creation of a federal state.

The implementation of the neo-functionalist strategy has resulted in important achievements in Western Europe, as we will see especially in Part IV of this book. The potentiality of functional collaboration as a stepping stone toward federa-tion in Europe and elsewhere will be explored in Part VI. Let us now return to the task of analyzing the process of the creation of international organizations.

THE THEORY OF PUBLIC GOODS

Even international organizations dealing with economic and social activities, with which functionalism does deal, have not been established and have not de-veloped according to a uniform pattern. Particular cases, of course, would have to be explained by particular circumstances. However, a helpful general insight into the process can be found in the theory of public, or collective, goods. The theory deals with a seeming paradox: contrary to the assumption that rational self-interest would lead the members of a group having a common interest to or-ganize and to act collectively to promote their common interest, this does not happen.

The explanation expounded with particular clarity by Mancur Olson relates first to the hiatus between individual efforts and collective action.[7] If the group is large, individual efforts will seem inconsequential and incapable of achieving the overall objective; hence the individual will concentrate on more proximate objec-tives even though their achievement may be counterproductive toward the group goal. An example is the individual who increases immediate income by increas-ing production even though the long-run effect of all producers doing this is to drive prices down and reduce the aggregate profits of the group. In world politics an individual state temporarily may increase security by increasing armaments, but all states may be less secure at the end of the resulting arms race.

A second part of the explanation concerns the nature of the services that would result from collective action. Some services have the character of being public goods; that is, if they are available to anyone, they must be available to everyone. Thus, with large organizations, individual efforts will have no noticeable effect on the organization, and the individual will receive the benefits of the organization with or without contributing to it. To return to the earlier example, should all but one producer restrict production in the interest of gaining a higher price, that higher price cannot be denied to producers who ignore the group edict and increase their own production. Or in world politics, the benefits of general disarmament cannot be denied to the state that ignores the overall agreement and increases its own armaments. These properties of public goods are particularly relevant to international organizations since they are largely in the business of providing such goods.

Several ancillary arguments flow from these basic postulates. One is that to insure wide participation, large organizations must utilize coercive sanctions or benefits other than the public good that can be allocated selectively. Compulsory membership tends to be a corollary of the efficient production of the collective good by a large organization.

Another argument is that small groups operate according to fundamentally different principles than do large groups. In a small group it is likely that there will be at least a few members who would be better off if the public good were provided even if they had to provide it themselves. This is because the smaller the number of members that share in the benefits of the public good, the greater the proportion going to any individual. If the size of the members of the group is unequal, there will be a tendency for smaller members to rely on voluntary, self-interested actions of larger members. The largest member would receive the largest benefit, and consequently would be willing to make the largest contribution. The smallest member, since it would enjoy some of the benefits of the public good in any case, and since its contribution would make little difference to the total public good, would have little incentive to contribute even its proportional share. Consequently, in small groups there is a tendency for small members to exploit large members, to seek a free ride, and there is also a tendency toward suboptimal production of the public good. But small groups are much more likely to organize to provide public goods than are large groups. The larger the group, the less adequate the rewards for individual action, the less likely that any subset or individual will be willing to bear the entire or a substantial proportion of the burden of providing the public good, and the greater the initial costs of creating an organization.

Earlier, drawing from federalism, the point was made that for an international organization to be created, the perceived benefits would have to outweigh the perceived costs. The theory of public goods helps explain how such benefits and costs are calculated and why the creation of general purpose organizations with broad membership has been so slow and difficult compared with the creation of limited membership, specific purpose organizations. The theory may also help in understanding how international organizations function.

MARXISM-LENINISM

Marxism-Leninism provides the final element in a theoretical framework for understanding the development of international organizations. International organizations have never been a central concern of Marxist-Leninist thought. Nevertheless, the theories that Marxist-Leninist writers have developed are important to understanding the development of contemporary international organizations for several reasons. First, they provide an alternative vision of how the world might be organized to pose against the vision prevalent in the West of a pluralistic community of nation-states tied together through networks of voluntary associations. Second, since they start from different premises, they can provide a different angle of vision and consequently can yield a broadened understanding. Finally, since the governments of roughly a third of the world's population subscribe at least formally to Marxist-Leninist theories, it is important to see how this may influence their attitude toward international organizations.

Marx and Engels

The class struggle rather than the struggle among nations and states was the central focus of Karl Marx's writings. His interest centered on the exploitation of man by man—why and how it occurred and how it could be eliminated. He saw states as reflections of their ruling classes and as instruments of class oppression. In the *Communist Manifesto* (1848) he posed the slogan "the workers have no country," and throughout his writings he stressed the solidarity of the interests of the proletariat.

Unlike the anarchists, however, Marx recognized the necessity of organization, and he was a centralist for economic reasons. He wanted to organize production for the benefit of the proletariat. He did not question the goal of a growing and highly productive economy; indeed, achieving this goal was crucial to advancing the welfare of the proletariat. Marx reasoned that specialization and large-scale industry were essential to a highly productive economy, and these in turn necessitated an integrated and centralized society. Furthermore, Marx felt that the proletarian revolution would occur within the framework of existing nation-states. As he put it, "The proletariat of each country must, of course, first of all settle matters with its own bourgeoisie."[8] The first stage after the revolution would be the establishment of the dictatorship of the proletariat, but after man and society were eventually transformed, Marx forecast a new classless society wherein there would be no need for state power. Specialization and large-scale industry would still exist, but exploitative discipline would be replaced by self-discipline and voluntary cooperation.

Marx believed that the proletarian revolution would first occur in one or more of the industrially most advanced states and then be repeated in others that were less advanced. That it would be repeated, he felt, was both inevitable and essential. Similarly, the transformation of the dictatorship of the proletariat into a classless society would not occur everywhere simultaneously, but in one area after another. In this development Marx saw the basis for the formation of a true brotherhood of man. His collaborator, Frederick Engels, referred to this eventual condition as the "World Republic." Marx scorned federalism in general and particularly as an arrangement for governing after the proletarian revolution; its only role could be as a transitional phase toward complete centralism.

As the nineteenth century wore on, Marx was confronted with considerable evidence that the proletariat felt more closely identified with nation-states than with the world proletarian movement. However, this did not lead him to modify his views significantly. He continued to stress the primacy of the class struggle, which he saw as the ultimate cause of national conflicts. In his view, class affiliations were primary, while attachments to nations were secondary and ephemeral. National prejudices would disappear after the proletarian revolution.

Marx and Engels argued that only the proletariat could destroy nationalism. They held that the bourgeoisie in each country had special interests, and because of these could not go beyond the limitations of nationalism. In short, the nation-state was the highest form of political organization and authority of which the bourgeoisie were capable. Thus Marx and Engels scoffed at plans to preserve peace by federations of existing states. Marx did see capitalism moving in the direction of a world economy, and he saw that the forces involved in this move had a tendency to erode nationalism. He staunchly maintained, however, that only the proletariat could move beyond nationalism—the bourgeoisie were incapable of this.

Lenin and Stalin

Marxist writers have continued to deal with these issues. Both Lenin and Stalin devoted considerable attention to them. Their writings did not significantly modify the basic Marxist framework, but they did elaborate portions of it in considerable detail. Since Lenin and Stalin were concerned with promoting and guiding an actual revolution and with the problems of governance after the revolution, they focused on more practical issues than had Marx. Many of these issues are now mainly of historical interest, but it is important to note Lenin's attitude toward what were then mere proposals or newly established international institutions.

Lenin argued that under capitalism the United States of Europe would be either "impossible or reactionary."[9] He felt that in the long run capitalists could not suppress their individual nationalistic interests, although they might achieve temporary agreements. Such temporary agreements among European states, he argued, could be:

> only for the purpose of jointly suppressing socialism in Europe, of jointly protecting colonial booty *against* Japan and America, which feel badly treated by the present division of the colonies, and which, for the last half century, have grown infinitely faster than backward, monarchist Europe, which is beginning to decay with age.[10]

Stalin saw the Pan-European movement in the 1920s and 1930s, and particularly Aristide Briand's proposal for the creation of a European union, as designed to undertake an anti-communist intervention in the Soviet Union.

The League of Nations, which was created two years after the Russian Revolution, was initially seen by the new Bolshevik government as a worldwide trust among bourgeoisie governments, with the purpose of suppressing revolution. Lenin and Stalin felt that the way to world peace was through the development of the Russian Revolution. In their view, now that the proletariat had seized power in Russia, that country could become the nucleus for a world socialist state. This concept was embodied in the 1924 Constitution of the U.S.S.R., which included the provision "that access to the Union is open to all Republics, already existing as well as those that may be born in the future." This constitution also proclaimed that the U.S.S.R. should serve "as a new decisive step toward the union of workers of all countries in one World Soviet Socialist Republic."[11] Lenin saw the Communist International, or Comintern, which was founded in March 1919, as a counter-organization to the League of Nations. The executive committee of the Comintern proclaimed that the organization was an "international association of the proletariat of all countries for the purpose of overthrowing the bourgeoisie and of laying foundations for an International Soviet Republic."[12] In Lenin's view, the aims of the Comintern and those of the League of Nations were mutually exclusive.

Communism and International Organizations

According to the classification scheme used in this book, the Comintern and the Communist Information Bureau (Cominform), which succeeded the Comintern after World War II but was dissolved in 1956, would be international nongovernmental organizations since they were established by and composed of Communist parties rather than governments. In the Soviet Union, however, the Communist party and the government are tightly interconnected. The new constitution that was adopted by the U.S.S.R. in 1977 proclaims: "The Communist Party of the Soviet Union is the leading and guiding force of Soviet society and the nucleus of its political system. The party defines the long-term development of society and outlines domestic and foreign policy."[13] In communist states governmental and nongovernmental institutions are generally closely connected, and individuals in communist states often tend to assume that the same situation prevails elsewhere.

In view of the extent to which the basic positions found in early Marxist writing have been repeated, it is striking how little they have affected the practice of communist states. In 1934 the U.S.S.R. joined the League of Nations. At that point, despite its earlier attack on the League, membership was important for the conduct of its relations with noncommunist states. And in its desire to gain security against Germany, the Soviet Union became one of the foremost advocates of joint action through the League. When it became apparent that this would not occur, the Soviet Union switched to the strategy of negotiating a bargain with

Germany, and after its attack on Finland in 1939, the U.S.S.R. was expelled from the League. But when a new universal membership, general purpose organization, the United Nations, was created, the Soviet Union was among its founders, and despite repeated rebuffs within the organization in the 1940s and 1950s and rumors of withdrawal, the U.S.S.R. has remained a member of the U.N. Moreover, given the opportunity of membership, no other communist state has chosen to remain outside of the U.N. The U.S.S.R. and other communist states also participate actively in several other universal membership IGOs, and individuals and groups within communist countries have joined INGOs.

That communist states should find international organizations necessary for handling their relationships with noncommunist states is not too surprising. But it is striking that communist states have also chosen international governmental organizations as a way of handling relationships among themselves. When communist regimes were established in several countries after World War II, not once was there a move toward taking advantage of the open character of the Soviet Constitution that would have allowed new Soviet republics to join the U.S.S.R. Instead, the communist regimes took over existing state apparatuses, and despite some early seemingly different arrangements, eventually relations between communist states resembled more closely relations between noncommunist states than they did early Marxist theories. In these circumstances international governmental organizations were a logical way of dealing with issues of common interest.

In the end, then, the basic Marxist proposition that horizontal (class) affiliations are more potent than vertical (national) affiliations has no more proven correct since World War I than it did before that war. Nevertheless, Marxist ideas have left a residue of distrust of international organizations among communist states, as is evidenced by the fact that these states belong to significantly fewer IGOs than do noncommunist states of comparable size and level of economic development. Communist states are also underrepresented in INGOs.

Marxist ideas should alert one to examine the class bases of international organizations and to consider the class consequences of their actions. Although international organizations may be neutral instruments, particular international organizations always have particular structures of influence, and this affects who benefits from what they do.

The Neo-Marxist Position

Contemporary writers of a neo-Marxist persuasion have frequently argued that particular international organizations have as their principal purpose and consequence maintaining the position and the perquisites in the global political system of the presently dominant states. According to these writers, certain international organizations are primarily instruments for keeping the relatively less developed states in a dependent position. It is impossible to give a single or simple response to these allegations. A major purpose of this book is to examine how international organizations affect the authoritative allocation of values. The evidence amassed in this examination should give readers a basis for making their own judgments about who benefits from particular organizations and from the ensemble of organizations.

We have sought to explain both historically and analytically how the webs of international organization networks came into being and evolved to their present dimensions. In Chapter 3 we explored proximate causes and immediate occasions for the creation of international organizations, while in this chapter we have considered broader theories. The contribution of these theories may be summarized as follows. Federalism spells out the requirements for the formal merger of sovereignties and by implication the conditions for limited surrenders of autonomy. Functionalism shows how developments in technology and the structure of society can relate to organized cooperation among states. The theory of public goods contains general propositions about the propensity of states to cooperate. Marxism-Leninism reminds us that political institutions are linked to societal structures and that institutions and the policies formulated in them have value consequences. Marxism-Leninism also provides a utopian vision of world order as an alternative of that of nation-states peacefully cooperating.

These several explanations should help us understand how international organizations have become a prominent feature of the contemporary global political system. They should contribute to clarifying the role of international organizations in this system and stimulate thought about how the webs of international organizations might contribute to transforming this system, but clearly they do not adequately cover or settle these issues. Thus both short- and long-run questions remain open. To tackle them we must consider first how international organizations operate as political institutions—how decisions are made. Then we must examine what international organizations have done in particular fields. Knowing more about these issues is essential to speculating about the future.

NOTES

1. William H. Riker, *Federalism: Origin, Operation, Significance* (Boston: Little, Brown, 1964), p. 11.

2. Ibid., p. 12.

3. David Mitrany, *A Working Peace System* (Chicago: Quadrangle, 1966), p. 70.

4. Ibid., p. 78.

5. Ibid., p. 98.

6. Volker Rittberger, *Evolution and International Organization: Toward a New Level of Sociopolitical Integration* (The Hague: Nijhoff, 1973).

7. Mancur Olson, Jr., *The Logic of Collective Action: Public Goods and the Theory of Groups* (New York: Schocken, 1968).

8. Karl Marx and Frederick Engels, *The Manifesto of the Communist Party (1848)*, pp. 477–519 in Vol. 6 of Karl Marx and Frederick Engels, *Collected Works* (London: Lawrence and Wishart, 1976), p. 495.

9. V. I. Lenin, "The United States of Europe Slogan," pp. 413–417 in Vol. 1 of V. I.

Lenin, *Selected Works in Two Volumes* (Moscow: Foreign Languages Publishing House, 1952), p. 414.

    10. Ibid., p. 416.

    11. Constitution of the U.S.S.R., January 31, 1924, Part 1, Declaration.

    12. "Long Live the First of May. Long Live Communism," *Communist International* (London ed.), 1 (May 1, 1919), 24.

    13. Constitution of the U.S.S.R., 1977, Article 6.

FOR FURTHER READING

Caporaso, James A., ed. "Dependence and Dependency in the Global System," *International Organization*, 32 (Winter 1978), 1–300.

Goodman, Elliot R. *The Soviet Design for a World State.* New York: Columbia University Press, 1960.

Haas, Ernst B. *The Uniting of Europe: Political, Social, and Economic Forces.* Stanford: Stanford University Press, 1958.

Jessup, Philip C., Joseph Chamberlain, Adolf Lande, and Oliver J. Lissitzyn. *International Regulation of Economic and Social Questions.* New York: Carnegie Endowment for International Peace, 1955.

Mitrany, David. *The Progress of International Government.* New Haven: Yale University Press, 1933.

——— . *A Working Peace System.* Chicago: Quadrangle, 1966.

Olson, Mancur, Jr. *The Logic of Collective Action: Public Goods and the Theory of Groups.* New York: Schocken, 1968.

Riker, William H. *Federalism: Origin, Operation, Significance.* Boston: Little, Brown, 1964.

Rittberger, Volker. *Evolution and International Organization: Toward a New Level of Sociopolitical Integration.* The Hague: Nijhoff, 1973.

Zimmerman, William. "The Transformation of the Modern Multistate System: The Exhaustion of Communist Alternatives," *The Journal of Conflict Resolution*, 16 (September 1972), 303–317.

DECISION MAKING IN INTERNATIONAL ORGANIZATIONS

5

THE POWERS, FUNCTIONS, AND STRUCTURES OF INTERNATIONAL ORGANIZATIONS

We turn now to analyze how decisions are made within international organizations. Our purpose is not to describe how decisions are taken within any particular organization, or set of organizations, but rather to generalize about the political processes that are typical of international organizations. Given our central focus on political issues, we will concentrate on international governmental organizations. However, the political processes of international nongovernmental organizations that are composed of national associations—and the majority of INGOs are of this nature—are similar to those of IGOs. INGOs will also enter the scene as participants in the processes of IGOs.

Our analysis of decision making in international organizations must inevitably start with consideration of legal and institutional issues. What authority are international organizations typically given? Through what types of actions is this authority typically exercised? How are the institutions of international organizations typically structured? Only after examining these issues can we consider those who participate in making decisions in international organizations and the way that they interact and behave. The mandate and structure of organizations provide a framework within which decisions must be taken, and they inevitably shape the process of decision making.

THE LACK OF AUTONOMY OF INTERNATIONAL ORGANIZATIONS

It is essential at the outset to recognize that the authority of international organizations is limited, and their functions are generally very restricted. Just as international organizations are created by voluntary action, they also have to rely on

77

voluntary action to achieve their purposes. In this sense, international organizations are not autonomous political systems.

In the case of IGOs, sovereignty, as has already been noted, rests with states. States have the capacity for action: they can apprehend and punish individuals within their jurisdiction who break their rules; they can levy taxes; and they can compel their inhabitants to perform military service. International governmental organizations generally cannot do these things. Should they seek to do them, ordinarily they would rely on governments. In the few instances when IGOs can act directly on individuals, it is only on the basis of authority delegated by governments for strictly defined purposes. Since in the end governments will bear the responsibility for executing decisions made within IGOs, they tend to keep a tight rein on these decisions. However, many governments will not be significantly concerned with large categories of decisions adopted by the IGOs to which they belong, and consequently they may allow IGO officials considerable freedom in making these decisions. Another instance of apparent autonomy is that on occasion governments will establish broad parameters and then allow IGOs substantial leeway within these parameters. But IGOs ultimately derive their capacity for action from governments, and governments are crucial to their decision-making process.

The relationship between INGOs and their constituent national associations is similar to that between IGOs and national governments. INGOs that are constituted on the basis of individual memberships are somewhat different and could have greater autonomy. Such INGOs, however, are a minority. Moreover, the majority of individual members of these INGOs tend to regard their affiliation as secondary. For instance, most individuals who belong to international professional associations also belong to national organizations, and their primary commitment is to the latter.

The terminology most frequently used in international organizations reflects the basic lack of autonomy of the institutions. *Delegates* or *representatives* participate in *conferences* which adopt *resolutions*. These conferences and the organizations of which they are a part are serviced by *secretariats* headed by *secretaries-general*.

The lack of autonomy is also apparent in their budgetary arrangements. For instance, the General Assembly of the United Nations can apportion the expenses of the organization among member states, but should a member state fail to pay its assessed contribution, the only penalty that it could suffer is the loss of voting privileges in the assembly, and this could occur only when the state was more than two years in arrears.[1] Some international governmental organizations lack even this sanction, and others have virtually abandoned it by always excusing members who plead that their delinquency can be explained by extraordinary circumstances. Thus IGOs generally lack the financial resources available to national and subnational governments because they have no way of imposing taxes.

As if to underscore the control of member states over the activities of international governmental organizations, during the 1950s and 1960s the practice developed of financing a considerable proportion of these activities not from the organizations' regular budgets, which are based on so-called mandatory assessments, but from voluntary contributions. In the early 1980s more than 60 percent of the funds expended by the United Nations and its related agencies came from voluntary rather than assessed contributions. Table 5.1 shows expenditure of the various U.N. agencies and programs in 1981 and indicates whether the source of the funds is assessed or voluntary contributions. (Only those agencies and programs with the largest budgets are listed separately.) It is striking that some of the U.N.'s most prominent programs have been financed by voluntary contributions. These include peacekeeping and economic development activities as well as those concerned with food, population, and refugees. While governments may feel a moral commitment to contribute, they are legally free to discontinue their voluntary contributions to IGOs. In administering programs financed in this manner, IGO executives cannot risk ignoring the views of the major contributing states.

The lack of autonomy of international governmental organizations is also reflected in the fact that the funds available to them are relatively limited. In 1981 the regular budget of the United Nations totaled approximately $716 million, and the total amount available to the U.N. family of agencies was about $4.7 billion. The expenditures of the United States national government for the fiscal year 1981, which ran from October 1, 1980, through September 30, 1981, were roughly $655 billion. In other words, the funds available to the entire U.N. system were only about seven-tenths of 1 percent as large as those available to the United States national government. The budgets of the European communities are also small in comparison with those of their members. In 1980 the expenditures of the national governments of the nine member states of the communities totaled about $650 billion, while the receipts of the communities were roughly $28 billion, less than 5 percent of the former. Other international governmental organizations have even smaller budgets than the U.N. family and the European communities. The World Bank and the International Monetary Fund may disperse greater amounts of money annually, but since the largest share of their disbursements is in the form of loans, the expenditures of these agencies are not comparable with the expenditures of other IGOs.

Just as the budgets of international governmental organizations are minuscule in comparison with those of national governments, so are their staffs. In 1981 the United States federal government employed 2,896,000 individuals, and the U.N. family of agencies and programs about 42,000, or approximately 1.4 percent.

As small as they are compared with those available to the governments of major states, the budgets and bureaucracies of the agencies of the U.N. system and of the European communities far exceed those of other international organizations. In the 1960s the average budget of other IGOs was less than $8 million, and the average number of paid staff was about 150.[2] INGOs were even smaller. Their average budget in the 1960s was less than $1 million, and their average number of paid staff was less than ten. Although comparable data are not available for the 1970s, there is no reason to believe that the numbers would be significantly larger, either for budgets or personnel. What international organizations can do is sharply restricted because of the limited resources at their disposal.

Because of the lack of autonomy of international organizations, it is important in considering decision making in them to see how they are linked with the political systems of their constituent units, states in the case of IGOs and national associations in the case of most INGOs. The basic mechanism for the linkage is the representative subsystem, which is a subsystem both of the international organization and of the constituent units.[3] Delegates, delegations, and permanent missions to IGOs form one component of their representative subsystems. The bu-

TABLE 5.1

Expenditures of Agencies and Programs of the U.N. System, 1981,
from Assessed and Voluntary Contributions*
(Thousands of Dollars)

A. *Regular Budgets (Assessed)*	
United Nations	716,300
Food and Agriculture Organization	147,300
International Atomic Energy Agency	68,200
International Labor Organization	104,100
United Nations Educational, Scientific and Cultural Organization	176,900
World Health Organization	235,800
Other Specialized Agencies	127,700
Subtotal	1,576,300
B. *U.N. Peacekeeping Operations*	
United Nations Disengagement Observer Force and United Nations Interim	
Force in Lebanon (Assessed)	176,100
United Nations Force in Cyprus (Voluntary)	100,200
Subtotal	276,300
C. *Voluntary Programs*	
United Nations Children's Fund	311,000
United Nations Development Program	937,500
United Nations Capital Development Fund	50,200
United Nations Food and Agriculture Organization, World Food Program	578,000
United Nations Fund for Population Activities	138,000
United Nations High Commissioner for Refugees	365,400
Special Refugee Programs	118,300
United Nations Relief and Works Agency for Palestinian Refugees in the Near East	197,000
World Health Organization Special Programs	83,900
Other voluntary programs	97,900
Subtotal	2,877,200
GRAND TOTAL	4,729,800

*Agencies and programs with annual budgets of less than $50 million have not been listed separately but have been lumped together.

Source: U.S. Department of State, *United States Contributions to International Organizations: Report to the Congress for the Fiscal Year 1981* (Washington, D.C.: Government Printing Office, 1982).

reaucracies that draft the instructions for these delegates are another essential component. But others who participate in determining the policies that the states pursue in the IGOs must also be included. Depending on the issues involved, these other elements may include one or more of the following: the head of state, other ministries than those dealing with foreign affairs (for instance, the economic or the health ministry), the legislative body or members of it, and interest groups or their spokespersons. It is through these representative subsystems that limits are set on what international organizations can do, and it is through them that decisions taken in IGOs are transmitted back to states for implementation. Although the formal titles of the individuals would differ slightly, the representative subsystems of INGOs are similar. Representative subsystems will have an important place in our considerations because they are crucial to international organizations.

A TAXONOMY OF THE DECISIONS AND FUNCTIONS OF INTERNATIONAL ORGANIZATIONS

To show what international organizations do, it will be useful to develop a taxonomy of the types of functions of international organizations and of the decisions that relate to these functions. However, not all activities of international organizations will be of equal concern to us. These bodies spend a considerable—some might even say, an inordinate—amount of time deciding where meetings should be held and where buildings should be located; electing conference officials; and choosing states or individuals for places on councils, committees, and other such organs. Then too, salaries have to be set and contracts for purchases negotiated. Decisions like these that relate primarily to matters internal to organizations are not generally of great concern to us. We are mainly interested in the decisions of international organizations that relate to international public policy, decisions that have consequences for the distribution of values in the global political system. Of course, some internally oriented decisions have important consequences for external outputs. They may shape procedures, skewing influence so as to insure certain results. Thus we cannot completely ignore internally oriented decisions, but our interest in them stems primarily from their consequences for other types of decisions.

The Range of Functions

The policy output of international organizations is varied, though modest. IGOs and INGOs make information available. They collect, analyze, and publish data. Sometimes they merely serve a facilitative function, bringing together in one convenient place material that is already publicly available but in scattered locations throughout the world. On other occasions they produce new materials, sometimes based on new concepts. The League of Nations started a statistical service, which soon gained a reputation throughout the world for careful and useful work. The United Nations has continued this tradition and publishes a number of widely used statistical compilations, such as the *Statistical Yearbook*. Other international organizations have performed similar functions.

International organizations also help disseminate information by serving as forums where differing points of view may be exchanged. The annual discussion—or "confrontation," as it is sometimes called—of members' economic policies and plans that occurred from 1948 through 1960 in the Organization for European Economic Cooperation (OEEC) and was continued after 1960 in OEEC's successor, the Organization for Economic Cooperation and Development (OECD), is an example. Indeed, many INGOs do nothing more than promote the dissemination of information or facilitate its exchange. The principal activity of Amnesty International and the International Commission of Jurists is to publicize violations of human rights. INGOs in various professional fields have publications to disseminate the latest technical developments to their members.

Another category of output of international organizations consists of normative affirmations. International organizations adopt declarations of principles and statements of goals. One of the best known of these is the Universal Declaration of Human Rights, adopted by the United Nations in 1948. This document, which is contained in Appendix E, has been widely recognized as a comprehensive statement of the fundamental human rights of all human beings.

IGOs have frequently gone further and proposed or enacted rules for the conduct of states. For example, they may prepare treaties that will be binding on the states that ratify them. The International Labor Organization (ILO) has adopted more than 150 conventions concerning diverse aspects of working conditions, and the United Nations has adopted several conventions designed to promote human rights and the control of armaments. Tariff reductions agreed to in conferences of the General Agreement on Tariffs and Trade (GATT) are included in a protocol which then must be ratified by states. In exceptional cases IGOs may be given the authority in limited spheres to enact regulations that will be binding without any further action by states. For instance, the commission of the European Economic Community can establish antitrust regulations, and the assembly of the World Health Organization (WHO) can adopt regulations that are binding unless states reject them or lodge specific reservations within a limited period of time. A few INGOs, such as the International Air Transport Association, also formulate rules for the conduct of their constituent units.

International organizations are also charged with supervising compliance with rules. The International Atomic Energy Agency (IAEA) has responsibilities to see that fissile materials are not diverted for weapons purposes. The International Cycling Association regulates all forms of competitive cycling.

Finally, international organizations make decisions about the allocation of the resources at their disposal. The International Monetary Fund (IMF) and the International Bank for Reconstruction and Development (IBRD) make loans. The United Nations Development Program (UNDP) must assign fellowships and technical assistance experts. The North Atlantic Treaty Organization (NATO) and the Warsaw Treaty Organization (WTO) make decisions about the deployment of military forces, and from time to time the U.N. has had to do so. The Oxford Committee for Famine Relief, which was founded in 1942 and since 1965 has been known as OXFAM, in the early 1980s allocated some $35 million annually for development and relief activities, and several other INGOs engage in similar activities.

These functions of international organizations can be grouped into five major categories: informational, normative, rule-creating, rule-supervisory, and operational.

Informational functions involve the gathering, analysis, exchange, and dissemination of data and points of view. The organization may use its staff for these purposes, or it may merely provide a forum where representatives from constituent units can do these things.

Normative functions involve the definition and declaration of standards. This function does not involve instruments that have legally binding effect, but rather proclamations that are designed to affect the milieu in which domestic and world politics are conducted.

Rule-creating functions similarly involve the definition and declaration of standards; however, the purpose is to frame instruments than can have a legally binding effect. In the case of IGOs, to have legally binding effect, such instruments usually must be signed and ratified by some number of member states, and the instruments generally apply only to those states that have taken such action. In a few IGOs, however, some decisions can be taken that are legally binding without the necessity of implementing action by the member states. Several INGOs can adopt rules that are binding for the constituent units.

Rule-supervisory functions involve measures taken to insure compliance with the rules that are in force by those subject to them. This function could entail several steps, ranging from detection of evidence that a violation had occurred, through verification of that evidence, to the imposition of sanctions.[4]

Operational functions involve the use of the resources at the organization's disposal. Financial and technical assistance and the deployment of military forces are examples.

This list is intended to provide a comprehensive typology of functions. Hardly any international organization actually performs all five, and many concentrate on only one or two. Nevertheless, international organizations may take decisions relating to each of the five categories of functions. International organizations must also make decisions about which functions to undertake and the balance among the functions they do undertake. These may be called *programmatic* decisions. And, as we have already noted, international organizations also make decisions about the formal allocation of power and authority within their structures. These may be called *representational* decisions. In all, then, seven types of decisions may be taken within international organizations. Both because of formal procedures and informal practices, different patterns of decision making frequently prevail for different types of decisions.

Distinguishing Functions and Decisions

The discussion thus far has mixed functions and decisions without too much concern for either legal or logical niceties. Now some distinctions must be made. Functions involve actions, doing something. Certain decisions may be included within this concept of functions. For instance, when the United Nations General Assembly adopted the Universal Declaration of Human Rights, it engaged in a normative function. Other decisions of the General Assembly—for instance, to undertake and publish a study of the economic consequences of disarmament— merely involve a commitment to engage in a function. The function itself may be carried out by a different organ.

The U.N. charter empowers the General Assembly to adopt resolutions. Such resolutions are decisions, but not all decisions of the U.N.—as the term is used here—are embodied in resolutions. Similarly, while the U.N. often performs functions by adopting resolutions, it performs functions in other ways as well. For instance, a U.N. secretariat official could decide to award a fellowship, which would be an operational function, and the decision would be taken by the secretariat offical under the authority of a resolution adopted by the General As- sembly. Finally, it must be stressed that rule-creating decisions of the General As- sembly involve the adoption of conventions that must be ratified by national governments before they take effect.

These statements about the United Nations would apply to most international organizations. The most significant exception is that the institutions of the Euro- pean communities can adopt regulations that are self-executing and conse- quently have the direct effect of law in every member state. Even in this case, though, national governments and courts must enforce the communities' regula- tions.

THE STRUCTURE OF INTERNATIONAL ORGANIZATIONS

The basic institutional features of international organizations—assemblies, councils, secretaries-general, and secretariats—have already been alluded to. Now they must be examined in detail.

Constitutional Documents

IGOs are generally created by treaties that set out the structures to be estab- lished. These treaties also specify the basic procedures for decision making, and sometimes they establish doctrines to guide the institutions' decisions and rules to govern the conduct of members. We have already noted how the U.N.'s charter outlawed the use of force against the territorial integrity or political indepen- dence of any states.[5] The charter of the Organization of American States (OAS) prohibits individual or collective intervention in the internal or external affairs of any other state.[6] The original articles of agreement of the International Monetary

Fund postulated the goals of fixed exchange rates for all members' currencies and unrestricted multilateral convertibility.[7] The treaty establishing the European Economic Community committed the member states to eliminate tariffs among themselves on industrial goods within fifteen years from its coming into force.[8] A cynic might observe that at least some of these obligations have been honored mainly in the breach. The point is that the constitutional documents of IGOs, like those of states, frequently go beyond creating institutions and try to establish principles to govern conduct. These principles at least create an agenda for decision making and sometimes establish an ideological atmosphere within which decision making must be conducted.

The constitutions of INGOs are usually like international treaties; they are formal documents that the constituent units of the INGOs negotiate and accept. Like the constitutions of IGOs, those of INGOs, in addition to specifying institutional structures, often proclaim norms designed to guide the conduct of members.

Some IGOs have been created by decisions taken in other IGOs. The United Nations Children's Fund (which still uses the acronym UNICEF derived from its original name, the United Nations International Children's Emergency Fund), the United Nations Conference on Trade and Development (UNCTAD), and the United Nations Industrial Development Organization (UNIDO) were all created by U.N. General Assembly resolutions. One important difference between the two modes is that when the constitutional document of an IGO is embodied in a treaty, the more powerful states have somewhat greater leverage in shaping the institution according to their desires. Their participation will probably be necessary to achieve the aim of the organization, and their bargaining position is strengthened by the knowledge that they could refuse to sign or ratify the treaty. They are in a somewhat weaker position with respect to a resolution of a body that is already in existence. Not surprisingly, the structures of UNCTAD and UNIDO are considerably more populist than those of several universal membership, specific purpose organizations created by treaties.

A few INGOs have also created other INGOs. For instance, the International Statistical Institute created three more or less autonomous bodies—the International Association of Municipal Statisticians, the International Association for Statistics in Physical Sciences, and the International Association of Survey Statisticians.

The basic constitutional documents of IGOs make provisions for amendments, and the most frequent use made of these provisions has been to alter structural features.[9] In the wake of the decolonization of the 1960s, and the sudden and substantial increases in their memberships, most of the universal membership organizations adopted amendments increasing the size of some of their smaller bodies, such as councils and commissions. Changes not involving structure have more frequently come about as a consequence of practice. An example is the shift in the relative importance in the United Nations of the Security Council and the General Assembly. When the Security Council was stymied because of the inability of the five permanent members to achieve the unanimity that the charter required for decisions, the General Assembly increasingly took action on matters that would have seemed, according to the charter, to be the exclusive preserve of the Security Council. There is a general tendency for organs with more inclusive membership to seek the prerogatives assigned to those with less inclusive membership. This has happened in most of the U.N.'s specialized agencies. Because of the provisions of the charter, however, in the 1970s, after the tide of decolonization and in the atmosphere of Soviet-American detente, the Security Council was able to regain some of its former importance in relation to the General Assembly.

Structural Features

However they were created, international organizations tend to have similar structures. Without exception they have a conference or an assembly in which all states or constituent units are represented. Those with large memberships tend to have one or more smaller bodies—usually called councils or boards—with certain specified tasks. Frequently other tasks can be delegated by the all-inclusive assembly to these smaller bodies. In some IGOs, particularly those with limited membership, the term "council" may be used to designate the body in which all member states are represented, but we shall use it here only for less-inclusive organs. To service the meetings of these bodies and carry out other designated activities, bureaus, offices, and secretariats or staffs have been created, and these are usually headed by one person, designated as secretary-general or director-general. Occasionally secretariats are headed by corporate groups. A few IGOs and an even smaller number of INGOs also have judicial bodies. All frequently create temporary organs, such as ad hoc committees, working parties, and expert groups, and they convene conferences. The only IGOs that differ substantially from this broad pattern are those that have been characterized as supranational, the European communities. The ways in which they differ are of considerable interest, but the importance of these differences will be clearer after we consider the institutions that conform to the general pattern.

The assemblies of IGOs are usually based on the international law doctrine of the sovereign equality of states. In conformity with this doctrine, each state is entitled to equal representation and usually to equal voting power, hence the axiom "one state, one vote." Only a few IGOs have deviated from this principle. In the International Monetary Fund and in the World Bank and its affiliated institutions, the International Development Association (IDA) and the International Finance Corporation (IFC), the voting power of member states is weighted according to their financial contributions. Voting is also weighted in the Council of Ministers of the European communities. For many types of decisions, the Federal Republic of Germany, France, Italy, and the United Kingdom each have ten votes, Belgium, Greece and the Netherlands five, Denmark and Ireland, three, and Luxembourg two. Forty-five affirmative votes are required for a decision to be taken. The weighting roughly accords with the size of the states' populations. Virtually all IGO assemblies are composed of representatives of governments, but in the International Labor Organization employers and workers organizations are also represented.

The assemblies of INGOs too have been affected by the doctrine of sovereign equality. Usually INGOs will allow only one national association from each state to hold membership, and more often than not each state's national association will have one vote in the assembly. Some INGOs have systems of proportional representation. For instance, representation in the congress of the International Confederation of Trade Unions (ICFTU) is based on the number of members a national trade union has, with unions having ten million members or more being given a maximum of twenty delegates.

The doctrine of sovereign equality could also be interpreted to mean that decisions must be made unanimously, and that was the rule in the League of Nations and continues to be the rule in the councils of OECD, CMEA (Council for Mutual Economic Assistance), NATO, and WTO and in other IGOs. Many IGOs and most INGOs, however, now require only a simple or a qualified majority, and even those that require unanimity usually interpret only negative votes as preventing decisions, not abstentions or absences.

The list of IGOs that either have weighted voting or require unanimity clearly indicates a strong relationship between the importance of the subject matter and the authority of the IGO on the one hand and the formal skewing influence on the other. Having a weighted voting scheme and requiring a qualified majority can mean that the concurrence of certain key states is a formal precondition for decisions. As a practical matter, since IGOs have had little success in compelling powerful member states to take actions that they oppose, even without weighted voting or other special provisions, the concurrence of key states is always a precondition for decisions that require the use of their resources. Rather than submit to majority rule in the council of the European Economic Community in 1965-1966, France blocked progress in all areas of EEC activity and threatened to disrupt the system permanently. Such obstinacy can bring substantial concessions to the point of view of the recalcitrant state, and in this instance it did. Since 1966, despite formal majority rule in the European communities, member states have a veto in matters that they perceive would affect their vital interests.

Finally, the doctrine of sovereign equality usually requires that, in legal theory at least, ultimate authority should be vested in the organ where all member states or constituent units are represented; this applies particularly to budgetary matters.

Assemblies normally meet at specified intervals. The usual pattern is annual or biannual meetings, but some assemblies meet more frequently and others less frequently. The U.N. General Assembly meets regularly every fall, the conference of ILO every spring, and UNESCO's general conference every other year. The commission of the Central Commission for the Navigation of the Rhine meets twice a year, but since World War II sessions of the plenipotentiary conference of the International Telecommunication Union (ITU) have been convened at average intervals of more than six years. Congresses of the International Confederation of Free Trade Unions are held every three years, and the congress of the

World Federation of Trade Unions (WFTU) meets every four years. Some IGOs vary the composition of their meetings. The Organization of African Unity (OAU) holds one meeting of heads of states and governments each year and two meetings of foreign ministers. Almost all assemblies can be convened for extraordinary sessions, and extraordinary sessions of IGO assemblies can be convened easily and very rapidly when governments maintain permanent representatives at the headquarters site.

The practice of having permanent representatives and missions at the headquarters of IGOs started in Geneva during the days of the League of Nations. Now almost all states maintain permanent missions in New York at the headquarters of the U.N. and in Geneva, where the headquarters of several specialized agencies and the European office of the United Nations are located. Several states also maintain permanent missions in many other locations, particularly at the headquarters of important regional organizations. All of the member states of the European communities, and several nonmember states as well, maintain permanent representatives in Brussels. Permanent representation is essential for assemblies being in permanent session, as are NATO's council and several other bodies.

Councils or boards are a second organ common to international organizations. The councils of IGOs, like their assemblies, are usually composed of representatives of states, normally governmental delegates, but employer and worker delegates are also included in ILO's governing body. The difference between assemblies and councils is that while all member states are represented in the former, only some are represented in the latter. The method of choosing states for representation in councils varies. Sometimes it is simply done on the basis of election by the assembly. Often, however, the constitutional document creating the organization specifies at least part of the membership. China, France, the Soviet Union, the United Kingdom, and the United States are designated in the U.N. charter as permanent members of the Security Council,[10] and the constitution of the International Labor Organization requires that the ten member states of "chief industrial importance" be represented on the governing body.[11] By specifying criteria rather than naming states, ILO's formula allows changes over time.

Even when there are not specific constitutional provisions requiring it, the most powerful states tend to be chosen again and again for membership on councils. Clearly their cooperation is thought to be essential for achieving the purposes of the organization. WHO is unusual among IGOs in that members of its executive board are elected as individuals rather than as representatives of states. The practice of electing individuals as council members rather than electing constituent units, which would in turn designate individuals to represent them, is more common among INGOs.

Councils almost invariably meet more frequently than assemblies. They tend to have responsibility for overseeing the administrative aspects of their organizations. Frequently they have the power to nominate the secretary-general, even though the election of this official is the responsibility of the assembly. Sometimes they even have the power of election, although in practice the right of nomination usually amounts to that. Constitutions frequently give councils special powers. In the United Nations, only the Security Council can order the deployment of military force. Assemblies also often delegate powers to councils. This has been done frequently in the World Bank and the International Monetary Fund. In both agencies most policy issues are settled by the respective boards of executive directors. Councils are a recognition that smaller groups tend to be more efficient decision-making bodies than larger ones. They also contravene the doctrine of sovereign equality by giving those states or constituent units that are members greater opportunity for influence than those that are represented only in the assemblies.

Secretariats are a third common organ. Originally they were created to service conferences—to make the necessary physical arrangements, record debates and decisions, prepare documentation, and provide translation facilities. Although these and similar activities remain an important part of the duties of secretariats, in some international organizations their responsibilities have become much broader. Secretariats now have roles in all five of the categories of functions of international organizations.

The Department of Economic and Social Affairs of the U.N. Secretariat prepares the annual *World Economic Survey*, and many other secretariats of international organizations gather, analyze, and publish data on their own responsibility. Publications are a principal activity of INGOs, and secretariats do most of the work involved. Many of the hortatory resolutions that have been adopted at the periodic UNCTAD conferences were based on preliminary papers prepared by the secretariat, and this is also true in other IGOs. The ILO Office (secretariat) writes preliminary drafts of conventions, and it gathers and publishes information about the implementation of conventions in various states. The staffs of the IBRD and IMF do most of the negotiation of the terms of the loans that are granted by these agencies, and UNDP officials select, assign, and give policy guidance to technical assistance experts in the field. UNDP officials also do the preliminary screening of project proposals and establish the technical requirements for these projects. The secretariats of ICFTU and WFTU have organized training courses for labor leaders. These examples could be multiplied several times. In view of their substantial responsibilities, it is not surprising that the personnel of many IGO secretariats now number in the thousands, and that the secretariats of a few INGOs now exceed fifty paid staff. Perhaps it is more surprising that so few do so much.

Staffing Secretariats

Early secretariats were frequently composed of nationals of the state in which an organization's headquarters was located. It was not long, however, before virtually all secretariats were internationalized. Now most constitutions of IGOs specify that in recruiting staff, even though efficiency should be a prime consideration, attention should also be paid to obtaining broad geographical representation in the secretariat. The constitutions of many INGOs contain similar provisions.

Geographic, political, and ideological considerations become particularly important in the appointment of higher-level officials. Thus in the United Nations, even though the secretary-general has always been the national of a smaller country, nationals of the permanent members of the Security Council are always included among the under and assistant secretaries-general. The president of the International Bank for Reconstruction and Development has always been a citizen of the United States, while the managing director of the International Monetary Fund has always been a Western European national. NATO's supreme allied commanders in Europe and the Atlantic have always been United States military officers, just as the supreme commander of the joint armed forces of the Warsaw Treaty Organization has always been a Soviet military officer. Many other examples of the reservation of key positions in the secretariats of international organizations for citizens of particular countries could be cited.

As secretariats of IGOs developed, so did the doctrine of the international civil service. This doctrine, which has been articulated by international officials and academic writers, was based on an understanding of the British civil service. According to this view, the British civil service impartially and loyally served the government of the day; composed on a career basis, it implemented policies that were determined by elected officials. In a similar fashion the secretariat of an IGO was seen as the servant of all of the member states, not of any particular state or group of states. In keeping with this view, members of secretariats customarily pledge not to seek or to receive instructions from governments, and the governments of member states are adjured not to seek to influence secretariat officials in the performance of their duties.[12] These elemental principles seem to be so logically essential to the functioning of the secretariat of an international governmental organization as to be self-evident, and generally they have been honored. Beyond these basic principles, however, the matter becomes more complex.

Some writers have maintained that to insure their impartiality members of secretariats should have permanent contracts. Others have argued that this is not necessary and that advantages can be gained from having a regular turnover in the staff of a secretariat. This is a way, they maintain, of keeping the scientific proficiency of the staff at a high level, and the largest portion of the staff in IGOs that work in technical fields, such as the World Health Organization and the International Atomic Energy Agency, have term contracts. The argument is that the work of an international governmental organization is largely administrative and that technical specialists performing such tasks will soon fall behind in their field; to maintain their expertise they need contact with operations, something that few IGOs can provide. Another argument for term appointments is that IGOs can benefit from having alumni from their secretariats working in bureaucracies of member states.[13] Consciously or unconsciously, this strategy seems to have been employed by the North Atlantic Treaty Organization: there has been frequent and regular circulation between the NATO secretariat and the defense ministries.

Another complicated and controversial issue is how much attention should be paid to nationality. Constitutions tend to require that secretariats be recruited on a wide geographical basis. But what exactly should this mean? The most powerful states, on which IGOs depend for support, have without exception required that some of their nationals be included among the higher-level staff of the organizations to which they belong. In the 1960s, in response to pressures particularly from the African states that had just gained sovereignty and joined IGOs, the concept that secretariats should include at least a few nationals from each member state and that beyond this the number of nationals holding secretariat posts should be roughly proportional to their state's financial contribution gained considerable acceptance among the agencies in the U.N. system. Although the new states contributed only a minuscule proportion of the budgets of the U.N. agencies, this principle still gave them a claim on more positions than they held at the outset.

Some states, particularly the United States and the Soviet Union, have insisted that their nationals serving in secretariats should be loyal to the regime. United States citizens must be processed under Executive Order 10422 before being appointed to a position in the secretariat of an international governmental organization. Under this executive order the U.S. Civil Service Commission must make a negative or affirmative determination about the loyalty to the United States of the individual involved, and this determination is given to the executive head of the IGO concerned. Presumably the United States government would be deeply distressed if an executive head insisted on appointing an individual whom the Civil Service Commission determined was not loyal to the United States. From 1953 until 1975 the Commission's determination was based on a full field investigation; since then only a national agency check has been involved, unless that check yields derogatory information, in which case a full field investigation is undertaken. The U.S.S.R. nominates its citizens for U.N. appointments and in practice allows them to accept only fixed term appointments. Governments throughout the world are far from willing to accept the idea that the secretariat of an international governmental organization would be impartial, regardless of how it were composed. Instead, they feel much more confident when at least some of their own nationals are included among the personnel.

The Role of Executive Heads

The secretariats of international organizations tend to be headed by a single individual, who is usually designated secretary-general or director-general. The title "managing director" is also used, and academic writers frequently prefer "executive head" as a generic term. Executive heads are generally elected through votes of one or more of the representative bodies of the organization for fixed terms of four or five years. Some executive heads have been reelected one or more times, so that their total tenure in office may even exceed twenty years.

Elected to office at about the same time, Sir Eric Drummond, the first secretary-general of the League of Nations, and Albert Thomas, the first director-general of the International Labor Organization, have often been characterized as representing two opposite conceptions of the role of the executive head of an international organization. Drummond has been portrayed as being inspired by the traditions of the British civil service, keeping himself and the secretariat as much as possible in the background, distrusting enthusiasm, and avoiding responsibility.[14] Thomas, on the other hand, saw his task as that of providing articulate and dynamic leadership.[15] In fact, the contrast is overdrawn. Certainly there were substantial differences in the styles of the two men. Drummond came from the British civil service. Thomas came from the French labor movement, and he had been actively involved in French politics. As executive heads of their respective agencies, both continued the habits that they had developed in their earlier careers.

Whatever style an executive head might adopt, the constitutional powers of the office are usually limited. Executive heads can appoint the secretariat and oversee its work. They usually have the responsibility of making reports to the representative bodies of the organization and sometimes have the right of introducing agenda items.[16] Other formal powers that executive heads may have tend to be delegated to them by representative bodies, which may also retract them. The extent to which powers have been delegated varies substantially with the organization, the function, and the historical period. It would be correct to state as a general rule that the greater the delegation of authority, the less important and less controversial the issue.

The number of international organizations that do not conform to the pattern of having a single executive head is small. The International Telecommunication Union (ITU) has several elected officials heading different sections of its staff. The European communities are, however, probably the most significant exception. They are headed by a commission, which has substantial powers conferred by the EEC, Euratom, and ECSC treaties. The commission consists of fourteen members, no more than two of whom may be of the same nationality. By common agreement France, the Federal Republic of Germany, Italy, and the United Kingdom each have two nationals as members of the commission, and Belgium, Denmark, Greece, Ireland, Luxembourg, and the Netherlands each have one. These individuals are nominated by their governments, and to be renominated after the conclusion of their four-year terms, they must retain the confidence of their governments.[17]

In the midst of the Congo imbroglio, and as part of his attack on the person and policies of Dag Hammarskjold, Nikita Khrushchev, chairman of the Council of Ministers and first secretary of the Communist Party of the Soviet Union, proposed that henceforth the secretariat of the United Nations should be headed by three individuals, one each from Western, Socialist, and neutral states. This "troika" proposal, as it was called, was anathema to those states that had backed Hammarskjold's policy in the Congo crisis, and it was roundly defeated. But the "troika" proposal and the commission of the European communities show the difficulty that governments have, in the world of sovereign nation-states, in accepting the proposition that a single individual should be entrusted with power to make decisions that could have significant consequences.

Judicial Organs

This same hesitancy is evident with respect to judicial bodies. Very few international governmental organizations have judicial arms. To allow a matter to be settled by adjudication is a more substantial renunciation of the ability to influence the outcome than to agree that it should be submitted to a representative body for consideration and discussion. In those instances where international governmental organizations have a judicial organ, it is invariably a collective body. The Court of Justice of the European communities is composed of eleven judges (which insures that there will be one from each member country), while the International Court of Justice (ICJ), a principal organ of the United Nations, has fifteen judges. Significantly, the statute of the ICJ allows judges having the nationality of one of the parties to a case before the court to sit in that case, and also provides that if the bench contains a judge of the nationality of one of the parties, any other party may choose a person to sit as judge in that case. If the court includes upon the bench no judge of the nationality of the parties, each of these parties may proceed to choose a judge.[18] Such specially appointed judges are added to the bench for the particular case. Governments are apparently far from convinced that there are not national points of view with respect to the interpretation of international law.

The only prominent INGO that has a judicial body is the International Chamber of Commerce (ICC). The Court of International Arbitration of the ICC was established to facilitate the quick settlement of business disputes among individuals and organizations residing in different countries.

The typical institutional structure of an international governmental organization, then, would include an assembly composed of representatives of all of the member states, one or more smaller councils composed of fewer of the member states, and a secretariat under the direction of an executive head. Figure 5.1 portrays the structure of the United Nations. The U.N.'s structure is somewhat atypical in that there is a judicial organ, the International Court of Justice, and there are several permanent councils—the Security Council, the Economic and Social Council, and the Trusteeship Council. In addition, several other IGOs are attached to the U.N. The basic institutions of the United Nations, however, are those that IGOs generally have.

The European Communities

Many of the structural features that differentiate the European communities from other international governmental organizations have already been alluded to. Now it is time to examine them more systematically and also bring out the other points of difference.

FIGURE 5.1
The Structure of the United Nations, 1983.

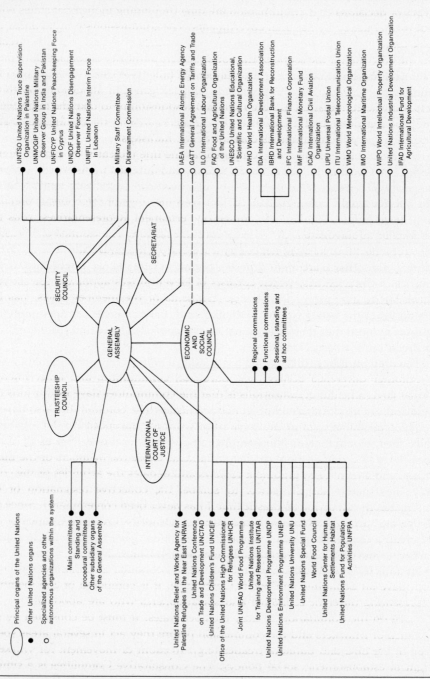

One of the most substantial differences between the communities and other IGOs is that community institutions have considerably greater power. Certain types of decisions of the commission are directly binding in member states without further action by national governments. The commission's powers under the EEC and Euratom treaties are not as profound as they are under the ECSC treaty; on the other hand, the scope of the commission's authority is considerably more extensive under the EEC treaty than under the other two treaties. Under the EEC and Euratom treaties, final decisions are the prerogative of the Council of Ministers, but the commission has the right and responsibility to take the initiative in proposing actions, and the Council of Ministers can alter the commission's proposals only by the unanimous consent of the ministers.

The Council of Ministers is composed, as the title indicates, of cabinet ministers. The council meets about once a month, and different ministers (e.g., of foreign affairs, agriculture, economics, transportation) participate depending on the subject matter being considered. Between meetings of the council, preparatory work is done by the Committee of Permanent Representatives; thus the council or its surrogate is in virtually constant session. The Council of Ministers has a secretariat of its own, headed by a secretary-general. Decisions of the council in specified fields are binding in the member states. The Court of Justice of the European communities, which consists of eleven judges appointed for six-year terms by common accord of the governments of the member states, has the power to review the legislation and actions of the organs of the communities and of member states to insure that they are in conformity with the treaties. In no other IGO do institutions have as significant power as do the commission, the Council of Ministers, and the Court of Justice.

Another difference between the European communities and other international governmental organizations is that the communities have institutions not found elsewhere. The Court of Justice is unusual. The communities also have as an integral part of their institutional framework the European Parliament. Since 1979 the 434 members of the European Parliament have been chosen by direct election. Before that date, national parliaments chose the members of the European Parliament. The Parliament reviews and debates the activities of the communities, and it has the power to compel the collective resignation of the commission—an action so drastic that it has never been contemplated. Since the 1970s the Parliament has also had budgetary authority. Only the Council of Europe has a comparable body—the Consultative Assembly—and both the organization's and the organ's powers are much less substantial.

In addition to the Parliament, the European Economic Community and Euratom have an Economic and Social Committee. It is composed of 156 members representing different economic and social spheres who are appointed by the council on the nomination of their member states. It must be consulted by the Council of Ministers and the commission before they act in several areas specified in the EEC and Euratom treaties (e.g., freedom of movement for workers, right of establishment, social policy). The Consultative Committee is a similar body for ECSC. These institutions reflect the corporatist strain in European po-

FIGURE 5.2
The Institutions of the European Communities, 1983

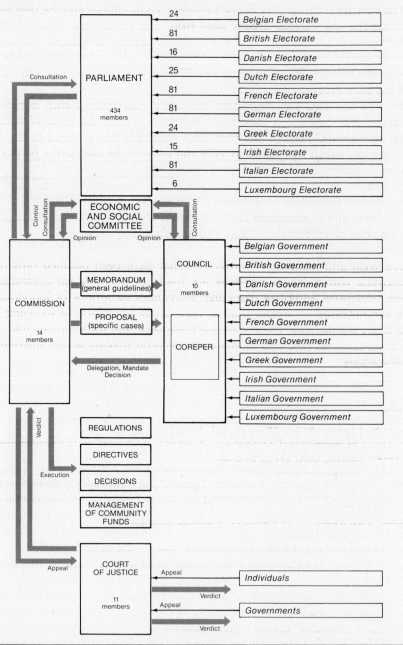

Source: European Communities Commission, *The Courier: European Community-Africa-Caribbean-Pacific*, No. 48 (March–April 1978), p. 36, modified to reflect subsequent changes.

litical thought. The European Investment Bank is another unusual institution of the communities.

The structural complexity of the European communities and the delicate balance among the various organs stem from and reflect how much authority hitherto exercised only by the governments of states was assigned through the three treaties to a supranational level. The treaties created unusually powerful international governmental organizations. The structure of the European communities is portrayed in Figure 5.2.

Because the EEC has negotiated association agreements with nonmember states, several institutions have been created to oversee the implementation of these agreements. Perhaps the most important are those related to the Lomé Convention, which was signed in 1975 and governs the association between the European Economic Community and the African, Caribbean, and Pacific states. (The Lomé Convention replaced earlier agreements between the EEC and these states.) There is a council of ministers (composed of members of the EEC Council of Ministers and Commission and ministers of the sixty-three associated states), a committee of ambassadors, and a consultative assembly.

The legal and institutional provisions that have been outlined provide the framework within which decisions are made in international organizations. These provisions authorize particular individuals or groups of individuals to take certain types of action; that is, they define authority. In so doing, they also shape interactions. Understanding these legal and institutional characteristics is an essential first step to analyzing decision making within international organizations.

NOTES

1. U.N. Charter, Article 17, paragraph 2, and Article 19.
2. Union of International Associations, *Yearbook of International Organizations*, Vol. 15, 1974 (Brussels, UIA, 1974), p. S 35.
3. This concept and many others in this chapter are drawn from a collective investigation in which I participated and to which I gratefully acknowledge my intellectual debts. The results of the investigation have been published in Robert W. Cox and Harold K. Jacobson, and Gerard Curzon, Victoria Curzon, Joseph S. Nye, James P. Sewell, and Susan Strange, *The Anatomy of Influence: Decision Making in International Organization* (New Haven: Yale University Press, 1973).
4. The stages outlined here are drawn from Fred C. Iklé, *Alternative Approaches to the International Organization of Disarmament* (Santa Monica, Calif.: RAND Corporation, 1962).
5. Chapter 1, Article 2, paragraph 4.
6. Article 15.
7. Articles 4 and 8.
8. Title 1. Chapter 1, Section 1, and Chapter 2.
9. See Leland M. Goodrich, Edward Hambro, and Anne Patricia Simons, *Charter of the United Nations: Commentary and Documents* (New York: Columbia University Press, 1969), pp. 641–647; and Lester H. Phillips, "Constitutional Revision in the Specialized Agencies," *The American Journal of International Law*, 62 (July 1968), 654–678.

10. Article 23.

11. Article 7.

12. Such commitments are contained in Article 100 of the U.N. Charter.

13. See David A. Kay, "Secondment in the United Nations Secretariat: An Alternative View," *International Organization*, 20 (Winter 1966), 63–75.

14. See F. P. Walters, *A History of the League of Nations* (London: Oxford University Press, 1952), p. 559.

15. See E. J. Phelan, *Yes and Albert Thomas* (London: Cresset Press, 1936).

16. U.N. Charter, Article 99. The secretary-general of the United Nations has the authority to "bring to the attention of the Security Council any matter which in his opinion may threaten the maintenance of international peace and security."

17. See Roy Pryce, *The Poliltics of the European Community* (London: Butterworths, 1973), p. 62.

18. Article 31.

FOR FURTHER READING

Bowett, D. W. *The Law of International Institutions.* London: Stevens and Sons, 2nd ed. 1970.

Goodrich, Leland M., Edward Hambro, and Anne Patricia Simons. *Charter of the United Nations: Commentary and Documents.* New York: Columbia University Press, 1969.

Keesing's International Publications. *Treaties and Alliance of the World: An International Survey Concerning Treaties in Force and Communities of States.* New York: Scribner, 1968.

Kirgis, Frederic L., Jr. *International Organizations: Their Legal Setting, Documents, Comments and Questions.* St. Paul: West Publishing, 1981.

Meron, Theodor. *The United Nations Secretariat.* Lexington, Mass.: D. C. Heath, 1977.

Peaslee, Amos J. (prepared by Dorothy Peaslee Sydis). *International Governmental Organizations: Constitutional Documents.* 6 vols. The Hague: Martinus Nijhoff, 1974–1976.

Robertson, A. H. *European Institutions: Cooperation, Integration, Unification.* London: Stevens and Sons, 3rd ed. 1973.

Schermers, Henry G. *International Institutional Law.* 2 vols. Leyden: A. W. Sijthoff, 1972.

Stein, Eric, Peter Hay, and Michael Waelbroeck. *European Community Law and Institutions in Perspective.* 2 vols. Indianapolis: Bobbs Merrill, 1976.

Stosic, Borko D. *Les organisations non gouvernmentales et les nations unies.* Genève: Librarie Droz, 1964.

Szawlowski, Richard. *The System of International Organizations of the Communist Countries.* Leyden: A. W. Sijthoff, 1976.

White, Lyman Cromwell. *International Non-governmental Organizations: Their Purposes, Methods, and Accomplishments.* New Brunswick, N.J.: Rutgers University Press, 1951.

Wionczek, Miguel S. (ed.) *Economic Cooperation in Latin America, Africa, and Asia: A Handbook of Documents.* Cambridge: M.I.T. Press, 1969.

6

THE PARTICIPANTS IN DECISION MAKING: THEIR INFLUENCE AND INTERACTIONS

Having discussed the basic legal features and the institutional structures of international governmental organizations, we may now shift our attention to the individuals who participate in these institutions, to consider their capabilities, sources of power, and influence, and to analyze how they interact.

THE DRAMATIS PERSONAE

For purposes of formal analysis, the individuals who participate in decision making in international organizations can be grouped into seven broad categories:

1. *Governmental representatives.* This category includes delegates of states to assemblies and councils and their deputies and assistants, representatives of states in ad hoc committees and other bodies, and officials of states who in their official capacity have contact with international organizations without being formally appointed as delegates or members of committees.

2. *Representatives of private associations.* As used here, the term "private associations" includes national and international nongovernmental organizations, transnational organizations, and some national enterprises. This category includes employer and worker delegates in the International Labor Organization and representatives of enterprises in the international consultative committees of the International Telecommunication Union. It also includes the representatives of INGOs who participate in the decision-making processes of IGOs as a consequence of consultative relationships. Finally, and most importantly, it includes the representatives of national as-

sociations who generally make up the assemblies and councils of INGOs. These individuals play the same role within INGOs as representatives of states play in IGOs.

3. *Representatives of international governmental organizations.* This category consists of officials of IGOs who represent their IGO in another IGO or in an INGO or who participate in the performance of functions conducted by more than one IGO.

4. *Executive heads.* The secretaries-general and directors-general of international organizations constitute the bulk of this category, which also includes the members of collective executive bodies, such as the commission of the European communities and the board of the Andean group.

5. *Members of secretariats.* This category consists of the staff members of international organizations.

6. *Individuals acting in their own capacity.* This category is made up of the individuals who are appointed in their own right to expert and ad hoc committees or other such bodies of international organizations. It also includes members of arbitral tribunals and courts.

7. *Publicists.* Persons employed by the mass media may affect decision making in international organizations by the way they report events or by their commentaries. Others who observe international organizations and have access to wide audiences—authors, public speakers, television personalities, and so on—can similarly affect decision making in international organizations. All individuals with this capacity are included in this category.

Not all of these categories of actors are involved in every decision in every international organization, but this list does cover reasonably well the variety of individuals who could be involved.

GOVERNMENTAL REPRESENTATIVES

Governmental representatives can play a role as observers or consultants in INGOs, but their more prominent role—on which our analysis will concentrate—is in IGOs. Since there are more than 150 states and several hundred international governmental organizations, many with two or more representative bodies, governmental representatives to IGOs obviously exhibit considerable differences. Some generalizations, however, are possible.

The Role of Delegate

As an initial point, governmental representatives are—in legal theory at least—just that. The title "delegate" is significant. Governmental representatives are agents of their governments and act on their behalf. They are not—again, at least in legal theory—free to act as they themselves might choose, but instead are charged with the responsibility of presenting and upholding the positions of their governments. Reality, of course, is considerably more complex than legal theory. The extent to which governmental representatives will be bound by detailed instructions varies with the individuals in question, their position, their state, the IGO, and the issue under consideration. Furthermore, delegates, like most diplomats, generally have an opportunity to influence the drafting of their instructions.

Sometimes heads of government serve as delegates. They would clearly be expected to have considerably more latitude than junior bureaucrats, but even heads of government may be bound by understandings reached with their colleagues or by limits that they know other governmental organs, such as legislatures, will not allow them to exceed. Cabinet ministers, who serve regularly as delegates to the Council of Ministers of the European communities and often participate in other IGOs, are in a similar position. Frequently members of the permanent missions that states maintain at the headquarters of IGOs serve as delegates. As the scope of IGO activity has broadened, increasing numbers of delegates have been drawn from government ministries other than foreign affairs—economics, health, transportation, and the like. Lower ranking officials, other things being equal, usually have less discretion than their superiors. However, who the individual is may make a difference.

The United States has often been represented at the United Nations by individuals who had considerable domestic political standing in their own right, such as Henry Cabot Lodge, Adlai Stevenson, Arthur J. Goldberg, and Andrew Young. Although these men held the rank of ambassador, they also sat in the cabinet. On one occasion, when Lodge voted "no" although his instructions had been to vote "yes," Robert D. Murphy, the assistant secretary of state for international organization affairs, called to remonstrate with him about this failure to follow instructions. Lodge retorted, "Instructions? I am a member of the President's Cabinet and accept instructions only from him." Murphy countered, "You are head of an embassy and our ambassadors take instructions from the Secretary of State." To which Lodge replied, "I take note of the department's opinions."[1] Individuals of lesser political stature might find it hard to be so cavalier.

As a general rule, the more highly developed economically and the larger the state, the more detailed its delegates' instructions. Given the vast number of issues that are considered in international governmental organizations (the annual agenda of the U.N. General Assembly alone usually contains about a hundred items), a state must have a fairly substantial bureaucracy to issue detailed instructions to all its delegates, and such bureaucracies are most generally found in the advanced industrial states. States with extensive territories and big populations can also easily staff substantial bureaucracies. Moreover, regardless of their general level of economic development, the large states tend to be among the most powerful in world politics, and their governments tend to perceive events throughout the world as potentially having consequences for their interests. For these reasons the size of a state also affects the extent to which its delegates' instructions are detailed. The distance between the site of a meeting and the state's capital can also be a factor. The performance of the U.S. representative at the U.N. in New York is often monitored on closed circuit television in Washington, and a tie line between the U.S. mission and the State Department insures instant communications. There is consensus among many observers that in the IGOs to which the United States and the Soviet Union belong, their delegates tend to receive more detailed and inflexible instructions than representatives of other states.

Beyond executing the instructions they are given, delegates from all states also report on developments in the organization to which they are accredited. In other words, they perform many of the same functions that all diplomats do. Like other diplomats, delegates can influence what they are told to do by what they report and how they report it; they also can ask to have their instructions changed and argue the case for doing this.

Interestingly, diplomats who have had experience both in bilateral diplomacy and as representatives to international governmental organizations generally feel that they have greater freedom in the latter capacity than in the former.[2] One explanation is that IGO meetings, simply because they are multilateral and involve many different points of view, tend to be less predictable. Some diplomats and writers have gone further and argued that diplomats who participate in the institutions of IGOs have a greater opportunity to influence the policies of their governments than do their counterparts who are accredited to national governments and practice bilateral diplomacy.[3]

Of course, different states behave differently in different organizations and on different issues. Even the United States' delegate may have only brief instructions, such as to insure that the organization's budget does not exceed a certain level. On other occasions instructions may be limited to matters peripheral to the substantive activities of the organization. For instance, in the 1960s U.S. delegates to the U.N. specialized agencies often had as their principal instruction to block the seating of the People's Republic of China, and delegates from other states have merely been instructed to vote with or against certain countries.

The factor most strongly determining how detailed instructions are seems to be whether or not a state's interests, as perceived by its government, are likely to be seriously affected by the organization or the issue in question. Almost all the decisions of some IGOs, such as the European communities, are regarded with great seriousness by the governments of all member states. The most powerful of their member states also take seriously the majority of the decisions of the International Atomic Energy Agency, the International Telecommunication Union, the International Bank for Reconstruction and Development, and the International Monetary Fund, which could have significant consequences for the security and economic interests of these states. Under such circumstances governments tend to issue their delegates detailed instructions. The most powerful member states see their own interests as being much less directly at stake in such IGOs as the United Nations Educational, Scientific and Cultural Organization and the World Health Organization, and consequently the instructions of their delegates to these bodies may be less detailed. The governments of the less economically advanced and less powerful states behave similarly in matters relating to their own interests; when the issues under consideration are deemed important, they undoubtedly issue precise instructions.

Key Member States

Our discussion will concentrate on a relatively small group of industrially advanced and powerful states because of their crucial importance for the functioning of international governmental organizations. This small group of states controls the intellectual and material resources on which IGOs depend. When they choose to issue detailed instructions to their delegates, what goes on in the capitals of these countries is much more important for the outcome of decision making in IGOs than what goes on at the site of the meeting of the assembly or council. To put the matter more technically, decision making in these organizations is dominated by the representative subsystems of a few key member states.

Even when these governments do not issue detailed instructions on every item on the agenda of an IGO, they nevertheless control the general level and broad outlines of the organization's activities. When this situation prevails—that is, when the most powerful states limit their influence to the broad parameters of an organization's activities—day-to-day decision making tends to be dominated by a political subsystem composed of those delegates, international officials, and others who actually participate in the political processes of the organization. Again, technically, decision making in these organizations is dominated by the participant subsystem.

The states that have the capacity to be of crucial importance to international governmental organizations are not numerous. Although they would certainly not agree about the precise ranking, most observers would probably consider the following ten states the most powerful in world politics since the conclusion of World War II: the United States, the Union of the Soviet Socialist Republics, the People's Republic of China, Japan, the Federal Republic of Germany, France, the United Kingdom, Italy, Canada, and India. Throughout most of the years since World War II, these states had the world's largest gross national products. Contributions to the United Nations' regular budget are assessed on the basis of "capacity to pay," a concept that takes into account total economic production, level of economic development, and other factors. Table 6.1 gives the assessments of these states for 1954, 1968, and 1982 in percentages of the total assessments. It is striking that those of the ten states that were members of the U.N. at the time consistently contributed more than 75 percent of the U.N.'s regular budget. The decline in the assessments of India and the United Kingdom is also notable, as is the increase in Japan's. At various times the United States has insisted that it should not pay more than a fixed proportion of the U.N.'s budget, and acting in response to U.S. proposals, the General Assembly successively enacted prohibitions against any one state being assessed more than one-third and then more than one-quarter of the budget.[4]

TABLE 6.1

Assessed Contributions of Selected States to the Regular Budget of the United Nations
(In Percentages of Total Assessments)

State	1954	1968	1982
Canada	3.30	3.02	3.28
China [a]	5.62	4.00	1.62
France	5.75	6.00	6.26
Germany, Federal Republic of [b]			8.31
India	3.40	1.74	0.60
Italy [c]		3.24	3.45
Japan [d]		3.78	9.58
U.S.S.R.	14.15	14.61	11.10
Byelorussian S.S.R.	0.50	0.51	0.39
Ukrainian S.S.R.	1.88	1.93	1.46
Total for U.S.S.R. and Soviet Republics	16.53	17.05	12.95
United Kingdom	9.80	6.62	4.46
United States	33.33*	31.57	25.00*
Total	77.73	77.02	75.51

[a] Both governments of China claim to be the government for the entire country. The government of the Republic of China represented China in the United Nations until October 1971. After that date China was represented by the government of the People's Republic of China.
[b] The Federal Republic of Germany was admitted to the U.N. in September 1973.
[c] Italy was admitted to the U.N. in December 1955.
[d] Japan was admitted to the U.N. in December 1956.
*Maximum permissible assessment set without reference to ability-to-pay formula.

Source: John P. Renninger and others, *Assessing the United Nations Scale of Assessments: Is It Fair? Is It Equitable?* (New York: United Nations Institute for Training and Research, 1982).

In 1982, only 8 states besides the leading 10 had assessed contributions of more than 1 percent: Australia (1.83%), Belgium (1.22%), Brazil (1.27%), German Democratic Republic (1.39%), the Netherlands (1.63%), Poland (1.24%), Spain (1.70%), and Sweden (1.31%). The remainder of the U.N.'s budget, 12.9 percent, was contributed by the remaining 139 member states, 70 of which paid the minimum assessed contribution of .01 percent.

Clearly the ten leading states are essential to any organization to which they may belong. In the case of the U.N. system our analysis actually understates their financial contribution because these ten states contribute an even larger portion to the budgets of certain of the voluntary programs. In the late 1970s the United States was contributing about 25 percent of the money available for the United Nations Fund for Population Activities, about 20 percent of the funds for the United Nations Force in Cyprus and 30 percent for the United Nations Relief and Works Agency, and about 50 percent of the money for the United Nations Fund for Drug Abuse Control. There can be no question about the ascendancy of the United States in this group of ten states. Simply using gross national product (GNP) as a measure, in the early 1950s the United States' GNP was three times that of the U.S.S.R., the state with the next largest GNP, and although its lead had narrowed by the mid-1970s, the United States' GNP was still about twice that of the U.S.S.R.

Since the capacities of the ten leading states can be crucial to international governmental organizations, it is important to consider the policies that they have pursued toward IGOs in the post–World War II period. Only a few of the ten have been very active. The People's Republic of China was largely excluded from international governmental organizations until it entered the United Nations in 1971. As of 1970 it was a member of only two organizations, and these were composed principally of African and Asian states and their functions were largely normative. Japan, Italy, and the Federal Republic in Germany, the principal defeated states in World War II, did not become active in many international governmental organizations until the 1950s. As of 1977, in the UIA's restrictive tabulation, these three states belonged to seventy-one, eighty-seven, and seventy-six IGOs respectively. The two Germanys joined the U.N. only in 1973. Italy and the Federal Republic of Germany were active in the European community organizations from the outset, and in the late 1960s Japan and the Federal Republic of Germany began to take an active part in the International Monetary Fund and the Organization for Economic Cooperation and Development—IGOs important in the functioning of the world market economy. In 1972 Japan began a campaign to obtain a permanent seat on the U.N. Security Council.

In 1977 Canada belonged to seventy-five IGOs and India to sixty-five, and at various times both states had played active roles in many of them. The governments of Lester Pearson in Canada and Jawaharlal Nehru in India, in particular, saw IGOs as a major vehicle for foreign policy. But by the mid-1970s, based on their GNPs, Canada and India would have ranked at the bottom of the list of the ten states, and starting in 1973 India's GNP was exceeded by that of Brazil. Furthermore the governments in power in both countries in the 1970s gave less priority to foreign affairs than had their predecessors. For all these reasons the role of Canada and India in IGOs declined starting in the late 1960s.

Four states then remain—the United States, the Soviet Union, France, and the United Kingdom. At the conclusion of World War II the United States saw the establishment and successful functioning of international governmental organizations as an essential goal, and it devoted substantial resources to the support of IGOs. Perhaps the United States did this to atone for its unwillingness to become involved in international governmental organizations in the years after World War I, and particularly its refusal to join the League of Nations. Or the reason may have been its ascendant position in the global political system, or perhaps simple and honest conviction that new forms of political authority were essential. Most likely the United States' position can be attributed to all of these motivating factors and others.

During World War II the United States had devoted considerable energy to planning for new universal membership IGOs, and it played a major role in seeing that they were established when the war ended. Then in the late 1940s and the 1950s, it also came to favor limited membership organizations, and took steps to create and support such bodies. Throughout the 1950s and 1960s, the United States played a leadership role in most of the IGOs to which it belonged. By 1977 these numbered seventy-eight. But toward the end of the 1960s, under the pressure of complex domestic problems and in the face of sometimes hostile majorities in IGOs, the United States' enthusiasm for leadership waned. By then its relative capacity for influence in world politics was also less. Figure 6.1 shows the percentage of times that the United States and the Soviet Union voted with the winning side on roll call votes in each session of the U.N. General Assembly through the thirty-sixth in 1981. The declining tendency for the United States to vote with the winning side is clear. An aggregate figure, however, masks the fact that the United States found itself at odds with the majority in the General Assembly on issues involving decolonization and economic development much more often than on issues concerning security. Nevertheless, the United States became deeply concerned by the tendency of some IGOs to adopt normative resolutions that it strongly disapproved. Dismay with such resolutions was a factor in the United States' decision in 1977 to withdraw from the International Labor Organization. Only in 1980 did the United States decide to return to the ILO.

The Soviet Union, the second most powerful state in the global political system, has played a very different role from that of the United States in the years since World War II. Although it participated in planning and creating the United Nations, the U.S.S.R., perhaps because of its minority status in the 1940s and 1950s, did not evince much enthusiasm for that organization until the 1960s. And it did not even join many of the existing universal membership, specific pur-

FIGURE 6.1

The Position of the United States and the Soviet Union in Relation to the U.N. Majority

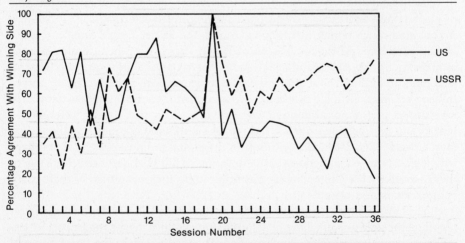

Source: Inter-university Consortium for Political and Social Research, P.O. Box 1248, Ann Arbor, Michigan 48106. ICPSR Study Number 5512, *United Nations Roll Call Data.*

pose IGOs until the mid-1950s. It was also during this early postwar period, however, that the Soviet Union began to create a web of IGOs among the communist states. Then in the 1960s its position in universal membership IGOs such as the U.N. improved, as is evidenced in Figure 6.1 by the increasing number of times that it voted with the winning side in the General Assembly on roll call votes. Its shifting positions were exactly the opposite of those of the United States.

By 1977 the Soviet Union belonged to forty-three IGOs. Considering the views of the early Marxist writers about international governmental organizations, it is significant that the U.S.S.R. was as deeply enmeshed in the web of IGO networks as it was. Starting in the 1930s the U.S.S.R. had found that international institutions were useful and probably even essential for the conduct of its relations with noncommunist states. In the period after World War II, perhaps to their surprise, Soviet leaders discovered that international institutions were necessary even among communist states.[5] Even so there has been a substantial difference in attitude between the leaders of the United States and those of the Soviet Union. The former have regarded international governmental organizations as a solution to the problem of world order, while the latter have seen IGOs as a temporary expedient at best. The improved position of the Soviet Union in institutions such as the U.N. General Assembly has not been due to Soviet leadership initiatives but rather because the Soviet Union found it easy to vote for the positions on decolonization advocated by the U.N.'s anticolonial majority, a majority that became increasingly impatient with the continuation of colonialism as time went on and as its ranks were swelled each year with newly independent states. The increased Soviet role in IGOs, then, should be seen not as signifying a commitment to the development of international institutions but rather as an acceptance of their inevitability in the present historical period.

Both France and the United Kingdom have been prominent in IGO affairs in the post–World War II period. In 1977 France belonged to 104 IGOs, more than any other state, and the United Kingdom belonged to 91. Though partly because of the absence of certain other states, Britain and France were the two most important states in the League of Nations. Perhaps because of their disappointment with the role of the League in the events of the 1930s, the two countries have often approached the U.N. and its specialized agencies with attitudes that appeared to have a *déjà vu* cast. Moreover, in the struggle over decolonization that has so preoccupied the United Nations, France and the United Kingdom were often placed in a defensive position. The Suez crisis in 1956 was the most extreme example. As the decolonization crises passed, however, the special ties that France and the United Kingdom were able to maintain with their former colonies gave them a source of influence on which they could draw in universal membership organizations. Yet despite this perhaps unanticipated resource, neither France nor the United Kingdom has ever in the period since World War II viewed universal membership organizations with the same enthusiasm as the United States.

France, however, played a leading role in the creation of the European communities. The United Kingdom, torn by its ties to the Commonwealth countries and to the United States, initially held back from a commitment to the European communities. Although it joined them in 1973, it remains to be seen how much importance the United Kingdom will give to this attachment. Before joining the European communities the United Kingdom took the initiative in the creation of the European Free Trade Association, and it stressed Commonwealth institutions.

Since World War II the United States, the Soviet Union, the United Kingdom, and France have, without question, been the most important members of the IGOs to which they have belonged. As Table 6.1 shows, from the 1940s through the 1960s they contributed more than 60 percent of the U.N.'s regular budget, and in the 1980s they contributed about 50 percent. They have been the source of important initiatives, and programs initiated by others could not be adopted without at least considering their views. No IGO which included these four states could act so as to seriously harm the clearly defined vital interests of either the United States or the Soviet Union, and it could act against Britain and France only if the two most powerful states agreed that such action should be taken, as they did when the U.N. acted in the Suez crisis in 1956. These states have also been crucially important for limited membership organizations. The United States plays a major role in NATO and OECD, as do Britain and France in the European communities. The Soviet Union dominates WTO and is crucial to CMEA.

The Influence of Smaller States

Despite the overwhelming resources of the leading ten states, delegates from smaller states can also be influential in international organizations. The delegates of smaller states, particularly those with advanced industrial economies, often can exercise influence because of expert knowledge that they have or acquire or because of abilities that they develop as negotiators or mediators.

In universal membership IGOs the delegates of smaller states that are in the process of economic development can also gain influence through their ability to mobilize the delegates of similar states to vote as a bloc. Less developed states from Africa, Asia, and South America now constitute a greater proportion of the member states of most major universal membership IGOs than the two-thirds required to pass substantive resolutions.

Starting with the first United Nations Conference on Trade and Development in 1964, these states began to caucus to attempt to achieve a common position on economic issues. Because there were originally seventy-seven such states, the caucus is known as the Group of 77, even though in the 1970s it came to include more than a hundred states. Figure 6.2 shows the member states that have participated in the caucuses of the Group of 77 as a percentage of the U.N.'s total membership.[6] Note that the future members of the Group of 77 came to constitute two-thirds of the U.N.'s membership during the seventeenth session of the General Assembly, two full years before the group's first formal attempt at caucusing.

FIGURE 6.2

The Group of 77 as a Percentage of the U.N. Membership*

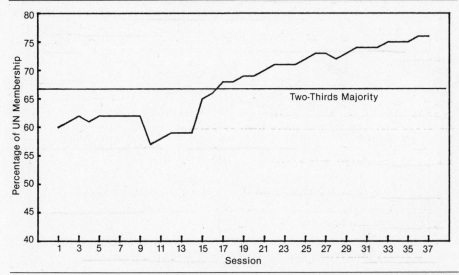

*The line represents the percentage of the U.N.'s total membership that the future (before 1964) or actual (starting in 1964) members of the Group of 77 comprised at each General Assembly session.

The states that make up the Group of 77 tended to take similar positions on many issues in the General Assembly even before their caucus started. This was especially true with issues concerning decolonization and economic development. When the caucus of the Group of 77 was initially formed in 1964, it had little immediate effect on increasing the cohesion of the group, but starting in 1971, at the twenty-sixth session, the group's cohesion increased substantially. These trends are shown in Figure 6.3. It is interesting that as the number of states that became members of the Group of 77 increased, the dispersion in voting also increased until the formal caucus was instituted. Given their numerical strength, if most of them vote together, the Group of 77 states can pass virtually any resolution that they wish in the U.N. General Assembly and in other similar institutions of universal membership organizations in which each state has one vote.

In addition to the Group of 77, several other caucusing groups operate within IGOs. Those in the U.N. General Assembly include the Afro-Asian Group, the African Group, the Latin American Group, the Nonaligned Group, the Scandinavian Group, the Western European Group, and the members of the European communities. The Soviet Union and other communist states also meet regularly to coordinate their positions. During the 1960s, when the budgets of the U.N. and the specialized agencies started to rise rapidly, the Western states plus Japan constituted what came to be known as the Geneva Group, the main purpose of which was to restrain the budgetary growth of the specialized agencies. The members of the OECD also often meet together during the sessions of more inclusive IGOs.

FIGURE 6.3
*Cohesion of the Group of 77 in Roll Call Votes of the U.N. General Assembly**

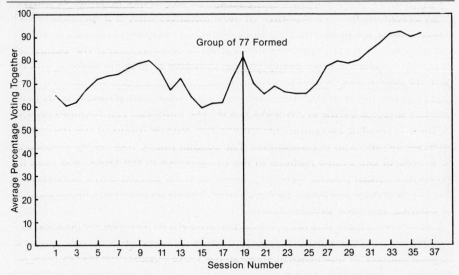

*The horizontal line represents the average percentage of the Group of 77 states voting identically at each Assembly session. The nineteenth session, the first after formation of the caucus, was abnormal in that there were only two roll call votes during the session; the usual number is around 150.

Source: Inter-university Consortium for Political and Social Research, P.O. Box 1248, Ann Arbor, Michigan 48106. ICPSR Study Number 5512, *United Nations Roll Call Data.*

At a minimum, the members of caucusing groups exchange information concerning one another's positions on various agenda items. They may go beyond this and attempt to coordinate the policies of the participating states, or even to frame common positions that all can adopt. However, only the Eastern European Group succeeds in achieving virtually uniform voting among its member states; the success of the other groups in this respect varies sharply.

Representative Subsystems

The mechanism for linking states with IGOs, as has been mentioned, is the representative subsystem. These subsystems are component parts of the political systems of both states and international governmental organizations. The delegate is at one end of the subsystem. An official who issues instructions is at the other end; this official is generally located in the national capital. The nature and extent of these instructions have already been discussed. How the instructions are formulated, however, needs to be analyzed. Again, with so many different possible combinations of states and IGOs, no generalization could conceivably apply to all instances.

Usually the process of formulating instructions is confined to bureaucrats. Publics seldom have detailed knowledge of the day-to-day activities of international governmental organizations. In most instances there is a "permissive consensus" among the public that the work of the IGO in question should go on. Of course in all societies, regardless of their form of government, the public sets broad limits on the foreign policy choices available to decision makers, and the more the public sees its direct interests at stake, the more sharply defined those limits will be. But it is not often that the public sees its direct interests as being seriously affected by the activities of IGOs. The European communities provide the most consistent exception. Exceptions can also be found in the histories of universal membership organizations. The Belgian public was deeply aroused by the actions of the United Nations in the Congo crisis in the 1960s, and both the French and British publics were very aware of U.N. actions in the Suez crisis in 1956. Even in these instances, though, public moods dictated only broad outlines for policies, not their precise content.

Legislatures too are generally not deeply involved in formulating policies. Particularly in countries with competitive forms of government—about a third of the total number of independent states in the 1970s—legislative bodies must appropriate contributions for IGOs, and they usually have to be involved in some way in the acceptance of norms and rules. Again, however, the legislature's function generally tends to be a matter of setting limits—albeit considerably more precise ones than those established by the public—rather than determining detailed content. Congress, for example, has set limits on U.S. financial contributions to IGOs. One reason that legislatures cannot do more to affect their states' policies in IGOs is that decision making in international institutions necessarily involves continual adjustment among the points of view of several states. Although individual legislators can and do participate in this process, it would be almost impossible for legislatures as collective bodies to be involved regularly and deeply.

It is executive officials and bureaucrats, then, who are most important in determining exactly what policy a state will pursue in an international governmental organization. Top executive officials have the final say, but many matters are not sufficiently important to warrant their involvement. On most issues the bulk of the work of preparing instructions is done by an office in a department or ministry or by several offices working together.

In the United States, the Bureau of International Organization Affairs in the Department of State has overall responsibility for providing guidance and support for American participation in international governmental organizations, and the assistant secretary in charge of the bureau has the legal responsibility for transmitting approved position papers to U.S. delegations to most IGOs.[7] For some items on the agenda of the U.N. General Assembly, the bureau would do almost all the work in the preparation of the position paper for the U.S. delegation. More frequently, the bureau would consult extensively with other bureaus in the Department of State and perhaps with offices in other departments. The Treasury Department is responsible for American participation in international financial institutions.

With respect to technical matters, an office in the relevant department might take primary responsibility for formulating the United States position, with the Bureau of International Organization Affairs playing only a coordinating and formal role. For example, the Department of Health and Human Services has the main responsibility for formulating United States policy concerning technical matters being considered by the World Health Organization, and the Labor Department plays a similar role in the case of the International Labor Organization.

Occasionally, interested private associations are involved. When the American position is being formulated for an administrative conference of the International Telecommunication Union at which the allocation of the radio frequency spectrum will be considered, the Federal Communications Commission holds hearings so that interested parties (e.g., radio and television broadcasters, amateur radio operators, police, and radio astronomers) can make their views known. The AFL-CIO and the Chamber of Commerce are generally consulted concerning United States policy with respect to the International Labor Organization.

To insure appropriate interbureaucratic consultation, interdepartmental committees are often used to formulate policy. By act of Congress, United States policy concerning monetary and financial matters must be considered by the National Advisory Council, which is chaired by the Treasury Department and includes representatives of the Departments of State and Commerce, the Board of Governors of the Federal Reserve, and the Export-Import Bank.

The elaborate process of interdepartmental coordination that has been developed in the United States is one of the reasons why the instructions of its delegations tend to be so rigid. Achieving consensus among representatives of various departments is such a substantial task that, once it is gained, the participants are not eager to have matters disturbed so that they will have to start over again. Few other governments have such an elaborate process of internal coordination, but none can completely avoid it. The American process can be regarded as an extreme example; other governments follow similar procedures that deviate only in the direction of greater simplicity. The crucial point is that in all governments the process is under the control of, and largely confined to, bureaucracies.

Furthermore delegates are primarily drawn from bureaucracies, be they ministries of foreign affairs, economic affairs, health, or social welfare, or some other department. Diplomats predominate at the United Nations, the Organization of American States, the Organization of African Unity, and similar general purpose IGOs, but in specific purpose organizations more than two-thirds and sometimes all of the delegates are from functional ministries. For example, from two-thirds to four-fifths of the participants in the various representative bodies of the World Health Organization are medical doctors employed by ministries of health. Occasionally, delegations include individuals who are not drawn from their state's bureaucracy. The United States delegation to the U.N. General Assembly regularly includes a senator or a congressman and some public figures, such as prominent educators, industrialists, and union officials. All of these individuals, however, are bound by their official instructions. This practice is sometimes followed in other international governmental organizations and by other states, but the delegate who is not part of her or his state's bureaucracy is the exception rather than the rule. And, formally at least, during the time that such individuals serve as delegates, they are assimilated into the bureaucracy.

Participant Subsystems

Shifting our consideration from the representative to the participant subsystems of IGOs, the part that delegates or governmental representatives play in decision making within international governmental organizations varies with the type of decision, the particular issue under consideration, and the individual government. Because legal authority rests with the sovereign member states, governments seek to and do control decisions affecting their vital interests by insuring that such decisions are made within the representative bodies of IGOs. Often, however, governments are willing to allow more or less routine decisions about many issues before IGOs to be taken without their extensive participation. Some generalizations are then possible about the types of decisions in which governmental representatives are most likely to play a predominant role and the types they may allow to be settled without their extensive participation. However, it is essential to keep in mind the reservation that there are many exceptions to these generalizations. And of course some governments will be interested in hardly anything occurring in an IGO to which they belong.

Governmental representatives generally insist on exercising final authority with respect to representational, normative, rule-creating, and programmatic decisions. In decisions involving posts within or ancillary to the conference machinery of IGOs, governmental representatives are almost the only actors to exercise influence. Secretariat officials, including secretaries-general, may be involved, but if they are, it is usually as go-betweens or "honest brokers." Sir Eric Wyndham White, the director-general of the General Agreement on Tariffs and Trade for its first two decades, took an active part in representational decisions in his organization, but such decisions were regarded as being of little significance by all concerned. U.N. Secretary-General Trygve Lie was more daring when in the early 1950s he urged that the People's Republic of China should be seated in the United Nations. David Morse, as director-general of ILO, took actions that contributed to driving the Republic of South Africa out of that organization, but he was clearly striving for what a substantial number of the governments of ILO's member states wanted. And actions such as his are the exception rather than the rule.

Decisions about high posts in secretariats are another matter; here formal authority is usually assigned exclusively to the secretary-general. But few secretaries-general would make a major appointment without at least conducting informal soundings among governmental representatives, and in some cases secretaries-general merely reserve the right to reject persons whom governments nominate. Since the functions of high ranking secretariat officials often include maintaining liaison—particularly with the governments of the most powerful countries—it would hardly be useful to have in such a post an individual who was regarded as *persona non grata* by these governments. The under-secretaries-general of the United Nations have always included citizens of France, the U.S.S.R., the United Kingdom, and the United States—all appointed by their own governments subject to the consent of the secretary-general.

Normative and rule-creating decisions ultimately have to do with the conduct of governments; consequently it is not surprising that governments should insist that their representatives have final responsibility in these areas. Ideas about codes of conduct, of course, can come from many sources, and frequently secretariats supply them. Secretariat officials may also be called in to draft resolutions, but in the end governmental representatives make the substantive decisions.

Programmatic decisions involve choices about how the resources at the disposal of an IGO should be allocated. Sometimes governments insist on being deeply involved, and their representatives surely must play a substantial role when costly new programs are being considered. But after settling broad outlines, governments are often willing to let secretariat officials have a predominant say about detailed decisions.

The involvement of governmental representatives in informational, rule-supervisory, and operational decisions varies greatly. If the informational decisions relate to exchanges of the points of view of various governments, as is the case in OECD's annual confrontation about member states' economic policies, governmental representatives are naturally deeply involved. What should be included in the U.N.'s *Statistical Yearbook*, however, is largely a secretariat decision.

In general, international governmental organizations do not have extensive rule-supervisory functions. With respect to those that they do have, however, secretariats are most often involved in detection aspects. The U.N. secretariat, for example, compiles statistics about the production and trade of narcotics, and the secretariat of the International Atomic Energy Agency was given substantial inspection responsibilities under the 1968 Non-Proliferation Treaty. When violations of rules are obvious, as when a state reneges on a tariff reduction agreed to in GATT, governments themselves can handle detection, although they may choose to ask for a secretariat study as a way of procrastinating. Secretariats are much less likely to be involved in verification, and decisions about sanctions are the sole preserve of governmental representatives.

Sources of Influence

Within this framework of differential participation in different types of decisions, several factors determine the influence of a governmental representative. A governmental representative's power—or capacity for influence—is derived from two basic sources, position and personal attributes. Position means the formal post that the individual holds, the representative of Algeria, Kuwait, the Union of Soviet Socialist Republics, the United States, and so on. Beyond this basic position, the individual may also hold an office in the IGO, the presidency of the U.N. Security Council, for example. Such offices may be useful supplements, but power or influence derived from position is basically a function of the standing of the individual's state in world politics generally or in the specific field in which the organization functions. Personal attributes that might contribute to an individual's influence are charisma, charm, negotiating ability, ability to mobilize coalitions, expert knowledge, language skills, experience, and reputation.

For representatives of the most powerful states, position is the crucial factor. Whatever their personal qualities, these representatives will be influential. Their states probably make major financial contributions to the organization and control resources that are so important that they give these states a virtual veto power in certain areas. For example, there is no point in the International Telecommunication Union's recommending a technical specification for telephones—for instance, relating to the placement of numbers in the dial—that the United States is unwilling to accept, since about half of the telephones in service in the world are located in the United States. Some normative decisions, of course, have been taken despite the opposition of a key state, in the hope of ultimately changing the state's position, but, contrary to impressions derived from the publicity given such actions, this is not done often. In addition to the control of resources in the specific field in question, the broad industrial and military might of the most powerful states is constantly in the background. Furthermore these states have large bureaucracies that can insure that their delegations are thoroughly prepared. They also tend to have larger delegations and missions, so that many people are available for contacts and discussions during meetings. And they have large foreign services, which can be mobilized to try to influence opinions in national capitals.

However, influence in world politics does not always mean influence in particular fields. Because the volume of its foreign trade is limited, the U.S.S.R.'s ability to influence trade negotiations is considerably less than its general ability to influence world politics. Conversely, states that have relatively limited capacity for influence in world politics may have substantial capacity in particular fields because of unique assets. For instance, Switzerland, because of the strength of its currency and its banking institutions, and the Middle Eastern oil-producing states, because of the essential role their exports play in the economies of the Western industrial states, have greater capacity for influence in economic negotiations than in negotiations concerning broader aspects of world politics.

Individual attributes are more important for representatives of less powerful states. For normative decisions, charismatic qualities and the ability to mobilize votes are important; in rule-creating decisions about technical matters, relevant knowledge is critical. Because of the importance of the particular qualities of individual representatives, the influence of less powerful states tends to vary among organizations and over time.

REPRESENTATIVES OF PRIVATE ASSOCIATIONS

Representatives of private associations participate in decision making in international organizations in several different capacities. The assemblies and councils of international nongovernmental organizations are composed of delegates from the national constituent units. Representatives of private associations thus play the same role in INGOs that representatives of governments play in IGOs.

In addition, private associations have formal rights to extensive participation in a few international governmental organizations. The International Labor Organization and the International Telecommunication Union are examples. ILO's constitution provides for a tripartite system of representation whereby member states are represented by delegates from employers' and workers' organizations as well as from governments. ITU allows private operating agencies (e.g., the American Telephone and Telegraph Company) to participate fully in the work of its international consultative committees—where recommendations concerning the standardization of equipment and operating practices are framed—and it allows scientifc and industrial organizations to participate in an advisory capacity. The Economic and Social Committee of the European communities is composed exclusively of nongovernmental delegates.

With respect to INGOs and to those instances where private associations have full voting participation in IGOs, generalizations about the character and capacities of the representatives of private associations would be virtually the same as those that have been made about governmental representatives to IGOs. The extent to which representatives are instructed varies, but on some issues representatives of private associations are clearly under no less rigid instructions than IGO delegates of the United States and the Soviet Union. Some private associations maintain offices—the equivalent of permanent missions—at the site of the headquarters of INGOs. For instance, both the American Federation of Labor–Congress of Industrial Organizations (AFL-CIO) and the Communications Satellite Corporation (Comsat) maintain offices in Geneva, Switzerland, where the headquarters of various IGOs and INGOs are located. Representatives of private associations tend to be drawn from the association's bureaucracy. The way their participation varies among types of decisions approximates that of governmental representatives. And, like governmental representatives, they derive their capacity for influence from both their positions and their individual characteristics.

Private associations are more generally allowed to participate in decision making in international governmental organizations as consultants. Usually their representatives have the right of making written and oral presentations, and sometimes they are permitted to introduce items into the agenda. In the 1970s about 400 international nongovernmental organizations had some type of consultative status with the United Nations and its specialized agencies; about 130 had consultative status with the Council of Europe; and about 62 with the Organization of American States.

Although in many ways the position of a representative of a private association which has consultative status with an IGO resembles that of a representative who has full rights of participation, consultative status is an incomparably weaker base for influence. Even though voting is not always the most important aspect of decision making in international governmental organizations, it is significant, and consultative privileges do not carry voting rights. In addition, the right to make written and oral presentations under consultative status is usually restricted compared to the freedom of governmental representatives to circulate documents and intervene in debates. Furthermore, unlike lobbyists who can threaten electoral and other pressure against individual legislators and other officials in national governments, representatives of INGOs and other private associations seldom have comparable leverage in IGOs with governmental delegates and secretariat officials. Finally, decisions in the representative bodies of IGOs are determined by much more than merely what goes on during the meeting: convincing those individuals who are in the room of the wisdom of a certain course of action may be totally without effect if they have unalterable instructions to favor a contrary course. For all of these reasons, when private associations feel that their interests are seriously involved in a decision being taken within an international governmental organization, unless they have full rights of participation, and perhaps even then, they tend to give more emphasis to their efforts to influence decisions taken in national capitals than to those taken at the headquarters of the IGO.

The European communities, however, because of their extensive powers, are an exception. Whether or not a private association has a formal right to be involved, when its interests are at stake it will certainly make its views known in Brussels—a frequent occurrence since many decisions of community institutions have binding effect within member states. Further, the commission of the communities, to advance political integration among member states, actively encouraged the formation and subsequent activities of European interest groups. More than 400 interest groups exist at the community level, and almost that many have offices in Brussels. Among the more important of these interest groups are the *Comité des Organisations Professionelles Agricoles* (COPA), the federation of agricultural producers; the *Union des Industries de la Communauté* (UNICE), the federation of manufacturers; and two trade union groups, the *Confédération Européene des Syndicats Libres dans la Communauté* (CESLC), which is affiliated with the International Confédération of Free Trade Unions, and the *Confédération Mondial du Travail* (CMT), which is composed of Christian trade unions.

REPRESENTATIVES OF INTERNATIONAL GOVERNMENTAL ORGANIZATIONS

Representatives of IGOs participate in decision making in international organizations principally in two ways, either in representative bodies through the exercise of consultative privileges granted to their organizations or in carrying out tasks within the framework of joint projects. Organizations collaborate on projects in various ways. The United Nations Development Program finances many activities that are conducted by specialized agencies; the UNDP provides the money and general supervision, while the agencies provide personnel and technical guidance. The United Nations Children's Fund has a similar relationship with the World Health Organization. The U.N. Fund for Population Activities (UNFPA) provides funds to both IGOs and INGOs.

When exercising consultative privileges, IGO representatives behave very much in the manner of governmental representatives and representatives of private associations. In the framework of collaboration on projects, they act in a fashion similar to members of bureaucracies. Through these two modalilties an extensive web of inter-IGO relationships and a more modest web of IGO-INGO relationships have been developed.

These webs undoubtedly have important consequences for many detailed decisions taken by international organizations. And through such detailed decisions UNICEF and WHO have each had an impact on the other's philosophy about the best approach to protecting the health of children in developing countries. By offering financial incentives and threatening to withhold financial support, the UNDP particularly—but UNFPA, the World Bank, and some other IGOs also—have been able to affect the priorities of various IGOs and INGOs. With this exception, however, IGOs have had very little impact on one another or on INGOs. Representatives of other IGOs tend not to be important actors in decision making in international organization.

The basic explanation for this is again the crucial importance of the governments of states—they control the resources necessary for action. If governments were monolithic entities, they could set priorities in one IGO and then help that organization enforce these priorities in other organizations. Governments, however, are not monolithic entities, but rather conglomerates of ministries, departments, and bureaus, whose members may have different priorities. Decision making in IGOs, then, tends to be a dialogue among segments of governments and the executive head and permanent staff of the IGO. What counts is what governments say in the particular IGO, not what they say in another; hence the relative unimportance of representatives of other IGOs. If governments wished or were able to enforce coordination among their departments concerning IGO policy, they would do this in national capitals, not through other IGOs. The lack of coordination within governments permits and indeed fuels considerable rivalry among IGOs. And jurisdictional disputes among IGOs are frequent.

EXECUTIVE HEADS

Compared to representatives of governments and private associations, whose principals control the resources that are vital for action, international officials appear to be in a relatively weak position, incapable of having a significant impact on decision making in their organizations. In a formal legal sense, this is generally true. Yet here, as in many instances, political reality is often more complex and nuanced than legal formulations would indicate.

The formal powers of executive heads are not extensive. They may appoint staff, though this prerogative is often hedged by civil service regulations and political considerations. Sometimes they have primary responsibility for allocating some of the resources at the disposal of the organization, such as technical assistance experts. Executive heads always have the right to make their views known in representative bodies, and they usually have the responsibility of taking the initiative in certain decisions, particularly those relating to budgets. Some executive heads preside at meetings of the representative bodies of their organizations, and many have the privilege of introducing agenda items. These, though, are only the formal sources of power of executive heads. They also have other sources of power that are informal and more subtle.

One extremely useful asset for executive heads is their position at the center of a sensitive communications network, which can be used to gain influence. Another asset is the permanency of executive heads and secretariats in contrast to the periodic nature of representative bodies. Because of this, executive heads often come to be perceived by publics as symbols of international organizations. In certain circumstances, particularly when dealing with budgets and operational matters, executive heads have virtual monopolies of information, and they can use this to enhance their influence. Finally, representative bodies often find it hard to frame coherent policies. Sometimes there are just too many points of view; on other occasions the differences may be sharp. In such circumstances representatives frequently turn to executive heads to seek points of agreement, to mediate differences, or even to define policies within broad limits.

To be able to capitalize on these assets, executive heads need to be attentive to certain key relationships. First, they need to insure that they control their own bureaucracies, at least to the extent of guaranteeing that these bureaucracies do not work against them. Few bureaucracies in whatever context are reliable, sensitive, and unfailing instruments of their chiefs, but the bureaucracies of international organizations pose particular difficulties. Many of these stem from their international composition. Their personnel have a diversity of native tongues, cultural backgrounds, and working habits. This at the least complicates internal communication processes, and it may lead to woeful misunderstandings. If there are conflicts among an IGO's member states or an INGO's constituent national associations, emotions connected with nationalism may cause some staff members to carry out their duties less than enthusiastically. And as in other bureaucracies, executive heads can find their policies sabotaged by subordinates who act according to their own designs or who form alliances with elements in the representative bodies to block the heads' initiatives. Executive heads can adopt various strategies for exercising control over their bureaucracies, but they can ignore the problem only at the peril of risking their ability to exercise influence.

Executive heads also need to be attentive to their relationships with two groups of member states or constituent national associations—those that have control of the resources that are essential in the organization's field of activities and those that constitute a voting majority in the organization's representative bodies. Sometimes these are the same states or associations, but often this is not the case. When it is not, the executive head's task is complicated considerably, for the voting majority will frequently want to go farther than the few most powerful states would wish. Under some circumstances the executive head can work with the majority to lead the powerful along, but this is a perilous task.

In the case of the United Nations, to ensure that, at least at the outset, the secretary-general will have the confidence of the most important states, the appointment is made by the General Assembly on the recommendation of the Security Council, and this recommendation requires the concurrence of the permanent members. The requirement that the appointment be made by the General Assembly is designed to insure that the secretary-general will have the confidence of the majority of the member states as well as of the most powerful states. The members of the commission of the European communities are appointed by common accord of the governments of the member states, which in effect means that the government of each state appoints the one or two members of the commission to which it is entitled, taking into account the attitude of the other member governments toward the individuals concerned. Again, the objectives are to gain the support of the most powerful states and the majority. In addition, this procedure insures there is someone on the commission from each member country who is acceptable to that country, an essential condition given the powers of the commission.

In trying to achieve their objectives, executive heads often have to go beyond formally prescribed relationships with the representatives of member states or national associations. This may mean entering into contact with domestic bureaucracies, or even with domestic interest groups—courses that may be risky. David Morse, an American who was director-general of the International Labor Organization for about two decades, relied on the support of the AFL-CIO, but this position became tenuous when his policies ran counter to the wishes of AFL-CIO head George Meany. When his successor, C. Wilfred Jenks, who was British, became involved in a sharp clash with Meany, the United States withheld its financial contribution to ILO. Although Jenks' successor, Francis Blanchard, sought to mend the rupture with Meany, he was unable to prevent the United States from withdrawing from ILO in 1977. It was only in 1980, after Meany's death, that the United States returned to ILO. Executive heads are most unlikely to go beyond attempting to gain the support of domestic interest groups. To appeal overtly and directly to the public of a member state for a policy opposed by its government would be a venture almost certainly destined to fail. Executive heads, then, must frame their strategies in the mold of interbureaucratic politics.

Given these basic parameters, it is not surprising that most executive heads have tended to emphasize a rational, or bureaucratic, rather than a charismatic style. They have generally preferred quiet private meetings to public pronouncements and have written carefully couched rather than polemical prose.

There have, however, been some notable exceptions. Albert Thomas, the first director-general of the International Labor Organization, has already been mentioned. Raul Prebisch, the first secretary-general of the United Nations Conference on Trade and Development (UNCTAD), is another. Both men had exceptional oratorical skills, forceful and dynamic presences, and a flair for clear, sharp exposition, and they enjoyed using these talents. Both traveled extensively to maintain contacts with governments; and both sought to create a normative role for their organizations in broad areas of economic and social policy. Particularly after the Congo crisis began, Dag Hammarskjold also adopted a charismatic style. He argued the case for his policies openly and forcefully. Interestingly, the successors to all three of these men have been much more inclined to the bureaucratic style. Charismatic leadership in international governmental organizations—as in states—seems to be particularly associated with the initial years of the organization or with periods of crisis.

Executive heads almost inevitably use whatever capacity for influence they have to attempt to increase the functions, role, and authority of their organizations. In this they behave like the heads of most organizations. Moreover, they are public figures and their historical role (a subject of some concern to most of them) will ultimately be related to the fate of the organization they lead.

Exactly which strategies an executive head employs and the functional objectives that he or she pursues will vary with individuals, organizations, and time. During the 1960s the heads of the U.N. agencies stressed the capacities of their organizations to render technical assistance to economically less developed states, and since the United States and other economically developed states were willing to provide the resources for such activities, the budgets and staffs of the U.N. agencies soared. During the 1960s the budgets of the agencies almost trebled.

Heads of the North Atlantic Treaty Organization and the Arab League have attempted to contribute to their organizations through efforts to resolve conflicts among member states. NATO head Dirk Stikker played an important part in mediating the Cyprus dispute between Greece and Turkey in the early 1960s, and Mahmoud Riad of the Arab League attempted to mediate in the Lebanese crisis in the 1970s. In proclaiming the doctrine of "preventive diplomacy," Dag Hammarskjold sought to develop a role for the United Nations as an instrument for settling conflicts at an early stage and without involving the most powerful states. Using this rationale he developed a major role for the U.N. and for himself as secretary-general in the Suez and Congo crises. Members of the International Committee of the Red Cross—the collective executive head of that organization—have frequently served as mediators. But while examples of success have been cited, there have also been cases of failure. The budgets of the agencies of the U.N. family stopped growing so rapidly in the 1970s as proposed increases were cut back, and many attempts at mediation have been rebuffed.

Whatever their strategies and objectives, the tactics that executive heads employ of necessity have several common elements. Executive heads use their position to speak privately to governments and associations and their representatives. They insert their priorities into budgets. And they articulate their concepts in their annual reports on the activities of their organizations. Although they may have formal authority only for narrowly defined categories of decisions, they have the opportunity of influencing many other decisions, and the record shows that their influence has been extensive and significant.

With its extensive legal authority the commission of the European communities has played a particularly vital role. Especially in the early years of the communities, by constantly advancing initiatives, by formulating package deals, which combined programs that appealed to different member states, and by forming alliances with member states and with interest groups, the commission was a vital catalyst in developing programs and promoting economic integration among the member states. Each of the fourteen members of the commission is responsible for one or more of the communities' main fields of activity and supervises the directorates or directorates-general dealing with these. Sicco Mansholt, a Dutch socialist, was a member of the commission from 1958 through 1972. For many years he was in charge of agricultural affairs. He worked assiduously with the agricultural ministers of the member states, and he stimulated the creation of community-level farmers' organizations and worked to involve them in the decision-making processes of the communities. His constituents in turn provided strong support for the policies that he preferred.[8] Examples of commissioners in other fields working with their constituents could also be cited; however, none has been as successful as Mansholt. The board of the Andean group has sought to perform a role similar to that of the commission of the European communities.

MEMBERS OF SECRETARIATS

Much of what has been said about executive heads applies by extension to the members of secretariats of international organizations. Whether or not members of secretariats have the capacity for influence in their own right depends on the formal structure and the political configuration of the organization.

In the case of the International Telecommunication Union, there are several elected officials and each is chosen by a slightly different constituency. Although in principle the Secretary-General has responsibility for all of the administrative and financial aspects of the Union's activities, this system insures each of the elected officials some capacity for independent influence, at least within his or her own sphere of reference. In other instances, such as ILO, where there are divisions among the member states about the proper function of the organization, different segments of the bureaucracy have formed alliances with coalitions in the representative bodies in attempts to further the cause of activities with which they are associated.

Sectoral alliances are also likely to occur where there is a collective executive head, such as the commission of the European communities. Even when single executive heads exercise firm control over their bureaucracies, those in charge of key departments have a capacity for some influence.

Operational decisions tend to offer the greatest scope for members of the secretariats of international organizations to exercise influence independently. The assignment of fellowships and technical assistance experts, the granting of loans, and the tactical deployment of military forces, for example, all involve a myriad of small decisions, far too many to be settled by the executive head alone or by consultation between the executive head and the representative bodies. Broad guidelines can be established, of course, but these inevitably must leave some discretion for practical application, and sometimes a right to interpret policy is used as a right to make policy.

The record of executive heads and representative bodies in making their views prevail exhibits considerable variation. When Dr. Marcolino G. Candau was director-general of the World Health Organization, it was clear that all WHO projects were executed according to policies that he had personally approved. David Morse, on the other hand, as director-general of ILO, was more inclined to allow subordinates wide discretion.

INDIVIDUALS ACTING IN THEIR OWN CAPACITY

The members of judicial or arbitral bodies of international organizations are generally chosen as individuals, even in cases where positions are formally or informally reserved for persons of particular nationalities. Individuals are also often appointed to perform ad hoc tasks of mediation. In these roles the individuals have substantial autonomy. They normally gain appointment only after having had distinguished careers outside the international organization. Because of their independent stature and the fact that frequently such assignments are the culmination of their careers, these individuals are in a strong position to resist pressures from governments, and realizing this governments seldom try to exert pressure. The authority and independence of the individuals appointed to the Court of Justice of the European communities is particularly impressive, as is the importance of the court. It is clear from the voting record of the judges of the International Court of Justice, however, that nationality does have an influence on the way judges approach problems. In instances where an issue has been considered by both bodies, the distribution of the votes of the ICJ judges often resembles the distribution of votes in the U.N. General Assembly. Judges and arbitrators perform rule-supervisory functions, and this tends to be the role of mediators also.

Individuals also become involved in decision making in international organizations when they serve as expert consultants. Sometimes governmental representatives and members of international secretariats are genuinely baffled by an issue and they need someone with specialized knowledge or at least with a different perspective to advise them on possible courses of action. In other instances, however, which actually may be more numerous, experts are called in to lend weight and legitimacy to a position that is already held by some actors within the participant subsystem—in other words, as a tactic to gain support for a particular position. Of course, the actual behavior of consultants may be quite different from that which was expected of them.

Normative and rule-creating decisions offer the greatest scope for the influence of expert consultants. In some fields and types of activity, experts may have virtually the final say. For instance, WHO convenes expert committees to prepare reports on the care and treatment of patients suffering from particular diseases, and the organization's ability to control these committees is extremely limited. Alterations in a committee's report may be made only with its consent. Although these reports do not have binding effect, they are widely regarded by physicians and health services throughout the world as standard guides to practice. Experts serving in other IGOs may have as much freedom to publish their views, but these are unlikely to be given as much weight as the WHO report. More often the report of an expert committee becomes one of the items considered by governmental representatives in drafting a resolution. Nevertheless, particularly with respect to normative decisions, individual experts can make a vital input.

PUBLICISTS

Publicists can play a role in decision making in international organizations only when the issues under consideration have some saliency for the public, and the agendas of international organizations generally contain few such items. Nevertheless, some issues considered by IGOs in particular are of broad public concern. The Korean War, the Suez crisis, and the Congo crisis were important events at the time. Matters concerning the world monetary system have been followed intently by a sizeable group of specialists and less intently by a much broader segment of the general public. Of course, what is of interest in one area of the world may seem of little consequence in another, so public attention and coverage varies.

There were some 400 newspaper and other media correspondents accredited at the New York headquarters of the United Nations, some 300 accredited at the European office of the U.N. in Geneva, and more than 200 at the headquarters of the European communities and NATO in Brussels in the early 1980s. These individuals and other publicists can influence decision making in international organizations by serving as go-betweens, by transmitting information among individuals involved in the participant subsystem. They can also reveal information or cast their stories to emphasize certain features and not others, strengthening the hand of some decision makers or embarrassing others. How they gain influence is not hard to see; it is a commonplace of politics within states. Making generalizations about the process, however, is more difficult. The influence of publicists in decision making within international organizations tends to be episodic. At its best, their influence is a means of enforcing public accountability. At its worst, it may represent a mischievous and irresponsible use of power, unchecked by public accountability.

THE DYNAMICS OF DECISION MAKING:
SOME CONSEQUENCES AND ISSUES

To this point we have described the powers accorded to international organizations, their institutional structures, and the characteristics and capabilities of the actors who participate in decision making within these institutions. Now we must probe how these various components interact and the consequences of this interaction. What we want to know is how decisions that are made within international organizations differ from those that might be made outside these structures. Do international organizations make a difference to decisional processes, to the distribution of influence, and to outcomes? If the growth of international organizations can be viewed as the increasing institutionalization of the global political system, what are the consequences of this? What values are served by the increasing role of IGOs in the global political system?

Unfortunately, there are no definitive answers to these questions. IGOs have developed in response to felt needs and pressures. Decisions that are made in them are not made elsewhere, and few decisions made in different settings are comparable enough to permit valid generalization. Nevertheless, reasoned speculation about the consequences of the decision-making processes of international organizations is possible.

To start with, decisions that are made within international organizations tend to be more open to public scrutiny than they would be if they were the result of traditional diplomacy. Many decisions are made in parliamentary settings, and although such bodies can hold closed meetings, there is a tendency toward open sessions. By definition, decisions made in international organizations almost always involve several individuals of different nationalities. The greater the number of persons involved, the more difficult it is to keep matters secret. Increasingly the number of nationalities magnifies this tendency because it enhances the probability that there will be differences in viewpoints.

A second major consequence is that positions not associated with any nation-state or national association can be introduced in decisional processes within international organizations. Indeed four of the seven categories of actors we have discussed—executive heads, members of secretariats, representatives of IGOs, and individuals—can act independently of the governments of states, and at least two of these categories—executive heads and members of secretariats—were shown to have the potentiality of substantial influence in certain circumstances. Of course, individuals cannot be separated from their cultural background and early socialization, but even with these qualifications the record is clear that executive heads, members of secretariats, representatives of other IGOs, and individuals acting in their own capacity have frequently taken positions that were different from those of the official representatives of the governments of their states.

Often such persons feel that their role demands that they take certain positions. Dag Hammarskjold, for example, felt that as secretary-general there were occasions when he had to act, even though the representative organs of the U.N.

were unable to provide specific instructions. He expounded these views in defending the actions he took during the Congo imbroglio in a now classic lecture that he delivered at Oxford University. He argued that it was the secretary-general's duty to execute the decisions of the representative bodies of the United Nations. However, the resolutions of the Security Council and the General Assembly could neither foresee nor provide for all possible contingencies. It could also happen, as it did, that in the new circumstances the representative organs of the U.N. would be unable to reach agreement. He argued that in this event the secretary-general could not refuse to act, even though his actions might run counter to the views of some member states. He maintained that "it is possible for the Secretary-General to carry out his tasks in a controversial political situation with full regard to his exclusively international obligations under the Charter and without subservience to a particular national or ideological attitude."[9] Hammarskjold argued that in acting the secretary-general should be guided first by "the principles and purposes of the Charter which are the fundamental law accepted by and binding on all States." [10] Secondly, in his view those principles were "supplemented by the body of legal doctrine and precepts that have been accepted by States generally and particularly as manifested in the resolutions of U.N. organs."[11] In addition, he supplemented his own judgment by conducting consultations with members of the permanent missions to the U.N. and by constituting and consulting advisory committees.

While few executive heads have been as bold as Hammarskjold was perhaps forced to be by the unprecedented events in the Congo, virtually all of them have had to take some actions without specific directions from representative organs. It is a safe guess that most of them would argue that they did what they did to defend the principles of their organizations. Even on a more modest level, when members of secretariats collectively prepare analyses and recommendations for action, the blend of nationalities that may be involved works to ensure that national viewpoints are surpassed. The result can be blandly dull. Nevertheless, nonnational viewpoints can be an important corrective to national biases.

A third major consequence is that small, weak, and poor states have greater influence in IGOs than they do outside of these institutions. The same is true for small national associations in INGOs. This stems from the emphasis in international organizations on settling matters by some form of majority voting and the tendency derived from the doctrine of sovereign equality to accord each state (or national association) one vote, whatever its geographical size, population, wealth, or income. Earlier we emphasized that whatever the formal arrangements, given the nature of IGOs the more powerful states have a greater potential for influence than the less powerful states. And the greater the immediate significance of the decisions, the more the powerful states will exercise their potential. The point here, however, is that the formal voting procedures of international governmental organizations give small, weak, and poor states resources that they would not otherwise have. Even if these resources are mainly useful with respect to representational, informational, and normative decisions, the long-run consequences of such decisions can be significant.

Of course the one state–one vote (or one national association–one vote) system is not a perfect method of representation. Table 6.2 compares the voting strength of the various geographic areas represented in the U.N. with their share of the world's population. As can be seen, in proportions of the world's population, the one state–one vote system results in the underrepresentation of Asia and the overrepresentation of Africa and the Americas. The reason for this is that Africa and Central and South America have many small states with limited populations while Asia has several large states with substantial populations.

The geographic divisions that we have been using, however, do not really reflect the major divisions in contemporary world politics. These divisions are more ideological and economic than geographic. Although no categorization of the world's states reflects these divisions perfectly, a reasonable approximation of the principal divisions can be achieved by dividing states into three broad categories: the members of the Organization for Economic Cooperation and Development (OECD), the members of the Warsaw Treaty Organization (WTO), and a group consisting of the remaining states, which can be called "others." The members of OECD include the developed states with market economies—those often referred to as "the West." The members of WTO are communist states with developed economies. The group called "others" includes the developing states with both market and planned economies, as well as some residual states that are hard to classify, such as Albania, Israel, and South Africa. With such exceptions, the category "others" is roughly synonymous with the Group of 77. Table 6.3 compares these groups' voting strength in the United Nations with their share of the world's population.

So viewed the one state–one vote system much more accurately represents the division of the world's population. The two groupings of developed states,

TABLE 6.2
A Comparison of the Voting Strength of Geographical Groupings in the United Nations with Their Population

Area	Number of States in U.N. 1982	Percentage of Votes in U.N. 1982	Population in Millions 1980	Percentage of Total World Population
Africa	51	32.4	468	10.7
Americas	34	21.7	613	13.9
Asia	34	21.7	2409	54.8
Europe	31	19.8	790	18.0
Oceania	7	4.4	22	.5
Total	157	100.0	4302	97.9

Source for population: International Bank for Reconstruction and Development, *World Bank Atlas: 1981, Gross National Product, Population, and Growth Rates* (Washington, D.C.: IBRD, 1982). Some 94 million people live in states and territories that do not have U.N. membership. The most populous territorial units are North Korea (17 million), South Korea (38 million), and Taiwan (17 million).

OECD and the Warsaw Treaty Organization, are underrepresented, and the developing countries are overrepresented, but these distortions are not nearly as extreme as those for the geographical groupings of states. Considering the divisions that actually prevail in contemporary world politics, then, the doctrine of the sovereign equality of states produces a representational system that roughly reflects the world.

Earlier in this chapter we distinguished between those international governmental organizations in which the representative subsystems dominate decision making and those in which the participant subsystem dominates. If the decisions of an IGO have consequences that have immediate importance for its member states, particularly the more powerful ones, it will tend to be in the first category, while IGOs that take decisions of lesser importance or with more remote consequences will tend to be in the second. Thus decision making in the International Monetary Fund, the General Agreement on Tariffs and Trade, and the International Atomic Energy Agency is dominated by their representative subsystems, while decision making in the World Health Organization, the International Labor Organization, and the United Nations Educational, Scientific and Cultural Organization is dominated by their participant subsystems. Small, weak, and poor states have a greater opportunity for influence in the organizations in the second category than they do in those in the first, but even organizations in the first category provide them with greater influence than they would have if decisions were taken outside of the structural framework. This is why such states press to have decisions made in IGOs.

TABLE 6.3

A Comparison of the Voting Strength of Ideological and Economic Groupings in the United Nations with Their Population

Grouping	Number of Countries 1982	Percentage of Votes in U.N. 1982	Population in Millions 1980	Percentage of Total World Population
OECD [a]	23	14.7	775	17.6
WTO [b]	9	5.7	377	8.6
Others [c]	125	79.6	3150	71.7
Total	157	100.0	4302	97.9

[a] Members of OECD: Australia; Austria; Belgium; Canada; Denmark; Finland; France; Germany, Federal Republic of; Greece; Iceland; Ireland; Italy; Japan; Luxembourg; the Netherlands; New Zealand; Norway; Portugal; Spain; Sweden; Turkey; United Kingdom; United States; and Switzerland, which is a member of OECD but not of the United Nations.
[b] Members of WTO: Bulgaria; Czechoslovakia; German Democratic Republic; Hungary; Poland; Romania; and the U.S.S.R., including the Byelorussian S.S.R. and the Ukrainian S.S.R.
[c] Others: all other 125 member states of the United Nations as of 1982.

Source for population: International Bank for Reconstruction and Development, *World Bank Atlas: 1981, Gross National Product, Population, and Growth Rates* (Washington, D.C.: IBRD, 1982).

The broad features of decision making in international organizations that we have outlined point in the direction of promoting greater rationality (in the sense of making available as much relevant information for decisions as is possible) and greater equity, qualities that many would seek to enhance. But the processes of decision making in international organizations also have other consequences.

Decision making in international organizations, whether dominated by the representative subsystems or the participant subsystem, tends to be mainly an interaction among bureaucrats. Secretariats are clearly international bureaucracies, but so too are the representative bodies of international organizations; the conferences and councils are composed of bureaucrats. This makes international organizations different from the political systems of states, where bureaucracies usually constitute only one element of the system. In competitive domestic political systems, bureaucracies tend to be counterbalanced by elected representatives in legislatures and elected executive leaders who are ultimately responsible to their constituents. If a majority of constituents feels that government is not properly responsive to their interests, they can replace their representatives in the hope that the new individuals will make the government more responsive. Even in noncompetitive systems, leaders must be attentive to maintaining public support. The European communities will be unique in having an organ, the European Parliament, in which there is an electoral link between representatives in an international institution and constituents. The significance of this, of course, will depend upon the powers that the parliament ultimately acquires. At present they are not substantial.

Because of their composition international organizations can be regarded as *meta-bureaucracies;* they are composed of their own bureaucracies and elements of the bureaucracies of other political systems. This term implies a good bit about the political style that prevails in international organizations and their strengths and weaknesses as political systems. International organizations may promote greater rationality and greater inter-state equity, but they are also removed from popular control and thus risk being unresponsive to popular opinion. To the extent that international organizations have gained authority in particular issue areas, they have increased the difficulty of maintaining democratic control in these areas. Should international organizations gain greater authority, finding ways of promoting popular control of their activities will become more acutely important; it may also be a condition of their gaining greater authority.

NOTES

1. Robert D. Murphy, *Diplomat Among Warriors* (New York: Doubleday, 1964), p. 367.

2. See Gary Lee Best, "Diplomacy in the United Nations" (unpublished Ph.D. dissertation, Northwestern University, 1960), p. 158, and also Chadwick F. Alger, "Personal Contact in Intergovernmental Organizations," in Herbert C. Kelman (ed.), *International Behavior* (New York: Holt, Rinehart and Winston, 1965); pp. 523-536.

3. Arnold Beichman, *The "Other" State Department: The United States Mission to the United Nations—Its Role in the Making of Foreign Policy* (New York: Basic Books, 1968), pp. xv, 202–209, and passim.

4. U.N. General Assembly Resolutions 665 (VII) and 2961 B (XXVII).

5. See William Zimmermann, "The Transformation of the Modern Multistate System: The Exhaustion of Communist Alternatives," *The Journal of Conflict Resolution,* 16 (September 1972), 303–317.

6. Thirty-one of the original fifty-one members of the U.N. became members of the Group of 77 when it was formed. They were Argentina, Bolivia, Brazil, Chile, Colombia, Costa Rica, Cuba, Dominican Republic, Ecuador, Egypt, El Salvador, Ethiopia, Guatemala, Haiti, Honduras, India, Iran, Iraq, Lebanon, Liberia, Mexico, Nicaragua, Panama, Paraguay, Peru, Philippines, Saudi Arabia, Syria, Uruguay, Venezuela, and Yugoslavia. Others that have joined the Group of 77 are listed in order of the year in which they became members of the U.N.: Afghanistan and Thailand in 1946; Pakistan and Yemen in 1947; Burma in 1948; Indonesia in 1950; Kampuchea (Cambodia), Jordan, Laos, Libya, Nepal and Sri Lanka (Ceylon) in 1955; Morocco, Sudan, and Tunisia in 1956; Ghana and Malaysia in 1957; Guinea in 1958; Cameroon, Central African Empire, Chad, Congo, Cyprus, Benin (Dahomey), Gabon, Ivory Coast, Madagascar, Mali, Niger, Nigeria, Senegal, Somalia, Togo, Upper Volta, and Zaire (Congo) in 1960; Mauritania, Mongolia, Sierra Leone, and Tanzania in 1961; Algeria, Burundi, Jamaica, Rwanda, Trinidad and Tobago, and Uganda in 1962; Kenya and Kuwait in 1963; Malawi, Malta, and Zambia in 1964; Gambia, Maldives, and Singapore in 1965; Barbados, Botswana, Guyana, and Lesotho in 1966; Democratic Yemen in 1967; Mauritius, Equatorial Guinea, and Swaziland in 1968; Fiji in 1970; Bahrain, Bhutan, Oman, Qatar, and the United Arab Emirates in 1971; Bahamas in 1973; Bangladesh, Grenada, and Guinea-Bissau in 1974; Cape Verde, Comoros, Mozambique, São Tomé and Príncipe, Surinam, and Papua–New Guinea in 1975; and Angola, Seychelles, and Western Samoa in 1976; Djibouti and Vietnam in 1977; Dominica and the Solomon Islands in 1978; Saint Lucia in 1979; Saint Vincents and the Grenadines and Zimbabwe in 1980; and Antiqua, Belize and Vanuata in 1981. Cuba did not participate in the Group of 77 until 1971 and Romania became a member of the Group of 77 in 1976. As of 1982 125 states and territories participated in the Group of 77, of which 121 were members of the U.N. For the purposes of this analysis, we included both states among the members and potential members of the Group of 77 from the session of their entry into the U.N.

7. A detailed description of the American system can be found in Donald G. Bishop, *The Administration of United States Foreign Policy Through the United Nations* (Dobbs Ferry, N.Y.: Oceana Publications, 1967).

8. Leon N. Lindberg and Stuart A. Scheingold, *Europe's Would-Be Polity: Patterns of Change in the European Community* (Englewood Cliffs, N.J.: Prentice-Hall, 1970), pp. 172–177.

9. Dag Hammarskjold, "The International Civil Servant in Law and Fact," Lecture delivered at Oxford on May 30, 1961, as reprinted in David A. Kay (ed.), *The United Nations Political System* (New York: Wiley, 1967), pp. 142–196. The quotation is on p. 158.

10. Ibid.

11. Ibid.

FOR FURTHER READING

Alker, Hayward R., Jr., and Bruce M. Russett. *World Politics in the General Assembly.* New Haven: Yale University Press, 1965.

Beichman, Arnold. *The "Other" State Department: The United States Mission to the United Nations—Its Role in the Making of Foreign Policy.* New York: Basic Books, 1968.

Cox, Robert W. "The Executive Head: An Essay on Leadership in International Organizations," *International Organization,* 23 (Spring 1969), 205–230.

——— , and Harold K. Jacobson and others. *The Anatomy of Influence: Decision Making in International Organization.* New Haven: Yale University Press, 1973.

Hadwen, John D., and Johan Kaufmann. *How United Nations Decisions Are Made.* Leyden: A. W. Sijhoff, 1962.

Hovet, Thomas, Jr. *Bloc Politics in the United Nations.* Cambridge: Harvard University Press, 1960.

Kaufmann, Johan. *Conference Diplomacy: An Introductory Analysis.* Leyden: A. W. Sijhoff, 1968.

Lador-Lederer, J. J. *International Non-Governmental Organizations and Economic Entities.* Leyden: A. W. Sijhoff, 1963.

Lindberg, Leon N., and Stuart A. Scheingold. *Europe's Would-Be Polity: Patterns of Change in the European Community.* Englewood Cliffs, N.J.: Prentice-Hall, 1970.

Pryce, Roy. *The Politics of the European Community.* London: Buttersworth, 1973.

Sauvant, Karl P. *The Group of 77: Evolution, Structure, Organization.* Dobbs Ferry, N.Y.: Oceania Publications, 1981.

Sharp, Walter. *The United Nations Economic and Social Council.* New York: Columbia University Press, 1969.

Siotis, Jean. *Essai sur le secretariat internationale.* Genève: Droz, 1963.

Stoessinger, John G. *The United Nations and the Superpowers.* New York: Random House, 1973.

INTERNATIONAL
ORGANIZATIONS
AND
SECURITY

7
CONCEPTS AND CONSTITUTIONAL MANDATES

As we turn to examine what international organizations have done, what activities they have undertaken in the global political system and with what effects, it is appropriate to start with the issue area of security. The first proposals for international governmental organizations were advanced in the hope that such bodies would contribute to the security of their member states, but this is only one reason for choosing security as a starting point. As it turned out, IGOs with manifest functions directly related to security were latecomers rather than the first to be established, and the number of contemporary IGOs with mandates in this field, including those with general mandates, is smaller than the number working in the economic or social fields.

The explanation developed in Chapter 3 for why it was so relatively late before attempts were made to implement the "peace plans," and why IGOs in this field constitute such a relatively small proportion of the total, is that security functions impinge clearly and obviously on sovereignty. Nothing is more fundamental to sovereignty than the issue of the security of the state. Until the early twentieth century the right to go to war was generally regarded as an inherent part of sovereignty, and war was viewed as a normal human occurrence. That security functions confront sovereignty so directly, and with it broader questions of order and status in the global political system, provides another reason for starting an examination of the functioning of international organizations with the field of security. What has been done in this field is a backdrop for activities in other fields. Still another reason for starting with security is that it is generally regarded as the most elemental aspect of political order and therefore as a prerequisite to attaining other goals.

Because the security of states is so intimately connected with sovereignty, international governmental organizations play a particularly dominant role in this field. IGOs have set the basic legal framework and have taken the most prominent actions. However, INGOs have also been involved. They have been forceful advocates for the creation of IGOs that would promote security, and they also have performed a number of functions that deal with security, sometimes in concert with IGOs and at other times by themselves.

THE MANY AND COMPLEX MEANINGS OF SECURITY

At the outset it is important to stress that "security" is an ambiguous concept. According to a common dictionary definition, security means being free of danger, free from fear and anxiety. To specify the meaning of security in greater detail, most people would agree that it involves an absence of violence and of menaces to one's person and rights. In this sense security means not having to endure or fear physical coercion. For some writers, however, security involves more than merely an absence of violence. They call security as we have defined it merely negative security; their goal is broader. They would seek positive security, which involves, in addition to an absence of violence, economic and social justice. They argue that without justice, freedom from physical violence is worthless. They regard hunger and racial or sexual discrimination as being at least as abhorrent as physical violence. Ethically, they have a point, but to make our analysis manageable, we will deal simply with the narrow concept of security in Part III. Parts IV and V will consider the attributes of positive security.

Furthermore, this chapter will examine only the relationship between military force and security. In the present era of interdependence, fear or anxiety could have several sources in addition to concern about military force. Countries that are heavily dependent upon imported food or oil could be concerned about continued access to these imports. Direct television broadcasts from communications satellites owned and operated by the United States could be viewed as threatening by a developing country. These are sources of genuine insecurity. Again, they are excluded from the following analysis only to make it manageable, and with the understanding that the issues involved will be treated in Parts IV and V.

Security of Nation-States

In the context of world politics even the narrow concept of security is complex. And even when viewed from the perspective of a single state, this concept of security does not provide a clear guide to action. To begin with, the issue of what should be made secure usually leaves at least some room for debate. Most states have a core territory that almost all inhabitants in this nationalistic era would feel should be governed by an indigenous system, and most citizens would agree to defend their state's core territory and its right to autonomy at practically any cost, but beyond this the consensus soon dissolves. Even with respect to core territories, particularly if their defense could involve a holocaust, a state's citizenry might not be unanimous. Questions concerning the defense of colonies, protectorates, allies, zones of influence, and economic investments hardly ever evoke unanimous responses among a state's populace, especially if insuring their security could involve substantial costs. How much should be expended is almost always a controversial issue. And in the global political system, non-core areas are much more frequently in jeopardy than core areas.

Another source of debate is how much security a state should seek to achieve, whether for its core territory or for non-core areas. Although superficially security appears to be an absolute concept, in reality a state can have more or less security. To illustrate this point, a modest concept of security might suggest that a state should simply have military forces sufficient to offer substantial resistance to the forces of a potential attacker, while a more ambitious concept would require forces adequate to overcome and conquer a potential attacker. Judging which concept is appropriate depends on, among other things, an estimate of what would be required to deter a potential attacker. This is always an issue of some uncertainty, and the amount of force required for deterrence may fluctuate over time. Moreover, since security is to a certain extent a subjective condition, different countries, or the same country at different times, might feel equally secure under quite different objective conditions. Not surprisingly, states that have recently suffered invasions are more likely to want far-reaching measures to enhance their security than those that have never had this experience or have had it only in the distant past. In sum, widely accepted objective measures or indicators of security have yet to be found.

Still another difficulty is that alternative and even opposing courses of action can be advanced as being the most efficacious means of gaining security. It can be argued that powerful military forces are necessary to deter potential attackers and are therefore essential to a state's security. But it can also be maintained that powerful military forces in one state are likely to be viewed as threatening by other states and will tend to induce the latter to increase their own forces, thereby setting in motion a spiraling arms race that could make all states less secure. Some might even argue that powerful military forces could provoke an attack.

If one could assume that all states were interested merely in insuring their own security, defined basically as the autonomy and integrity of their core territories, and if there were no conflicting definitions of core territories, it might be possible to conceive a scheme that would achieve this objective. To oversimplify grossly, the military forces of all states might be limited to those that were essential to insure domestic order. The theory of public goods, however, shows how difficult it is for large groups—and there are more than 150 states in the contemporary global system—to collaboratae to obtain goods that all desire and from which all would benefit. The circumstances with respect to security sharply illustrate the general problem. In a situation of mutual suspicion caused by inevitable uncertainty about others' intentions, it is difficult for a state to unilaterally reduce its military forces because such a course might prove disastrous if other states did have expansionist aims. On the other hand, joint action is hard to arrange since in the prevailing mistrust only comparable cuts would be acceptable to all par-

ties. Yet no two states are identically endowed, and at least partly as a consequence of different physical characteristics, their military forces are not identical.
In these circumstances, defining comparable cuts is exceedingly difficult.

Global Security

The problem of insuring the security of all states in the global system is even
more complicated. In every historical period the leaders of some states have had
objectives that involved changing the existing distribution of values, and more
often than not the leaders of other states have seen these objectives as threatening
their security. This tendency has led observers of the state system to divide states
into two categories—those interested in self-preservation and those interested in
self-expansion—and to explain the dynamics of the system in terms of the clash
between states in these two categories. Of course, not all instances of clashing
objectives have led to violence. The probability of violence has depended on a
variety of factors, including the relative strength and determination of the parties
to the dispute, their knowledge of each other, and the nature of the values
at stake.

At one time, the distribution of values meant essentially the control of territory, and this continues to be the central issue when large-scale violence is involved. But disputes concerning economic and social issues, such as foreign
investments and human rights, can also lead to violence. In some ways this
broadening of the agenda eases the problem of resolving conflicts by nonviolent
means. The supply of territory is fairly fixed. Consequently, one state's gain of
territory must usually be another's loss. In contrast, the supply of other values,
particularly wealth, is not necessarily fixed, and it is possible to frame solutions
to disputes so that all can gain.

The broad point, however, is that a global security system cannot assume that
all states are interested merely in guaranteeing the autonomy and integrity of
their own core territories; such a scheme must also take account of the real possibility of extensive and powerful pressures for change in the existing distribution
of values. It would be possible to design a security system that had as its primary
purpose repressing such pressures, but in the long run such a system would
surely fail to contain either change or violence.

To endure, a system of security would have to achieve consensus on the basic
rights of the units within the system, but it would also have to allow the possibility of change in the distribution of values. It would have to (1) define the circumstances under which change would be possible, (2) specify the procedures that
would be employed, and (3) make clear the type of change that would be allowed. Some domestic political systems appear to have made substantial progress toward achieving this goal. Unfortunately, its realization in world politics
seems much more problematic.

To evaluate the extent to which international organizations have contributed to
a viable system of security in international politics is a complex task, even using
as narrow a definition of security as we have chosen. Given the uncertainty

about the appropriate way to gain security from military violence, it is not surprising that despite initial pressure toward a single approach emphasizing a hierarchically structured command system, international organizations have
attempted a multiplicity of approaches, and little hierarchical structure has
emerged. To understand these several approaches, we must first consider them
on an abstract level.

SECURITY FOR WHOM?

Defining the units in the system and the characteristics that give them legitimacy
has been a perennial problem in international politics; indeed, it has probably
been the principal issue that has occasioned the use of violence. Thus thoughts
and theories about legitimacy must be our first concern.

Various criteria of legitimacy have been mooted. During the nascent period of
the European state system, religion was the principal criterion. Among the six
"peace plans" that we reviewed, those of Dubois and Poděbrad proposed organizations that would provide security for Christian states. Religion, though, gradually faded as an issue in international politics. Different forms of Christianity
were recognized as having equal status in the Peace of Westphalia (1648), and
eventually even the distinction between Christian and non-Christian states lost
salience.

Three other criteria for determining the legitimacy of states have at different
times and in different places been widely accepted: nationalism, democracy, and
communism. Because the writing about each of these concepts is voluminous,
the following brief discussions are not meant as thorough analyses, but rather as
synopses essential to insuring at least a minimal basis of common understanding.

Nationalism, the most elusive of the three concepts, is extremely difficult to
define or measure with precision. Broadly, nationalism means that people have a
sense of belonging together and feel that they ought to control the government of
the state that encompasses them. Karl W. Deutsch has described the phenomenon as involving "interlocking habits of communication."[1] Whether or not individuals speak the same language, they can understand one another, and their
behavior tends to be mutually predictable. A people's desire to control their governance is also essential to nationalism; without it the feeling of belonging together would have much less political force. Nationalism, defined in this way,
began in the later Middle Ages and gained momentum after the French Revolution. As it gained force, so did the doctrine of national self-determination. Hark-
ing back to Rousseauist ideas of consent, the doctrine of national
self-determination holds that "each nation has a right to constitute an independent state and determine its own form of government."[2] Plebiscites are a means of
determining the wishes of peoples in these matters, and boundaries could be
drawn according to the results of plebiscites.

Democracy, as an ideal, also emphasizes consent and in this sense is related to
nationalism. It goes beyond nationalism, however, in that it deals with the oper-

ation as well as the constitution of government. Democracy is generally taken to mean rule by the majority, either directly or indirectly through a system of representation. Thus concepts of democracy in the modern era of states with substantial populations emphasize the election of officials, and sometimes such procedures as popular initiative and referenda. Most concepts of democracy also include the notions that there should be limits on governmental power and that citizens should be protected against the arbitrary exercise of governmental authority. Democracy stresses that, in determining the course a people should take, the views of individuals should be weighted equally. It rejects the right of one individual, or a select few, to decide governmental policy.

Communism, again as an ideal, extends the notion of equality to the economic sphere. According to communist theories, the means of production should be owned and administered in common, and the goods produced should be distributed to individuals according to their needs.

Those who have advocated that nationalism, democracy, or communism should be used as criteria for determining the legitimacy of states have generally done so because they felt that realization of the concepts was important in its own right and also an essential prerequisite to peace. Arguments have been elaborated maintaining that states that did not meet the standards involved in these concepts would be likely either to invite violence against themselves or, conversely, to initiate violence against others.

International nongovernmental organizations have been created with the ultimate purpose of promoting the security of particular categories of states. The International Movement for Atlantic Union, for instance, is dedicated to uniting the peoples of the Atlantic community in an effective democratic union. The underlying assumption is that the security of the states in the Atlantic basin will be strengthened if they are united. Both the interwar Communist International (Comintern) and the postwar Communist Information Bureau (Cominform) regarded only countries with communist regimes as legitimately deserving security. These INGOs, though, are exceptions. Most INGOs that have some direct concern with security and all IGOs have taken a different course.

Whatever their personal commitments, the founders of international governmental organizations have avoided the concepts of nationalism, democracy, and communism in defining security functions. Instead, they have taken the position that international governmental organizations should promote the security of existing states, whatever their origins and present status. Thus Article 10 of the covenant of the League of Nations declared:

> The Members of the League undertake to respect and preserve as against external aggression the territorial integrity and existing political independence of all Members of the League.

Article 2, paragraph 4, of the United Nations charter, although it states the obligation differently, takes a similar approach of accepting states as they are, without reference to their domestic economic and political institutions or to whether or not their boundaries coincide with those of nationalities:

All Members shall refrain in their international relations from the threat or use of force against the territorial integrity or political independence of any state...

The constitutional documents of other international governmental organizations, such as the Organization of American States and the Organization of African Unity, contain similar statements.[3]

In part this approach has reflected a pragmatic realization that large numbers of states would not meet criteria formulated on the basis of nationalism, democracy, or communism. There has been a determination to deal with the world as it is, rather than as one might like it to be. This approach has also reflected a value preference elevating the absence of violence above the realization of the goals of national self-determination, democracy, and communism.

Not that participants in international organizations have abandoned these goals. On the contrary, they have continued to promote them, and within the context of international organization, as subsequent chapters will show, but they have taken the position that the use of force against the territorial integrity and political independence of existing states is not a legitimate way of doing this. The sole exception to this norm is that the overwhelming majority of members of contemporary international organizations came to agree that the colonial possessions of Western states (and later South Africa) should not be included within the prohibition against the use of force; wars of national liberation against these states have been regarded as legitimate. With this exception, though, present doctrine has answered the question of which states international organization should make secure by saying those presently in existence, whatever their history and characteristics.

CONFLICT RESOLUTION AND DISPUTE SETTLEMENT

In practice it is hard to conceive how it would be possible to eliminate threats or the use of force against the territorial integrity and political independence of states without at the same time eliminating the use of force in conflicts and disputes among states, and indeed international organizations have generally been oriented toward the latter goal. The Institute of International Law (*Institut de droit international*) was founded in 1873 to promote the peaceful resolution of disputes among states, and it continues to work for this aim. The institute has been instrumental both to development of international law and to the creation of IGOs. The constitutional instruments of IGOs dealing with security have generally required that member states should settle their disputes by peaceful means, a requirement foreshadowed by the "peace plans." Article 2, paragraph 3, of the United Nations charter ordains that:

All members shall settle their international disputes by peaceful means in such a manner that international peace and security, and justice, are not endangered.

The constitutional documents of other international governmental organizations contain similar statements.[4]

Mandating the peaceful settlement of disputes among states is but the first step toward achieving this goal; its realization requires much more. International governmental organizations have been seen as a way of providing modalities for the peaceful resolution of disputes. Early ventures emphasized a legal approach to conflict resolution: disputes should be settled by impartial persons on the basis of preestablished principles. Thus the first universal IGO with a mandate in the security field was the Permanent Court of Arbitration, established in 1899, and arbitration was one of the modes envisaged in the League covenant for the peaceful settlement of disputes. The covenant established the Permanent Court of International Justice, and it also provided that disputes that were not submitted to arbitration or adjudication should be submitted to the council, which could make recommendations for their settlement.

Historical development has been in the direction of increasingly making war, or the resort to force, an illegal act, and of broadening the array of instruments of peaceful settlement. While the League covenant allowed the possibility that under certain circumstances it would be legal for a state to go to war, the United Nations charter only sanctions the use of force in circumstances approved by the U.N. The U.N. charter also devotes its entire sixth chapter, consisting of six articles, to the pacific settlement of disputes and sets forth a whole spectrum of techniques, ranging from bilateral negotiations through formal adjudication, and including the catchall of "other peaceful means" of the parties' own choice. The charter of the Organization of American States contains a similarly inclusive list of acceptable techniques of peaceful settlement.[5]

Virtually all the techniques assume, however, that in the modern era war is not an instrument of policy that would rationally be chosen by states. They therefore rely on delays, so that decisions will not be taken hastily, the assumption being that while emotions might prevail in a decision that was taken quickly, if there were time for tempers to cool, rational thought would come to the fore. Contemporary techniques also frequently introduce third parties to facilitate communication, and they try to make decision processes more open, so that the bases for decisions will be subject to wider scrutiny.

THE MANAGEMENT OF FORCE

Issues relating to the peaceful settlement of disputes must necessarily be seen in the context of how force is managed. There are three broad approaches to the management of force in a multistate system: the balance of power, collective security, and disarmament and arms control. Traditionally, international organization has been considered to have functions only with reference to the latter two approaches, but in reality, as will be seen, it is involved in all three. Before demonstrating this, though, it is important that the three approaches should be understood on an abstract level.

The Balance of Power

Although it may have other meanings, "balance of power" most often refers to an equilibrium in distribution of power or force, and it is in this sense that the term is of interest to us. In essence, the balance of power in its pure form is a decentralized way of managing force. It does not interfere with sovereignty, and it leaves decisions about the management of force to states. It assumes that states should or will take steps by themselves to protect their own territorial integrity and political independence.

Alliances have been the classical mechanism of the balance of power, and if states were not too disparate in power, it is conceivable that equilibrium could be achieved through shifts in the membership of alliances. After World War II, however, two states overwhelmed all others in power, and their armament levels became the determinants of equilibrium.

Supporters of the balance of power argue that it tends to maintain peace and discourages the use of force. They reason as follows: if there were an equilibrium in distribution of power, the chances of obtaining gains through the use of force would seem slight and the risks substantial. Although the balance of power has not always prevented the outbreak of war—and its advocates have generally accepted war as the ultimate means of achieving equilibrium—supporters claim that it has served to maintain the political independence of the major states in the system.

The balance of power was the technique used to manage force from the creation of the state system through the early twentieth century. During this period there was a broad consensus that, in an imperfect world and given the acceptance of war as a normal human phenomenon, the balance of power was as effective a way of managing power as could be conceived. However, as technology made warfare more and more destructive, increasing thought came to be given to alternative techniques.

Collective Security

Woodrow Wilson was among the most prominent of the critics of the balance of power and an articulate advocate of the alternative of collective security. He argued that the balance of power had been "found wanting, for the best of all reasons that it does not stay balanced inside itself, and a weight which does not hold together cannot constitute a makeweight in the affairs of men."[6] He maintained that as a consequence of its instability, the balance of power invariably led to the violation of what he considered to be the rights of some states and also to war. Collective security, in his view, would be a better way of managing power. As he put it in a speech delivered during World War I:

> There must now be, not a balance of power, not one powerful group of nations set off against another, but a single overwhelming group of nations who shall be the trustee of the peace of the world.[7]

Wilson expressed the idea of collective security well. In essence, the theory postulates that there should be an agreed status quo, and that an organization should be formed whose members would agree to oppose, with force if necessary, any attempt to change the status quo by the use of force. The image is that of the entire community arraigned against a lonely aggressor.

The distinguishing characteristic of collective security is that it is directed against any state that might become an aggressor. The target of collective security is not identified in advance, unlike the situation in an alliance, which is explicitly or implicitly directed against a state or group of states. In Wilson's view, as in that of many of the supporters of collective security, the threat of such a coalition would be sufficient to deter aggression. Thus they gave little thought to what would happen if the collective forces should have to be deployed against those of an aggressor. Such issues as how the collective forces should be directed and whether or not their mission should be limited to the restoration of the status quo were unexplored. Nevertheless, collective security involves an attempt to manage force in a more centralized manner than in a balance of power system.

The League of Nations was generally perceived as an attempt to replace the balance of power with a collective security system. As we have seen, Article 10 of the League covenant defined the status quo; Articles 12 through 15 spelled out various mechanisms for the peaceful settlement of disputes. Should war nevertheless occur, Article 16 provided for a boycott and embargo against the aggressor and also authorized the council to recommend that the armed forces of member states be used to stop the aggression.

Despite "gaps" in the covenant—situations in which war might be regarded as legal or in which the council might be unable to act—it provided more than a rudimentary basis for the establishment of a collective security system; yet in a real sense it was never tested. Two major states, the Soviet Union and the United States, were not members of the League at the outset, and their absence diminished the credibility of collective deterrence. The most powerful original members, Britain and France, were unwilling to entrust their security entirely to the League. And one state, Germany, was strongly opposed to the status quo. For all these reasons, no sooner had the League been established than alliances and armaments, the traditional mechanisms of the balance of power, began to appear. In the end, neither the new mechanisms of collective security nor the traditional modalities of the balance of power were able to prevent the holocaust of World War II.

The founders of the United Nations hoped to create a stronger instrument of collective security than the League had been. The U.N. charter, therefore, is much more detailed and specific than the League covenant, and responsibility for the operation of collective security is focused on the permanent members of the Security Council—China, France, the Soviet Union, the United Kingdom, and the United States. Each of these states can veto any decision on enforcement actions. An entire chapter, 7, is devoted to specifying the manner in which the U.N. might take "action with respect to threats to the peace, breaches of the peace, and acts of aggression." The Security Council is empowered to decide on measures short of the use of force, such as the complete or partial interruption of economic relationships and the severance of diplomatic relationships. In Article 43 the charter envisaged that members of the United Nations would negotiate agreements with the Security Council under which they would make available military forces and other facilities for use should the Security Council decide to undertake enforcement actions.

In conceptual terms the arrangements provided for under the United Nations charter can be viewed as a limited collective security system designed to operate against any state other than the five permanent members of the Security Council and such states as these five should choose to use their veto to protect. Beyond unaligned small and weak nations, the only states against which the system could have been expected to operate were those that were defeated in World War II—Germany, Italy, and Japan.

In the period after World War II, however, the two most powerful of the permanent members of the Security Council, the Soviet Union and the United States, came to regard each other as the principal threat to their security. As a result, each resorted to the traditional mechanism of the balance of power, alliances, as a way of enhancing its security. Unlike what happened in the interwar period, however, these alliances, particularly the North Atlantic Treaty and the Warsaw Treaty, involved the establishment of substantial international governmental organizations, and consequently international organization became involved in the management of force through balance of power strategies. In a way, the U.N. charter sanctioned this development because Article 51 states:

> Nothing in the present Charter shall impair the inherent right of individual or collective self-defense if an armed attack occurs against a Member of the United Nations, until the Security Council has taken measures necessary to maintain international peace and security.

Both the North Atlantic Treaty and the Warsaw Treaty, as well as the constitutional documents of other alliances, refer to this article.

In Chapter 8 the charter also envisaged that regional collective security organizations might be created, and several have been, including the Organization of American States and the Organization of African Unity. The OAS can function both as a collective security system against an aggressor within the region and as an alliance against a state outside the region. Members have treated it in both ways.

The broad point is that as the twentieth century developed, many international governmental organizations came to be involved in a variety of approaches to the management of force. Although individuals such as Woodrow Wilson may have thought that it was possible to create a system in which the management of force was entrusted to a single central authority, reality has proved much more complex. The management of force is no longer completely decentralized, nor is it entrusted to a single collective security system. Instead, although ultimate control of force continues to rest with sovereign states, several international governmental organizations are also involved and in a variety of ways.

Disarmament and Arms Control

Disarmament and arms control have been viewed as another alternative to the balance of power. Literally, disarmament means giving up or reducing a military establishment. On the most elementary level the connection between armaments and violence is obvious: the greater the armaments, the greater the damage that can be done, and the smaller the armaments, the less the damage. But advocates of disarmament believe that there may be a more complicated connection, and that armaments in themselves may be a cause of war. They suggest that in a system in which the management of force is decentralized, the existence of armaments will be a source of insecurity. Each state, being uncertain of the intentions of others, will fear their armaments. And because of this fear, each state will be pressured to maintain its own armaments at a high level and to increase them. The cycle works as follows: as some states increase their armaments, they make other states feel insecure, and these states increase their armaments in response, reinforcing the fears of the first group of states. Viewed in this manner, arms races are inexorable spirals bred by insecurity. The theory goes on to postulate that war is a likely outcome of arms races, because a miscalculation may occur, or one state will feel that it must act to take advantage of a temporary and diminishing margin of superiority or because its position can only worsen.

There is also a connection between disarmament and collective security. A major problem of collective security is insuring that the forces subject to collective decisions are large enough actually to deter a potential aggressor. If disarmament and arms control measures succeeded in reducing the forces available to individual states, the force requirements for collective security would be lessened. Moreover, if an effective system of collective security were in existence, states might be more willing to enter into disarmament and arms control arrangements.

The theory of arms control stresses the need to lessen the dangers associated with the possession of large arsenals, especially of nuclear weapons. Arms control efforts may or may not involve actually reducing armaments. Measures aimed at increasing communications could lessen the possibility of egregious miscalculations. Other measures such as limits on the development and deployment of certain weapons could serve to avoid destabilizing developments, and thus lessen mutual fears, which are likely to trigger dangerous decisions. Even more importantly, contemporary strategists assume that one of the major deterrents to the use of nuclear weapons—if not the principal deterrent—is the fear of devastating nuclear retaliation, and arms control measures could be designed to insure that a state's armaments programs were not aimed at achieving invulnerability to retaliation.

The League covenant was the first attempt to give an IGO a mandate with respect to disarmament and arms control. Article 8 stated that the member states recognized "that the maintenance of peace requires the reduction of national armaments to the lowest point consistent with national safety and the enforcement by common action of international obligations." It directed the council to formulate plans for achieving this objective with respect to each state, and decreed that after these plans had been accepted by the several governments, the limits on armaments should not be exceeded without the concurrence of the council. The covenant also expressed the view that "the manufacture by private enterprise of munitions and implements of war is open to grave objections," and directed the council to "advise how the evil effects attendant upon such manufacture can be prevented..."

Not surprisingly, Article 8 produced few concrete results. Its significance is more in the concept it represented. It was a strong commitment to disarmament, and it envisaged that this could be managed for the entire globe by one central institution.

The founders of the United Nations took a different approach. Article 26 of the charter directs the Security Council to formulate "plans to be submitted to the Members of the United Nations for the establishment of a system for the regulation of armaments." This is the principal provision of the charter that relates to disarmament, and note that the word "disarmament" is not even used. Believing that the relatively low level of the armaments of Britain and France tempted Hitlerian Germany to launch World War II, the founders of the U.N. were more concerned with having sufficient military forces available to deter aggression than they were with disarmament. On the other hand, they were not unmindful of the dangers of an unlimited arms race, and thus the concern for regulation.

As additional international governmental organizations were created in the security field after World War II, they followed the mixed approach to disarmament that characterized the United Nations charter. The Western European Union (WEU) was founded in 1955 to make the rearmament of the Federal Republic of Germany possible, but the WEU is also charged with responsibility for enforcing arms limitations regarding Germany. In a sense, the more international organizations have become involved in disarmament and arms control activities, the more their approach has come to encompass elements of a balance of power strategy.

The involvement of international organization in security issues has not resulted, as some may have hoped, in the creation of a single hierarchical structure for the management of force, a structure that would gradually supplant national control of military force. International organizations have not ended the attraction of balance of power strategies; on the contrary, they have themselves adopted these strategies. And states remain in control of military force. Nevertheless, international organizations have attempted to restrict and control the use of force in a variety of ways, and they have established bureaucratic structures to perform these functions. What exactly has been accomplished is the subject of the next chapter.

NOTES

1. Karl W. Deutsch, *Nationalism and Its Alternatives* New York: Knopf, 1969), p. 14.
2. Alfred Cobban, *National Self-Determination* (Chicago: University of Chicago Press, 1944), p. 4.
3. See Article 5 of the OAS Charter and Article 3, paragraph 3, of the OAU Charter.
4. See Article 1 of the North Atlantic Treaty, Article 1 of the Warsaw Treaty, Articles 1 and 2 of the Inter-American Treaty of Reciprocal Assistance, and Article 3, paragraph 4, of the Articles of the Organization of African Unity.
5. See Chapter 4; see also the Pact of Bogota.
6. Woodrow Wilson, *War and Peace*, edited by Ray Stannard Baker and William E. Dodd (New York: Harper and Brothers, 1927), Vol. 1, p. 364.
7. Ibid., p. 343.

FOR FURTHER READING

Brown, Seyom. *New Forces in World Politics.* Washington: Brookings, 1974.

Claude, Inis L., Jr. *Power and International Relations.* New York: Random House, 1964.

Haas, Ernst B. "The Balance of Power: Prescription, Concept or Propaganda," *World Politics,* 5 (July 1953), 442–477.

——— ."Types of Collective Security: An Examination of Operational Concepts," *The American Political Science Review,* 49 (March 1955), 40–62.

Hinsley, F. H. *Nationalism and the International System.* London: Hodder and Stoughton, 1973.

Kaplan, Morton A. *System and Process in International Politics.* New York: Wiley, 1957.

Levine, Robert A. *The Arms Debate.* Cambridge: Harvard University Press, 1963.

Martin, Laurence. *The Two-edged Sword: Armed Force in the Modern World.* New York: Norton, 1982.

Schelling, Thomas C., and Morton Halperin. *Strategy and Arms Control.* New York: Twentieth Century Fund, 1961.

Wolfers, Arnold. *Discord and Collaboration: Essays on International Politics.* Baltimore: Johns Hopkins, 1962.

8
ACTIVITIES TO PROMOTE SECURITY

Having discussed the theories underpinning various approaches to international security problems, and the ways in which the mandates of international organizations reflect these approaches, we may now examine what IGOs and INGOs have done in this field. Using the typology developed in Chapter 5, we will consider activities in each of the five categories of actions that concern issues external to the organization—informational, normative, rule-creating, rule-supervisory, and operational. The listing is intended to be illustrative, not comprehensive, but the most important activities are included.

INFORMATIONAL ACTIVITIES

Information is important for all the approaches to security. However the management of force may be arranged, it is vital to have knowledge about both the intentions and the capabilities of states. And given the rationalistic assumptions involved in the various theories of conflict resolution and dispute settlement, information is also essential to the success of efforts to promote security. International organizations have consequently undertaken substantial activities in this sphere.

Clarifying Positions

The League of Nations started a practice—the general debate—that has since been adopted by several of the INGOs and virtually all of the IGOs that function in the security field. The general debate is the most formal and stylized exchange of information that occurs within international organizations. It generally takes place in the early stages of the meetings of one or more of the principal organs, and the structuring rubric is usually comments on the report of the executive head. These reports tend to cover developments with respect to all the issues that are important to the organization, but delegates feel free to go beyond the report in their comments and to discuss issues they consider important that were not mentioned in it.

The nature of these debates varies. INGOs that have them, such as the Afro-Asian People's Solidarity Organization, tend to open them to the public and indeed to seek publicity for them. In the League and the U.N. general debates have been public, and this has often been the case in the Organization of American States as well. On the other hand, the equivalents of the general debate that occur in the bi-annual meetings at the ministerial level of the council of the North Atlantic Treaty Organization and in periodic and irregular sessions of the Political Consultative Committee of the Warsaw Treaty Organization are held behind closed doors, although usually a communique is issued at their conclusion. In NATO general exchanges are virtually continuous. They occur in formal sessions at the weekly meetings of the council at the level of permanent representatives and informally at weekly luncheons of the same group. Like the ministerial sessions, these meetings, too, are closed.

In the League and the U.N. the subject matter covered in the general debate is all inclusive. In the institutions of the alliances, although the greatest attention tends to be devoted to the partners' attitudes toward states in the opposite camp, interallied disputes are also considered, as are aspects of member states' foreign policies that might impinge on issues directly related to the alliances' purposes. General debates in other specific purpose international organizations follow the pattern of NATO and WTO in being relatively limited in scope, but because general debates *are* general, they frequently wander afield. The records of ILO, ITU, UNESCO, WHO, and other specialized bodies show how the burning controversies of the day can easily be connected to the most technical issues.

More focused exchanges of views occur in debates and discussions of specific topics. These topics may involve particular disputes or broad issues such as the effects of nuclear weapons. Again, these discussions tend to be public in INGOs and universal membership IGOs and private in limited membership IGOs, particularly organizations associated with alliances.

Opinions on the value of general debates and other exchanges of views vary. Many observers have been particularly critical of public discussions and skeptical of their utility. These individuals argue that most of the statements by delegates tend to be set pieces, often highly nationalistic in tone and frequently more oriented toward the speaker's domestic audience than toward the other delegates in the organization. They go on to assert that such statements are as likely to exacerbate conflicts as to ameliorate them, and that they are also likely to inhibit compromise. On the other hand, one distinguished scholar, Inis L. Claude, sees the U.N.'s public debates as potentially the organization's greatest contribution.[1] In his view:

[The] general debate has served to dramatize the peril of atomic war, to point up the threats posed by the arrogance and irresponsibility of expansive states, to reveal the growing strength of neutralism, to demonstrate the sensitivities of newly emergent states, and to indicate the dynamism of ationalist movements among colonial peoples.

Undoubtedly, discussions are more frank and candid when they are conducted privately among allies, but whether open or closed to the public, general debates give delegates an opportunity to state their positions on all issues and to hear the positions of all other delegates. Although delegates' statements are not an infallible guide to intentions, they provide substantial clues and consequently could contribute to making the behavior of associations and, more importantly, of states more mutually predictable.[2]

Clarifying Capabilities

International organizations have also attempted to increase the information available about the military capabilities of states. One of the early steps that the League of Nations took was to inaugurate the publication of the *Armaments Yearbook*, which attempted to provide comprehensive coverage of all states' military forces.

The United Nations did not continue this effort in the period after World War II. Some U.N. member states, such as the U.S.S.R., regarded information about military capabilites as confidential and would not supply it for publication by the U.N. In general the greater heterogeneity of the U.N.'s membership and the consequent larger number of controversies among member states would have made continuing the League's publication activities difficult. Instead, since World War II agencies of national governments and INGOs have undertaken the publication of data similar to that contained in the League series. The *Strategic Balance*, an authoritative publication issued annually by the London-based Institute of Strategic Studies (ISS) is the most comprehensive and well-known series, but the Stockholm International Peace Research Institute (SIPRI) and the United States Arms Control and Disarmament Agency (USACDA) also collect and regularly publish data concerning military forces throughout the world. These organizations are not subject to the same constraints that an IGO would be. On the other hand, in many parts of the world ISS and SIPRI are probably given greater credibility than USACDA.

Within NATO, gathering information about the military forces of the Warsaw Pact is a joint responsibility, and the member states of the alliance share intelligence information. There is a Defense Review Committee which regularly updates and extends a comparative analysis of the forces available to WTO and NATO. Presumably the Warsaw Treaty Organization has similar procedures. In contrast to the interwar period, then, the general publication of data on military forces has shifted from an IGO to INGOs and national governments. In addition, more detailed information is circulated within limited membership IGOs.

Beyond these activities, as new weapons have been developed, information has been circulated within international organizations. One INGO, the Pugwash Conferences on Science and World Affairs, was founded expressly for the purpose of allowing scientists to discuss problems that arose as a result of scientific progress, and in particular the dangers created by the development of weapons of mass destruction. For several years after its creation in 1957, it was the principal channel for discussion of these important and controversial issues among participants from NATO and WTO countries. The meetings are private, but the proceedings of the conferences are distributed to heads of states and other interested individuals. The private exchanges at the Pugwash Conferences are undoubtedly the organization's most important contribution. The conferences involve individuals with access to decision makers in the major countries. It is clear that the information exchanged in the Pugwash Conferences was instrumental in persuading decision makers to attempt to limit the spread and growth of arsenals of nuclear weapons.

IGOs have also undertaken activities in this field. In 1955 the General Assembly of the United Nations established the Scientific Committee on the Effects of Atomic Radiation. This committee has periodically published reports dealing with the general mechanisms through which ionizing radiation affects human life and observed levels of ionizing radiation and radioactivity in the environment. The committee's reports provided an effective assessment of the effects of radioactive fallout from the large-scale testing of nuclear weapons by the Soviet Union and the United States in the late 1950s and early 1960s. Within NATO detailed information about nuclear weapons and their effects is shared within the Nuclear Planning Group, a seven-state suborgan ultimately responsible to the council. Given the limited number of states that have developed the new weaponry, these informational activities of international governmental organizations have insured that knowledge about the effects of nuclear weapons would not be restricted to those states alone. In addition, the U.N. committee has made information about the effects of nuclear weapons more available to the publics of all states, countering governmental efforts to restrict the dissemination of such information.

It is reasonable to believe that the circulation of information on military forces and weaponry within international organizations has made egregious miscalculations less probable and contributed to more realistic assessments of the dangers of violence.

Fact Finding

Fact finding is another informational activity undertaken by international governmental organizations. Fact finding as a technique for the settlement of disputes received considerable support in the period between the two world wars. In using this technique an IGO appoints an individual or a group of individuals to investigate at the site of an incident the issues in a dispute between states and to report their findings to the IGO. The assumption is that if the facts are widely known, the parties to the dispute will somehow resolve their differences.

The most prominent fact-finding effort was the commission of inquiry that the League of Nations dispatched to investigate the Japanese invasion of Manchuria in 1931. The commission was slow in completing its mission, and although it reported that the Japanese attack was not an act of self-defense as had been claimed, and the League assembly eventually approved the report, the commission had virtually no impact on events. Perhaps as a consequence, since then fact finding has found less favor as a technique of peaceful settlement. In addition, with improvement in communications and transportation, information about events in remote areas has become more readily available, lessening the need for fact-finding missions.

NORMATIVE ACTIVITIES

Normative activities are the principal function of almost all the INGOs working in the security field, and they also constitute a substantial portion of what IGOs do. Many INGOs were founded essentially for the purpose of propagating particular doctrines or points of view. Often, as in the case of the International Confederation for Peace and Disarmament, this is evident in their names. Once created, such INGOs devote their resources to publicizing their tenets. The constitutional documents of several IGOs, as we have seen, also contain normative pronouncements—for instance, exhorting states to settle their disputes peacefully—and exhortations of this nature are a regular feature of the activities of IGOs.

The resolutions that make up such a large portion of the output of the assemblies and councils of international organizations are perfect vehicles for normative pronouncements. The prominence that international organizations give to normative activities can be seen as a corollary of their lack of authority. If international organizations cannot order individuals or states, they can attempt to influence them by expressions of approval or disapproval. Normative activities do not have immediate, direct effects in committing resources to particular actions. They may, however, affect attitudes and thereby behavior. Given the broad membership of the U.N., its pronouncements probably carry more weight than those of any other international organization.

The most salient normative activities of international organizations concerning security may be grouped into five broad categories. The first involves attempts to refine the basic principles stated in the U.N. charter and elsewhere concerning the prohibition against interference with the territorial integrity and political independence of states. The second category consists of activities directed toward the delegitimization of Western colonialism; these activities have in essence excluded Western colonial territories from the basic protection given to the existing territorial division of the world. Normative pronouncements relating to specific situations constitute a third category of activities. Those urging disarmament and expressing sentiments against the further development of new weaponry are a fourth category. The final category is quite different in that instead of urging states to disarm, it has taken the opposite approach and exhorted them to maintain forces that would be sufficient to insure deterrence.

Refining Principles against the Use of Force

Even though the constitutional documents of many international governmental organizations have pledged members not to use force against the territorial integrity or political independence of states, the governments of many states have felt that this norm needed refinement and reinforcement. The movement for refinement began almost as soon as the League of Nations started functioning, and it continues to this day. As the twentieth century has advanced and new technologies and forms of social organization have been created, the complexity of the task has increased, along with growing awareness that the crossing of borders with massed troops is not the only way in which force can be used against a state.

Thus efforts to refine basic principles have often focused on defining aggression. Both the League covenant and the U.N. charter directed these organizations to take action against aggression, but neither defined aggression in detail. First steps toward a definition were taken during the League period, and a definition was finally adopted by the U.N. General Assembly in 1974. The assembly's resolution defines as acts of aggression:

1. The first use of armed force in contravention of the Charter [unless the Security Council concludes that such a determination] would not be justified in the light of prevailing circumstances.
2. The invasion or attack by the armed forces of a State of the territory of another State. . .
3. Bombardment. . . or the use of any weapon against the territory of another state.
4. Blockade of the ports or coasts of a State. . .
5. An attack by the armed forces of a State on the land, sea or air forces, marine and air fleets of another State.
6. [The use of armed forces stationed in another country with its consent] in contravention of the conditions provided for in the agreement or any extension of their presence. . . beyond the termination of the agreement.
7. The action of a State which has placed its territory at the disposal of another State to be used by that other State for perpetrating an act of aggression.
8. The sending by or on behalf of a State of armed bands, groups, irregulars or mercenaries, which carry out acts of armed force against another State of such gravity as to amount to the acts listed above. . .[3]

The resolution also states that the Security Council may determine that other acts constitute aggression.

Parallel with the movement to define aggression, international organizations have sought to erect additional barriers against coercion that might fall short of an armed attack against the territorial integrity or political independence of a state, but that would nonetheless seriously constrict the ability of a people to determine its own course. Efforts have been directed to give legitimacy to the doctrine of nonintervention in domestic matters. Not surprisingly, these efforts have been led and sustained by the citizens and governments of less powerful states. Their purpose has been to restrain more powerful states. Latin American states, reacting to the United States interventions in the early twentieth century, sought formal approval for the principle and finally succeeded in gaining this at the Pan-American Conference in Montevideo in 1933. At their insistence the principle was enshrined in Article 15 of the charter of the Organization of American States:

> No State or group of States has the right to intervene, directly or indirectly, for any reason whatever, in the internal or external affairs of any other State. The foregoing principle prohibits not only armed force but also any other form of interference or attempted threat against the personality of the State or against its political, economic and cultural elements.

The principle of nonintervention is also proclaimed in the charters of the League of Arab States and the Organization of African Unity.[4] Resolutions affirming the principle have been adopted at conferences of nonaligned states and congresses of the Afro-Asian Peoples' Solidarity Organization. In 1965 the U.N. General Assembly adopted a Declaration on the Inadmissability of Intervention in the Domestic Affairs of States and the Protection of Their Independence and Sovereignty.[5] Beyond restating the broad prohibition, the declaration proscribes economic, political, and other measures designed to coerce states, and enjoins states not to "organize, assist, foment, finance, incite or tolerate subversive, terrorist or armed activities directed towards the violent overthrow of the regime of another State, or interfere in civil strife in another State." The assembly adopted another declaration restating these principles in 1981.[6]

Delegitimizing Western Colonialism

At the same time that INGOs and the majority of states in IGOs have sought to elaborate the prohibition against attacks on the territorial integrity and political independence of states, they have also sought to insure that this prohibition should not apply to the colonial territories of Western countries, or to South Africa. This has involved first delegitimizing the notions of colonialism and of racial discrimination as practiced in South Africa, which the majority of states associate with colonialism. Anticolonialists have orchestrated a careful campaign that has made effective use of both INGOs and IGOs. As decolonization progressed in the period after World War II, the new states were unified in their determination to end colonialism. Meeting together at the first conference of nonaligned states in Bandung in 1955, they sounded a clarion call against colonialism. Following this conference and as a direct result of it, in 1957 an INGO, the Afro-Asian Peoples' Solidarity Organization (AAPSO), was founded with the express purpose of coordinating the struggle against colonialism and imperialism. Resolutions condemning colonialism have regularly been adopted at AAPSO's periodic conferences.

In certain respects both the League covenant and the U.N. charter can be regarded as steps toward the delegitimization of colonialism. The provisions concerning the mandate system in Article 22 and the general statement in Article 23(b) pledging the League's member states to "undertake to secure just treatment of the native inhabitants of territories under their control" sought to place international responsibilities on the colonial powers. The U.N. charter went farther and established the general goal of "self-government" for all colonies and dependent territories.[7] It was only in 1960, however, that the General Assembly, its ranks infused with the delegates of seventeen new member states, adopted the Declaration on the Granting of Independence to Colonial Countries and Peoples.[8] The resolution declared "colonialism in all its manifestations" to be a denial of fundamental human rights and contrary to the U.N. charter. It mandated the cessation of armed action or repressive measures of all kinds against dependent peoples. This resolution bore a sharp resemblance to those that had been adopted at Bandung and at the AAPSO conferences. Leaders in African and Asian states accorded great importance to the General Assembly's action. The head of Ghana's permanent mission to the United Nations, Ambassador Alex Quaison-Sackey, wrote that he had no doubt that Resolution 1514 (XV) was "as important to Africa as the Charter of the United Nations and the Universal Declaration of Human Rights."[9]

Since 1960 resolutions of the same character have been adopted in the U.N. and other IGOs, and all resolutions dealing with the protection of states from aggression and interference in their internal affairs have carefully enunciated that their prohibitions did not sanction the continuation fo colonialism. One could even infer from the resolutions of the early 1960s a right to support movements directed against colonialism and racism actively and with armed force. In 1961 when India seized Goa, a Portuguese territory, the majority in the U.N. refused to condemn the action. In the 1970s the U.N. General Assembly went so far as to regularly call on all states to extend to national liberation movements "all the moral, material, political and humanitarian assistance necessary in their struggle for the restoration of their inalienable rights."[10] These and other resolutions virtually sanction peacebreaking to end colonialism and apartheid.

Pronouncing on Specific Situations

Proclamations regarding specific situations constitute a third category of normative actions. The executive heads of INGOs that were created to advance a particular cause, such as the Afro-Asian Peoples' Solidarity Organization, frequently make statements and issue proclamations about particular events or situations. This can legitimately be seen as a part of their official responsibilities. The issue can be more complex for the executive heads of IGOs. Sometimes these officials do make strong statements about particular situations, either in their annual reports or in other public pronouncements. There is no difficulty when the executive head merely reiterates the substance of resolutions that have been adopted by the conference machinery of the organization. Occasionally, however, an executive head may feel strongly about an issue that has not been considered by the organization's assembly or council or concerning which no resolution could be adopted. The executive head could feel compelled to speak because of his or her sense of obligation to the purposes of the organization. When he was secretary-general of the U.N., U Thant regularly spoke about the Vietnam War and expressed his hope for a peaceful resolution of the conflict and his hope that the settlement would reflect the interests of the Vietnamese people rather than those of other states—even though it was unlikely that the member states of the organization would agree to a resolution expressing these sentiments. Such pronouncements involve obvious risks for executive heads and for that reason do not occur with great frequency.

The more usual form of normative action with respect to specific situations is the adoption of resolutions by the assemblies and councils of international organizations. Such resolutions are the principal product of conferences of organizations like the Afro-Asian Peoples' Solidarity Organization. AAPSO has regularly condemned particular colonial regimes in strident terms; it has also supported the Palestine Liberation Organization and condemned Israel. Similar resolutions have been adopted in certain IGOs, such as the Organization of African Unity. The U.N. General Assembly has also adopted resolutions on a variety of situations involving decolonization. Before the assembly's anticolonial group gained its present preponderant majority, these tended to be bland and went no further than expressing the hope that the conflict would be settled in accordance with the principles of the charter. As the strength of the anticolonial group grew, however, the resolutions became increasingly bold in their support of rapid and complete decolonization. Starting in the mid-1960s, assembly resolutions have regularly called for the cessation of the use of armed force against independence movements, and directed administering states to yield to nationalist demands and establish time-tables for rapidly granting independence. These resolutions come much closer to those of AAPSO.

International governmental organizations have also made pronouncements about actions of states in situations that did not involve Western colonialism. In 1956 the U.N. General Assembly condemned the Soviet occupation of Hungary.[11] In 1968 the principal Western states sought to have the Security Council take similar action with respect to Czechoslovakia, but this effort was frustrated by a Soviet veto. NATO did condemn the invasion and occupation of Czechoslovakia.[12] Conversely, the Political Consultative Committee of the Warsaw Treaty Organization regularly condemned the American involvement in Vietnam.[13] In 1980, 1981, and 1982, the General Assembly called for the withdrawal of foreign (i.e. Soviet) troops from Afghanistan.[14]

The significance of such pronouncements is difficult to gauge. It is clear, however, that governments devote substantial efforts to trying to prevent them. Obviously it is more of an embarrassment for a state to be condemned by an organization to which it belongs than by one with membership limited to the other side, and a collective condemnation carries more force than the words of a single individual or a single state.

Often what is involved in these pronouncements is the application to particular circumstances of a norm previously articulated in general terms. Further evidence that states are sensitive to being pilloried in this fashion is provided by the fact that when states find themselves in situations that involve broad norms of behavior, they have increasingly sought collective approval for their acts. After U.S. military forces invaded the Dominican Republic in 1965, the United States sought to have them incorporated as the principal element of an OAS force, and the Soviet invasion of Czechoslovakia was more or less a multilateral operation of WTO. Both the United States and the Soviet Union, however, had to make significant concessions in their original positions to obtain whatever collective sanction they gained.

International organizations can also take less formal action. Merely agreeing to hear a party to a dispute can sometimes confer a status that is important. This has been true particularly in cases involving decolonization in which the Western metropolitan state has regarded individuals in the nationalist movement as rebels. When such individuals are heard by the U.N. General Assembly or some comparable body, they gain a certain legitimacy and also obtain access to a world audience that they would not otherwise have.

What is involved in all of these actions is "collective legitimization," the bestowing of approval.[15] And the giving of collective approval also implies the function of registering collective disapproval. Both with respect to broad principles and in particular circumstances, international organizations have become important articulators and defenders of norms.

Urging Disarmament and Arms Control

International organizations have performed similar functions with respect to disarmament generally and to efforts to control new weapons in particular. As its name implies, this is the principal purpose of the International Confederation for Disarmament and Peace, and other INGOs have also acted in this field.

Several IGOs, including the U.N., have adopted resolutions on these matters. The General Assembly has urged that there should be disarmament. It has expressed the hope that the testing of nuclear weapons could be ended, and it has condemned particular nuclear weapons tests. The assembly has also asked states not to deploy nuclear weapons in outer space, on the deep sea bed, or in Antarctica, Africa, and Latin America. Other General Assembly resolutions have taken a stand against the development of chemical and bacteriological weapons. Limited membership organizations have taken similar stands on many of the same issues. Sometimes these hortatory resolutions have been as far as states have been willing to go, but they have often served as a prelude to the preparation and adoption of a legally binding convention.

Exhorting States to Arm

The final category of normative actions is different from those that have been considered to this point, and it is peculiarly the province of IGOs. This category involves efforts urging states to arm rather than disarm. To accept that these actions are related to security, one must agree that many approaches to the problem of security are possible, that ensuring that states have sufficient arms can be an important ingredient in security, and that simultaneous pursuit of different approaches to security is not necessarily counterproductive.

The North Atlantic Treaty Organization provides the most important example of the process. NATO is a crucial factor in determining the military forces of its member states. Many of the smaller states, such as Belgium, the Netherlands, Denmark, and Norway, can rationally envisage their own defense under modern conditions only within the context of a broader coalition. A unilateral program, given the geographical location of these states and the limited size of their territories and populations, would have little rationale. Another consequence of NATO is that it makes possible the permanent stationing of United States troops in Europe, which is acceptable both to the Europeans and to the Americans only in the context of a joint effort. So NATO provides a framework for a joint military effort.

The alliance's normative activities give substance to this framework. Starting in the early 1950s, attempts were made to establish overall "force goals" that could serve as a basic structure for targets for individual member states. Countries' efforts were regularly reviewed by the alliance. Starting in 1966, force goals were set for the five coming years, and target contributions were set for each of the participating countries. Establishing the force goals is a complex process that involves the preparation of guidelines by the Council of Ministers, estimates of military requirements by NATO military commanders, review by several committees, and ultimate adoption by the Defense Planning Committee. According to the official NATO handbook, in setting the goals for each country an attempt is made:

> . . . to ensure that there is an element of challenge in the goals which each country is being asked to accept: a reasonable and realistic challenge in all the circumstances, but still a challenge which goes somewhat beyond the countries' supposed intentions, in the interests of collective defense planning for the Alliance.[16]

After the force goals are established, individual countries formulate their own force and financial plans, and these are then forwarded to NATO, where they are analyzed by both the NATO international staff and its military authorities. Eventually, the Defense Review Committee conducts a "multilateral" examination of all countries' plans and attempts to eliminate differences between these plans and NATO's force goals. The Defense Review Committee then reports to the Defense Planning Committee on the extent to which countries have been able to meet the force goals and why they have fallen short if they have. Although the alliance cannot legally compel countries to maintain military establishments of particular levels and character, this process brings considerable moral suasion to bear. It involves responsible national governmental officials at all stages; it forces them to contribute to setting targets and then to explain their country's behavior in light of these targets. The process has undoubtedly contributed to the NATO countries' maintenance of a relatively high and stable level of military armaments since the alliance's formation.

Although the procedures of the Warsaw Treaty Organization are not as widely publicized, a similar process presumably occurs in that organization with rather similar results. In this way, the two alliance structures have maintained a rough military balance between themselves. Table 8.1 shows the total forces of the members of NATO and WTO. The figures in Table 8.1 include the entire military establishments of the United States and the Soviet Union, not all of which would be available for combat in Europe. The point made earlier that different countries have different force structures can be seen from the fact that NATO has more personnel than WTO but fewer division equivalents. The principal feature suggested by the table, however, is the strong pressure toward stable and mutually balanced forces.

RULE-CREATING ACTIVITIES

The rule-creating activities of IGOs concerning security have as their end product conventions that have legally binding effect on states that ratify them. In this sense, they are more analogous to the domestic legislative and administrative

TABLE 8.1
Military Forces of NATO and WTO Members

	1962	1967	1972	1977	1982
Military Personnel					
NATO	5,914,000	6,278,800	5,141,231	4,762,300	4,998,000
WTO	4,579,000	4,271,000	4,393,000	4,751,500	4,821,000
Division Equivalents					
NATO	81	89	91	99	145
WTO	221	203	220	223	176
Tanks					
NATO	16,000	Not Available	Not Available	25,428	28,779
WTO	38,000	38,200	48,775	57,700	64,790
Combat Aircraft					
NATO	11,805	9,359	9,494	9,239	10,067
WTO	16,000	16,800	16,676	10,495	8,347
Strategic Missiles					
NATO	650–700	1,710	1,808	1,856	1,716
WTO	775	1,375	2,052	2,386	2,387

Source: Various issues of the annual publication of the Institute for Strategic Studies, *The Military Balance* (London: ISS).

processes that result in the enactment of laws and regulations than are normative activities. But unlike laws, which generally apply automatically to all individuals within the jurisdiction of the issuing agency, conventions still must be accepted voluntarily by states.

The constitutions of international governmental organizations with mandates in the security field contain some rules about the conduct of states. But, as we have seen, these are vague, and the founders of IGOs saw international institutions as providing the mechanisms for the preparation of conventions giving detailed content to these general statements. IGOs have attempted to perform this role, particularly with reference to disarmament and arms control.

Given the formal monopoly that states have on the legitimate control of force in international politics, the role of INGOs in rule-creating activities has been limited. They have, however, often served as sources of proposals for rules, and once conventions have been proposed by IGOs, INGOs have lobbied states to ratify them.

The Interwar Period

The League covenant envisaged an important role for the organization in preparing disarmament agreements, but despite substantial efforts, the League's accomplishments were minimal. The Treaty of Versailles had placed severe restrictions on German military forces and armaments, proclaiming that this would be the first step toward general disarmament. Because of this, from the outset the problem of achieving arms control in Europe was defined as either reducing the military establishments of other countries to the low levels set for Germany or allowing Germany to increase its armaments to some agreed level. During the 1920s Germany's goal increasingly became to achieve equality in armaments. France, on the other hand, in view of Germany's superior industrial base, felt that to allow Germany to have equal mobilized military forces would give that country an edge that would threaten French security. Although this dispute ran through all of the League's efforts, it was most evident in the General Disarmament Conference, which formally opened in 1932 and was to have been the culmination of the League's activities. The contradictory demands soon produced a stalemate. In October 1933, after Adolph Hitler had become chancellor, Germany withdrew from the conference and the League of Nations, striking a mortal blow to the chances of general disarmament.

Some arms control agreements were negotiated during the period of the League, however, but generally outside its auspices. At the Washington Conference in 1922, the United States, Great Britain, Japan, France, and Italy agreed that no new capital ships would be built for ten years and established a ratio for such ships (5:5:3:1.67:1.67, respectively). In 1930, at the London Naval Conference, this agreement was extended, and regulations were also adopted concerning submarine warfare.

The most enduring of the arms control agreements signed during the interwar period is the Protocol for the Prohibition of the Use in War of Asphyxiating, Poisonous or Other Gases, and of Bacteriological Methods of Warfare. This treaty, which was a byproduct of a 1925 League conference on international arms traffic, entered into force in 1928, and it remains in force. Even though the United States originally proposed the treaty, it did not ratify it until 1975.

U.N. Arms Control Efforts

Although the U.N. charter placed less emphasis on disarmament, by the time the United Nations came into being, many government officials and informed observers felt that the advent of nuclear weapons had given new urgency to the task. The first resolution that the General Assembly adopted dealt with this issue. The assembly created the Atomic Energy Commission and instructed it to make specific proposals for the control of atomic energy to insure its use only for peaceful purposes, for the elimination of atomic weapons and all other weapons of mass destruction, and for effective safeguards against the diversion of nuclear materials designated for peaceful purposes. At that time, only the United States had detonated nuclear weapons.

The commission's negotiations centered on proposals submitted by the United States and the Soviet Union. The United States proposed that the production of atomic energy should be managed by an international authority under majority rule and with extensive powers to insure that atomic materials were not being used for unauthorized purposes, and that there should be no veto in Security Council decisions about sanctions in the event that agreements concerning atomic materials were violated. Once the international authority was created, the United States would give up its nuclear materials. The Soviet Union, in contrast, proposed that a convention should be drafted immediately outlawing the use, production, and stockpiling of nuclear weapons. International inspection would be limited. Violations of the convention would be punishable under domestic laws, and any international decisions would have to be taken within the framework of the Security Council, where the veto would apply. The two proposals reflected the mutual distrust of the two states, a distrust that could not be overcome, and in 1949 the commission suspended its work. That same year the Soviet Union detonated its first atomic device.

In 1947 the Security Council established the Commission on Conventional Armaments, but it too soon became deadlocked in a division between East and West and was dissolved in early 1952. At the outset of this period, the United States had had a nuclear monopoly, and the Soviet Union, a great lead in conventional armaments. By 1952 the Soviet Union had created a nuclear arsenal, and indeed had even detonated a hydrogen device before the United States. On the other side, the United States and its allies had begun a substantial program within NATO to regain the conventional strength that had been demobilized after World War II.

In 1952 the General Assembly created the Disarmament Commission, which consisted of the eleven states that were represented on the Security Council plus Canada. Six of these states (Canada, Denmark, France, Greece, the United Kingdom, and the United States) were members of NATO, and four others (Colombia, Chile, the Republic of China, and Pakistan) were or would become allied with the United States. Lebanon and the U.S.S.R. were the other members. This commission assumed jurisdiction for negotiations with respect to both nuclear and conventional armaments. Negotiations in this body and in its subcommittees also proved fruitless, and in 1957 the Soviet Union refused to participate further, claiming that membership was stacked in favor of the West.

The following year the General Assembly enlarged the Disarmament Commission to include all members of the United Nations, but it was obvious that a body with eighty-two members was too large for detailed negotiations. The sole meeting of the commission that year was held to endorse the decision of the foreign ministers of France, the United Kingdom, the United States, and the Soviet Union to create a ten-nation disarmament committee, consisting of five states each from NATO and WTO. The equality of membership reflected the substantial balance that had been achieved by NATO and WTO in armaments.

That fall the General Assembly directed the secretary-general to provide facilities and assistance to the ten-nation committee. Thus the U.N. began a practice, which it has continued, of allowing the parties principally involved to determine the membership of the negotiating body and of limiting its own role to endorsing their decision. In 1961 the Soviet Union and the United States agreed that eight neutral states should be added to the ten states that had been named originally, and in 1969 they agreed that an additional eight states should be added and that the name of the body should become the Conference of the Committee on Disarmament (CCD). In 1974, following the admission of the German Democratic Republic and the Federal Republic of Germany to the United Nations the previous year, these two states and three others were added to the CCD. In 1978 the committee was renamed the Committee on Disarmament (CD) and negotiations were initiated to again expand its membership. This modification was designed to induce the participation of the People's Republic of China and France. France had not participated in the CCD, although it had been a member. The forty states that have been members of the CD since 1979 are:

NATO Members: Belgium, Canada, France, Federal Republic of Germany, Italy, the Netherlands, the United Kingdom, and the United States;

WTO Members: Bulgaria, Czechoslovakia, German Democratic Republic, Hungary, Poland, Romania, and the U.S.S.R.

States that are not members of NATO or WTO: Algeria, Argentina, Australia, Brazil, Burma, Cuba, Egypt, Ethiopia, India, Indonesia, Iran, Japan, Kenya, Mexico, Mongolia, Morocco, Nigeria, Pakistan, People's Republic of China, Peru, Sri Lanka, Sweden, Venezuela, Yugoslavia, and Zaire.

The membership of the CD reflects a carefully negotiated balance. In addition to the members from each of the two alliances, the CD includes all of the most populous states. The CD includes all of the states capable of major military efforts. The CD is the principal body for the conduct of disarmament and arms control negotiations that is connected with the U.N. It meets in virtually permanent session in the *Palais des Nations* and reports annually to the General Assembly. The assembly gives instructions to the CD and endorses the agreements reached there.

The first arms control agreement concluded after World War II, however, was not negotiated in the CD or its forerunners but in an even less formal way. The United States invited the states that participated in the International Geophysical Year (IGY) to attend a conference in Washington in 1959, with the purpose of preparing a convention that would insure that the Antarctic would be reserved for peaceful uses, as had been the case during the IGY. The convention that was signed gave all parties to the treaty the right to inspect one another's activities in the Antarctic to determine whether or not the prohibitions in the treaty were being violated. All the states that have activities or interests in Antarctica are parties to the treaty, and it has been in force since 1961.

In 1963, in negotiations in Moscow, the United States, the United Kingdom, and the Soviet Union agreed to the Treaty Banning Nuclear Weapons Tests in the Atmosphere, in Outer Space, and Under Water. Although the final agreement was signed at this trilateral meeting, and the earliest negotiations were also trilateral, from 1961 on, the eighteen-nation disarmament committee, forerunner of the CCD, played an important role. Provisions of the agreement were thoroughly aired in that setting. In contrast to early proposals advanced by both sides, the treaty in its final form is extremely simple. There is no international organization to monitor the ban. This reflects the judgment of the states principally involved that they themselves have adequate detection mechanisms. States that do not have nuclear weapons, such as Sweden, also have detection capabilities that are important sources of verification. Similarly, there is no provision for imposing sanctions against a violator of the ban. States may withdraw from the treaty should they decide that "extraordinary events" related to the subject matter of the treaty have jeopardized their "supreme interests." The test-ban treaty went into effect as soon as it was signed by the United Kingdom, the United States, and the Soviet Union. As of 1982, 111 states had deposited either instruments of ratification or of accession to the treaty. This list, however, did not include France or the People's Republic of China. In addition to limiting radioactive fallout, the treaty was designed to halt the proliferation of nuclear weapons, and in this respect the large number of states that have adhered to it is significant. It also has the effect of precluding the testing of anti-ballistic missile systems.

Four additional treaties have resulted from negotiations conducted at least in part in the Conference of the Committee on Disarmament. The first is the Treaty on the Non-Proliferation of Nuclear Weapons, which was signed in 1968. Under the terms of this treaty nuclear-weapon states agree not to transfer nuclear weapons or explosives to any nonnuclear-weapon state, and nonnuclear-weapon states agree not to acquire nuclear weapons or explosives. The nonnuclear-weapon states also agree to accept safeguards implemented by the International Atomic Energy Agency to prevent the diversion of nuclear material from peaceful to military purposes.

In combination with the partial nuclear test ban, this treaty is a strong inhibition against the proliferation of nuclear weapons. Because of this, before they would sign the treaty, nonnuclear-weapon states insisted that they should have some protection against nuclear threats. The protection ultimately given was a trilateral declaration by the United Kingdom, the United States, and the Soviet Union in the U.N. Security Council which contained a warning that "any State which commits aggression accompanied by the use of nuclear weapons must be aware that its actions are to be countered effectively by measures to be taken in accordance with the United Nations Charter to suppress the aggression or remove the threat of aggression."[17] The three states also co-sponsored a resolution containing the same warning which was adopted by the Security Council with all members voting affirmatively except France, which abstained.[18] This assurance proved sufficient to induce many nonnuclear-weapon states to sign the treaty, which entered into force in March 1970. As of 1982, 118 states had deposited instruments of ratification or accession. Again, neither France nor the People's Republic of China had signed the treaty. India, Israel, Argentina, Brazil, Pakistan, and South Africa also had not signed the Treaty.

The second treaty that the CCD played a major part in drafting prohibits the emplacement of nuclear weapons and other weapons of mass destruction on the seabed and the ocean floor and in the subsoil thereof. This prohibition does not apply to a twelve-mile coastal zone, but even with this exclusion the treaty bars nuclear weapons from emplacement on almost 70 percent of the earth's surface. This treaty, which was signed in 1971, entered into force in 1972, and as of 1982, seventy states had deposited instruments of ratification or accession.

The third treaty, which was signed in 1972, prohibits the development, production, and stockpiling of bacteriological (biological) and toxin weapons and pledges the signatories to destroy whatever such weapons they may have. This treaty entered into force in 1975. As of 1982, ninety-two states had deposited instruments of ratification or accession.

In 1977 the CCD completed work on a fourth treaty, the Convention on the Prohibition of Military or Any Other Hostile Use of Environmental Modification Techniques, and it was opened for signature. It came into effect the following year, and by 1982 thirty-four states had deposited instruments of ratification or accession. A draft version of the treaty had been discussed extensively in the General Assembly during the thirty-first session. In this case, as in the case of the nonproliferation treaty, the negotiation process began when the co-chairs of the CCD, the Soviet Union and the United States, tabled identical proposals. Concerting the positions of these two states has always been an essential prelude to meaningful negotiations in the CCD and its successors.

Since the late 1970s, there have been negotiations in the Committee on Disarmament directed toward a treaty that would ban the production and stockpiling of chemical weapons. Thus far, these negotiations have foundered on the issue of designing appropriate measures of verification and insuring compliance. There have also been talks on a comprehensive text ban and on creating nuclear-free zones in various regions.

As a result of a U.S. initiative in 1974, in 1979 the Convention on the Physical

Protection of Nuclear Material was completed. States that ratify the treaty are committed to take steps in conformity with their national laws and procedures to avert the dangers posed by unlawful taking and use of nuclear materials, for instance, by terrorists. The treaty was supported in the review conferences provided for in the nonproliferation treaty and in the International Atomic Energy Agency and is an element in the nonproliferation regime. It will enter force when it has been ratified by twenty-one states.

The General Assembly has endorsed and given its approval to other arms control agreements that have been negotiated outside of the U.N. framework. After an initiative by Bolivia, Brazil, Chile, Ecuador, and Mexico, negotiations ensued which culminated in 1967 with the signature at Tlateloco, Mexico, of the Treaty for the Prohibition of Nuclear Weapons in Latin America. The purpose of the Tlateloco Treaty is to make Latin America a nuclear-free zone. Although only Latin American states may sign the treaty, other states that control territories situated within the Latin American geographical zone may undertake the same obligations by signing Protocol I. Nuclear-weapon states may sign Protocol II, by which they undertake to respect the denuclearized character of Latin America and not to use or threaten the use of nuclear weapons against the parties to the treaty. As of 1982, twenty-four Latin American states had ratified the treaty. Argentina had signed the treaty but had not ratified it. Although Brazil had signed and ratified the treaty, since it had neither negotiated a safeguards agreement with IAEA nor exercised its right to waive this requirement, the treaty was technically not in force with respect to Brazil. The United Kingdom, the Netherlands, and the United States had ratified Protocol I and France had signed it. The People's Republic of China, France, the U.S.S.R., the United Kingdom, and the United States had ratified Protocol II.

Bilateral Soviet-American Agreements

In 1969 the Soviet Union and the United States began bilateral negotiations on the limitation of defensive and offensive strategic weapons. The two states have regularly reported to the United Nations on these negotiations, and the General Assembly has adopted resolutions encouraging their efforts and approving the results.

The Strategic Arms Limitations Talks, or the SALT negotiations, resulted in several agreements. Two of these are directed toward avoiding misunderstandings that might result in war. One is the 1971 agreement to revise and modernize the Direct Communications Agreements of 1963, under which two direct communications circuits are maintained between Moscow and Washington. The other (also signed in 1971) is the Agreement on Measures to Reduce the Risk of Outbreak of Nuclear War, under which the parties pledge to take steps to guard against unauthorized or accidental use of nuclear weapons. This treaty provides arrangements for rapid communications should the danger of nuclear war arise from an accidental or unauthorized incident involving a possible detonation of a nuclear weapon or from detection of unidentified objects on early-warning systems. It also provides for advance notification by each state of planned missile launches that go beyond its territory in the direction of the other state.

Two major agreements were achieved in 1972. One was the Treaty on the Limitation of Anti-Ballistic Missile Systems. This agreement prohibits nationwide ABM deployment and limits ABM deployment for the defense of particular regions to two widely separated areas in each country. The treaty also limits the weapons that may be deployed in these areas. The other principal achievement in 1972 was not put in treaty form, but in the form of an executive agreement. This "interim agreement," as it has been called, provided for a freeze of up to five years on the deployment of strategic missile launchers. In effect, this agreement was extended until the SALT II treaty was completed in 1979. In addition, the two states signed a general pledge to take measures to prevent nuclear war. A principal feature of this agreement is the commitment to have "urgent consultation" if there appears to be a risk of a nuclear conflict.

The ABM treaty and the interim agreement on the limitation of strategic offensive arms provided for the establishment of a Standing Consultative Commission, a permanent joint U.S.S.R.-U.S. body which meets in Geneva and has as its purpose implementing the provisions and objectives of the two agreements. Among other things this body has formulated procedures for destroying or dismantling weapons systems that are in excess of the agreements or that are being replaced by newer systems, as is allowed under the agreements. It is also a forum for discussion of evidence that could indicate violations of the several agreements.

In 1974 the Soviet Union and the United States signed two additional agreements, both protocols to treaties already in force. The first extended the partial test-ban treaty to underground tests of nuclear weapons in excess of 150 kilotons, and the second limits the deployment of ABM systems to one site in each country. In 1976 the Soviet Union and the United States reached agreement on a Treaty on Underground Nuclear Explosions for Peaceful Purposes and on a protocol to this treaty. The treaty and protocol establish a regime for the conduct of underground nuclear explosions for peaceful purposes (PNEs), to ensure that PNEs are not used to obtain weapons-related benefits. The principal innovation of the treaty is that it establishes on-site inspection procedures so that the other side can observe the explosion and the preparations for it. As of 1982 the United States had not ratified either of these supplementary underground testing treaties, consequently neither was in effect.

In 1979 the United States and the Soviet Union completed and signed the Treaty on the Limitation of Strategic Offensive Arms. The treaty established limits on the number of intercontinental ballistic missile and sea-launched ballistic missile launchers, heavy bombers, and air-to-surface ballistic missiles. Some influential political figures in the United States argued that the limits that were established in the treaty disadvantaged the United States, and others expressed doubts about the verifiability of Soviet observance of these limits. After the U.S.S.R.'s invasion of Afghanistan and the establishment of the military regime in Poland, the likelihood of the U.S. Senate giving its advice and consent to the treaty seemed extremely problematic. Both President Carter and President Reagan, nevertheless, pledged that as long as the Soviet Union abided by the treaty, the United States would do nothing to jeopardize it. Thus, even though the treaty has not been ratified, both the Soviet Union and the United States have observed its basic provisions.

Despite the U.S. failure to ratify the underground testing treaties and the 1979 SALT treaty, the search for limitations on nuclear weapons continued. In 1982 the United States and the Soviet Union launched the Strategic Arms Reduction Talks (START). Reflecting criticisms that candidate Ronald Reagan had made of the 1979 SALT Treaty, the Reagan administration proposed substantial reductions in the numbers of Soviet and U.S. strategic weapons. The U.S.S.R. tabled an equally radical although substantially different proposal. That same year the two powers also began negotiations to eliminate or limit intermediate-range nuclear forces stationed in Europe. Popular pressures to avoid nuclear war compelled governments to take nuclear arms control negotiations seriously.

Controls on German and Japanese Rearmament

Other arms control agreements have been reached since the end of World War II without any reference to the United Nations, yet they do involve IGOs. The most important of these relate to Germany. Germany's surrender was unconditional, and the terms of surrender provided for the complete disarmament and demilitarization of the country. Before a final peace settlement could be negotiated, the four occupying powers—France, the United Kingdom, the United States, and the Soviet Union—were at loggerheads. The cold war ensued, and Germany was in effect divided into two countries, the larger portion occupied by the three Western powers and the smaller portion by the Soviet Union.

As cold war tensions increased, rearming Western Germany appeared to be essential to any meaningful Western defense effort. This possibility was first discussed in the NATO council in September 1950, after the Korean War had broken out. After two years a plan was elaborated that would allow German rearmament, but only as a part of an integrated European force. As the European Coal and Steel Community, which had been negotiated in 1950 and 1951 and had come into being in 1952, had merged these industries, and thereby merged a major component of the war potential of Belgium, France, Italy, Luxembourg, the Netherlands, and Western Germany, so it was planned that the European Defense Community would merge their military forces. The other five partners would give up independent control of their military forces in return for gaining some collective control over the prospective German forces. This scheme, however, had to be abandoned in August 1954, when the French National Assembly refused to ratify the treaty.

Intensive negotiations ensued until an alternative way was found to allow German rearmament but to control the process. The final solution was embodied in a series of agreements signed in Paris in October 1954. France, the United Kingdom, and the United States ended their occupation regime and the Federal Republic of Germany gained sovereignty. The Federal Republic and Italy acceded to the Brussels Treaty, a collective defense agreement signed in 1948 by Belgium, France, Luxembourg, the Netherlands, and the United Kingdom. The organizational structure under the treaty was expanded. The new organization, to be known as the Western European Union (WEU), would have a council that would be capable of functioning continuously and a body under the council known as the Agency for the Control of Armaments, which would have the functions that its title implies. The Federal Republic of Germany signed a separate agreement undertaking not to manufacture in its territory nuclear, chemical, or biological weapons. It also undertook not to manufacture other specified weapons such as missiles, tanks, large warships, and submarines except under controlled conditions. The Agency for the Control of Armaments was given authority to monitor these agreements.

The Federal Republic of Germany was admitted to NATO, and it was understood that its entire military force would be put within the NATO command and would be subordinate to the supreme allied commander in Europe. Germany agreed that France, the United Kingdom, and the United States would have the right to station their troops within the Federal Republic up to the level prevailing at the time the agreements were signed. The United Kingdom pledged in a protocol to the Brussels Treaty to continue to maintain its forces in Western Germany as long as this was the desire of the majority of the parties to the treaty. The United States also pledged to maintain its troops in Germany. Finally, the Federal Republic declared that it would never have recourse to force to achieve the reunification of Germany or modification of the present boundaries of the Federal Republic.

The way in which the Federal Republic of Germany's military forces are integrated into the NATO command structure effectively limits their use to purposes authorized by NATO. All of the Federal Republic's land forces are assigned to the Allied Command in Europe. The supreme allied commander has always been an American army general. Eleven German divisions are assigned to the Allied Forces Central Europe, the commander-in-chief of which is a German general. Four of these divisions are in the Northern Army Group and seven are in the Central Army Group. Neither group is commanded by a German. One German division is assigned to Allied Forces Northern Europe, the commander-in-chief of which has always been British. Thus all German division commanders report to non-German superiors, and the highest ranking German general cannot issue commands directly to German division commanders, but instead must issue them through non-German generals. Furthermore, divisions of other NATO members are placed so that they physically separate the German divisions in the Northern and Central Army Groups. Although France withdrew its forces from the formal NATO structure in 1966, the two divisions that it maintains in Germany in fact cooperate with the command.

Shortly after the Paris agreements were announced, the Soviet Union and Albania, Bulgaria, Czechoslovakia, Hungary, Poland, Romania, and Eastern Germany signed the Warsaw Treaty. This created the Warsaw Treaty Organization and also formally allowed East Germany's rearmament. Although the rearmament of the German Democratic Republic (GDR) was not accompanied by the same number of protocols as was that of the Federal Republic, in practice the results have been somewhat similar. The GDR's military forces are integrated in the WTO structure, the GDR does not have a complete armaments industry, and Soviet forces are regularly stationed on its territory.

In both West and East the rearmament of Germany had been accomplished under controlled conditions, and the control was as important to the new allies of each of the two Germanys as it was to the other side. A goal that had eluded negotiations during the League period was finally achieved in the mid-1950s in a very decentralized manner. Given the centrality of the German problem in the nineteenth and twentieth centuries, this achievement may well be the most significant arms control agreement reached since the end of World War II.

Japan, the other defeated state with an industrial base to support a major military force, imposed restrictions on itself. Article 9 of the Japanese Constitution provides that "the Japanese people forever renounce war as a sovereign right of the nation and the threat or use of force as means of settling international disputes." The article further provides that "land, sea, and air forces as well as other war potentials will never be maintained." Japan's basic law on atomic energy limits its research and development activities to those with peaceful purposes.

Cold war tensions eased in the late 1960s, and in 1970 the Federal Republic of Germany and the U.S.S.R. signed a treaty normalizing their relations. In 1973 the members of NATO and WTO began negotiations on the mutual reduction of forces and armaments and associated measures in Central Europe. As of 1978 these negotiations had not produced any concrete agreements. However, the Helsinki Agreement, which resulted in 1975 from the Conference on Security and Cooperation in Europe, did provide for a voluntary commitment to prior notification of major military maneuvers in Europe.

The Ensemble of Arms Control Agreements

Table 8.2 lists the major arms control agreements that have been negotiated since the conclusion of World War II. The Geneva Protocol, the one treaty from the League period still in force, is also listed. As can be seen, the treaties prohibit the manufacture, stockpiling or use of bacteriological weapons, and they prohibit the use of asphyxiating, poisonous, or other gases. They prohibit the stationing of weapons of mass destruction in the Antarctic, in outer space, on the deep seabed, and in Latin America. They attempt to inhibit the proliferation of nuclear weapons. The Soviet Union and the United States have sought to limit their arms race and to insure that accidents or other events would not impel them into a nuclear war. German rearmament has been closely controlled, and Japan has imposed severe restrictions on its rearmament. Surely there is much more to be done to limit arms races, but the accomplishments that have been made in the years since World War II are significant.

RULE-SUPERVISORY ACTIVITIES

Contrary to what was envisaged in early disarmament and arms control plans, the rule-supervisory activities of international organizations have been minimal in this field. In part this is because not many rules have been created. But even those agreements that are in effect generally do not assign important rule-

TABLE 8.2
Major Arms Control Agreements in Force in 1982.

MULTILATERAL AGREEMENTS

Treaty and Date Opened for Signature	Number of Ratifications or Accessions, 1982
Geneva Protocol, 1925	118
Western European Union, 1954	7
The Antarctic Treaty, 1959	23
Limited Test-Ban Treaty, 1963	111*
Outer Space Treaty, 1967	82*
Treaty for the Prohibition of Nuclear Weapons in Latin America, 1967	24*
Protocol I	3
Protocol II	5
Non-Proliferation Treaty, 1968	118*
Seabed Arms Control Treaty, 1971	70*
Biological Weapons Convention, 1972	92*
Environmental Modification Convention, 1977	34
Convention in Physical Protection of Nuclear Material, 1980	4

BILATERAL AGREEMENTS, U.S.S.R.–U.S.

Treaty, Date of Signature, and Status

"Hot Line" Agreement, 1963, in force
"Accidents Measures" Agreement, 1971, in force
"Hot Line" Modernization Agreement, 1971, in force
ABM Treaty, 1972, in force
Interim Agreement Limiting Strategic Offensive Arms, 1972, in force
Prevention of Nuclear War, 1973, in force
ABM Protocol, 1974, in force
Threshold Testban and Protocol, 1974, not ratified
Underground PNE Ban and Protocol, 1976, not ratified
Treaty on the Limitation of Strategic Offensive Arms, 1979, not ratified

*The totals for the ratifications and accessions listed here differ from those listed by ACDA because the Byelorussian SSR and the Ukrainian SSR are included here while they are not included in ACDA's totals.

Source: United States, Arms Control and Disarmament Agency, *Arms Control and Disarmament Agreements: Texts and History of Negotiations* (Washington, D.C.: Government Printing Office, 1982).

supervisory roles to international organizations. The partial test ban, the outer space treaty, the treaty on the deep seabed, and the SALT agreements are monitored by the parties to the agreements. International organizations are not formally involved in the detection or verification of violations, and the basic sanction against violations is the right of the aggrieved party to withdraw from the agreement.

The United Nations did, however, become involved in investigating allegations raised by the United States in 1981 that the Soviet Union used or made possible the use of chemical weapons in Afghanistan and chemical and toxin weapons in Southeast Asia. In 1982 a group of experts appointed by the U.N. secretariat concluded that available evidence indicated that toxins had been used in Asia.

A major reason neither INGOs nor IGOs have been given significant rule-supervisory functions is the difficulty of creating institutions in which all affected states would have confidence. The problem arose early in the negotiations on nuclear weapons when the Soviet Union made it clear that it would feel confident in giving the Security Council extensive powers only if it retained the right of veto, a condition that the United States considered unacceptable to its security interests. The U.S.S.R. claimed that it feared a hostile majority in the Security Council would take unwarranted action against it. The United States asserted that it feared the veto would be used to block justified action against a violator. No way could be found to satisfy both sides, and the broad problem has proved most intractable.

An INGO plays a minor role in monitoring the partial nuclear test ban treaty in that the Stockholm International Peace Research Institute collects and publishes material on nuclear tests that are conducted. SIPRI relies heavily on the work of the Swedish seismic detection center at Uppsala and the Swedish Institute for National Defense. The United States announces most of the tests that it conducts and also most of the tests of other states that it detects. SIPRI reports supplement and confirm those of the United States.

Only three agreements involve international governmental organizations in substantial ways in rule-supervisory activities: the Treaty for the Prohibition of Nuclear Weapons in Latin America, the Treaty on the Non-Proliferation of Nuclear Weapons, and the protocol and related agreements that brought the Federal Republic of Germany into the Western European Union.

The Treaty of Tlateloco established the Agency for the Prohibition of Nuclear Weapons in Latin America to operate a control system specified in the treaty. This control system provided that all of the parties to the treaty should enter into safeguards agreements with the International Atomic Energy Agency. And it allowed both the IAEA and the council of the agency to conduct on-site investigations in the territories of the signatories under specified circumstances. As of 1982, no such on-site investigations had been conducted.

The nonproliferation treaty committed the nonnuclear-weapon states to accept the IAEA safeguards system to verify that they are fulfilling their obligations under the treaty. Essentially the safeguards aim at insuring that nuclear materials used in power reactors and for other peaceful purposes are not diverted for use in the construction of weapons. The safeguards are accomplished through auditing procedures and direct inspection. As of mid-1980, IAEA safeguards agreements with sixty-nine countries that were parties to the nonproliferation treaty had entered into force. IAEA was negotiating agreements with several other states, and under other arrangements, it administered safeguards agreements in several additional countries. The European Atomic Energy Community also maintains a safeguards system for its members.

The rule-supervisory body with the most substantial historical record is the Agency for the Control of Armaments (ACA) of the Western European Union; it has conducted its activities since January 1956. The ACA monitors the Federal Republic of Germany's compliance with the agreements that it made not to manufacture various types of weapons by inspecting the manufacturing establishments that could undertake such production. It also monitors all of the military forces and equipment of all of the member states of the Western European Union.

ACA, which has its offices in Paris, has a modest staff of about fifty citizens of the seven WEU countries, of whom twenty are at the professional level. The director of ACA has always been a retired French general officer. The governments of the member states of WEU submit statistical material to ACA annually in response to a detailed questionnaire prepared by the agency. ACA examines this material and also conducts about seventy unannounced and randomly chosen on-site inspections each year to verify its accuracy. ACA has never inspected the nuclear weapons of United States forces in Europe or those held by the United States and another NATO country under the so-called "double key" control, by which the consent of both countries would be required before the weapons could be used. With the exception of monitoring German nonproduction of weapons, ACA exercises mutual supervision within the framework of an alliance. By the late 1960s its functioning had become routine, but in earlier years its work was vital to making people in both Western and Eastern Europe confident that the Federal Republic of Germany was rearming in a controlled manner. Presumably it could provide assurances again if they were needed.

The rule-supervisory role of international organizations in the security field is modest. It is most extensive with respect to technologies that can be used for peaceful as well as military purposes and with respect to the less powerful countries (especially the nonnuclear-weapon states) and those that have been defeated in major wars (such as the Federal Republic of Germany). Its function is primarily that of giving reassurances that states are observing their obligations, rather than ferreting out violators.

Similarly, the international courts have not become a major force in dispute settlement. During its existence (1922–1946) the Permanent Court of International Justice ruled on thirty-seven contentious cases and twenty-eight advisory cases, and from 1946 through mid-1980 the International Court of Justice had rendered opinions in forty contentious cases and sixteen advisory cases. Few of these involved the most serious issues of the times.

OPERATIONAL ACTIVITIES

The operational activities of international organizations in the area of security fall into three broad categories: those relating to mediation and conciliation efforts, those relating to the imposition of economic sanctions, and those relating to the deployment of military forces. INGOs have been involved in activities in the first category, but various IGOs have undertaken activities of each of the three types.

Mediation and Conciliation Efforts

In the contemporary global political system, both INGOs and IGOs have been used as instruments for mediation and conciliation efforts. During military conflicts the International Committee of the Red Cross (ICRC), or its agents, tries to have regular contact with officials of all sides to fulfill its mandate of insuring that military and civilian casualties receive protection and assistance. Through these contacts, and its links with national Red Cross societies, the ICRC can sometimes serve as a go-between and facilitate communication between opposing sides. The ICRC's efforts and accomplishments, however, have been given little publicity for fear of compromising the committee's ability to perform its primary function of providing humanitarian assistance.

International governmental organizations are more frequently and prominently engaged in conciliation and mediation. Often the executive head serves as mediator or go-between. U Thant did this during the 1962 Cuban missile crisis; he appealed personally to President Kennedy and Chairman Khrushchev and then visited Cuba. U.N. Secretary-General Javier Perez de Cuéllar sought to mediate between the United Kingdom and Argentina in the Falkland/Islas Malvinas crisis in 1982. The secretary-general of NATO, Dirk U. Stikker, mediated between Greece and Turkey with respect to Cyprus in 1967. The secretary-general of the Arab League attempted to mediate in the civil war that erupted in Yemen after the 1962 revolution and in other disputes. The executive heads of other international governmental organizations have made similar efforts. Sometimes, rather than being personally involved, executive heads appoint, either on their own initiative or with the authorization of a council or an assembly, personal or special representatives to undertake mediatory functions. In the 1950s Ralph Bunche served as the U.N.'s mediator in the Palestinian disputes, and a decade later Gunnar Jarring performed somewhat similar functions in the Middle East.

Instead of appointing a single mediator, an international governmental organization may appoint a commission, naming either individuals or states, which will then in turn name individuals. The League council frequently resorted to this device, appointing a commission in the Greece-Bulgarian incident (1925) and in the conflict between Colombia and Peru (1932–1934). There have been numerous U.N. commissions and committees attempting to ease the Arab-Israeli conflict in the Middle East and the various conflicts between India and Pakistan, among others. The Organization of American States has a standing body, the

Inter-American Peace Committee, which has been an instrument of conciliation in numerous disputes in the Caribbean and in Latin America. And the Organization of African Unity has from time to time deputized one or a small number of its members to mediate in various intra-African disputes.

The nature of conciliation and mediation efforts varies with the circumstances. At a minimum, representatives of international organizations make communication between the parties to a dispute possible or easier. They may go beyond this by interpreting information. Sometimes they even suggest compromise solutions. Their efforts carry the moral force of the organization they represent; they can remind the parties to the dispute of the normative standards of the organization and the legal obligations that the parties may have undertaken. In this respect, international organizations now perform functions similar to some of those that in an earlier era were performed by the pope. When governmental representatives serve on mediation or conciliation commissions, they may discreetly bring the pressure of their government to bear on a solution.

Imposition of Economic Sanctions

The second type of operational activity in the security field, ordering and managing economic sanctions, has been undertaken exclusively by international governmental organizations. This was first attempted in the fall of 1935 when the League assembly voted to impose economic sanctions against Italy because of its attack on Ethiopia. These sanctions included embargoes on arms, credit, and raw materials (although not petroleum) and a prohibition against imports from Italy. The sanctions had little effect—Italy's conquest of Ethiopia was consummated the following spring—and they were eventually dropped.

After it had called for a cease-fire in the Palestinian dispute in May 1948, the U.N. Security Council imposed a nondiscriminatory embargo on shipments of arms to both Israel and the Arab states. In 1949 the General Assembly sought to cut off the assistance that the Greek guerrillas were receiving by calling on all states to refrain from sending arms or other materials of war to Albania and Bulgaria until a U.N. organ determined that their assistance to the guerrillas had ceased. In neither case was an effort made to monitor or coordinate the policies of the U.N.'s member states, and the resolutions had little effect.

After the People's Republic of China intervened in the Korean War, the General Assembly called for an embargo on shipments of strategic goods to that country. This embargo was enforced largely outside U.N. machinery and as a consequence of pressure by the United States. In 1963 and 1964 the Security Council called for an embargo on all military material to South Africa that might be used to advance its national policy of racial discrimination. In 1965, immediately after Southern Rhodesia's unilateral declaration of independence, the Security Council imposed an embargo on military equipment and petroleum against the recalcitrant colony, and in 1966 it called for a boycott of selected exports from Rhodesia. Starting in 1968, the Security Council adopted a series of resolutions that added up to a comprehensive program of mandatory economic sanctions against Rhodesia. Moreover, machinery was established to coordinate and monitor the application of these sanctions. The Security Council voted to lift the sanctions only after an agreement was reached in 1979 for the independence of Rhodesia, or Zimbabwe as the new state would be called, and the establishment of a government through majority rule.

Limited membership IGOs have also carried out programs of economic sanctions since the end of World War II. The members of NATO have sought to maintain an embargo against the shipment of strategic goods to the Soviet Union and for a time against the People's Republic of China, and in the 1960s the Organization of American States maintained economic sanctions against Cuba.

The economic sanctions of the League against Italy and the U.N. against Rhodesia were adopted under constitutional provisions that made them mandatory on the member states, and although the NATO decisions were not legally binding, they were expressed in a form and forum that exerted considerable pressure on member states to comply. In each of the three cases machinery was established within the international governmental organization to coordinate and manage the application of the sanctions, and in each case there was widespread, although not total, compliance by the member states of the organization. Yet in at least two of the cases the sanctions fell short of forcing the countries against which they were directed to change their policies significantly. Italy and Rhodesia both found some countries with which they could trade. (From 1971 to 1977 a provision of an act of Congress, the so-called Byrd amendment, named after Senator Harry Byrd of Virginia who introduced it, explicitly forbade the United States to participate in the boycott of Rhodesian chrome.) The Soviet Union and the People's Republic of China also found countries with which they could trade, and in addition they were able to make internal adjustments to compensate for the trade that was lost. Indeed, some analysts have even suggested that the Western embargo against the Soviet Union, rather than cutting off that country's supply of strategic goods, may have had the effect of accelerating its ability to produce such materials. How much the sanctions contributed to the ultimate collapse of the breakaway Rhodesian government is debatable. They were certainly a factor, but their relative weight in relation to the military operations by indigenous forces opposed to the regime is virtually impossible to determine.

Deployment of Military Forces

The third type of operational activity in the security field, also undertaken exclusively by international governmental organizations, consists of the deployment of military forces. Except for the collaboration involved in allied operations in wartime, this is a phenomenon of the period since the end of World War II.

The founders of the United Nations thought that the failure of the League to have an enforcement capacity was one of its major weaknesses, and they were determined to rectify this. The U.N. charter thus went into great detail to specify how the organization might employ force. Basic responsibility was to rest with the Security Council, which could, under the terms of Article 42, "take such action by air, sea, or land forces as may be necessary to maintain or restore international peace and security." Article 43 provided that member states would negotiate special agreements to make armed forces available to the Security Council for such use.

The charter also established the Military Staff Committee as a subordinate body to the Security Council. This committee consists of the chiefs of staff of the permanent members of the Security Council, or their representatives, and representatives of such other members as the committee may decide would be essential to the conduct of its work. The Military Staff Committee was to be responsible for the strategic direction of any armed force placed at the disposal of the Security Council. Theoretically these provisions would have allowed centralized control of the deployment of military forces in the postwar world.

Obviously, this did not occur. One major reason was the early collapse of the Article 43 negotiations. Soon after the Military Staff Committee was established, the Security Council directed it to prepare plans for the implementation of this article. Since it was generally understood that the greatest military contributions would be made by the permanent members of the Security Council, the first task was that of securing agreement among these states on the nature of their contributions. A deadlock soon developed between the United States and the Soviet Union which could not be resolved.

One major disagreement concerned the size and strength of the forces that would be put at the disposal of the Security Council, an argument that had been foreshadowed in the difference between the peace plan of the Abbé de Saint-Pierre and that of the Duc de Sully. The United States favored forces of considerable size and strength, while the Soviet Union wanted relatively small forces. On this issue, the positions of the Republic of China, France, and the United Kingdom were closer to that of the Soviet Union than that of the United States. At the root of this disagreement was the issue of the prospective functions of the military forces to be put at the disposal of the Security Council. The 20 divisions, 3,800 aircraft, and 185 warships envisaged by the United States would have been a far more formidable force than the 12 divisions, 1,800 aircraft, and 36 warships envisaged by the Soviet Union. The larger force would have been a challenge for any state, including the permanent members of the Security Council.

Another major division concerned the composition of the contingents to be provided. The Soviet Union argued that the contributions of the permanent members of the Security Council should be equal and identical, while the United States—supported this time by China, France, and the United Kingdom—maintained that the contributions could reflect the differences in the composition of the military establishments of these states and needed only to be comparable. Specifically, the United States preferred to contribute mainly air and naval forces and wanted the Soviet Union to contribute predominantly land forces. This issue was related to that concerning the size and strength of the forces, for if they were to be at the level preferred by the United States, the contributions of the permanent members of the Security Council could not be equal and identical. Apparently the Soviet Union feared that the Western powers were attempting to create a powerful instrument from which the U.S.S.R. might be excluded, and which could be used to further Western interests. The Western states, on the other hand, clearly wanted to forestall the possibility that the Soviet Union might, through its participation in U.N. efforts, gain military access to areas in which it had previously not had influence.

In sum, the negotiations foundered on mutual mistrust. The Military Staff Committee reported to the Security Council in 1947, but the council proved unable to break the deadlock, and the Article 43 negotiations have not been pursued further since then. Although the Military Staff Committee has continued to exist, it has been largely inactive since 1948.

Despite the inability to implement the plan envisaged in the charter, as the U.N. began to deal with disputes that had involved violence and might erupt in violence again, an urgent need arose to deploy at least limited military forces. The response was tentative and ad hoc, but it was a beginning. Between 1946 and 1949 the United Nations created four military instruments to monitor agreed cease-fires and carry out related services and to engage in fact-finding: the United Nations Special Committee on the Balkans (UNSCOB), the United Nations Truce Supervisory Organization (UNTSO) in Palestine, the United Nations Commission for Indonesia (UNCI), and the United Nations Military Observer Group in India and Pakistan (UNMOGIP). All of these groups were of modest size, and although composed of military personnel, their function was not to employ force but to act as observers and by their presence to be a deterrent to the use of force by the parties to the dispute.

The following year, however, the United Nations deployed a military force in a radically different way. On June 25, 1950, North Korean troops invaded the territory of the Republic of Korea. That same day the Security Council determined by a vote of 9 to 0, with one abstention (Yugoslavia) and one member absent (the U.S.S.R.), that the attack was a breach of the peace and called for an immediate cessation of hostilities and withdrawal of North Korean forces. The resolution was without effect; the North Korean attack continued.

On the morning of June 27, 1950, President Truman ordered General Douglas MacArthur to use American air and sea forces in the area to assist in the defense of the Republic of Korea. Eleven hours later, the Security Council adopted a resolution which noted that the North Koreans had neither ceased hostilities nor withdrawn their forces and recommended that member states furnish such assistance to the Republic of Korea as might be necessary to repel the attack and restore peace and security to the area. On June 30 the United States ordered a naval blockade of Korea and authorized the use of its ground forces in Korea. On July 7 the Security Council requested all member states providing military forces in pursuance of its earlier resolutions to make them available to a unified command under the United States. The next day, General MacArthur was designated commanding general.

Eventually sixteen member states of the U.N. provided combatant units. In addition, the Republic of Korea placed its military forces under the unified command. Thus began the most extensive use of military force under the auspices of an international governmental organization yet to occur. At first the U.N. forces were pushed back, but then the tide turned and they advanced north. As they rushed toward the border of North Korea, the Yalu River, forces from the People's Republic of China entered the fray, and eventually a stable dividing line was achieved near the 38th parallel, which had originally been the border between North and South Korea. A cease-fire was concluded in July 1951, and an armistice agreement was signed in July 1953.

Did this episode indicate that despite the failure of the Article 43 negotiations the United Nations could nevertheless deploy military units for major enforcement activities? Perhaps, but close inspection indicates that the circumstances under which the U.N. took action in Korea were unusual and unlikely to be repeated.

The Security Council was able to take the decisions that it did in June and July only because of the absence of the Soviet Union. Starting in January 1950 the U.S.S.R. boycotted most U.N. organs because of their refusal to seat the representatives of the People's Republic of China rather than those of Nationalist China. Soviet delegates were actually in New York in June and July; why they did not attend the Security Council meetings remains unexplained. When the Soviet delegates did return to the Security Council in August 1950, they blocked further action by that body through the use of the U.S.S.R.'s veto.

In the face of this situation in fall 1950, the General Assembly adopted the Uniting for Peace Resolution, which allowed it to make recommendations to member states with respect to the use of armed force to restore international peace and security even though the issue was on the agenda of the Security Council. Although this resolution provided a modality for continuing to prosecute the war in Korea, and it has since been used for setting in motion other peacekeeping activities, whether or not it would provide a way of inaugurating a major enforcement effort is debatable. Such an authorization would be sought in the General Assembly only if it had already failed to gain acceptance in the Security Council because of the veto of one of the permanent members, and it is not at all clear that the necessary two-thirds majority could be found in the assembly for strong military actions that were opposed by a powerful state.

As the Korean War went on, support for it in the U.N. waned. A General Assembly resolution decrying Chinese intervention in the war and declaring the People's Republic of China an aggressor was adopted by a vote of 44 to 7 with nine abstentions. India and Burma joined the five communist states then members of the U.N. in opposing the resolution, and Afghanistan, Egypt, Indonesia, Pakistan, Saudi Arabia, Sweden, Syria, Yemen, and Yugoslavia abstained. Since 1950 the number of U.N. member states that take positions on world problems similar to those of the states that abstained has increased substantially. Therefore, it is not at all certain that a decision to undertake a major enforcement activity would command the requisite majority in either the Security Council or the General Assembly.

Furthermore, the Korean effort was possible only because a powerful country, the United States, was willing and able to make a major contribution. At one point there were some 740,000 military personnel under the unified command.[19] Although several countries contributed these personnel, as can be seen in Table 8.3, by far the largest proportion came from the United States and the Republic of Korea. And the United States contributed almost all of the naval and air forces. Clearly the enforcement action depended heavily on the American contribution. The United States government was willing to make such an extensive contribution in this instance because it saw the action as part of its broad effort to "contain" communism. Whether or not one or more powerful states would see their interests as being as identical with those of some future enforcement action is problematical.

To date, the Korean case stands as an isolated episode rather than a precedent. The U.N. has continued to deploy military forces, but more after the model of the actions it took before 1950 with respect to Greece, the Middle East, Indonesia, and the Indian subcontinent than those that it took with respect to Korea.

The next deployment of military force by the United Nations came in 1956. In October, in the wake of the Egyptian nationalization of the Suez Canal, France, Israel, and the United Kingdom attacked Egypt. Although British and French vetoes prevented the Security Council from taking action, the General Assembly, acting under the terms of the Uniting for Peace Resolution, called for an immediate cessation of hostilities and a withdrawal of military forces to positions behind established armistice lines. The General Assembly also created the United Nations Emergency Force (UNEF) to supervise implementation of its resolutions by interposing itself between the belligerent parties.

At peak strength, UNEF had about 6,000 personnel, drawn from ten of the twenty-four states that offered to contribute forces. None of these ten states was a permanent member of the Security Council. However, the United States supplied substantial logistical support for UNEF. The commander of the force was appointed by the secretary-general of the U.N. and reported directly to him. Because Israel was unwilling to have UNEF personnel stationed on its territory, they were deployed only on the Egyptian side of the armistice line, and when Egypt requested in 1967 that they be withdrawn, Secretary-General U Thant complied.

TABLE 8.3

Proportion of Military Forces Contributed by Various States to the Unified Command in Korea

State	Ground Forces Percentage	Naval Forces Percentage	Air Forces Percentage
United States	50.32	85.89	93.38
Republic of Korea	40.10	7.45	5.65
Others	9.58	6.66	.97
	100.00	100.00	100.00

Source: U.S. Department of State, United States Participation in the United Nations, Report of the President to the Congress for the Year, 1951 (Washington, D.C.: Government Printing Office, 1952), p. 228.

The expenses of UNEF were placed in a separate budget for which the General Assembly levied a special assessment.

As UNEF forces were deployed, British, French, and Israeli troops were withdrawn from Egypt and a modicum of peace was restored to the Middle East. American disapproval and pressures may have been a primary reason for the withdrawals, but the General Assembly's resolutions meant that the three countries could take the position that they were responding to the orders of an international governmental organization of which they were members rather than to the injunctions of a more powerful state. The creation and presence of UNEF also allowed the three governments to maintain that the purposes they had sought to achieve with their forces would now be accomplished by the international force.

UNEF seemed to suggest a new and remarkably successful approach to peacekeeping for the U.N., and when the United States landed marines in Lebanon in 1958 for the announced purpose of preventing infiltration of agitators from neighboring countries, the Security Council responded by creating the United Nations Observer Group in Lebanon (UNOGIL), which had as its mandate monitoring and presumably thereby preventing infiltration. The United States marines were then withdrawn.

Two years later, the U.N. again acted on the UNEF model. Shortly after Belgium granted the Congo its independence (on June 30, 1960), the Congolese *Force Publique* rebelled against its Belgian officers, civil strife broke out, and the Belgians landed paratroopers. The Security Council called upon Belgium to withdraw its troops and authorized the secretary-general to provide the Congolese government with such military and technical assistance as might be necessary until the Congolese security forces could fully meet their responsibilities. To implement this resolution, the secretary-general established the United Nations Operation in the Congo (*Operation des Nations Unies au Congo*, or ONUC), which was composed of two sections, civilian operations and an international armed peace force, the United Nations Force in the Congo. This force, which like UNEF was composed of military contingents from states that were not permanent members of the Security Council, ultimately reached a maximum strength of 20,000. Again, the United States provided substantial logistical support.

In setting out the mandate of the United Nations force, the secretary-general proposed and the Security Council concurred that its personnel should "not take any action which would make them a party to internal conflicts in the country."[20] Yet in the circumstances prevailing in the Congo, this was virtually impossible. Almost immediately after independence (on July 11, 1960), the province of Katanga seceded, in September a constitutional crisis arose, and later other provinces attempted to secede. As the most powerful military force on the scene, ONUC tended to affect political outcomes, and the various sides sought either to enlist the U.N. to support their causes or to restrict its activities so that it would not interfere with their efforts to promote their objectives. Successive U.N. officials, force commanders, and secretaries-general earnestly strove to pursue a neutral and impartial course, but inevitably various parties to the several disputes were antagonized, and ONUC troops ultimately had to use force to secure their own freedom of movement in Katanga. In the process the Katangese secession was broken. When the United Nations force was withdrawn in 1964, the Congo's territorial integrity had been maintained, and the country had a government that was reasonably stable and capable of maintaining order.

As the disputes in the Congo flared, however, the original consensus in the Security Council on which ONUC had been created soon evaporated, and the Soviet Union shifted its position from support for the U.N.'s activities in the Congo to strong opposition. The expenses of the United Nations Force in the Congo, like those of UNEF, were charged to a special account, for which special assessments were levied. The Soviet Union refused to pay these assessments, as it had those of UNEF, and France also refused to pay for ONUC's military activities. Both the U.S.S.R. and France took the position that they would not pay for U.N. peacekeeping activities of which they disapproved, and in the end they were not forced to do so.

The next two times the United Nations deployed military force it took account of this economic reality. When fighting broke out in Yemen in 1962 between royalist forces loyal to the Imam and the forces of the revolutionary council that had deposed him, the secretary-general obtained the agreement of Saudi Arabia and the United Arab Republic to discontinue aiding respectively the two sides in the conflict. Then the Security Council, with the Soviet Union abstaining, established the United Nations Observation Mission in Yemen (UNYOM) to verify that these agreements were being observed. The United Arab Republic and Saudi Arabia agreed to meet the costs of UNYOM, which operated for fourteen months in 1963 and 1964.

Somewhat similar arrangements were made for the United Nations Force in Cyprus (UNFICYP). Cyprus, which had been ruled by the United Kingdom since 1878, became independent in 1960 under special constitutional arrangements designed to preserve a legal distinction between the Greek and Turkish Cypriote communities and to maintain a balance between their rights and interests. (Although the island is considerably nearer Turkey than Greece, Greek Cypriotes constitute about 80 percent of the population.)

After independence the situation on Cyprus was relatively calm until 1963, when the president, Archbishop Makarios, submitted constitutional amendments that would have reduced Turkish Cypriote autonomy. Fighting broke out between the two communities. In early 1964 the Security Council authorized the establishment of UNFICYP with a mandate to attempt to prevent the fighting, to maintain law and order, and to contribute through these actions to a return to normal conditions. At one point UNFICYP contained more than 6,000 military personnel from Austria, Canada, Denmark, Finland, Ireland, Sweden, and the United Kingdom. All costs of UNFICYP were met by the governments supplying the military contingents and by voluntary contributions.

In 1974 President Makarios was ousted in a coup engineered by a Cypriote group that favored *enosis*, union with Greece. Turkey responded by invading Cyprus. The Turkish army quickly seized the eastern 40 percent of the island, concentrated the Turkish Cypriote population there, and drove Greek Cypriotes to the other part of the island. Turkish Cypriotes have insisted that the island should be partitioned into two separate units; Greek Cypriotes have insisted on a unified government. The U.N. force in Cyprus has remained throughout all of this, contributing to the minimization of violence. But as of mid-1983 negotiations between the two Cypriote communities remained at impasse, and the U.N. had been unable to bring the two sides to agreement.

In fall 1973, in the aftermath of the Yom Kippur war between the Arab states and Israel, the Security Council reactivated the United Nations Emergency Force (UNEF II). In this instance the Soviet Union agreed that all U.N. member states would be liable for the costs. Another difference between 1956 and 1973 was that on the second occasion UNEF (with a maximum authorized strength of 7,000 and an actual strength of about 4,000) was deployed in both Egypt and Israel. When Egypt and Israel concluded their peace treaty in March 1979, they and the United States sought the continuation of UNEF II to monitor the agreement. Because of the Arab states' and its own opposition to the Camp David agreement which formed the basis for the treaty, the Soviet Union opposed extending UNEF II's mandate and let it be known that it would use its veto to block any extension. Given this impasse, eventually the Multinational Force and Observers was formed outside the U.N. under United States leadership to patrol a buffer strip along the Egyptian-Israeli border.

Progress toward a settlement between Syria and Israel has been considerably slower than between Egypt and Israel. In May 1974 the Security Council, acting on the basis of a joint Soviet-American proposal, authorized the creation of the United Nations Disengagement Observer Force (UNDOF) to monitor the cease-fire line between the two states. This force, which has an authorized maximum strength of 1,250, has also been financed by assessments on all U.N. member states. Basically the personnel of UNEF II and UNDOF have been drawn from states other than the permanent members of the Security Council.

When Israel invaded southern Lebanon in March 1978, the U.N. Security Council immediately adopted a resolution calling for the withdrawal of Israeli forces from Lebanon and creating the United Nations Interim Force in Lebanon (UNIFIL). Twelve members of the Security Council voted in favor of the resolution, which was introduced by the United States; but Czechoslovakia and the Soviet Union abstained, and the People's Republic of China did not participate in the vote. The representatives of the U.S.S.R. and China expressed regret that the resolution did not condemn Israel, and the Chinese representative stated that his country was against U.N. peacekeeping forces in principle because they could pave the way for superpower intervention. Later, in April 1978, the General Assembly approved financial arrangements for UNIFIL, which had an authorized strength of 6,000, by a vote of ninety-nine to fourteen. Most of the countries that opposed the financial arrangements took the position that the aggressor should pay the costs of UNIFIL. China and the Soviet Union were among the fourteen states that were opposed to the financial arrangements, and they indicated that they would not be bound by them. The failure to maintain the consensus that prevailed in financing UNEF II and UNDOF could foreshadow another financial crisis similar to the one that the U.N. faced in financing the Congo operation.

When Israel invaded Lebanon a second time in 1982, the Israeli forces moved directly through UNIFIL positions, ignoring the U.N. peacekeeping force. Overwhelmed, UNIFIL offered no resistance. The Israeli government felt that UNIFIL had provided little protection against attacks on Israel by Palestine Liberation Organization groups based in Lebanon. When a cease-fire was finally negotiated, the Israel government insisted that the international force to supervise the maintenance of order in Beirut should be established outside of the U.N., and it was. The multinational force established at the request of the president of Lebanon was composed of French, Italian, and U.S. military personnel.

The record has demonstrated a capacity on the part of the United Nations to deploy military forces, although this capacity is quite different from that envisaged in the charter. Except in the Korean situation, the U.N.'s military forces have been small. They have tended not to involve personnel from the permanent members of the Security Council, but rather from less powerful states. Their financing is precarious. They are stationed on a state's territory only with its consent, and their mandates tend to be confined to observation. They are introduced after a period of hostilities, and usually only when the parties to the dispute are searching for a graceful way to extricate themselves. The U.N. force provides this modality. The occasions for the deployment of U.N. forces can all be traced to lingering problems that have carried over from the colonial period.

How much use will be made of such forces in the future is open to question. Problems associated with the end of colonialism are gradually being settled. The fact that two international forces established outside of the U.N. were operating in 1982 in the Middle East, where U.N. forces have traditionally been used, made it clear that the U.N. was not the only instrumentality through which such forces could be created. If U.N. members do not broadly share in the financing of U.N. peacekeeping forces, one of the arguments for using the U.N. framework is negated. The main attraction of establishing peacekeeping forces under U.N. auspices must be the legitimacy thereby accorded to the forces. If U.N. forces are seen as ineffective, or if the U.N. is seen as a partisan in the controversy, this attraction may be lost.

Other international governmental organizations have also deployed military forces in conflict situations. When a long-standing dispute between Honduras and Nicaragua reached a peak of intensity in 1957, the Organization of American States arranged a settlement which involved submitting the dispute to the International Court of Justice, and then in 1961 the OAS dispatched a force to oversee implementation of the court's decision.

In 1965 the United States, apparently fearing a communist take-over in the Dominican Republic, landed 32,000 marines and army troops on the island. Eventually, the OAS authorized that an Inter-American Peace Force (IAPF) should be dispatched to the island, and U.S. forces were integrated into the IAPF, which also included 2,000 troops from Brazil, Costa Rica, Honduras, Nicaragua, and Paraguay and was commanded by a Brazilian general. All foreign forces were withdrawn in 1966.[21]

The Arab League undertook peacekeeping operations in Kuwait in 1961 and in Lebanon in 1976. When Kuwait became independent, Iraq claimed it as a "lost province." The Arab League eventually, after admitting Kuwait as a member to prevent a takeover by Iraq, agreed to station a joint Arab force of 3,300 in Kuwait, composed of units from Egypt, Jordan, Saudi Arabia, the Sudan, and Tunisia under Saudi command. The force stayed in Kuwait until 1963 when the crisis had passed. The Arab League also established a force in Lebanon in 1976, when communal fighting threatened the disintegration of the country. Syria provided roughly two-thirds of the some 30,000 Arab League troops eventually stationed in Lebanon. This force, which also included troops from Saudi Arabia, Libya, and the Sudan, in effect disarmed the combatants and imposed a cease-fire. Its presence was instrumental in the reestablishment of a government in Lebanon. Its presence also appears to have facilitated the build-up in Lebanon of military forces of the Palestine Liberation Organization. In the aftermath of the Israeli invasion of Lebanon in 1982, Syria maintained its troops in Lebanon, which by then were estimated to number 60,000.

Of course, the most substantial military forces committed to international governmental organizations have been those of NATO and WTO. At the first NATO council meeting in September 1949, plans were initiated for an integrated defense effort, and the following year a NATO command structure was created and an armaments build-up begun. The Soviet Union had substantial military forces throughout Eastern Europe at the conclusion of World War II, and Soviet officers commanded some of the forces of Eastern European states in the early postwar years, but a unified command was not created until the Warsaw Treaty was signed in 1955. Both alliances have joint staffs, and both conduct joint exercises. As Table 8.1 indicated, the two sides have maintained broadly equivalent military power. The treaties establishing both organizations proclaim that their purposes are defensive, and to date, except for the use of WTO forces in Czechoslovakia in 1968, the military forces under the command of the two pacts have been deployed only in exercises.

In August 1968 troops from the U.S.S.R., Bulgaria, the German Democratic Republic, Hungary, and Poland invaded Czechoslovakia. The action was not conducted in the name of the Warsaw Treaty; however, Czechoslovakia's attitude toward the pact was cited as a reason for the intervention.[22] In October a treaty legalizing the status of WTO troops in Czechoslovakia was signed. But even if the invasion of Czechoslovakia is considered a use of WTO forces, neither these forces nor those of NATO have been used outside the boundaries of the two alliances. Rather, they have stood, poised against each other, for roughly a quarter of a century.

The deployment of military forces by international governmental organizations since World War II, then, is quite different from the early visions reflected in the United Nations charter. While the U.N., unlike its predecessor, has been able to deploy forces, these have been modest (except in Korea). Limited membership organizations—for example, the Organization of American States and the Arab League—have also deployed forces, although less frequently. Two limited membership IGOs, NATO and WTO, have had major forces at their disposal, but these have been used mainly to deter each other.

Even though military force remains basically under the control of sovereign states, international organizations have taken important steps toward limiting and controlling the way in which this force may be used. Government officials are more aware than ever before of the positions of other states and also of the potential dangers of conflicts with modern weapons. There have been strong normative pronouncements against the use of force, and the use of military force for aggressive purposes has been declared illegal. Agreements are in effect that limit the dispersion and deployment of nuclear weapons and brake the arms race between the nuclear superpowers, the Soviet Union and the United States. The two major alliances have to some extent bureaucratized the control of military force and have provided frameworks for German rearmament. Finally, the development of peacekeeping capacities by the U.N. and certain regional IGOs has provided a new and useful instrument for efforts to limit violence between the parties to disputes and to prevent conflicts from spreading to other parties. But what effects have all of these actions had? It is to this question whether or not security has been increased as a consequence of the actions of international organizations that we now turn.

NOTES

1. Inis L. Claude, Jr., *Swords into Plowshares: The Problems and Progress of International Organization*, 4th ed. (New York: Random House, 1971), pp. 336 ff.

2. See Chadwick F. Alger, "Non-resolution Consequences of the United Nations and Their Effect on International Conflict," *Journal of Conflict Resolution*, 5 (June 1961), 128–145, 139–140.

3. U.N. General Assembly Resolution 3314 (XXIX).

4. Article 8 and Article 3, paragraph 2, respectively.

5. U.N. General Assembly Resolution 2131 (XX).

6. U.N. General Assembly Resolution 36/103, "Declaration on the Inadmissibility of Intervention and Interference in the Internal Affairs of States."

7. U.N. Charter, Article 73 (b).

8. U.N. General Assembly Resolution 1514 (XV).

9. Alex Quaison-Sackey, *Africa Unbound: Reflections of an African Statesman* (New York: Praeger, 1964), p. 139.

10. This quotation is taken from Resolution 3396 (XXX), "Question of Rhodesia," but similar phraseology can be found in resolutions dealing with other territories.

11. U.N. General Assembly Resolutions 1004 (ES II), 1005 (ES II), 1006 (ES II), and 1007 (ES II).

12. "Final Communique of the Ministerial Meeting of the North Atlantic Council, 14–16 November 1968," *NATO: Facts and Figures* (Brussels: NATO, 1971), Appendix 16, pp. 368–371.

13. See Robin A. Remington, *The Warsaw Pact: Case Studies in Communist Conflict Resolution* (Cambridge: M.I.T. Press, 1971), pp. 223 ff.

14. U.N. General Assembly Resolution 35/37, 36/34, and 37/37.

15. For a broad analysis of the function of "collective legitimization," see Inis L. Claude, Jr., "Collective Legitimization as a Political Function of the United Nations," *International Organization*, 20 (Summer 1966), 367–379.

16. North Atlantic Treaty Organization, *NATO: Facts and Figures* (Brussels: NATO, 1971), p. 97.

17. U.N. Security Council, *Official Records*, 23rd year, 1430th meeting (June 17, 1968), pp. 2, 4, and 5.

18. U.N. Security Council, Resolution 255 (June 19, 1968), paragraph 2.

19. Rosalyn Higgins, *United Nations Peacekeeping: Documents and Commentary*, Vol. 2, Asia (London: Oxford University Press, 1970), p. 202.

20. U.N. Security Council, *Official Records*, 15th Year, 872nd meeting (July 7, 1960), p. 5.

21. Joseph S. Nye, *Peace in Parts: Integration and Conflict in Regional Organization* (Boston: Little, Brown, 1971), p. 145.

22. See Remington, *Warsaw Pact*, p. 106.

FOR FURTHER READING

Bechoeffer, Bernard G. *Postwar Negotiations for Arms Control.* Washington, D.C.: Brookings, 1961.

Claude, Inis L. Jr. "The United Nations and the Use of Force," *International Conciliation*, 532 (March 1961), 325–384.

Fabian, Larry L. *Soldiers Without Enemies: Preparing the United Nations for Peacekeeping.* Washington, D.C.: Brookings, 1971.

Fox, William T. R., and Annette Baker Fox. *NATO and the Range of American Choice.* New York: Columbia University Press, 1967.

Goodrich, Leland M. *Korea: A Study of U.S. Policy.* New York: Council on Foreign Relations, 1956.

——— , and Anne P. Simons. *The United Nations and the Maintenance of International Peace and Security.* Washington, D.C.: Brookings, 1955.

Gordenker, Leon. *The UN Secretary-General and the Maintenance of Peace.* New York: Columbia University Press, 1967.

Jacobson, Harold K., and Eric Stein. *Diplomats, Scientists and Politicians: The United States and the Nuclear Test Ban Negotiations.* Ann Arbor: University of Michigan Press, 1966.

Lefever, Ernest W. *Uncertain Mandate: Politics of the U.N. Congo Operation.* Baltimore: Johns Hopkins University Press, 1967.

Newhouse, John. *Cold Dawn: The Story of SALT.* New York: Holt, Rinehart and Winston, 1973.

Remington, Robin Alison. *The Warsaw Pact: Case Studies in Communist Conflict Resolution.* Cambridge: M.I.T. Press, 1971.

Renwick, Robin. *Economic Sanctions.* Cambridge: Center for International Affairs, Harvard University, 1981.

Rotbat, Joseph. *Scientists in the Quest for Peace: A History of the Pugwash Conferences.* Cambridge: M.I.T. Press, 1972.

Talbot, Strobe. *Endgame: The Inside Story of SALT II.* New York: Harper, 1979.

9

TOWARD A MORE SECURE AND PEACEFUL WORLD?

Has the growth of international organizations contributed to achieving greater local, regional, and global security? As we have seen, the activities of international organizations with respect to security are many and varied. Yet these activities are far from the original visions held by those who have worked to supplant sovereign states with hierarchically organized world government. States remain the centers of decision with respect to the use of military force, but international organizations have attempted to inhibit some forms of state behavior and forestall others. Have these activities contributed to the security of states? Is the world more secure because international organizations exist, and in increasing numbers, and as a consequence of the activities that international organizations have performed? Important as these questions are, they are not easy to answer.

METHODOLOGICAL PROBLEMS IN ANALYZING CAUSATION

There are major methodological problems that make it difficult to give clear anwers to these questions and to others that will be posed in subsequent chapters. Causation in human affairs is a complex phenomenon that social science grapples with and handles with varying degrees of success. In analyzing individual behavior, it is often possible to create relatively controlled conditions, so that the effects of different variables can be carefully scrutinized—even laboratory experiments are possible. Dealing with individuals as their basic unit of analysis, psychologists have learned a great deal about human motivation, perception, and conditioning. Following the lead of psychologists, political scientists have become very sophisticated in analyzing electoral behavior. Through careful research, it has been possible to determine the relative potency of factors such as

family background, education, social and economic status, ideology, party identification, and the perception of issues in affecting an individual's decision to
vote for one candidate rather than another.

Analyzing the behavior of large groups of individuals is more difficult simply
because more people are involved and it is harder to establish controlled conditions for observation. Analysis of states is further complicated by significant differences in political structures, levels of economic development and wealth, and
physical characteristics, such as the size of territories and populations, borders,
terrain, and resources. Although states are the basic units in world politics, they
are so different that it is not always appropriate to treat them as if they were the
same, and it is often difficult to group them into meaningful categories.

Another problem is that the behavior in which we are interested does not consist of discrete, repetitive, easily observable acts. A state's going to war is a significantly different action from an individual's casting a ballot. Furthermore, the
number of events in which we are interested is relatively small, and thus applying
the techniques of statistical inference, which have proved such powerful tools in
analyzing individual social and political behavior, is more difficult.

For all of these reasons it is much harder to isolate the effects of different variables on the behavior of states than on the behavior of individuals. In both cases
multiple factors frequently, if not always, contribute to behavior, but when dealing with individuals, it is much easier to ascertain the importance of particular
factors.

We are interested in the effects of international organizations on security, but
we know that factors other than the number of international organizations and
the nature of their activities have changed over time. And changes in certain of
these other factors have also undoubtedly had profound consequences for security. For instance, the increase in destructive capabilities, especially the development of nuclear weapons, has surely had an impact on the willingness of
governments to employ violence. The character of governments and the nature
of their relationships with their subjects have also changed as a consequence of
higher levels of education, the concentration of populations in urban areas, and
greater political and social mobilization. In addition, the interdependence of
states has grown as a result of increasing international trade. Under these conditions, we must assume multiple causation and become resigned, at least in the
existing state of knowledge, to not being able to isolate the effects of any single
variable. We must settle for assessing broad trends and attempting to see patterns
of interrelationships.

THE OUTBREAK OF WAR

A major impetus for the early "peace plans" was the desire to limit interstate violence, and this has been a potent factor in the creation of both INGOs and IGOs.
The opening words of the charter of the United Nations are: "We the peoples of
the United Nations determined to save succeeding generations from the scourge

of war, which twice in our lifetime has brought untold sorrow to mankind..."
There can be no doubt that, in the minds of its founders and initial supporters,
the primary purpose of the U.N. was to prevent war. International organizations
will have achieved one of their major purposes if in some way they contribute to
limiting war.

Even though only a tiny minority of the international organizations in existence have direct mandates in the field of security, there are several reasons why
all international organizations are relevant to the issue of security. One object of
international organizations working in the economic and social fields is to antici-
pate difficulties and solve problems before they reach the stage of armed conflict.
Thus these organizations can be seen as having a conflict-avoidance function. In
domestic politics within states, success in limiting violence has always been accompanied by the creation of institutions for solving problems and allowing
change to occur peacefully. It is reasonable to assume that these processes should
also be linked on the international level.

Functionalist theory gives additional reasons for believing that all international organizations, whatever their mandates, are relevant to security. Functionalists argue that habits of cooperation learned in dealing with relatively technical
and noncontentious problems, such as those involving mail and telecommunications, will be transferred to other areas. They also envisage states becoming involved in networks of collaborative activity through international organizations
and predict that the desire to preserve and expand these networks will lessen the
willingness of governments to go to war.

Finally, international organizations increase the possibilities for communications among states. The greater the number of international organizations, the
greater the communications among states and the smaller the chance for misper-
ceptions. To the extent that incorrect perceptions lead to violence, fewer misper-
ceptions should contribute to security.

Warfare can be measured in various ways. For a first effort, perhaps the best
measure is simply the frequency of outbreaks of interstate violence. Scholars
have used other measures, such as the number of battle deaths in a war and the
duration of a war calculated as the number of months that it lasted multiplied by
the number of states that were involved. Battle deaths, however, are heavily dependent on the weapons technology available at the time, and the duration of
wars can be seriously affected by the levels of economic development of the participating states.

Figure 9.1 shows the percentage of sovereign states engaged in international
war in each of the years from 1816 through 1980. Since the number of sovereign
states in the global political system has expanded over the years, increasing the
number of states that could go to war, the percentage of states engaged in war
rather than the absolute number would appear to be a better measure of whether
states have become more or less prone to settle their disputes by violence.

As is apparent in Figure 9.1, there have been three periods in the years since
1815 when a substantial percentage of the sovereign states in the global political
system have been engaged in war: the period that began in 1853 with the Cri-

mean War and ended in 1871 with the Franco-Prussian War, the period that began in 1914 with the outbreak of World War I, and the period that began in 1939
with the commencement of World War II. The first of these periods involved the
unifications of Italy and Germany, and several of the belligerents were Italian
and German states that were eventually joined together. Therefore, in view of the
subsequent configuration of the global political system, the relatively high proportion of states engaged in war during this period is somewhat misleading. Certainly the common intuitive understanding is that with World Wars I and II the
twentieth century witnessed more organized interstate violence than did the
nineteenth century. After World War II fairly substantial percentages of states entered the Palestinian War in 1948 and the Korean War in 1950 and 1951.

Chapter 3 pointed out that the number of international organizations increased sharply after World War I and even more dramatically after World War
II. Whatever the effects of the international organizations that were in existence
in the 1920s and 1930s, World War II nevertheless occurred. But what about the
period since 1945? Figure 9.1 gives hope that states have become less prone to attempt to settle their disputes by violence. World War II broke out in 1939 just
twenty years after the conclusion of World War I, but more than thirty years
have passed since the end of World War II without the inauguration of another

FIGURE 9.1
Percentage of Sovereign States Engaged in International Wars

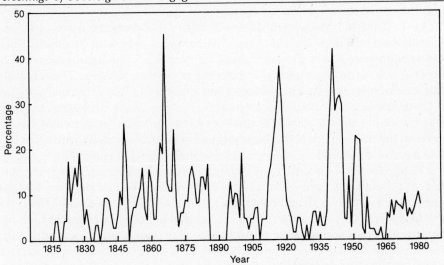

Source: The data on which the figure is based are drawn from Melvin Small and J. David
Singer, *Resort to Arms: International and Civil Wars, 1816–1980* (Beverly Hills: SAGE, 1982),
pp. 118–122.

major war.

Moreover, the participation of the great powers in wars has been limited. Great powers are those states with a capacity to play a major role in international security issues. During the period since 1816 the states that have met the criteria for great power status have been: Austria-Hungary until 1918; China since 1949; France, Prussia/Germany/the Federal Republic of Germany; Japan until 1945; Russia/the U.S.S.R.; Great Britain/the United Kingdom; and the United States. Given the military capacity of great powers, their involvement in war carries the greatest risks for the global system. When all of the great powers were engaged during World Wars I and II, the resulting violence was enormous. Until World War I, great powers frequently clashed. Since World War II, only the Korean conflict saw great powers fighting on opposing sides in an interstate war. Great powers have continued to be involved in wars, but only on one side, as in the case of the United States in Vietnam. Although during any given year since 1965 roughly 10 percent of the states in the global system have been involved in international wars, those have mainly been lesser powers.

Undoubtedly several factors have contributed to the relative lack of organized interstate violence in the global political system in the years since 1945. With the development of modern technology, particularly nuclear weapons, the potential destructiveness of war has increased enormously. Government leaders in all of the major states have frequently spoken of the awesome character of modern weapons, and they have indicated great reluctance to undertake any action that might result in these weapons being used. In addition, as the protests in the United States about the Vietnam war, in France about the Algerian conflict, and in Portugal about that country's African wars demonstrated, better educated and increasingly urbanized populations appear to be less willing to bear the costs of war than were earlier generations.

It is possible that the evolving webs of international organizations have also contributed to the declining use of organized violence in interstate relations. Each of the arguments advanced earlier about how international organizations might contribute to lessening violence is plausible in varying degrees. The relatively low level of interstate violence in the period since World War II charted in Figure 9.1 is of course not proof of the proposition that the tendency of states to resort to violence has decreased as the number of international organizations has increased, but it does suggest that international organizations along with other factors have contributed to a more peaceful global political system.[1]

The argument that international organizations have made a positive contribution to promoting security is strengthened by several studies showing that the greater the number of shared memberships in IGOs two states might have, the less likely they are to go to war.[2] The relationship is complicated by the fact that contiguous states are the ones most likely to go to war against each other, and they also tend to have the highest number of shared memberships in international organizations. Controlling for this, however, we find a slight tendency for states with more shared memberships in international organizations to be less prone to become engaged in significant military violence against one another.

EXPENDITURES ON ARMAMENTS AND NUCLEAR PROLIFERATION

The extent and type of armaments possessed by states provide another index of global security. Uncontrolled arms races and the spread of nuclear weapons to vast numbers of states would cause substantial insecurity. The chance of violent military conflict would increase, as would the probability that nuclear weapons would be used. Expenditures on armaments indicate the extent of armaments possessed by states, and it is possible to count the number of states that have nuclear weapons in their arsenals.

Newspaper readers must be aware that military expenditures have increased in the 1970s and early 1980s, and for some countries at a seemingly sharp rate. However, these expenditure data need to be put in perspective. Figure 9.2 compares world military expenditures with the world product—the sum of goods and services estimated to have been produced in the world—each year from 1960 through 1980. Figures for both categories have been adjusted for inflation and are in constant 1979 U.S. dollars. As is clear from the chart, although both world military expenditures and gross world product have grown during the decade and a half, the latter has increased more rapidly. In 1960 world military expenditures were $298 billion or 6.8 percent of the gross world product of $4,380 billion. By 1980 world military expenditures had risen to $495 billion, but they were only 4.6 percent of the gross world product of $10,792 billion. Figure 9.3

FIGURE 9.2
World Product and World Military Expenditures

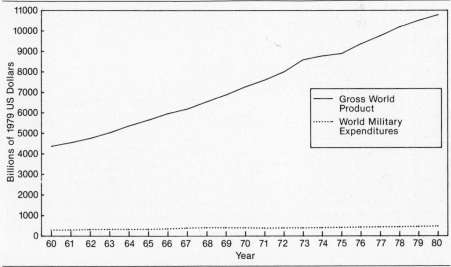

Source: Data drawn from Ruth Leger Sivard, *World Military and Social Expenditures,* 1982 (Leesburg, Va.: World Priorities, 1982), p. 26.

portrays the general trend and disaggregates this trend to show how developed and less developed countries have pursued divergent policies. Activities of NATO and WTO would be particularly relevant to the military expenditures of the developed countries, while those of the U.N., the OAS, and OAU would be more important for those of the less developed countries. Until the late 1970s the developed countries were devoting a decreasing share of their gross national products to military expenditures while less developed countries were devoting an increasing share, but in the late 1970s these trends were reversed. Since in 1980 the military expenditures of the developed countries were more than three and a half times greater than those of the less developed countries, a trend toward increased military expenditures by the developed countries would rapidly drive the world total upward. A much sharper change than has been projected, however, would be required to reverse the fact that, as of the early 1980s, a substantially smaller portion of the world product was devoted to military expenditures than had been the case two decades earlier.

A not unrelated development is that the proliferation of nuclear weapons has been much more limited than typically had been predicted. The United States was the first to develop nuclear weapons, and its atomic bombs, dropped in August 1945 on Hiroshima and Nagasaki, are the only nuclear weapons to have been used in warfare. The Soviet Union detonated its first nuclear weapon in 1949. The United Kingdom detonated a nuclear weapon in 1952, France in 1960, and the People's Republic of China in 1964. Only these five states, which are also the permanent members of the U.N. Security Council, have developed extensive

FIGURE 9.3
Military Expenditures as a Percentage of Gross Product.

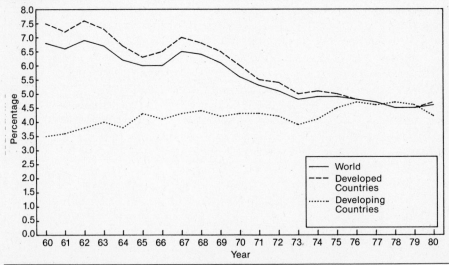

Source: Data used for the figure are drawn from Ruth Leger Sivard, *World Military and Social Expenditures, 1982* (Leesburg, Va.: World Priorities, 1982), p. 26.

arsenals of nuclear weapons. India detonated a nuclear device in 1974. The Indian government insisted, however, that it was interested only in the scientific and economic aspects of nuclear energy and that it did not intend to develop a nuclear weapons program. In 1981 Israel acknowledged that it has the capacity to make nuclear weapons in a short time. There is suspicion that South Africa detonated a nuclear device in the South Atlantic in 1979, but this suspicion has never been confirmed. Whether the number of nuclear weapons states in 1983 was five, six, seven, or eight, it was far lower than many officials and many informed observers feared it might be, and so was the number of states that had the technical capability to make nuclear weapons.

It is impossible to know whether the decline in the proportion of the world product being devoted to military expenditures and the limited extent of the proliferation of nuclear weapons will continue. It is also impossible to prove that international organizations have contributed to these developments. However, the developments accord with the broad objectives frequently expressed in IGOs and INGOs. In addition, there can be no doubt that international organizations have played a major part in keeping arms control and arms limitation considerations in the forefront of public attention. The enhanced public concern with limiting armaments has probably served as a brake on military expenditures. IGOs and their activities are unquestionably crucial components of the nonproliferation regime.

THE CONSEQUENCES OF IGO INVOLVEMENT IN CONFLICTS

To this point we have simply been looking at broad trends to which international organizations and their activities may have contributed. It is time now to focus more directly on the actions of international organizations and attempt to ascertain their direct and immediate consequences.

IGOs have increasingly been brought into disputes and conflicts in the global political system. One study, by Kal J. Holsti, compared the handling of conflicts that arose from incompatible objectives between two or more states and involved the threat or the use of force, and then analyzed how the outcomes varied with the modalities of their handling.[3] Thirty-eight conflicts were identified in the period starting in 1919 and running through 1939, and thirty-nine in the period starting in 1945 and running through 1965. International governmental organizations became involved in sixteen (42 percent) of the cases in the interwar period and in twenty-three (59 percent) of the cases in the period after World War II. The Permanent Court of International Justice was also involved in six cases during the interwar period, and the International Court of Justice in five cases in the postwar period, but five of the former and two of the latter were cases in which IGOs were also involved. Adding the cases in which only the courts were involved, international institutions played a role in seventeen cases (45 percent) in the first period and twenty-six cases (67 percent) in the second.

Another study, by Ernst B. Haas, found that of the 217 disputes that involved fatalities resulting from military activities in the period between July 1945 and September 1981, 138 (64 percent) were brought before one or more of five international governmental organizations—the United Nations, the OAS, the OAU, the Arab League, and the Council of Europe—and another 65 disputes that did not involve fatalities were also brought before these bodies.[4] An even higher proportion, 72 percent, of the 103 disputes that Haas classified as serious were brought before one or more of the IGOs. Moreover, the proportion of serious disputes referred to IGOs increased from 46 percent in the period 1945–1950 to 95 percent in the period 1976–1981.

Still another study, by William D. Coplin and J. Martin Rochester, discovered that a higher proportion of the cases considered by the U.N. and the International Court of Justice involved hostilities than of those considered by the League of Nations and the Permanent Court of International Justice, suggesting that in the post–World War II period more salient cases were being brought before international institutions.[5] Furthermore, despite the veto provision, 23 percent of the disputes involving fatalities considered by the U.N. between 1945 and 1981 involved as a party either the U.S.S.R. or the United States.[6]

Although the figures from these three studies are not totally comparable because of differences in the definitions of "conflict" and "dispute," the evidence seems clearly to indicate that a substantial number of situations that could involve a threat to the security of states have been brought before international governmental organizations and that this number has been greater in the period since World War II than in the period between the two world wars.

Holsti's study of conflicts also showed that forcible conquest or annexation was the outcome in fewer of the cases in the 1945–1965 period. Sixteen (42 percent) of the cases in the interwar period had such an outcome, but only six (15 percent) in the postwar period. Significantly, in both periods the chances of this being the outcome were diminished if the conflict was brought before an international governmental organization or an international court. In the interwar period 45 percent of the cases in which international institutions were not involved resulted in forcible conquest or annexation, but when international institutions were involved, this figure was reduced to 39 percent. Corresponding figures for the 1945–1965 period are 23 percent and 12 percent. If these data can be taken as evidence, the protection of the territorial integrity of states that has been an important goal of international organizations appears to be increasingly respected in the global political system; and the chances of this norm being respected appear to improve when international institutions undertake actions to ameliorate the conflict or dispute.

The empirical studies that have been cited seem to suggest that there are important differences between the disputes and conflicts brought before the Permanent Court of International Justice or the International Court of Justice and those brought before the League of Nations or the United Nations.[7] States in Western Europe, North America, and Oceania that are economically developed and have competitive polities are more likely to initiate cases before the courts than are other states, and the cases that are brought before the courts are less likely than others to involve hostilities. African and Asian states, on the other hand, clearly prefer to bring cases before the nonjudicial institutions. These differences at least partially explain why in the postwar period the tendency to bring disputes to the ICJ has not increased parallel to the tendency to bring matters before the U.N. Western states have constituted a decreasing proportion of the states in the global political system: the system has become more heterogeneous, and to be successfully utilized as an instrument of conflict resolution, law tends to require a certain homogeneity among the affected parties.

Differences between international institutions also appear if the cases brought before them are categorized according to the issues they involve. Using a typology of three categories of issues—decolonization, cold war, and other—Haas found that 38 percent of the eighty-seven cases that involved fatalities and were brought before the U.N. between 1945 and 1981 involved decolonization issues and 17 percent the cold war.[8] In contrast, of the fifty-one cases brought before the four regional organizations—the OAS, the OAU, the Arab League, and the Council of Europe—only 4 percent involved decolonization issues and only 14 percent cold war issues; 80 percent involved other issues. Almost by definition, decolonization and cold war issues involve parties from more than one region; thus the division between the disputes dealt with by regional and global organizations reflects the differences in their memberships.

The fact that a conflict or dispute is brought before an international governmental organization of course does not insure that it will be solved, or if it is solved, that the activities of the organization contributed to the solution. In fact, Haas found that in only 56 percent of the 203 cases brought before the U.N. and the four regional international governmental organizations between 1945 and 1981 did IGO involvement appear to have made even a modest contribution to managing the dispute.[9] He defined success in managing a dispute as (1) having an impact on abating the conflict for a period of at least three years, (2) stopping the hostilities, (3) isolating the conflict so that additional parties did not become involved, and (4) settling the conflict so that the parties did not raise it again. In his coding technique, even a modest contribution to any of these dimensions constituted some success. Using an index based on averaging the total composite scores for each of the four dimensions for each case before an IGO, Haas concluded that the ability of the U.N. and the OAS to manage conflicts had decayed in the periods starting respectively in 1970 and in 1965.[10] There was not a sharp difference in the percentages of cases in which the organizations scored some success, but the average extent of success measured across the four dimensions dropped.[11] This finding coincides with the demonstration in Figure 9.1 that the percentage of states involved in war has increased since 1965.

Both the U.N. and the regional organizations have been most successful with the categories of disputes that have been before them more frequently than other categories; that is, the U.N. has been most successful in decolonization cases, and the regional organizations have been most successful in cases that involved issues other than decolonization and the cold war.[12] The regional organizations had a somewhat higher success rate than the United Nations, but they were involved in only 80 cases while the U.N. was involved in 123. Moreover, the U.N. has consistently been involved in a higher proportion of the more serious disputes. Of the 103 disputes involving fatalities that Haas classified as serious, 52 were referred to the U.N. and only 22 were referred to one of the four regional IGOs.

Of all the variables that might be linked to the possibility of success, United States' leadership seems to be the most important. In an earlier study covering the period between 1945 and 1970, Ernst B. Haas, Robert L. Butterworth, and Joseph S. Nye found that when the United States took the lead in the OAS, the organization achieved some success in 82 percent of the cases, and when it took the lead in the U.N., the organization was successful in two-thirds of the cases.[13] With respect to all five organizations, the more the action taken had a substantial, as opposed to a procedural, character, the greater the chances of some success. Finally, the weaker the protagonists, the greater the chances that a regional organization would be successful.[14]

The apparent decay in the effectiveness of some international organizations in managing conflict in the period since 1965 may be explained by the decline in the number of decolonization issues and the pulling back of the United States from exercising leadership in the conflict management activities of the U.N. and the OAS. Nevertheless, as the 1980s began, more serious disputes were being referred to IGOs than ever before. And although it was true that a higher percentage of states was involved in war than had been a decade and a half before, these disputes were not ones that seriously threatened the global political system. For better or worse, the system appeared to have come to accommodate a relatively low level of conflict, largely confined to its geographic and political periphery.[15]

None of this, of course, proves that international organizations have made a decisive contribution to security. What we do know is that the percentage of states engaged in international war has been relatively low since World War II, and the proportion of the gross world product devoted to military expenditures has declined since 1960. There also appear to be fewer cases of forcible annexation and conquest. Furthermore, disputes and conflicts have increasingly been brought before international governmental organizations, and in at least some of the cases this appears to have contributed to settling the conflict. But if progress has been made in these spheres, what we have considered is merely negative security. We now turn to the elements of positive security, those relating to economic and social issues.

NOTES

1. After conducting a similar analysis of the relationship between the number of IGOs and the amount of violence in the global political system, J. David Singer and Michael Wallace in their article, "Intergovernmental Organization and the Preservation of Peace, 1816–1964: Some Bivariate Relationships," *International Organization*, 24 (Summer

1970), 520–547, concluded (p. 540) that "the amount of IGO has almost no effect on the amount of war which the system experiences." This conclusion could be an artifact of the analytical techniques that they used. They computed rank order and product moment correlations between the number of IGOs in the system and the amount of war in the following five-year period. The correlations were extremely low. There is, however, little in the theoretical arguments about the relationship between international organizations and war that would lead one to accept this as an appropriate test. Five-year time periods seem excessively short for any institution to have significant effects, and one would not necessarily expect there to be a close-fitting linear relationship between the number of IGOs and the amount of war in the global political system. Instead, theoretical arguments about the consequences of international organizations deal with broad historical movements. Dividing the century and a half covered by the data into six twenty-five-year periods, which accords with an intuitive periodization of the time span, and using averages for the number of sovereign states and IGOs in each period, as is done in Table 9.1 below, the data would appear to support the argument that as the number of IGOs has grown, the amount of violence in the global political system has decreased. Arranged in this manner, the data show that the period since World War II has been remarkably peaceful.

TABLE 9.1
IGOs and War

Time Period	Average Number of States	Average Number of IGOs	Wars Begun	Ratio of Wars Begun to States	Ratio of State Months of War to States	Battle Deaths per Hundred Population
1816–1839	24.6	1.2	3	.122	6.057	.747
1840–1864	37.8	2.4	14	.370	9.643	.5609
1865–1889	34.8	10.0	7	.201	7.83	1.45730
1890–1914	41.2	33.2	11	.267	18.337	2.21910
1915–1939	59.6	76.2	8	.134	21.862	5.0896
1940–1964	78.4	140.6	6	.076	6.945	.3631

2. See Bruce M. Russett, *International Regions and the International System: A Study in Political Ecology* (Chicago: Rand McNally, 1967); Kjell Skjelsbaek, "Shared Memberships in Intergovernmental Organizations and Dyadic War, 1865–1964," pp. 31–61 in Edwin H. Fedder (ed.), *The United Nations: Problems and Prospects* (St. Louis, Center for International Studies, University of Missouri, 1971); and David Morse Hopkins, *Conflict and Contiguity: An Empirical Analysis of Institutionalization and Conflict in Contiguous Dyads* (Ph.D. dissertation, Syracuse University, 1973, available through University Microfilms).

3. Kal J. Holsti, "Resolving International Conflicts: A Taxonomy of Behavior and Some Figures on Procedures," *Journal of Conflict Resolution*, 10 (September 1966), 272–296. The findings reported here are either taken from this article or are derived from data presented there.

4. Ernst B. Haas, "Regime Decay: Conflict Management and International Organizations, 1945–1981," *International Organization*, 37 (Spring 1983), 189–256. The findings presented here are either taken from this article or derived from data presented there.

5. William D. Coplin and J. Martin Rochester, "The Permanent Court of International Justice, the International Court of Justice, the League of Nations and the United Nations: A Comparative Empirical Survey," *The American Political Science Review*, 66 (June 1972), 529–550.

6. Haas, "Regime Decay," p. 243.

7. Coplin and Rochester, "Permanent Court."

8. Haas, "Regime Decay," p. 242.

9. Ibid., pp. 243, 247, 248, 252, and 253.

10. Ibid., pp. 203, 207, and 213.

11. Ibid., p. 249.

12. Ibid., p. 252.

13. Ernst B. Haas, Robert L. Butterworth, and Joseph S. Nye, *Conflict Management by International Organizations* (Morristown, N.J.: General Learning Press, 1972), pp. 27–30.

14. Ibid., p. 34.

15. See Haas, "Regime Decay," pp. 234–235.

FOR FURTHER READING

Butterworth, Robert Lyle. *Managing Interstate Conflict, 1945–1974: Data with Synopses.* Pittsburgh: University Center for International Studies, 1976.

——— . *Moderation from Management: International Organizations and Peace.* Pittsburgh: University Center for International Studies, 1978.

Coplin, William D., and J. Martin Rochester. "The Permanent Court of International Justice, the International Court of Justice, the League of Nations and the United Nations: A Comparative Empirical Survey," *The American Political Science Review,* 66 (June 1972), 520–550.

Haas, Ernst B., Robert L. Butterworth, and Joseph S. Nye. *Conflict Management by International Organizations.* Morristown, N.J.: General Learning Press, 1972.

Haas, Ernst B. "Regime Decay: Conflict Management and International Organizations, 1945–1981," *International Organization,* 37 (Spring 1983), 189–256.

Holsti, Kal J. "Resolving International Conflicts: A Taxonomy of Behavior and Some Figures on Procedures," *Journal of Conflict Resolution,* 10 (September 1966), 272–296.

Janowitz, Morris. "Toward a Redefinition of Military Strategy in International Relations," *World Politics,* 26 (July 1974), 473–508.

Levy, Jack S. "Historical Trends in Great Power War, 1945–1975," *International Studies Quarterly,* 26 (June 1982), 278–300.

Nye, Joseph S. *Peace in Parts: Integration and Conflict in Regional Organization.* Boston: Little, Brown, 1971.

Singer, J. David, and Michael Wallace. "International Governmental Organization and the Preservation of Peace, 1816–1964: Some Bivariate Relationships." *International Organization,* 24 (Summer 1970), 520–547.

Small, Melvin, and J. David Singer. *Resort to Arms: International and Civil Wars, 1816–1980.* Beverly Hills: SAGE, 1982.

Zacher, Mark W. *International Conflicts and Collective Security, 1946–1977.* New York: Praeger, 1979.

IV

INTERNATIONAL ORGANIZATIONS AND THE GROWTH AND DISTRIBUTION OF THE WORLD PRODUCT

10

INTERNATIONAL ORGANIZATIONS IN THE CONTEMPORARY GLOBAL ECONOMY

The activities of international organizations in the economic field need to be seen in the perspective of the development and nature of the contemporary global economy. Roughly in the middle of the nineteenth century, a new and distinct epoch in history began in which the quantity and diversity of goods produced in some areas of the world increased enormously. In Western Europe, North America, Australia, New Zealand, and Japan, per capita product measured in constant 1965 prices rose from $200 or $250 per year in the early and mid-nineteenth century to $2,000 or more in 1965. This rapid rise contrasts sharply with the slow quintupling of per capita product in Western Europe between 900 and 1850.[1]

THE REQUISITES AND CONSEQUENCES OF ECONOMIC GROWTH

Simon Kuznets, the foremost student of modern economic growth, has ascribed this phenomenal increase in productivity to "the extended application of science to problems of economic production."[2] Science—the empirical study of phenomena, the testing of hypotheses, and the formulation of generalizations that can be used as the basis for predictions—has made possible the development of technology, and science-based technology has been the source of modern economic growth. The development of new sources of energy, such as the steam boiler, internal combustion engine, electrical generator, and nuclear reactor, and the improvement or development of materials such as iron, steel, aluminum, alloys, and plastics have been essential to modern economic growth. Increases in productivity have depended upon and continue to depend upon technological innovations such as these.

But while technology has been essential to modern economic growth, this growth could not have occurred had there not been appropriate ideological and societal changes. Science could not have flourished had there not been a climate of opinion that permitted, encouraged, and rewarded scientific inquiry. More generally, human attention had to shift and regard what happened in an individual's life on earth as crucial, rather than seeing earthly life as a brief episode in a much longer existence. This shift implied increasing the attention devoted to the material conditions of life and placing much greater emphasis on material goods. Equally essential was the shift from evaluating individuals by their ascribed characteristics to evaluating them by their activities and achievements. In other words, modern economic growth has depended upon the widespread acceptance of the attitudes of secularism and egalitarianism.

Societal changes were also required. When the bulk of human production consisted of subsistence agriculture, relatively uncomplicated forms of social organization could suffice, but as technology increasingly came to be applied to production, social organization had to permit and facilitate specialization in production. And as technology developed, the potential gains increased from taking advantage of economies of scale; that is, the cheaper costs per unit made possible through larger production runs.

The changes in social organization stemming from these factors have been dramatic during the past hundred years. In the developed countries agriculture's share of the total labor force generally declined from more than 50 percent to 20 percent or less, and in some of these countries it fell to less than 10 percent. Conversely, the share of the total labor force employed in the industrial and service sectors increased, and a shift in population from agricultural to urban areas accompanied this transition. In the United States, for instance, in 1870 only a quarter of the population lived in towns with 2,500 persons or more but by 1960 almost two-thirds of the population lived in such areas.

In addition, the sustained economic growth that has occurred since the mid-nineteenth century has required the continual introduction of technological innovations, and their application has involved social changes; new techniques have resulted in the displacement of older industries and the workers in these industries. Increasing specialization and urbanization and continual change have put substantial strains on social cohesion. Agricultural communities could be held together by family bonds and the ties forged in face-to-face contacts, but as modern economic growth progressed, more impersonal means of attaining social cohesion became necessary. Nationalism came to be the primary social cohesive and its intensity often appears to have varied directly with the quantity, depth, and speed of the social dislocations occasioned by the application of technological innovations.

The process of modern economic growth started in the nineteenth century in Britain, spread to Western Europe, then to North America, Australia, Japan, and New Zealand, and after that to Eastern Europe. The application of technology in still other areas of the world is occurring increasingly, but the process has just begun and progress so far is limited and spotty. The achievement of large per capita products has occurred mainly in what are commonly termed "Western states" and in the communist states in Eastern Europe. The consequence of this limited spread has been a substantial increase in international stratification. Even when the process of modern economic growth started, the now developed states had higher per capita products than the rest of the world, but the phenomenal economic growth that has occurred in these states has widened the gap. As of 1979 roughly a quarter of the world's population lived in countries which had per capita products of $3,500 or more, while half lived in countries where the per capita product was less than $350.[3] Put another way, almost 60 percent of the world's product accrued to countries that contained only a quarter of the world's population. Modern economic growth has been accompanied by increasing international economic inequality.

Modern economic growth has also increased the interdependence among states. The effects, of course, have not been uniform and have varied with the size and natural-resource endowment of states. A few states have sufficient natural resources so that they need not be overly dependent upon other areas for materials, and large enough territories and populations to permit considerable specialization and allow advantage to be taken of economies of scale without going beyond their own borders. The United States, the Soviet Union, China, and India are examples, but few other states even come close to being so fortunately endowed. As of 1980, of the more than 150 sovereign states in the global political system, only these four had populations of more than 200 million, and only thirty-three states had populations of more than 20 million.[4] Three-fourths of the states have limited populations, and most of these have relatively small territories.

For the vast majority of states, economic growth has meant increasing interactions with other states. Most states that now are termed "developed" have had to import raw materials, and even with the development of synthetic substitutes, they have been unable to end their dependence on external sources of supply. As industrialization proceeded, trade with other states became an essential condition of achieving the advantages of specialization and economies of scale. Small countries have been able to achieve significant economic growth only through heavy reliance on foreign trade. Many countries, even the largest, have had to rely on external capital to promote their economic development, and all have drawn from the transnational pool of scientific and technological advances. Interdependence also has other less benign aspects. Sometimes the harmful side effects of technologies cannot be confined within the borders of the states where they are deployed; atmospheric and water pollution are prime examples. And in the case of finite or nonrenewable resources, use of a resource by one state may preclude use by other states.

Interdependence in all of the senses just described has made states increasingly sensitive to occurrences beyond their borders. Sometimes this sensitivity is mutual and symmetrical, but more frequently, since states are unequal in size and endowments, it is asymmetrical and affects some states considerably more than others. Some are particularly dependent upon the import of a vital raw material, petroleum, for example. Others are dependent upon the export of a commodity or a few commodities to one or a few states for a substantial portion of their gross national products, and thus are particularly vulnerable to shifts in the demand for these commodities in these countries. Still others are dependent upon trade with larger countries in the sense that this trade is a much larger proportion of their gross national products than it is of their trading partners'; consequently the former are more vulnerable than the latter to shifts in the other's level of economic activity. Interdependence thus often means dependence, but this dependence differs in degree and with issues. Some countries are more dependent than others, and while some countries are dependent with respect to certain issues, other countries may be dependent on them with respect to different issues. France is highly dependent upon the importation of Middle Eastern petroleum, but France's former colonies in Africa are dependent upon French purchase of the commodities they export.

To summarize, the contemporary epoch has been characterized by the application of science and technology to the processes of production. In the regions of the world where this process has been carried furthest—Europe, North America, Australia, New Zealand and Japan—the result has been phenomenal economic growth and unparalleled standards of material welfare. But as a consequence of this economic growth, the gap between the average standard of living in these areas and that in the remainder of the world has widened substantially; international stratification and inequality have been magnified. An equally important consequence has been increasing interdependence among states, but this interdependence has seldom been symmetrical.

The activities of contemporary international organizations must be seen against this background of the development of the modern global economy.

INTERDEPENDENCE AND TRADE: THE INTERACTIONS OF STATES

The nature of the activities of international organizations has been shaped by the fact that states have provided the organizing frameworks for modern economic growth. Thus it is essential to understand what states have done and how they have interacted economically. States were the units within which specialization originally occurred, and they have been the source of policies that facilitated economic growth. States minted currencies, which made it possible to conduct commerce on a basis other than barter. They have allowed or promoted the creation of institutions that made possible the amassing of capital for investment purposes. They have also promoted the development of transport and communications and other aspects of infrastructures, and they have facilitated the enhancement of human resources through education.

The Balance of Payments

As states have grown economically their interactions with other states have generally increased. These interactions are measured in the accounting statement known as the balance of payments, which summarizes the economic transactions of a country with the rest of the globe during a given period, usually a year. It includes the income received from the export of goods and services and the expenditures made on the import of goods and services. This portion of the statement is generally called the current account. Flows of money relating to loans and investments are also included, and this portion of the statement is called the capital account.

Like other accounting statements, the balance of payments must balance. If a state's income from exports does not cover its expenditure on imports, the deficit must be made up by receipts gained from services, income from investments abroad, or a loan or gift from abroad. Since charity is seldom boundless, over some period of time (frequently shorter rather than longer), a state's exports must cover its imports. However, as will be seen, a good bit of effort has been devoted to making it possible for states to balance their exports and imports on a global rather than a one-to-one basis and to extending the time period for achieving balance. The thrust of these efforts has been to make international commerce possible on a basis other than barter. Within states these functions are performed by having a single currency and credit mechanisms.

Exchange Rates

Since states have all developed their own currencies, if there is to be trade among them on a basis other than barter, there must be some way of relating currencies to one another. For didactic purposes it is useful to conceive of two very different ways of determining the value of one currency in terms of another, or more precisely, the exchange rate.

One method would be to rely exclusively on the market forces of supply and demand. This system would involve freely fluctuating exchange rates. Thus, if the demand in the United States for French goods and consequently for French francs rose more rapidly than the French demand for U.S. goods, the value of the franc would rise and the exchange rate might shift from, say, five francs to a dollar to four francs to a dollar.

A system based on the gold standard would be quite different: the value of each currency would be fixed in terms of gold, and all currencies would be freely convertible into gold. Exchange rates would fluctuate only within the narrow range determined by the price of shipping gold, for beyond that range it would be more economical to settle accounts by transferring gold. Under a gold standard, if the demand in the United States for French goods were rising more rapidly than the French demand for U.S. goods, although the value of the dollar would fall in relation to the franc, it would not fall beyond the point at which it would be cheaper to convert dollars to gold and then ship the gold to France in payment for the goods.

Either freely fluctuating exchange rates or a gold standard would tend to promote equilibrium between countries' exports and imports, since under each system adjustments would occur automatically. As exchange rates shifted, so presumably would the demand for exports and imports. If the value of the dollar dropped from five francs to four, U.S. goods would be cheaper in France, which should increase their sale there, and French goods would be more expensive in the United States, which should reduce sales. Thus the shift in the exchange rate would promote equilibrium between the exports and imports of the two countries. If the gold standard were in effect, and gold were transferred from the United States to France, there would be an economic contraction in the United States and an expansion in France since each country's currency supply would be tied to its gold reserves. This general alteration of the level of economic activity in the two countries—deflation in the United States and inflation in France—would decrease the demand for French goods in the United States and increase the demand for U.S. goods in France.

Either system, however, would have substantial disadvantages, and therefore neither has ever been fully implemented. Uncertainty about exchange rates could discourage trade, for individuals would be unwilling to make contracts when they could not be certain what their liabilities or rewards would be. The gold standard would eliminate this uncertainty, but it would also mean that the level of domestic economic activity would be significantly affected, if not determined, by external events—a situation unacceptable to governments increasingly held accountable by their constituents for full employment.

A government could also set the value of its currency arbitrarily and unilaterally. To maintain the exchange value that it established, however, unless the country's income and expenditures abroad were fortuitously in equilibrium, the government would have to control all foreign transactions to insure the achievement of equilibrium. It could do this by licensing all foreign transactions or by having a state monopoly of foreign trade. Intervention of this nature would allow the government to discriminate as it wished among buyers and sellers at home and abroad, and it probably would not result in an optimal international division of production. Were all states to operate in this manner, maximum world production would not be achieved since the structured pattern of trade would prevent full advantage being taken of opportunities for specialization.

Tariffs and Other Barriers to Trade

There are other techniques besides exchange controls through which governments can regulate the economic transactions between their own and other countries. Tariffs and quotas will affect the level of imports; the former by adding a charge that will increase the price of an item for the purchaser, and the latter by limiting the quantity of an item that can be imported. Governments may impose tariffs to raise revenues, to protect domestic industries (because they believe these industries need time to establish a costly infrastructure before they are exposed to global competition or because they think that these industries, even though inefficient in global terms, are essential to national defense or welfare), or for other reasons. Quotas can serve the same protectionist purposes. Exports can be limited quantitatively or by forcing the exporter to pay a duty, and they can be stimulated by providing subsidies. Beyond these relatively obvious techniques, there are numerous other ways in which governments can restrict commerce with other states. The list of non-tariff barriers to trade is long and includes health and sanitary regulations, licensing requirements, and purchasing regulations. Again, all or any of these techniques could create distortions that would work against an optimal international division of production.

Matters relating to exchange rates are generally referred to as monetary issues. Those relating to efforts designed to restrict or promote trade in goods and services are generally termed commercial issues. International investments and loans are usually treated under the rubric of capital flows. International organizations have been involved in all three areas, as well as in efforts to promote scientific developments and other activities that do not fit in these three categories but nevertheless relate to the growth and distribution of the global product.

Levels of Interstate Cooperation in Trade

Issues concerning economic interactions among states can be approached on a global basis or by selected groups of states, usually a regional group of contiguous states. In the latter instance, a terminology has been developed to categorize the ways in which states might attempt to work together. Table 10.1 portrays the five conceptually different levels of cooperation.

As can be seen, the levels of cooperation move from what might be termed regional economic disarmament—the elimination of barriers to trade within the group by means of a free trade area—to increasingly elaborate cooperation. The customs union, the next step after economic disarmament, adds a common external tariff to be applied to nonparticipating states. After that, in a common market, the factors of production, labor and capital, are allowed to move freely from one member state to another. In an economic union, policies dealing with such

TABLE 10.1
Levels of Economic Cooperation Among States

	No Tariffs or Quotas Internally	Common External Tariff	Free Flow of Factors	Harmonization of Economic Policies	Unification of Policies and Institutions
1. Free Trade Area	X				
2. Customs Union	X	X			
3. Common Market	X	X	X		
4. Economic Union	X	X	X	X	
5. Total Economic Integration	X	X	X	X	X

Source: Drawn from Bela Balassa, *The Theory of Economic Integration* (Homewood, Ill.: Irwin, 1961), p. 2; and Joseph S. Nye, Jr., *Peace in Parts: Integration and Conflict in Regional Organization* (Boston: Little, Brown, 1971), pp. 28–29.

matters as social security, transportation, and monetary issues are harmonized. And in the final stage of full economic integration, the several states have become one for all economic purposes. These five different levels provide useful benchmarks, but in practice states have refused to be bound by such a rigid categorization. When groups of states have decided to cooperate, they have simply picked those devices that seemed suitable, whether or not they fitted this logical categorization.

HOW MUCH INTERVENTION IN ECONOMIC FORCES?

To a large extent, the debate about what activities international governmental organizations should undertake with respect to economic matters parallels the debate about what governments should do in this realm. This is hardly surprising, since IGOs are extensions of governments.

The Role of Governments

One aspect of the debate may be framed conceptually in two polar extremes. One polar position would be advocacy of complete laissez faire. In this view, market forces, supply and demand, should determine what is produced and how, and how products are distributed. Private companies should organize production, with no or minimal governmental intervention. The rationale undergirding this position is that reliance on market forces, and implicitly on competition, insures efficiency; the argument is that production will be maximized in this manner and that welfare will thereby be maximized too. Exponents of this position tend to place emphasis on the size of the total product and its growth over time.

The diametrically opposite view would be that all economic activity should be organized and controlled by the government. This position is often taken because of a critical evaluation of the results of market allocations. Too little attention, it is felt, is devoted to basic public services, to esthetic values, or to equity considerations. Proponents of governmental intervention argue that in a laissez-faire economy vital resources are squandered while essential needs are left unmet, and the income disparities that develop are too great. The list of criticisms could be expanded, but these illustrate the general argument that market allocations may accord insufficient weight to values deemed to be important, and government should intervene to promote those values.

In the Soviet Union and the People's Republic of China and in the other communist countries of Eastern Europe, governmental control over the economy is virtually complete. The term "planned economies" is appropriately applied to these countries. The government owns and controls the means of production; prices are determined by governmental decisions rather than market forces; and state monopolies are responsible for foreign trade.

Although the term "market economies" is generally applied to the other states

state shall be represented by delegates from labor and business organizations as well as by government delegates, was designed to facilitate its task of drafting conventions to deal with bettering the conditions of labor. The founders of ILO felt that for the conventions to reflect real conditions, it was essential that representatives of all three elements should participate in their drafting. Clearly, ILO's founders assumed that economies would be organized according to market principles and that the means of production would be owned and operated by private companies. If governments organized production and owned and operated the means of production, the rationale for tripartite representation would not exist.

The collapse of the global economy in the 1930s and the so-called Keynesian revolution in economics were both instrumental in changing the outlook of governments still further. On the one hand, governments found that their constituents were simply unwilling to tolerate the massive unemployment that accompanied the worldwide depression. On the other, Keynesian theories indicated ways in which governmental intervention in the economy might reduce unemployment. Governments throughout the world began to move in the direction of applying Keynesian prescriptions.

At least partly as a consequence, they also erected new barriers to international trade; if the planning prescriptions were to have their hoped-for effect, extraneous forces could not be allowed to disturb them. Keynesian economics merged with traditional nationalist and protectionist pressures to promote national at the expense of international solidarity. In 1930 the United States adopted the Smoot-Hawley tariff, which raised tariffs to unprecedented levels: in some instances the new rates were 50 to 100 percent greater than the old ones. Other governments, seeing prospects of declining exports to the United States because of the new tariff levels, retaliated by raising their own tariffs. In 1931 Great Britain abandoned the gold standard, and other countries, including the United States, soon followed suit. As a concomitant of its efforts to stabilize agricultural prices, the United States established import quotas for basic commodities. Britain abandoned free trade, erected a tariff wall, and then adopted a system of preferential rates for commonwealth countries.

During this period vocal and increasingly enfranchised citizens in all of the industrialized countries demanded governmental intervention to insure a minimum standard of living. Full employment was part of this, but it also involved other measures, such as provisions for income during retirement and benefits for workers' survivors. Responding to these demands involved taxation for the redistribution of wealth.

Thus governments added to the goal of promoting economic growth, which they continued to espouse, new goals of income stability through full employment and a greater measure of equity through the redistribution of wealth. These goals carried over to their view of what international governmental organizations could do, although in the 1930s there were few practical consequences of this expanded vision. When the time came to reestablish an international economic order after World War II, most governments were willing to give IGOs a larger role. In addition, because of the actions that they were committed to take domestically to counter unemployment and promote redistribution, the dimensions and difficulties of international collaboration in the economic field had expanded considerably.

Influenced by the rise of Hitler and Mussolini and the experience of World War II, governments also increasingly came to believe that there was a link between economic conditions and domestic and international strife. The theory that bad economic conditions bred violence gained credence. Thus governments became interested in dealing with economic problems not only because they were viewed as being important in their own right, but also because good economic conditions were seen as a prerequisite to obtaining security.

THE U.N. SYSTEM: A BROADENED MANDATE

The provisions of the United Nations charter reflected these new understandings and conditions. Article 55, on international economic and social cooperation, begins by asserting the link between economic conditions and security:

> With a view to the creation of conditions of stability and well-being which are necessary for peaceful and friendly relations among nations . . .

It then goes on to proclaim that the organization shall promote:

> a. higher standards of living, full employment, and conditions of economic and social progress and development;

> b. solutions of international economic, social, health, and related problems; and international cultural and educational cooperation.

Through these phrases the U.N. is committed to attempting to achieve growth in the global economic product and also to many of the goals of the modern welfare state.

Nongovernmental organizations (NGOs) were pushing governments toward a more interventionist posture in national economic affairs, and national and international nongovernmental organizations exerted a similar pressure at the international level. At the same time that the U.N. charter was being drafted in San Francisco, an INGO, the World Federation of Trade Unions (WFTU), was meeting across the bay in Oakland. WFTU's request to participate in the San Francisco Conference was not granted, but this request contributed to the pressure to include a provision in the charter to allow INGOs to take part in the U.N.'s economic and social activities. The American Congress of Industrial Organizations (CIO), which had an observer attached to the United States delegation, also pressed hard for such a provision, as did other American NGOs that were present at San Francisco. Article 71, the result of this pressure, allows both national and international nongovernmental organizations to be brought into consultative relationships with the U.N. It was clear at San Francisco that labor NGOs would use this privilege to insist that the U.N. take seriously the commitments contained in Article 55.

Despite the far-reaching nature of the U.N.'s goals as stated in Article 55, the policy instruments with which the organization was endowed by the charter are extremely modest. Paragraph 7 of Article 2 precludes the organization from intervening "in matters which are essentially within the domestic jurisdiction of any state..." The U.N.'s powers are to undertake studies and prepare reports, to make recommendations, to prepare conventions for consideration and ratification by states, to convene conferences, and to create specialized agencies and make recommendations for their coordination. In the broad design of its founders, the U.N. was to play a general coordinating role, and operational activities were to be undertaken by functionally defined specialized agencies, some of which were already in existence while others were to be created.

Several of the U.N.'s specialized agencies continue the tradition of the Central Commission for the Navigation of the Rhine; their purpose is primarily that of facilitating international trade by insuring that there are minimal obstacles to making maximum use of modern means of communication and transport. The International Telecommunication Union, the Universal Postal Union, the International Civil Aviation Organization, the International Maritime Consultative Organization, and the World Intellectual Property Organization, a central purpose of which is to facilitate transnational utilization of intellectual achievements through harmonization of policies concerning proprietary rights. These organizations all deal with the infrastructure of international trade. The Food and Agricultural Organization was created in 1945 in recognition of the fact that the agricultural sector is essential to survival but also has special problems amidst modern industrial growth. FAO's purpose is to increase the production and improve the distribution of agricultural products and to improve the conditions of rural populations.

Three U.N. specialized agencies were proposed to deal directly with international trade—one in the field of monetary policy, another dealing with capital flows, and a third in the area of commercial policy. The International Monetary Fund (IMF) was created at the Bretton Woods Conference in 1944. IMF's central purpose is to contribute to the expansion and growth of international trade by promoting exchange liberalization; that is, currencies that would be freely convertible and would have relatively stable values. In the original conception, states were to set the exchange rate for their currencies in consultation with IMF and not change the rate without engaging in prescribed discussions with the organization. In turn, IMF was assigned an amount of money that it could lend to member states so that they could engage in open-market operations to support the value of their currencies. IMF can be seen as an international agency created to assist governments that found themselves in temporary balance-of-payments difficulties, and it was mandated to work toward eliminating exchange restrictions and toward making currencies freely convertible. It was an attempt to avoid both the domestic costs of the gold standard and the uncertainties of a system of freely fluctuating exchange rates. Its function was to allow countries having temporary deficits on their current accounts a period of time to attempt to correct these deficits—to see whether fundamental adjustments were truly necessary.

IMF functioned according to the original conception until 1971. Since then, although IMF's objective has continued to be to promote exchange liberalization, its role with respect to exchange rates has been altered, as will be described in Chapter 11.

The International Bank for Reconstruction and Development (IBRD), which was also created at Bretton Woods, was to deal with longer-term issues, as its name implies. Membership in IMF is a condition of membership in IBRD, or the World Bank as it is often called. Paragraph iii of Article I of IBRD's Articles of Agreement summarizes the bank's purposes:

> To promote the long-range balanced growth of international trade and the maintenance of equilibrium in balances of payments of encouraging international investment for the development of the productive resources of members, thereby assisting in raising productivity, the standard of living and conditions of labor in their territories.

The events of the 1930s, the currency devaluations and the defaulting on loans, had undermined the confidence of international investors, yet international investment was assumed to be essential to the long-run growth of the world economy. IBRD was assigned funds that it could use for loans to member states and, more importantly, to guarantee loans that it would arrange for member states through the usual investment channels, that is, through private capital markets.

The third specialized agency envisaged in the original scheme, that dealing with commercial policy, was stillborn. But a less elaborate and less powerful and extensive organization, the General Agreement on Tariffs and Trade (GATT), emerged from the effort to create an international trade organization. The General Agreement was originally envisaged primarily as a code of conduct for commercial policy. It commits contracting parties to maintain most-favored-nation treatment toward one another; that is, to grant all contracting parties the most favorable treatment extended to any country with respect to tariffs and other obstacles to trade. Using this basic obligation as a framework, GATT came to sponsor several negotiations in which bilateral bargains about mutual reductions in tariffs were extended to all contracting parties. Some exceptions to most-favored-nation treatment are permitted under the General Agreement, but in principle these must be justified before the contracting parties. In the event of violations of the code, the General Agreement permits affected contracting parties to engage in retaliation by imposing higher tariffs or other sanctions against the violator.

Despite the acknowledgment of other economic goals in the U.N. charter and the constitutional documents of the specialized agencies, the primary commitment remained to economic growth, and to reliance on market mechanisms as the most effective means of achieving this growth. This was presaged as early as August 1941 in the joint declaration of President Franklin D. Roosevelt and Prime Minister Winston Churchill known as the Atlantic Charter. The fourth point of the charter, which was a statement of principles concerning a future peace settlement, proclaimed that the two leaders, on behalf of their countries, would endeavor:

...to further the enjoyment by all States, great or small, victor or vanquished, of access, on equal terms, to the trade and to the raw materials of the world which are needed for economic prosperity.

Basically the U.N. system was designed to promote international trade globally and on as free a basis as possible. It was assumed that states would pursue welfare goals, and a substantial function of the U.N. system was to mitigate the restrictive effects on international trade of the pursuit of these goals.

It was also assumed that the means of production would be owned predominantly by private companies and that these companies would be responsible for organizing the bulk of production. Lending by the World Bank was not designed to replace private capital as the principal mode of investment, but instead to encourage private capital to perform its traditional role and to facilitate the operation of private capital markets. The founders of the U.N. system undoubtedly thought primarily of national private companies and national capital markets, but their vision could be applied to transnational corporations and capital markets, and they clearly had as an objective a global free-market economy.

THE GROWTH OF LIMITED MEMBERSHIP IGOS AMONG DEVELOPED STATES

As in the case of security, events in the post–World War II world soon departed from this relatively clear and uncluttered vision of a global economic order. The same political disagreements that contributed to the formation of opposing limited membership IGOs in the security field also had an impact on economic issues. The Soviet Union and most of the communist countries of Eastern Europe did not join FAO, the International Monetary Fund, the World Bank, or GATT. Since the last three particularly were oriented primarily toward facilitating the international trade of market economies, the communist countries' refusal to become involved reflected among other things the difficulty of bringing planned economies into a market-based framework. More importantly, it reflected a basic disagreement with the philosophy of these IGOs about how production should be organized.

When the true dimensions of the task of reconstructing and rehabilitating the economies devastated by World War II became apparent, the principal contributor to the effort, the United States, preferred to administer its aid by itself rather than give it to the United Nations or the World Bank to administer. The United States also insisted that the European states prepare joint requests for the aid and coordinate plans for its use. The framework for this activity was the Organization for European Economic Cooperation (OEEC), which was created in 1948. The Soviet Union and the communist countries of Eastern Europe refused to join the OEEC, thereby barring themselves from receiving United States Marshall Plan, or more formally, European Recovery Program, assistance. Consequently whether or not Congress would have appropriated funds that would be allocated to communist states cannot be known. OEEC became a lively forum for cooperation among the states of Western Europe. In the 1960s, after the task of reconstruction had been completed, OEEC's name was changed to the Organization for Economic Cooperation and Development (OECD), and the United States, Canada, and Japan became members. OECD became the center of economic cooperative activities among the industrialized states with market economies.

After the creation of OEEC, the communist states of Eastern Europe formed their own organization, the Council for Mutual Economic Assistance (CMEA, or Comecon), in 1949.

Both OECD and CMEA have as a major purpose the promotion of economic growth, but the phraseology in the latter case is distinctive. Article 1 of the CMEA charter states the aim of the organization to be:

> ...contributing, through the union and coordination of the forces of the member countries of the Council, to the planned development of the national economy and an acceleration of the economic and technical progress of these countries; raising the level of industrialization of the underdeveloped countries; an uninterrupted growth in labor productivity; and a steady rise in the well-being of the peoples of the member countries.

The stress on planning is in sharp contrast to the reliance on market mechanisms in other international organizations. The creation of OEEC and CMEA marked the division of the global economy into market and planned segments, each with its own economic international governmental organizations.

REGIONAL ECONOMIC INTEGRATION ATTEMPTS

The international organizational mosaic became even more complicated as the years passed. The regional economic integration movement added several new organizations. The first step in this direction was taken in 1951 with the signing of the treaty establishing the European Coal and Steel Community (ECSC). Under the terms of the treaty, Belgium, the Federal Republic of Germany, France, Italy, the Netherlands, and Luxembourg created a common market among themselves for coal and steel. Six years later, the same six countries committed themselves to establish an all-inclusive common market by signing the Treaty of Rome creating the European Economic Community (EEC). In 1973 the United Kingdom, Ireland, and Denmark joined the EEC, and Greece joined in 1981.

INGOs, particularly the European Movement and the Action Committee for the United States of Europe, provided a crucial impetus for the formation of ECSC and EEC. They mobilized elite and general public opinion to support the drafting and ratification of the treaties.

The creation of the European Economic Community was followed by efforts in the direction of regional economic integration among other states in Europe and among states in Latin America and Central America, in the Caribbean, and in East, West, and Central Africa; among the Arab states; among Turkey, Iran, and Pakistan; and among Southeast Asian countries.[5] All of the regional economic integration schemes stress economic growth as their primary goal. All accept varying commitments to economic integration, ranging from the creation of free trade areas through distant commitments to economic union. Since all grant more favorable trading conditions to members than to nonmembers, all involve a contravention of the GATT principle of most-favored-nation treatment, but this is an exception allowed under the GATT code of conduct in specified circumstances. In a broad sense, the regional economic integration schemes involve attempts to alter the distribution of the global economic product by accelerating economic growth among their members. They can be seen as an attempt by their members to improve their economic lot. Interestingly, the constitutional documents of some of them also proclaim the goal of promoting equity among their members.[6]

OTHER INTERNATIONAL ORGANIZATIONS WITH REDISTRIBUTIVE, REGULATORY, AND OPERATIONAL FUNCTIONS

Additional organizations have been added in even more explicit attempts to alter the distribution of global economic production. The first such effort was the U.N.'s Expanded Program of Technical Assistance, instituted in 1949. The idea behind the program was that economic growth in the poorer states of the world could be accelerated through the infusion of training programs and expert advice. This transfer of technical knowledge was to be financed by voluntary contributions from the richer members of the United Nations. In 1957 the U.N. Special Fund was created to support on the same basis of voluntary contributions larger projects of longer duration, more explicitly designed to stimulate capital investment, and in 1965 the two programs were merged into the United Nations Development Program.

In 1964 the United Nations Conference on Trade and Development was created with the explicit purpose of bettering trading conditions for less developed countries.[7] In 1966 the United Nations Industrial Development Organization was established with the mandate of "encouraging the mobilization of national and international resources to assist in, promote and accelerate the industrialization of the developing countries, with particular emphasis on the manufacturing sector."[8]

The 1960s saw the formation of a number of regional development banks, which attempted to mobilize capital both within and outside the regions to promote more rapid development of poor areas. The European Investment Bank was created as part of the EEC; supporting projects for developing less advanced regions within the community is among its principal functions. CMEA has two banks associated with it. Other regional development banks are the Inter-American Development Bank, the African Development Bank, the Asian Development Bank, the Central American Bank for Economic Integration, the West African Development Bank, the Caribbean Development Bank, and the Andean

Development Corporation. The purpose of all of these banks is to promote redistribution, either within the region itself or from other regions to the region or both.

Another category of organizations established with the explicit purpose of promoting redistribution is made up of what are, in effect, cartels of raw-materials-producing countries. The first of these was the Organization of Petroleum Exporting Countries (OPEC), which was established in 1960 in the wake of a sharp decline in the prices of petroleum products. OPEC's immediate objective was to recoup this loss; its longer-term purposes were to stabilize and increase the exporting countries' earnings by means of the regulation of production. Other commodity organizations have been formed among the countries that produce bauxite, copper, phosphate, tin, chrome, natural rubber, iron, mercury, timber, coffee, and bananas. Some of these organizations also include the principal consumers of the products.

Whether the fisheries organizations should be regarded as cartels created to regulate production for economic purposes or regulatory attempts to promote conservation depends partly on one's point of view. Such organizations date from the nineteenth century, and several of them existed in the 1980s.[9] It is clear that unrestricted competition using modern technology could result in rapid depletion of the oceans' resources, and the need for regulation for conservation purposes is obvious. But it is also obvious that regulation has economic effects: under market conditions the number of fish that are harvested will affect their price, and if the total amount to be harvested is to be limited, shares of the harvest must be allocated.

International nongovernmental organizations perform similar roles of regulating competition in various fields of transport. For example, the International Air Transport Association regulates the fares that member airlines may charge on international routes, and the so-called liner conferences have an influence on the rates charged for ocean freight.

The regulations of international governmental organizations in the environmental field also have economic effects, although the impact here may be less immediate and apparent. Less developed areas and countries fear that environmental regulations could hamper their efforts to achieve economic growth. This fear was expressed forcefully by the less developed countries during the United Nations Conference on the Human Environment in 1972. To allay this fear the Declaration on the Human Environment adopted by the conference asserted that:

> Economic and social development is essential for insuring a favorable living and working environment for man and for creating conditions on earth that are necessary for the improvement of the quality of life[10]

This constituted an essential condition for achieving the principal normative goal articulated by the conference:

Man has the fundamental right to freedom, equality, and adequate conditions of life in an environment which permits a life of dignity and well-being, and bears a solemn responsibility to protect and improve the environment for present and future generations.[11]

The conference adopted a detailed and elaborate action program to achieve this goal and created within the U.N. structure a governing council for environmental programs, an environment secretariat headed by an executive director, and an environment fund (to be raised by voluntary contributions) for financing environmental projects.

Finally, in 1964 what is in effect an international public utility, the International Telecommunication Satellite Organization, was established. INTELSAT's purpose is to operate a global communication satellite system. It operates in the global context much as a national common carrier would within a state. Intersputnik is a similar system, though with more limited membership, which uses satellites manufactured by the Soviet Union. In 1982, under the provisions of the newly negotiated Law of the Sea Convention, steps were taken toward creating an institution that would conduct deep-sea mining. It would in effect be an international governmental-owned enterprise that would operate commercially and compete with transnational corporations.

Like governments, international governmental organizations have moved from more or less passively attempting to facilitate economic growth to increasing intervention in economic processes to achieve various social goals. Economic growth has continued to be foremost among these, but income stability, a more equitable distribution of wealth, and environmental protection are growing in importance.

No economy in the world today is completely laissez faire, but most continue to allow private ownership of the means of production and to rely substantially on market mechanisms to determine what shall be produced and how it shall be distributed. Only in communist countries has private ownership of the means of production been abolished and planning completely substituted for market mechanisms. International governmental organizations have followed a similar pattern. Most IGOs rely on interventions in market mechanisms to achieve their goals and assume that the ownership and organization of production will be in the hands of private companies. Of course, IGOs composed of states with planned economies play a different role, that of meshing the results of national planning processes. Exactly how IGOs function in these respects and with what degree of success, and what role INGOs and transnational organizations (principally transnational corporations) play, are the next questions to address.

NOTES

1. See Simon Kuznets, *Economic Growth of Nations: Total Output and Production Structure* (Cambridge: Belknap, 1971), pp. 10–27.

2. Simon Kuznets, *Modern Economic Growth: Rate, Structure, and Spread* (New Haven: Yale University Press, 1966).

3. International Bank for Reconstruction and Development, *World Bank Atlas, 1981* (Washington, D.C.: IBRD, 1982), pp. 4–7.

4. Ibid., p. 8.

5. The European Free Trade Association, the Latin American Free Trade Association, the Andean Group, the Central American Common Market, the Caribbean Free Trade Association, the East African Community, the Central African Customs and Economic Union, the West African Economic Community, the Arab Common Market, the Maghreb Group, Regional Cooperation for Development, and the Association of South-East Asian Nations.

6. See Article 2, paragraph e of the treaty establishing the Caribbean Free Trade Association; Chapter 5 of the Treaty for East African Cooperation; and the entire *Acuerdo de Cartagena*, the Act of Cartagena which created the Andean Group.

7. For a broad statement of the programmatic goals of UNCTAD see the final act of the first conference, U.N. Document E/Conf. 46/L. 28.

8. Paragraph II, 1, U.N. General Assembly Resolution 2152 (XXI).

9. Inter-American Tropical Tuna Commission, International Commission for the Northwest Atlantic Fisheries, International Commission for the Southeast Atlantic Fisheries, International North Pacific Fisheries Commission, International Pacific Salmon Fisheries Commission, International Whaling Commission, North Pacific Fur Seal Commission, Northeast Atlantic Fisheries Commission.

10. Declaration on the Human Environment, Article 8.

11. Ibid., Article 1.

FOR FURTHER READING

Blake, David H., and Robert S. Walters. *The Politics of Global Economic Relations.* Englewood Cliffs, N.J.: Prentice-Hall, 2nd ed., 1983.

Dell, Sydney. *Trade Blocs and Common Markets.* New York: Knopf, 1963.

Gardner, Richard N. *Sterling-Dollar Diplomacy.* New York: McGraw-Hill, 1969.

Jacobson, Harold K. "Labor, the UN and the Cold War," *International Organization,* 11 (February 1957), 55–67.

Kuznets, Simon. *Modern Economic Growth: Rate, Structure, and Spread.* New Haven: Yale University Press, 1966.

Lagos, Gustavo. *International Stratification and Underdeveloped Countries.* Chapel Hill: University of North Carolina Press, 1963.

Lorwin, Lewis L. *The International Labor Movement: History, Policies, Outlook.* New York: Harper, 1953.

Myrdal, Gunnar. *An International Economy: Problems and Prospects.* New York: Harper, 1956.

———. *Beyond the Welfare State: Economic Planning and Its International Implications.* New Haven: Yale University Press, 1960.

Okun, Arthur M. *Equality and Efficiency: The Big Tradeoff.* Washington, D.C.: Brookings, 1975.

Rappard, William E. *The Quest for Peace Yesterday and Today.* London: David Davies Memorial Institute of International Studies, 1944.

Shotwell, J. T. (ed.) *The Origins of the International Labor Organization.* 2 vols. New York: Columbia University Press, 1934.

Spero, Joan E. *The Politics of International Economic Relations.* New York: St. Martin's, 2nd ed., 1981.

Viner, Jacob. *International Economics.* Glencoe, Ill.: Free Press, 1951.

11

STEPS TOWARD
THE CREATION OF A
WORLD ECONOMY

It should not be surprising that international organizations are more active in the economic field than in any other. The first modern international governmental organization, the Central Commission for the Navigation of the Rhine, was created to facilitate commerce among states, and there have always been more IGOs and INGOs with mandates in the economic field than in the fields of security or social welfare. A larger portion of IGO budgets is allocated to economic tasks than to any other tasks. The IGOs with the greatest formal authority, the European communities, were created to perform economic functions. This field also has more substantial INGOs, measured by staffs and budgets, than the others. Finally, it is the sphere of activity of a type of transnational organization, the multinational or transnational corporation. Transnational corporations have become, in the eyes of many, the principal vehicle for the internationalization of the world economic system.

Chapter 10 outlined different basic approaches to dealing with economic issues and introduced the principal IGOs in this field and their mandates. Generally the membership and purpose of INGOs are clear from their titles; consequently the various INGOs can be introduced along with the consideration of their activities. In this chapter, we will examine what international organizations have done with respect to the growth and distribution of the world product, especially in the period since World War II. As we analyze the activities of international organizations, we need to attempt to understand the relationship between these activities and the rapid growth since the 1950s of transnational corporations. We need also to consider whether international organizations have followed basically laissez-faire approaches to economic issues, as their mandates appeared to indicate that they would, or whether they have sought to promote planning and public ownership of production facilities.

In considering the economic activities of international organizations, we will employ again the categories of action that were set forth in Chapter 5 and used as a framework for Chapter 8. In this instance too, the activities that are analyzed should be regarded as an illustrative sample rather than as a comprehensive listing.

INFORMATIONAL ACTIVITIES

As production processes and economic relationships have become more complex, the need for gathering data and exchanging information about these processes and relationships has grown substantially. Some of the most significant tasks with respect to economic issues involve increasing the supply and availability of economic data and facilitating the exchange of information about economic activities.

Collecting and Disseminating Data

The League of Nations was the first IGO to devote substantial efforts to increasing the supply and availability of economic data. The League secretariat included a distinguished group of economists who did pioneering work in compiling and publishing statistics dealing with the domestic economies and international trade of the states that then made up the global political system. Since World War II the League's activities in this field have been further developed by the IGOs that have been created with mandates to deal with economic issues. Several serial publications started by the League have been continued and expanded by contemporary IGOs. The United Nations publishes a number of annual compendiums of basic statistical data: the *Statistical Yearbook*, the *Demographic Yearbook*, the *Yearbook of International Trade Statistics*, the *World Trade Annual*, *World Energy Supplies*, and the *Yearbook of National Account Statistics*, among others. Other IGOs also publish various statistical series.

Of course the quest for data about economic matters long antedates international organizations. Rudimentary governmental censuses date from antiquity, but with the phenomenal economic growth of the modern epoch, governments and private agencies have sought more and more data. The role of international organizations has not been to originate the quest for data or to supplant the efforts of private agencies and governments to collect data. On the contrary, international organizations are responsive to the desires of their members, and the data that IGOs publish have generally been collected by governments. The role of international organizations has been more complex and subtle.

The collection of data depends first on development of an understanding that certain facts might be important and also on the development of concepts. The relevance of population data is obvious, as is some of the potentially useful disaggregations of this data, such as sex and age distributions. Scientific work was essential, however, so that rather than getting totals by physically counting everyone, accurate estimates could be made through the use of sampling techniques. Other types of data—for instance, the widely used measure of economic performance, gross national product (GNP)—have depended on the development of basic concepts. International organizations have been important in crystalizing notions of relevance, and sometimes they have also been the source of scientific innovations with respect to the conceptual basis for data and techniques for its collection.

More frequently, however, the role of international organizations has been to establish internationally accepted definitions and standards of accuracy, so that data collected by their members would be relatively uniform and comparable. For example, if data concerning the gross national products of different countries are to be useful in shaping international policies, they must be collected according to a common notion of what GNP means and by uniform sampling techniques. International organizations have devoted tremendous efforts to these seemingly mundane but extremely important tasks. They have developed standard definitions and set norms for accuracy. They have trained statisticians and facilitated the exchange of information on a personal basis among statisticians. IGOs have sought an upgrading and a harmonization of the practices of the statistical services of governments. In some instances, this has meant little change in what was being done and would have been done in the absence of IGO activities; in other extreme instances, it has meant inaugurating and developing statistical services. The result has been a vast harvest of increasingly accurate and useful data about the global economy and its many components.

The range of this data is impressively broad. The six standard publications of the U.N. mentioned previously give an indication, but the totality of data resulting from the efforts of international organizations is much broader than even the titles of these six serial publications would indicate. Organizations with broad mandates to deal with economic issues, such as the United Nations, the Organization for Economic Cooperation and Development, and the Council for Mutual Economic Assistance, compile comprehensive data, and these compilations are supplemented in special fields by organizations working in those fields, such as the U.N.'s specialized agencies. The International Labor Organization publishes employment data, and the IMF and GATT publish data on international trade. Over the years the geographical coverage of the data has also become more comprehensive. The League concentrated mainly on Europe and North America, but by the 1970s the total effort of all international organizations covered the entire globe.

As the concerns of governments and their subjects have broadened, new types of data have been added to the basic core of demographic, production, and trade statistics and national accounts. The World Weather Watch came into existence in 1968, and this global meteorological observation effort has been steadily upgraded since then. The Weather Watch, which is coordinated by the World Meteorological Organization (WMO), insures that national meteorological services use standard measurements and data collection techniques and provides for the global transmission of data gathered at each point in the system. In 1972 steps were taken in the U.N. toward the creation of Earthwatch; this involved systems of environmental assessment covering evaluation, research, monitoring, and information exchange. Several components of Earthwatch were functioning by the mid-1970s. Much of the impetus for the creation of the World Weather Watch and Earthwatch came from an INGO, the International Council of Scientific Unions (ICSU), which also facilitated the research that made these monitoring efforts feasible. ICSU organized the International Geophysical Year in 1957–1958, the first attempt to measure geophysical phenomena simultaneously throughout the world, and it is a co-sponsor with the World Meteorological Organization of the Global Atmospheric Research Program.

In the 1960s and 1970s the role of transnational corporations in the world economy became an increasingly salient and controversial issue. The United Nations first appointed a group of "eminent persons" from all areas of the globe to hold what in effect amounted to public hearings about the activities of transnational corporations. Acting on the basis of recommendations contained in the reports of this group, in 1974 the U.N. created a Commission and a Center on Transnational Corporations, with a principal purpose of monitoring their activities.

Several glaring and significant conclusions with important implications for national and international policies have emerged simply from the availability of the data collected by international organizations. U.N. data collection efforts played an essential role in creating an awareness of the accelerating rate of increase in the world's population, a phenomenon that began in the nineteenth century, gained momentum in the early years of the twentieth, and achieved an incredible pace after 1950. Thanks also to the work of international organizations, the world's growing population can be compared to the available food supplies, in gloomy counterpoint. The data collection efforts of IGOs have also brought out the gap between the gross national products of the relatively rich countries and those of the relatively poor and the widening of this gap over time.

Making Forecasts

International organizations have used the data that have been gathered as a basis for both short- and long-term forecasts, and forecasting is a second category of informational activity. A good deal of the popular concern about the current rate of population growth stems from projections of the consequences of this growth rate given projections about the availability of food supplies.

Short-run economic forecasts are prepared by many organizations. Among the most important are those of the Organization for Economic Cooperation and Development. In the early 1980s OECD countries accounted for more than 60 percent of world trade, and more than 70 percent of this total was trade among OECD members. Receipts from foreign trade constitute an important share of the gross national products of most OECD countries. The forecasts are based on government data, but preparing them jointly forces differing assumptions into the open. Contradictory assumptions must be resolved, for in the end no country can export more than its trading partners will purchase. Since so much of OECD member countries' trade is with one another, making a joint forecast for all of the economies quickly reveals discrepancies in national plans.

Analyzing Economic Issues

Analyzing economic issues is a third informational function of international organizations, and like the compilation and publication of data and forecasting, it is largely the domain of secretariats—the involvement of delegates is minimal. A number of important studies have been completed under the auspices of international organizations, either by consultants brought in specifically for the task or by secretariats.

International organizations have several unique advantages as sponsors for economic analyses. Under their auspices problems can be approached from an international rather than a national perspective, and because IGOs are presumably politically uncommitted and commercially disinterested, the findings of studies done for them often have greater legitimacy and acceptability than do studies conducted under other auspices. Studies conducted by IGOs can be particularly important for the governments of smaller and poorer countries, which do not have bureaucracies capable of preparing independent analyses.

Several analyses conducted under the auspices of international organizations have been of seminal importance and have had a major impact on national and international policies. League of Nations publications clearly identified the mechanisms by which a major economic depression can be spread from one country to another,[1] and many of the activities of post-World War II international governmental organizations have been devoted to attempting to prevent these mechanisms from having that effect. Another League study probed the advantages that could be gained from regional economic integration under certain conditions,[2] and it too has had a profound impact on events in the postwar period. Early in its history the United Nations published *Measures for the Economic Development of Underdeveloped Countries*,[3] and this document, the first widely publicized attempt to analyze the problems of the less developed countries and to propose actions to accelerate their economic growth, significantly affected the development of the organization and of its policies. Countless other studies have been conducted by the United Nations, its specialized agencies, and other international organizations, and many of these have also had major consequences for policy.

One of the most important topics for the contemporary world economy, the issue whether or not limits to global economic growth exist in the form of resource constraints and the build-up of damaging pollution, was first broached by an INGO, the Club of Rome. Founded in 1968, the Club of Rome immediately sponsored studies to explore the future, raising questions that had not been raised, or perhaps could not be raised, in the more formal and bureaucratic settings of IGOs. Its first major publication, *The Limits to Growth*,[4] was controversial, but attracted worldwide attention and stimulated broad debate and numerous further studies—by the Club of Rome itself, other INGOs, and IGOs. Perhaps the most notable of these was conducted by Harvard's Nobel Laureate economist Wassily Leontief, who headed a team of consultants to the U.N. Their computer simulation analysis of various possible future courses of action showed that with planning and cooperation global economic growth and a more equitable distribution of the world product were both possible.[5]

Exchanging Information and Views

A fourth category of informational activities conducted by international organizations with reference to economic issues involves exchanges of information and views. This is the principal function of many INGOs; they exist to keep their members abreast of current developments in their fields. Exchanges of information can take place through publications or through informal and formal meetings.

Within IGOs, particularly, the data compiled and published by the organization, the forecasts, or the analyses often provide the basis for carefully structured and organized discussions. The most serious of these discussions are those conducted in private among officials who have important responsibilities for economic policy within their own states. Such officials from the market economies are most likely to come together for frank private discussions in sessions organized by the International Monetary Fund, the Bank for International Settlements (BIS), the Organization for Economic Cooperation and Development, and the European communities. CMEA is the principal forum where individuals with similar responsibilities in the planned economies meet for private discussions.

The IMF and the BIS have organized private discussions to deal with the various crises that have developed over monetary issues. Private discussions occur routinely in the European communities and in the periodic sessions of OECD and CMEA.

OECD has also adopted the custom of annually reviewing the economic policies and performance of each of its member countries. The secretariat prepares a basic analysis; then there is a "confrontation" in which representatives of the country involved are questioned by specially designated reporters from other member countries. After this, the secretariat study is revised and published. Preparing for and participating in such exercises forces governments to examine the premises underlying their policies, the appropriateness of the means they have chosen to the goals they have articulated, and the international consequences of their actions. The function of OECD confrontations is to encourage governments to pursue complementary rather than competitive policies. Governments could adopt policies, such as erecting barriers to imports, that might gain certain short-term advantages by easing difficult internal problems, but which in the long term would be costly to all OECD members, including the state that initiated them. By exchanging information, however, governments might be able to make mutual adjustments that would benefit everyone.

Different governments have different problems. Some societies are extremely concerned about unemployment, while others fear inflation. Policies framed on the bases of these different concerns inevitably have conflicting, and perhaps contradictory, elements. The point to the exchanges of views and information is to allow countries to formulate their economic policies in light of the projected consequences for other countries, and with awareness of the problems of these countries and the policies they are likely to pursue.

Exchanges of information and of views also occur in the United Nations. These discussions are usually conducted in public, and they are often conflictual, serving mainly to highlight major economic issues. Their immediate impact on policy is much less frequent than that of the discussions in limited membership or specific purpose IGOs. Since the mid-1960s these discussions in the General Assembly and other U.N. bodies have concentrated particularly on the problems of less developed countries, and they have become a principal vehicle for shaping and maintaining the unity of the Group of 77 on economic issues.

Convoking Public Conferences

A final informational activity, the convocation of large public conferences to consider particular issues, is principally a technique for dramatizing major problems. The United Nations has convened conferences on the peaceful uses of atomic energy in 1953, 1958, 1963, and 1983; on new sources of energy in 1961 and 1981; on the application of science and technology for the benefit of less developed countries in 1963 and 1979; on the least developed countries in 1981; on population in 1954, 1965, and 1974; on food in 1970 and 1974; on the environment in 1972; and on water in 1977. The purpose of such conferences is generally not to effect short-term changes in policies but rather to work toward global consensus about what should be done in the hope of promoting changes in policies in the longer term and the ultimate adoption of complementary, adaptive policies.

NORMATIVE ACTIVITIES

With the purpose of promoting long-run changes in policy, U.N. conferences have frequently adopted hortatory statements of principle, and this is a prominent normative activity of international organizations. Hortatory statements of principle, which have covered many issues, are intended to have a broad impact on the climate of opinion that surrounds policy making. Many have reaffirmed the goal of global economic growth and have suggested actions that might facilitate achieving this goal. Others have sought to delineate costs that ought not to be paid in the quest for growth, and still others have attempted to mandate principles to guide the distribution of gains from future growth.

Population Growth and Economic Development

The United Nations convened the World Population Conference in Bucharest in 1974 to dramatize the consequences of the rapid growth in the world's population and the implications for the future, particularly with respect to inhibiting growth in per capita income and straining the capacity of resources and productive systems to support life, if existing trends were not altered.

The first principle of the plan of action adopted at the conference read:

> Countries which consider that their present or expected rates of population growth hamper their goals of promoting human welfare are invited, if they have not yet done so, to consider adopting population policies, within the framework of socio-economic development, which are consistent with basic human rights and national goals and values.[6]

The plan of action went on to specify policies that have generally moderated fertility levels. It also suggested that countries consider adopting quantitative goals for the reduction of their fertility rates and policies to achieve these goals. In a most tentative way it suggested that less developed countries should attempt to reduce their birth rates from 38 per 1,000 in 1974 to 30 per 1,000 in 1985, and that developed countries should attempt to keep their birth rates in the neighborhood of 15 per 1,000. The plan reflected the concerns of the developing nations that efforts to limit population growth should not be substituted for efforts to promote economic growth. However, it did affirm the principle that access to information about, and means of, family planning is a basic human right and essential to maternal and child health—a principle that has legitimized many government-sponsored birth control programs in less developed countries. In view of the sensitivity of the subject, the background of centuries of religious and ideological doctrines concerning it, and the fact that traditionally population is mainly a domestic rather than an international matter, the plan was a significant achievement.

International nongovernmental organizations, such as the International Planned Parenthood Federation, took much firmer stands against population growth considerably earlier. INGOs face fewer constraints than do IGOs in making normative pronouncements about such controversial issues as population. However, their pronouncements are less likely to have the same authority as those of IGOs, particularly when the action that is desired must be implemented by governmental policies. For this reason, INGOs often attempt to induce IGOs into adopting their positions.

Protecting the Environment

The most comprehensive statement delineating costs that ought not to be paid in achieving economic growth is the Declaration on the Human Environment, which was adopted in 1972 at the U.N. Conference on the Environment. This declaration proclaimed that:

The natural resources of the earth including the air, water, land, flora and fauna and especially representative samples of natural ecosystems must be safeguarded for the benefit of present and future generations through careful planning or management, as appropriate.

The capacity of the earth to produce vital renewable resources must be maintained and, wherever practicable, restored.

Man has a special responsibility to safeguard and wisely manage the heritage of wildlife and its habitat which are now gravely imperilled by a combination of adverse factors. Nature conservation including wildlife must therefore receive importance in planning for economic development.

The non-renewable resources of the earth must be employed in such a way as to guard against the danger of their future exhaustion and to ensure that benefits from such employment are shared by all mankind.

The discharge of toxic substances or of other substances and the release of heat, in such quantities or concentrations as to exceed the capacity of the environment to render them harmless, must be halted in order to ensure that serious or irreversible damage is not inflicted upon ecosystems. The just struggle of the peoples of all countries against pollution should be supported.

States shall take all possible steps to prevent pollution of the seas by substances that are liable to create hazards to human health, to harm living resources and marine life, to damage amenities or to interfere with other legitimate uses of the sea.[7]

Twenty other principles are also included in the declaration. All are very general, and, of course, none is binding on states. This does not, however, diminish the importance of the declaration. Its function is inspirational and educational, and its stature in this respect is enhanced by its having been adopted unanimously.

Setting Targets for Growth

Other normative statements have been directed toward accelerating economic growth in less developed countries. In 1961 the U.N. General Assembly declared the 1960s to be the "development decade," and proclaimed the objective of achieving no later than the end of the decade a minimal annual rate of growth of 5 percent in the gross national products of the less developed countries.[8]

For the U.N.'s second development decade, the 1970s, this objective was increased to an annual growth rate of 6 percent, and it was increased to 7 percent for the third development decade, the 1980s.[9] Several more specific goals were also established for the third development decade: an annual rate of growth in the per capita GNPs of the less developed countries of 4.5 percent, an annual rate of expansion in their agricultural output of 4 percent, and an annual rate of expansion in their industrial output of 9 percent.[10]

A number of measures have been recommended to implement these objectives. Developed countries have been urged to grant less developed countries generalized, nonreciprocal, and nondiscriminatory tariff preferences. They have also been asked to provide financial resource transfers to less developed countries of a minimum net amount of 1 percent of their gross national products (a minimum of .7 percent of this to be official governmental development assistance). These targets have been widely accepted as goals to be met. For instance, the Organization for Economic Cooperation and Development uses the resource transfer targets as criteria for evaluating its members' aid policies. OECD has also adopted recommendations with respect to the terms on which its members should give development assistance, and these have in turn been endorsed by the United Nations General Assembly.[11]

In the mid-1970s hortatory declarations adopted by the General Assembly and other U.N. bodies became even more assertive about the need to accelerate economic growth in the less developed countries (LDCs). There were several reasons for this. Even though in the aggregate the goals of the first development decade were met, the position of some poor LDCs and of poor people in virtually all LDCs did not improve very much. Moreover, the gap between the average income in the less developed and developed countries increased substantially, provoking envy, anger, and frustration in LDCs. As new states joined the U.N. and swelled the ranks of the Group of 77, mustering majorities for strong resolutions became easier and easier. Finally, the Group of 77 was emboldened by the actions of the OPEC countries in 1972 in starting to take control of the oil companies' operations in their territories and increasing the price of oil by more than a factor of four the following year. The decision for the increase was taken in late 1973, and the new higher price went into effect January 1, 1974.

In 1974 the General Assembly called for the creation of a new international economic order, one that would be more favorable to the less developed states. That same year it adopted the Charter of Economic Rights and Duties of States.[12] The second article of this document proclaimed:

> Every state has and shall freely exercise full permanent sovereignty, including possession, use and disposal, over all its wealth, natural resources and economic activities.

Subsidiary points included the rights to exercise authority over foreign investment, to regulate and supervise the activities of transnational corporations, and to nationalize, expropriate, or transfer ownership of foreign property. The article made no mention of international law standards concerning nationalization, but instead asserted that the national law of the host country could govern the procedure and that disputes about compensation should be settled according to the host country's national law unless both parties agreed to use other peaceful means. The fifth article, reflecting the success of OPEC, proclaimed the right of states to associate in organizations of primary commodity producers in order to develop their economies and achieve stable financing of their exports.

The charter was adopted by a vote of 126 to 6 with ten abstentions. Belgium, Denmark, the Federal Republic of Germany, Luxembourg, the United Kingdom, and the United States were all opposed, and Austria, Canada, France, Ireland, Israel, Italy, Japan, the Netherlands, Norway, and Spain abstained. In other words, the charter was not supported by the most important countries with market economies, countries which accounted for almost 65 percent of global production.

As of the early 1970s the less developed countries accounted for less than 7 percent of global industrial production. The second general conference of the United Nations Industrial Development Organization, held in Lima in 1975, proclaimed that the share of industrial production generated in LDCs should be increased to at least 25 percent by the year 2000. The conference called on the governments of developed countries to take actions to make this possible. This target of 25 percent has been reaffirmed several times, including in the international development strategy for the third U.N. development decade.

The U.N. General Assembly and the United Nations Conference on Trade and Development in the mid-1970s urged the developed countries to provide relief from the mounting external debt burden of developing countries through cancellation or rescheduling of their debts to governments and private creditors in the developed countries. The two bodies also called for the conclusion of trade agreements to stabilize the prices of primary commodities at reasonably high levels, compensatory finance facilities to stabilize export earnings, and other measures to improve and diversify the productive capacity of developing countries. The General Assembly and UNCTAD also endorsed the concept that the prices LDCs receive for the primary goods they export should be indexed to the prices they have to pay for the manufactured goods they import from the developed countries.

None of these resolutions pleased the developed countries. The United States was particularly opposed to them and voted against virtually all of them.

In summary, the normative activities of the U.N. and other similar institutions concerning the economic development of less developed states provoked a major confrontation in the mid-1970s between the LDCs and the developed countries. Whether this confrontation would lead to negotiations that would ultimately result in significant changes in the world economy for the benefit of less developed countries remained to be seen.

In a step that in some ways paralleled what had happened earlier in the arms control negotiations, the principal protagonists in what had come to be called the North-South dialogue agreed in 1975 to the creation of an ad hoc body to continue the discussions that had been launched in the various universal membership forums. Just as the Soviet Union and the United States had agreed to the creation of the ten-nation committee in the hope that more serious arms control discussions might occur in a smaller body, the principal members of OPEC and selected important LDCs agreed to the creation of the Conference on International Economic Cooperation (CIEC). This body consisted of representatives of seven developed countries plus the EEC (whose nine members agreed to speak with one voice) and nineteen less developed countries.[13] After a year and a half of negotiations, CIEC reached an inconclusive end, having achieved little more than a further clarification of the issues in the North-South dialogue and a general commitment of the developed countries to continue the discussion in other existing international bodies. It was not clear whether or not this experimental body had been useful or would be repeated. However, serious arms control negotiations were also very slow in starting.

In less publicized forums the developed countries have set targets for their own growth. In 1961 the member states of OECD set a target of a 50 percent expansion in their combined gross national products by 1970. Although this meant a somewhat lower annual increase (4.1 percent) than that projected for the less developed countries, it actually meant a higher annual rate with respect to per capita GNP because a more rapid growth in population was projected for LDCs. OECD's target for the 1970s is even higher, an increase of 65 percent in the combined gross national products of the member countries by the end of the decade.[14] Faced with the bleak and uncertain condition of the world economy in 1980, OECD's member states refrained from setting targets for growth for the coming decade and instead pledged through their economic policies "to restore price stability and to promote in both the short and the medium term the conditions for investment-led supply-oriented growth in output and employment."[15]

The CMEA countries have also surely set targets for growth in the process of coordinating their national plans, which began with the plans for the 1966–1970 period and was repeated for the 1971–1975 period. In 1976 economic goals were set for the coming fifteen years. Although the figures have not been publicized, it is reasonable to assume that they are at least as high as those set for the OECD member states.

Among other reasons for the serious concern of the governments of the developed countries with insuring their own growth is the fact that since World War II they have been under strong pressure by national and international labor movements to minimize unemployment and to produce regular increases in workers' standards of living. The ability of governments to remain in power in the developed countries is strongly affected by their publics' perception of their ability to manage economic affairs. Worker demonstrations in Poland are not the same thing as an election in a Western European country, yet their effect in ending the government's tenure in office can be the same.

The principal pressure for altering the distribution of the world product comes from international governmental organizations; the principal pressure for altering the distribution of national products within developed countries comes from international and national nongovernmental organizations. As was pointed out in Chapter 3, LDCs hold proportionately more memberships in IGOs than they do in INGOs. Consequently, they are much more likely to press their point of view in IGOs, and the U.N. and its agencies with their universal membership and capacity to draw public attention have been principal instruments in the LDCs' campaign. On the other hand, the developed countries, and particularly those with pluralistic societies, hold a disproportionately large number of memberships in INGOs. Therefore many INGOs are inclined to take positions that reflect those of groups within developed countries.

Facilitating International Trade

The normative activities that have been discussed to this point have been intended to affect the climate within which the public policies of states are framed; other normative activities of international organizations have been meant to have a more immediate effect. In a very general sense, the charters of IMF, GATT, and OECD commit member countries to relatively stable exchange rates and convertible currencies and to liberalizing conditions for the exchange of goods, services, and capital; in other words, to free trade, to open competition, and in general to applying the principles of the market economies to international trade. Substantial progress has been made toward these goals in the years since World War II. OECD has adopted many normative declarations that have been taken very seriously by its member governments and have consequently been instrumental in attaining these goals. In particular, in the early 1960s OECD adopted a Code on the Liberalization of Capital Transactions. Foreign investment in the OECD member countries became considerably easier as a consequence of actions that their governments took to comply with this code.

Progress toward the liberalization of world trade, however, has been severely threatened because of the economic crises that erupted in the early 1970s, particularly after the Yom Kippur War and subsequent sharp increase in the price of petroleum in 1973–1974. In attempting to make certain that its member countries did not try to cope with the crises by taking actions that might jeopardize the progress that had been achieved, in 1974 the OECD council adopted a "pledge" committing the member states not to take unilateral action in the next twelve months to restrict imports,[16] and this pledge was renewed annually through 1979. The fear was that if one country started restricting imports because of a deficit on its current account, this could create balance-of-payments problems for the other countries, and they would also have to restrict their imports, causing a general decline in international trade.

Just as progress seemed to be made toward resolving the economic crises, petroleum prices again shot up in 1979. This time, as a result of OPEC decisions and the cutback in Iranian production because of the revolution, prices were doubled. As countries attempted to adjust to the second petroleum price shock and pressures against liberal trade surged again, OECD's "pledge" took on renewed relevance. In 1980, the council adopted a broad declaration on trade which incorporated the pledge, and since then this declaration has been periodically reaffirmed.

OECD has also attempted to "guide" the policies of its member countries in numerous other fields. Environmental policies provide an example. When environmental concerns became salient and there was a rash of governmental policy making in this field, in 1972, OECD adopted the "polluter pays" principle. According to this principle the costs of pollution and of its abatement should be borne by the polluter, who in most instances would be the producer.[17] The producer could adjust the prices of the products produced accordingly. The principle commits member countries not to use public subsidies to cover the costs of lessening pollution. The underlying rationale for the principle is the notion that prices should reflect the scarcity of natural resources, specifically of water and air. Manufacturers should not treat water and air as if they were free goods. As a guide to public policy in the market economies, the principle is extremely important. Among other things, it is an attempt to insure equal competition among goods that are exported by the market economies, for if the pollution abatement efforts of manufacturers in one country were supported by a public subsidy, these manufacturers would have a competitive advantage.

Member countries which violate officially adopted OECD principles may be called before the council to justify their actions.

CMEA has served a similar function for the planned economies of the Soviet Union and Eastern Europe. In 1962 the CMEA council adopted the Basic Principles of the International Socialist Division of Labour, which was intended to guide CMEA's future work and the national plans of its member states.[18] Starting with this base, CMEA has adopted increasingly detailed recommendations with respect to the various sectors of the economies of its members, and the overall result has been greater specialization among them.

Some normative activities of this nature also are directly oriented toward affecting the distribution of wealth between the developed and less developed countries. OPEC adopts decisions about the amount of petroleum its member states should produce and export and also the price at which it should be sold. Legally these decisions can only be recommendations. They are not self-executing; the member governments must act to implement them. The sanction for not following them—as in the case of OECD's pledge against unilateral restrictions of imports—can only be that other governments also would not follow them, but since this would weaken everyone's position, it is a powerful sanction. On the other side of this particular issue, the International Energy Agency (which was created within the framework of OECD and includes the major consumers of OPEC's petroleum except France) when faced with the 1974 price increases, recommended that its members follow policies of conservation designed to reduce the demand for petroleum and consequently to reduce its price.

Encouraging Standardization

A final category of normative activities of international organizations in this field involves technical standardization. If communications are to occur by means of telephonic equipment or by means of radio, the equipment must be compatible. To facilitate this, the International Telecommunication Union has over the years adopted various recommendations concerning technical specifications for telecommunication equipment.

In a more general way, a strong case can be made for standardization with respect to all goods. For instance, if different types of screws, nuts and bolts, and bearings were used in manufacturing goods in various areas of the world, finding replacement parts and repairing goods imported from other areas would be difficult. An INGO, the International Federation of National Associations of Standardization, was formed in 1926 to recommend standards. This body was discontinued during World War II, but the International Organization for Standardization (ISO—an acronym that does not correspond to the initial letters of the organization's name in any language, and therefore can be used in all languages without change) was created in 1946 to continue its work. There were eighty-nine members of ISO in 1982, and they reflected the full diversity of the world's economic systems. Some members, such as that from the United States, were nongovernmental bodies, while others, such as that from the Soviet Union, were governmental ministries or sections of ministries.

The early work of ISO concentrated on industrial products, but starting in the 1960s its scope was broadened to include medical equipment, furniture, sizing of clothes, air and water quality, dairy products, and other areas. By the 1970s ISO's efforts covered virtually all fields of human activity, and this expansion is reflected in the number of standards adopted. There were only fifty-seven at the end of 1956, but by 1982 there were more than 4,600, and another 1,500 were in the process of being drafted.

Other IGOs and INGOs have undertaken similar activities in their fields of specialized competence. The basic function of these activities is to facilitate international specialization and trade. Once adopted, standards tend to be followed, even though in international law they are not legally binding. Representatives of the concerns that will employ the standards are generally extensively involved in their formulation. Moreover, it is in everyone's long-term interest to observe the standards. A company manufacturing machinery would only limit the potential sales of its product if it used bolts that were not of a standard size that would be readily available elsewhere.

Thanks to standardization activities, progress has been made toward the universal adoption of the metric system. The standardization activities of international organizations may seem prosaic, but they have made a profound contribution toward the creation of a global market.

RULE-CREATING ACTIVITIES

Rule-creating activities—those which result in the adoption of instruments that could have legally binding force—are particularly the province of international governmental organizations. As has been mentioned, the International Air Transport Association is one of the few INGOs to be prominently involved in creating rules. Rule-creating activities in the economic field fall into seven major categories, divided primarily according to the states to which the rules are intended to apply. The first two categories involve rules with potentially universal application. The third and fourth categories concern rules meant primarily for all market economies. The fifth category includes rules intended to apply to regionally defined groups of states. Rules intended for planned economies constitute a sixth category, and those designed for states involved in trade in particular commodities, a seventh.

Communications and Transport

To date, the rule-creating activities that are intended to produce instruments with potentially universal application have been confined principally to the areas of communication and transportation. The reasons for this are relatively obvious. At least minimal agreement concerning technical issues and operating procedures in these areas is essential for there to be any commercial contact among states. In addition, the nature of a state's economy has little impact in these areas: all governments operate postal and meteorological services, and whatever the form of a state's economy, the frequency spectrum that its radio stations must use, the high seas that its ships must sail, and the air space that its planes must traverse are the same. Not surprisingly, some of the specialized agencies with mandates in these fields have had the largest memberships of any international organizations. In 1982, when the U.N. had 157 members, the Universal Postal Union had 164 and the International Telecommunication Union 157. The World Meteorological Organization had 154 members, the International Civil Aviation Organization had 150, and the International Maritime Organization had 121. Considering the technical and specialized nature of the last two organizations and their limited interest for states that do not have airlines or merchant marines, even their memberships were quite large, and they included all of the states that did have substantial facilities.

The Universal Postal Convention and its detailed regulations, which have periodically been revised since their initial preparation in 1875, must be implemented by all members of the Universal Postal Union. They regulate the basic mail services and fix the basic charges, weight limits, and dimensions for articles of correspondence. Other postal services are regulated by special agreements that are binding only on UPU members that have acceded to them.

Allocations for uses of the radio frequency spectrum are agreed to in the administrative conferences of the International Telecommunication Union, and they are embodied in the Radio Regulations, which are revised periodically. The regulations reserve various segments of the spectrum for specific purposes—for instance, maritime mobile, broadcasting, aeronautical, radio navigation, land mobile, amateur, and space. Assigning specific frequencies to stations or users within the broad allocations is the responsibility of member states, and these assignments must be registered with ITU's International Frequency Registration Board (IFRB). However, a state may not assign a frequency to a station if it is likely to cause interference with a station already registered with IFRB.

Conventions relating to maritime safety, the transport of dangerous goods at sea, and maritime pollution are among those that have been negotiated under the auspices of the International Maritime Organization. The International Civil Aviation Organization (ICAO) has been responsible for the elaboration of conventions and standards relating particularly to safety and operational aspects of civil aviation. Member states that are unable to put into effect ICAO's standards covering such matters as pilot licensing, rules of the air, and airworthiness of aircraft must notify ICAO of the differences between their practices and the standards, and the ICAO council passes this information on to the other member states. It may or may not reach those who travel by air. The International Air Transport Association deals with air fares and the liability of carriers.

Road transport and transport by inland waterways raise somewhat different issues. In contrast to ocean shipping and aircraft transport, standardization among the road and inland waterway systems used in different continents is not obligatory. Many of the important activities with respect to road transport and inland waterways have been conducted in the U.N.'s Economic Commission for Europe. These activities, however, have had universal import. From the outset they were intended to apply to both the market economies of Western Europe and the planned economies of Eastern Europe. Moreover, the standards that have been developed in Europe have tended to be adopted subsequently in other geographical regions.

There has not been the same tendency toward creating universal rules with respect to railways. Among the several organizations with activities in this field, only the International Railway Congress Association has broad membership including several of both the principal market and planned economies, and its activities are confined to exchanges of information. Those organizations involved in the creation of rules with respect to technical standards for railways and the exchange of railway equipment have narrower memberships.

The International Labor Code elaborated by the ILO also is applicable to all states, but we will consider the activities undertaken in connection with this code in the chapters dealing with social welfare and human rights.

Rules for the Economic Use of New Environments

As it became apparent that with modern technology petroleum and minerals could be taken from the seabed and as commercial fishing became more important, the traditional law of the sea, which dealt mainly with shipping, increasingly appeared to require modification to take account of the new economic possibilities. The U.N. convened a conference on the law of the sea in 1958. This conference adopted four conventions, one of which, by extending national jurisdiction to the continental shelf, created a legal framework for the development of off-shore oil wells. Another law of the sea conference began in 1973 and finally concluded in 1982. The new convention that resulted from these prolonged negotiations extended the national jurisdiction of coastal states to 200 miles from their shores, and created an international regime to govern the economic use of the deep seabed beyond these limits that would involve an international authority with licensing powers, and an enterprise that could conduct sea bed mining operations.

Progress in the law of the sea negotiations was slow, and for those who hoped for the creation of a powerful international authority with a vast domain, it was disappointing, particularly because the United States refused to accept the convention that finally resulted from the negotiations. On the other hand, the convention established rules that limited and regulated assertions of national authority and would dampen conflicts arising from competing claims. Even the creation of an international authority with a modest domain would mean that for the first time states were not the sole political entities to exercise political jurisdiction over economic resources. The general acceptance by most states that these resources were the common heritage of humankind was an important step.

IMF and GATT

The third category of rule-creating activities of international organizations—those involving rules primarily intended to apply to all market economies—has taken place mainly within two U.N. agencies, the International Monetary Fund and the General Agreement on Tariffs and Trade. Even though IMF's membership is large—146 in 1982—Hungary, Romania, Yugoslavia, Laos, Vietnam, and the People's Republic of China were the only states with centrally planned economies to belong. GATT's membership in 1982 was only eighty-eight, but this number also included six states with centrally planned economies: Cuba, Czechoslovakia, Hungary, Poland, Romania, and Yugoslavia. Neither organization, however, includes the U.S.S.R., and the planned economies that have joined the agencies have not deflected their basic orientation toward the problems of market economies.

IMF's mandate was to promote exchange liberalization. Article IV of its constitutional document required members to establish a par value for their currency in terms of gold. Having set this value, they were required to see that transactions in their currency did not vary from it by more than 1 percent above or below. Member states were allowed one unilateral change in the value of their currency of up to 10 percent, but after that they were only to change the par value in consultation with the fund. The articles of agreement also provided that member states that abided by these agreements should have access to the resources of the fund; that is, a state could borrow foreign currency to engage in open-market operations to insure the stability of its currency.

Although it took some time for this system fully to be established in the years following World War II, once in place it was maintained until August 1971. Most member countries established par values with the IMF. The most notable exception was Canada, which maintained a floating exchange rate. Currency convertibility among the industrial countries was achieved in 1958. Less developed countries pegged their currencies in terms of the dollar, the pound sterling, or the French franc, and the dollar was convertible into gold. In effect, the world was on a dollar standard. Because the dollar was the common unit of value, there was no way for the United States to change the value of its own currency other than by inducing other countries to change the value of their currencies.

This system worked reasonably well through the 1960s, even though during several of the later of these years the United States had deficits on the current account of its balance of payments. What happened was that countries that were in surplus to the United States (i.e., were earning more dollars than they spent) simply added dollars to their reserves. In essence, foreign countries were giving the United States short-term credit. This accumulation of dollars grew at a disturbing rate when the United States' deficits expanded in the late 1960s. Some currency adjustments were made by other countries, but adjustments also had to be made in domestic policies to maintain the fixed exchange rates, and the feeling grew in the United States that other currencies, particularly the German mark and Japanese yen, were undervalued in relationship to the dollar, making German and Japanese imports to the United States too inexpensive and American exports to these countries too expensive. In addition, the accumulation of dollars abroad grew to be far greater than the American gold reserve. The United States could not redeem all of the dollars held abroad. Although negotiations were conducted to attempt to alter and ease the situation, they failed to produce an agreement.

The differences were essentially political rather than technical. Table 11.1 shows the U.S. balance of payments for 1970. As can be seen, although exports exceeded imports, military expenditures abroad exceeded arms sales. Unilateral transfers (essentially foreign aid) constituted a substantial expenditure, and capital flows also accounted for a net deficit of considerable magnitude. The United

TABLE 11.1
U.S. Balance of Payments, 1970
(Millions of Dollars)

	INCOME	EXPENDITURE
CURRENT ACCOUNT		
Merchandise	$42,469 (exports)	$39,866 (imports)
Military Transactions	1,501 (arms sales)	4,855 (direct expenditures)
Net Investment Income		
Private	3,631	
Government		112
Net Travel and Other Transportation Expenditures		2,023
Other Services, Net	2,220	
Remittances, Pensions, and Other Unilateral Transfers		3,248
CAPITAL ACCOUNT		
Long-term Capital Flows, Net		
Private		1,434
Government		2,045
Short-term Capital Flows, Net		482
Liquid Private Catpital Flows, Net		5,988
Allocation of SDRs	867	
Changes in Liabilities to Foreign Official Agencies	7,362	
Changes in U.S. Official Reserve Assets, Net	2,477	
Subtotal	60,527	60,053
Errors and Omissions		476
Total	$60,527	$60,529*

*Difference due to rounding.

Source: Economic Report of the President, 1976 (Washington, D.C.: Government Printing Office, 1976), pp. 274–275.

States made up these deficits by giving up some of its official reserves (essentially selling gold), by gaining some IMF special drawing rights (SDRs, which will be explained subsequently), and by foreign governments holding dollars (essentially making short-term loans to the United States). The United States argued that because of the rates of exchange it could not export enough to cover its expenditures. Several European nations, in contrast, maintained that the United States was having balance-of-payments difficulties because it was spending too much on foreign military ventures (Vietnam) and making too many long-term foreign investments. As foreign governments became increasingly restive about amassing quantities of dollars that they knew could never be redeemed for gold, the crisis deepened.

In August 1971 President Richard Nixon announced that the United States would suspend the convertibility of dollars into gold, and he also put into effect other measures to protect the country's balance-of-payments position. Renewed negotiations led in December 1971 to the so-called Smithsonian Agreement. Agreement was reached on a realignment of the major currencies, a realignment which effectively devalued the dollar. Agreement was also reached to allow currencies to fluctuate within a wider range (± 2.25 percent in relation to intervention currencies such as the dollar, the pound sterling, and the French franc and up to ± 4.5 percent in relation to nonintervention currencies) than in the past. The agreements were ratified by the executive directors of the IMF, but this new regime was short-lived. By June 1972 the United Kingdom, because of balance-of-payments difficulties, had decided that it would no longer attempt to maintain a fixed value for the pound, but instead would allow its value to float. In early 1973 eight other European countries announced that although they would try to maintain relatively fixed relationships among their own currencies, their currencies would float in relation to the dollar.

Since then, the international monetary regime has been one of managed floating exchange rates. Fixed rates do not exist between the major European currencies and the Japanese yen and the dollar, but at the same time governments intervene to insure that radical changes do not occur precipitously. The basic problem in the 1970s and early 1980s has been that the major industrial countries with market economies have had different rates of inflation, and this has immensely complicated the problem of maintaining currency stability.

Meanwhile, an important new development had occurred. For some time governments had been concerned about the international supply of liquidity. The ability of governments to deal with the monetary aspects of temporary balance-of-payments difficulties was dependent upon their reserves—gold and the intervention currencies they held—and on their capacity to borrow. Governments became concerned that international liquidity was not increasing rapidly enough to keep pace with the expansion in international trade. They worried that increases in international liquidity were determined by factors that were at best marginally related to the issues at stake. Whether or not increases occurred depended upon the willingness of producing states (particularly the Soviet Union and the Republic of South Africa) to sell gold and the willingness of the United

States to continue to have balance-of-payments deficits and of other countries to hold dollars.

To remedy this, a movement began in the 1960s to create an international reserve unit, and in 1969 the International Monetary Fund created a special drawing account. States were given special drawing rights with respect to this account. These rights are proportional to the contributions that countries make to the IMF, which in turn are proportional to countries' shares in world trade. Other members of IMF participating in the scheme are obliged to accept SDRs up to specified amounts in settlement of a country's debts. Originally the value of SDRs was defined by the dollar value of gold, but starting in July 1974 their value was defined by the weighted averages of the currencies of the sixteen countries each of which had a share of world exports of goods and services in excess of 1 percent on the average over the five-year period 1968–1972. In 1981 the IMF began to use a simplified basket of five currencies—the U.S. dollar, German mark, yen, French franc, and pound sterling—for determining the value of SDRs. In short, through creation of the special drawing account, the IMF is moving into the position of becoming a central bank for the central banks of the market economies—it is able to create a reserve asset. Under present rules, the creation of new assets requires a majority that, in effect, must include the votes of both the United States and the members of the European Economic Community.

Since the demise of fixed exchange rates in 1971, the rule-creating function of IMF has been in a sense diminished, yet at the same time, with creation of the special drawing account, the potential of a larger rule-creating and operational role exists. Starting in mid-1972 the ad hoc Committee on the Reform of the International Monetary System and Related Issues, more commonly known as the Committee of Twenty, and which was composed of ten developed and ten less developed countries, searched for agreement on a new international monetary regime. Finally in January 1976 the committee formulated proposed amendments to the articles of agreement. Under the amendments, which IMF's board of governors accepted in April 1976 and which formally came into effect in 1978, IMF members became free to make whatever monetary arrangements they wished; they could either set the rate of exchange or let their currencies float. In return for this freedom, member governments undertook to cooperate to maintain orderly economic and financial conditions and to promote international monetary stability. IMF can make recommendations about countries' exchange rate policies, and if a country fails to adhere to these recommendations, it could lose access to IMF loans.

The amendments seek to demonetize the role of gold. They end the requirement that currencies should be valued in terms of gold and also end the official price for gold. The price of gold is determined by the market, and IMF is not required to make or receive payments in gold. IMF took steps to return one-sixth of the gold that member countries had contributed to it and to auction off another one-sixth of its gold holdings. The proceeds from this auction will be used for the benefit of developing countries. As a counterpoint to the deemphasis on the role of gold, the amendments give increased emphasis to the role of SDRs. To a large extent the amendments legalize the monetary arrangements that came into being after 1971. The present monetary regime, at least for the major industrial countries with market economies, is one in which the value of currencies is determined by a system of managed floating. This system requires frequent consultation and cooperation among finance ministers and their deputies and among the central bankers of the principal countries.

The present monetary regime is far from perfect, and many problems remain to be solved. What is impressive is that the system has continued to function despite major changes in the world economy. Even though its operations were not the way that they had been envisaged at Bretton Woods, the system functioned when the United States played a dominant role in the world economy in the 1950s and early 1960s. It then adjusted to the growing role of other states, particularly the members of the European communities and Japan, and the diminished role of the United States. Finally, it survived and accommodated the suddenly increased role of the OPEC countries. Despite substantial problems, basic exchange stability and convertibility have been maintained.

This record of accomplishments stands in stark contrast to the failure of the League of Nations to achieve currency stabilization. The League's final attempt was the International Economic Conference convened in London in 1933. Its collapse was determined when the United States refused to agree to a fixed value for the dollar. From then until the post–World War II period, there were competitive devaluations and currencies were not freely convertible.

Just as the International Monetary Fund has provided the framework for the negotiation of the international monetary regime, the General Agreement on Tariffs and Trade has provided a framework for the negotiation of the international commercial regime. As in the case of IMF, the basic instrument of GATT contains a number of norms for conduct to which states are committed when they join the organization. The most fundamental of these is the rule of nondiscrimination, the obligation to grant all other members of GATT most-favored-nation treatment. A second rule is that member states should use only tariffs to protect their domestic industries, not other restrictions on trade. Quantitative restrictions are generally prohibited, as are internal taxes that discriminate against imports. The General Agreement also calls for the elimination of export subsidies. The basic purpose of these norms is to promote trade liberalization and eliminate as many obstacles to competition as possible. Permissible exceptions to the broad norms include a general exception for less developed countries, permission to create customs unions and free trade areas, and authorization to take emergency action in the event of serious market disruptions.

The General Agreement also includes a mechanism for tariff reductions. These occur as a result of multilateral conferences held under GATT auspices in which bilateral agreements are made to reduce particular tariffs, or whole tariff schedules, and these reductions are then extended to all GATT members on the basis of the most-favored-nation principle. The final reductions are included in a schedule which is annexed to the General Agreement, and consequently they become part of the agreement itself. Because of the importance of the United States as a market for world exports, and the necessity for congressional authorization to reduce U.S. tariffs, the rhythm of GATT tariff-cutting conferences has been tied to the periodic extensions of the U.S. Trade Agreements Act of 1934 and its successors. These acts allow the president to negotiate tariff cuts up to specified percentages in return for reciprocal concessions from other countries. The idea of negotiating reciprocal tariff reductions embodied in the original Trade Agreements Act was the conceptual basis for GATT.

From 1947 through 1979 seven major trade negotiations took place under GATT's auspices: in 1947 (Geneva), in 1949 (Annecy, France), in 1951 (Torquay, United Kingdom), in 1956 (Geneva), in 1960 and 1961 (Geneva, the "Dillon Round"), from 1964 through 1967 (Geneva, the "Kennedy Round"), and from 1973 through 1979 (Tokyo and Geneva, the "Tokyo Round").

The results of bilateral negotiations in the 1930s and the GATT negotiations in the post–World War II period have been substantial: the tariff levels on all dutiable imports to the United States have dropped from about 59 percent in 1932 to 25 percent in 1946 to 9.9 percent at the conclusion of the Kennedy Round.[19] Thanks to GATT's rule-creating activities, by the conclusion of the Kennedy Round the market economies had moved very close to having free trade among themselves in manufactured and semi-manufactured goods, and this process continued in the Tokyo Round. Given the economic difficulties of the 1970s, the continuation of the process of trade liberalization was a significant accomplishment. The weighted average tariff rate of the United States, the EEC, and Japan on such items will be less than 5 percent when the last of the cuts agreed to in the Tokyo Round are implemented in 1987.[20] GATT negotiations also resulted in the progressive elimination of import quotas on almost all nonagricultural products.

Again, this record contrasts sharply with that of the League of Nations. The last major effort of the League in this area was the 1930 International Conference for a Tariff Truce, a futile attempt to halt the upward spiral of tariffs. As a consequence of this failure, and the failure to achieve monetary stabilization, a large part of international trade came to be conducted on a bilateral basis, and the overall total of global trade declined.[21]

GATT's record in areas other than tariffs or quotas on manufactured and semi-manufactured goods, however, is much less impressive. Until the Kennedy Round, agricultural products had largely been exempted from the negotiations, and although these products were considered during that round, little progress was made toward liberalizing trade in them. There are several explanatory factors. Starting in North America and extending to other temperate zones, agricultural productivity has undergone revolutionary increases in the mid-twentieth century. A simple statistic illustrates the point: in 1970 one farm worker in the United States could feed thirty-five persons, compared with eight in 1920. Such an increase has brought social problems. The number of farm workers required has declined, and overproduction could easily result in a loss of farm income. Western governments tend to be particularly sensitive to agricultural issues because agricultural areas tend to be overrepresented in their legislatures and because food self-sufficiency is highly valued. Starting in the 1930s the United States moved to manage its agricultural sector, employing import quotas among other devices. In the early 1950s Congress insisted that GATT regulations should not apply to several agricultural commodities. The contracting parties to GATT acquiesced by granting a waiver in 1955, the only permanent waiver ever given by the organization. With the United States market thus excluded, other countries were not interested in dealing with agricultural issues.

By the Kennedy Round, however, the situation had changed. The European Economic Community had adopted its Common Agricultural Policy, which the United States felt tended to limit the access of its agricultural exports to the European market. Thus in the Kennedy Round negotiations the United States pressed for the inclusion of agricultural products, but the EEC was unwilling seriously to modify its agricultural policy, and little was accomplished. The Tokyo Round also failed to produce significant results for agricultural products, although arrangements were negotiated for bovine meat and dairy products. These arrangements provided for exchange of information and market monitoring and allowed the possibility of cooperative action to counter market disciplines.

A second area in which GATT had made little progress by the end of the Kennedy Round concerned nontariff barriers, such measures as customs classification and valuation, and public procurement policies. Until tariffs had been substantially lowered and quotas eliminated, these barriers did not seem so significant. Furthermore, they are less visible than tariffs, which are normally published in one public comprehensive schedule. Finally, bargaining equivalencies are much more difficult to determine in this area than with tariffs. The Kennedy Round did begin to deal with nontariff barriers, and they were one of the major topics on the agenda for the negotiations that began in Tokyo in 1973.

Among the Tokyo Round's major accomplishments were codes of conduct specifying rules concerning: customs valuation, government procurement, import licensing procedures, subsidies and countervailing duties, and technical barriers or standards. Beyond specifying binding rules that apply among signatories, each agreement establishes procedures for dealing with complaints by parties to the agreement about violations of the rules and mechanisms for obtaining redress if the complaints are upheld. All of the agreements had entered force by January 1, 1981, and they were being overseen by GATT committees or councils. These codes of conduct were a major step toward reducing the impact on international trade of nontariff barriers. In addition, the antidumping code (which had been adopted in 1967) was revised during the Tokyo Round to bring it into conformity with the code on subsidies and countervailing duties and to rectify problems that had arisen implementing it. Finally, an agreement was negotiated that committed those states that ratified it to allow free trade in civil aircraft and component parts and their repairs.

Finally, instead of eliminating restrictions on trade in textiles, the contracting parties to GATT moved to manage this trade. Again, the impetus came from the United States. Textiles can easily be produced competitively in less industrialized countries, but sharp increases in imports of textiles could result in substantial unemployment in the more industrialized countries. In the 1950s the United States Congress became deeply concerned about rapid increases in imports of cotton textiles from Japan and threatened to enact quotas. Instead, an agreement was negotiated in 1955 according to which Japan undertook voluntarily to limit its export of cotton textiles to the United States. At the same time, the United States sponsored Japan's membership in GATT.

It was soon discovered in the United States that although this agreement limited imports of Japanese cotton textiles, it did not stop increases in the imports of cotton textiles from other areas, such as Hong Kong. With United States prompting, a broad Cotton Textiles Arrangement was negotiated within the framework of GATT which allowed importing countries to establish quotas. Theoretically, the arrangement was to allow the controlled expansion of the cotton textile markets. It did that, but many criticized the slow pace of expansion. In 1974 this arrangement was replaced with a broader one covering almost all textiles, the Multi-Fiber Agreement. This agreement mandated that no new restraints should be created unless specifically authorized, and that existing unilateral and bilateral restraints should be phased out, and it established a surveillance body to oversee implementation of these provisions. How satisfactory this more elaborate arrangement will be remains to be seen. It must at the same time satisfy the desire of the less developed countries to expand their exports and the desire of the developed countries to insure that their low-skill industries do not suffer socially and politically disruptive competition. The Multi-Fiber Agreement was negotiated in 1977 and again in 1981.

If the target that has been proclaimed of having 25 percent of industrial production occur in less developed countries by the end of this century is to be met, a substantial number of low-skill industries will have to be developed in LDCs. Unrestricted exports of the goods of these industries to the developed countries could cause considerable social disruption. Unemployment in such industries in the United States and Europe is already a serious problem. Should unemployment increase further, allowing increased imports would probably become politically impossible. Regulating the flow of imports so that both less developed and developed countries will be satisfied will be an extremely difficult task, one that will require political leadership of the highest order.

GATT has had little effect on the conditions of trade between market and centrally planned economies. States with the largest planned economies, the U.S.S.R. and the People's Republic of China, are not members of GATT. Even though Czechoslovakia has always been a member, when the United States suspended the application of most-favored-nation treatment for the country, GATT merely took note of the situation. Since the late 1950s other communist countries have joined GATT—Poland, Yugoslavia, Hungary, and Romania—but their presence has not had a significant impact on the negotiations. Should East-West trade increase further, there will be greater pressure to regularize the conditions that govern this trade, either through the GATT regime or through some other institutional arrangement. This too will require political leadership.

Crafting arrangements for East-West trade and accommodating increased exports from LDCs will not be the only tasks related to international trade that will require farsighted leadership. As barriers to trade have been reduced and as exchange rates have fluctuated markedly, trade patterns have become increasingly volatile. Trade competition among themselves has exacerbated Western countries' problems in accepting increased exports from LDCs and centrally planned economies.

According to classical economic theory, structural adjustments should occur in national economies to allow production to take place wherever comparative advantage is greatest. Western governments, however, cannot allow structural adjustments without intervening in some way to minimize the consequences for employment. Abrupt and deep structural adjustment could produce unemployment levels that would be intolerable for Western societies. Western governments have consequently resorted to quantitative restrictions to control the pace of structural adjustment; these restrictions sometimes almost seem calculated to avoid structural adjustment.

As we have seen, the quantitative restrictions in the textile sector have been organized within the framework of GATT. Such restrictions in other sectors have grown up outside the framework of GATT. Countries, particularly the United States and the members of the European communities, facing surges of imports that have threatened domestic industries, have pressed exporting countries to accept Voluntary Export Restraints (VERs) or more Orderly Marketing Agreements (OMAs) in case of the United States and Voluntary Restraint Agreements (VRAs) in the case of the European communities. Because these are quantitative restrictions on exports and not imports, technically they do not violate GATT rules, but they certainly contravene GATT's broad goal of trade liberalization. The proportion of world trade affected by VRAs and OMAs is certainly substantial, although it is impossible to estimate it accurately. It includes trade in footwear, steel, automobiles, and ships, among other sectors.

In their present form, VERs are neither based on agreed rules nor are they subject to any organized multilateral surveillance. If they are not abandoned or somehow brought within the framework of the fundamental principles of the GATT regime and made to serve its basic goals, they could lead to its demise.

Direct Foreign Investment and Transnational Corporations

The relative exchange liberalization that has resulted from the IMF's activities and the reduction in obstacles to trade as a consequence of the activities of GATT have facilitated an enormous growth in international trade since World War II. Currency convertibility, relative exchange stability, and reduced obstacles to trade have also facilitated the growth of transnational corporations. As tariffs and quotas were reduced, firms could think about locating the production of goods wherever this would be least expensive. It even became possible to consider producing different components of finished products in several countries and bringing them together for final assembly in yet another country. Currency convertibility and relative exchange stability were prerequisites for firms' thinking and acting in this way: sudden and sharp changes in exchange rates could easily undermine the cost calculations. The development of more rapid and less costly transport and the lessening of restrictions on capital transactions also contributed to expanding corporate managers' horizons.

Direct foreign investment, the purchase of facilities to be controlled substantially by the investing unit, is perhaps the best measure of the growth of transnational corporations. Table 11.2 compares the growth of United States exports and direct foreign investment between 1950 and 1980. As can be seen, during the thirty-year span, both exports and direct foreign investment grew about twenty times. During the decades of the 1950s and 1960s, U.S. direct foreign investment grew relatively more rapidly than U.S. exports, but this situation was reversed in the 1970s. Much of the surge in U.S. direct foreign investment resulted from U.S. corporations establishing manufacturing facilities within the European communities in order to take advantage of the newly expanded market there. As of 1980, 36 percent of U.S. direct foreign investment was located in the then nine member states of the European communities. Another 21 percent of U.S. direct foreign investment was located in Canada. In all, the member countries of OECD accounted for more than 72 percent of U.S. direct foreign investment. Less than a quarter of U.S. direct foreign investment was in less developed countries. The direct foreign investment of other Western countries has also grown rapidly, although this growth started somewhat later than that of the United States. The OECD Code on the Liberalization of Capital Movements undoubtedly facilitated the great expansion of direct foreign investment. By the late 1970s transnational corporations were a major factor in global production.

The rapid growth of transnational corporations provoked attempts in various forums to create rules to regulate foreign investment. The less developed countries have pressed, particularly in the Commission on Transnational Corporations, for negotiation of a code of conduct to govern the operations of transnational corporations. The corporations, in contrast, have argued that the behavior of host countries should also be regulated by a code of conduct.

TABLE 11.2
U.S. Exports and Direct Foreign Investment
(Value in Billions of Current U.S. Dollars)

	1950	1960	1970	1980
Exports	10.3	20.6	43.2	216.7
Direct Foreign Investment				
(book value)	11.8	32.0	78.1	213.5

Source: United States Senate, 93rd Congress, 1st Session, Committee on Finance, *Implications of Multinational Corporations for World Trade and Investment and for U.S. Trade and Labor* (Washington, D.C.: Government Printing Office, 1973), p. 95; U.S. Department of Commerce, *Survey of Current Business*, Vol. 61, No. 8 (August 1981), p. 21; and U.N. Speretariat, *Statistical Yearbook, 1979/1980* (New York: U.N., 1981), p. 440.

Following the disclosures in the mid-1970s about payments made by Lockheed and other companies to government officials, the United States called for preparation of an agreement to outlaw corrupt practices of transnational corporations. Thus far the only completed general agreement is the Convention on the Settlement of Investment Disputes, negotiated under the auspices of the International Bank for Reconstruction and Development, which entered into force in 1966 and by June 1981 had been signed by eighty-three states and ratified by seventy-eight. In addition, as will be described below, the Andrean Group has adopted a joint regulation to govern the conditions of direct foreign investment in the member countries.

In 1976 OECD adopted a normative Declaration on International Investment and Multinational Enterprises. This declaration was intended to guide governments in their dealings with transnational corporations and transnational corporations in their dealings with governments, groups, and individuals. It urged governments to give transnational corporations the same treatment that they would give to national corporations. On the other hand, obligations were spelled out for transnational corporations in eight areas: (a) general policies, (b) disclosure of information, (c) competition, (d) financing, (e) taxation, (f) employment, (g) industrial relations, and (h) science and technology. Transnational corporations were urged to be responsive to governmental policies with respect to such issues as regional development and to make public information such as would be required by the Securities and Exchange Commission in the United States on their operations so that realistic tax policies could be implemented.

In Europe corporations rather than individuals are expected to bear the primary burden of production shifts; lay-offs are to be avoided at almost any cost, and the declaration followed this philosophy. It also called on companies to follow nondiscriminatory hiring policies and not to take advantage of their global mobility to avoid collective bargaining. Transnational corporations were encouraged not to pursue predatory competition policies and to insure that all countries in which they operated benefited from research and development activities. OECD created a Committee on International Investment and Multinational Enterprises to monitor the consequences of the declaration, which it determined would be reviewed in three years. When the OECD Council in 1979 reviewed the functioning of the regime created by the declaration, it concluded that the declaration provided a satisfactory framework and made only modest modifications. Given the fact that most transnational corporations have their headquarters and their most extensive operations in OECD countries, the declaration is very important. It is also clear that the members of OECD think that it is a model statement that could be applied to the entire world.

Regional Economic Integration among Market Economies

A fifth major category of rule-creating activities concerns rules that are intended for regionally defined groups of states. The European Economic Community is by far the most important of these regional groupings, both in the extent of the rules that have been created and in the role of the group in global trade. In 1980 the EEC's nine member countries had a total population that was 16 percent larger than that of the United States, and their combined gross national products were almost equal to that of the United States. Their exports, excluding intra-community exports, constituted more than 16 percent of global exports, exceeding the United States' share by more than 5 percent.[22] The EEC is the largest single exporting and importing unit in the world economy.

The treaty establishing the European Economic Community committed the six original member states to establish a customs union according to a fixed time schedule. In fact, this achievement was gained eighteen months before it was required. All tariffs and quota restrictions on intracommunity trade in nonagricultural products were eliminated by July 1, 1968, and the Common External Tariff went into effect on the same date. External actors had a role in setting the Common External Tariff in that what its level should be was a subject negotiated by GATT's Kennedy Round. When Denmark, Ireland, and the United Kingdom became members of the EEC on January 1, 1973, they began the process of gradual adjustment to participation in the customs union, a process which was completed July 1, 1977. Greece's accession, which took effect on January 1, 1981, will be spread over a five-year transition period.

The creation of the customs union, first among the original six countries and then among the nine, is one of the major explanations for the enormous increase in U.S. direct foreign investment in Europe during the 1960s and 1970s. American firms wanted to develop manufacturing facilities in Europe so that they could take advantage of the enlarged European market. Some leaders in the European communities encouraged U.S.-based transnational corporations to invest in Europe in the belief that this would contribute to European economic integration. They thought that American management would move more quickly to take advantage of the enlarged European market than would more conservative European management. They also believed that the example set by American transnational corporations would stimulate European management to a broader vision. Experience has substantiated their beliefs.

The EEC treaty also provided that the common market should be extended to agriculture and to trade in agricultural products, but that this should be accompanied by the establishment of a common agricultural policy. The EEC's Common Agricultural Policy (CAP) was elaborated during the course of the 1960s; it was put into effect for most commodities by mid-1966 and was completely in effect by mid-1968. The system involves common support prices throughout the community for basic agricultural commodities. Target prices are set at levels designed to insure a reasonable return to farmers. When actual prices that are paid for particular products fall a certain percentage below target prices, government agencies intervene in the market to support prices by buying commodities. Threshold prices are set for imports from noncommunity sources. Their level is designed to insure that once transport costs from the port of entry are added, the price of imported commodities should be at or above the level of the target price. Variable levies are charged on imports. These are supposed to make up the difference between world prices and threshold prices. As a consequence of the variable levies, effective protection on some products ranges from 50 percent to over 100 percent. To enable community producers to sell on world markets, restitution payments, or export refunds, are paid.

The policy in its broad orientation is not unlike that adopted by the United States in the 1930s. As was the case in the United States, it has served to spur agricultural production, and it has resulted in an increased level of agricultural self-sufficiency within the EEC. It has also similarly produced surpluses and increased community agricultural exports, and as of the early 1980s, it swallowed up two-thirds of the communities' funds.

To insure that the stimulus to competition provided by creation of a larger market would not be lost because of collusive arrangements among firms, the EEC treaty contained several rules on competition, which community agencies have acted to implement. The resulting antitrust policy must be numbered among the major accomplishments of the EEC. Substantial progress has also been made toward the creation of a single labor force by allowing workers to move freely within the community in search of employment, and some restrictions imposed on capital movements have been eliminated. There has also been progress in cooperation in the areas of tax policy, transport policy, energy policy, and monetary policy.

The European Monetary System (EMS) was created in 1979. The purpose of the EMS is to create a zone of relative monetary stability within the European communities. Without such stability, many of the communities' achievements, especially the Common Agricultural Policy, would be at risk. Those members of the European communities that chose to participate agree to limit the fluctuation of their currencies in relation to the currencies of the other participating members to a band of plus or minus 2.25 percent (except Italy, which is permitted to allow the lira to fluctuate within a band of plus or minus 6 percent). All members of the communities except the United Kingdom and Greece chose to participate. The system also involved the creation of a new kind of money, the European currency unit (ECU). The ECU is a basket of the currencies of the member countries that has become part of the reserves of their central banks. They receive ECUs for depositing 20 percent of their gold and dollars with the European Monetary Cooperation Fund (EMCF). The United Kingdom participates in this aspect of the EMS. The European currency unit is also the *numéraire* or denominator for the exchange-rate mechanism and the unit of account for the communities. The EMCF is slated to become the European Monetary Fund. It will be a mini-IMF for the European communities. EMCF can loan funds to member states to maintain the value of their currencies within the permissible bands. EMF in effect would be a central bank for the communities; it would issue ECUs against national currencies and intervene on behalf of all EEC members against currencies like the U.S. dollar and the Japanese yen.

Community policies have gradually superseded national policies with respect to external commercial matters. Since 1973 there have been common commercial policies toward the communist states of Eastern Europe. Commercial relations between the EEC's nine member states and sixty-three countries in Africa, the Caribbean, and the Pacific (ACP)—most of them former colonies of EEC members—are governed by the Lomé Convention, which provides for tariff-free and quota-free entry into the community for all manufactured goods from the sixty-three and for 96 percent of their agricultural products. The convention further provides mechanisms for stabilization of the earnings from exports of specified primary commodities by the ACP countries to the EEC countries. Under these arrangements, commonly known as the STABEX system, if earnings from the export of a particular commodity constitute more than a certain percentage (2.5 to 7.5 percent depending on the circumstances) of an ACP country's gross national product, and if the country's earnings from this commodity in any given year falls more than 2.5 to 7.5 percent (again depending on the circumstances) below the average earnings received during the last four years, the country would be entitled to a transfer payment up to the amount of the difference between the earnings received and the reference level. Depending on subsequent developments concerning the price of the exported commodity and the ACP country's balance of payments, this transfer payment might not have to be repaid. In any case, interest would not be charged.

Additional preferential trading agreements have been negotiated between the European Economic Community and Turkey (1963) and Spain (1970); the six countries that are members of EFTA, Austria, Iceland, Norway, Portugal, Sweden, and Switzerland (1973); Finland, an associate member of EFTA (1974), and ten other countries bordering the Mediterranean.[23] In short, the European Economic Community is a partially completed common market that has elements of economic integration and that as a unit has preferential trading relationships with more than eighty other countries.

In 1983 fourteen other regional groups of market economies had taken some steps toward establishing free trade areas, customs unions, or common markets:

1. *Andean Group*—formed in 1969; comprising Bolivia, Chile, Colombia, Ecuador, Peru, and Venezuela. Chile withdrew in 1976.
2. *Arab Common Market*—formed in 1964; comprising Egypt, Iraq, Jordan, and the Syrian Arab Republic.
3. *Association of South-East Asian Nations*—formed in 1967; comprising Indonesia, Malaysia, the Philippines, and Singapore, and Thailand.
4. *Caribbean Community and Common Market*—formed in 1973 to replace the Caribbean Free Trade Association which had been established in 1968; comprising Antigua and Barbuda, Barbados, Belize, Dominica, Grenada, Guyana, Jamaica, Montserrat, St. Kitts-Nevis-Anguilla, St. Lucia, St. Vincent-Grenadines, and Trinidad and Tobago. The American Bahamas are an associate member. Integration attempts in the Commonwealth Caribbean date from the colonial period.
5. *Central African Customs and Economic Union*—formed in 1964, but with a history of collaboration dating to the colonial period; comprising Cameroon, Central African Republic, Chad, Congo, and Gabon. Chad

withdrew in 1968.

6. *Central American Common Market*—formed in 1960; comprising Costa Rica, El Salvador, Guatemala, Honduras, and Nicaragua. Honduras discontinued participation in 1969.

7. *Council of the Entente*—formed in 1959; comprising Benin (Dahomey), Ivory Coast, Niger, Togo, and Upper Volta.

8. *East Caribbean Common Market*—formed in 1968; comprising Antigua, Dominica, Grenada, Montserrat, St. Kitts-Nevis-Anguilla, St. Lucia, and St. Vincent.

9. *Economic Community of West African States*—formed in 1975; comprising Benin (Dahomey), Cape Verde, Gambia, Ghana, Guinea, Guinea-Bissau, Ivory Coast, Liberia, Mali, Mauritania, Niger, Nigeria, Senegal, Sierra Leone, Togo, and Upper Volta.

10. *European Free Trade Association*—formed in 1959; comprising Austria, Denmark, Norway, Portugal, Sweden, Switzerland, and the United Kingdom. An Agreement of Association was signed between Finland and EFTA in 1961 and Iceland became a full member of EFTA in 1970. Denmark and the United Kingdom withdrew from EFTA December 1972, the day before they became members of ECSC, EEC, and Euratom.

11. *Latin American Integration Association*—formed in 1960; comprising Argentina, Bolivia, Brazil, Chile, Colombia, Ecuador, Mexico, Paraguay, Peru, Uruguay, and Venezuela (known as the Latin American Free Trade Association until 1980).

12. *Maghreb Group*—formed in 1964; comprising Algeria, Morocco, and Tunisia.

13. *Regional Cooperation for Development*—formed in 1964; comprising Iran, Pakistan, and Turkey.

14. *West African Economic Community*—formed in 1973, but with a history of collaboration dating to the colonial period; comprising Ivory Coast, Mali, Mauritania, Niger, Senegal, and Upper Volta.

The success of these groupings in undertaking rule-creating activities directed toward economic integration varies. Some have made considerable headway; others have barely progressed beyond the initial treaty; and still others have foundered.

Probably the Andean Group, the Central American Common Market, the Central African Customs and Economic Union, and the European Free Trade Association have the most substantial achievements. The Andean Group has moved toward establishment of a customs union, approved industrial development programs for the metalworking, petrochemical, and automobile industries, and also set up a common code for foreign investment. However, in 1976 Chile withdrew from the group because it felt that adherence to this code interfered with its ability to attract foreign investment. The Central American Common Market has freed its internal trade and established a common external tariff, although there are some exclusions to both. Remarkably, the Central American

Common Market continued to function in the 1980s despite the turmoil in Central America. The Central African Customs and Economic Union has created a customs union. There are no internal barriers to trade in industrial goods among the members of the European Free Trade Association, and, thanks to EFTA's agreement with EEC, industrial goods circulate freely among both members of both organizations.

The East African Community, which was comprised of Kenya, Tanzania, and Uganda, was formed in 1967. Before the creation of the community there had been a long history under colonialism of integration among the three countries. The three states, however, found it impossible to preserve this legacy of common services and a customs union, and the community completely collapsed in 1977. This is the only integration institution to have disintegrated.

Like the European Economic Community, all of the regional groupings of states infringe on GATT's most-favored-nation principle in varying degrees. They create enclaves of preferential trading arrangements. Although free trade areas and customs unions constitute permissible exceptions to GATT's rule of nondiscrimination, they are subject to scrutiny by the contracting parties.

CMEA

There is one final grouping of states, CMEA, but since it links centrally planned rather than market economies and therefore raises different issues and problems, it merits treatment in a separate category.

Given the decentralized nature of market economies, economic integration can be accomplished by removing tariffs, quotas, and other obstacles to trade. Enlarging the size of the market in this manner will promote efficiency by allowing more widespread competition and by permitting firms to take advantage of economies of scale. Governmental officials collaborating in the institutions of the regional groupings do not have to decide where production facilities will be located and how much will be produced; these matters can be left to private entrepreneurs and market forces.

With centrally planned economies, however, the situation is different. Integration can be achieved only through planning. The process of sharing information and voluntarily coordinating plans within CMEA has already been mentioned. This process is intended to permit larger production runs by reducing duplication. When successful, it results in bilateral and sometimes multilateral agreements for the delivery of goods. CMEA has also provided a forum in which agreements about joint projects can be negotiated. The most notable of these are the Druzhba oil pipeline, which transports oil from the Soviet Union to Hungary, the German Democratic Republic, Poland, and Czechoslovakia; the integrated power grid linking the power systems of the member countries; and the railway freight-car pool, a common pool drawn upon by member countries.

In 1962 Nikita Khrushchev proposed that CMEA should go even further and that the organization's institutions should be endowed with appropriate authority for "building the socialist world economy as a single entity."[24] Exactly what this would involve was never publicly clearly developed, but it could well have meant the creation of a unified plan covering all member countries. Moving in this direction was unacceptable to Romania and other smaller Eastern European communist countries, and Khrushchev's initiative foundered. For his initiative to have been successful, the member countries essentially would have had to delegate economic sovereignty to CMEA. Since in market economies, governments do not control so much to start with, moving in the direction of integration does not appear to involve giving up so much, and since basic decisions about the location of production are left to the private sector, matters which are salient controversies among centrally planned economies need not arise.

One of the explanations for the fact that the regional economic integration schemes among the less developed countries have made slower progress than the European Economic Community is that the governments of LDCs are relatively more involved in economic activities, and consequently even though they are formally classified as market economies, the integration process among them in some respects resembles that among centrally planned economies.

Commodities

A final category of rule-creating activities involves commodities. One type of agreements are those negotiated among the principal consumers and producers of particular commodities. Since the end of World War II such agreements have been negotiated covering seven commodities—coffee, olive oil, sugar, tin, natural rubber, cocoa, and wheat—all under the auspices of the United Nations or the United Nations Conference on Trade and Development. Their broad purpose is to eliminate excessive fluctuations in the price of these commodities. The demand and supply curves for basic commodities tend to be relatively inelastic in the near term: the supply of commodities offered for sale does not change rapidly in response to price shifts, and thus a slight change in demand is likely to produce sharp increases or decreases in price. For countries whose GNPs are heavily dependent upon the export of one basic commodity, a decline in demand can have disastrous consequences. Commodity agreements could set ceiling and floor prices which would be maintained by governmental intervention in markets; they could involve the creation of buffer stocks; and they also could involve quantitative controls on production and trade. The agreements that have been in effect have employed these techniques, either alone or in combination.

In policy instruments employed, international commodity agreements are not unlike the agricultural policies pursued in the United States and the European Economic Community. Despite this, the United States has been wary of entering into such agreements. This opposition has an ideological basis stemming from a basic preference for a free market. It also reflects a fear that commodity agreements would be used to transfer resources from the richer to the poorer countries and that they would involve a substantial commitment for the United States.

Throughout the 1950s and 1960s, when the demand for basic commodities was relatively soft, the less developed countries that were producers of primary commodities pushed for commodity agreements and by 1970 succeeded in obtaining five covering coffee, tin, olive oil, sugar, and wheat.

Spurred by the North-South dialogue, efforts to reach similar agreements on other primary commodities began in the mid-1970s. The cocoa agreement was signed in 1975. In 1977 representatives of developed and developing countries met under the auspices of UNCTAD to begin negotiations on a proposed "common fund," which would be a new instrument for financing the buffer stocks created under commodity agreements and a further step toward organizing the system of international trade in primary commodities. The Articles of Agreement for the Common Fund were signed in 1980; the agreement covering natural rubber came into effect that same year. In the difficult economic climate of the early 1980s, however, the existence of all of the commodity agreements appeared precarious. Those for olive oil and wheat had in fact lapsed and as of 1982 the Common Fund had failed to achieve sufficient ratifications to enter into force.

As the 1970s developed, it became clear that commodity agreements arrived at between producing and consuming countries would not bring benefits to the developing countries nearly as impressive as those gained by the Organization of Petroleum Exporting Countries, a cartel of producing countries founded in 1960. In 1973-1974, by carefully organized collaboration, OPEC was able to achieve price increases of four and a half times, from $2.59 to $11.65 per barrel. Despite the example set by OPEC, it was also clear that the cartel strategy would not be as effective in other commodities where market conditions were not as favorable as in petroleum. Nevertheless there could be little doubt that other commodity-producing countries would be prepared to use this strategy in the future if market conditions changed, for example, if shortages developed in key industrial raw materials.

RULE-SUPERVISORY ACTIVITIES

The rule-supervisory activities of international organizations tend to be concentrated in the same IGOs as are the rule-creating activities. INGOs and transnational organizations are little involved, except as plantiffs and defendants before the Court of Justice of the European communities. Labor INGOs do play an important role with respect to the conventions negotiated in ILO, but these activities will be treated as part of the discussion of human rights in Chapter 14.

ITU

The IGOs with universal memberships that have mandates relating to transport and communications engage in certain rule-supervisory activities. They constitute a first category. Among these IGOs, the International Telecommunication Union has the most highly developed rule-supervisory functions, and these relate to the utilization of the radio frequency spectrum. The International Frequency Registration Board maintains a register of frequency assignments. States must notify the IFRB of assignments of frequencies to particular stations. Before placing an assignment in the register, the IFRB must first determine that the station is not likely to interfere with assignments already registered. If the IFRB so determines, the assignment can then be placed in the register and it has international recognition.

In the event of disputes about interference, the Radio Regulations urge the states involved to attempt to settle the matter through bilateral or multilateral negotiations, but if these fail, the IFRB can be asked to study the case and to make recommendations. Clearly the authority is modest, but states have been unwilling to go further. In general, however, it is in everyone's interest to comply with the regulations. There is little point to broadcasting if the transmissions cannot be received because of interference. Thus the function of the international organization can be limited to maintaining a registry. If the basic principle of operation were more complicated than the first-come first-served rule that now applies, however, the arrangement might prove less satisfactory. Even as it is, there is substantial interference in radio reception in Europe because of the crowding of the frequency spectrum, and neither ITU nor national states have been able to regulate or stop the pirate stations that have evaded control by transmitting from the North Sea.

IMF and GATT

Secondly, there are the two IGOs with mandates that relate to trading relationships among market economies, the International Monetary Fund and the General Agreement on Tariffs and Trade. The original articles of agreement of the International Monetary Fund required member states to consult the fund about changes in the value of their currencies. In fact, states whose currencies were of substantial importance for world trade tended to decide and announce changes in their par values first and then consult the IMF later. At best, the processes occurred simultaneously. The reasons for this are obvious. Countries do not change the value of their currencies frivolously—serious issues have to be involved—and the decision will have important consequences for their domestic economies. A country might try devaluation as a strategy for dealing with a deficit in its balance on current account. If it were not allowed to devalue, it might have to take steps to deal with the deficit that would involve increasing the level of unemployment, something governments do not want to be determined by external forces. Furthermore, if news of a change in the par value of a currency were to leak and circulate in advance, speculative transfers of funds could weaken or negate the effectiveness of the action.

For these reasons, governments have not been willing to transfer substantial authority in the determination of the par values of their currencies to an international agency, and the 1978 changes in IMF's Articles of Agreement recognize this and legitimate the freedom of governments to make their own choices. On the other hand, because of the continuing requirement for consultation, these matters have constantly been discussed within the framework of IMF, and as

IMF's membership has expanded, there has been an increasing tendency for there to be preliminary discussions in other settings, such as the Organization for Economic Cooperation and Development. Because of the exchange of information involved in these discussions, governments inevitably are deeply aware of the interaction of their foreign trade with that of other states, and of the consequences for other states of any changes in the value of their currencies. Here too, the logic of the situation commands a measure of cooperation. A devaluation could have no effect if all other states implemented equivalent devaluations in retaliation.

Through its ability to provide funds for states to ease their temporary balance-of-payments difficulties, IMF has gained some authority over countries' economic policies. Since its loans must be repaid, IMF maintains, as any prudent lender would, that its borrowers ought to pursue policies that will facilitate this. Thus, when lending money beyond that amount to which governments are more or less automatically entitled, the IMF scrutinizes the borrower's domestic and foreign economic policies, and it may make recommendations for changes. In certain instances, it may refuse to lend funds unless changes are made. Thus the ability to loan money has given IMF a type of surveillance authority. This authority substantially increased in significance in the 1980s as the debt problems of the less developed countries mounted. The funds that IMF could provide were, of course, important in their own right; in addition, private lenders more and more would only agree to provide additional funds for less developed countries on the condition that these countries negotiate agreements with IMF about their basic economic policies. The extent of IMF's surveillance authority obviously varies with countries and their circumstances. In general, the smaller the country, the more desperate its plight, and the fewer alternative sources of financial assistance it has, the more responsive it must be to IMF's views. Among the major countries, the IMF has particularly scrutinized the policies of the United Kingdom because of its persistent balance-of-payments problems, and has frequently insisted on alterations in British policy before granting loans. On the other hand, debtors also acquire a certain power over their creditors. Because a default by a major debtor country could seriously jeopardize international financial arrangements by weakening confidence, IMF and other creditors are very anxious to avoid this possibility and will go to considerable lengths in efforts to avoid it.

GATT also exercises supervisory functions. Its contracting parties can authorize waivers in the application of the organization's rules, and they have done so on several occasions. The waiver granted to the United States with respect to the operation of its agricultural price support program has already been mentioned. Waivers have also been allowed with respect to regional economic integration schemes, to temporary tariff surcharges erected because of balance-of-payments difficulties, and to restrictions designed to deal with market disruptions. GATT can also appoint a working party to determine whether or not a country's charge that it has suffered economic injury through the action of another member state is justified and, if the finding is affirmative, to authorize the injured country to take appropriate retaliatory action. The codes concerning nontariff barriers that were negotiated during the Tokyo Round enlarged GATT's supervisory functions substantially. GATT is the forum for the settlement of disputes.

GATT has been a gentle overseer, and the secretariat is exceedingly unobtrusive. Infractions are readily visible; therefore, there is no need for special efforts to discover them. The initiative in bringing cases forward rests either with the party seeking a special dispensation or the party that considers itself wronged. The decision essentially rests with the country's trading partners. The system assumes that states have mutual self-interest in increasing opportunities for trade and in keeping barriers to trade as low as possible. The sanction, increases in the restrictions to trade, if applied competitively, could in the end result in diminished welfare for everyone. The goal of the system is to induce compliance with the rules rather than to punish wrongdoers. To date, the system has been reasonably effective.

Arrangements for the conduct of rule-supervisory activities within several of the regionally defined groupings of states and those consisting of producers and consumers of particular products resemble those of IMF and GATT; the mode of proceeding has more in common with negotiations than with adjudication. Whenever possible, decisions are avoided and efforts are made to achieve mutually satisfactory adjustments. The available sanction, retaliation in kind, tends to be a step that all parties are reluctant to take.

The European Communities' Court of Justice

There are, however, some exceptions to this general tendency toward negotiation rather than adjudication, and the most prominent involves the European communities. The Court of Justice of the European communities was created by the treaty establishing the European Coal and Steel Community, and its jurisdiction was expanded when the EEC and Euratom came into being. The court's function is complex and unique. It might be described as a composite of an international court, a constitutional court, an administrative court, a civil court, and a court of appeal.

It is an international court in that member states may bring before it alleged violations by other member states of the communities' rules. It is a constitutional court because it is the sole judge of the rights and obligations of community institutions and member states under the treaties. Its functions as an administrative court derive from its authority to review the legality of acts of the EEC's council and commission and to annul them if they are *ultra vires.* The civil jurisdiction of the court extends to cases in which an individual or a company seeks damages for a wrongful act involving community responsibility. Action may be brought before the Court of Justice by a member state, the council, or the commission. In addition, "natural or legal persons" (individuals or corporations) may institute proceedings against decisions of the communities that are of direct and individual concern to them. This access is an essential corollary of the power of community institutions to act directly on private parties. Although private parties may not sue their own government before the court alleging that it has applied community law to their prejudice, individuals may under such circumstances sue in their national courts, and when the case reaches the highest national court, that body is bound to refer to the European Court any question of the interpretation of community law. In these instances and in others, under Article 177 of the EEC treaty, the court is allowed to render a preliminary ruling interpreting community law.

From 1952 through 1981, 3,800 cases had been brought before the Court of Justice, of which 1,542 were pending.[25] Since 1960 the European Commission has brought more cases before the court than member states, and private parties have brought more than either the commission or member states. The cases in the later years have dealt primarily with agricultural, antitrust, social security, and personnel matters.

When private parties are involved, the court relies on their national governments to enforce its decisions. As mentioned above, the court can annul decisons of community institutions and award damages. In the case of member states, however, no sanctions are provided to insure compliance with the court's decisions. Nevertheless, no member state has yet acted in defiance. The court's principal function has been in delineating the meaning of community law for private parties, and this has been extremely important, especially in the antitrust field, where community law is having a determining influence on the nature of European industrial structures and the operations of transnational corporations.

As a consequence of a convention negotiated within the World Bank, an arbitral tribunal for investment disputes, the International Center for the Settlement of Investment Disputes, exists, but very few cases have been submitted to it.

OPERATIONAL ACTIVITIES

The operational activities that international organizations have thus far undertaken in the economic field have principally been conducted by IGOs, and they may be grouped into four broad categories. The first category, that of serving as a clearing house for financial transactions, involves the least complex tasks. The second category is that of serving as a vehicle for the provision of financial and technical assistance. International organizations make loans and grants and provide training opportunities. In financial resources and personnel involved, this is by far the most substantial operational task of international organizations in the latter part of the twentieth century. The third category is that of operating buffer stocks of commodities to insure the availability of reserve supplies and to promote price stability, and the fourth is that of managing commercial and scientific undertakings.

Managing Clearing Arrangements

Because it provides greater opportunities for specialization and thus for efficiency, multilateral trade is more likely to promote a greater total product than trade that must always be balanced on a bilateral basis. Yet if currencies are not convertible, it is difficult to have anything other than bilaterally balanced trade. Regional groups of states, however, have sought to gain the benefits of at least limited multilateralism by having IGOs serve as clearing houses for the payments stemming from trade among the members of the group.

The members of the Organization for European Economic Cooperation created the European Payments Union (EPU) to serve this purpose. Under this arrangement, each participating state's currency was denominated in terms of an accounting device, a European Currency Unit (not to be confused with the European currency unit that was established as part of the European Monetary System). Each state's transactions with all other participating states were consolidated. The Bank for International Settlements was assigned the task of managing the accounts. Limits were established on the deficits and surpluses that states could accumulate within given periods, and ultimately countries with deficits had to settle their accounts. The system was extremely successful in freeing participating states from the constraints of balancing their external transactions bilaterally, and its establishment was a major step in the post–World War II liberalization of global trade.

The CMEA countries attempted to achieve the same results by creating the International Bank for Economic Cooperation (IBEC) in 1963 and assigning it payments-clearing functions. Because of the centralization of planning within CMEA countries, however, a strong proclivity toward bilateral trading arrangements remains, and IBEC has not provided the same catalyst toward multilateralism as EPU did within OEEC.

Providing Financial and Technical Assistance

The second, and by far the largest, category of operational economic activities of international organization involves serving as a vehicle for financial and technical assistance. Activities of this nature were inaugurated in the 1920s when the League of Nations arranged reconstruction loans for Austria, Hungary, Estonia, and Danzig. An essential part of the arrangement was that League-appointed commissions were given extensive control over the domestic economic and financial policies of the recipient country or territory.

It was only after World War II, however, that this task really became a major activity of international organization. The first step was the creation of the United Nations Relief and Rehabilitation Administration, a multilateral effort to provide postwar relief. The moves in 1944 to create the International Monetary Fund and the International Bank for Reconstruction and Development were a second step, and in the postwar period the number of institutions and programs performing assistance functions rapidly multiplied.

Contemporary international organizations render financial and technical assistance for two broad purposes, to promote stability in exchange rates and to promote economic and social development. The activities of the International Monetary Fund directed toward the first purpose have already been discussed.

The other institution created at the Bretton Woods Conference in 1944, the International Bank for Reconstruction and Development, or World Bank, inaugurated activities directed toward the second purpose. Although over the years the bank has been joined in providing financial assistance by several other international organizations, its program remains by far the largest. Thus there is an important link between the two purposes for which financial assistance is given, since the bank only provides financial assistance to its member states (142 as of 1982) and membership in IMF is a prerequisite to membership in IBRD. The substantive meaning of the link is that to benefit from the financial assistance of the bank, a state must make a commitment toward monetary stability.

By the 1970s IBRD's lending activities were oriented exclusively toward less developed countries. It was joined in these activities by several other international organizations, of which two, the International Development Association and the International Finance Corporation, were its own affiliates. The World Bank provides funds for less developed countries mainly by raising money in capital markets, using its own subscribed capital as a guarantee, and then lending the money at an interest rate that is about half a percentage point above the rate it paid to raise the money—which puts the bank's lending rate very close to the commercial level.

The International Finance Corporation, which was established in 1956, operates much like the World Bank, except that its purpose is to promote the growth of private enterprise in developing member countries. It provides equity and loan capital for private enterprises. It also holds shares in national and regional development finance corporations.

The International Development Association (IDA) is the "soft money" window of the World Bank. Established in 1960, it provides capital on exceptionally favorable terms for less developed member states. Most of its loans have been for a term of fifty years, with a ten-year initial grace period and no interest charge, only a service charge of three-quarters of one percent per year. IDA relies primarily on contributions from its richer member states for its funds, and these states have periodically replenished them.

Several regional banks have also been established. When the European Economic Community came into being in 1958, the European Investment Bank (EIB) was one of its institutions, and the bank's mandate was eventually broadened to include lending to developing countries associated with the communities. In addition, each of the agreements that the EEC has had with the former colonial dependencies of its member states has involved providing resources for the European Development Fund, which makes grants and loans on advantageous terms to the associated countries. The Inter-American Development Bank (IDB) was established in 1959, the African Development Bank (AfDB) in 1963, the Asian Development Bank (AsDB) in 1966, and the Caribbean Development Bank (CarDB) in 1969.

After the quantum jump in oil prices in 1973–1974, several members of OPEC established three funds to make loans to less fortunately endowed developing countries: the Arab Fund for Economic and Social Development (AFESD), the

Organization of Arab Petroleum Exporting Countries Special Account (OAPEC), and the Special Arab Fund for Africa (SAFA). These three funds started operations in 1974.

In 1981 these several multilateral organizations (excluding the EIB) made "net" loan disbursements (broadly, loans minus repayments) that totaled $25 billion. Their outstanding loans amounted to $180 billion.[26]

The capital-providing institutions render some technical assistance in the course of their lending operations. Multilateral agencies responsible for relief operations also provide technical assistance. The main multilateral source of technical assistance, however, is the United Nations Development Program (UNDP). The components of this program, which involves the U.N. itself and its associated agencies, date from 1950. In the biennium 1980–1981 the gross expenditures of the UNDP were $248.5 million.[27] While the Soviet Union is not a member of IBRD and its affiliates or of the regional development banks, it has contributed to the UNDP and certain other U.N. funds.

INGOs such as Caritas Internationalis, the International Confederation of Catholic Charities, and OXFAM, the Oxford Committee for Famine Relief, also provide substantial technical assistance. National nongovernmental organizations like the Ford Foundation and the Rockefeller Foundation have played an important role too. Nongovernmental organizations have frequently been less inhibited than IGOs in undertaking projects in fields that might be controversial.

The net flow of assistance resources from both bilateral and multilateral sources in 1981 was $104 billion. Of this, 85 percent came from OECD countries, 2 percent from CMEA countries, 10 percent from OPEC countries, and 3 percent from other countries.[28] The flow of funds from OECD countries was divided as follows: contributions to multilateral institutions, 9 percent; official bilateral development assistance and other official flows, 28 percent; private flows (direct investment, portfolio investment, and export credits), 61 percent; and grants by voluntary agencies, 2 percent.[29]

In absolute terms, the flow of resources to the developing countries channeled through multilateral institutions has increased substantially over the years. This is mainly because Western governments chose to channel an increasing proportion of their official development assistance through such institutions. In the period 1964–1966, aid channeled through multilateral institutions averaged about 6 percent of the net official development assistance of the members of the Development Assistance Committee of OECD; in 1981 it was 23 percent. In 1980 and 1981 Canada, Finland, Japan, Italy, Norway, and the United States all channeled more than 30 percent of their official assistance in this manner.[30]

The share of multilateral institutions in the total net flow of resources to less developed countries, however, has not risen equally sharply. The reason is that private flows in the form of direct and portfolio investment from Western countries have also increased substantially. Private flows from OECD countries in 1971 were $8.4 billion; by 1981 they were $53.7 billion.[31] While OECD countries' contributions to multilateral institutions increased by more than five times during this period, the private flow of resources (which in 1981 was more than seven times larger than the flow of resources from multilateral institutions) increased by more than six times. Given the larger absolute amounts involved in the private flows of resources, and with a more rapid rate of increase, they have come to constitute a sharply increased share of the total. For those who saw one of the principal purposes of multilateral assistance as being that of inducing private investment in the less developed countries, these figures could be read as indicating substantial success.

International organization has also been involved in lending operations oriented toward inducing economic growth within the industrialized world. Many of the early loans of the International Bank for Reconstruction and Development had this purpose. The European Investment Bank, which operates like the World Bank, has as its principal purpose making and guaranteeing loans to stimualte the growth of less developed regions of the European community. In the early 1980s its loans totaled more than $3 billion a year. The European communities have also established special funds which make grants for particular purposes, though with the same general end. In 1971 CMEA created an International Investment Bank (IIB), which makes loans to stimulate growth in the less developed regions of the member countries of that organization.

Operating Buffer Stocks of Commodities

The third and fourth categories of operational activities of international organization in the economic field are not nearly as well developed or as extensive as the first two. The third category, the operation of buffer stocks of basic commodities, is an essential aspect of the agricultural policies of many governments. The purpose of such stocks is to moderate price fluctuations and to provide reserve supplies for emergencies. In theory, these stocks buy commodities when there are surplus conditions to insure that the price does not fall too low and store the commodities until such time as there is a shortage, when they are then sold to insure that the price does not rise too high. How well practice corresponds with theory depends upon the price levels set for market interventions. If they are set too high in terms of market conditions, the result can be a continual accumulation of surplus commodities.

Since the mid-1930s there have been numerous efforts to create international buffer stocks. There have been proposals both for the creation of stocks that would be held and managed by international institutions and for the creation of stocks that would be held by national governments and managed by cooperation among these governments in international institutions, as well as different combinations of these two basic variants. Under the Common Agricultural Policy of the European Economic Community, decisions about intervention prices are made by international institutions, but actual stocks are held by national institutions. The agreements for coffee and sugar essentially involve coordination of policies concerning nationally held and managed buffer stocks. Only the agreements for cocoa, rubber, and tin provide for internationally operated buffer stocks, though the sugar agreement provides for an international fund to finance the nationally held stocks. These five were the only commodity agreements that were legally in force during the early 1980s.

Managing Scientific and Commercial Undertakings

The fourth category of operational activities consists of managing scientific and commercial undertakings. Scientific laboratories have been created or sponsored by the International Atomic Energy Agency, the United Nations Educational, Scientific, and Cultural Organization, and Euratom.

INTELSAT, the International Telecommunications Satellite Organization, is the principal example of an international governmental organization managing a commercial enterprise. Created in 1964, INTELSAT operates a global tele-communications system utilizing communications satellites. The organization has more than a hundred members. The satellites can be used for the transmission of telephone messages, television programs, and other related purposes. In essence, INTELSAT is a global public utility. Because of the nature of the technology, this was virtually the only practicable way to manage its exploitation. Intersputnik, sponsored by the U.S.S.R., is a similar system. Perhaps INTELSAT is a forerunner of other similar institutions. The Law of the Sea Treaty, which was signed in 1982, provided for the establishment of an enterprise to engage in deep-sea mining.

International organizations are clearly taking steps toward the creation of a world economy. They have moved the developed market economies farthest in this direction, but much of what has been done has also applied to the less developed countries with market economies. Some links have been established between the planned economies—in particular the U.S.S.R. and the Eastern European countries—and the market economies, but the institutional connections between the two types of economies are far less extensive than those among the market economies.

The most important steps taken so far have essentially involved laissez-faire principles. The market economies have moved toward opening their borders to trade and capital investment from abroad, and the European communities have even established an open market for labor. Thanks to the rule-creating activities of international organizations, the states with market economies have engaged in what can be termed economic disarmament, and the nascent world economy is the result of this.

As one would expect, private firms have seized the opportunity. Starting in the late 1950s transnational corporations quickly moved to internationalize production, and they have grown rapidly and substantially in subsequent years.

Thus far, the extent to which international organizations have attempted to intervene to channel and direct market forces has been extremely limited. The European communities have taken more extensive steps than any other international governmental organization; however, the intervention of international organizations generally falls far short of the current practices of even the most laissez-faire governments. On a global level, INTELSAT and Intersputnik may be regarded as international public utilities, and perhaps they will be followed by other similar organizations established for the exploitation of joint resources such as the deep seabed.

The less developed countries have argued that much more intervention is essential to promote their own more rapid economic and social development. Universal membership organizations, spurred by the Group of 77, have endorsed the LDCs' position on a variety of issues through hortatory resolutions. But the governments of states with the greatest international economic strength—the United States, the Federal Republic of Germany, and Japan—have strongly resisted moves toward internationally organized intervention in market forces. Some of the normative activities of IGOs such as the setting of targets for economic growth, however, can be seen as tentative moves in the direction of global indicative planning of the type that occurs in many developed market economies in Western Europe.

Though steps have been taken toward the creation of a world economy, strong central institutions to direct that economy have not been established. Instead, states remain the units with greatest political authority concerning economic issues, but a complex overlay of international organizations has been added to facilitate voluntary cooperation among them. We must now explore the results of this system.

NOTES

1. League of Nations, *The Course of Phases of the World Economic Depression* (Geneva: League of Nations, 1931), and Gottfried Haberler, *Prosperity and Depression* (Geneva: League of Nations, 1941).

2. League of Nations, *Customs Union: A League of Nations Contribution to the Study of Customs Union Problems* (Lake Success, N.Y.: League of Nations, 1947).

3. U.N. Secretariat, Department of Economic Affairs, *Measures for the Economic Development of Underdeveloped Countries* (New York: U.N., 1951).

4. Donella H. Meadows *et al.*, *The Limits to Growth* (New York: Universe, 1972).

5. Wassily Leontief *et al.*, *The Future of the World Economy: A United Nations Study* (New York: Oxford University Press, 1977).

6. U.N. Document E/Conf. 60.19, p. 9.

7. Principles 2, 3, 4, 5, 6, and 7 of the Declaration on the Human Environment, U.N. Document A/Conf. 48/14/Rev. 1, pp. 3–5.

8. U.N. General Assembly Resolution 1710 (XVI).

9. U.N. General Assembly Resolution 2626 (XXV), and U.N. General Assembly Resolution 35/56.

10. U.N. General Assembly Resolution 35/56.

11. OECD, *Development Assistance, 1969 Review* (Paris: OECD, 1970), Annex III, and U.N. General Assembly Resolution 2626 (XXV), paragraph 44.

12. U.N. General Assembly Resolution 3281 (XXIX).

13. The seven developed countries were Australia, Canada, Japan, Spain, Sweden, Switzerland, and the United States. The nineteen less developed countries were Algeria, Argentina, Brazil, Cameroon, Egypt, India, Indonesia, Iran, Iraq, Jamaica, Mexico, Nige-

ria, Pakistan, Peru, Saudi Arabia, Venezuela, Yugoslavia, Zaire, and Zambia.

14. OECD, *Activities of OECD in 1970: Report of the Secretary-General* (Paris: OECD, 1971), p. 81.

15. OECD, *Activities of OECD in 1980: Report of the Secretary-General* (Paris: OECD, 1981), p. 8.

16. OECD, *Observer,* 70 (June 1974), 41.

17. OECD, *Activities of OECD in 1972: Report of the Secretary-General* (Paris: OECD, 1973), p. 117.

18. CMEA, *A Survey of 20 Years of the Council for Mutual Economic Assistance* (Moscow: CMEA Secretariat, 1969), p. 22.

19. Robert E. Baldwin and David A. Kay, "International Trade and International Relations," *International Organization,* 29 (Winter 1975), 99–131, on p. 100.

20. GATT, *The Tokyo Round of Multilateral Trade Negotiations:* vol. 2, *Supplementary Report* (Geneva: GATT, 1980), p. 6.

21. Lamartine Yates, *Forty Years of Foreign Trade* (London: Allen and Unwin, 1959), p. 28.

22. U.N. Secretariat, Department of Economic and Social Affairs, Statistical Office, *Statistical Yearbook, 1979/80* (New York: U.N., 1981).

23. Israel (1975), Algeria (1976), Tunisia (1976), Morocco (1976), Malta (1976), Egypt (1977), Jordan (1979), Syria (1977), Lebanon (1977), and Cyprus (1977).

24. N. S. Khrushchev, "Vital Questions of the Socialist World System," *World Marxist Review* (Toronto), 5 (September 1962), 9.

25. European Communities, Commission, *Fourteenth General Report on the Activities of the European Communities* (Brussels: ECSC/EEC/EAEC, 1982), p. 338; see also Stuart A. Scheingold, *The Law in Political Integration: The Evolution and Integrative Implications of Regional Legal Processes in the European Community* (Cambridge: Center for International Affairs, Harvard University, 1971), pp. 12–14, and Emile Noel, *Comment fonctionnent les institutions de la Communauté Européenne* (Bruxelles: CEE, 1977).

26. OECD, *Development Cooperation: Efforts and Policies of the Members of the Development Assistance Committee: 1982 Review* (Paris: OECD, 1982), p. 52.

27. U.N. Document DP/550, 17 April 1981, p. 3.

28. OECD, *Development Cooperation, 1982,* p. 52

29. Ibid., p. 178.

30. Ibid., pp. 73 and 178.

31. Ibid., 1972, p. 221, and 1982, p. 178.

FOR FURTHER READING

Aubrey, Henry G. *Atlantic Economic Cooperation: The Case of OECD.* New York: Praeger, 1967.

Bergsten, C. Fred. *The Dilemmas of the Dollar: The Economics and Politics of United States International Monetary Policy.* New York: New York University Press, 1975.

Curzon, Gerard. *Multilateral Commercial Diplomacy: The General Agreement on Tariffs and Trade and Its Impact on National Commercial Policies and Techniques.* London: Michael Joseph, 1965.

Dam, Kenneth W. *The Rules of the Game: Reform and Evolution in the International Monetary System.* Chicago: University of Chicago Press, 1982.

Gardner, Richard N., and Max F. Millikan (eds). *The Global Partnership: International Agencies and Economic Development.* New York: Praeger, 1968.

Johnson, D. Gale. *World Agriculture in Disarray.* London: Macmillan, 1973.

Kaser, Michael. *Comecon: Integration Problems of the Planned Economies.* London: Oxford University Press, 1965.

Kindleberger, Charles P. *American Business Abroad: Six Lectures on Direct Investment.* New Haven: Yale University Press, 1969.

Kohnstamm, Max, and Wolfgang Hager (eds.) *A Nation Writ Large? Foreign Policy Problems Before the European Community.* London: Macmillan, 1973.

Mason, Edward S., and Robert E. Asher. *The World Bank since Bretton Woods.* Washington, D.C.: Brookings, 1973.

Mikdashi, Zuhayr. *The Community of Oil Exporting Countries: A Study in Governmental Cooperation.* Ithaca: Cornell University Press, 1972.

Pearson, Lester B. *Partners in Development: Report of the Commission on International Development.* New York: Praeger, 1969.

Pincus, John. *Trade, Aid and Development: The Rich and Poor Nations.* New York: McGraw-Hill, 1967.

Preeg, Ernest H. *Traders and Diplomats: An Analysis of the Kennedy Round Negotiations Under the General Agreement on Tariffs and Trade.* Washington, D.C.: Brookings, 1970.

Robson, Peter. *The Economics of International Integration.* London: George Allen and Unwin, 1980.

Seers, Dudley, and Leonard Joy. *Development in a Divided World.* Harmondsworth: Penguin, 1971.

Solomon, Robert. *The International Monetary System, 1945–1976: An Insider's View.* New York: Harper & Row, 1977.

Triffin, Robert. *Our International Monetary System: Yesterday, Today and Tomorrow.* New York: Random House, 1968.

Vernon, Raymond. *Sovereignty at Bay: The Multinational Spread of U.S. Enterprise.* New York: Basic Books, 1971.

Warnecke, Stephen J. (ed.). *The European Community in the 1970s.* New York: Praeger, 1972.

A WORLD ECONOMY: FOR WHOSE BENEFIT?

Steps have been taken toward creating a world economy, and international organizations have played a major role in this development. We have examined what international organizations have done; now it is appropriate to attempt to assess the consequences of these actions. Have the manifest economic goals articulated in the constitutions and resolutions and decisions of international organizations been achieved? Have the activities of international organizations also served latent functions? Has world trade increased? What has happened to the gross world product in both its overall growth and its distribution among and within countries since World War II? Who has benefited as a result of progress toward a world economy? Can the trends established in the years since World War II be projected into the future? Are new strategies required to realize either old or new goals?

As we saw in Chapter 9, it is difficult if not impossible to establish causal links between the activities of international organizations and global developments. Too many factors are involved, and it is too difficult to isolate the effects of particular actions. The most we can do is consider what has happened and see how this is related to what international organizations have done. If developments have been contrary to the proclaimed aims and policy goals of international organizations, it seems reasonable to conclude that however well-intentioned their activities, they have not been effective. It also seems reasonable, in the event there has been some concordance, to think that international organizations may have contributed to the outcome.

WORLD TRADE

The first data that we should examine concern international trade. A primary purpose of a large number of international organizations—including the first modern IGO—has been to facilitate the expansion of international trade, and the activities in this area are extensive.

Growth of Trade

The growth of world imports and exports between 1950 and 1980 is traced in Table 12.1. The figures are current rather than constant dollars. Because of inflation they exaggerate the increase in world trade. This is particularly a problem for the 1970s because of the high rates of inflation experienced by most market economies then. The problem is compounded by the devaluation of the dollar in 1971 and the absence of fixed exchange rates among the currencies of the most important trading countries after that date. Even allowing for inflation, however, the growth in world trade since World War II has been phenomenal. As can be seen, between 1950 and 1980 the value of global trade increased more than thirty times. The absolute volume of world trade increased more than five times. At no other period in history has world trade grown so rapidly. Previous record growth was in the neighborhood of 50 percent per decade. In the decade of the 1950s the value of trade doubled, and in the 1960s and 1970s it grew even more rapidly. Since international organizations were much more active in this field in the later period, this comparison supports the belief that their activities may have contributed to the increase in trade.

Changes in Distribution

States have not, however, shared equally in the growth of world trade. Figure 12.1 shows how world exports were divided among three major groups of states—the members of OECD, the members of the Warsaw Treaty Organization, and the remaining states (mostly LDCs)—at fifteen-year intervals, in 1938, 1953, and 1968. In addition, the exports of the six original members of the EEC are given as a subdivision of OECD's share. The three years include the last relatively normal year for trade before World War II as well as a postwar year before

TABLE 12.1
The Growth of World Trade, 1950–1980
(Value in Millions of Current U.S. Dollars)

Year	Imports	Exports
1950	62,738	60,785
1955	97,462	92,978
1960	135,113	128,275
1965	197,493	187,010
1970	328,543	313,868
1975	902,434	873,567
1980	2,047,459	1,988,005

Source: U.N. Secretariat, Department of Economic and Social Affairs, *Statistical Yearbook, 1979/1980* (New York: U.N., 1981), pp. 440–441.

the full implementation of the European communities. As can be seen, the developed countries, the members of OECD and WTO, increased their exports more rapidly than did the less developed countries. The growth in the WTO countries' relative share of world exports can be seen as early as 1953; it continued through 1968. The growth in the OECD countries' relative share of exports occurred particularly between 1953 and 1968, the period in which international organizations among the OECD countries increased their activities. Over the thirty-year period the exports of OECD and WTO countries became an increasingly larger proportion of the growing total, while the exports of other countries became a relatively smaller proportion.

The exports of the developed countries have also grown at differential rates. Table 12.2 shows the rates of growth in the exports of major developed states and groups of states from 1958 through 1978, a period in which international organizations were very active. Most importantly, the European Economic Community began to function on January 1, 1958. In addition, Japan became a member of GATT in 1955, thereby obtaining greater access to the markets of GATT member countries. The figures in Table 12.2 are percentage increases for each five-year period. As can be seen, Japan's performance outdistanced that of all the others, but the increase in the exports of the original six members of the European Economic Community is also impressive. The exports of Japan and the six original

FIGURE 12.1
Shares of the World Exports, 1938–1968

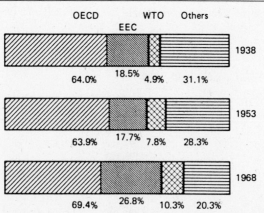

Source: U.N. Secretariat, Department of Economic and Social Affairs, *Statistical Yearbook, 1976* (New York: U.N., 1977), pp. 424–425.

It can be observed that the principal change that occurred was that the OPEC countries received more money for their exports, but this tremendously increased their ability to purchase goods and make investments abroad. In terms of rapidly altering the economic position of a group of developing countries, the sharp increase in the price of oil was the most effective action that had been taken. OPEC's gains came at the expense of both less developed and developed countries. In loss of shares of world exports, non-OPEC LDCs suffered relatively even more than the member states of OECD. These shifts in the distribution of shares of world exports, however, must be viewed in the context of the enormous increase in the value and volume of world trade in the 1970s.

THE FLOW OF FUNDS TO LDCS

A great deal of what international organizations have done since World War II has been oriented toward accelerating the economic and social development of the less developed countries. In budgeted funds, the most extensive operational activities of IGOs are of this character, and international organizations have also attempted to stimulate the flow of public and private funds to LDCs. How this flow of funds has increased was described in Chapter 11. The increase has been substantial and significant. Nevertheless, the total flow of funds continues to fall short of some of the normative targets that have been established by the U.N. and accepted by other bodies. As noted in Chapter 11, the U.N. has set two targets for the developed countries: (1) developed countries should transfer each year .7 percent of their gross national products as official governmental development assistance, either bilaterally or through multilateral institutions, and (2) the total annual flow of funds, including private funds, from the developed countries should equal 1 percent of their GNPs. In 1975, for the first time, the member countries of OECD's Development Assistance Committee (DAC) achieved and even exceeded the 1 percent target; however, they fell short by a considerable margin of the .7 percent target.[1] This pattern of achievement has continued since. The total net flow of capital to LDCs from all sources (OECD, OPEC, and communist countries) in 1975 was $46.8 billion. By 1981 the total net flow of funds had reached 104 billion.

Table 12.3 shows the 1981 total flow of funds and the flow of Official Development Assistance to LDCs from various states as a percentage of their GNPs. Interestingly, it includes funds from OPEC countries, states that were not thought of as being in the category of developed countries at the time that the normative resolutions were adopted. More importantly, it demonstrates that very few of the developed states have met the longstanding U.N. target that official development assistance (ODA) should equal .7 percent of their GNPs. In 1975 the Netherlands and Sweden were the only two of the seventeen DAC member countries that met the target. This was the first year that the Netherlands had met it and the second for Sweden. In 1981 Denmark, France, and Norway also met the target. The OECD states that were not members of DAC—Greece, Iceland, Ireland, Luxembourg, Portugal, Spain, and Turkey—were not significant sources of funds for LDCs; indeed, some of them required assistance themselves.

Had all of DAC's members met the ODA target, presumably the flow of funds to LDCs would have been substantially larger, because an increase in ODA should not have led to a decrease in the flow of private funds. There was, however, little popular support in most of the DAC countries for a substantial transfer of public funds to LDCs. Had the Soviet Union and the other communist states in Eastern Europe with relatively high per capita gross national products also met the norms, this too would have increased the total flow of funds. Even with these shortfalls, however, the fact that the total net flow of funds to the less developed countries was as large as it was must be marked as a major accomplishment, for which international organizations merit at least some of the credit.

DIRECT FOREIGN INVESTMENT

During the same period that global trade grew at such an extraordinary rate and a significant transfer of funds to LDCs was set into motion, another development also occurred: the role of transnational corporations (TNCs) expanded rapidly. Although international organizations have undertaken only minimal programs directly oriented toward transnational corporations, the consequences of many

TABLE 12.3
The Flow of Funds to LDCs from Various States
and Groups of States as a Percentage of Their GNPs, 1981
(In Terms of Net Disbursements)

	Official Development Assistance	Total Flow
DAC Countries*	.35	1.21
Of which:		
Canada	.43	1.50
France	.73	2.01
Federal Republic of Germany	.47	1.18
Italy	.19	1.07
Japan	.28	1.09
Netherlands	1.08	1.59
Sweden	.83	1.32
United Kingdom	.44	2.01
United States	.20	.90
OPEC Countries	1.46	1.59
U.S.S.R.	.15	.15

*The DAC member countries are Australia, Austria, Belgium, Canada, Denmark, Finland, France, Federal Republic of Germany, Italy, Japan, Netherlands, New Zealand, Norway, Sweden, Switzerland, the United Kingdom, and the United States.

Source: OECD, *Development Cooperation: Efforts and Policies of the Members of the Development Assistance Committee, 1982 Review* (Paris: OECD, 1982), pp. 160, 161, 182, 183.

of their activities were to facilitate the operations and growth of TNCs.

Unfortunately, reliable figures on transnational corporations and their growth are limited. The U.N. Center on Transnational Corporations was established only in 1974, and the OECD Committee on International Investment and Multinational Enterprises was not created until 1976. Moreover, there is no agreed single definition of a transnational, or multinational, corporation. In preparing its 1976 Declaration on International Investment and Multinational Enterprises, OECD eventually took the pragmatic course of not trying to achieve an agreed definition, which would have to deal with the murky issue of the extent of autonomy of local branches, but simply adopted the commonsense position that the declaration should apply to operations of companies outside of their home countries. Despite all these difficulties of definition and lack of information, however, some general observations are possible about the magnitude of transnational corporations and their location.

By 1971, according to U.N. estimates, the book value of direct foreign investment (a rough measure of TNCs already utilized in Chapter 11) totaled $165 billion, representing a 52 percent increase in half a decade, and by 1976 it had reached $287 billion.[2] Thus the spectacular growth in world trade coincided with an equally spectacular growth of transnational corporations. As has already been mentioned, there are several reasons for the two phenomena occurring simultaneously. Exchange liberalization facilitated foreign investment; reductions in tariffs made it possible for corporate managers to think of locating production in areas of low factor costs; and the creation of customs unions provided an incentive for placing new investment within the free trade zone and inside the common external tariff. Consequently, starting in the 1960s, there has been substantial movement in the direction of the internationalization of production.

Transnational corporations are essentially extensions of enterprises within Western states. In book value, 96 percent of direct foreign investment in 1971 was held by transnational corporations headquartered in fourteen Western countries: the United States, the United Kingdom, France, the Federal Republic of Germany, Switzerland, Canada, Japan, the Netherlands, Sweden, Italy, Belgium, Australia, Portugal, and Denmark. Transnational corporations with headquarters in the United States accounted for 52 percent of the total, those with headquarters in the six original EEC member countries accounted for 16 percent, and those with headquarters in the United Kingdom accounted for 15 percent. The United States' share was somewhat less than it had been five years previously because of the extremely rapid growth of direct foreign investments from Japan, the Federal Republic of Germany, and Sweden, and the U.S. share declined further during the 1970s.

More than half of the total direct foreign investment has always been in the developed market economies, and their share appears to have increased with the recent growth of transnational corporations. For instance, Canada and Europe accounted for 56 percent of U.S. direct foreign investment in 1960, and for 60 percent in 1971.[3] Only transnational corporations headquartered in the Netherlands—which account for just 2.2 percent of the total—had more than half of their direct foreign investment in developing countries. What direct foreign investment there is in developing countries tends to be concentrated in certain geographical areas. In the 1960s, 43 percent of the direct foreign investment of OECD members in less developed countries was concentrated in Argentina, Brazil, India, Mexico, Nigeria, Venezuela, and certain Caribbean islands.[4] Nevertheless, the United States and many other OECD member countries have continued to maintain that transnational corporations should be and would be the principal engine to promote global economic growth.

WORLD PRODUCTION

World production has also grown phenomenally since the end of World War II. International organizations have attempted to stimulate the growth of world production and modify its distribution in a variety of ways. Many normative activities have addressed these issues directly. Operational activities involving a transfer of funds have been intended to accelerate the economic and social development of the recipients and to increase the rate of growth of their gross national products and per capita GNPs. Finally, all of the activities relating to international trade have directly or indirectly affected countries' GNPs.

Growth of the Global Product

Given the differences in methods of calculating national accounts (particularly between planned and market economies) and the difficulties of converting different currencies into one common measure, especially since 1971 when fixed exchange rates were ended, estimates of the global product contain considerable possibilities for error. Working with slightly different assumptions, different economists have arrived at estimates that vary by 10 percent or more. Any discussion of the world product and its distribution must acknowledge the substantial uncertainties that are involved. With these caveats, let us examine how world production has grown since 1945 and how it has been distributed among major groups of states.

Table 12.4 shows the growth in the global product between 1950 and 1980, as calculated by a consultant of the U.S. Department of State. The basic data were drawn from U.N. publications, but were adjusted to take account of inflation, and the numbers are equivalent to the value of the dollar in 1980. Because so much economic activity—for instance, subsistence farming—in less developed countries is not part of the monetary economy and thus is not captured in estimates of LDCs' gross national products, supplements have been added to their GNPs. Without these supplements, which are larger for LDCs with lower per capita GNPs, the world product would be smaller, as would the share accruing to the LDCs. The United Nations has been attempting for several years to devise a system for comparing countries' GNPs that would take account of the different extent of economic activity conducted in the monetary sector. The preliminary

TABLE 12.4
The Growth of the Global Product, 1950–1980

Year	Global Product (In Billions of 1980 U.S. Dollars)	Percentage Increase in 5-year Period
1950	2,939,537	
1955	3,781,275	28.6
1960	4,678,310	23.7
1965	5,985,920	28.0
1970	7,673,252	28.2
1975	9,422,251	22.8
1980	11,269,078	19.6

Source: U.S. Department of State, Bureau of Public Affairs, Herbert Block, *The Planetary Product in 1980: A Creative Pause?* (Washington, D.C.: Department of State, 1981), pp. 30–31.

conclusions of this project would give even larger supplements to LDCs than do the figures published by the Department of State.[5]

As can be seen from Table 12.4, in the three decades between 1950 and 1980 the global world product more than tripled. The growth in world production was particularly impressive during the 1960s, when the annual aggregate growth rate was 5 percent or more. During the 1960s the overall growth rate of the GNPs of the less developed countries exceeded that of the developed countries, as indeed it has throughout the period since the conclusion of World War II. Thus the broad target of the U.N.'s first development decade—an annual growth rate in the GNPs of less developed countries of 5 percent—was more than met. OECD's broad target of a 50 percent expansion during the decade of the 1960s in the combined GNPs of its member states was also met. Neither the U.N.'s second development decade target (6 percent annual growth rate for LDCs) nor OECD's target for the 1970s (65 percent for the decade), however, was met. Table 12.4 shows the slowdown in the growth of world production.

Distribution of the Global Product

The fact that the GNPs of less developed countries have consistently grown more rapidly than those of developed countries has meant that the LDCs' share of the world product has gradually increased over the years. Figure 12.3 portrays the distribution of the global product in 1950, 1960, 1970, and 1980. Even though the percentages in the figures are carried to one decimal point, this should not be taken as indicating that the data from which the percentages were calculated are that accurate. The data are consistent and the changes in the shares of groups of states are relatively small. Of course, our grouping of "Others" would not completely coincide with everyone's intuitive notion of what is meant by the term "less developed countries," nor would our OECD and WTO groupings completely coincide with intuitive understandings of the meaning of "developed countries." Unfortunately, there are no generally accepted definitions of these categories. The groupings used here properly place the major states: the United

FIGURE 12.3

Shares of the Global Product, 1950–1980

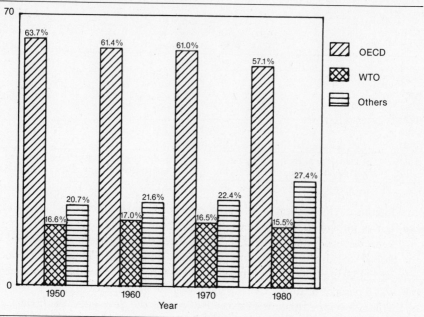

Source: U.S. Department of State, Bureau of Public Affairs, Herbert Block, *The Planetary Product in 1980: A Creative Pause?* (Washington, D.C.: Department of State, 1981), pp. 30–31.

States, the members of the European Economic Community, and Japan are in OECD; the Soviet Union is in WTO; and Bangladesh, Brazil, India, Indonesia, Mexico, Nigeria, Pakistan, and the People's Republic of China are in Others. These units account for roughly three-quarters of the world's population. To shift the placement of a few small states would not make much difference in the totals and would make comparisons between economic and other issues difficult.

The gradual effects of differential rates of growth among the three groups of states can be seen in Figure 12.3. During the 1950s the economies of both WTO and LDC countries grew more rapidly than those of the members of OECD. During the 1960s and 1970s, in contrast, while the economic growth of the LDCs continued to exceed that of the members of OECD, the economic growth rate of WTO members fell to roughly the level of OECD members.

Those favoring a more equalitarian distribution of the world product among countries could take some encouragement from the gradual increase in the LDCs' share of the global product. And in fact, as a consequence of the vastly improved status of the OPEC countries this trend accelerated in the 1970s. As Figure 12.4 shows, however, in 1980 the relatively small proportion of the world's population living in developed countries gained the lion's share of the global product. Together the member countries of OECD and WTO accounted for 25.8 percent of the world's population in 1980, but 72.6 percent of world production accrued

FIGURE 12.4
Shares of Exports, Global Product, and Population, 1980

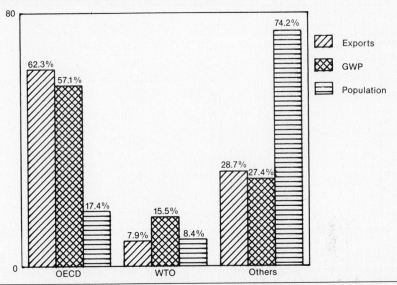

Source: U.S. Department of State, Bureau of Public Affairs, Herbert Block, *The Planetary Prod-uct in 1980: A Creative Pause?* (Washington, D.C.: Department of State, 1981), pp. 30–45 and U.N. Department of Economic and Social Affairs, *Statistical Yearbook, 1979/1980* (New York: U.N., 1981), pp. 440–441.

to these states, while the other states in the global political system, which ac-counted for 74.2 percent of the world population, gained only 27.4 percent of the global product. The unequal distribution of trade (which is related to the un-equal distribution of income because those with higher incomes can buy more from abroad and greater specialization in production contributes to greater effi-ciency and thus a greater product) is also apparent from Figure 12.4. Despite the advances that less developed countries made during the three decades from 1950 to 1980, the disparity between their share of the world population and their share of world exports and the global product continued to be dramati-cally large.

From one perspective, the gap between the less developed countries and the developed countries increased during this thirty-year period. Because population growth was more rapid in the LDCs, even though in the aggregate their GNPs grew more rapidly than those of the developed countries, their per capita GNPs grew less rapidly. Figure 12.5 compares the growth of the per capita GNPs of the three groups of states from 1950 to 1980. The growth in the per capita GNPs of the OECD states tapered off in the early 1970s with the slowing of their eco-nomic growth, but even so the gap between the average per capita GNP of the OECD states and that of those states in the Others category grew from about $3,000 in 1950 to more than $7,000 in 1980.

FIGURE 12.5
Per Capita GNP Compared

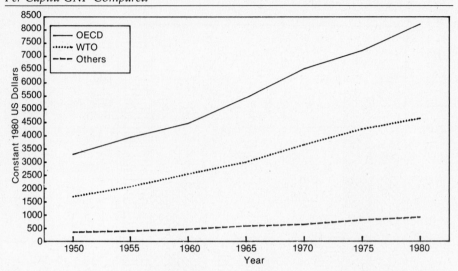

Source: U.S. Department of State, Bureau of Public Affairs, Herbert Block, *The Planetary Product in 1980: A Creative Pause?* (Washington, D.C.: Department of State, 1981), pp. 60–73.

Figure 12.6 shows how much this this growing gap was affected by population growth in the countries in the Third World, the Others category. During the two decades between 1960 and 1980, the GNPs of these countries grew by 206 percent, almost twice as fast as that of the members of OECD and WTO, but because their population grew more than two times as fast, their per capita GNPs grew at only a marginally more rapid rate.

Of course these aggregate figures mask considerable differences among individual states. For instance, in 1980 the per capita GNP of the United States was $11,231, while that of Sweden was $11,028. That same year the per capita GNP of other OECD members was: Federal Republic of Germany, $10,487; United Kingdom, $5,232; Spain, $3,097; and Greece, $3,096. Within the Warsaw Treaty Organization, Czechoslovakia's per capita GNP was $5,340, that of the U.S.S.R. was $4,822, and that of Romania was $3,230. In the Others category, tiny Qatar, with a population of 220,000 persons, had a per capita GNP of $25,026; Brazil, with a population of over 100 million, had a per capita GNP of $2,687; and India, with a population of over 680 million, had a per capita GNP of $444.[6] Nevertheless, the group averages do give a broad sense of how the absolute gap between the average income in the relatively rich countries and in the relatively poor countries has grown in the years since World War II, even though comparatively the gap may have narrowed. It was the growing absolute gap, of course, that LDC delegates stressed in their calls for the creation of a new international economic order.

FIGURE 12.6

Change in GNP, Population, and Per Capita GNP, 1960–1980

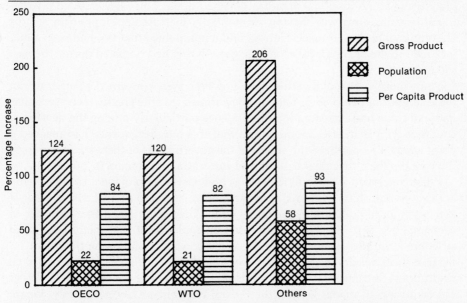

Source: U.S. Department of State, Bureau of Public Affairs, Herbert Block, *The Planetary Product in 1980: A Creative Pause?* (Washington, D.C.: Department of State, 1981).

Data on the distribution of income within countries are much less readily available than data on the distribution of the world product among countries. In his pioneering studies of the process of economic growth, Simon Kuznets discovered that during the early stages of growth the processes of industrialization and urbanization led to a less equalitarian distribution of income, but that at later stages the distribution of income became more equalitarian through income transfers.[7] More recent studies for the period 1950–1970 have confirmed these findings.[8] In the 1970s a consensus developed within international organizations that whatever economic progress less developed countries may have made in the 1960s, it had had little impact on the poorest sectors of the populations of these countries. For this reason, attempts were made in the 1970s, especially in the universal membership IGOs, to target assistance to LDCs so that it would be of more direct benefit to the poorest LDCs and to the poorest persons within all LDCs.

ASSESSMENTS OF THE RECORD AND PRESCRIPTIONS FOR THE FUTURE

Attitudes toward the economic activities of international organizations may be grouped into five broad categories, and in the early 1980s none of these were complacent. One view, held essentially in the developed market economies, applauded what international organizations had done. This view credited international organizations with having substantially increased the opportunities for international trade and specialization, and it maintained that this had been a major factor in the phenomenal economic growth that had occurred during the past three decades.

Many individuals holding this view, however, were concerned whether or not these conditions could be sustained. They argued that the greatly increased international trade had increased interdependence particularly among the developed countries with market economies, and that this interdependence had reached a point where it jeopardized the ability of the governments of these states to pursue the welfare goals that they had set and must attain to remain in power.

What concerned these individuals was how fast unemployment could develop because of real shifts in comparative advantage and also of artifacts of the system, such as rapid shifts in exchange rates. They maintained that in order to avoid nationalistic reactions to increased unemployment that might lead to restrictions on trade, greater economic policy coordination among the major industrial states would be essential, as would increased authority for international institutions. Starting in 1974, the heads of government of the seven major Western countries—Canada, France, the Federal Republic of Germany, Italy, Japan, the United Kingdom, and the United States—and the president of the Commission of the European communities began to hold annual economic summits. The institutionalization of coordination, however, did not proceed beyond this.

The concerns of this group were heightened as a consequence of the 1973–1974 increase in the price of petroleum, which enormously raised the import bill of the developed countries. Table 12.5 shows the United States balance of payments for 1974. In contrast to the situation in 1970 (shown in Table 11.1, p. 241), when American exports exceeded imports by more than $2.6 billion, in 1974 imports exceeded exports by almost $5.3 billion. For many other countries, the situation was considerably worse, and indeed it grew worse for the United States as its oil imports continued to mount in subsequent years. In 1981 U.S. imports exceeded exports by a record $39.6 billion.

Petroleum exports, of course, were not the only cause of this difficulty. Inflation and a loss of competitive advantages were also factors. From 1971 through 1981, U.S. exports exceeded U.S. imports only in 1973 and 1975. Although other items in the U.S. balance of payments compensated for this situation, the overall international payments position of the United States was problematic during several years in the 1970s. With the United States in a weakened position and less able to bear special burdens of leadership, some observers doubted that the free trading system that had been so carefully crafted after World War II could stand the strain imposed by the new situation. The value of world exports actually declined in 1981; it had not done this since the 1950s, and then only in 1952 and 1958. Moreover, as a consequence of the increased flow of private resources to LDCs, the international debt of these countries zoomed upward. In the early

TABLE 12.5
U.S. Balance of Payments, 1974
(Millions of Dollars)

	Income	Expenditure
CURRENT ACCOUNT		
Merchandise	98,309 (exports)	103,586 (imports)
Military Transactions	2,944 (arms sales)	5,103 (direct expenditures)
Net Investment Income		
Private	13,351	
Government		3,229
Net Travel and Other Transportation Expenditures		2,692
Other Services, Net	3,830	
Remittances, Pensions, and Other Unilateral Transfers		7,182
CAPITAL ACCOUNT		
Long-term Capital Flows, Net		
Private		8,463
Government	1,119	
Non-liquid Private Short-term Private Capital		
Flows, Net		12,936
Liquid Private Capital Flows, Net	10,543	
Changes in Liabilities to Foreign Official Agencies, Net	9,831	
Changes in U.S. Official Reserve Assets, Net		1,434
Subtotal	139,927	144,625
Errors and Omissions	4,698	
Total	144,625	144,625

Source: Economic Report of the President, 1976 (Washington, D.C.: Government Printing Office, 1976), pp. 274–275.

1980s several major LDCs faced extremely painful choices in their efforts to manage their external debts.

Some holding the views just described, and other people as well, were deeply concerned about the rapid growth of transnational corporations. Many felt that TNCs, through their capacity to shift operations from one country to another, had evaded national regulation. On the other hand, the loose and decentralized system of international organizations was no match for the centralized and purposeful control exercised within transnational corporations. Thus, according to this view, there were no existing political institutions capable of insuring socially responsible behavior on the part of transnational corporations. Various examples of corporate acts were cited to support the argument: plants that were closed when governments were attempting to combat unemployment, and investments made with capital raised outside the host country when its government was attempting to pursue a deflationary policy. It was also alleged that the actions of the treasurers of transnational corporations in shifting funds from one currency to another contributed to the international monetary difficulties of the 1970s and early 1980s. Those who held these views also called for greater policy coordination among states and more authority for international institutions. Otherwise, they argued, the course of world economic development would be left to be determined mainly by TNCs, acting primarily to realize their private goals. Many wished to build up both IGOs and INGOs, seeing international labor movements as being particularly important to counter the power of transnational corporations.

Attitudes in a third category were particularly concerned that more progress had not been made toward alleviating the plight of the poorest sectors of the world. This group was not particularly interested in creating new international institutions or altering those that exist, but simply in channeling a greater amount of funds to poorer countries. Individuals in this group usually maintained that the flow of private funds was unlikely to increase rapidly enough to meet their goals and therefore more public funds would be needed, and they generally argued that these funds should be channeled through international institutions rather than handled through bilateral arrangements.

Attitudes in a fourth category were more critical of existing international organizations. Persons in this group argued that the major IGOs in the economic field were principally designed to protect and promote private enterprise, and they did not believe that private enterprise could be a satisfactory vehicle for promoting the economic and social development of the less developed countries. Private enterprise, they felt, brought inappropriate capital-intensive technology to LDCs, and as a consequence, instead of increasing employment, fostered unemployment by luring workers to urban areas in search of jobs that did not exist. Private enterprise, in their view, also distorted consumption tastes in LDCs, shaping them to be like those in the developed market economies.

Individuals holding those views argued that a substantial portion of the benefits of economic growth derived from the activities of private enterprise would be channeled into luxury consumption for a minority, while the poor majority would receive few benefits and might be even further impoverished. They claimed that transnational corporations perpetuated the underdevelopment of less developed countries by siphoning off profits and transferring them to the developed countries, and therefore a strategy that relied on direct foreign investment and TNCs to promote development would maintain the less developed countries in a position of dependency on the developed countries. People of this persuasion also claimed that aid channeled through the World Bank and other international institutions had been and would be distributed so as to insure governmental behavior favorable to private enterprise. The principal prescription of this group was self-reliance. This would imply a more limited role for universal membership IGOs like the World Bank and perhaps a broader role for limited membership IGOs, such as regional economic integration schemes.

Supporters of transnational corporations, of course, denied the allegations of the critics, and they pointed to the efficiency of TNCs and to the rapid economic growth of LDCs that had attracted substantial direct foreign investment. They contrasted the economic performance of these countries with that of countries which had chosen to rely more heavily on government planning and government ownership of production facilities. Although cases and episodes were cited to support the argument that existing economic IGOs rewarded LDCs favorable to private enterprise and disciplined those that were hostile, broadly convincing empirical proof of the allegation has yet to be achieved. Cases and episodes were also cited to prove the contrary.

Holders of views constituting a fifth and final category were mainly concerned about what they perceived to be the finite capacity of the world to support human activity. These individuals were skeptical of the vision of accelerated economic growth for the less developed countries and continued economic growth for developed states. They feared that efforts to achieve this vision would rapidly deplete supplies of nonrenewable resources and create untenable levels of environmental pollution, thereby provoking catastrophe. Their prescription involved setting limits on aspirations, significant redistribution of wealth and income from richer to poorer states, and significant regulation of economic activity based on an enhanced planning capacity. Implementing this prescription would clearly require substantially augmenting the authority of international institutions.

What is significant about the debates we have just outlined is not that they exist, but that they are conducted in international as well as national institutions, and that the proper role of international institutions is a central element in them. As the twentieth century draws to a close, economic issues are no longer the exclusive prerogative of states and private enterprises, but instead are increasingly the concern of international organizations. Just as during the first half of the twentieth century national governments increasingly exercised their suzerainty over economic affairs within their borders, in the second half international organizations have been increasingly exercising suzerainty over the growth and distribution of the global product.

NOTES

1. OECD, *Development Cooperation: Efforts and Policies of the Members of the Development Assistance Committee: 1982 Review* (Paris: OECD, 1982), p. 177. The discussion that follows is based on information from this survey.

2. U.N. Secretariat, Department of Economic and Social Affairs, *Multinational Corporations in World Development* (New York: U.N. [Sales Number E 73 II A 11], 1974), p. 139; and *Transnational Corporations in World Development: A Re-examination* (New York: U.N. [Sales Number E 78 II A5], 1978), p. 36

3. U.S. Senate, 93rd Congress, 1st Session, Committee on Finance, *The Multinational Corporation and the World Economy* (Washington, D.C.: Government Printing Office, 1973), p. 45.

4. U.N. Secretariat, *Multinational Corporations in World Development*, p. 19.

5. See Irving B. Kravis, Zoltan Kenessey, Alan Heston, Robert Summers, and assistants, *United Nations International Comparison Project: Phase One, A System of International Comparisons of Gross Product and Purchasing Power* (Baltimore: Published for the World Bank by the Johns Hopkins University Press, 1975).

6. These data are taken from U.S. Department of State, Bureau of Public Affairs, Herbert Block, *The Planetary Product in 1980: A Creative Pause?* (Washington, D.C.: Department of State, 1981). All of the data can be found in Tables 1, 2, and 3, pp. 30–73.

7. Simon Kuznets, "Economic Growth and Income Inequality," *American Economic Review*, 49 (March 1955), 1–28.

8. Hollis Chenery and Moises Syrquin with the assistance of Hazel Elkington, *Patterns of Development, 1950–1970* (London: Published for the World Bank by Oxford University Press, 1975), pp. 60–63.

FOR FURTHER READING

Bergsten, C. Fred, and Lawrence B. Krause (eds.). *World Politics and International Economics.* Washington, D.C.: Brookings, 1975.

Brandt, Willy, and others. *North-South: A Program For Survival: Report of the Independent Commission on International Development Issues.* Cambridge, Mass.: MIT Press, 1980.

Cooper, Richard N. *The Economics of Interdependence: Economic Policy in the Atlantic Community.* New York: McGraw-Hill, 1967.

Cox, Robert W. "Labor and the Multinationals," *Foreign Affairs*, 54 (January 1976), 244–265.

Goulet, Denis, and Michael Hudson. *The Myth of Aid: The Hidden Agenda of the Development Reports.* Maryknoll, N.Y.: Orbis, 1971.

Hansen, Roger D. "The Political Economy of North-South Relations: How Much Change?" *International Organization*, 29 (Autumn 1975), 921–948.

Hayter, Teresa. *Aid as Imperialism.* London: Penguin, 1971.

Krasner, Stephen D. "The Tokyo Round: Particularistic Interests and Prospects for Stability in the Global Trading System." *International Studies Quarterly*, 23 (December 1979), pp. 379–478.

Libby, Ronald T. "External Co-optation of a Less Developed Country's Policy Making: The Case of Ghana, 1969–1972," *World Politics*, 29 (October 1976), 67–89.

Magdoff, Harry. *The Age of Imperialism: The Economics of U.S. Foreign Policy.* New York: Monthly Review Press, 1969.

Rosen, Stephen J., and James B. Kurth. *Testing Theories of Economic Imperialism.* Lexington: Lexington Books, 1974.

Schmidt, Helmut. "The Struggle for the World Product," *Foreign Affairs*, 52 (April 1974), 437–451.

Vernon, Raymond. *Sovereignty at Bay: The Multinational Spread of U.S. Enterprises.* New York: Basic Books, 1971.

INTERNATIONAL ORGANIZATIONS AND SOCIAL WELFARE AND HUMAN RIGHTS

13

INTERNATIONAL ACTION TO PROMOTE HUMAN DIGNITY AND JUSTICE: THE SEARCH FOR ROLES

Beyond security and material goods, human beings seek social welfare and human rights, or in more abstract terms, dignity and justice. From time immemorial philosophers and theologians have been concerned with defining and perfecting concepts of human dignity and justice. At least some individual lives have always been regarded as precious, to be protected and nurtured, and there have always been ideas about how individuals should be treated, about what was fair and what was not fair. From these basic postulates normative understandings have been derived about how social relations should be organized and conducted.

TOWARD AN UNDERSTANDING AND DEFINITION OF HUMAN DIGNITY AND JUSTICE

All political systems claim to be founded on prevailing concepts of human dignity and justice. But the interaction between such concepts and political systems is more complex than this. Beyond putatively being based on such concepts, political systems also contribute to defining them. Many of the most profound statements about human dignity and justice are found in the constitutions, laws, and other political documents of states. And efforts to achieve and preserve different conceptions of human dignity and justice have occasioned wars and violence.

Although no one would oppose human dignity and justice in the abstract, there has never been complete agreement on what these concepts involve. Moreover, the concepts have varied with the historical epoch. As society has become more complicated, the commonly understood components of human dignity and justice have grown more complex. Perhaps the core of the notions of human dignity and justice is the same, but certainly the way these basic norms are applied in an isolated community with a subsistence economy is vastly different from the way they are applied in an interdependent world that relies heavily upon advanced technology for production.

The Historical Heritage

Concepts of human dignity and justice are central to defining the rights and duties of individuals in their societies and the responsibilities of governments toward their subjects. The evolution of these concepts is familiar in broad outline. They have been influenced by the beliefs and values of Judaism, Christianity, Islam, Hinduism, and Buddhism, and by the long effort to discover or to establish natural law. Codes of conduct concerning the relations of individuals to one another and governing the relations between individuals and their governments have existed throughout history.

The codes on which modern international organizations most clearly draw, however, date from the medieval period. The great documents of English constitutional history—the Magna Carta (1215), the Petition of Rights (1628), and the Declaration of Rights (1689)—gradually established restrictions on the arbitrary exercise of governmental authority and power. Government was forbidden to imprison individuals without a trial or to arrest them without specifying charges. Excessive bail was prohibited. The right of citizens to bear arms and the right not to have soldiers billeted in one's home were proclaimed. The right of petition was established, and elections were mandated for the House of Commons. The supremacy of Parliament in relation to the King was declared, and the necessity of frequent meetings of Parliament was specified. The Virginia Bill of Rights (1776) and the United States Bill of Rights (1789) proclaimed in addition the rights of freedom of speech, of the press, of assembly, and of religion, and set limitations on search and seizure. This list of civil and political rights is familiar and is an important part of the heritage that accrues to contemporary international organizations.

The heritage, however, is broader. In 1789, the same year that the United States Congress adopted the Bill of Rights, the French National Assembly adopted the Declaration of the Rights of Man. This declaration, echoing the proposition held to be self-evident in the American Declaration of Independence (1776), began with the ringing assertion that "Men are born and remain free and equal in rights. Social distinctions can be based only upon public utility."[1] It enunciated the doctrine that laws should only prohibit such actions as are injurious to society, and it reiterated the by then familiar civil rights that have been listed above. The first French Constitution adopted after the Revolution mandated that all citizens should be eligible for all offices and employment without any distinction other than of virtue and talent. It also directed that a system of public relief should be created that would bring up abandoned children, support infirm paupers, and provide work for the able-bodied poor, and that a system of free public education open to all citizens should be established. These provisions reflected the broadened understanding of the meaning of human dignity and justice that accompanied the increasing complexity of society. The ideas that all individuals should be entitled to the minimal prerequisites for effectve functioning in society and to the minimal necessities of existence were gaining adherents. This involved a fundamental philosophical shift. Early notions about human dignity and justice led to the creation of restraints on the power and authority of government; these newer notions created obligations for governments to provide services to their subjects.

The Constitution of the U.S.S.R. adopted in 1936 provided another landmark. In a detailed statement, the Fundamental Rights and Duties of Citizens, it declares that citizens have the right to work and to payment for work in accord with its quality and quantity; to rest and leisure; to maintenance in case of disability or sickness and in old age; and to education. The Constitution pledges that women shall have equal rights with men and that all citizens shall have equality irrespective of race and nationality. It affirms the traditional civil rights, including freedom of speech and of the press and the inviolability of persons and homes, and it also establishes the right of Soviet citizens to unite in mass organizations such as trade unions and youth organizations.

Thus the heritage of international organization in this field is extensive. Whether or not governments actually practiced what they proclaimed in declarations and in their constitutions is at this stage not the issue. What is important is that their proclamations reflected the evolving political content given to philosophical understandings of human dignity and justice. Other examples could have been used to illustrate the same points. Those that have been cited here were chosen because of their salience. The British, American, French, and Russian constitutional documents are milestones in the long process of giving political and legal meaning to understandings of human dignity and justice.

The Application of Concepts

One aspect of this process, treated implicitly to this point, merits explicit mention. Most early political definitions of human dignity and justice were intended to be applied in a restricted manner. In general, rights were conceived as applying only to citizens and citizenship was limited in different ways. Usually men were treated more generously than women. But as time wore on, the philosophical basis for differentiation among individuals weakened, and the norms of equality and nondiscrimination found increasing adherents. It became harder and harder to justify why all human beings should not be treated equally regardless of creed, sex, or race. And even the justification for distinguishing between citizens and noncitizens suffered erosion in several spheres.

Notions of human dignity and justice thus have led to the understandings that there should be restraints on the exercise of governmental power and authority

and that governments should provide the basic necessities of life for their subjects. Furthermore, it has increasingly been accepted that the detailed specification of rights that emerged from these understandings should apply without
discrimination to all individuals within the jurisdiction of a state.

In practical circumstances, of course, none of these rights could be realized
completely, among other reasons because various elements of the concepts were
contradictory. Governments were instructed to treat individuals equally and
without discrimination, but at the same time to give special treatment to those
with particular need. Free speech was to be allowed, yet one person's shouting
could make it impossible for others to be heard. If the state is to prepare citizens
for life, some education should probably be compulsory, but at what age should
further education become a matter of choice? How far should the state go in attempting to protect the health of its citizens when this involves limiting their
choice in such matters as alcohol, tobacco, and safety? To what extent should individuals be forced through taxation to restrict their present consumption so as
to provide for the contingencies of catastrophic illness and old age? Another difficulty is the limited material means available to many present-day societies with
which to meet the basic needs of their members. Even the most affluent societies
face difficult choices. For example, should additional resources be allocated to
health care or education? The application of human rights and the provision of
basic entitlements by states, therefore, always involve the exercise of judgment in
the balancing of conflicting claims and the use of limited resources.

Although he used only the term "human dignity," Herbert C. Kelman has expressed with great clarity a contemporary vision of what we have termed human
dignity and justice. Human dignity in his view refers "to the status of individuals
as ends in themselves, rather than as a means toward some extraneous ends."[2] He
distinguished two components to human dignity, identity and community:

> To accord a person identity is to perceive him as an individual, independent and distin-
> guishable from others, capable of making choices, and entitled to live his own life on
> the basis of his own goals and values. To accord a person community is to perceive
> him—along with one's self—as part of an interconnected network of individuals who
> care for each other, who recognize each other's individuality, and who respect each oth-
> er's rights.[3]

He then specified that:

> ...to maximize human dignity, a society needs institutions designed to expand the
> range of individual choices; to create opportunities for self-development and self-
> utilization; to promote widespread participation in decision-making; to assure freedom
> of expression and the right to dissent; to protect individuals against arbitrary treatment
> by authorities; to enable them to give free expression to their ethnic, cultural, and reli-
> gious traditions; and to protect their right to organize themselves into groups devoted to
> the achievement of all of these purposes. At the same time, maximization of human dig-
> nity also calls for institutions designed to meet the population's basic needs for food,
> housing, clothing, health care, and education; to protect the society as a whole against
> violence, starvation, disease, and disaster; to protect individuals against the disabilities

arising from unemployment, sickness, and old age; to provide compassionate care for those who are unable to care for themselves; and to assure that all segments of the society have equal access to all of the benefits.[4]

Kelman's vision can serve as a useful benchmark against which to measure contemporary national and international institutions, actions, and policies.

How to Involve International Organizations: Conceptual Issues

Establishing the role of international organizations with respect to security and economic issues is much simpler and more direct than establishing their role with respect to social welfare and human rights. War is clearly a phenomenon that involves relations among states; consequently, it is reasonable and logical to assume that collective action in international organizations might find ways to prevent or limit war. Similarly, the role of international organizations in economic issues is derived from the basic fact that specialization and the division of labor in production extend beyond the borders of states. The matters discussed in this chapter, however, are much less obviously international in character. They pertain to the relations between individuals and between governments and their subjects. In the cases of security and economic issues, it can easily be argued that international collaboration is essential to realize the goals of minimizing violence and maximizing economic production. With respect to social welfare and human rights, superficially at least, the same argument is not as compelling. Why should an international organization be necessary to insure free basic education or trial by jury?

Of course, the role of international organizations could be seen as that of appellate courts, places where individuals could go for redress when they felt that they had been unjustly treated by their government. The problem is that according to the doctrine of sovereignty the authority of a state is held to be supreme within the territory under its jurisdiction, and in these matters states are likely to insist on the prerogatives of sovereignty.

The reasons for this are not simply form and protocol, although these motivations can be important. As was noted above, no contemporary political system can insure that all rights are realized completely. Rights have to be balanced against each other and one individual's rights against those of others, and limited resources must be allocated among competing needs. Which compromises seem desirable will vary; different cultures will evaluate the importance of different rights in different ways, and the evaluation may vary with time and circumstances. Freedom of the press may seem less important to those who are poorly fed and chronically ill than it does to those with a more fortunate existence. One of the reasons that governments tend to insist on the prerogatives of sovereignty in this sphere is to insure that their acts are judged by the standards of their own people and not by those of other societies. Because governments insist on maintaining their own prerogatives of sovereignty, they are often reluctant to breach those of another government. Consequently, INGOs have frequently been more effective critics of governmental practices than have IGOs.

Even if governments were willing to have their actions in this sphere judged by an international organization—and, as will be described later, in the years since World War II an increasing number have proved to be willing—the question of implementing corrective actions would pose an intricate and difficult problem. Suppose it were determined on the petition of an individual that a government had acted in an arbitrary manner clearly violating broadly accepted restrictions on state authority or that the individual had not received some entitlement. How would an international organization insure that the individual's grievances were redressed? Only governments have the means of physical action. Would the international organization ask the offending government to force itself to change its ways, or would it ask other governments to take such action? If other governments were to take such action, it could ultimately involve war. The moral gain of enforcing compliance through war could well be ambiguous, and in any case the willingness of states to take actions that could involve serious costs to protect individuals in territories other than their own has been problematic at best. Publicity and persuasion must be important instruments for international organizations in this sphere. International organizations must rely on and seek to develop and stimulate the consciences of government officials. Their task is easier in the case of open and pluralistic societies where there is already strong public support for the values at stake.

The involvement of international organizations in social welfare and human rights issues has been hesitant and cautious. First, there was a groping to discover aspects of problems that were international, and then a gradual movement toward international action. Some individuals have always been concerned about the fate of humankind throughout the world, not just in their immediate society, and this has provided a continual impulse toward the formation of international nongovernmental organizations in this field. Most people, however, whether acting alone or in groups have tended to be concerned first with the situation in their own society and to seek improvements in the realization of human dignity and justice there. Various early transnational exchanges and international private associations emphasized separate action within national societies to achieve common goals. Only as the connections among societies increased did it become apparent that these seemingly national social and legal matters had international aspects and that international action could be essential for achieving solutions at the national level.

There has also been a close conceptual connection between the actions of national governments and those of international governmental organizations. What IGOs have done has tended to have a base in some national experience; international governmental organizations have found it difficult to effectively promote concepts that are in advance of those of all national governments. However, they have been able to take advanced concepts prevalent in some areas and encourage their application elsewhere, promoting a general advance and also a general homogenization of concepts.

International organizations can encourage and exhort states to adopt particular practices, they can provide technical and material assistance, and they can condemn practices that they do not approve. But it is exceedingly difficult for them to force recalcitrant states to take actions that they do not wish to take.

STEPS TOWARD INTERNATIONAL INVOLVEMENT

Slavery is a basic affront to human dignity. In the eighteenth and nineteenth centuries slavery was also an international phenomenon: men, women, and children were captured in Africa and transported to other parts of the world to be sold as slaves. Because it was odious, and because it also had international aspects, slavery was the first area in which international involvement in social welfare and human rights issues occurred. An international nongovernmental organization, the British and Foreign Anti-Slavery Society (which still exists under the name Anti-Slavery Society for the Protection of Human Rights), played an essential role in prompting governments to act. Throughout the nineteenth century it campaigned against slavery.

As early as 1815, at the Congress of Vienna, the principal states of the time acknowledged the need and duty to suppress the slave trade. (Slavery itself had been abolished in France, Britain, and Denmark around the turn of the century.) Despite this early moral commitment, however, it was only in 1890 at the Brussels Conference that a comprehensive treaty was signed providing effective measures for ending the slave trade, including a limited right to board and search ships suspected of carrying slaves. The fact that the United States did not abolish slavery until the 1860s helped postpone adoption of effective measures to end the trade. Beyond this, states generally were reluctant to allow the breach of sovereignty that the search of vessels in time of peace implied.

Other nineteenth-century actions were even more limited and tentative. The 1890 Brussels Conference also adopted regulations for the control of liquor and firearms in Africa, the motivation being that unsophisticated indigenous inhabitants should be protected from some of the more obviously dangerous aspects of life in the industrializing countries. Again an INGO, the Aborigines Protection Society, which was founded in 1837 and merged with the Anti-Slavery Society in 1909, played an important role in urging governments to act. Numerous conferences were held on health, mainly because new techniques of transportation made it possible to bring diseases easily from southern hemisphere countries to Europe and North America, and the industrializing countries wanted to avoid this risk while at the same time minimizing interference with commerce. At several of these conferences the creation of international governmental organizations was discussed, but few of the plans that were put forward came to fruition.

A conference was also held on protecting the working class. In the states where industrialization was occurring, increasing support was being mobilized for the proposition that labor should be protected against abusive management practices. Early national labor movements and the formation of the Socialist International in 1864 created pressures for governmental action to protect labor.

However, states feared that if they adopted progressive legislation, they would be placed at a competitive disadvantage in the world market in relation to those states that did not adopt such legislation, and hence it seemed that for there to be progress some way would have to be found so that all states would adopt similar social legislation. With respect to slavery, health, and the protection of labor, then, international trade provided the rubric that made possible contemplating breaching state sovereignty and eventually allowing a role for international organizations. Finally, two INGOs were formed to provide measures of relief to those afflicted by natural and human-caused disasters or otherwise in distress: the International Committee of the Red Cross, which was created in 1863, and the Salvation Army, which was founded two years later.

Health was the first field in which international governmental organizations were actually created. The *Conseil supérieur de santé* was established early in the nineteenth century to instigate and supervise port quarantines. Organizations with broader membership and functions came early in the twentieth century. The Pan American Sanitary Bureau (which later became the Pan American Health Organization) was created in 1902 with members from both North and South America, and the International Office of Public Health *(Office international d'hygiène publique)* was created in 1907 and included member states from Europe as well as from North and South America. Advances in scientific knowledge about health care and the establishment of national health offices in several states undoubtedly contributed to and facilitated the creation of IGOs in this field, but increasing commerce and opportunities for commerce also stimulated action. Still, the involvement of international organization was modest.

THE LEAGUE OF NATIONS AND THE INTERNATIONAL LABOR ORGANIZATION

The year 1919 marked a major change. Although social welfare and human rights activities were seen as a minor aspect of the functions of the League of Nations, the tasks assigned to the League and to the International Labor Organization, which was also created through the Treaty of Versailles, so broadened the involvement of international governmental organizations in these matters as to constitute a sharp departure from previous tradition. The League covenant created the mandates system, which provided a measure of international supervision over colonial rule. The International Labor Organization was established as an effort to protect workers and to promote humane conditions of work. The covenant committed League member states to mitigate suffering and to promote health and efforts to prevent disease throughout the world. Finally, the League was given responsibility for protecting the rights of minorities in the newly created states in central and Eastern Europe.

In each instance, although the goals for international action were often phrased in lofty terms, the commitments that governments undertook were narrowly defined, and the means put at the disposal of IGOs were modest. Nevertheless, the overall effect was to broaden vastly the involvement of international governmental organizations in the task of promoting human dignity and justice.

Just as slavery is odious to human dignity, so is the only slightly different concept embodied in some types of colonialism that holds that certain races should rule others indefinitely and without restrictions. Thus it was a logical progression in the nineteenth century to move from outlawing slavery and the slave trade to attempting to insure that certain standards of conduct would be observed in colonies, even if these standards only involved protecting the indigenous inhabitants from their own weaknesses. The League built upon this tradition, but went considerably farther. The covenant committed members of the League "to secure just treatment of the native inhabitants under their control,"[5] but means were provided for checking on the implementation of this obligation only with respect to the former colonies of the states that were defeated in World War I. Their colonial territories were detached from them in the peace settlement and placed within the mandates system, and responsibility for the governance of the mandated territories was assigned to the victorious states. The covenant stated that the "well-being and development" of peoples in the mandated territories formed a "sacred trust of civilization," and it required the states responsible for administering these territories to report annually to the council. A permanent commission was set up to receive and examine the reports and to advise the council on the way in which these states were observing their obligations.

The International Labor Organization was established to promote humane working conditions through facilitating the passage of labor legislation. The annual conference of the organization, at which member states would be represented by worker, employer, and government delegates, was given power to adopt conventions which would then be submitted to national legislatures for ratification. This was seen as a way of working toward eliminating inhumane conditons by making it possible for states to adopt protective legislation without fear of worsening their manufacturers' competitive position in international trade.

The League covenant also committed members of the League to establish and maintain international organizations "to secure and maintain fair and humane conditons of labor" and "to take steps in matters of international concern for the prevention and control of disease."[6] The member states agreed to encourage and promote voluntary national Red Cross organizations. Finally, the League itself was given responsibility for "the general supervision over the execution of agreements with regard to the traffic in women and children, and the traffic in opium and other dangerous drugs."[7]

A series of peace treaties and declarations concluded during or immediately after the Paris Peace Conference placed further responsibilites upon the League. Eventually, fourteen states accepted obligations to protect the rights of national minorities within their borders. These rights included basic equality; freedom to use their mother tongue; freedom to maintain their own charitable, educational, religious, and social institutions; instruction in state elementary schools in their own language; and an equitable share of public funds provided for charitable, educational, and religious purposes. Individuals could petition the council of the League about infringements of their rights, and other states could also register complaints.

These several tasks assigned to the League and ILO established that the relationships between a government and its subjects and relationships among a government's subjects were legitimate topics for consideration and action by international organizations. The right of petition in the case of the minorities was a radical innovation. The council's responsibilities both in this instance and with respect to the mandates system created a mechanism for supervision by an IGO. Moreover, although international trade, which had originally provided the justification and rationale for IGOs' entering the field of social welfare and human rights, continued to be prominent, it no longer was the only justification. Gradually, the world community was moving toward an understanding that these issues were sufficiently important that action concerning them was justified whether or not international trade was involved.

Of course, a cynic could observe that even though some general obligations had broad application, those obligations that were phrased in precise detail and for which mechanisms for international supervision were created applied only to a very limited number of territories. Those governments that accepted the extensive obligations to protect the rights of their minorities in reality had little choice about accepting them, since the obligations were embodied in the treaties or understandings that accompanied their birth as states. No already established state accepted such obligations. Similarly, the only colonies that were placed in the mandates system were those that had been held by the states defeated in the war. During the war the Allies had made secret treaties dividing these colonies among themselves, and the actual assignment of states to administer the mandated territories followed these plans. Given the moral slogans the Allied states had proclaimed as they prosecuted the war, they were hardly in a position to prevent the interposition of the modest international supervision that the mandates system involved. With respect to labor legislation, labor movements were powerful and commanded governmental attention and respect in the countries of Western Europe and North America, and these movements were in a strong position to insist that the peace settlement include provisions to protect their interests. In addition, many government officials felt that the modest concessions involved in the creation of the International Labor Organization could possibly stave off demands for a radical restructuring of societies on the pattern of the Russian Revolution. The spectre of Bolshevism was a powerful stimulus for being responsive to the requests of labor.

Even though the tasks and powers assigned to the League and ILO were limited and could be viewed cynically, they constituted an important precedent, one that could and would be drawn on later. Moreover, important work could be inaugurated, and it was. The various assigned tasks were indeed performed and others were quietly added. One of the human tragedies of World War I was the large number of refugees it created, people who for one reason or another were unwilling to return to their native country. The League soon became involved in attempts to ease their plight. A high commissioner for refugees was appointed, and he developed a small staff to assist in the resolution of refugee problems. Work was also conducted within the League toward the adoption of agreements that states could accept granting refugees certain rights. In addition, the League created the International Organization for Intellectual Cooperation, which undertook modest programs with respect to science and education, and was a forerunner of the United Nations Educational, Scientific and Cultural Organization.

Important international nongovernmental organizations were also formed during the period between World Wars I and II. In 1919 the non-confessional European trade unions formed the International Federation of Trade Unions, which was the forerunner of the International Confederation of Free Trade Unions (ICFTU). The International Federation of Christian Trade Unions (IFCTU) was founded in 1920. (Its name was changed to the World Confederation of Labor (WCL) in 1968.) The International Federation for the Rights of Man was established in 1922.

THE U.N.'S BROAD MANDATE

The years at the end of and immediately after World War II brought further significant changes in the approach of international organizations to questions of social welfare and human rights. Perhaps the most important reason for the change was that many journalists, historians, government officials, and common citizens had come to believe that the international community must do more to promote human dignity and justice. They were appalled by the inhuman acts of Nazi Germany and determined that no state should ever again be permitted to perpetrate such atrocities. Many were also convinced that Nazi Germany might not have wreaked such international violence had it been made to pursue more humane standards of conduct within its own borders.

The preamble of the United Nations charter reflected these feelings and beliefs. It began:

> We the people of the United Nations determined to save succeeding generations from the scourge of war, which twice in our lifetime has brought untold sorrow to mankind, and to reaffirm faith in fundamental human rights, in the dignity of the human person, in the equal rights of men and women and of nations large and small, and to establish conditions under which justice and respect for the obligations arising from treaties and other sources of international law can be maintained, and to promote social programs and better standards of life in larger freedom...

Promoting the realization of human rights became one of the prominent tasks of the United Nations, which was given a much broader mandate than the League had possessed. While the League was authorized to be concerned with the rights and status of individuals in the mandated territories and of national minorities in certain countries, the charter clearly stated that the United Nations was "to achieve international cooperation...in promoting and encouraging respect for human rights and for fundamental freedoms for all without distinction as to race, sex, language, or religion."[8] The same paragraph also pledged the United Nations to achieve cooperation in solving international problems of social, cultural, or humanitarian character. Two whole chapters of the charter, 9 and 10, were devoted to elaborating these obligations and creating mechanisms for their implementation.

Following the directive contained in the charter, at its first session in February 1946 the U.N.'s Economic and Social Council (ECOSOC) created the Commission on Human Rights. Eleanor Roosevelt, the late president's widow, was chosen to chair the commission, and it immediately outlined an ambitious program of activities. ECOSOC also created a Subcommission on the Status of Women, a Social Commission, and a Commission on Narcotic Drugs.

The U.N. charter also set forth, in Chapter 11, far-reaching goals for all member states administering non-self-governing territories, including insuring "with due respect for the culture of the peoples concerned, their political, economic, social, and educational advancement, their just treatment, and their protection against abuses."[9] In terms of historical development, the obligation to insure political, economic, social, and educational advancement had been added to the nineteenth-century admonition against abuses and the League obligation for just treatment. Another departure with respect to colonial matters was that the successor to the mandates system, the trusteeship system, which was established in Chapters 12 and 13, was in principle applicable to any non-self-governing territory.

The national and international nongovernmental organizations represented at San Francisco played a major role in insuring that the U.N. charter would provide such an expansive mandate for social welfare and human rights activities. The United States delegation had representatives of more than forty nongovernmental organizations associated with it. Various INGOs were represented at the conference as observers, and (as mentioned in Chapter 10) the World Federation of Trade Unions (WFTU) was meeting across the bay in Oakland. The representatives of nongovernmental organizations wanted to be able to continue to pressure governments to achieve social welfare and human rights objectives, and to this end they worked for and eventually succeeded in writing into the charter provision for international and national nongovernmental organizations to have consultative status with the Economic and Social Council of the U.N.[10] The Soviet Union and the World Federation of Trade Unions played a leading role in this struggle, and Soviet demands for recognition of WFTU as the principal labor organization were a contributing factor in the decision to include this charter provision for consultative status. Such consultative privileges were soon extended by many other IGOs.

Even though the obligations on member states set forth in the U.N. charter concerning issues of human dignity and justice were much more far-reaching and broadly applicable than those contained in the League covenant, the means of insuring their implementation put at the disposal of the U.N. were not significantly different from those that the League had had. They continued to be collecting information, conducting research, issuing publications, convening conferences, and preparing conventions that states could adopt. With respect to colonial territories, the powers of the United Nations were somewhat more extensive in that the states that were responsible for non-self-governing territories were required to transmit regularly to the secretary-general "statistical and other information of a technical character relating to economic, social, and educational conditions in these territories."[11] In the case of trust territories, the Trusteeship Council had the right to receive, accept, and examine petitions and to visit the territories to investigate conditions there.

How confining the broad restriction contained in paragraph 7 of Article 2 would be only time would tell. This paragraph, which was referred to in Chapter 10, stated:

> Nothing contained in the present Charter shall authorize the United Nations to intervene in matters which are essentially within the domestic jurisdiction of any state or shall require the Members to submit such matters to settlement under the present Charter. . . .

Not only was "domestic jurisdiction" not defined in the charter, no procedure was established there for defining it. Thus the practical meaning of the injunction would depend upon how the organs of the United Nations interpreted it. The juxtaposition of this restriction alongside the extensive goals proclaimed in the charter neatly framed the basic dilemma of how an international governmental organization composed of sovereign states and dependent upon them for the means of action might insure that the governments of these same states treated their inhabitants and regulated interpersonal conduct within their borders so as to achieve human dignity and justice.

UNESCO AND WHO: MANDATES FOR OPERATIONAL ACTIVITIES

In two areas, health and education, U.N. member states sought to extricate themselves from this quandary by creating international organizations with operational as well as more traditional responsibilities.

The constitution of the United Nations Educational, Scientific and Cultural Organization (UNESCO) was signed in November 1945. Its preamble asserted more clearly than any other constitutional document the perceived connection between violations of human dignity and international violence. It began with the declaration that "wars begin in the minds of men," and it asserted that World War II had been "made possible by the denial of the democratic principles of the dignity, equality and mutual respect of men, and by the propagation, in their place, through ignorance and prejudice, of the doctrine of the inequality of men and races." The preamble also declared that "the wide diffusion of culture, and the education of humanity for justice and liberty and peace are indispensable to the dignity of man and constitute a sacred duty which all the nations must fulfill in a spirit of mutual assistance and concern."

To give substance to these broad goals, the organization was empowered to advance knowledge and understanding of peoples through the use of mass communications; to promote popular education and the spread of culture by assisting the governments of member states to develop educational programs and through other techniques; and to work to maintain, increase, and diffuse knowledge. But these extensive functions were also hedged in the following paragraph with the familiar prohibition against intervening in domestic jurisdiction.[12]

The constitution of the World Health Organization (WHO), which was signed in July 1946, took an approach as lofty as that of UNESCO. It proclaimed that "the enjoyment of the highest attainable standard of health is one of the fundamental rights of every human being without distinction of race, religion, political belief, economic or social condition," and set this as the objective of the organization.[13] To achieve this objective, some twenty-two specific functions were enumerated, including assisting "governments, upon request, in strengthening health services."[14]

AN EXPANDING WEB OF INTERNATIONAL ORGANIZATION NETWORKS FOR HUMAN DIGNITY AND JUSTICE

The creation of both UNESCO and WHO had been envisaged in the planning for the postwar period, but in the first year of its existence the United Nations concluded that it was also necessary to create two additional specialized organizations to provide operational assistance for particular groups of individuals. In 1946 the General Assembly authorized the creation of the International Refugee Organization (IRO) and the United Nations International Children's Emergency Fund (UNICEF). IRO was to provide assistance for the many refugees who as a consequence of the war and postwar changes found it impossible to return to their home countries. UNICEF was to provide relief for suffering children in war-devastated Europe. Both organizations were envisaged as temporary bodies, and IRO was indeed terminated. But there has been a need for permanent institutions to assist refugees and children, and so the post of United Nations High Commissioner for Refugees (UNHCR) was created in 1951 to take the place of IRO, and UNICEF's mandate was broadened to include children in Asia, Africa, and Latin America as well as Europe.

New international nongovernmental organizations were also established to provide relief. OXFAM was formed in the United Kingdom in 1942 as the Oxford Committee for Famine Relief, and in the postwar years it was swiftly transformed into a permanent INGO. CARE, the Cooperative for American Relief Everywhere, with members in the United States and Canada, was established in 1945. Over the years its principal focus has shifted from providing relief to helping poor people in less developed countries, particularly by supplying food and medical care. Caritas Internationalis, the International Conference of Catholic

Charities, was formed in 1951, although it built on organizational activity that had existed since 1924.

As happened in the security and economic fields, in the years after World War II the panoply of IGOs in this field with potentially universal membership was soon supplemented by IGOs with restricted membership. The charters of the two most prominent among these, the Council of Europe and the Organization of American States (OAS), were both completed in 1948. The OAS was open to any American state. The Council of Europe was open to those European states that "accept the principles of the rule of law and of the enjoyment by all persons within its jurisdiction of human rights and fundamental freedoms."[15] The broad mandates of both institution allow ample scope for work concerning issues related to human dignity and justice. The statement of objectives and goals in the OAS charter, however, is considerably more extensive than that in any other IGO constitutional document written in the immediate postwar period. It proclaims that: "All human beings, without distinction as to race, nationality, sex, creed, or social condition, have the right to attain material well-being and spiritual growth under circumstances of liberty, dignity, equality of opportunity, and economic security."[16] Later it proclaims that work is "a right and a social duty," and declares that elementary education should be compulsory and without cost and that higher education should be "available to all, without distinction as to race, nationality, sex, language, creed, or social condition."[17]

The principal novelty of the Council of Europe and the Organization of American States, however, was that they were initial attempts of regional IGOs to deal with human rights, and, as will be seen, these organizations have been responsible for some of the most significant accomplishments in this area. Both the Council of Europe and the OAS have developed appellate procedures, and those of the Council of Europe have been used extensively. Other regional organizations have also entered the fields of social welfare and human rights. For instance, when the Organization of African Unity was created in 1963, it was given a mandate to assist governments to achieve "a better life for the peoples of Africa" and "eradicate all forms of colonialism from Africa."[18] Acting to fulfill this mandate, in 1981 the OAU adopted the Banjul Charter of Human and People's Rights. In the 1980s, consideration also began to be given to the creation of arrangements to protect and promote human rights in the Asian region.

Finally, several additional nongovernmental organizations have been established since World War II to advance social welfare and human rights. Two of the most prominent of these work exclusively in the area of human rights, and they were created as INGOs precisely so that they could avoid the inhibitions that IGOs face in criticizing governments. The International Commission of Jurists resulted from the Congress of Jurists held in West Berlin in 1952. Its purpose is to promote the realization of the rule of law, and when it has discovered and documented systematic violations of human rights, it seeks to mobilize public opinion against these violations. Amnesty International, founded in London in 1961, seeks particularly to guarantee freedom of religion and opinion and other basic human rights. It works to mobilize public opinion in favor of these rights; it attempts to secure the release of political prisoners held by governments; and it tries to aid the families of these prisoners.

The heightened concern with issues of human dignity and justice that arose out of World War II thus led to a more extensive involvement of international organizations in this field. The mandates given to new international governmental organizations were more far-reaching, and more IGOs were given authority to do work in this field than ever before. The coverage provided by the new mandates was ample. The goals, if one includes those articulated by regional IGOs, were clearly as broad as those subscribed to by national governments. But despite the ringing declarations that gave legitimacy to a vastly expanded role for international organizations in this field, little was done to resolve the fundamental quandary of determining exactly what international organizations could do to promote human dignity and justice.

In a limited number of cases, IGOs were authorized to serve as appellate bodies, but even in these instances, the right to obtain information on which to base a judgment was limited, and no means was provided for enforcing judgments. Instead, the mandates of IGOs allowed them to collect information, formulate norms, and draft conventions and to provide assistance for the development of national educational and health systems and for sustaining refugees and children. INGOs were also formed to undertake activities with respect to social welfare and human rights, and although their powers were no more extensive than those of IGOs, they could be free of some of the inhibitions that IGOs suffer. The aims and goals of international organizations were lofty, but the powers and authority assigned to them were modest. How these modest powers have been utilized and, indeed, expanded is the subject of the next chapter.

NOTES

1. The French Declaration of the Rights of Man as well as the English Declaration of Rights, the United States Bill of Rights, the 1936 Constitution of the U.S.S.R., and several other basic documents can be found in Ian Brownlie (ed.), *Basic Documents on Human Rights* (Oxford: Clarendon Press, 1971). The text of the French declaration is on pp. 8–10.
2. Herbert C. Kelman, "The Conditions, Criteria, and Dialectics of Human Dignity: A Transnational Perspective," *International Studies Quarterly*, 21 (September 1977), 529–552, on p. 531.
3. Herbert C. Kelman, "Violence Without Moral Restraint: Reflections on the Dehumanization of Victims and Victimizers," *Journal of Social Issues*, 29, 4 (1973), 25–61, on pp. 48–49.
4. Kelman, "The Conditions, Criteria, and Dialectics of Human Dignity," pp. 532–533.
5. Article 23.
6. Ibid.
7. Ibid.
8. Article 1, paragraph 3.
9. Article 73a.
10. Article 71.
11. Article 73, paragraph e.
12. Article 1, paragraph 3.

13. Preamble and Article 1.
14. Article 2.
15. Article 3.
16. Article 29(a).
17. Ibid., Articles 29 and 30.
18. Article 2.

FOR FURTHER READING

Beitz, Charles R. *Political Theory and International Relations*. Princeton, N.J.: Princeton University Press, 1979.

Cantril, Hadley (ed.). *Tensions That Cause War*. Urbana: University of Illinois Press, 1950.

Center for Study of the American Experience. *Rights and Responsibilities: International, Social, and Individual Dimensions*. Los Angeles: University of Southern California Press, 1980.

Claude, Inis L., Jr. *National Minorities: An International Problem*. Cambridge: Harvard University Press, 1955.

Cranston, Maurice. *What Are Human Rights?* New York: Basic Books, 1962.

Haas, Ernst B. "The Reconciliation of Conflicting Colonial Policy Aims: Acceptance of the League of Nations Mandate System," *International Organization*, 6 (November 1952), 521–536.

——— . "The Attempt to Terminate Colonialism: Acceptance of the United Nations Trusteeship System," *International Organization*, 7 (February 1953), 1–21.

Holcombe, Arthur N. *Human Rights in the Modern World*. New York: New York University Press, 1948.

Lauterpacht, Hirsch. *International Law and Human Rights*. New York: Praeger, 1950.

Lorwin, Lewis L. *The International Labor Movement: History, Policies, Outlook*. New York: Harper, 1953.

Mander, L. A. *Foundations of Modern World Society*. Stanford: Stanford University Press, 1948.

Maritain, Jacques. *The Rights of Man and Natural Law*. New York: Scribner, 1943.

Rawls, John. *A Theory of Justice*. Cambridge: Harvard University Press, 1971.

Senghor, Leopold. *African Socialism*. New York: Praeger, 1964.

Wright, Quincy. *Mandates Under the League*. Chicago: University of Chicago Press, 1930.

14

ACTIVITIES TO PROMOTE SOCIAL WELFARE AND HUMAN RIGHTS

As international organizations began activities in the fields of social welfare and human rights in the years immediately after World War II, it quickly became apparent that the priorities of individuals and of states with respect to these issues differed significantly. These conflicting priorities led to different approaches. The consensus that existed at the conclusion of the war that international organizations would have to play a major role to promote human dignity and justice disappeared as soon as international organizations began to decide what was to be done, and in what order. The conflicts that came to the surface then have continued and have pervaded all of the activities undertaken by international organizations in these fields.

CONFLICTING PRIORITIES AND DIFFERENT APPROACHES

One conflict concerns colonialism. Many individuals and states see colonialism as the most abhorrent of all affronts to human dignity and are willing to subordinate all other concerns in this area to efforts to end colonialism. The states that are most firmly committed to this position are largely to be found in Africa and Asia. South American states have also generally taken anticolonial positions, though not as stridently. Both the Soviet Union and the United States have anticolonial traditions, and each went on record early in the postwar period as being opposed to colonialism. Many of the Western European states were also in principle opposed to colonialism. The difference between these Western European states and the United States, on the one hand, and the African and Asian states and the Soviet Union, on the other, was that the latter group wanted to end colonialism immediately, while the former envisaged a gradual process of decolonization that would extend over varying time periods and would allow economic, social, and political development to occur in the meantime. African, Asian, and Soviet representatives argued that colonialism should be ended immediately, regardless of economic and social conditions and prospects, and that in any case independence would produce greater economic and social progress than would continued colonial rule.

A second conflict concerns the relative importance of civil and political, as opposed to economic and social, rights. In the immediate postwar period the United States and the United Kingdom, following their traditions, sought to emphasize civil and political rights, and they saw the question of promoting human dignity and justice largely as one of protecting individual freedoms and creating restraints on the exercise of governmental authority. Western European states shared this view in varying degrees. The Soviet Union, on the other hand, gave much greater emphasis to economic and social rights and consequently to the obligation of governments to provide for the welfare of their subjects. Other countries with communist governments sided with the U.S.S.R., and most of the newly independent states of Africa and Asia also came to take this position.

Both conflicts have been apparent throughout the period since World War II in the activities in this field undertaken by universal membership organizations. Since the Group of 77 states gained a numerically dominant position in these institutions, their activities have increasingly reflected the priority that these states give to the struggle against colonialism and all forms of racial discrimination and their emphasis on the promotion of economic and social development. Those states, such as the United States and the United Kingdom, that have traditionally stressed the importance of civil and political rights have continued to argue their position in universal membership institutions, though sometimes almost as a beleaguered minority. They have also placed more and more emphasis on limited membership IGOs as forums where more far-reaching action could be taken. Individuals in these states and elsewhere who have been interested in advancing civil and political rights have concentrated much of their effort in international nongovernmental organizations.

Despite this diversity of views among individuals and states, there has been an increasing tendency toward general recognition of the legitimacy of the values that all are seeking to promote. The acrimony of the debates, however, has not been dampened by this development; on the contrary, it may even have been increased. With the broadening of the, at least rhetorical, agreement on the legitimacy of all of the values at stake, governments whose performance was being criticized could not take refuge in a denial of the importance of the goal. Accusations that a government has fallen short of a goal that it has in principle accepted have provoked heated verbal defenses and arguments that are at least as vigorous as those about the importance of the goal. That activities in this field should be so conflictual stems from the fact that the issues involved are central to human ethical systems and to the self-defined purposes of societies and states.

INFORMATIONAL ACTIVITIES

In several respects the informational activities of international organizations with respect to social welfare and human rights parallel similar activities in the economic field.

Gathering Data and Developing Social Indicators

International organizations have first been involved in a large and important data-gathering effort. ILO has long published its *Bulletin* and *Yearbook of Labor Statistics*, which contain data on employment, hours of work, wages, and other related matters. UNESCO's *Statistical Yearbook* contains data on enrollment in educational institutions, literacy, cultural facilities such as libraries, and mass media. The World Health Organization collects epidemiological information and vital statistics as well as information concerning medical and paramedical personnel, hospitals, and public health practices; it publishes some of these on a weekly basis, others monthly, and most of them annually. FAO and the U.N. collect and publish data on nutrition.

The problems of standardizing concepts and data collection procedures that we noted with respect to economic data also arise in these fields. In one area, however, the task is easier here. The constitution of the World Health Organization empowers the World Health Assembly to adopt regulations concerning "nomenclatures with respect to diseases, causes of death and public health practices."[1] Regulations adopted pursuant to this provision come into force for all WHO member states except those that notify the director-general of their rejection or reservations within a specified period. This procedure has facilitated the task of obtaining standardization in the collection of health data.

However, there is a broader problem that has complicated considerably the task of data collection with respect to social welfare: social indicators have simply not been as well developed as economic indicators. Between the two world wars the concepts of gross national product and per capita GNP were developed, and during the 1940s and 1950s they came to be widely accepted as measures of economic performance. But despite great interest in the subject, particularly since the mid-1960s, similar agreement on social indicators has not been achieved.[2] Consequently, reports on the world social situation have lagged behind, and have had less impact than, reports on the world economic situation. The first U.N. report on the world social situation was not published until 1952, and they are now published on a triennial basis.

The concern with measuring social welfare has, however, produced agreement that several social indicators—as opposed to two main economic indicators—will be required. Progress has also been made toward identifying the key concepts that the indicators should represent. In 1973 OECD agreed on a list of nine key social concerns: health, individual development through learning, employment and quality of working life, leisure time, personal economic situation, physical environment, social environment, personal safety and the administration of justice, and social opportunity and participation. The breadth of the list is impressive, yet it accords with the broad understanding developed in Chapter 13 of the contemporary meaning of human dignity and justice.

Since 1973 work has been going on within OECD on the development of appropriate indicators to measure attainment with respect to these concerns.[3] Some of the indicators, such as life expectancy, are already available. Others, such as those involving internationally agreed standards for assessing access to health care, are in the process of development. Still others, relating for instance to primary and secondary social attachments, remain at the conceptual stage. Although OECD will use several social indicators, one of the ways in which they will be brought together will be to see whether disadvantages are dispersed or accumulate to particular groups within societies. This should provide a much better understanding than has previously been possible of the extent of inequality within societies.

Given the essentiality of material means to the provision of social welfare and the importance of political and social culture to the determination of what aspects of social welfare should receive emphasis, it may well be that limited membership organizations will make more rapid progress in this area than universal membership organizations.

Monitoring Performance

Several of the data that have been mentioned, such as those concerning health, education, and nutrition, are relevant to concepts of economic and social rights and can be used to monitor performance with respect to these rights. Moreover, the collection of such data has generally been uncontroversial. Civil and political rights present a different problem. Since 1946 the United Nations has published a *Yearbook on Human Rights.* This includes constitutional provisions, legislative acts, executive orders, and judicial decisions concerning the observance of human rights and also international conventions and agreements. The crucial issue, however, is often how various legal provisions are implemented. IGOs have generally avoided attempting to collect and disseminate data on such issues unless authorized to do so by a specific convention.

International nongovernmental organizations have been less constrained. Both the International Commission of Jurists and Amnesty International have published detailed, specific, and highly critical analyses of the practices of governments of all political persuasions in all parts of the world. Both INGOs have serial publications: the International Commission of Jurists publishes a biannual review, and Amnesty International publishes the monthly *Amnesty International Newsletter,* the bimonthly *Chronicle of Current Events,* and the yearly *Annual Report.* In addition, each organization has issued scathing special reports on particular countries and territories, such as South Africa, East Pakistan, Paraguay, Northern Ireland, the U.S.S.R., Czechoslovakia, Brazil, and Indonesia. Both organizations have been meticulous in checking allegations, and each has developed an amazing capacity to obtain information. In 1972 Amnesty In-

ternational launched a global campaign against the use of torture by governments, and in 1973 it published its classic *Report on Torture.*[4] The goal of eliminating torture dates from the earliest attempts to put restrictions on
governmental power, but Amnesty International was the first international organization to systematically collect and publish information on the practice. It
was awarded the 1977 Nobel Prize for Peace for its efforts to protect
political prisoners.

In the case of non–self-governing territories, IGOs have used the collection of
data as a technique for exercising a measure of international surveillance over colonial rule. Under the terms of the League covenant, states administering mandated territories were required to submit annual reports on them to the
Permanent Mandates Commission, which then rendered modest judgments. The
U.N. charter continued this procedure for the trust territories, and Article 73e required member states to transmit regularly to the secretary-general "statistical
and other information of a technical nature relating to economic, social, and educational conditions" in all other non–self-governing territories for which they
were responsible. The United Nations immediately created a committee to examine these reports, and through this technique extended surveillance to all non–
self-governing territories.

Exchanging Information

Another informational activity of international organizations consists of exchanges of scientific information and information about the application of particular policies. ILO, UNESCO, WHO, and OECD all facililtate information
exchanges among their member states. ILO circulates information on social security systems, UNESCO on pedagogical techniques, and WHO on the treatment
of diseases, to cite only a few examples. The 1974 World Food Conference created a World Food Council to provide a forum for the regular discussion of
global food needs and the global food supply. This council was meant to be a
small body involving the principal food exporting and importing states; the
U.S.S.R. became a member even though it was not a member of FAO. Within
OAS and the Council of Europe exchanges of information occur in regular meetings of ministers of education and of labor. For hundreds of INGOs the exchange
of information is their sole or principal function. Through their information-
exchange activities, international organizations promote the wide circulation of
the results of social research and experience with particular social policies. As a
consequence, innovations in social policy can spread quickly through regions or
the entire world.

Research

International organizations also conduct research, although most research in
these fields is done by national governments and private agencies. In 1968 OECD
established the Center for Educational Research, which among its several func-

tions has the task of exploring ways of maximizing equality of educational opportunity. OECD also regularly conducts reviews of its member countries' educational policies. OAS sponsors an Inter-American Indian Institute and an Inter-American Children's Institute which do research on problems in their fields. WHO sponsors an International Center for Research on Cancer. In the 1970s the International Labor Organization began a world employment program; initial aspects of the program involved many analyses of how to promote more jobs throughout the world. The United Nations International Research and Training Institute for the Advancement of Women began its programs in 1982. These programs seek to promote links between general development activities and issues that affect women.

Publicizing Issues

Finally, international organizations have sought to publicize social welfare and human rights issues by convening conferences. A few examples are the International Conference on Human Rights (Teheran, 1968), the World Conference of the International Women's Year (Mexico City, 1975), the Conference on Human Settlements (Vancouver, 1976), the World Employment Conference (Geneva, 1976), the International Conference on Assistance to Refugees in Africa (Geneva, 1982), and the World Assembly on Aging (Vienna, 1982).

NORMATIVE ACTIVITIES

Both because social welfare and human rights issues concern human aspirations and because of the limited means at the disposal of international organizations, normative activities have received considerable prominence.

Declarations: Enunciating Principles

Declarations loom large among the activities of INGOs and IGOs, and United Nations declarations are perhaps the most important. In an imperfect yet plausible way they represent the aspirations of humanity. The U.N. is the only universal membership, general purpose international governmental organization in existence. Despite the distorting effects of the doctrine of sovereign equality that accords each state one vote and the authoritarian character of so many of the governments whose delegates make up the U.N. General Assembly, it remains the only body that has a semblance of a claim to express world public opinion. U.N. declarations are formal and solemn instruments, reserved for rare occasions when principles of great and lasting importance are being enunciated.

The first declaration of major importance to be adopted by an IGO after World War II was the American Declaration of the Rights and Duties of Man, which was adopted by the ninth conference of American states held at Bogota, Colombia, in the spring of 1948. This declaration was an important prelude to the subsequent activities of OAS with respect to human rights.

Later that same year, the United Nations adopted the Universal Declaration of Human Rights, which remains the most important of the U.N.'s declarations.[5] In the preamble the General Assembly proclaimed that the declaration should be "a common standard of achievement for all peoples and all nations."

The thirty articles of the declaration deal with both civil and political rights and economic, social, and cultural rights. The first article declares: "All human beings are born free and equal in dignity and rights. They are endowed with reason and conscience and should act towards one another in a spirit of brotherhood." The other articles are equally clear and ringing, and the declaration, which is reprinted in Appendix E, merits reading in full.

The norm of equality is salient throughout the text. The early articles state the traditional civil and political rights: the right to life and liberty, the prohibition of slavery, freedom from arbitrary arrest, the right to be presumed innocent until proven guilty according to law in a public trial, the prohibition of cruel and unusual punishment, the right to privacy, the right to freedom of conscience and of opinion and expression, the right to assembly, and the right to participate in government. In addition, the declaration also contains innovative provisions concerning civil and political rights. It proclaims that "everyone has the right to a nationality." It also holds that individuals should have freedom of movement within states and should be free to leave states including their own. With respect to cultural, economic, and social rights, the declaration states that everyone has the right to marry and found a family, to own property, to social security, to education, to work and rest and leisure, and "to a standard of living adequate for the health and well-being of himself and of his family, including food, clothing, housing and medical care and necessary social services." The declaration also states that individuals have duties to their communities.

The Universal Declaration of Human Rights is a powerful and moving document, setting forth the highest human aspirations. No state voted against it, although eight—Byelorussia, Czechoslovakia, Poland, Saudi Arabia, the Ukraine, the Union of South Africa, the Soviet Union, and Yugoslavia—abstained, and two—Honduras and Yemen—were absent.

The declaration has attained the status that its authors hoped. It has become a common standard for achievement in this field, a standard against which the actions of states and international institutions have been measured. The declaration also set the direction for much subsequent work. Other declarations have been drafted to elaborate points mentioned briefly in it, and conventions have been prepared so that there would be legally binding instruments covering the rights proclaimed in it.

In 1960 the U.N. General Assembly adopted another declaration of fundamental importance—the Declaration on the Granting of Independence to Colonial Countries and Peoples.[6] This declaration, General Assembly Resolution 1514 (XV), sounded the death knell of colonialism. Throughout history until well into the twentieth century, the imposition of colonial rule by a nation over alien territories was regarded as a legitimate act. Even in the nineteenth century, though, there was an emerging consensus that colonial powers should not be free to do completely as they pleased, that they had obligations with respect to the inhabitants of the territories that they ruled.

This notion was strengthened in the mandates provisions of the League covenant, although these provisions applied to only a limited number of territories. The League's actions with respect to the Italian attack on Ethiopia marked a new stage in the slowly emerging consensus against colonialism. Although the steps that the League took were ineffective in stopping the conquest, they succeeded in delegitimizing it. The League's action symbolized that the world community no longer regarded colonial conquest as legitimate. The United Nations charter extended the notion that colonial powers should regard their rule over non–self-governing territories as a "sacred trust" to all such territories and obligated the colonial powers to take action to promote the well-being of the inhabitants of their territories.

The 1960 General Assembly declaration went farther and pronounced that colonialism should cease:

> The subjection of peoples to alien subjugation, domination and exploitation constitutes a denial of fundamental human rights, is contrary to the Charter of the United Nations and is an impediment to the promotion of world peace and co-operation.

In other words, colonialism itself was no longer legitimate. The preamble made this clear. One paragraph stated that the General Assembly was "convinced that the continued existence of colonialism prevents the development of international economic cooperation, impedes the social, cultural and economic development of dependent peoples and militates against the United Nations ideal of universal peace." Another paragraph of the preamble proclaimed the belief "that the process of liberation is irresistible and irreversible and that, in order to avoid serious crises, an end must be put to colonialism and all practices of segregation and discrimination associated therewith." An operative paragraph asserted that "inadequacy of political, economic, social or educational preparedness should never serve as a pretext for delaying independence." The declaration called for ending armed action against dependent peoples and for taking immediate steps to grant them their complete independence and freedom.

Again, no state voted against this declaration, but nine abstained—Australia, Belgium, the Dominican Republic, France, Portugal, Spain, the Union of South Africa, the United Kingdom, and the United States. A comparison between the states that did not vote for this declaration and those that did not vote for the Universal Declaration of Human Rights points up the different approaches that they have had concerning which activities should be given priority in efforts to promote human dignity and justice. For some states, such as Belgium, France, the United Kingdom, and the United States, advancing traditional civil and political rights was a much more important goal than ending colonialism, while for others, such as the Soviet Union, the priority was exactly the opposite. Interestingly, South Africa abstained on both declarations.

The U.N. General Assembly has adopted several other declarations. In 1959 it adopted the Declaration on the Rights of the Child,[7] and four years later, the Declaration on the Elimination of All Forms of Racial Discrimination.[8] The latter was closely linked with the declaration that had been adopted previously decrying colonialism, and it was aimed particularly at the practice of apartheid. It called for efforts "to prevent discrimination based on race, colour or ethnic origin, especially in the fields of civil rights, access to citizenship, education, religion, employment, occupation and housing," and it decried all practices of racial segregation. In 1965 the General Assembly adopted the Declaration on the Promotion among Youth of the Ideals of Peace, Mutual Respect and Understanding between Peoples.[9]

Two declarations were adopted in 1967, one on Territorial Asylum and the other on the Elimination of Discrimination against Women.[10] The first article of the latter declaration proclaimed:

Discrimination against women, denying or limiting as it does their equality of rights with men, is fundamentally unjust and constitutes an offense against human dignity.

Later articles condemned particular widely prevalent discriminatory practices and called for specific legislative action to insure women's equal rights with men. The declaration was an early and important step in the worldwide women's movement that gained much greater strength in the 1970s. Two years later, in 1969, the General Assembly adopted a very broad Declaration on Social Progress and Development.[11] In 1975 it adopted a Declaration on the Rights of Disabled Persons and a Declaration on the Protection of All Persons from being subjected to Torture and Other Cruel, Inhuman or Degrading Treatment or Punishment.[12] In 1981, after almost two decades of work, the General Assembly adopted the Declaration on the Elimination of All Forms of Intolerance and of Discrimination Based on Religion or Belief.[13] Several of these declarations repeated and elaborated sections of the Universal Declaration of Human Rights.

Resolutions: Making Specific Recommendations and Judgments

The adoption of resolutions is another type of normative activity. Although the legal instrument for adopting a resolution is the same as is involved in adopting a declaration, resolutions that do not contain formal declarations are less significant pronouncements and tend to be taken less seriously.

The U.N. General Assembly adopts several resolutions dealing with social welfare and human rights each year. Some of these concern particular topics, such as the treatment of migrant workers. In this instance, the thirtieth session, in 1975, appealed to governments to remind their administrative agencies of the obligation to respect the human rights of migrant workers.[14] Other resolutions deal with particular countries; for instance, the thirtieth session expressed its distress at the violation of human rights by the militiary government in Chile and called upon the Chilean government to cease certain practices and to respect human rights and fundamental freedoms.[15]

In the 1970s and early 1980s the General Assembly regularly condemned Israel for the policies that it pursued in the territories it occupied as a consequence of the 1967 war.[16] Similar resolutions have been adopted by the conferences of UNESCO and ILO. In the 1970s these conferences devoted so much time to resolutions dealing with the Arab-Israeli conflict and other disputes that several Western states became disenchanted with the organizations, and this was one of the factors behind the United States' decision to withdraw from ILO.

By far the largest number of normative resolutions adopted by the General Assembly in the fields of social welfare and human rights in the years since the Group of 77 states attained a two-thirds majority have dealt with racial discrimination, continued colonialism, apartheid, and, broadly, the situation in southern Africa.

International nongovernmental organizations also often adopt resolutions condemning particular situations and countries. The International Commission of Jurists regularly issues judgments after conducting investigations, and Amnesty International issues pronouncements about specific countries. The trade union internationals—the World Federation of Trade Unions, the International Confederation of Free Trade Unions, and the World Confederation of Labor—frequently take clear stands, especially when they feel that rights of affiliated trade unions and their members have been violated.

International organizations have also adopted more technical recommendations. WHO, UNESCO, ILO, the Organization of American States, and the Committee of Ministers of the Council of Europe all do this regularly, as do other international institutions. Even though these might involve the same broad topics as the resolutions mentioned in the preceding paragraphs, the treatment here is considerably more specific. The Committee of Ministers of the Council of Europe has adopted recommendations outlining several specific actions that should be taken with respect to migrant workers. In this instance, the organization includes as members almost all of the host and home countries of migrant workers in Western Europe; therefore the governments with a direct interest in the problem have been involved in drafting the recommendations. Given the composition of the Committee of Ministers, foreign ministers or their designates, the Western European governments are in effect agreeing to tell themselves what action to take. A different procedure is involved in WHO, where groups of experts prepare reports that contain recommended ways of treating particular diseases or public health problems. These too are taken very seriously, not because of the official position of the authors but rather because of their reputation for technical expertise.

RULE-CREATING ACTIVITIES

Since the central issue with respect to social welfare and human rights is the behavior of governments, rule-creating activities, that is, the preparation of international conventions that can establish legally binding obligations on governments, have assumed an extremely important role in the activities of international organizations in this field. Almost by definition, rule-creating activities are peculiarly the province of international governmental organizations, particularly in this field, where the goal is to establish obligatory standards for the conduct of governments. The role of international nongovernmental organizations has been mainly to raise issues and to prompt governments and IGOs to act.

Over the years many international conventions have been prepared within the framework of IGOs. The process of adopting a convention can take several years. The first step may be the preparation of a draft by the secretariat, or it may be the circulation by the secretariat of a questionnaire to governments to determine what existing practices are. Initial drafts are considered by committees and ad hoc groups and sometimes are referred to governments for their comments. Finally, the convention can be "adopted" by the international organization, which is to say that the organization endorses the convention and recommends it to governments for signature and ratification. Conventions come into force only when a certain number of governments (always specified in the text) have ratified them. The number varies depending on the subject matter, and if the adhesion of particular states is essential to implementation of the convention, this too can be specified as a condition for the convention's taking effect.

When states ratify conventions, they are legally bound to implement their provisions. However, if they fail to observe this obligation, the sanction is somewhat problematic. Usually states which do not comply with a convention they have ratified lose whatever privileges they may have gained under the convention, but in the fields of social welfare and human rights, conventions confer many obligations but few privileges. A convention could allow the other signatory states to impose sanctions against a state that was not fulfilling its obligations, but states are not strongly inclined to take actions that could be costly to protect the inhabitants of another country against the actions of their government. Thus in many instances the most substantial sanction for noncompliance with the terms of a convention is adverse publicity.

The difficulty of enforcing compliance affects the attitudes of states as they draft conventions, but not in uniform ways. Some states react to the situation by agreeing to provisions that they cannot implement; others have a tendency to be very cautious and to try to restrict provisions to those for which there is a clear consensus and a high probability of implementation.

The International Labor Code

Although the convention is a legal instrument of long standing, it first gained extensive use as a means of promoting social welfare and human rights with the creation of the International Labor Organization in 1919. ILO was created explicitly for the purpose of adopting international labor conventions, and six were adopted at ILO's first conference, in 1919. Each annual conference of ILO during the interwar period adopted additional conventions, so that on the eve of World War II, in 1939, the International Labor Code consisted of sixty-seven conventions. The code covered many aspects of working conditions, and the conventions were, by and large, relatively technical and specific, although one, Number 29, outlawed forced labor. A few other conventions were adopted by the League of Nations during this period, but these were confined to the control of drugs, the abolition of the slave trade, and the suppression of traffic in women and children.

What happened after World War II was vastly different. There was much more concern with the issues of human dignity and justice, and a much broader approach was taken. ILO continued and expanded its activities related to the International Labor Code. From 1946 through 1981 another eighty-nine conventions were adopted, so that as of January 1982 the International Labor Code consisted of 156 conventions. Of these, only eighteen had not received sufficient ratifications for entry into force, and thirty-eight, including eight of those that lacked sufficient ratifications, had been revised by subsequent conventions.

The International Labor Code covers virtually all aspects of working conditions. In addition, several conventions deal with special groups of workers, such as women, children, fishermen, seafarers, and those engaged in agriculture and commerce. A limited number of conventions deal with broad civil rights, and all but one of these were adopted after World War II. Conventions 29 and 105, adopted in 1930 and 1957, concern the abolition of forced labor, and Conventions 87 and 98, adopted in 1948 and 1949, concern the right to organize and collective bargaining. In the 1970s and 1980s, ILO adopted additional instruments, Conventions 135, 141, and 154, extending, refining, and amplifying the broad general principles established in these basic conventions. Convention 100 mandates equal remuneration for equal work; this was adopted in 1951. Seven years later, in 1958, the International Labor Conference adopted Convention 111, which prohibits discrimination in employment and occupations.

The World Federation of Trade Unions and the American Federation of Labor, each of which has consultative status with the Economic and Social Council of the United Nations, were instrumental in prompting ILO to adopt these conventions dealing with broad civil rights. WFTU led off by raising the issue of equal pay for equal work and by demanding that action should be taken to implement this goal. The AFL, which was bitterly opposed to WFTU, viewing it as communist-dominated and a tool of Soviet foreign policy, countered by raising the issues of forced labor and trade union rights. The AFL accused the U.S.S.R. of practicing forced labor and of permitting only government-controlled trade unions. WFTU in turn accused the United States, the United Kingdom, and other states with market economies of not paying equal wages to men and women doing the same jobs. The debates in ECOSOC and ILO were acrimonious, but eventually the relevant conventions were prepared and adopted, and they rank among the more important conventions in the International Labor Code. In 1954 the Soviet Union rejoined ILO, which it had left in 1939 when it was expelled from the League of Nations because of its attack on Finland. A tactic of the United States and others during the bitter debates on these issues had been to have the matters referred to ILO, where they could be debated without Soviet participation. The Soviet reentry into ILO undoubtedly had among its aims blocking the effectiveness of this tactic.

The U.N. Human Rights Covenants

Although ILO's activities since the end of World War II have been broader and more extensive than those that it undertook in the period between the two world wars, the record of the United Nations contrasts even more sharply with that of the League of Nations. The League's activities were confined to preparing conventions that aimed at eliminating certain social abuses by attempting to control their international aspects. From its first days, although the United Nations has continued to deal with these topics, it has also attacked squarely the central problems of human rights, which traditionally had been considered matters of domestic jurisdiction.

The Universal Declaration of Human Rights was regarded as a prelude to the preparation of legally binding instruments, and as soon as the declaration had been adopted, the drafting of human rights convenants began. The process was finally completed in 1966 with the adoption by the General Assembly of the International Covenant on Economic, Social and Cultural Rights, the International Covenant on Civil and Political Rights, and the Optional Protocol to the second covenant.[17]

In response to the Anglo-American argument that only civil and political rights could be defined with sufficient precision to be legally enforceable, at an early stage a decision was taken to prepare two covenants rather than one. Even this did not satisfy American objections. The United States continued to maintain that many of the norms being placed in the covenants—for instance, the right of national self-determination—could not be put in a form so as to constitute enforceable obligations. In addition, there was concern in Congress that U.N. conventions and perhaps even the charter would supersede United States laws. This concern contributed to the pressure for a constitutional amendment limiting executive agreements and restricting the application of conventions. Such an amendment proposed by Senator John Bricker gained substantial support. In opposing this amendment, to mollify those senators who supported it, Secretary of State John Foster Dulles committed the Eisenhower administration not to sign or to seek ratification of the human rights covenants, and from that point on the United States played a very modest role in their preparation.

The first article of each covenant proclaims that "all people have the right of self-determination." The International Covenant on Economic, Social and Cultural Rights includes articles dealing with the right to work and the right to "just and favorable" conditions of work, including equal remuneration, safe and healthy working conditions, equal opportunity for promotion, and provision for rest and leisure. Other articles deal with the right to form and participate in trade unions, the right to social security, the right to special protection for children and mothers, the right to an adequate standard of living, the right to "the highest attainable standard of physical and mental health," the right to education, and the right to take part in cultural life and in the benefits of scientific progress. States that are parties to the covenant are obliged to submit reports on the measures they have taken and the progress they have achieved in implementing the rights recognized in it. The covenant was to take effect when thirty-five states had ratified it, and it came into force on January 3, 1976.

The International Covenant on Civil and Political Rights has articles dealing with all of the traditional civil rights, including the right to life, liberty, and security of person; to fair, public, and speedy trials; to freedom of thought and religion; to freedom of association; to participate directly or indirectly in the conduct of public affairs; and to vote and be elected at periodic free elections conducted by secret ballot and according to universal and equal suffrage. In addition, other articles provide for freedom of movement and freedom to choose one's residence for all persons legally within a territory. The covenant states that "everyone shall be free to leave any country, including his own." Still other articles provide for the right to marry and to found a family and give children the right to acquire a nationality. One article allows members of a minority to enjoy their own culture, to profess and practice their own religion, and to use their own language. The covenant requires that signatory states prohibit propaganda for war and also prohibit advocacy of national, racial, or religious hatred.

Exceptions to some of the rights are allowed when a national emergency is proclaimed. However, any state acting under this provision is required to notify the other states that are parties to the covenant through the secretary-general of the U.N. of the derogations and of the reasons for them.

The covenant provides for the establishment of a Human Rights Committee, which is empowered to consider reports by signatory states on the measures that they have taken to implement the provisions of the covenant. In addition, signatory states can declare that the committee may receive and consider communications from one signatory state that another is not fulfilling its obligations under the treaty. This procedure came into effect in 1978 when ten states parties to the treaty had made such a declaration. As of July 1, 1982, fourteen states had made the declaration. If states ratify or accede to the Optional Protocol to the treaty, they allow the Human Rights Committee to consider communications from individuals under their jurisdiction claiming to be victims of violations of the provisions of the covenant. Ratification by ten states was also required for the Optional Protocol to come into effect. The covenant itself came into force on March 23, 1976, three months after thirty-five states had deposited instruments of ratification or accession with the secretary-general of the U.N. The Optional Protocol came into force at the same time, thirteen states having ratified it, three more than the protocol specified as being necessary.

In 1977, in an address before the U.N. General Assembly, President Jimmy Carter reversed the long-standing U.S. official attitude and policy and announced that his administration would seek the advice and consent of the Senate in the ratification of the two covenants. As of 1983, the Senate had not acted.

Conventions against Discrimination and for Equality

The United Nations has also adopted conventions dealing with more limited topics. Several of these have been concerned with eliminating discrimination and promoting equality.

In 1965 the General Assembly adopted the International Convention on the Elimination of All Forms of Racial Discrimination. In ratifying the treaty states "condemn racial discrimination and undertake to pursue by all appropriate means and without delay a policy of eliminating racial discrimination in all its forms and promoting understanding among all races."[18] States that are parties to the convention agree not to engage in acts of racial discrimination and to prohibit and bring to an end racial discrimination by any person, group, or organization. The convention contains a long list of civil, economic, and social rights and freedoms in the enjoyment of which racial discrimination shall be prohibited. Signatory states are also enjoined to undertake positive steps to combat prejudices which lead to racial discrimination. The convention established a Committee on the Elimination of Racial Discrimination, which considers reports from the states parties to the treaty on the measures that they have taken to give effect to its provisions. It also can receive complaints from states that are parties that a signatory state has not given effect to the provisions of the convention. Should this occur, an ad hoc conciliation commission must be appointed to investigate the matter and report its findings to the committee. The convention entered into force on January 4, 1969, and as of July 1, 1982, 115 states had ratified or acceded to it and another 9, including the United States, had signed but not yet ratified it. South Africa has neither signed nor ratified the convention.

Given the voluntary character of the rule-making activities of IGOs, the rules often cannot be made to apply to the states most likely to break them. Few of the states most likely to wish to develop nuclear weapons have ratified the nonproliferation treaty, and the case with respect to South Africa and racial discrimination is similar. The U.N. convention, along with ILO's convention against discrimination in employment and occupation[19] and UNESCO's convention against discrimination in education,[20] constitute a comprehensive commitment to eliminate discrimination. In addition, in 1973 the General Assembly adopted the International Convention on the Suppression and Punishment of the Crime of Apartheid.[21] In the 1950s the United Nations also brought up to date previous conventions concerning the abolition of slavery and the slave trade.[22] South Africa has ratified all of the antislavery conventions, but none of the others.

Sexual discrimination is perhaps even more widespread than racial discrimination, and the United Nations has adopted several conventions aimed at eliminating sexual discrimination. In 1952 the General Assembly adopted the Convention on the Political Rights of Women.[23] Five years later, it adopted the Convention on the Nationality of Married Women,[24] and in 1962 it adopted the Convention on Consent to Marriage, Minimum Age for Marriage and Registration of Marriages.[25] These conventions came into effect in 1954, 1958, and 1964, and as of July 1, 1982, they had been ratified by ninety, fifty-four, and thirty-one states, respectively. The United States has ratified the Convention on the Political Rights of Women and signed but not yet ratified the Convention on Consent to Marriage. ILO's convention on equal remuneration is important in this area, as are ILO's and UNESCO's conventions on the elimination of discrimination, both of which cover sexual as well as racial discrimination. In 1949 the General Assembly adopted the Convention for the Suppression of the Traffic in Persons and of the Exploitation of the Prostitution of Others,[26] which revised and updated the convention on the same subject that had been adopted during the League period.

The U.N. Decade for Women, which was launched in 1975 with the Mexico City Conference, was intended to accelerate the pace of achieving equality for women. The major achievement of the first half of the decade was the adaptation by the General Assembly in 1979 of the Convention on the Elimination of All Forms of Discrimination Against Women.[27] This convention, which came into force in September 1981, enumerates the basic principles for achieving equal rights for women throughout the world. As of July 1, 1982, it had been ratified by thirty-nine states. Another fifty-one states, including the United States, had signed the convention but had not yet ratified it.

States ratifying the convention on the Elimination of All Forms of Discrimination Against Women commit themselves to take all appropriate measures to eliminate discrimination against the full participation of women in the political and public life of the country. Specifically, they agree to ensure, on equal terms with men, the right of women to vote, to participate in the formulation and implementation of public policy and to hold public office, and to participate in the nongovernmental organizations concerned with the public life of the country. Ratifying states also agree that women shall have equal rights with men to acquire, change, and retain their nationality. They agree to take appropriate measures to eliminate discrimination against women in the fields of education and employment. They pledge that discrimination against women in the field of health care shall be ended, and that women shall have equal access to health care facilities, "including those related to family planning" (Article 12).

Women are to be accorded equality before the law. Special attention is to be given to the particular problems faced by rural women. Women are to have full equality in matters related to marriage and family relations. These and other provisions provide a comprehensive blueprint for achieving equality between women and men.

Other U.N. Conventions

Several of the conventions that the United Nations has adopted stem in one way or another from the world wars. Determined to do everything possible to prevent a recurrence of anything like the outrageous conduct of the Nazi regime toward the Jews and others, in 1948 the General Assembly adopted the Convention on the Prevention and Punishment of the Crime of Genocide.[28] Genocide is defined as "acts committed with intent to destroy, in whole or in part, a national, ethnical, racial, or religious group, as such,"[29] and constitutionally responsible rulers, public officials, and private individuals are all subject to punishment for the crime. Punishment is to be provided for in national legislation, and in addition contracting parties may call upon any U.N. organ to take whatever action might be appropriate. The convention was in part a post-hoc justification for aspects of the international trial of war criminals at Nuremberg, but it was also a commitment for the future. Since 1948 there has been a clear legal basis for prosecuting public officials and others who engage in genocide.

In response to another war-related problem, the United Nations prepared a Convention relating to the Status of Refugees in 1951,[30] a Convention on the Status of Stateless Persons in 1954,[31] and a Convention on the Reduction of Statelessness in 1961.[32] The general principle underlying these treaties is that refugees and stateless persons should, insofar as possible, receive equal treatment with citizens and that in any case there should be no discrimination among refugees and stateless persons. In 1967 a protocol to the Convention relating to the Status of Refugees broadened the concept of refugees to include persons who found themselves in that status as a result of post-1951 events; in effect, it gave the U.N. High Commissioner for Refugees a continuing mandate.[33] Finally, in 1968 the General Assembly adopted a Convention on the Non-Applicability of Statutory Limitations to War Crimes and Crimes against Humanity.[34]

The United Nations has also continued the work that was started by the League of Nations with respect to the control of narcotic drugs. The most significant step of a legal nature taken by the U.N. was the consolidation of previous treaties on this matter and extension of the coverage they provided through the adoption of the Single Convention on Narcotic Drugs,[35] which was opened for signature in 1961 and came into effect in 1964. In addition, in an attempt to deal with substances not covered by the Single Convention, the United Nations adopted the Convention on Psychotropic Substances in 1971.[36]

In the mid-1970s in the wake of various terrorist attacks, the United Nations started work on drafting a convention on international cooperation to prevent the taking of hostages. Progress was slow. Individuals who were terrorists in the minds of some were national liberation fighters in the minds of others. In 1979, however, in the midst of the crisis caused by the Iranian seizure of the U.S. embassy in Tehran, the assembly adopted the International Convention against the Taking of Hostages.[37] Conventions to prevent the hijacking of aircraft were negotiated within the framework of the International Civil Aviation Organization, and the U.N. General Assembly urged states to ratify these conventions.

Finally, the United Nations has attempted to prepare conventions dealing with freedom of information, but this effort has been mired in a controversy between the United States, which supports almost total freedom of the press, and the Soviet Union and the majority of states in Africa, Asia, and South America, which favor strict control over the press. The only treaty to result from this effort is the Convention on the International Right of Correction,[38] which was adopted in 1952 and entered into force in 1962. As of July 1, 1982, only eleven states had ratified this convention.

Starting in the late 1970s, several less developed countries, joined by the communist countries, issued a call for a New World Information and Communication Order (NWICO). The call was motivated by the LDCs' perception that Western-based news agencies (United Press International, the Associated Press,

Reuters, and Agence France-Press) dominated the transmission of news across international borders and the LDC's disagreement with the way that their societies were portrayed in the Western media. Early NWICO proposals involved preparing codes with respect to the position of journalists and the role of the media. Western states saw these proposals as direct attacks on freedom of information and opposed them forcefully.

Ratification of Human Rights Conventions

The several important human rights conventions that the United Nations, ILO, and UNESCO have adopted are listed in Table 14.1. The conventions are grouped under major headings. The table includes the year that the conventions were adopted, the year that they entered into force, and the number of states that had deposited instruments of ratification, accession, or acceptance (the difference relates to the internal constitutional processes of the states and to the timing of the action in relation to the adoption of the convention; the legal effect of the action is the same) as of July 1, 1982.

Table 14.1 clearly shows that the greatest effort has gone toward establishing and protecting the norm of human equality. The conventions on discrimination, women's rights, and slavery all relate to this norm. More states have ratified the ensemble of conventions outlawing discrimination than any other convention, except the ILO convention outlawing forced labor, which has also received more than one hundred ratifications. Freedom of information is the area where the least progress has been made. Indeed, some journalists would even regard the one convention that has been adopted as a retrogressive step.

Most of the conventions entered into force within two or three years after they were completed, but the International Covenants on Civil and Political Rights and on Economic, Social and Cultural Rights and the Convention on the International Right of Correction did not come into effect for a decade after they were completed, and the time lapse before the Convention on the Reduction of Statelessness came into effect was fourteen years. The last convention contains important obligations concerning the way states give nationality, and the obligations in the two basic human rights covenants are very broad. These conventions impinge on sovereignty beyond the obligation to eliminate discrimination or to outlaw some specific practice such as forced labor.

The propensity of states to ratify human rights conventions varies significantly. Table 14.2 (p. 330) shows how many of eleven important human rights conventions of the U.N. and ILO the ten states that have contributed the most to the U.N.'s budget over the years have ratified. The United States has argued that many of the matters covered in the conventions are determined by the separate states under its federal system, and thus it would be inappropriate for it to ratify certain conventions. It has also maintained that its standards are generally above those specified in international conventions. Table 14.2 would seem to indicate that international conventions as instruments for achieving human dignity and justice are most congenial to Western European states as a group.

TABLE 14.1
Human Rights Conventions of the United Nations, ILO, and UNESCO

Type and Title of Convention and Year Opened for Ratification	Number of Ratifications, Accessions, or Acceptances (1982)	Year of Entry into Force
Basic Human Rights		
International Convenant on Civil and Political Rights, 1966	70	1976
Optional Protocol to the International Covenant on Civil and Political Rights, 1966	27	1976
International Covenant on Economic, Social and Cultural Rights, 1966	73	1976
Prevention of Discrimination		
International Convention on the Elimination of All Forms of Racial Discrimination, 1965	115	1969
International Convention on the Suppression and Punishment of the Crime of Apartheid, 1973	67	1976
ILO Equal Remuneration Convention, 1951	100	1953
ILO Discrimination (Employment and Occupation) Convention, 1958	101	1960
UNESCO Convention against Discrimination in Education, 1960	69	1962
Women's Rights		
Convention on the Political Rights of Women, 1952	90	1954
Convention on the Nationality of Married Women, 1957	54	1958
Convention on Consent to Marriage, Minimum Age for Marriage and Registration of Marriages, 1962	31	1964
Convention on the Elimination of All Forms of Discrimination against Women, 1979	39	1981
Slavery, Servitude, Forced Labor, and		
Similar Institutions and Practices		
Slavery Convention, 1926 as amended in 1953	77	1955
Protocol Amending the Slavery Convention, 1953	46	1955
Supplementary Convention on the Abolition of Slavery, the Slave Trade, and Institutions and Practices Similar to Slavery, 1956	96	1957
Convention for the Suppression of the Traffic in Persons and of the Exploitation of the Prostitution of Others, 1949	53	1951
ILO Abolition of Forced Labor Convention, 1957	107	1959

TABLE 14.1 *Continued*
Human Rights Conventions of the United Nations, ILO, and UNESCO

Type and Title of Convention and Year Opened for Ratification	Number of Ratifications, Accessions, or Acceptances (1982)	Year of Entry into Force
War Crimes and Crimes Against Humanity,		
Including Genocide		
Convention on the Prevention and Punishment of the Crime of Genocide, 1948	89	1951
Convention on the Non-Applicability of Statutory Limitations to War Crimes and Crimes against Humanity, 1968	23	1970
Nationality, Statelessness, Asylum, and		
Refugees		
Convention on the Reduction of Statelessness, 1961	10	1975
Convention relating to the Status of Stateless Persons, 1954	32	1960
Convention relating to the Status of Refugees, 1951	90	1954
Protocol relating to the Status of Refugees, 1966	89	1967
Freedom of Information		
Convention on the International Right of Correction, 1952	11	1962

*For U.N. conventions the figure is the number of ratifications, accessions, or acceptances as of July 1, 1982; for ILO conventions, January 1, 1982, and for UNESCO conventions, January 1, 1981.

Sources: U.N. conventions: U.N. Document ST/HR/4/Rev. 4, "Human Rights International Instruments: Signatures, Ratifications, Accessions, etc., 1 July 1982"; ILO conventions: ILO, *International Labor Conventions Chart of Ratifications, January 1982*; UNESCO conventions; UNESCO, Circular Letter/2773.

Regional Human Rights Conventions

The efforts to promote human dignity and justice through the adoption of conventions in universal membership IGOs have been supplemented by similar actions within regional organizations. In 1950 the Council of Europe adopted the European Convention on Human Rights,[39] and this convention entered into force in 1953, a time-lag notably shorter than occurred with respect to the U.N.'s international covenants. By 1974 the European Convention had been ratified by all eighteen members of the Council of Europe: Austria, Belgium, Cyprus, Denmark, France, Federal Republic of Germany, Greece, Iceland, Ireland, Italy, Luxembourg, Malta, Netherlands, Norway, Sweden, Switzerland, Turkey, and the United Kingdom. Portugal ratified the convention in 1976 after it became a member of the Council of Europe. Spain ratified the convention in 1979. The Euro-

TABLE 14.2

The Propensity of Major Contributor States to Ratify Human Rights Conventions of the U.N. and ILO

(Ratifications Registered as of July 1, 1982)

State	Convention 1	2	3	4	5	6	7	8	9	10	11	Total Ratified	Percentage Ratified
Canada	X	X	X	X	X	X	X	X	X	X	X	11	100
China, People's Republic of				X			X					2	18
France	X		X	X	X		S	X	X	X	X	8	73
Germany, Federal Republic of	X		X	X	X	X	X	X	X	X	X	10	91
India	X		X	X	X	S	S	X	X			6	55
Italy	X	X	X	X	X		S	X	X	X	X	9	82
Japan	X		X		X		S					3	27
U.S.S.R.	X		X	X	X	X	X	X	X			8	73
United Kingdom	X		X	X	X	X	S	X	X	X	X	9	82
United States	S		S	S	X		S		X			2	18
Total	8	2	8	8	9	4	4	7	8	5	5		

X Ratification, accession, notification of succession, acceptance or definitive signature
S Signature not yet followed by ratification

Conventions:

1. International Covenant on Civil and Political Rights, 1966.
2. Optional Protocol to the International Covenant on Civil and Political Rights, 1966.
3. International Covenant on Economic, Social and Cultural Rights, 1966.
4. International Convention on the Elimination of All Forms of Racial Discrimination, 1965.
5. Convention on the Political Rights of Women, 1952.
6. Convention on the Nationality of Married Women, 1957.
7. Convention on the Elimination of All Forms of Discrimination against Women.
8. Convention on the Prevention and Punishment of the Crime of Genocide, 1948.
9. Supplementary Convention on the Abolition of Slavery, the Slave Trade, and Institutions and Practices Similar to Slavery, 1956.
10. ILO Abolition of Forced Labor Convention, 1957.
11. Convention relating to the Status of Refugees, 1951.

Sources: U.N. Document ST/HR/4/Rev. 4, "Human Rights International Instruments: Signatures, Ratifications, Accessions, etc., 1 July 1982"; and ILO, *International Labor Conventions, Chart of Ratifications, January 1, 1982.*

pean Convention on Human Rights provides comprehensive coverage of the traditional civil and political rights. Eleven years after its adoption, in 1961 the Council of Europe adopted the European Social Charter, which covers many of the rights that are included in the International Covenant on Economic, Social and Cultural Rights and some others as well, for instance, relating to migrant workers.[40] The mechanism for enforcement of the European Social Charter, like that of the U.N. covenant, is periodic reporting.

The European Convention on Human Rights, however, provided for the creation of a European Commission on Human Rights and a European Court of Human Rights. Under the terms of the convention the states that are parties may declare that the commission may receive petitions from individuals or groups claiming to be victims of violations of the treaty. By January 1980 all twenty Council of Europe member states that had ratified the convention had accepted this procedure except Cyprus, France, Greece, Malta, Spain, and Turkey. After receiving a petition, the commission then considers the situation and tries to reach a satisfactory adjustment. If this fails, and if the respondent state has accepted its jurisdiction, the commission or a state that is party may take the matter before the European Court of Human Rights. These parties may take a matter before the court even if there has not been a previous individual petition. Decisions of the court are binding, and the court may order redress. All twenty Council of Europe member states that had ratified the convention except Malta and Turkey had accepted the compulsory jurisdiction of the European Court by January 1980.

In 1948 the Organization of American States adopted the Inter-American Conventions on Granting Political and Civil Rights to Women,[41] and in 1969 it adopted the American Convention on Human Rights.[42] This latter convention contains several rights not included in the European Convention, for instance, concerning the right to legal personality and limiting capital punishment. States parties to the convention have no choice about accepting the right of the Inter-American Commisson on Human Rights to accept petitions from individuals alleging violations; their consent is necessary, however, for the Inter-American Court of Human Rights to gain jurisdiction. The Inter-American Commission on Human Rights was created in 1959 and has functioned since 1960. It acts as a mediatory body, using its power to issue reports as a potential sanction to induce compliance. In 1977 President Carter announced that his administration would seek ratification of this convention, and he urged other OAS members to ratify it. In July 1978 the convention finally received sufficient ratifications to come into force. As of July 1982, sixteen states had ratified the convention.

Finally, the Final Act of the Conference on Security and Cooperation in Europe, signed in August 1975 in Helsinki, Finland, included a broad section on human rights. This involved a new departure for the thirty-five states attending the conference, which included the members of both NATO and WTO as well as several European states that did not belong to either alliance. The rights involved were those particularly important in the perspective of the division of Europe, such as access to information and the right to travel. The conference held its follow-up meeting in 1977–1978; the second follow-up meeting began in November 1980 and finally completed its work in summer 1983. The follow-up meetings appeared to be moving in the direction of institutionalization, and discussions of the implementation of the human rights provisions of the Final Act apparently would become a regular feature of these periodic meetings.

These, then, are the legally binding obligations that international governmental organizations have established concerning social welfare and human rights. Let us turn to see how these obligations are supervised.

RULE-SUPERVISORY ACTIVITIES

The constitutions of some international governmental organizations and many of the rules created within IGOs have made explicit provision for the creation of rule-supervisory mechanisms. Chapter 13 of the United Nations charter, which details the composition, functions, and procedures of the Trusteeship Council, and sections 2, 3, and 4 of the European Convention on Human Rights, which provide for the European Commission on Human Rights and the European Court of Human Rights, are examples.

International governmental organizations have gone considerably beyond such explicit provisions. Standing organs and particularly the General Assembly of the United Nations have taken it upon themselves to exercise rule-supervisory functions, and they have created temporary and permanent bodies for this purpose. INGOs have entered the picture as complainants, often raising issues that governments would avoid, and INGOs such as Amnesty International and the International Commission of Jurists, as we have noted, have also been willing to issue clear judgments about violations. Both IGOs and INGOs have, furthermore, sought to exercise a substantial measure of supervision over norms concerning social welfare and human rights that have been pronounced as declarations and that they believe should be general rules of conduct, regardless of the fact that they have not been embodied in legally binding instruments.

Colonial Issues

This tendency to blur the distinction between the supervision of rules and of norms has been most pronounced on the part of IGOs with respect to colonial issues. This area is also an appropriate starting place for an analysis because it is the one in which the capacity of universal institutions for rule supervision has been most developed. Under the U.N. charter the Trusteeship Council was given extensive powers with respect to those territories placed within the trusteeship system. Governments of metropolitan countries responsible for trust territories were required to submit periodic reports responding to a questionnaire formulated by the Trusteeship Council concerning conditions in the territories. In addition, the U.N. could receive petitions from individuals in the trust territories, and the council could send visiting missions to them to examine conditions on the scene.

The General Assembly has constantly sought to create the same type of regime for dependent territories that were not placed within the trusteeship system. First, it created a Committee on Information from Non–Self-Governing Territories to consider the reports that metropolitan countries were required to submit under Article 73e of the charter. After the adoption of Resolution 1514 (XV), the Declaration on the Granting of Independence to Colonial Countries and Peoples, the General Assembly created a special committee to oversee implementation of the declaration, and this committee eventually replaced the Committee on Information. The General Assembly sought to endow both the Committee on Information and the Special Committee on the Implementation of Resolution 1514 (XV) with the same authority to require reports, receive petitions, and dispatch visiting missions that the charter gave to the Trusteeship Council.

The results have been mixed. On the one hand, the metropolitan countries responsible for trust territories have fully complied with the authority given to the Trusteeship Council under the charter, and they have generally sought to be responsive to the council's recommendations. The Union of South Africa, however, which under the mandates system was given responsibility for South-West Africa, refused to place the territory within the trusteeship system, and it has persistently defied the myriad efforts of the United Nations to establish a measure of supervision over its rule of the territory. Eventually, in 1966, the General Assembly declared that South Africa had failed to fulfill its obligations under the League mandate and that henceforth South-West Africa would be administered directly by the United Nations.[43]

South Africa refused to withdraw from the territory, which the General Assembly proclaimed in 1968 should be known as Namibia, and until the late 1970s it defied all actions by U.N. organs, including the Security Council, to establish the U.N.'s authority over the territory. The United Nations declared the national liberation movement, the South-West Africa People's Organization, to be the authentic representative of the Namibian people and called upon states to sever economic relations with South Africa that concern Namibia. It specifically sought to forestall and discourage the exploitation of uranium in Namibia, claiming that this can legitimately be done only with the consent of the people. It set up a fund for Namibia and sought to provide training for refugees from the territory. These actions had little effect on South Africa and only slight effect on countries and companies doing business with Namibia through South Africa. However, in the late 1970s South Africa moved toward granting Namibia independence. In July 1978, the Security Council approved a plan for bringing Namibia to independence, but South Africa refused the U.N.'s plan. Negotiations to bring Namibia to independence continued into the 1980s.

Eventually, Australia, New Zealand, Portugal, and the United Kingdom gave the Special Committee on the Implementation of Resolution 1514 (XV) the same measure of cooperation that they had accorded the Trusteeship Council; they submitted reports, allowed petitions, and permitted visiting missions in their non–self-governing territories. France, South Africa, Spain, and the United States have refused to permit visiting missions, though all but South Africa have submitted reports and all have been incapable of preventing the U.N. from receiving petitions. Portugal's consent to visiting missions came only after the Portuguese revolution in 1974; the previous regime had been very uncooperative. Because they concluded that the Special Committee was unable to approach issues objectively, the governments of several countries, including the United States, have refused to be members of the committee.

Southern Rhodesia was not one of the territories concerning which the United Kingdom submitted information to the U.N. under the terms of Article 73e of the charter, but the General Assembly declared Resolution 1514 (XV) to be applicable to the territory, and the Special Committee on the Implementation of Resolution 1514 (XV) included Southern Rhodesia within its cognizance. The committee's goal was a regime that would adequately represent the territory's 5 million Africans. The committee initially sought to have the United Kingdom, as the administering authority, repeal the 1961 constitution which excluded most blacks from political participation and reserved power to the roughly 600,000 white residents. Not only did this not happen, in November 1965 the minority government of Southern Rhodesia unilaterally declared its independence from the United Kingdom. The U.N. condemned this action, and in 1966 the Security Council imposed economic sanctions against Southern Rhodesia, which after 1968 the U.N. referred to as Zimbabwe, the African name for the territory.

The sanctions had some effect on Zimbabwe, even though not all states complied with the Security Council decisions. As noted in Chapter 8, in 1971 the United States Congress enacted a law, the so-called Byrd amendment, mandating the continued importation of chrome from Zimbabwe, which was not repealed until 1977. Despite the external pressure, the minority government in Zimbabwe gave little evidence of willingness to make significant compromises until 1977, when it began to attempt serious negotiations about a transfer of power. In 1978 an internal settlement was achieved, but nationalist guerrilla forces and the U.N. refused to accept this settlement. Agreement for the independence of Zimbabwe was finally achieved in 1979.

As one shifts from colonial to broader issues, the techniques and procedures of rule-supervisory activities change only slightly. In very few other instances, however, have governments given as extensive authority to international institutions.

Narcotics Control

Social defense would seem to be an area in which governments would have common interests and in which there would be strong incentives toward international cooperation. To a large extent this has been true. The 1961 Convention on Narcotic Drugs created the International Narcotics Control Board, a body consisting of eleven experts elected by the U.N. Economic and Social Council to serve in their personal capacity. The function of the board is to oversee governmental monitoring of the production and distribution of narcotic drugs so as to limit their use to medical and scientific purposes. The board receives and scrutinizes reports from governments. Keeping track of the licit trade in narcotic drugs helps to identify the sources of the illicit trade, and it contributes to the effectiveness of national systems of control. The board estimates that it receives approximately 90 percent of the data that it should receive, were all governments completely fulfilling their obligations.

The Narcotics Control Board can make visits to individual countries, and it can direct recommendations at particular governments. Thus its principal sanction is publicity. In its public pronouncements the board is generally more inclined to praise governments for the measures they have taken and their successes in establishing and maintaining control than it is to criticize them.

Labor Issues

The regime established by the International Labor Organization to verify compliance with international labor conventions predates even the bodies which preceded the International Narcotics Control Board. Governments are required to report on the measures they have taken to give effect to the conventions they have ratified. These reports are examined by a specially appointed Committee of Experts, which then reports to a committee of the International Labor Conference. The Committee of Experts makes "observations" on the governmental reports, which vary from mild to serious reprobations to the governments concerned. States that are repeatedly unresponsive to the committee's suggestions are called to the attention of the Conference Committee, and this may result in their being put on a list of particularly "uncooperative" states. The Committee of Experts estimates that it receives about 90 percent of the reports that it should receive. The committee attempts to keep track of the changes made in national legislation and practice in response to its observations.

In addition to this regular procedure, ILO has adopted a special procedure for two conventions, the Convention Concerning Freedom of Association and Protection of the Right to Organize (No. 87, 1948) and the Right to Organize and Collective Bargaining Convention (No. 98, 1949). In 1950 the U.N. Economic and Social Council established a Fact-Finding and Conciliation Commission which was to settle disputes over implementation of these two conventions. However, it could only assume jurisdiction over a case if a government expressly agreed. ILO's governing body then created a tripartite organ, the Committee on Freedom of Association, to investigate complaints to determine whether or not they should be referred to the Fact-Finding and Conciliation Commission. The ILO committee will consider complaints only from national and international nongovernmental organizations of workers and employers.

The International Confederation of Free Trade Unions, the World Confederation of Labor, and the World Federation of Trade Unions have all been active in filing complaints, as have national trade unions. From 1951 through 1982 the Committee on Freedom of Association received complaints concerning more than 1,000 cases. The committee can dismiss cases; it can make recommendations that the government concerned review certain practices; or it can take more severe steps, such as recommending that the matter be referred to the Fact-Finding and Conciliation Commission—in effect, a finding of guilty. Hardly any cases have gone before the Fact-Finding and Conciliation Commission. Most cases end in conclusions drawing the attention of the government concerned to infringements of particular principles embodied in the conventions.

Other Human Rights Issues

The United Nations' rule-supervisory activities with respect to human rights are varied. Special bodies have been created as a consequence of conventions that have come into effect, and in addition the U.N.'s regular organs have acted to induce states to comply with broad norms articulated in the charter as well as in declarations and conventions.

Several conventions require that states parties to them submit reports to the U.N. on the laws and regulations that they adopt to implement the convention concerned. Certain conventions have gone further. The International Convention on the Elimination of All Forms of Racial Discrimination provided for a special body that was created in 1969, the Committee on the Elimination of Racial Discrimination, which has the responsibility to receive and consider reports on legislative, administrative, judicial, or other measures that states parties to the convention have taken to give effect to its provisions. The committee may consider complaints from states that are parties to the convention against other states parties, and if and when ten states accept the option, it may also receive complaints from individuals in those states.

The Committee on the Elimination of Racial Discrimination is composed, in principle, of experts elected for their personal capacities by the states parties to the convention. Nevertheless, it is estimated that at least half of the individuals who have been members have concurrently held positions in their country's foreign service.[44] Perhaps for this reason, the committee has been reticent to pose awkward questions. Still, its work in reviewing reports has undoubtedly resulted in reforms in laws and practices of states parties. As of 1982 no interstate proceedings had been brought before the committee.

After the International Covenant on Civil and Political Rights came into effect, a similar committee was established to receive and consider the reports required under the treaty and to consider interstate complaints. The Economic and Social Council is responsible for considering the reports that are required under the International Covenant on Economic, Social and Cultural Rights. States party to the convention on the Elimination of All Forms of Discrimination Against Women submit reports to a committee of twenty-three experts established under the terms of the convention, the Committee of the Elimination of Discrimination Against Women.

As soon as the United Nations was created, it began to receive communications from individuals and groups containing complaints that states were violating human rights. In 1947 the Economic and Social Council ratified a decision of the Commission on Human Rights to the effect that the commission had no power to take any action in regard to any such complaints concerning human rights,[45] and by extension all other organs were similarly debarred from considering them. There has always been pressure, however, for the United Nations to do something about these communications, and gradually procedures were evolved for dealing with them. In 1959 the secretary-general was authorized to compile two lists of the communications: a public list that would indicate the human rights principles involved, and a confidential list for the Commission on Human Rights that would contain a brief indication of the substance of each communication and would not be confined to principles. In addition, the members of the commission may examine the original communications.[46]

The procedure was further liberalized in 1970 when the Economic and Social Council authorized the Subcommission on the Prevention of Discrimination and Protection of Minorities to appoint a working group of five to consider all communications received, including replies from the governments concerned, with a view to bringing those communications which appeared to "reveal a consistent pattern of gross and reliably attested violations of human rights and fundamental freedoms"[47] to the attention of the subcommission. The subcommission then must determine whether such communications should be brought to the attention of the Commission on Human Rights. If the communications are referred to the Commisson on Human Rights, it may appoint an ad hoc committee to investigate the situation. Such an investigation, however, can be undertaken only with the consent of the state concerned. Starting in 1978, the Commission disclosed the names of the countries whose human rights problems it had considered in closed session. The procedure is cumbersome and its effectiveness is far from established, yet it represents a milestone in giving individuals throughout the world access to international institutions to complain about their governments in the absence of a specific legal commitment providing for this.

The principal organs of the United Nations have also dealt with specific human rights issues involving the violation of widely accepted norms for conduct even when the country against which charges were made had not accepted specific obligations through the ratification of conventions. The issue that has appeared on the agenda of U.N. bodies most persistently is racial discrimination in South Africa. At the initiative of India the question of the treatment of Indians in South Africa was inscribed on the agenda of the General Assembly's first session, and that body undertook consideration of the broader question of racial conflict resulting from the apartheid policies of the South African government in 1952. In 1962 the two items were combined under the title "The Policies of Apartheid of the Government of the Republic of South Africa." This item has appeared on the agenda of successive General Assembly sessions since then. South Africa has consistently maintained that the issues involved are within its domestic jurisdiction, but this has not deterred the U.N. Both the General Assembly and the Security Council have condemned South Africa's apartheid policies, asserting that they violate provisions of the charter concerning human rights and fundamental freedoms and that they endanger international peace and security. Each body has called upon the government of South Africa to abandon these policies.

In 1962 the General Assembly requested member states to break off diplomatic and economic relations with South Africa.[48] It also asked the Security Council to impose sanctions against the country, and in 1963 the Security Council requested that states observe an arms embargo. These decisions were elaborated in subsequent resolutions, but U.N. members that sought substantially stronger action were unsuccessful until 1977 because France, the United Kingdom, and the United States blocked attempts in the Security Council to make the arms embargo mandatory. Finally, in 1977, after South Africa outlawed various domestic anti-apartheid and liberal organizations, the Security Council voted to adopt a mandatory arms embargo.

The United States substantially imposed an arms embargo starting in 1963, and in the 1970s even before the Security Council acted, the United Kingdom moved toward an arms embargo. In the 1970s and early 1980s France and Israel were South Africa's principal arms suppliers. The United States, the United Kingdom, and France have done little to interrupt normal economic relations, nor have South Africa's other major trading partners, the Federal Republic of Germany and Japan, taken steps toward breaking off economic relations.

The majority in the U.N. has sought to isolate South Africa diplomatically. It has succeeded in driving South Africa from some specialized agencies, and in 1974 suspended South Africa from the General Assembly. Although South Africa has made minor changes in its apartheid policies, their basic character has not been altered. And the South African government has been adamant that it would not under any circumstances conceive a one-person/one-vote formula for political participation that would allow blacks equal rights.

Regional Supervision

At the regional level some bodies charged with rule-supervisory activities have greater authority, and their proceedings more clearly resemble those of national judicial institutions under democratic governments. The European Convention on Human Rights, it will be recalled, provided for both a Commission on Human Rights and a Court of Human Rights. Cases that could not be resolved by the commission could be referred to the court, or if a state party had not accepted the jurisdiction of the court, the case would be considered by the Committee of Ministers. Decisions of both the Court of Human Rights and the Committee of Ministers are legally binding.

The Commission on Human Rights began functioning in 1955, and by 1982 it had received more than 9,000 complaints. The commission found some 200 of these admissible. The vast majority of complaints were declared inadmissible because national remedies had not been exhausted, because the complaint was "manifestly ill-founded" or an abuse of the right of petition, because the time limits between the last decision of a national court and presentation to the commission had been exceeded, or because the complaint was by an individual against a state that had not accepted the protocol giving individuals the right to petition. Some 30 cases had been brought before the court and somewhat more than 50 before the Committee of Ministers. The other cases that had been declared admissible had either been resolved at the commission stage, withdrawn or discharged, or were still in process.

The various Council of Europe institutions have obviously proceeded in a very conservative manner. One study in 1975 found that little more than 2 percent of the complaints had been declared admissible. Interpreting national law had been avoided; only the issue of whether or not national law contravenes the Convention on Human Rights had been considered. Forty-two of the fifty-eight decisions of the Committee of Ministers and the Court of Human Rights, or more than two-thirds, involved Austria and Belgium. Only a few of the decisions found national laws to contravene the convention. Governments respected these decisions, and some have even modified basic laws, but none of the decisions involved matters of major importance.[49]

The practices of the military regime that was installed in Greece in 1967 constituted the most significant case of violations of the European Convention. In 1969, after the Commission on Human Rights found it guilty of violations, Greece denounced the convention and withdrew from the Council of Europe. Perhaps the most significant sanction that Greece suffered was that from 1967—even before the judgment of the commission—until the overthrow of the military regime in 1974, the association agreement between Greece and the European Economic Community was suspended, causing real economic difficulties for Greece. Bringing Greece into the European communities was seen as a way of solidifying Greece's return to democracy.

The Inter-American Commission on Human Rights was created in 1959, a decade before the American Convention on Human Rights was drafted. As early as 1965 the commission was given authority to examine complaints from individuals about alleged violations of the American Declaration of the Rights and Duties of Man. It can investigate complaints, conduct on-site inspections with the consent of the state involved, and make recommendations. Now that the American Convention on Human Rights is in effect, it will provide a juridical framework comparable to that of the Council of Europe.

By 1983 the Inter-American Commission on Human Rights had received some 10,000 complaints. It sent about one-third as many communications to governments as it received complaints. Although only a few cases have resulted in public discussion, it would appear that some governments have willingly furnished information to the commission and have been responsive to its suggestions for changes in their law and practices. Others have refused to furnish information, while still others have gone so far as to allow on-site inspections but have been unwilling to contemplate seriously the commission's recommendations. The commission has been notably ineffective in influencing, at least in the short run, the conduct of the Cuban, Brazilian, and Chilean governments. On the other hand, it did have a considerable impact during the Dominican crisis of 1965, influencing both the conduct of the United States intervention and the nature of the new government that was formed.[50]

The record of the rule-supervisory activities of international organizations is mixed. Counting the efforts having to do with decolonization, there have been more activities concerned with enforcing the norm of racial equality than with any other norm. The regime created by the Council of Europe is the most advanced in formal juridical authority, but even here implementation of the legally binding decisions of the Court of Human Rights or the Committee of Ministers depends on the voluntary compliance of the government concerned. Should a state choose, it could even denounce the convention, as the military government of Greece did. If a violation of human rights were judged to involve a threat to peace, the Security Council of the United Nations would have the authority to issue binding decisions and to enforce them with sanctions. This, of course, would require the consent of the five permanent members of the Security Council, and the record indicates that this consent would not easily be given.

The main sanction then, whatever the juridical regime, appears to be adverse publicity. This can and has affected governments, forcing them to adjust their practices so as to bring them into conformity with internationally approved standards. Adverse publicity has also given strength to individuals and to opposition groups within countries where the governments were guilty of violating internationally approved norms. It has further forced other states to reconsider their policies toward the state concerned; the United States' voluntary arms embargo against South Africa is an example. In a few instances involving widely acknowledged egregious violations—Rhodesia, South Africa, and Greece—certain economic sanctions have also been applied, and the ruling regimes have been subjected to international opprobrium and isolation. The long-run effect of these efforts cannot now be known; in the case of Greece a more humane regime replaced the one that was condemned, and Zimbabwe has won its independence.

OPERATIONAL ACTIVITIES

The operational activities of international organizations relating to social welfare and human rights may appear humdrum in comparison with the more moving issues that are involved in the formulation and enforcement of norms and rules, yet they have made important contributions to human welfare and merit close attention. The operational activities of international organizations in these fields are many and varied.

Refugees and Relief

First, since the closing days of World War II, international organizations have been involved in major efforts to ameliorate the plight of those suffering from human-caused and natural calamities. Persons displaced by the events of the war needed temporary sustenance and then assistance in repatriation or resettlement. The United Nations Relief and Rehabilitation Administration had this as one of its main functions, and during its existence from November 9, 1943, through June 30, 1947, UNRRA expended almost $4 billion. At the peak of its operations, it had close to 30,000 employees. It provided for the total care of displaced persons, and helped from 9,000,000 to 14,000,000 (according to varying estimates) return to their homes. Nevertheless, more than a million displaced persons remained, most of whom sought resettlement rather than repatriation.

The International Refugee Organization (IRO) was created in 1946 to assist these persons, and from June 1947 to January 1952 it helped resettle more than a million, repatriated 73,000, and made arrangements for 31,000 who required institutional care.[51] Most of the individuals that IRO assisted came from Eastern Europe, and most refused to return to their countries of origin. The Soviet Union and other Eastern European states were bitterly critical of IRO. After 1951 those remaining refugees who owed their status to events connected with World War II were taken care of by the United Nations High Commissioner for Refugees, and their resettlement was facilitated by the Intergovernmental Committee on European Migration, an IGO that had been created in 1938 to assist refugees from Austria and Germany.

Events in the post-World War II period brought new displaced persons and refugees. The partition of Palestine in 1948 created a whole new community of persons unable to return to their homeland. After various temporary expedients were attempted, in 1949 the United Nations Relief and Works Agency for Palestine Refugees in the Near East (UNRWA) was created to care for this Arab community of somewhat under a million people. The original mandate envisaged the termination of direct relief by the end of 1950, but as of 1982, reflecting the still unsettled conditions of the Arab-Israeli dispute, the population in UNRWA's camps had grown to more than 1.9 million persons and its annual budget was running to more than $271 million.

As has already been mentioned, in 1966 the mandate of the Office of the United Nations High Commissioner for Refugees (UNHCR) was extended to cover post-1951 refugees. The function of the High Commissioner is to provide international protection for refugees and to assist in their voluntary repatriation or assimilation within new national communities. In the 1960s and 1970s the greatest proportion of the High Commissioner's assistance budget generally went to Africa, where the total refugee population was more than a million persons. UNHCR also attempted to respond to emergency situations—for example, in Cyprus after the 1974 conflict, in Southeast Asia after the conclusion of the Vietnam War, and in South Asia after the Soviet invasion of Afghanistan. In the early 1980s, Asia accounted for the largest share of the UNHCR budget.

Most of the funds available to the High Commissioner come from voluntary contributions. Table 14.3 shows UNHCR expenditures during 1981. Only those countries where the expenditures amounted to more than $10 million are listed separately. The figures should not be taken to represent the number of refugees in each area, since the cost of providing for the basic needs of refugees was considerably less in Africa and Asia than in Europe. In Africa the effects on neighboring countries of the exodus from the turmoil in Angola, Chad, Ethiopia, and Uganda is evident. Refugees from Vietnam continued to populate camps in the countries of Southeast Asia, and Pakistan was burdened with a huge number of refugees from Afghanistan. The effects of the conflict in Cyprus are also apparent.

Various INGOs have also provided relief to refugees and displaced persons. The International Committee of the Red Cross (ICRC) regularly provides assistance in combat zones, and it has had significant programs in southern Africa. In geographic concentration ICRC relief expenditures closely parallel those of UNHCR. Such organizations as CARE are also active in providing relief.

In 1965 the United Nations made financial provisions to enable it to provide, on the decision of the secretary-general alone, emergency relief assistance for countries that suffered natural disasters. Under the procedures that were authorized, between 1965 and 1970 the United Natons provided emergency assistance to Iran, Peru, and Turkey following earthquakes; to Algeria, Iraq, Mongolia, Niger, and Syria following floods; and to Costa Rica following a volcanic eruption. In 1971 the General Assembly created the position of Disaster Relief Coordinator to become the focal point of U.N. activities in this area, and two years later it es-

TABLE 14.3
UNHCR Expenditures, 1981
(Thousands of U.S. Dollars)

AFRICA	
Cameroon	11,848.9
Somalia	49,078.2
Sudan	19,817.1
Zaire	21,123.1
Others	64,564.7
Total	166.432.0
AMERICAS	
Total	18,921.3
ASIA	
Indonesia	11,587.3
Malaysia	10,994.7
Pakistan	109,482.5
Philippines	13,560.2
Thailand	61,578.7
Others	43,649
Total	250,852.4
EUROPE	
Cyprus	12,678.9
Others	8,817.4
Total	21,496.3
OCEANIA	
Total	178.4
GLOBAL AND REGIONAL PROJECTS	
	16,376.1
Grand Total	474,256.5

Source: U.N. General Assembly Official Records, 37th Session, Supplement 12, *Report of the United Nations Commissioner for Refugees* (A/37/12), pp. 69–70.

tablished a special voluntary fund to be available for use in emergency situations. Beyond providing emergency relief, the Office of the Disaster Relief Coordinator (UNDRO) assists countries in pre-disaster planning and in disaster prevention. In the 1970s, UNDRO provided emergency assistance to countries in the Sahelian region, Ethiopia, Peru, Mozambique, and Tonga, among other states. Again, INGOs, and particularly the ICRC, have active programs of disaster relief.

Technical Assistance

The United Nations family of agencies also conducts substantial technical assistance programs to help governments raise health standards, increase nutritional levels, and increase educational attainments—in other words, to meet what came to be called in the 1970s basic human needs. UNESCO has set as its goal achieving world literacy, and a large portion of its technical assistance projects are designed to work toward this goal. FAO's technical assistance projects seek to increase both the quantity and quality of food produced. WHO has concentrated on improving basic health services and also on the eradication of particular diseases; by 1976 its campaign to eradicate smallpox had virtually eliminated the disease. WHO collaborates with the United Nations Children's Fund in a global program to assist governments in improving maternal and child care.

The United Nations has provided help in establishing drug abuse programs and assistance for countries attempting to have farmers shift from the cultivation of drug sources to other crops. The International Labor Organization and the United Nations provide technical assistance to help governments improve their social services. ILO's program includes such matters as labor statistics, social security services, and occupational health. ILO also attempts to assist countries implement the International Labor Code, and it sponsors a workers' education program which has consciousness-raising aspects. In the 1970s and early 1980s, technical assistance projects by UNESCO, FAO, WHO, and ILO regularly accounted for more than 50 percent of the expenditures of the United Nations Development Program. These agencies also financed some technical assistance projects from their own regular budgets.

The broad purpose of all of these operational activities is to work toward providing individuals of whatever condition and in whatever circumstances throughout the world with the basic necessities for life in the late twentieth century. Some operational activities of international organizations go beyond this. For instance, the United Nations provides technical assistance in the area of human rights. Regional seminars that bring together local leaders for discussions of particular human rights topics are the most frequent form of this U.N. activity. However, most of the operational activities of international organizations have had a less abstract orientation.

Precisely because operational activities have tended to concentrate on concrete tasks, providing assistance essential to survival or to life at minimally acceptable standards, except for the years immediately after World War II when there was an acrimonious debate between communist and noncommunist countries about the activities of IRO, there has been an impressive consensus concerning the operational activities of international organizations in this field. The overwhelming majority of governments throughout the world have clearly become committed to the proposition that there are basic necessities to which all individuals should be entitled. In the 1980s, however, this commitment still received modest financial backing. In all, annual expenditures by international organizations on these operations activities probably amounted to less than $1 billion, a relatively modest sum.

The consensus on operational activities sharply contrasts with the acrimony that has surrounded many of the other activities of international organizations concerning social welfare and human rights. Throughout the period since World War II there has been bitter disagreement about what should be done and which tasks should receive priority. Yet if the record is viewed retrospectively, the emerging consensus is perhaps as impressive as the controversy. By the 1970s broad agreement had been achieved concerning the priority to be given to the principle of human equality. Much disagreement, of course, remains, but the multiplicity of international organizations—IGOs and INGOs, and universal membership and limited membership bodies—has allowed a multiplicity of approaches. Groups interested in promoting certain goals concerning human dignity and justice who have encountered obstacles in particular international organizations have not been blocked, but have been able to shift to other institutions where they could proceed without hindrance. The result has been an unprecedented number of activities. Now we should try to ascertain the consequences of these activities.

NOTES

1. Article 21, paragraph b.
2. For a glimpse of the academic debate concerning these matters, see Raymond A. Bauer (ed.), *Social Indicators* (Cambridge: MIT Press, 1966). See also UNESCO, *International Social Science Journal*, 27 (1975), which is entitled "Socio-Economic Indicators: Theories and Applications."
3. This is described in OECD, *OECD Observer*, 85 (March 1977), 24–27.
4. Amnesty International, *Report on Torture* (London: Amnesty International, 1973).
5. U.N. General Assembly Resolution 217 A (III).
6. U.N. General Assembly Resolution 1514 (XV).
7. U.N. General Assembly Resolution 1386 (XIV).
8. U.N. General Assembly Resolution 1904 (XVIII).
9. U.N. General Assembly Resolution 2037 (XX).
10. U.N. General Assembly Resolutions 2312 (XXII) and 2263 (XXII), respectively.
11. U.N. General Assembly Resolution 2542 (XXIV).
12. U.N. General Assembly Resolutions 3447 (XXX) and 3452 (XXX).

ASSESSING
THE ATTAINMENT
OF HUMAN DIGNITY
AND JUSTICE

All of the activities of international organizations with respect to social welfare and human rights potentially could contribute to the attainment of human dignity and justice, yet various activities pose quite different issues and are susceptible to different treatments. Gaining perspectives on international organizations' activities in these fields is therefore an essential preliminary step to attempting to assess their consequences.

PERSPECTIVES CONCERNING INTERNATIONAL ORGANIZATIONS' ACTIVITIES

First, it is notable that the character of the various activities of international organizations concerning social welfare and human rights has been distinctly skewed. The preponderance of the informational and operational activities concern relatively concrete matters such as education, nutrition, health, and social security, while the normative, rule-creating, and rule-supervisory activities are more frequently concerned with more abstract issues of human rights. Naturally this is not an exclusive dichotomy; the U.N. provides technical assistance in the field of human rights, and some of the norms enunciated and rules created within international organizations deal with the right to education and to health care. It is a marked tendency, however, and it stems from the nature of the subjects. Medical and educational personnel require specific training. Information about this training or the training itself can be provided from an external source.

Instituting racial equality or freedom of speech and association within a polity, however, is something for which no certain formulas have been found; rather, it is a matter of imbuing individuals with attitudes that respect these concepts and inhibit their violating them, an issue of gradual learning and internalizing basic norms.

A second major point is that in these fields the distinction between the products of normative and of rule-creating activities—that is, between resolutions and declarations on the one hand and conventions on the other—is not nearly as pronounced as it is in other areas. The reason that this is so relates to the nature of the sanction that is most likely to be used, publicity. Military and economic coercion are much more likely to be used in a case involving security or economic issues than in a case involving social welfare or human rights issues. In contrast to these sanctions, publicity involves few costs for those who criticize a regime for its failures of commission and omission with respect to human rights, and publicity can be as effective in enforcing a declaration as in enforcing a convention. International organizations, or more properly the majority of nation-states in the contemporary global system, have given greatest priority to attempting to achieve racial equality. This has meant efforts to eliminate slavery, then colonialism, then racial inequality within states. The outlawing of genocide must also be seen as part of the struggle for racial equality. Gaining equality with men for women has also received substantial attention. The global community seems to have ranked attaining minimum standards of health care and educational opportunities slightly below the basic goal of human equality, but has nonetheless given these matters considerable importance. Insuring that all individuals have the minimal requirements for subsistence is another broad goal that has received wide support, and this has led international organizations to undertake activities with respect to refugees and to provide disaster relief. Finally, the global community has also sought to promote the traditional civil and political rights of individuals, but when this goal has conflicted with any of the other goals of the global community, the latter have almost always been given priority.

In part, this relative ranking of goals—first equality, then basic needs, then civil and political rights—stems from the nature of international activity. IGOs in particular have generally found it easier to deal with issues that concern relationships among states than with issues involving relationships within states, especially those between a government and its subjects. The ranking also reflects a broad global consensus that some problems should be solved before others are tackled.

The list of the major human rights conventions adopted by the U.N., ILO, and UNESCO presented in Table 14.1 (pp. 324–325) clearly showed that there have been more conventions devoted to establishing the norm of human equality than to any other single goal and that these conventions have achieved more ratifications than any other group of conventions. Moreover, the activities directed toward achieving human equality have been far more numerous and extensive than those directed toward any other goal. Let us begin, then, by considering the effects of activities to end colonialism and promote racial and sexual equality.

DECOLONIZATION AND HUMAN EQUALITY

In 1945, when the charter of the United Nations was signed, almost a quarter of the world's population lived in dependent territories. By 1970 less than 1 percent of the world's population inhabited territories that had not attained self-rule, and by 1983 the number had been reduced to just over two-tenths of 1 percent. From 1945 through 1983, ninety-one states gained independence. Table 15.1 lists these states and gives the date of their independence and their population. The table makes apparent the temporal course of decolonization, starting in the Middle East in the immediate aftermath of World War II, concentrating in Asia in the remaining years of the 1940s and in the early 1950s, then shifting to Africa in the late 1950s and the 1960s. Decolonization has been one of the major developments of the period since the end of World War II. It has involved a significant restructuring of the global political system, and this restructuring has been achieved with remarkably little violence.

Clearly, international institutions cannot claim to have caused or managed this transformation. They have, however, played an important and constructive role that started even before World War II. Their normative pronouncements, including the Covenant of the League of Nations and the Charter of the United Nations, delegitimized the concept of colonialism and gave legitimacy to the struggle for self-rule. Through the mandates and the trusteeship system, the League and the U.N. provided a measure of supervision for a limited number of dependent territories, and in certain instances this supervision appears to have prevented abuses of colonial power. In what is now Tanzania, for instance, land alienation schemes were blocked by the actions of the League.[1] International institutions also provided a forum which anticolonial leaders could use to gain publicity and advance their cause. The institutions provided moral encouragement for these leaders and their followers, and also some material assistance. Frequently, international institutions became involved in the process of decolonization at crucial points, and when this occurred, their influence was always oriented toward hastening rather than prolonging colonial rule. Indonesia provides a case in point.[2] U.N. actions on balance favored the Indonesian nationalists rather than the Dutch who were attempting to reassert colonial control. The role of international institutions in decolonization should not be exaggerated, yet it is clear that they have been deeply involved in the process and have made important contributions to it.

With respect to racial discrimination more broadly, there is no measure of accomplishment comparable to the number of states that have gained independence or the proportion of the world's population living in dependent territories. We know that more states have ratified the Convention on the Elimination of All Forms of Racial Discrimination than any other U.N. human rights convention and that the signatory states have been relatively faithful in submitting the required reports to the Committee on the Elimination of Racial Discrimination. But racism is a broad phenomenon that pervades many aspects of life, including education, employment, housing, and social services. Careful contextual analy-

TABLE 15.1

Progress of National Independence, 1946–1982

State	Date of Independence	Population, 1980 (In Thousands)
Jordan	Mar. 22, 1946	3,190
Philippines	July 4, 1946	48,400
Pakistan	Aug. 14, 1947	82,411
India	Aug. 15, 1947	663,586
Burma	Jan. 4, 1948	35,289
Sri Lanka	Feb. 4, 1948	14,738
Israel	May 15, 1948	3,878
Korea, Republic of (South)	Aug. 15, 1948	38,197
Korea, People's Democratic Republic of (North)	Sept. 9, 1948	17,914
Vietnam	Mar. 8, 1949	52,299
Laos	July 19, 1949	3,721
Kampuchea (formerly Cambodia)	Nov. 8, 1949	8,872
Indonesia	Dec. 28, 1949	151,894
Libya	Dec. 24, 1951	2,977
Sudan	Jan. 1, 1956	18,691
Morocco	Mar. 2, 1956	20,242
Tunisia	Mar. 20, 1956	6,363
Ghana	Mar. 6, 1957	11,450
Malaysia	Aug. 31, 1957	13,436
Guinea	Oct. 2, 1958	5,014
Cameroon	Jan. 1, 1960	8,503
Togo	Apr. 27, 1960	2,699
Madagascar	June 27, 1960	8,742
Zaire (formerly Congo)	June 30, 1960	28,291
Somalia	July 1, 1960	3,645
Benin (formerly Dahomey)	Aug. 1, 1960	3,567
Niger	Aug. 3, 1960	5,305
Upper Volta	Aug. 5, 1960	6,908
Ivory Coast	Aug. 7, 1960	7,937
Chad	Aug. 11, 1960	4,524
Central African Republic	Aug. 13, 1960	2,294
Congo	Aug. 15, 1960	1,537
Cyprus	Aug. 16, 1960	628
Gabon	Aug. 17, 1960	551
Senegal	Aug. 20, 1960	5,661
Mali	Sept. 22, 1960	6,906
Nigeria	Oct. 1, 1960	77,082
Mauritania	Nov. 28, 1960	1,634
Sierra Leone	April 27, 1961	3,474
Kuwait	June 19, 1961	1,372
Tanzania	Dec. 9, 1961	17,934
Western Samoa	Jan. 1, 1962	156
Burundi	July 1, 1962	4,512
Rwanda	July 1, 1962	5,046
Algeria	July 5, 1962	18,594
Jamaica	Aug. 6, 1962	2,192

TABLE 15.1 *Continued*

State	Date of Independence	Population, 1980 (In Thousands)
Trinidad and Tobago	Aug. 31, 1962	1,139
Uganda	Oct. 9, 1962	13,201
Kenya	Dec. 12, 1963	16,402
Malawi	July 6, 1964	5,968
Malta	Sept. 21, 1964	364
Zambia	Oct. 24, 1964	5,645
The Gambia	Feb. 18, 1965	601
Maldives	July 26, 1965	148
Singapore	Aug. 9, 1965	2,391
Guyana	May 26, 1966	884
Botswana	Sept. 30, 1966	821
Lesotho	Oct. 4, 1966	1,339
Barbados	Nov. 30, 1966	253
Yemen (Aden)	Nov. 30, 1967	1,890
Nauru	Jan. 31, 1968	8
Mauritius	Mar. 12, 1968	957
Swaziland	Sept. 6, 1968	547
Equatorial Guinea	Oct. 12, 1968	363
Tonga	June 4, 1970	97
Fiji	Oct. 10, 1970	619
Bahrain	Aug. 14, 1971	364
Qatar	Sept. 3, 1971	220
United Arab Emirates	Dec. 2, 1971	796
Bangladesh	Apr. 4, 1972	88,656
The Bahamas	July 10, 1973	237
Grenada	Feb. 7, 1974	98
Guinea-Bissau	Sept. 12, 1974	573
Mozambique	June 25, 1975	10,473
Cape Verde	July 5, 1975	324
São Tomé and Príncipe	July 10, 1975	85
Papua New Guinea	Sept. 16, 1975	3,082
Angola	Nov. 11, 1975	7,078
Suriname	Nov. 25, 1975	389
Comoros	Dec. 21, 1975	335
Seychelles	June 29, 1976	65
Djibouti	June 27, 1977	119
Solomon Islands	July 7, 1978	221
Tuvalu	Oct. 1, 1978	7
Saint Lucia	Feb. 22, 1979	120
Kiribati	July 12, 1979	58
Saint Vincent	Oct. 27, 1979	122
Zimbabwe	April 18, 1980	7,360
Vanuatu	July 30, 1980	109
Belize	Sept. 21, 1981	162
Antigua	Nov. 1, 1981	75
Total States = 91		Total Population = 1,607,021

Sources: Based on data from the U.S. Department of State, Bureau of Intelligence and Research, *Status of the World's Nations* (Washington, D.C.: Government Printing Office, 1980); and International Bank for Reconstruction and Development, *World Bank Atlas*, 1981 (Washington, D.C.: IBRD, 1982).

ses would be required to determine the actual amount of racial discrimination in various countries, and given the absence of a common measure, it would be difficult to make meaningful comparisons. The studies that have been done indicate that almost all countries have enacted legislation, adopted administrative orders, and had judicial decisions to ban racial discrimination[3]; and most of these countries claim to have made progress in implementing programs to eliminate racial discrimination. However, it was clear as of 1982 that in the country where racial discrimination was most blatant, South Africa, very little progress had been made despite the condemnation of the international community and the sanctions that had been imposed.

The convention on genocide has also received a large number of ratifications. Nevertheless, in the late 1960s and early 1970s willful destruction of human life on a massive scale occurred in Bangladesh, Uganda, Biafra, and Burundi, and the most that international governmental organizations did was to hold discussions and adopt cautious resolutions. Of the four states that were involved— Pakistan, Nigeria, Burundi, and Uganda—only Pakistan had ratified the Convention on the Prevention and Punishment of the Crime of Genocide. INGOs, in contrast, were forthright in their condemnations of these states.

Conventions relating to equality for women have also been ratified by a substantial number of countries. As of 1982 the Convention on the Political Rights of Women had been ratified by ninety countries, and ILO's Convention on Equal Remuneration by one hundred countries. (As of 1956 only ten countries had ratified the Convention on Equal Remuneration, and as late as 1969 there were only sixty-five ratifications.) There have also been advances in national law and practices. As of 1973 women were eligible to vote in all elections and to compete for office on a basis of equality with men in 124 countries. In only six countries were women ineligible to vote or to stand for office. Progress was also being made toward implementation of the principle of equal pay for equal work.[4]

ACHIEVING BASIC HUMAN NEEDS

Progress is easier to document with respect to basic human needs.

Health, Education, and Nutrition

Between 1960 and 1970 the number of medical facilities and trained medical personnel increased substantially. In 1960 in less developed countries, when the ratio was worst, there was one hospital bed for every 881.2 persons; by 1970 despite a sizeable increase in the world's population, this ratio had dropped to one for every 812.1 persons and in the late 1970s it was 799.8.[5] In 1960 there was only one doctor for every 8,043.5 persons, by 1970 there was one doctor for every 6,642.7 persons, and in the late 1970s there was one for every 4,638.3 persons. The ratio of hospital beds and doctors to population improved throughout the world. In what the World Bank refers to as the industrialized countries with market economies (all OECD members except Greece, Portugal, Spain, and Turkey) the number of persons per doctor dropped from 830.7 in 1960 to 639.4 in the late 1970s.

According to World Bank figures, life expectancy rates increased throughout the world. In less developed countries, the life expectancy of an infant at birth jumped from forty-two years in 1960 to fifty-seven years in 1980. In industrialized countries with market economies it increased from seventy to seventy-four years, and in centrally planned industrial economies from sixty-eight to seventy-one years.[6] The high rate of infant mortality in the less developed countries was the most important factor explaining the low life expectancies in these regions, and as the increasing life spans indicate, significant progress was made during the 1960s and 1970s in lowering infant mortality rates. The incidence of some diseases dropped sharply, and one, smallpox, was virtually eliminated.

Between 1960 and the late 1970s a significant expansion of educational opportunity occurred. The total number of persons enrolled in the three levels of education (primary, secondary, and post-secondary) rose from 325 million to 802 million.[7] In 1960 slightly less than 11 percent of the world's population was enrolled in school; by 1980 over 18 percent was enrolled. The largest increase was in primary education, and the world was clearly moving toward the goal of universal primary education. As of 1980, at least seven years of education was compulsory in 161 countries; only 33 had not made some amount of education compulsory. The overall percentage of persons over fifteen who were illiterate declined from 39 percent in 1960 to 29 percent in 1980.[8] Again, there were substantial differences among major groups of countries.

School enrollment ratios are given in Table 15.2 according to economic categories used by the World Bank in its monitoring of global development. The low income developing countries had per capita GNPs in 1980 of $410 or less. The thirty-three countries in this category include populous countries such as Bangladesh and the People's Republic of China. Almost half of the world's population lived in these thirty-three countries. The middle income developing countries had per capita GNPs of more than $410 in 1980. Three members of OECD—Greece, Portugal, and Turkey—and one member of the Warsaw Treaty—Romania—are among the sixty-three states included in this category. A little more than a quarter of the world's population lived in these states. Four countries are included in the category of high income oil exporters—Kuwait, Libya, Saudi Arabia, and the United Arab Emirates. The industrial market countries include the remaining members of OECD, and the non-market industrial economies include the remaining members of WTO. The percentage of male and female children of the relevant age group enrolled in primary education has been given separately so that the gains in the proportion of females receiving primary education can be seen. Since children under or above the age group are enrolled in primary or secondary school, the percentages are in some cases more than 100.

All groups of economies have made progress in most categories. The developing countries have made major gains in students enrolled in primary and second-

TABLE 15.2
School Enrollment Ratios by Economic Category, 1960–1979

| | Number Enrolled in Primary School as a Percentage of Age Group (6–11 years) | | | | Number Enrolled in Secondary School as a Percentage of Age Group (12–17 years) | | Number Enrolled in Higher Education as a Percentage of Population Aged 20–24 | |
| | Male | | Female | | | | | |
	1960	1979	1960	1979	1960	1979	1960	1979
Low Income Developing Economies (Per Capita GNP of 410 or less in 1980)	68	98	34	84	15	49	2	3
Middle Income Developing Economies (Per Capita GNP of more than $410 in 1980)	84	104	68	93	15	39	4	11
High Income Oil Exporting Countries	44	92	12	70	5	44	—	7
Industrial Market Economies	107	104	112	104	64	88	17	37
Non-Market Industrial Economies	101	95	101	96	48	93	11	20

Source: International Bank for Reconstruction and Development, *World Development Report, 1982* (New York: Oxford, 1982), pp. 154–155.

ary education. The industrial countries—both market and non-market—have significantly expanded the proportion of students enrolled in higher education. The dramatic increase in the proportion of female students enrolled in primary education is particularly striking. It is an important step toward greater equality for men and women.

The general increase in school attendance during the 1960s was paralleled by an increase in the proportion of the world's adult population that was literate. Table 15.3 provides a summary. As can be seen, the industrialized countries had already achieved virtual complete adult literacy by 1960. In the less developed countries in 1960, in contrast, less than half of the adult population was literate, and in the poorer LDCs, only slightly more than a quarter was literate. The progress that these countries made in the following years is impressive. By the end of

TABLE 15.3
Adult* Literacy by Economic Category, 1960–1979
(Percentages)

	1960	1979
Low Income Developing Economies (Per Capita GNP of $410 or Less in 1980)	26	51
Middle Income Developing Economies (Per Capita GNP of More than $410 in 1980)	49	68
High Income Oil Exporters	14	32
Industrial Market Economies	97	99
Non-market Industrial Economies	98	100

*Persons 15 years or older

Source: International Bank for Reconstruction and Development, *World Development Report, 1982* (New York: Oxford, 1982), pp. 24, 154–155.

the 1970s, for the first time in world history, more than half of the world's population was literate. Again there are vast differences among the countries included in the various groups. Among countries included in the low income category in 1977, only 5 percent of the adult population of Niger and Upper Volta was literate while in the People's Republic of China and Tanzania the proportion was 66 percent, and in Burma 70 percent.

It is worthy of note that in 1980 on a global basis public expenditures on health and education were almost twice as large as military expenditures.[9] Sadly, however, the military expenditures of the less developed countries as a group were almost as large as their public expenditures on health and education, and even though the population of the less developed countries was more than three times that of the developed countries, the public expenditures of the former on health and education were only about one-sixth of those of the latter.

Global developments with respect to nutrition have been positive, for the world but not for all regions or countries. Table 15.4 gives average annual growth rates for total and for per capita food production for the major geographical regions for the two decades between 1960 and 1980. Less developed countries are divided first into low- and middle-income categories and then by geographical region. The world and a majority of its regions made more progress in increasing food production in the 1960s than in the 1970s. The per capita figures show how difficult the rapid rate of population increase in the LDCs makes the task of increasing the level of nutrition in these countries. As can be seen, on a per capita basis, in South Asia food production just kept pace with population growth in the 1970s and in Africa food production on a per capita basis actually declined during this decade. The 1982 *Report on the World Social Situation* commented on the food production record in the 1970s of African countries:

TABLE 15.4
*Average Annual Growth Rates of Food Production by Region
(excluding China), 1960–1980*

	Total		Per Capita	
	1960–1970	1970–1980	1960–1970	1970–1980
Developing Countries	2.9	2.8	0.4	0.4
Low Income	2.6	2.2	0.2	-0.3
Middle-income	3.2	3.3	0.7	0.9
Africa	2.6	1.6	0.1	-1.1
Middle East	2.6	2.9	0.1	0.2
Latin America	3.6	3.3	0.1	0.6
Southeast Asia	2.8	3.8	0.3	1.4
South Asia	2.6	2.2	0.1	0.0
Southern Europe	3.2	3.5	1.8	1.9
Industrial Market Economies	2.3	2.0	1.3	1.1
Non-market Industrial Economies	3.2	1.7	2.2	0.9
Total World	2.7	2.3	0.8	0.5

Source: International Bank for Reconstruction and Development, *World Development Report,
1982* (Washington, D.C.: IBRD, 1982), p. 41.

The long-run experience of many countries in Africa has been very different from the over-all trend. In the African region as a whole, the food supply per inhabitant shrank on an average by one-tenth over the decade. Given the initial situation, the effect on millions has proved catastrophic. Recurrent cycles of political instability, civil disorders and prolonged drought have all contributed to keeping millions in hunger and to depressing further the general level of nutrition on the continent.[10]

To some extent the progress in regions other than Africa was attributable to the introduction of new technologies in crop production. Realizing such technological advances in Africa remained an unmet challenge. As the 1980s began, there was evidence that governments of African countries would devote greater attention to agricultural development and food production.

Figures on food production provide only a most rudimentary indication of global progress toward meeting human nutritional needs. To understand properly the extent to which these needs are being met, the available supplies would have to be compared to nutritional norms.

The World Bank estimated that in 1977 on an aggregate basis, available food supplies (including net supplies gained from foreign trade as well as from domestic production) constituted 97 percent of the daily per capita calorie requirements in low-income economies, 107 percent in middle income economies, 131 percent in industrial market economies, and 137 percent in non-market industrial economies.[11] In addition, more would have to be known than is at present about the distribution of food consumption within countries. Because of internal inequalities, country aggregates can be extremely misleading and aggregates of several countries even more so. The Food and Agriculture Organization estimates that in 1980 430 milllion people were undernourished; that would be about 10 percent of the world's population.[12] Only marginal progress, if any, has been made in lowering this figure.

Either to give international organizations full credit for the progress that has been achieved with respect to health, education, and nutrition or to blame them for the shortcomings in these fields would be inappropriate. International organizations have certainly not played a central directing role in any of these fields; they have been at most an important catalyst. Through their informational activities they have gathered the data essential to identifying problems, and they have insured that information about techniques to meet these problems would be transmitted rapidly throughout the global political system. They have set goals, which they have encouraged governments to meet, and they have provided assistance to governments. Developments in health, education, and nutrition have been in accord with the professed aims of international organizations; consequently, it seems fair to give them a share of the credit for what has happened.

Refugee and Disaster Relief

In the years since World War II major steps have been taken toward developing institutions and procedures for meeting the needs of refugees and for being responsive to the needs of those whose lives were adversely affected by disasters. In the 1970s and 1980s the Office of the U.N. High Commissioner for Refugees and the U.N. Relief and Works Agency for Palestine Refugees in the Near East had substantial programs, and the Office of the U.N. Disaster Relief Coordinator was ready to assist in the event of disasters. INGOs, and particularly the International Committee of the Red Cross, also had major programs in both areas.

With respect to disaster relief, the control of communicable diseases, and nutrition, the necessity to rely on self-reporting by governments constituted a weakness. The governments of various countries that were dependent on tourist expenditures were sometimes reluctant to notify WHO about cholera outbreaks. Some governments were unwilling to admit the existence of food crises. IGO and INGO employees, dependent as they were upon governmental cooperation, at times did not report facts that governments preferred to hide. However, some notable failures of reporting by governments and by international organizations in the 1960s and 1970s seemed to cause sufficient embarrassment for all concerned to make all parties more responsible. Food crises such as in Ethiopia and the Sahel cannot be hidden forever, and governments discovered that for the sake of their external and internal positions they would ultimately have been better off to have announced the situation sooner rather than later. Similarly, newspaper stories about cholera based on partial accounts by travelers probably have done more to deter tourism than an official notification to WHO with all of the facts. Moreover, prompt reporting brings prompt assistance, a fact of which governments became increasingly aware.

Unemployment and Inflation

As one goes beyond these basic elements of social welfare, charting developments becomes considerably more difficult. The concepts used are less uniform, and comparable data are not available for large parts of the world. What data there are indicate problems with respect to unemployment and price stability. Unemployment seems to have risen generally in the 1970s, reaching a high in 1980, for instance, in Jamaica of 27.4 percent, 12.2 percent in Chile, and above 7 percent in most OECD countries.[13] Japan and Switzerland seemed like exceptions to the general trend with unemployment rates of 2 and .2 percent respectively. The rate of inflation was also high during the 1970s. For instance, in the United States, using 1970 as a base year, the general price index had risen to 212.4 by 1980. But the situation was significantly worse in many LDCs. Again using 1970 as a base year, by 1980 the general price index was 1,339 in Zaire, 2,950 in Ghana, 259,090 in Argentina, and 419,601 in Chile.[14]

These problems were constantly on the agendas of international organizations, and they were the subject of numerous studies, analyses, and conferences. International organizations, by providing forums in which international cooperation could occur, undoubtedly contributed to preventing the world economy from entering the downward spiral that was so disastrous in the 1930s. They also provided forums in which information about social security and employment programs could be exchanged. Nonetheless, unemployment and inflation remained, with their painful consequences.

POLITICAL AND CIVIL RIGHTS

To this point, with the exception of the discussion of decolonization and efforts to promote human equality, the issues we have considered have involved economic and social rights. With respect to civil and political rights, whether progress has been made or whether there has been a general decline is debatable.

The most responsible comprehensive research on civil and political rights is the survey and ranking of states and territories done each year by Freedom House, an American nongovernmental organization that has its office in New York. Experts rank each state or territory on a seven-point scale, those states regarded as "most free" receiving 1 and those regarded as "least free" receiving 7. Each state or territory is ranked separately according to its realization of political rights and civil liberties. Civil liberties include "freedom from political censorship, open public discussion, the maintenance of a rule of law (especially as signified by the ability of the courts to decide against the government), and freedom from government terror.[15] Political rights refer essentially "to the extent to which the people of a country are able to play an active and critical role in choosing their leaders, and thus ultimately in determining the laws and means of enforcement under which they will live."[16] The Freedom House survey does not use the term "freedom" in the sense of national independence. Thus it would have rated Uganda more free before independence than after independence when the regime of Idi Amin was in power. The concepts that are used in the Freedom House surveys are clearly those that are involved in the European and the American Conventions on Human Rights, and with the exception of the right of national self-determination, they cover those that are involved in the International Covenant on Civil and Political Rights. Beyond publishing separate rankings for each country with respect to political rights and civil liberties, the Freedom House survey makes an overall judgment of "free," "partly free," or "not free." "Generally, states rated (1) and (2) in the two categories of political and civil liberties will be 'free'; those at (3), (4), and (5), 'partly free'; and those at (6) and (7), 'not free.'"[17] Cases where ratings for political rights and civil liberties differ are decided by averaging and judgment.

Freedom House has been conducting its annual survey since 1972, and the results are published in the January-February issue of its magazine, *Freedom at Issue*. Table 15.5 gives an eleven-year record of the survey. Over the eleven-year period the percentage of the world's population living in countries that are judged by the Freedom House survey to be "free" has increased, and the percentage living in countries that are considered "not free" has decreased. When a single country with a large population, such as India, shifts from one category to another it can make a tremendous difference to the proportions of the world's population in the two categories. The emergency regime instituted in India in 1975 put that country in the "partly free" category, and when the election of 1977 ended the emergency regime, India moved back to the "free" category.

Taking a longer time perspective, one's attitude toward whether or not progress has been made toward a more complete realization of civil and political

TABLE 15.5
Results of Freedom House Surveys
(Population in Millions)

	Free		Partly Free		Not Free	
Survey Date	Number of People	Percentage of World Population	Number of People	Percentage of World Population	Number of People	Percentage of World Population
Jan. 73	1,029	30.88	720	21.61	1,583	47.51
Jan. 74	1,351	35.73	812	21.48	1,618	42.79
Jan. 75	1,366	35.32	899	23.25	1,602	41.43
Jan. 76	803.6	19.78	1,435.8	35.34	1,823.4	44.88
Jan. 77	789.9	19.65	1,464.0	36.42	1,765.9	43.93
Jan. 78	1,454.5	35.63	874.3	21.41	1,753.9	42.96
Jan. 79	1,483.2	35.09	1,042.7	24.67	1,700.9	40.24
Jan. 80	1,601.3	37.02	921.2	21.29	1,803.6	41.69
Jan. 81	1,613.0	35.88	970.9	21.59	1,911.9	42.53
Jan. 82	1,631.9	35.86	916.5	20.14	2,002.7	44.00
Jan. 83	1,665.1	35.32	918.8	20.04	2,000.2	43.64

Source: Raymond D. Gastil, "The Comparative Survey of Freedom VIII," *Freedom at Issue, 44,* (January–February, 1978), pp. 3–19, at p. 2, and "The Comparative Survey of Freedom," *Freedom at Issue,* 70 (January–February, 1983), pp. 3–14 at p. 4.

rights throughout the world in the years since World War II depends in part upon how one evaluates decolonization and the achievement of independence. This is a positive accomplishment, and it must be so regarded under the terms of the International Covenant on Civil and Political Rights, the first article of which proclaims the right of national self-determination. On the other hand, decolonization has not resulted in a striking increase in the number of democratic governments in independent states. Instead, former colonies have much more frequently adopted various forms of authoritarian rule.

In the 1980s democracies were largely concentrated in Western Europe, North America, and Oceana. The January 1983 Freedom House survey ranked all OECD member states as "free" except Turkey, which was scored "partly free." In contrast, all of the member states of WTO were regarded as "not free." Of the 134 states that are included in the group that we have identified as Others and were included in the Freedom House survey, 23.9 percent (thirty-two) were ranked as being "free," 33.6 percent (forty-five) as being "partly free," and 42.5 percent (fifty-seven) as being "not free."[18] Such statistics bring into question the role of international organizations, and particularly that of IGOs, in promoting the greater realization of civil and political rights.

These questions would not apply to the activities of the Council of Europe. Twenty of its twenty-one member states (all except Liechtenstein) have ratified the European Convention on Human Rights, and all except Cyprus and Turkey were ranked by the Freedom House January 1983 survey as being "free." (Cyprus was given a score of 4 on political rights and 3 on civil liberties and Turkey scores of 4 and 5.) The activities of the Council of Europe, however modest they may seem to have been, must have served to reinforce democratic traditions in Western Europe, and ostracism by the Council of Europe and the economic sanctions imposed by the European Economic Community deserve some of the credit for the restoration of democracy in Greece. Furthermore, the potential prize of membership in the Council of Europe and then in the European Economic Community may have been among the stimuli that produced the transformation toward democracy in Portugal and Spain. Establishment of a democratic regime clearly was a prerequisite to Spain's acceptance as a member of the North Atlantic Treaty Organization in 1982.

Universal membership IGOs and regional organizations outside of Western Europe are different. None of them has a membership as homogenous in respecting political and civil rights as the members of the Council of Europe. Of the seventy states that had ratified the International Covenant on Civil and Political Rights as of July 1, 1982, the 1983 Freedom House survey ranked thirty-one (44.3 percent) as being "free" with respect to civil and political rights; fifteen (21.4 percent) as being "partly free," and twenty-four (34.3 percent) as being "not free." In contrast, however, eighteen or two-thirds, of the twenty-seven states that had ratified the Optional Protocol (giving the Human Rights Committee the right to consider communications from individuals within their jurisdiction alleging violations of the covenant) were considered "free" in the Freedom House 1983 survey, and only two were judged as being "not free."

It could be argued that the long-run effect of states' adhering to conventions that commit them to maintaining civil and political rights that they have not yet attained will be to induce the governments of these states to move toward granting these rights. Once a government has ratified a treaty, it can legitimately be criticized by dissident groups of its own citizens, by national and international nongovernmental organizations, and by other states for not meeting the standards of the treaty. In support of this argument, Solidarity's first demand was that the government fully implement ILO Convention 87 on Freedom of Association, which Poland had ratified. The question of the full implementation of this convention was an issue throughout the struggle for reform in Poland.

Ernst Haas, however, after a careful study of the consequences of this same ILO convention, where there is a fairly elaborate mechanism for supervision, concluded that on balance international efforts to protect freedom of association have had little effect on changes with respect to governmental practices concerning trade union freedoms.[19] The danger is that the ratification of treaties by a large number of states which do not uphold their standards could breed substantial cynicism in the global community. Even worse, the activities of international organizations could be perverted to rationalize what in commonsense terms would surely constitute violations of human rights.

Since internal groups, nongovernmental organizations, states, and IGOs seem to have been as free in criticizing governments for not adhering to standards proclaimed in declarations as they have in criticizing states for not fulfilling obligations specified in treaties, an argument could be made that until states are ready to fulfill the obligations specified in a treaty, as the members of the Council of Europe were, international organizations might better concentrate on normative rather than rule-creating activities. When in the late 1970s, as a result of congressional mandates and decisions by the executive branch, the United States began to take judgments about the human rights performance of governments into account in allocating economic assistance, those judgments took note of the views of such nongovernmental groups as Amnesty International and Freedom House, but they were made unilaterally by the U.S. administration.

Perhaps the most optimistic interpretation that can be put on all of the developments concerning the attainment of human dignity and justice throughout the world in the years since World War II is to accept the proposition that achieving racial and sexual equality and meeting basic human needs are essential preliminary steps to obtaining the more abstract civil and political rights. This has certainly been the position argued explicitly or implicitly by the majority of states within the United Nations. Substantial progress has been made in these areas, and in the meantime the continual reassertion of civil and political rights goals may have helped to insure that they are not forgotten or abandoned. Moreover, during the 1960s and 1970s significant forces were mobilized in support of these goals. The activities of INGOs concerning civil and political rights gained momentum. Furthermore, individuals began to gain access to international institutions to complain about conditions in their own countries, whether or not their states had accepted this in a formal treaty. This was a major step toward giving international institutions broad appellate jurisdiction. One could hope that in the long run these developments would yield more tangible results than they have thus far.

NOTES

1. See B. T. G. Chidzero, *Tanganyika and International Trusteeship* (New York: Oxford University Press, 1969), pp. 214–247.

2. Alastair M. Taylor, *Indonesian Independence and the United Nations* (Ithaca: Cornell University Press, 1960).

3. See the report of the U.N.'s special rapporteur Hernan Santa Cruz, *Racial Discrimination* (New York: U.N., 1971).

4. See International Labor Office, *Equal Remuneration: General Survey* by the Committee of Experts on the Application of Conventions and Recommendations (Geneva: ILO, 1975).

5. This material concerning health care is taken from the International Bank for Reconstruction and Development, *World Bank Tables, 1980* (Washington, D.C.: IBRD, 1980), p. 448.

6. International Bank for Reconstruction and Development, *World Development Report, 1982* (Washington, D.C.: IBRD, 1982), p. 151–152.

7. Compare: U.N., Department of Economic and Social Affairs, *1974 Report on the World Social Situation* (New York: U.N., 1975), p. 224, and *1982 Report on the World Situation* (New York: U.N., 1982), pp. 103, 105, and 107.

8. Ibid., 1974, p. 225, and 1982, p. 116.

9. Ruth Leger Sivard, *World Military and Social Expenditures, 1982* (Leesburgh, Virginia: World Priorities, 1982), p. 27.

10. U.N. Department of International Economic and Social Affairs, *1982 Report on the World Social Situation* (New York: U.N., 1982), p. 67.

11. International Bank for Reconstruction and Development, *World Development Report, 1982* Washington, D.C.: IBRD, 1982), pp. 152–153.

12. U.N. Department of International Economic and Social Affairs, *1982 Report on the World Social Situation* (New York: U.N., 1982), p. 64.

13. International Labor Organization, *Yearbook of Labour Statistics*, 1981, (Geneva: ILO, 1981), pp. 315–327.

14. Ibid., pp. 515–524.

15. Raymond D. Gastil, "The Comparative Survey of Freedom VII," *Freedom at Issue*, 39 (January-February 1977), 5–17, at p. 6. Gastil is responsible for the preparation of the annual survey, and he works in conjunction with several individuals who are experts on particular geographical regions.

16. Ibid.

17. Raymond D. Gastil, "The Comparative Survey of Freedom VIII," *Freedom at Issue*, 44 (January-February 1978), 3–19, at p. 8. The way in which the rankings are assigned is also described in the 1977 survey, "Freedom VII," pp. 6–8.

18. Raymond D. Gastil, "The Comparative Survey of Freedom," *Freedom at Issue*, 70 (January-February, 1983), pp. 3–14.

19. Ernst B. Haas, *Human Rights and International Action: The Case of Freedom of Association* (Stanford: Stanford University Press, 1970).

FOR FURTHER READING

Davis, Morris. Audits of International Relief in the Nigerian Civil War: Some Political Perspectives," *International Organization*, 29 (Spring 1975), 501–512.

——— . "Some Political Dimensions of International Relief: Two Cases," *International Organization*, 28 (Winter 1974), 127–140.

Emerson, Rupert. *From Empire to Nation: The Rise to Self-Assertion of Asian and African Peoples.* Cambridge: Harvard University Press, 1960.

——— . "The Fate of Human Rights in the Third World," *World Politics*, 27 (January 1975), 201–226.

Fraser, Donald. "Human Rights at the UN: The Double Standard," *The Nation*, September 21, 1974, 230–232.

Haas, Ernst B. *Human Rights and International Action: The Case of Freedom of Association.* Stanford: Stanford University Press, 1970.

Jacobson, Harold K. "The United Nations and Colonialism: A Tentative Appraisal," *International Organization*, 16, (Winter 1962), 37–56.

Landy, Ernest A. *The Effectiveness of International Supervision: Thirty Years of I.L.O. Experience.* London: Slaves, 1966.

Schreiber, Anna P. *The Inter-American Commission on Human Rights.* Leyden: A. W. Sijhoff, 1970.

Scoble, Harry M., and Laurie S. Wiseberg. "Human Rights NGOs: Notes Towards Comparative Analysis," *Revue de droits de l'homme*, 9 (1976), 630–644.

Sohn, Louis B., and Thomas Buergenthal. *International Protection of Human Rights.* Indianapolis: Bobbs-Merrill, 1973.

Wainhouse, David. *Remnants of Empire: The United Nations and the End of Colonialism.* New York: Harper & Row, 1964.

INTERNATIONAL ORGANIZATIONS AND FUTURE WORLD ORDER

16

WEBS OF COMMUNICATIONS NETWORKS AND THE EROSION OF SOVEREIGNTY: A FORMULA FOR AN ERA OF INTERDEPENDENCE

International organizations have clearly become an integral part of the contemporary global political system, and they have had a demonstrable effect on the distribution of values within this system. But what of the future? How is the global political system evolving, and what are the roles of international organizations in this evolution?

THE GLOBAL POLITICAL SYSTEM AND THE CLASSICAL VISION OF ITS FUTURE EVOLUTION

There have been many changes in the multistate system since its inception in the seventeenth century. The relative capacity, or power, of states within the system has constantly shifted. Because of its pioneering industrialization, Great Britain attained the status of the most powerful state within the system early in the nineteenth century, and then roughly at the beginning of the twentieth century, the United States overtook Great Britain. Now other states are gaining in stature in relation to the United States. Such changes, however, need have little impact on the basic modalities of the multistate system; its principal elements could continue to be sovereign, independent, territorially defined units which would interact on the basis of their own decisions.

The extension of the multistate system, which initially began in Europe, to the entire globe, as new means of transportation and communications narrowed distances and as new states emerged with the breakup or collapse of European empires, is another important change. But increasing the number of units also need have little impact on the functioning of the multistate system. Like the more established states, the new states are territorially defined and claim sovereign independence. Whether the multistate system consists of 50 or 150 units need not affect the modalities of its functioning.

International organizations have contributed to both of these changes, as we have seen in preceding chapters, but what is of particular interest here is whether or not the global political system itself is undergoing some fundamental alteration; whether or not the world is moving from the multistate system that was established by the Peace of Westphalia in the seventeenth century, and what role, if any, international organizations are playing in this process and might play in a new world order.

The classical image of how the multistate system would be transformed has been patterned on the development of the state, and it has basically involved the hierarchical arrangement of political authority. Thus, states might be superseded by larger states. These larger states, however, would continue to claim sovereign independence, and they would be territorially defined. If this process were continued long enough, eventually the entire world might be under the rule of one government. World government achieved by voluntary federation has typically been the ultimate goal of those who have found the multistate system so deficient as to be unacceptable; their principal argument has usually been that this is the only way in which war could be avoided.

International organizations could easily be seen as fitting this classical image: way-stations toward the creation of larger territorially defined political systems. The European Economic Community could be viewed as the forerunner of the United States of Europe, and the League of Nations and the United Nations as early, halting steps toward the creation of a world government at some distant time. Often these institutions have been criticized from this perspective: the EEC has been condemned because its member states have not yet achieved full economic integration, and the U.N. has been castigated because of its inability to control conflict.

INGOs could also be viewed in this perspective; their role would be that of emerging interest groups for larger polities. The International Confederation of Free Trade Unions, the World Confederation of Labor, and the World Federation of Trade Unions could be viewed as incipient global labor movements, and the International Chamber of Commerce could be seen as ultimately playing a role in a global political system equivalent to that which the Chamber of Commerce now plays in the United States' political system. Transnational corporations have already made dramatic progress in internationalizing production processes. It could be argued that governmental authority with a domain as extensive as that of the transnational corporations will have to be developed to control TNCs to insure that their impressive capacities are directed toward broad public goals rather than narrow private ones. The growth of global trade unions could be seen as essential to insuring that power existed that could countervail that of TNCs.

Perhaps this perspective is correct. Perhaps international governmental organizations are forerunners of larger territorial units that would resemble existing states as ways of organizing political authority, and perhaps INGOs are emerging interest groups with a larger domain. It may simply be that the process of uniting several states into larger units by their own voluntary action is slow. Even when force was used in the unification of Germany and of Italy during the nineteenth century, the process took more than two decades; in a more complex age one could reasonably expect voluntary federation to be slower.

Such a vision would see states as the principal units in the global political system in the immediate future. There would be fewer states than there now are, and many of them would be geographically larger than those that presently exist, but the global political system would for some time continue to follow the Westphalian pattern, and interaction in the global system in the early part of the twenty-first century might well resemble that in the European multistate system of the nineteenth century. But according to this vision there would eventually be one world federal government.

To consider whether or not current developments accord with an image of the future involving dominant political authority being held by larger and larger territorially defined units requires, at a minimum, analyzing how contemporary nation-states gained their sovereign authority. This background is needed so that present developments can be measured against abstract theories of how several political units, through their own voluntary action, might merge into a larger unit—that is, how international integration might occur.

The Development of States

Let us return to points raised in Chapter 1 and consider the historical development of states. As typically conceived and in international law, a state is a territorially defined political unit the government of which is supreme in internal affairs and independent with respect to external affairs. The government of a state has this authority because the inhabitants of its territory accord it legitimacy. Formal definitions of sovereignty assign a monopoly of the legitimate use of coercion to the government of a state, and in fact a measure of coercion is always an element in insuring compliance with a government's commands, but compliance generally must be achieved through voluntary obedience. Citizens usually obey their government's orders because they believe that these orders are legitimate and not because they fear coercion; to have to resort to coercion to enforce every command would obviously overwhelm any government.

How governments gain authority and legitimacy as a general phenomenon is not well understood empirically. At one time subjects accepted the divine right of monarchs to rule. In the modern era the development of the authority and legitimacy of states and their governments has been associated with the growth of nationalism. Nationalism is a crucial ingredient in individuals' giving their loyalty to their states. The essence of nationalism is the development among a group of people of a sense of common identity and a feeling that the group ought to constitute a political unit that should manage its own affairs.

As Karl W. Deutsch has shown, nationalism depends upon the development of complementary habits and facilities of communication.[1] A common language helps, but nationalism has developed in places like Switzerland even in the absence of a common language, and different nationalisms exist among people who share the same language. Shared historical experiences have probably been the most crucial element in the rise of nationalism. Such experiences nurture a sense of common values and of a common destiny, and they lead to the development of symbols that represent this awareness of a common identity.

The growth of nationalism has both followed and preceded the establishment of states. Great Britain and France existed as states before the development of nationalism, and in these cases the existence of states contributed to the emergence of nationalist sentiment. A German sense of identity, on the other hand, apparently antedated the establishment of modern Germany and abetted the process of political unification in the nineteenth century. Many newly established states in Latin America in the nineteenth century and in Africa and Asia in the mid-twentith century have sought to create a sense of nationality among their inhabitants. Whether institutions have been established first and then attempts made to create loyalties, or whether common sentiments have led those who held them to demand the creation of political institutions, it is clear that the creation of institutions and the development of loyalties have been closely linked.

There can be many mechanisms accounting for an individual's loyalty to a state and its institutions. An individual may have a sentimental attachment to the symbols of a state, or to the collective identity of the people encompassed in the state. One's loyalty could also be derived from the sense that the state embodies and enhances the realization of values that one treasures. An even more pragmatic source of loyalty can be the belief that one's personal fortunes are inexorably linked with those of the state. Probably the loyalty of most individuals to their states is derived in varying degrees from all of these sources. Leaders attempting to build and maintain nationalism have typically utilized both sentimental and rational pragmatic appeals.

Historically, the development of nationalism has been associated with the shift from subsistence agriculture to exchange economies, with urbanization, and with social mobilization.[2] At first nationalism was a sentiment confined to elites; then with the increasing demands that governments put on their subjects and with the development of communications facilities, it became a mass movement.

To this point our discussion of nationalism has considered the consolidation of existing states or the creation of larger states. It must be remembered, however, that the growth of nationalism has also led to the breakup of states. In the early part of the twentieth century, nationalism clearly contributed to the collapse of the Austro-Hungarian and Ottoman empires. Later in the century, nationalism was an important factor in the separation of Bangladesh from Pakistan. Nationalism among large minorities in such states as Canada, Belgium, Nigeria, Spain, Yugoslavia, and even the United Kingdom of Great Britain and Northern Ireland has threatened the unity of these states. Wherever there is a group of people possessing a culture distinct from that of the majority of the inhabitants of a state

the less developed countries. More than 40 percent of the population of LDCs will probably live in urban areas by the end of the twentieth century, while considerably less than 10 percent lived in such areas at the beginning of the century. Providing meaningful employment and necessary services for this enormous and rapid increase in urban populations throughout the world, and especially in the LDCs, has already caused substantial problems. These tasks will surely continue to test the capacity of political institutions. There can be no question, though, that the trend toward urbanization will continue until a substantial majority of the population in virtually every country lives in urban areas.

The world's growing population is also becoming increasingly literate. By 1980 fewer than 30 percent of the world's population over fifteen years of age was illiterate.[7] If the same progress toward eliminating adult illiteracy that was made between 1960 and 1970 continues until the end of the century, by 2000 only about one out of five persons over fifteen years of age will be illiterate.

If historical patterns are a precedent, growing urban and literate populations will be increasingly articulate and effective in expressing political demands. One should not expect decreasing political volatility, especially within less developed countries.

The world's growing population and the demand of this population for higher standards of material welfare seem certain to strain global capacities. Food and energy crises have already occurred and seem likely to recur unless action is taken to alter present trends. Shortages of non-renewable resources appear inevitable. Clearly, at some point in the not too distant future, supplies of some non-renewable resources will be exhausted. As industrialization proceeds and spreads, unsupportable levels of air and water pollution can also be foreseen unless present trends are checked. Gloomy forecasts make catastrophic systemic breakdowns resulting in millions of deaths and perhaps irreversible damage to the human environment seem inevitable.[8] Other analyses show that despite global interdependence different regions will be affected differently by the continuation of present trends and that human intervention to alter these trends could avert catastrophes.[9] In general, the sooner the human intervention, the less damage will have been done.

Some more optimistic studies of the future argue that various resource and production crises can be solved through cooperation to maximize the gains of all, rather than confrontation in which all parties seek only to maximize their own self-interest. They maintain that different problems can be solved by cooperation at different levels. However, they also argue that a holistic, global approach is essential because everything is interrelated and at least the outline of a master plan must exist to guide the solution of discrete problems.

Our discussion has implied that the world product will continue to expand, as it has so sharply since the end of World War II. If present trends continue without change, the benefits of this increased global production will be disproportionately gained by the inhabitants of those countries that have high levels of economic development. The gap between the average per capita income in the developed countries and that in the developing countries has grown since World

War II, and if present trends are continued, it will increase in ratios and dramatically in absolute terms. As of 1979, 49 percent of the world's population living in the thirty-three countries that had per capita GNPs of less than $330 received less than 5 percent of the world product, while 13 percent of the world's population living in the twenty-six countries that had per capita GNPs of $7,590 and over received 58 percent.[10] Unless corrective measures are taken, as of the end of the twentieth century, the gap between material standards in the rich countries and in the poor countries could be even greater.

Changes in the structure of national and governmental societies are also occurring, and they can be expected to continue. With improvements in transportation and communications, there has been a substantial increase in transnational participation.[11] A growing number of persons travel, study, or establish temporary residences outside their own countries. During the 1960s and especially during the 1970s the number of international nongovernmental organizations increased even more rapidly than the number of international governmental organizations. As of 1980, according to the Union of International Associations' conservative count, there were 4,265 INGOs.[12] In all forms of transnational participation, growth has been concentrated particularly among the developed countries of Europe and North America. As of 1980 these countries accounted for just under 50 percent of the participation in international organizations.

Production processes have also become significantly internationalized since the end of World War II. Transnational corporations have been in existence for some time, but it was only in the 1950s and 1960s that they grew so spectacularly. A few examples of how United States-based TNCs grew illustrate the point.[13] Enterprises engaged in the extraction and distribution of raw materials led the way. From 1930 to 1938 the seven major U.S. oil companies expanded their operations from twenty-four to forty countries, but by 1957 the total had reached sixty-three, and by 1967 ninety-six.[14] In 1939 these seven companies had 351 foreign subsidiaries; they had 786 in 1957 and 1,442 in 1967. The 187 manufacturing enterprises that comprise the major American transnational corporations had 715 foreign manufacturing subsidiaries in 1939.[15] By 1950 they had 988 foreign manufacturing subsidiaries. Then came the period of explosive growth. By 1959 the total had reached 1,891 and by 1967, 3,646. In 1974 the sales of the world's fifty largest corporations (of which twenty-four have their headquarters in the United States) amounted to more than 8 percent of the world product, and these corporations employed about 2 percent of the world's population.[16] Considering that the operations of these enterprises are concentrated in the noncommunist countries, this concentration is even greater than the figures indicate, and immediate past trends suggest that these proportions should grow. Surely economic interdependence among states will continue to increase.

In a very general way, it can be argued that the entire world may, for the first time, be coming to participate in a coherent global social system. Beyond the increases in various forms of transnational participation that have already been cited, there is evidence that in quite diverse developing countries contact with modern institutions tends to result in individuals' adopting common modern attitudes and values.[17] As human life experiences become more similar, so should attitudes, values, and basic dispositions.[18] There is a convergence in attitudes toward the utilization of science and technology and toward bureaucratic procedures. Populations are increasingly being incorporated into new social roles. There is a broad movement toward attitudes that can be identified as modern and post-modern. Clearly, the growing consensus on the essentiality of human equality is part of the trend. This does not necessarily mean, however, that there will be convergence among states with respect to economic and political forms, and systems of economic and political control. The evidence of the continuing differences between the economic and political systems of such countries as the United States, France, and the Soviet Union suggests that modern attitudes can thrive within a variety of frameworks.

Institutional Issues: Universal Membership IGOS

With this sketch of developments and trends concerning general societal phenomena, we can turn to a consideration of institutional issues. What has happened with respect to the locus of political authority in the global system? As decolonization proceeded in the post-World War II period, a point was reached in the 1970s when nearly all of the world's territory was under the jurisdiction of sovereign, independent states, and there is no reason to expect that this process will not be carried to its ultimate conclusion.

For the more than eighty states that have gained their independence since 1945, their first task has been the consolidation of their political authority within their own boundaries. Few of these states began with ready-made nationalism; most have had to devote considerable efforts to nation building. Given the fragility of these states, the distinction between opposition and treason has often been blurred, and most have adopted regimes that are authoritarian in varying degrees.

At the same time that the nation-state pattern has been extended to the entire globe, however, international governmental organizations have also been created at an impressive pace. Using the conservative figures of the Union of International Associations, there were 118 IGOs in 1954, 154 in 1960, 242 in 1970, and 337 in 1980.[19] One estimate, made in 1966, projected that there would be from 380 to 545 IGOs by 1985.[20] It seems likely that the lower number will be exceeded, and using UIA's more liberal counting rules, there were already 1,039 IGOs by 1980. Interestingly, in contrast to the situation with respect to international nongovernmental organizations, participation in IGOs by states in Africa, Asia, South and Central America, and Oceania has grown more rapidly than participation by states in North America and Europe.

The many international organizations that now exist have begun to make an impact on the consciousness of the world's population. Almost all IGOs and many INGOs have information offices that work to publicize the organization and its activities. The news media throughout the world regularly carry items dealing with international organizations. A systematic survey of 1,000 daily newspapers published in fifty countries revealed that any issue of any newspaper throughout the world would be likely to carry one or two items dealing with the United Nations.[21] (Newspapers with a tradition of extensive coverage of world affairs, such as *Le Monde* and the *New York Times*, give much greater coverage to the U.N. than do other newspapers.) Television stations provide somewhat more extensive coverage of the U.N., and radio stations considerably more extensive coverage. Interestingly, all media in less developed countries give greater attention to the United Nations than do the media in developed countries. However, since the media are so much more plentiful in the developed world, the general populations of the developed countries receive more exposure to items about the United Nations than do the general populations of the LDCs. Less developed and developed countries also give attention to different aspects of the United Nations. The developed countries give greatest emphasis to political and security questions, while the less developed countries stress the U.N. in general and economic and social questions.[22]

At least partly as a consequence of media attention, awareness of the United Nations within the developed countries has been high.[23] In public opinion surveys in Western Europe and North America, more than four out of five respondents have indicated that they have some knowledge of the United Nations. Public satisfaction with the U.N.—affirming that the U.N. is doing a "good job"—has varied among these countries and with time from a low of about one out of five to a high of more than three out of five respondents. Despite dissatisfaction in various countries at different times with the manner in which particular issues have been treated in the United Nations, in general a majority of the public within Western European and North American countries has felt that the U.N. has justified its existence. In addition, a majority in some of these countries and a substantial minority in others have favored giving the United Nations more power, including its own military forces. U.N. peacekeeping efforts have met with widespread approval, even in Britain and France at the time of the Suez imbroglio.[24] Many people, often a majority, would favor their country's conducting more of its foreign relations through IGOs than has been the practice.[25] At the same time, there has long been a broad appreciation of the limited relevance of the United Nations to the Soviet-American conflict. And only a minority has felt that the U.N. by itself could provide an adequate guarantee for the security of their own country.[26]

We have little systematic data on public opinion in the communist countries and the less developed countries. There is no reason, however, to believe that public attitudes in these countries would be significantly more favorable toward giving the United Nations or other universal membership IGOs greater political authority. The data that are available about public attitudes in LDCs indicate that there is less awareness of the United Nations, but that among those who are aware of the U.N., a higher proportion have a favorable attitude toward what it has done than in the developed countries.

There is no possibility, then, of the U.N. soon supplanting the nation-state as a focus for the primary loyalty of human beings. The United Nations and other universal membership IGOs are seen as useful adjuncts to the nation-state, not as substitutes for it. Increasing economic interdependence and greater social homogeneity have not yet made significant numbers of people more willing to transfer important political authority to universal membership international governmental organizations.

Regional IGOS

But what of regional IGOs? Are these not more plausible successors to the nation-state? The European communities particularly must be considered, for their institutions have supranational powers and many writers and political activists have hoped or even perhaps believed that the communities would serve federalist objectives. Actually, the community institutions of various regional economic integration schemes now perform some of the functions that governments previously performed.

Table 16.1 presents a modified version of a system developed by Leon N. Lindberg for measuring the scope of the political authority of the European communities.[27] The functional areas that are listed are those that typically occupy governments, especially those of economically developed countries. Each functional area is ranked from low to high integration according to how decisions are made in the area. The criteria used in assigning scores are:

1. All policy decisions are made by individual governments by means of purely internal processes or are made in other non-national settings.
2. Only the beginnings of community-level decision authority have appeared.
3. Substantial regular policymaking goes on at the community level, but most matters are still decided by purely domestic processes.
4. Most decisions must be taken jointly, but substantial decisions are still taken autonomously at the nation-state level.
5. All choices are subject to joint decision in the community system.

Scores are given in Table 16.1 for five regional economic integration efforts—the Andean Group, Association of South East Asian Nations, the Central American Common Market, the Central African Customs and Economic Union, and the European communities—for the year in which the community was inaugurated and for 1982. As a point of comparison, rankings are also given for the United States for 1982.

The Andean Common Market was created in 1969 by the signing of the Cartagena Agreement by Bolivia, Chile, Colombia, Equador, and Peru. Venezuela joined the group in 1973, and Chile withdrew from the group in 1976. The Cartagena Agreement aims both at the creation of a common market and at common investment and development policies. The 1980 population of the five states was 72.6 million. Without Chile the population of the Andean Group was about that of Mexico; however, its area is more than twice as large as that of Mexico. Integration among the Andean Group of states was seen as essential to counter the economic hegemony in South America of Argentina, Brazil, and Mexico.

TABLE 16.1
The Changing Scope and Level of Political Authority in Selected Regional Economic Integration Schemes and in the United States.*

	Andrean Common Market		Asean		Central American Common Market		Central African Customs and Economic Union		European Communities		United States
	1969	1983	1967	1983	1960	1983	1964	1983	1951	1983	1983
External Relations											
1. Military security	1	1	1	2	1	1	1	1	1	1	5
2. Commercial relations	1	3	1	3	2	3	1	2	1	4	5
3. Diplomatic relations	1	2	1	3	1	2	1	1	1	3	5
Political and Civil Rights Functions											
4. Public safety	1	1	1	1	1	1	1	1	1	2	3
5. Political participation	1	1	1	1	1	1	1	1	1	3	4
6. Civil rights	1	2	1	1	1	1	1	1	1	3	4
Social and Cultural Functions											
7. Culture	1	2	1	2	1	1	1	1	1	1	2
8. Health	1	1	1	1	1	1	1	1	1	2	3
9. Social welfare	1	1	1	1	1	1	1	1	1	2	4
10. Education	1	2	1	1	2	2	1	1	1	2	3
Economic Functions											
11. Free movement of goods	1	3	1	2	3	3	1	4	1	5	5
12. Free movement of capital	1	3	1	2	1	1	1	2	1	4	5
13. Free movement of labor	1	1	1	1	1	1	1	2	1	5	5
14. Transport policy	1	1	1	2	2	3	1	2	1	4	3
15. Agricultural policy	1	2	1	1	1	3	1	2	1	4	5
16. Economic planning	1	2	1	1	1	2	1	1	1	2	4
17. Monetary policy	1	1	1	1	1	1	1	2	1	3	5
18. Natural resources	1	2	1	1	1	2	1	1	1	2	4

TABLE 16.1 *Continued*

	Andrean Common Market		Asean		Central American Common Market		Central African Customs and Economic Union		European Communities		United States
	1969	1983	1967	1983	1960	1983	1964	1983	1951	1983	1983
External Relations											
19. Counter-cyclical policy	1	1	1	1	1	1	1	1	1	2	5
20. Research and development	1	2	1	1	2	2	1	2	1	2	4
Percentage of Scores at Various Levels											
1	100	45	100	65	75	55	100	60	100	10	—
2	—	40	—	25	20	25	—	35	—	45	5
3	—	15	—	10	5	20	—	—	—	20	20
4	—	—	—	—	—	—	—	5	—	15	30
5	—	—	—	—	—	—	—	—	—	10	45

*The scoring was done by the author and Professor Dusan Sidjanski of the University of Geneva. The scoring system benefited from discussions in Professor Sidjanski's seminar on regional economic integration during the academic year 1977–1978.

Source: The measuring instrument is a modified version of that presented in Leon N. Lindberg, "Political Integration as a Multidimensional Phenomenon Requiring Multivariate Measurement," *International Organization 24* (Autumn 1970), 649–731, at pp. 663–678.

The Association of South East Asian Nations was created in 1967 at a meeting of the heads of state of Indonesia, Malaysia, the Philippines, Singapore, and Thailand. The governments of the five states hoped that the conflicts among their states could be surmounted through economic cooperation. As the United States withdrew from Vietnam, the five states also became increasingly concerned about security in the region. Although ASEAN has moved toward the creation of a customs union, many of its accomplishments relate to bargaining in international economic negotiations and to coordination of the five countries' policies on issues considered in the U.N. affecting security in Southeast Asia. Because the five countries had a combined population of 258.9 million—almost as large as that of the ten members of the European communities and greater than that of the United States—and included some of the world's fastest growing economies, ASEAN had considerable stature in international negotiations. At the same time, the difficulty of transportation among the countries complicated efforts to develop internal trade.

The five Central American states—Costa Rica, El Salvador, Guatemala, Honduras, and Nicaragua—were administered as a unit under the Spanish crown, and they were united in a confederation for almost two decades after they gained independence in the early nineteenth century. They have flirted with the idea of political integration frequently since the dissolution of this early confederation. The Central American Common Market came into existence in 1960, and it has functioned with varying degrees of success since then. After the so-called soccer war between Honduras and Nicaragua in 1969 Honduras withdrew from the common market, and as of 1982 a modality had not been found for this country to resume full participation. The political crises and conflicts in the region in the 1980s further complicated the situation. Somewhat surprisingly, a considerable measure of economic cooperation continued among the member states despite all of the obstacles. The five states are relatively small in size, form a compact geographical unit, and in 1980 had a total population of about 20.3 million, somewhat less than the population of California.

The Central African Customs and Economic Union, or the *Union Douanière et Economique de l'Afrique Centrale* (UDEAC), was created in 1964 with Cameroon, the Central African Republic, Chad, the People's Republic of the Congo, and Gabon as members. All of these states had been administered jointly under colonial rule as part of French Equatorial Africa, and the Central African Republic, Chad, the People's Republic of Congo, and Gabon had formed the *Union Equatoriale* in 1959. The UDEAC treaty provided for the creation of a common market and a certain coordination of development and investment policies. Chad withdrew from UDEAC in 1968. In 1980 the four remaining countries had a combined population of approximately 12.9 million, somewhat less than that of Texas. But the area of the UDEAC states is more than twice as large as that of Texas.

Belgium, France, the Federal Republic of Germany, Italy, Luxembourg, and the Netherlands took the first step toward economic integration in Western Europe in 1951 when they signed the treaty creating the European Coal and Steel Community. In 1957 these same six states signed treaties creating the European Atomic Energy Community and the European Economic Community. In 1973 Denmark, Ireland, and the United Kingdom joined the three communities, and Greece joined in 1981. The combined 1980 population of the nine states of about 269.9 million was exceeded only by that of China and India; it was greater than that of all other states, including the Soviet Union and the United States.

In each of the five areas a strong, and perhaps even a compelling, case existed for regional economic integration. In each area, having a larger territory with a greater population than any of the individual states had would offer significant economic advantages. A larger market would facilitate achieving economies of scale and encourage both domestic and foreign investment. In several of the areas, there was a history of common rule, and all of them have several of the background characteristics thought to be essential to achieving regional integration.

As can be seen from Table 16.1, in all five regions community institutions have played a role in decision making in several issue areas, although in none of the five cases have community institutions gained the same overall authority as the national government of the United States. Reflecting the purposes of the regional economic integration schemes, in all five cases community institutions have gained greatest authority with respect to economic functions. None of them has gained substantial authority with respect to military security. In 1983 the institutions of the European communities had a more substantial role in decision making than did community institutions in any other region. Both the Andean Group and UDEAC have made slow but steady progress. Scorings for more points in time would show that integration in the Central American Common Market apparently reached a plateau in the late 1960s and further progress has not occurred. ASEAN has made more progress in external relations than it has in internal cooperation. The record is mixed, but over time the political authority of the community institutions in all of the integration efforts has grown.

INSTITUTIONS AND PUBLIC OPINION

This analysis of the scope of integration, particularly with respect to the European communities, provides some support for the thesis that in regional settings international institutions may be the forerunners of larger territorially defined units, and in Europe at least significant changes in public attitudes have accompanied the growth of institutional authority. As the institutions of the European communites have developed, public attitudes within the member countries toward other member countries have become more friendly.[28] Among the publics of the original six members of the European communities, Ronald Inglehart found that by the 1970s support for European integration was "relatively deep-rooted and stable."[29] In the newer three member states of the communities, such feelings were less widespread. Pro-European attitudes have generally grown with membership in the communities, and by the early 1970s some individuals even indicated that they identified with Europe more than with any other geo-political unit.[30]

On the surface, then, these phenomena would seem to support the notion that the European communities could well lead to the United States of Europe. Developments would seem to fit with all three approaches—the federalist, the communications, and the neo-functionalist—for as we have seen in earlier chapters, trading among the member states increased enormously with the progress of the European communities, and increases in communications accompanied this increase in trade.

But reality is more complex than this simple picture would have it. Table 16.1 also indicates that progress toward integration has not been uniform. Integration among the states of the Central American Common Market appears stalled. The East African Community, which is not included in Table 16.1 but which at one time had considerable integration, completely disintegrated in 1977. There also may have been some decline in the integration among the member states of the European communities in the period between 1973 and 1977, and significantly this decline occurred in the issue areas of the original integration efforts, areas in which one would have thought that the neo-functionalists' inexorable logic of expansive sectoral integration would have been compelling.[31] Instead, however, either the nation-state or some unit larger than the European communities has proved to be the better framework for attempting to deal with the problems of these modern industrial societies that were interdependent not only with one another but with other states in Western Europe that were not members of the communities and with North America and Japan. In the 1973–1977 period leaders and interest groups within the European communities did not behave in the manner predicted by the neo-functionalist approach.

The data with respect to public opinion are also more complex than a simplistic interpretation that would see a simple transfer of loyalty from nation-states to the European communities. Inglehart's analyses indicate that favorable attitudes toward the European communities appear to be associated with favorable attitudes toward internationalism generally, or what might be called a cosmopolitan approach to international affairs.[32] Furthermore, according to the data from the same 1973 survey on which Inglehart based many of his analyses, in France, the Netherlands, Italy, Denmark, Ireland, and the United Kingdom, more persons stated that they identified first with the world rather than first with Europe.[33] In all cases younger persons are more likely to identify with Europe or with the world than are older persons, and in all cases supranational identification is strongly associated with holding what have been described as post-materialist values.[34]

All this having been said, however, even in Europe individuals retained a strong sense of local and national identification. The 1973 survey data show that in all nine of the member states of the European communities, more than half of the respondents gave their nation as either their first or second identification, and in the Netherlands, Ireland, and the United Kingdom, the proportion giving such responses was more than 70 percent.[35] It was more than 60 percent in Denmark, France, and Italy. In Belgium, the Federal Republic of Germany, Denmark, and Luxembourg, more than half of the respondents gave their town as their first identification, and this choice was also the most popular in Italy, the Netherlands, and Ireland, being chosen in each of these three cases by about 40 percent of the respondents. The town was the second most popular first choice in France and the United Kingdom. In these two countries the nation was the most popular first choice, and it was the second most popular first choice in all of the others.

To the extent that such surveys represent an adequate test of national identification and nationalism, it would seem that even in Western Europe, where since the end of World War II there has been a broad, continual, and multifaceted drive to diminish and supplant nationalism, where transnational participation has been most developed, and where supranational institutions exist, the nation remains the most potent geo-political unit for identification. This is also true in the United States. Nationalism remains potent in the advanced industrial states, where post-materialist values are most widespread. In the less developed countries, which are often rent with deep social and cultural divisions, and face divisive issues in dealing with developmental problems and strategies, leaders must be expected to appeal to national sentiment and to attempt to develop nationalism to keep their countries together. The growth of national sentiment is also a likely consequence of the increase in urbanization and literacy that these areas will experience. Nationalism will probably become more rather than less potent among the LDCs than it now is.

We must therefore expect the nation-state to be the primary focus of political allegiance for the foreseeable future. But if nationalism will continue to be a dominant force structuring the global political system, it need not necessarily be the same destructive nationalism that has had such disastrous consequences in the past. Among the advanced industrial countries of Western Europe and North America, there has developed a strong revulsion against the use of military force for almost any purpose other than the defense of the nation-state itself. Beyond defending the United States, only an attack on Canada, Western Europe, or Japan would elicit support from a majority of the U.S. public in the early 1980s for U.S. military action.[36] In a public opinion survey conducted in 1970 in Belgium, the Federal Republic of Germany, France, Italy, and the Netherlands, avoiding another world war was desired more than anything else.[37] Although the evidence is sketchy, it may be argued that in the advanced industrial democracies nationalism is primarily pragmatic and welfare-oriented rather than emotional and jingoistic.

The Involvement of States in IGOS and INGOS

Present trends indicate a future world of increasing complexity—complexity caused by a more numerous, urban, literate, and sophisticated population that will demand material betterment, putting strains on the limited capacity of human institutions and world resources. Paradoxically, as the Westphalian system of sovereign states is extended over the earth's territory, it will be virtually impossible for states to isolate themselves from outside influences. The interdependence of states has grown significantly since the end of World War II, and it appears certain to increase even more in the coming years and perhaps at an even faster pace. The large and growing number of international governmental organizations and international nongovernmental organizations is testimony to this interdependence. The creation, existence, and growth of IGOs and INGOs clearly demonstrate how unsuitable the nation-state is as a unit for dealing with many contemporary problems. At the same time, the deepening desire for participation in political decisions means that for many problems some nation-states are simply too large to be satisfactory units. Decentralization has been essential to satisfy the desire for participation and also to deal more adequately with complexity. But even with these elements of erosion of its central authority—the creation of international organizations and decentralization—the nation-state remains and appears likely to remain the predominant focus for political allegiance.

Robert O. Keohane and Joseph S. Nye have urged that the "state-centric" model that has long been prevalent in studies of international politics should be replaced with a more complex image of reality.[38] Surely the evidence supports their plea. Sovereign states are not being superseded as the principal actors in world politics. Sovereignty, however, is rapidly being eroded. More and more states are bound in webs of networks of international organizations, and in more and more functional areas the freedom of states to make unilateral decisions is restricted. Some of the ties are universal, but for most states the greater number of ties and the stronger commitments are with limited membership IGOs. Clusters of states are bound together in organizations, but these groups of states do not seem to be merging into new territorially defined political units, larger states; or if they are, the process appears to be so slow that it will not reach fruition in the future with which we are concerned. Only in Western Europe is political integration even a remote possibility, and if the United States of Europe were formed, the new entity would itself be deeply enmeshed in a web of ties with other economically developed states through such IGOs as NATO and OECD, and with the entire world through the U.N. family of agencies.

Ernst B. Haas has coined the phrase "asymmetrical regional overlap" to describe the contribution of international institutions to the current organization of political authority in the regions within the global system.[39] Haas has described his concept in the following manner:

Asymmetrical overlapping involves a much more complex arrangement. Many units depend on many others but the pattern of interdependence is asymmetrical: For some purposes all may be equally interdependent, but for others a few of the units cohere closely with a few others while for still other purposes the pattern may again be different without involving all units equally. In short, while authority is certainly withdrawn from the preexisting units, it is not proportionately or symmetrically vested in a new center; instead it is distributed asymmetrically among several centers, among which no single dominant one may emerge, though one might imagine subtypes of this dependent variable involving various degrees of centralized authority. The ensemble would enjoy legitimacy in the eyes of its citizens though it would be difficult to pinpoint the focus of the legitimacy in a single authority center; rather, the image of infinitely tiered multiple loyalties might be the appropriate one.[40]

Haas ventured the opinion that present arrangements in Western Europe may be approaching this image, and I share his judgment.

In a careful review of historical cases of political integration, Karl W. Deutsch has distinguished between "amalgamated" and "pluralistic" security communities.[41] Security communities are groups of people with practices and institutions strong enough to assure expectations that change will be achieved by peaceful rather than violent means. "Amalgamated" security communities occur when two or more units unite into a larger unit, with some common government. "Pluralistic" security communities achieve the expectation of peaceful change without the units giving up their legal independence; the units formally retain sovereignty. Deutsch cited Canada and the United States and Norway and Sweden as examples of "pluralistic" security communities. Deutsch and his associates examined sixteen cases dating from the eleventh century through the nineteenth century and found that although both types of security communities were practicable approaches, "pluralistic security-communities turned out to be somewhat easier to attain and easier to preserve than their amalgamated counterparts.[42] Our analysis of the role of contemporary international governmental organizations points in a similar direction. The primary immediate contribution of IGOs would appear to be the formation of "pluralistic" rather than "amalgamated" security communities.

What we have, then, is a global political system that is already complex and growing even more complex. Nation-states retain sovereignty and consequently remain the principal actors in international politics. But all states are enmeshed in complex webs of international organizations, both governmental and nongovernmental, and their societies, rather than being sealed from one another, are linked by growing transnational connections. Although political authority continues to be centered in governments of nation-states, in reality it is widely dispersed. With respect to countless issues, to be effective governments must act together, but different issues elicit cooperation by different combinations of states. States entangled in webs of international organizations is the proper simile to describe the contemporary global political system, and international organizations, both IGOs and INGOs, are best seen as sophisticated communication devices, instruments for transmitting and relaying messages and coordinating actions. The global political system continues to consist of multiple sovereign centers of decision making, but effective power is increasingly being organized in a non-hierarchical manner.

THE FUNCTIONING OF A NON-HIERARCHICAL SYSTEM

The contemporary world political system, then, is one of growing interactions and complexity, but it is one in which power and authority are not organized in a hierarchical manner, and there is no immediate prospect of power and authority being organized in a hierarchical manner. States now have and for the foreseeable future will continue to have ultimate power and authority. International organizations have very little ability to force the compliance of states through the use of coercion. For millennia the world has operated without a single global center of power and authority. The global political system has always been decentralized, and although this has had substantial costs, within this decentralized framework humankind has made remarkable progress in raising material standards of life and in increasing the extent to which interpersonal relations and relations between governments and their subjects are governed by principles of humanity and civility.

Were it not for the horrendous dangers posed by recent scientific and technological developments, it might be possible for humankind to continue to exist on earth without a more elaborate global political system than has existed in the past. The webs of networks of international organizations that have been established are testimony, however, to the widespread consensus that the decentralization of the past is not adequate to the problems of the present and the future. But some argue, as we have seen, that existing international organizations are not adequate either, that some form of global government is needed. If apocalyptic catastrophes occur, this argument will have been proven correct, but such events cannot now be accurately foreseen. To the extent that the fear of such events underlies the call for world government, no real response to the argument is possible. Positions in such debates tend to be based on generalized feelings of pessimism or optimism. To the extent, however, that the call for organizing the world in a more hierarchical manner is based on the fear that a non-hierarchical system cannot function effectively, a response based on analogy is possible.

Considerable research has been conducted concerning the functioning of industrial organizations in modern society. Very broadly, this research has found that while all large organizations of human beings involve the potential for conflict, organizations that resolve such conflicts as may arise by means of coercion are less effective than those that resolve them through cooperative techniques. Both morale and productivity are higher in organizations that do not stress hierarchy and status than they are in those that do stress these organizational characteristics.

Effective organizations set goals collectively rather than by command. Communications and participation are deep and widespread. Integrative and mutually acceptable, rather than divisive, goals are sought. Facts are gathered cooperatively so that situational constraints are broadly understood and common definitions of problems can be achieved. Groups are kept small so that informal procedures may be used and trust can be developed, and these small groups are linked by individuals who have multiple group memberships. Peer leadership is stressed. The desire of individuals for self-esteem and a sense of worth is developed, and interpersonal relationships are structured to facilitate fulfillment of this desire. Rewards and involvement are used to motivate individuals rather than fear. Effective organizations, rather than stifling dissent, acknowledge the existence of differences and disagreements and seek to use this creatively to find innovative solutions to problems.

This research on industrial organizations would suggest therefore that the hierarchical organization of authority not only is not essential to getting things done, but may even be counterproductive, especially with reference to matters of some complexity.

Because of the informational activities of international organizations, an enormous amount of statistical data and other information has become available concerning developments throughout the world. IGOs and INGOs have facilitated the monitoring of developments in virtually all fields of human endeavor, and they have provided forums where developments and trends can be considered, discussed, and publicized. Both normative and rule-creating activities work in the direction of achieving consensus among the governments of states, and more remotely among peoples, for it is the governments of states that in the end will decide whether or not to accept the rules and to implement the standards articulated by international organizations. Sometimes governments can be pressed by their populations to accept standards that they would not have accepted otherwise, but there are limits to the ability of international organizations to mobilize public opinion without governmental support, and these limits are even more pronounced when there is governmental hostility.

The rule-supervisory activities of international organizations are properly called "supervisory" rather than "enforcement" activities; they rely on persuasion and publicity much more than on coercion. The operational activities of contemporary international organizations are to an extraordinary extent conducted on a voluntary basis. Funds are largely provided through voluntary contributions, and the consent of the state concerned is a prerequisite to any activity being conducted. In sum, international organizations hardly ever issue commands; instead, they facilitate voluntary cooperation. Therefore in some cases INGOs can be as effective as IGOs, and on occasion even more effective.

The policies of governments cannot help but be influenced by the extent to which their states are enmeshed in webs of networks of international organizations. Willingly or unwillingly, governments are exposed to the positions of the governments of other states and to information prepared by secretariats. The viewpoint of the secretariat may be international or it may be a mélange of national orientations, but in any case it is likely to be different from that of any single government. Few contemporary governments are impervious for long to information; most attempt to formulate their policies taking into account all of the information that is available.

Given the present extent of interdependence among states, there are many goals that even the most powerful states can achieve only in collaboration with other states. International organizations provide readily available frameworks for such collaboration. They also have fixed procedures for how decisions should be taken, and governments seeking to utilize these organizations to achieve certain goals must take these procedures into account. They must adjust their policies so that they will be supported by whatever proportion of the member states of the organization is required. Both features of the enmeshment of states in webs of international organization networks, the exposure to information, and the necessity of obtaining the consent of others, work toward influencing the policies of governments so that they are less ethnocentric and more moderate. Government policies are shaped in the direction of fitting global developments and taking account of the goals of other states.

In addition, international organizations facilitate the development of communication linkages among governmental officials whose primary responsibility is domestic programs, as David Mitrany postulated that they would. Since the goals of officials with domestic sectoral responsibilities are not always the same as those of foreign officers or even the same as those of presidents or prime ministers, these communications links in sectoral fields have been used to form coalitions to advance sectoral goals. Thus national goals become blurred and merged into more broadly determined sectoral goals.

Michel Crozier has described processes in the contemporary global political system with the term *apprentissage institutionel*.[43] In his view, the world is going through a period of learning how to use voluntary institutions to achieve cooperation and coordination in the performance of more and more complex tasks. The emerging processes facilitated by the growth of international organizations within the global political system bear a close resemblance to those processes that have been found to be effective in modern industrial organizations.

However, there are aspects of international organization that run counter to the principles derived from research on these organizations. The stress on parliamentary procedures, and on voting, and the rigid instruction of delegates can easily highlight and exacerbate conflict rather than contribute to its resolution. Even more important, some conflicts among countries still largely escape the webs of international organization networks, and in the settlement of all conflicts, whether or not they are treated by and within international organizations, the potential for recourse by states to economic and military coercion remains high.

The extent to which a cooperative, problem-solving approach can be applied to conflict resolution depends on the extent to which there is a broad consensus on basic values. In the absence of such a consensus, often the only solution is a hierarchical command, enforced if necessary by coercion. Clearly it would be myopic to ignore the many and deep disagreements concerning basic values that exist among the countries of the world today, but the argument of this book has been that international organizations by being, above all, communications networks have become effective instruments for narrowing the differences among countries concerning basic values and for working toward the development of a significant consensus. Indeed, it would appear that a genuine, broad, and deep consensus does exist concerning the need to prevent a nuclear holocaust, and that consensus is developing on other points as well, such as the illegitimacy of using military force to resolve disputes or to alter established boundaries of states and on the need to eliminate colonialism and racial discrimination. There is less consensus concerning the way in which economic production should be organized and how the fruits of productive processes should be allocated, but even with respect to such economic issues, because of the extent of economic interdependence, common interests are developing in the continued smooth functioning of the global economy. Disagreement is perhaps sharpest concerning the proper relationships between individuals and governments. How rapidly and to what extent the limited consensus that presently exists in global society can be expanded and deepened is problematic.

In the meantime, the task of global leadership should be to treat cooperatively the topics that can be so treated while working toward a broader consensus to isolate the disagreements that do exist and to attempt to prevent them from spilling over and destroying the limited consensus. The task of leadership rests particularly with the industrially developed countries, which have benefited so substantially from the existing world order. The growing gap between the standard of material welfare enjoyed by the minority of the world's population that lives in these countries and the majority of humankind that lives in less developed countries is becoming an increasing source of frustration for the latter group. Preserving and extending the limited consensus that presently exists in global society will require the relatively rich countries to be responsive to the sources of this frustration. If this can be achieved, one can be optimistic about the future; if it cannot, divisions within the world are certain to harden, and the chances for cooperation will lessen. Barring a nuclear holocaust, the distribution of the world product will surely be the dominant issue of world politics during the remainder of the twentieth century. Should there be an impasse in this issue area, the disagreement could well spread and contaminate cooperation in other areas. This could weaken the consensus that exists in the security field, and it certainly would not make progress in the fields of social welfare and human rights easier.

How the distribution of the world product will be treated and what the structure and dimensions of the global political system will be in the future cannot be foreseen in detail. Nothing is completely foreordained. Yet the basic elements of the global political system of the future are surely already in place. They are: states which will continue to have ultimate power and authority; international organizations of all types, governmental and nongovernmental with universal and limited memberships and with specific and general purposes; and transnational organizations, with TNCs being an especially important subdivision of this category. Undoubtedly, all of these bodies will be important in the future as they are at present, but the relative weight of their influence could be substantially different from what it is now. Governments can stress IGOs or INGOs and different types of each in their policies, and they can seek to exercise by themselves or with others more or less control over transnational corporations.

In the 1970s there appeared to be a real danger that the conflict between developed countries and less developed countries might become so intense within universal membership IGOs that the developed countries might either withdraw from some of these organizations or continue to participate in them but pay little attention to their activities and instead concentrate on pursuing their policies in IGOs limited to the developed countries. The United States' withdrawal from the International Labor Organization in 1977 could be seen as a harbinger of such a development. But its return to ILO in 1980 could indicate a rejection of the strategy of withdrawal. Were the developed countries to lessen their involvement in the web of universal membership international organizations, surely the potential of an important channel for the resolution of global conflict would be diminished.

The argument of this book has been that it is the enmeshment of states in international organizations that has facilitated the development of consensus on a broad range of important issues and cooperation to achieve the agreed goals. If this argument is correct, then it is to the interests of both the developed and the less developed states to preserve and indeed deepen the existing enmeshment of states in organizations that include both sides.

Richard A. Falk, in his *A Study of Future Worlds,* has called for the creation of an international organization before the end of the twentieth century that would provide effective "central guidance" for the global political system.[44] This would involve a universal membership, general purpose organization with a more elaborate structure and more substantial powers than those of the United Nations. In the short run, given the divisions that exist in the world, the possibility of such an organization's being created seems remote. The structural issues that have plagued the designers of international organizations since the authors of the early "peace plans" seem no easier to solve in the contemporary world—with the vast disparities in size, population, wealth, ideology, and political system that exist among the more than 150 sovereign states that constitute the present global political system—than they were at the time that the state system emerged. The insolubility of these problems explains the constant pressure to create limited membership, special purpose organizations. This pressure will undoubtedly persist.

Under the circumstances, the most powerful states, which would bear the greatest burden for the implementation of collective decisions, will surely be reluctant to give greater authority to any international organization in which they do not have a predominant voice. From the perspective of popular control of political institutions, international organizations should gain greater authority only when more is known about how to insure popular control of these "meta-bureaucracies."

The most important issue, then, is not building up the authority of a universal membership, general purpose organization, but rather insuring that there are open and ample communications links among the major groups of states today: the developed states with market economies, the developed states with planned economies, and the less developed states. Whether or not this will occur is up to governments and their peoples. International organizations are instruments. Whether they shall be used and how they shall be used will be determined by human beings. Humankind will decide its fate.

NOTES

1. Karl W. Deutsch, *Nationalism and Social Communication: An Inquiry into the Foundations of Nationality* (New York: Wiley, 1953).

2. See Karl W. Deutsch, "The Growth of Nations: Some Recurrent Patterns of Political and Social Integration," *World Politics,* 5 (January 1953), 168–195.

3. See Deutsch, *Nationalism and Social Communication,* and Karl W. Deutsch and others, *Political Community and the North Atlantic Area: International Organization in the Light of Historical Experience* (Princeton: Princeton University Press, 1957).

4. Ernst B. Haas authored the pioneering work following this approach; see his *The Uniting of Europe: Political, Social and Economic Forces, 1950–1957* (Stanford: Stanford University Press, 1958). Joseph S. Nye's *Peace in Parts: Integration and Conflict in Regional Organization* (Boston: Little, Brown, 1971) is the most comprehensive statement, including all of the refinements that have been built into the approach.

5. Bernard Berelson, "World Population: Status Report 1974," *Reports on Population/ Family Planning,* 15 (January 1974), 3–5.

6. See U.N., Department of Economic and Social Affairs, *Growth of the World's Urban and Rural Population, 1920–2000,* Population Studies, No. 44 (New York: U.N., 1969).

7. U.N. Secretariat, Department of International Economic and Social Affairs, *1982 Report on the World Social Situation* (New York: U.N., 1982), p. 115.

8. See Donella H. Meadows *et al., The Limits to Growth* (New York: Universe Books, 1972).

9. See Mihajlo Mesarovic and Eduard Pestel, *Mankind at the Turning Point: The Second Report of the Club of Rome* (New York: Signet, 1974).

10. International Bank for Reconstruction and Development, *World Bank Atlas: Gross National Product, Population and Growth Rates, 1981* (Washington, D.C.: IBRD, 1982), p. 4.

11. For a detailed analysis of these trends, see Robert Cooley Angell, *Peace on the March: Transnational Participation* (New York: Van Nostrand, 1969).

12. Union of International Associations, *Yearbook of International Organizations, 1981, 19th* ed. (Brussels: UIA, 1981), pp. 1981–1982.

13. The examples are taken from Raymond Vernon's study, *Sovereignty at Bay: The Multinational Spread of U.S. Enterprises* (New York: Basic Books, 1971).

14. Ibid., p. 32.

15. Ibid., p. 62.

16. The figures on the sales and employees of the world's fifty largest industrial companies are taken from *Fortune,* 90:2 (August 1974), p. 185.

17. See Alex Inkeles and David H. Smith, *Becoming Modern* (Cambridge: Harvard University Press, 1974).

18. This point is argued persuasivley in Alex Inkeles, "The Emerging Social Structure of the World," *World Politics,* 27 (July 1975), 467–495.

19. Union of International Associations, *Yearbook of International Organizations, 1981,* pp. 1981–1982.

20. Union of International Associations, *Yearbook of International Organizations, 1974, 15th* ed. (Brussels: UIA, 1974), p. S34.

21. See Alexander Szalai with Margaret Croke and associates, *The United Nations and the News Media* (New York: U.N. Institute for Training and Research, 1972), p. 15.

22. Ibid., p. 84.

23. See William A. Scott and Stephen B. Withey, *The United States and the United Nations: The Public View, 1945–1955* (New York: Manhattan, 1958), p. 32; and Richard L. Merritt and Donald J. Puchala (eds.), *Western European Perspectives on International Affairs* (New York: Praeger, 1968), p. 407.

24. Merritt and Puchala, *Western European Perspectives on International Affairs*, p. 410.

25. John E. Rielly (ed.), *American Public Opinion and U.S. Foreign Policy, 1975* (Chicago: Chicago Council on Foreign Relations, 1975), p. 21.

26. Ibid.

27. See Leon N. Lindberg, "Political Integration as a Multidimensional Phenomenon Requiring Multivariate Measurement," *International Organization*, 24 (Autumn 1970), 649–731, at pp. 663–678.

28. See Barry B. Hughes and John E. Schwarz, "Dimensions of Political Integration and the Experience of the European Community," *International Studies Quarterly*, 16 (September 1972), 263–294.

29. Ronald Inglehart, *The Silent Revolution* (Princeton: Princeton University Press, 1977), p. 342.

30. Ibid., p. 330–362.

31. See Ernst B. Haas, *The Obsolescence of Regional Integration Theory* (Berkeley: University of California, Berkeley, Institute of International Studies, 1975), p. 21.

32. See Ronald Inglehart, "The New Europeans: Inward or Outward Looking?" *International Organization*, 24 (Winter 1970), 129–139.

33. Inter-university Consortium for Political and Social Research, P. O. Box 1248, Ann Arbor, Michigan 48106, ICPSR Study Number 7330, *1973 European Communities Study*.

34. Inglehart, *The Silent Revolution*, p. 334.

35. ICPSR Study Number 7330, *1973 European Communities Study*.

36. John E. Rielly (ed.), *American Public Opinion and U.S. Foreign Policy, 1983* (Chicago: Chicago Council on Foreign Relations, 1983), p. 31.

37. Inter-university Consortium for Political and Social Research, P. O. Box 1248, Ann Arbor, Michigan 48106, ICPSR Study Number 7260, *1970 European Communities Study*.

38. Joseph S. Nye and Robert O, Keohane, "Transnational Relations and World Politics: An Introduction," *International Organization*, 25 (Summer 1971), 329–350.

39. Ernst B. Haas, "The Study of Regional Integration: Reflections on the Joy and Anguish of Pretheorizing," *International Organization*, 24 (Autumn 1970), 607–646, at pp. 634–635.

40. Ibid., p. 635.

41. Karl W. Deutsch and others, *Political Community and the North Atlantic Area*, p. 6.

42. Ibid., p. 29.

43. Michel Crozier, *Les possibilités d'utiliser les méthodes d'analyse de la sociologie des Organisations dans l'étude des Institutions internationales* (Geneva: Carnegie Endowment for International Peace, European Center, 1966. Mimeographed).

44. Richard A. Falk, *A Study of Future Worlds* (New York: Free Press, 1975), p. 156. The type of global political system that Falk would prefer is outlined in Chapter 4, "Designing a Preferred World Polity," pp. 224–276.

FOR FURTHER READING

Alting von Geusau, Frans A. M. *European Perspectives on World Order*. Leyden: A. W. Sijhoff, 1975.

Angell, Robert Cooley. *Peace on the March: Transnational Participation*. New York: Van Nostrand, 1969.

Bhagwati, Jagdish (ed.). *Economics and World Order: from the 1970s to the 1980s*. New York: Macmillan, 1972.

Black, Cyril E. *The Dynamics of Modernization: A Study in Comparative History*. New York: Harper & Row, 1968.

Brzezinski, Zbigniew. *Between Two Ages: America's Role in the Technetronic Era.* New York: Viking, 1970.

Deutsch, Karl W. *Nationalism and Its Alternatives.* New York: Knopf, 1969.

—— . *The Nerves of Government: Models of Political Communication and Control.* New York: Free Press, 1963.

Falk, Richard A. *A Study of Future Worlds.* New York: Free Press, 1975.

Fisher, Roger. *Improving Compliance With International Law.* Charlottesville, Virginia: University Press of Virginia, 1981.

Haas, Ernst B. "A Study of Regional Integration: Reflections on the Joy and Anguish of Pretheorizing," *International Organization,* 24 (Autumn 1970), 607–646.

—— . *Scientists and World Order.* Berkeley: University of California Press, 1977.

Huntington, Samuel P. *Political Order in Changing Societies.* New Haven: Yale University Press, 1968.

Jacobson, Harold K. "The Global System and the Realization of Human Dignity and Justice," *International Studies Quarterly,* 26 (September 1982), pp. 315–331.

Kahn, Herman, and Anthony Wiener. *The Year 2000.* New York: MacMillan, 1965.

Katz, Daniel, and Robert L. Kahn. *The Social Psychology of Organizations.* 2nd ed. New York: Wiley, 1978.

Kelman, Herbert C. "Patterns of Personal Involvement in the National System: A Social-Psychological Analysis in Political Legitimacy," in James N. Rosenau (ed.), *International Politics and Foreign Policy: A Reader in Research and Theory.* New York: Free Press, 1969.

Keohane, Robert O., and Joseph S. Nye. *Power and Interdependence: World Politics in Transition.* Boston: Little, Brown, 1977.

Likert, Rensis, and Jane Gibson Likert. *New Ways of Managing Conflict.* New York: McGraw-Hill, 1976.

Scott, Andrew M. *The Dynamics of Interdependence.* Chapel Hill: University of North Carolina Press, 1982.

The Web of IGOs, 1980

This list of international governmental organizations in existence in 1980 was compiled by the same principles as the list that appeared in the first edition of *Networks of Interdependence.* Like the lists compiled by Michael D. Wallace and J. David Singer, it includes IGOs that have only two member states; the Union of International Associations insists on a minimum of three. Unlike Wallace and Singer and UIA's restrictive list, this list also includes IGOs that are formally part of another IGO, such as the United Nations Conference on Trade and Development which is formally a part of the United Nations. The rationale for this is that several organizations of this type have substantial budgets and considerable autonomy; they seem as important as many formally independent IGOs.

I used the list of IGOs that appeared in the first edition of *Networks of Interdependence* as a point of departure. All new data came from the 19th, or 1981, edition of UIA's *Yearbook of International Organizations.* Over the years partly as a result of improved data collection, UIA has become much more inclusive in its listing. The 1970 list included in *Networks of Interdependence* contained 289 organizations. I deleted 39 IGOs from that list because the 19th edition of the *Yearbook of International Organizations* either indicated that they had been dissolved or did not list them. I added 371 new organizations, 120 of which had been established in 1970 or earlier; 238 of which were established after 1970; and 13 of which do not have a date of creation in the *Yearbook* entry. The number of member states for each IGO is that given in the *Yearbook* and is usually for 1980.

Clearly it is hard to know exactly how many international governmental organizations there are in the global political system. The point of this listing is not to be definitive, but rather to illustrate the extent and variety of IGOs that constitute the web of communications networks.

LIMITED MEMBERSHIP, SPECIFIC PURPOSE	DATE OF CREATION	NUMBER OF MEMBERS
ACP/EEC Consultative Assembly	1975	70
Administrative Centre of Social Security for Rhine Boatsmen	1950	6
African and Malagasy Coffee Organization	—	8
African and Malagasy Council on Higher Education	1968	11
African and Mauritian Common Organization	1964	11
African and Mauritian Office for Law Research and Studies	—	—
African and Mauritian Union of Development Bank	1962	11
African Civil Aviation Commission	1969	41
African Center for Applied Research and Training in Social Development	1977	—
African Cultural Institute	1971	17
African Data Processing Institute	1971	—
African Development Bank	1963	47
African Development Fund	1972	17
African Groundnut Council	1962	7
African Institute for Economic Development and Planning	1962	10
African Intellectual Property Organization	1962	13
African Postal Union	1961	12
African Postal and Telecommunications Union	1961	11
African Reinsurance Corporation	1976	—
African Society for the Development of the Millet-and-Sorghum-Based Food Industry	—	5
African Telecommunications Union	1961	—
African Timber Organization	1975	11
African Training and Research Center in Administration for Development	1964	33
Afro-Asian Rural Reconstruction Organization	1962	25
Agency for the Prohibition of Nuclear Weapons in Latin America	1969	21
Agency for the Safety of Aerial Navigation in Africa and Madagascar	1959	14
Agrarian Research and Intelligence Service	1963	—
Air Afrique	1961	10
AMCO Guarantee and Cooperation Fund	1977	—
Andean Development Council	1969	6
Andean Monetary Fund	—	—
Andean Reserve Fund	1976	5
Antarctic Club	1959	13
Anzus Council	1951	3
Arab Authority for Agricultural Investment and Development	1978	—
Arab Authority for Exhibitions	1964	—
Arab Bank for Economic Development in Africa	1974	17
Arab Bureau of Education for the Gulf States	—	7
Arab Common Market	1978	5
Arab Deterrent Force	1978	7
Arab Fund for Economic and Social Development	1968	21
Arab Fund for Technical Assistance to Arab and African Countries	1974	7
Arab Health Organization	—	—
Arab Human Rights Committee	—	—
Arab Institute for Forestal Studies	—	—
Arab Investment Company	1974	12
Arab Joint Defense Council	1950	—

LIMITED MEMBERSHIP, SPECIFIC PURPOSE Continued	DATE OF CREATION	NUMBER OF MEMBERS
Arab Labor Organization	1965	18
Arab League Educational, Cultural, and Scientific Organization	1964	20
Arab Literacy and Adult Education Organization	1966	20
Arab Loan Fund for Africa	1976	—
Arab Mining Company	—	14
Arab Monetary Fund	1976	14
Arab Oil Experts Committee	—	—
Arab Organization for Administrative Sciences	1969	16
Arab Organization for Agricultural Development	1970	—
Arab Organization for Industrial Development	1968	18
Arab Organization for Standardization and Metrology	1965	10
Arab Permanent Committee for Meteorology	—	—
Arab Postal Union	1946	17
Arab States Broadcasting Union	1969	20
Arab Telecommunications Union	1958	—
Arab Tourism Union	1954	16
Asian Cultural Fund	1978	—
Asian-African Legal Consultative Committee	1956	21
Asian and Pacific Center for Women and Development	1977	—
Asian and Pacific Coconut Community	1968	10
Asian and Pacific Development Administration Center	1973	—
Asian and the Pacific Development Center	1980	—
Asian and Pacific Development Institute	1964	—
Asian Cultural Documentation Center	1975	—
Asian Development Bank	1966	42
Asian Development Fund	1974	—
Asian Highway Coordinating Committee	1964	14
Asian-Oceanic Postal Union	1962	11
Asian Productivity Organization	1961	14
Asian Regional Center for Technology Transfer	1977	—
Asian Regional Coordinating Committee on Hydrology	—	—
Asian Reinsurance Corporation	1979	10
Asian Vegetable Research and Development Center	1971	6
Association for Iron Ore Exportive Countries	1975	9
Association for the Caribbean and Adjacent Regions	1975	16
Association of African Industrial Technology Organizations	1977	—
Association of African Trade Promotion Organizations	1974	26
Association of Natural Rubber Producing Countries	1970	7
Bank of Central African States	1955	5
Benelux Economic and Social Council	1961	27
Benelux Economic Union	1958	3
Board of Nordic Development Projects	1968	5
Broadcasting Organization of the Islamic States	1975	—
Bureau for the Placement and Education of African Refugees	—	—
Cafe Mundial	1973	3
Cairo Demographic Center	1963	—
Caribbean Aviation Training Institute	1975	14
Caribbean Community	1973	12
Caribbean Council for Science and Technology	1979	—
Caribbean Development and Cooperation Committee	1975	—
Caribbean Development Bank	1969	18

LIMITED MEMBERSHIP, SPECIFIC PURPOSE Continued	DATE OF CREATION	NUMBER OF MEMBERS
Caribbean Documentation Center	1977	—
Caribbean Examination Council	1972	15
Caribbean Food and Nutrition Institute	1967	17
Caribbean Information System for Agriculture	—	—
Caribbean Information System for Economic and Social Planning	1979	—
Caribbean Investment Corporation	1973	12
Caribbean Meteorological Organization	1973	12
Caribbean Regional Drug Testing Laboratory	1975	10
Cattle and Livestock Economic Community of the Council of the Entente States	1970	5
Center for Research and Documentation on Oral Traditions and African Languages	1977	10
Center for Research on New Methods of the Use of Coal	1972	6
Center for the Coordination of Social Science Research and Documentation in Africa South of the Sahara	1964	—
Central African Customs and Economic Union	1964	4
Central American Bank of Economic Integration	1961	5
Central American Clearing House	1961	5
Central American Common Market	1960	5
Central American Corporation for Air Navigation Services	1960	5
Central American Defense Council	1963	5
Central American Economic Cooperation Committee	—	—
Central American Education Coordination	—	—
Central American Energy Commission	1979	5
Central American Institute of Public Administration	1954	6
Central American Monetary Union	1964	5
Central American Research Institute of Industry	1956	6
Central Bank of West African States	1955	6
Central Commission for the Navigation of the Rhine	1815	6
Central Office for International Railway Transport	1890	33
Civil Aviation Council of Arab States	1967	20
Cocoa Producers Alliance	1962	8
Colombo Plan Council for Technical Cooperation in South and Southeast Asia	1950	26
Commission of the Cartagena Agreement	1969	5
Committee for Coordination of Joint Prospecting for Mineral Resources in the South Pacific Area	—	9
Committee for Coordination of Investigations of the Lower Mekong Basin	1957	3
Committee for Coordination of Joint Prospecting for Mineral Resources in Asian Offshore Areas	1966	9
Committee for Nordic Youth Cooperation	1976	5
Committee of Arab Experts on Cooperation	—	—
Commonwealth Advisory Aeronautical Research Council	1946	7
Commonwealth Agricultural Bureaux	1929	25
Commonwealth Air Transport Council	1945	—
Commonwealth Committee on Mineral Resources and Geology	1948	27
Commonwealth Defence Science Organization	1946	14
Commonwealth Foundation	1966	44
Commonwealth Fund for Technical Cooperation	1971	41

LIMITED MEMBERSHIP, SPECIFIC PURPOSE Continued	DATE OF CREATION	NUMBER OF MEMBERS
Commonwealth Regional Health Secretariat for East, Central, and Southern Africa	1974	10
Commonwealth Secretariat	1965	41
Commonwealth Science Council	1946	32
Commonwealth Telecommunications Organization	1967	25
Commonwealth War Graves Commission	1917	14
Conference of Chartering and Shipowning Organizations of CMEA Countries	1952	7
Conference of Commonwealth Postal Administrations	1971	—
Conference of Directors of Danube Lines	1953	8
Conference of East and Central African States	—	16
Conference of European Ministers Responsible for Local Government	—	—
Conference of Gulf States Ministers of Agriculture	1977	—
Conference of Ministers of Arab States Responsible for the Application of Science and Technology to Development	—	—
Conference of Ministers of France or Franc Zone Countries	1964	—
Conference of Ministers of the Civil Service of French-speaking Countries	—	—
Conference of Ministers of Youth and Sports of French-speaking Countries	1969	22
Consortium Interafrican de Distribution Cinematographique	1974	—
Coordination Committee for Fishing and the Industrialization of Fishing	1976	—
Coordinating Committee of South-East Asian Senior Officials on Transport and Communications	1967	—
Coordination Committee of the Broadcasting Organizations of Non-Aligned Countries	1977	—
Coordinating Committee of the Lagos-Nouakchott Highway	—	—
Coordinating Committee of the Trans-East African Highway	—	—
Council for Mutual Economic Assistance	1949	10
Council of Arab Economic Unity	1962	13
Council of Europe Resettlement Fund for National Refugees and Overpopulation in Europe	1956	16
Council of Ministers for Asian Cooperation	1968	27
Council of Nordic Ministers of Education and Culture	—	5
Council of Producers Associations of Non-aligned Countries	1976	—
Council on International Cooperation in Research and Uses of Outer Space	1970	9
Danube Commission	1948	7
Desert Locust Control Organization for Eastern Africa	1962	8
Development Bank of Central African States	1975	6
East African Agriculture and Forestry Organization	1948	3
East African Development Bank	1967	9
East African Industrial Licensing Council	1953	3
East African Marine Fisheries Research Organization	1951	3
East Africa Medical Research Council	1967	3
East African Meteorological Department	1929	3
East African Railways Corporation	1969	3
East Caribbean Common Market Council of Ministers	1973	12
East Caribbean Currency Authority	1965	7

LIMITED MEMBERSHIP, SPECIFIC PURPOSE Continued	DATE OF CREATION	NUMBER OF MEMBERS
East Caribbean Commission	—	6
Eastern Regional Organization for Public Administration	1958	10
Economic Community of the Great Lakes Countries	1976	3
Economic Community of West African States	1975	15
ECOWAS Fund	1975	—
Educational Innovations Program for Development in the Arab States	1979	—
European Agricultural Guidance and Guarantee Fund	1962	—
European and Mediterranean Plant Protection Organization	1951	34
European Atomic Energy Community	1958	10
European Center for Higher Education	1972	—
European Center for Medium Range Weather Forecasts	1973	14
European Civil Aviation Conference	1954	22
European Coal and Steel Community	1952	10
European Company for the Chemical Process of Irradiated Fuels	1957	12
European Company for the Financing of Railway Rolling Stock	1955	16
European Conference of Insurance Supervisory Services	1949	16
European Conference of Local Authorities	1957	—
European Conference of Ministers of Transport	1953	19
European Conference of Postal and Telecommunications Administrations	1959	26
European Conference on Satellite Communications	1963	26
European Development Fund	1957	—
European Documentation and Informational System for Education	1968	14
European Economic Community	1958	10
European Free Trade Association	1960	6
European Informatics Network	—	—
European Investment Bank	1957	9
European Molecular Biology Conference	1969	15
European Network for Scientific and Technical Information	1975	10
European Organization for Nuclear Research	1954	12
European Organization for the Safety of Air Navigation	1960	7
European Patent Organization	1973	16
European Safeguards Research and Development Association	1968	6
European Social Fund	1957	—
European Southern Observatory	1962	6
European Space Agency	1962	11
European Space Operations Center	—	—
European Space Research and Technology Center	—	—
European Space Research Institute	—	—
European University Institute	1972	—
European Youth Foundation	1972	21
Federation of Arab Scientific and Research Councils	1976	14
Fund for Solidarity and Economic Development of the West African Economic Community	1978	—
General Fisheries Council for the Mediterranean	1952	19
General Treaty on Central American Economic Integration	1960	5
Group of African, Caribbean and Pacific States	1975	58
Group of Latin American and Caribbean Sugar Exporting Countries	1976	22
Group of Ten	1962	10
Ibero-American Bureau of Education	1949	18

LIMITED MEMBERSHIP, SPECIFIC PURPOSE Continued	DATE OF CREATION	NUMBER OF MEMBERS
Indian Ocean Special Committee	1972	25
Indo-Pacific Fisheries Commission	1948	19
Indus Basin Development Fund	1960	7
Industrial Development Unit	—	—
Industrial Property Organization for English-Speaking Africa	1977	6
Information and Documentation Center of the Directorate of the Environment and Local Authorities	1967	14
Institute for Training and Demographic Research	—	—
Institute of Nutrition of Central America and Panama	1946	6
Inter-African Bureau for Animal Resources	1951	
Inter-African Bureau for Soils	—	—
Inter-African Coffee Organization	1960	21
Inter-African Committee for Hydraulic Studies	1960	12
Inter-African Phyto-Sanitary Council	—	—
Inter-American Center for Regional Development	1977	—
Inter-American Center of Biostatics	1952	—
Inter-American Children's Institute	1919	25
Inter-American Commission of Women	1928	25
Inter-American Committee for Agricultural Development	1961	—
Inter-American Committee on the Alliance for Progress	1963	23
Inter-American Conference on Social Security	1942	20
Inter-American Defense Board	1942	23
Inter-American Development Bank	1959	43
Inter-American Export Promotion Center	1967	—
Inter-American Indian Institute	1940	17
Inter-American Institute of Agricultural Sciences	1944	28
Inter-American Music Council	1956	22
Inter-American Nuclear Energy Commission	1959	21
Inter-American Research and Documentation Center on Vocational Training	1963	14
Inter-American Studies and Research Center on Educational Planning	1978	—
Inter-American Trade Center	1967	—
Inter-American Training Center in Communications for Population	1972	—
Inter-American Travel Congresses	1939	26
Inter-American Tropical Tuna Commission	1949	6
Inter-Arab Guarantee Corporation	1970	19
Intergovernmental Commission for Cooperation of Socialist Countries in the Field of Computer Technology	1969	8
Intergovernmental Commission on Central American River Basins	1969	6
Intergovernmental Committee on Science and Technology for Development	1979	—
Intergovernment Committee on the River Plate Basin	1971	5
Intergovernmental Coordinating Committee for Population and Family Planning in Southeast Asia	—	—
Intergovernmental Council of Copper Exporting Countries	1968	5
Intergovernmental Group of Non-Aligned Countries on Raw Materials	1974	17
International African Migratory Locust Organization	1955	17
International Association for Vine, Fruit, and Vegetable Growing Mechanization	1964	5

LIMITED MEMBERSHIP, SPECIFIC PURPOSE Continued	DATE OF CREATION	NUMBER OF MEMBERS
International Bank for Economic Cooperation	1964	8
International Bauxite Association	1974	11
International Boundary Commission (U.S.-Mexico)	1889	2
International Center for Advanced Mediterranean Agronomic Studies	1962	—
International Center for Agricultural Research in Dry Areas	1976	8
International Center for Diarrhoeal Diseases Research, Bangladesh	1960	—
International Center for Higher Studies in Journalism for Latin America	1959	—
International Center for Industrial Studies	—	—
International Center for Public Enterprises in Developing Countries	1976	24
International Center for Scientific and Technical Information	1969	10
International Center for Spanish-Speaking Countries for Training and Education in Environmental Sciences	1975	—
International Commission for Food Industries	1934	11
International Commission for the Conservation of Atlantic Tunas	1969	14
International Commission for the Protection of Lake Constance	1960	3
International Commission for the Protection of the Moselle against Pollution	1961	3
International Commission for the Protection of the Rhine against Pollution	1963	5
International Commission for the Scientific Exploration of the Mediterranean Sea	1919	17
International Commission for the Scientific Exploration of the Sea	1919	17
International Commission for the Southeast Atlantic Fisheries	1969	15
International Commission of Civil Status	1948	12
International Copyright Information Center	1971	—
International Customs Tariffs Bureau	1890	—
International Energy Agency	1974	24
International Information System on Research in Documentation	—	—
International Institute for Cotton	1966	11
International Institute for Integration of "Andres Bello" Treaty	1975	—
International Institute for the Study of Economic Problems of the Socialist World	1970	—
International Insurance Inspectorate of African States	1962	11
International Investment Bank	1970	10
International Joint Commission (US-Canada)	1911	2
International Microwave Control Center	—	3
International Moselle Company	1957	3
International Natural Rubber Organization	1979	—
International North Pacific Fisheries Commission	1952	3
International Nuclear Information System	1970	—
International Olive Oil Council	1948	19
International Organization for Cooperation in Light Chemicals Production	1969	8
International Red Locust Control Organization for Central and Southern Africa	1949	9
International Regional Organization against Plant and Animal Diseases	1953	7
International Rice Commission	1948	47
International Social Sciences Information System	1976	7

LIMITED MEMBERSHIP, SPECIFIC PURPOSE *Continued*	DATE OF CREATION	NUMBER OF MEMBERS
International Tea Promotion Association	1979	8
International Whaling Commission	1946	24
Inter-state Organization for Advanced Technicians of Hydraulics and Rural Equipment	—	—
Interstate School Veterinary Sciences and Medicine	1971	—
Inter-University Committee for East Africa	1970	3
IOC Association for the Caribbean and Adjacent Regions	1975	18
Islamic Commission for Economic and Social Affairs	—	—
Islamic Cultural, Education, and Religious Foundation	1970	—
Islamic Development Bank	1974	30
Islamic Educational, Cultural, and Scientific Organization	1979	—
Islamic Solidarity Fund	1974	—
Italian–Latin American Institute	1966	21
Jerusalem Committee	1979	13
Joint Anti-Locust and Anti-Aviarian Organization	1965	9
Joint Committee of the Nordic Natural Science Research Councils	1967	4
Joint Institute for Nuclear Research	1956	11
Joint Nordic Center for Labor Market Training	1971	3
Joint Nordic Organization for Lappish Culture and Reindeer Husbandry Affairs	1963	3
Joint Nordic Organization in the Field of Testing and Control	1973	5
Joint Railway Commission (Bolivia-Argentina)	1941	2
Joint Railway Commission (Bolivia-Brazil)	1937	2
Lake Chad Basin Commission	1964	4
Lake Victoria Fisheries Commission	1977	3
Latin America Cancer Research Information Project	1977	—
Latin American Center for Physics	1962	13
Latin American Demographic Center	1957	35
Latin American Economic System	1975	25
Latin American Energy Organization	1974	21
Latin American Faculty of Social Sciences	1957	—
Latin American Institute for Educational Communication	1956	20
Latin American Institute for Economic and Social Planning	1962	38
Latin American Integration Association	1961	11
Latin American Population Documentation System	1976	—
Latin Union	1951	—
Liptako-Gourma Integrated Development Authority	1971	3
Maghreb Permanent Consultative Committee	1964	4
Mediterranean Trust Fund	1980	—
Middle Eastern Regional Radioisotope Center for the Arab Countries	1962	—
Ministerial Conference of West and Central African States on Maritime Transport	—	—
Ministerial Conferences on Education, Youth and Sports in French-Speaking Countries	1968	22
Monetary Committee of the Franc Zone	1955	14
Multinational Center for Adult Education	1971	—
Mutual Aid and Loan Guarantee Fund Council of the Entente	1966	5
Mutual Assistance of the Latin American Government Oil Companies	1965	10
Niger Basin Authority	1964	9

LIMITED MEMBERSHIP, SPECIFIC PURPOSE Continued	DATE OF CREATION	NUMBER OF MEMBERS
Nordic Accelerator Committee	1974	5
Nordic Advisory Committee on Cultural Activities	1971	5
Nordic Art Center	1978	—
Nordic Committee on Disability and the Handicapped	1979	5
Nordic Committee on Foreigners	1957	5
Nordic Contract Organization for Fisheries Questions	1962	—
Nordic Cooperation Committee for International Politics, Including Peace and Conflict Research	1966	5
Nordic Council for Arctic Medical Research	1968	5
Nordic Council for Tax Research	1973	4
Nordic Council on Custom Administration	1975	5
Nordic Cultural Cooperation	1972	5
Nordic Cultural Fund	1967	10
Nordic Economic Research Council	1979	5
Nordic Forest Research Cooperation Committee	1972	4
Nordic Forestry Union	1946	5
Nordic Fund for Technology and Industrial Development	1973	5
Nordic Gene Bank for Agricultural and Horticultural Plants	1978	5
Nordic Government Officials' Committee on Environmental Questions	1973	5
Nordic Institute for Studies in Urban and Regional Planning	1968	5
Nordic Institute for Theoretical Atomic Physics	1957	5
Nordic Institute of Regional Policy Research	1966	5
Nordic Investment Bank	1976	5
Nordic Joint Committee for the Textile Industries	1949	5
Nordic Labor Market Committee	1954	4
Nordic Language and Information Center	1976	—
Nordic Language Secretariat	1978	5
Nordic Medicament Board	1974	5
Nordic Postal Union	1869	5
Nordic Road Safety Council	1971	4
Nordic School Cooperation	1972	—
Nordic Senior Officials' Committee for Agricultural and Forestry Questions	1979	—
Nordic Senior Officials' Committee for Cooperation in the Building	1973	—
Nordic Senior Officials' Committee for Cooperation in the Field of Food Legislation	1971	4
Nordic Senior Officials' Committee for Development and Questions	1977	—
Nordic Senior Officials' Committee for Legislative Questions	1974	—
Nordic Senior Officials' Committee for Monetary and Financial Questions	1974	—
Nordic Senior Officials' Committee for Regional Policy	1973	—
Nordic Senior Officials' Committee for Trade Policy Questions	1974	—
Nordic Senior Officials' Committee for Transport Questions	1972	—
Nordic Social Policy Committee	1974	5
Nordic Statistical Secretariat	1970	5
North American Air Defense Command (U.S.-Canada)	1958	2
North Atlantic Treaty Organization	1949	16
North-East Atlantic Fisheries Commission	1959	15
North Pacific Fur Seal Commission	1958	4
Northwest Atlantic Fisheries Organization	1979	13

LIMITED MEMBERSHIP, SPECIFIC PURPOSE *Continued*	DATE OF CREATION	NUMBER OF MEMBERS
OCAM Guarantee and Cooperation Fund	1977	—
OECD Center for Educational Research and Innovation	—	—
OECD Nuclear Energy Agency	1972	24
OECD Development Center	—	—
Office for Research on African Food and Nutrition	1956	5
Organization for Cooperation in the Field of Heavy Metallurgy	1964	6
Organization for Cooperation in the Roller Bearings Industry	1964	7
Organization for Coordination in Control of Endemic Diseases in Central Africa	1963	5
Organization for Cooperation of Socialist Countries in the Domain of Tele- and Postal Communications	1957	11
Organization for Economic Cooperation and Development	1961	24
Organization for the Development of the Senegal River	1972	3
Organization for the Planning and Development of Kagera River	1977	3
Organization of Arab Petroleum Exporting Countries	1968	9
Organization of Railways Cooperation	1956	13
Organization of the Petroleum Exporting Countries	1960	13
Pan African Telecommunictions Union	1977	—
Pan American Center for Foot-and-Mouth Disease	1978	—
Pan American Center for Human Ecology and Health	1975	—
Pan American Center for Sanitary Engineering and Environmental Sciences	1968	—
Pan American Health Organization	1902	29
Pan American Highway Congresses	1925	28
Pan American Institute of Geography and History	1928	21
Pan Arab Organization for Social Defense against Crime	1965	18
Pepper Community	1971	3
Permanent Commission for the South Pacific	1952	3
Permanent Executive Secretariat of the "Andres Bello" Convention	1969	6
Permanent Founding Committee of the Seerat Congress	1976	—
Permanent Inter-African Bureau for Tsetse and Trypanosomiasis	1949	—
Permanent Interstate Committee for Drought Control in the Sahel	1973	9
Permanent Joint Commission of Uruguay, Paraguay, and Bolivia	—	3
Permanent Secretariat of the Conference of the South American Agreement on Narcotic Drugs and Psychotropic Substances	—	—
Plant Protection Committee for the South East Asia and Pacific Region	1955	22
Population Information and Documentation System for Africa	1978	—
Postal Union of the Americas and Spain	1911	24
RCD Cultural Institute	1966	3
RCD International School of Insurance	1970	3
Regional Advisory Council for Scientific and Atomic Research	1972	—
Regional Arab Information Network for Social Sciences	—	—
Regional Center for Conservation of Cultural Property in the Arab States	—	—
Regional Center for Functional Literacy in the Arab States	1952	—
Regional Center for Solar Energy	1979	6
Regional Center for Specialized Services in Surveying and Mapping	1975	—
Regional Center for Training in Aerial Surveys	1972	—
Regional Cooperation for Development	1964	3

LIMITED MEMBERSHIP, SPECIFIC PURPOSE Continued	DATE OF CREATION	NUMBER OF MEMBERS
Regional Fisheries Advisory Commission for the South West Atlantic	1961	3
Regional Institute for Population Studies	1972	—
Regional International Organization for Plant Protection and Animal Health	—	—
Regional Mineral Resources Development Center	1973	—
Regional Oil Combating Center for the Mediterranean Sea	1976	16
Sahelian Scientific and Technological Information and Documentation	1976	—
Scandinavian Council for Drug Research	1974	—
Scandinavian Institute of Asian Studies	1965	4
SEAMEO Regional Center for Education in Science and Mathematics	—	—
SEAMEO Regional Center for Tropical Biology	—	—
Seameo Regional English Language	1968	—
SEATO Clinical Research Laboratory	1963	—
SEATO Medical Research Laboratory	1960	—
Secretariat for the Convention on International Trade in Endangered Species of Wild Fauna and Flora	1980	60
Secretariat for the Tourism Integration of Central America	1965	—
Senior Officials' Committee for Nordic Cultural Cooperation	1971	—
South-East Asia Lumber Producers Association	1974	3
South-East Asia Tin Research and Development Center	1977	3
South-East Asian Fisheries Development Center	1967	—
Southeast Asian Ministers of Education Secretariat	1965	8
Southern Africa Regional Tourism Council	1973	8
Southern African Customs Union	1969	8
Southern African Development Coordination Committee	1979	9
South African Regional Commission for the Conservation and Utilization of the Soil	1950	9
Southern African Transport Communication Commission	—	9
South Pacific Air Transport Council	1946	4
South Pacific Bureau for Economic Cooperation	1972	12
South Pacific Commission	1947	11
South Pacific Forum Fisheries Agency	1978	—
Special Fund for the Organization of Petroleum Exporting Countries	1976	—
Standing Committee of the Organization of African Unity and the League of Arab States	1977	14
Statistical, Economic, and Social Research and Training Center for Islamic Countries	1978	43
Stefan Banach International Mathematical Center for Raisins Research Qualifications	1972	7
Supreme Council for Sport in Africa	1965	—
Tanzania-Zambia Railway Authority	1968	3
The Regional Bureau of the Middle East Committee for the Affairs of the Blind	1973	14
Trans-African High Coordinating Committee	1971	6
Trans-Sahara Liaison Committee	1966	—
Tripartite Commission for the Restitution of Monetary Gold	1946	3
Tripartite Commission on the Working Conditions of Rhine Boatmen	1950	5

LIMITED MEMBERSHIP, SPECIFIC PURPOSE Continued	DATE OF CREATION	NUMBER OF MEMBERS
Tropical Pesticides Research Institute	1945	—
Typhoon Committee	1968	8
Union of Banana Exporting Countries	1974	7
Union of Central African States	1968	2
United Nations Center for Regional Development	1971	—
Warsaw Treaty Organization	1955	7
West African Rice Development Association	1970	15
West African Clearing House	1975	12
West African Development Bank	1973	6
West African Economic Community	1959	6
West African Examinations Council	1951	4
West African Health Community	1972	5
West African Insurance Institute	1978	5
West African Monetary Union	1962	6
West African Regional Group	1968	9
West European Union	1955	7
World Center of Islamic Education	1980	43
World Data Bank	1975	—

POTENTIALLY UNIVERSAL MEMBERSHIP, GENERAL PURPOSE

Agency for Cultural and Technical Cooperation	1970	28
AGLINET	1979	—
Bank for International Settlements	1930	30
Consultative Council for Postal Studies	1957	34
Customs Cooperation Council	1950	89
Diplomatic Conference of International Maritime Law	1905	—
Food and Agriculture Organization	1945	146
General Agreement on Tariffs and Trade	1948	85
Hague Conference on Private International Law	1893	27
Intergovernmental Committee for Migration	1951	32
Intergovernmental Copyright Committee	1952	18
Intergovernmental Council of the International Hydrological Programme	1974	30
Intergovernmental Oceanographic Commission	1960	92
International Accounting Standards Committee	1973	45
International Agency for Research on Cancer	1965	12
International Atomic Energy Agency	1956	110
International Bank for Reconstruction and Development	1945	139
International Bureau of Education	1925	74
International Bureau of Weights and Measures	1875	45
International Center for Advanced Technical and Vocational Training	1963	150
International Center for Settlement of Investment Disputes	1966	84
International Center for the Study of the Preservation and the Restoration of Cultural Property	1958	66
International Civil Aviation Organization	1944	147
International Civil Defense Organization	1931	36
International Coffee Organization	1962	45

POTENTIALLY UNIVERSAL MEMBERSHIP, SPECIFIC PURPOSE Continued	DATE OF CREATION	NUMBER OF MEMBERS
International Cocoa Organization	1973	49
International Committee of Military Medicine and Pharmacy	1921	87
International Cotton Advisory Committee	1939	48
International Council for ADP in Government Administation	1968	14
International Council For the Exploration of the Sea	1902	17
International Court of Justice	1942	157
International Criminal Police Commission	1923	126
International Development Association	1960	126
International Diplomatic Academy	1926	91
International Exhibition Bureau	1931	36
International Finance Corporation	1956	140
International Fund for Agricultural Development	1975	131
International Hydrographic Organization	1921	48
International Information Systems on Research in Documentation	—	—
International Institute for Educational Planning	1963	141
International Institute for the Unification of Private Law	1926	45
International Institute for Labor Studies	1960	145
International Institute of Refrigeration	1920	56
International Investment Bank	1970	10
International Labor Organization	1919	145
International Lead and Zinc Study Group	1959	30
International Maritime Organization	1948	120
International Maritime Satellite Organization	1979	34
International Monetary Fund	1945	141
International Narcotics Control Board	1961	13
International Office of Epizootics	1924	—
International Organization of Legal Metrology	1955	46
International Poplar Commission	1879	32
International Relief Union	1927	16
International Rubber Study Group	1944	28
International Sericultural Commission	1948	15
International Sugar Organization	1968	59
International Telecommunications Satellite Organization	1964	105
International Telecommunication Union	1865	155
International Tin Council	1971	31
International Trade Center	1964	248
International Tsunami Information Center	1964	74
International Union for the Protection of Industrial Property	1883	89
International Union for the Protection of Literary and Artistic Works	1886	72
International Union for the Protection of New Varieties of Plants	1961	12
International Union for the Publication of Customs Tariffs	1890	79
International Vine and Wine Office	1924	29
International Wheat Council	1949	48
International Wool Study Group	1947	42
Office of the United Nations Disaster Relief Coordinator	1971	—
Office of the United Nations High Commissioner for Refugees	1951	157
Organization for Coordination and Cooperation in the Control of Major Endemic Diseases	1960	9
Permanent Council of the International Convention for the Use of Appellations of Origin and Denominations of Cheese	1951	8

POTENTIALLY UNIVERSAL MEMBERSHIP, SPECIFIC PURPOSE Continued	DATE OF CREATION	NUMBER OF MEMBERS
Permanent Court of Arbitration	1889	74
UNCTAD Common Fund for Commodities	1980	—
United Nations Children's Fund	1946	103
United Nations Conference on Trade and Development	1964	163
United Nations Development Program	1965	157
United Nations Educational, Scientific and Cultural Organization	1945	153
United Nations Environment Fund	1972	—
United Nations Environment Program	1972	58
United Nations Fund for Drug Abuse Control	1971	70
United Nations Funds for Population Activities	1967	—
United Nations Industrial Development Fund	1978	—
United Nations Industrial Development Organization	1967	89
United Nations Institute for Training and Research	1963	157
United Nations Relief and Works Agency for Palestine Refugees in the Near East	1950	—
United Nations Research Institute for Social Development	1963	130
United Nations University	1973	24
Universal Postal Union	1874	162
World Food Council	1974	36
World Food Program	1961	157
World Health Organization	1946	157
World Heritage Committee	1976	21
World Intellectual Property Organization	1967	95
World Meteorological Organization	1873	153
World Tourism Organization	1975	103

LIMITED MEMBERSHIP, GENERAL PURPOSE

Amazonian Cooperation Council	1978	8
Andean Council	1979	5
Association of South East Asian Nations	1967	5
Coordination Bureau of the Non-Aligned Countries	1973	78
Council of Europe	1949	21
Council of the Entente	1959	5
Group of 77	1967	120
Institute for Latin American Integration	1964	24
Inter-Parliamentary Consultative Council of Benelux	1955	3
League of Arab States	1945	21
Nordic Council	1952	5
Nordic Council of Ministers	1971	5
Organization of African Unity	1965	49
Organization of American States	1890	28
Organization of Central American States	1951	5
Organization of the Islamic Conference	1971	43
South Pacific Forum	1971	9

POTENTIALLY UNIVERSAL MEMBERSHIP, GENERAL PURPOSE

United Nations	1945	157

INGOs with Extensive Consultative Relationships with IGOS

This list has been compiled from material contained in the Union of International Associations' *Yearbook of International Organizations*, Vol. 19, 1981 (Brussels: UIA, 1981). The INGOs included here have been ranked according to the number of international governmental organizations with which they had formal consultative relationships. Having formal consultative relationships with a large number of IGOs could be interpreted as indicating that the INGO in question plays a substantial role in international relations, although it must be kept in mind that many INGOs have working relations with IGOs without having formal consultative status. The scoring system used here is the same as that used by the UIA in compiling a similar list published in Vol. 15, 1974, of the *Yearbook*. The scoring system attempts to reflect the complexity of the different grades of consultative relationship by using a somewhat arbitrary point system. In the case of ECOSOC (which grants consultative status for the United Nations), ILO, FAO, and UNESCO, 3 points were given to those INGOs placed in the principal category, 2 points to those placed in the second category, and 1 to the others. In the case of UNCTAD, 2 points were given to those INGOs placed in the principal category and 1 to the others. Two points were given for each relationship an INGO had with other IGOs. INGOs are listed in order of the total number of points that they received. The maximum possible number of points is 60. Only INGOs that received 5 or more points have been listed.

37 points
International Organization for Standardization

33 points
International Chamber of Commerce

26 points
International Council of Voluntary Agencies
World Confederation of Labour

25 points
International Federation of Agricultural Producers

24 points
International Confederation of Free Trade Unions

23 points
World Confederation of Organizations of the Teaching Profession

20 points
International Cooperative Alliance
International Union for Conservation of Nature and Natural Resources
League of Red Cross Societies

19 points
Cooperative for American Relief Everywhere, Inc.
International Council of Women
International Council on Social Welfare

18 points
International Electrotechnical Commission
International Organization of Consumers Unions
World Federation of Trade Unions
World Federation of United Nations Associations

17 points
International Union of Architects

16 points
European Confederation of Agriculture
International Planned Parenthood Federation
World Veterans Federation

15 points
International Commission on Irrigation and Drainage
International Commission on Radiological Protection
International Council of Scientific Unions
International Council on Jewish Social and Welfare Services
International Federation for Home Economics

14 points
Commission of the Churches on International Affairs
International Chamber of Shipping
International Social Service
International Union for Child Welfare
International Union of Family Organizations

13 points
International Cargo Handling Coordination Association
International Union of Socialist Youth
Rehabilitation International

12 points
Catholic International Union for Social Service
International Union of Local Authorities
Soroptimist International Association
World Crafts Council
World Jewish Congress
World Union of Catholic Women's Organization
World Young Women's Christian Association

11 points
All-India Women's Conference
International Agency for the Prevention of Blindness
International Alliance of Women
International Astronautical Federation
International Automobile Federation
International Federation of Pharmaceutical Manufacturers Associations

International League for Human Rights
International League of Societies for the Mentally Handicapped
International Round Table for the Advancement of Counselling
International Youth and Student Movement for the United Nations
Inter-Parliamentary Union
Latin American Association of Finance Development Institutions
World Assembly of Youth

10 points
Friends World Committee for Consultation
International Phosphate Industry Association
World Association of Girl Guides and Girl Scouts

9 points
Associated Country Women of the World
International Christian Union of Business Executives
International Commission of Agricultural Engineering
International Committee of Catholic Nurses
International Federation for Information Processing
International Federation of Business and Professional Women
International Federation of Journalists
International Federation of University Women
International Federation on Aging
International Hotel Association
International Road Federation
International Society of Soil Sciences
World Alliance of Young Mens' Christian Associations
World Federation for Mental Health
World Federation for the Protection of Animals
World Federation of Democratic Youth
Zonta International

8 points
Airport Associations Coordinating Council
Consultative Council of Jewish Organizations
International Association of Schools of Social Work
International Catholic Migration Commission
International Council of Nurses
International Law Association
International Maritime Radio Association
International Union of Nutritional Sciences
Medical Women's International Association
Panafrican Institute for Development
United Towns Organization
Women's International Democratic Federation
Women's International League for Peace and Freedom
World Council for the Welfare of the Blind
World Energy Conference
World Federation of Catholic Youth

7 points
Association for Childhood Education International
Catholic International Education Office
Inter-American Planning Society

International Association for Educational and Vocational Guidance
International Association for Educational and Vocational Information
International Association of French-Speaking Parliamentarians
International Association of Logopedics and Phoniatrics
International College of Surgeons
International Confederation of Midwives
International Cooperation for Socio-Economic Development
International Council of Jewish Women
International Council of Societies of Industrial Design
International Council on Monuments and Sites
International Federation of Air Line Pilots Associations
International Movement of Catholic Agricultural and Rural Youth
International Savings Bank
International Union for Health Education
Jaycees International
Organization of African Trade Union Unity
Pan American Federation of Engineering Societies
World Movement of Mothers
World Organization of the Scout Movement
World University Service

6 points
Co-ordinating Board of Jewish Organizations
Council for International Organizations of Medical Sciences
European Insurance Committee
Inter-American Association of Broadcasters
International Air Transport Association
International Association for The Protection of Industrial Property
International Association for Water Law
International Association of Conference Interpreters
International Association of Lighthouse Authorities
International Association of Ports and Harbours
International Association of Students in Economics and Management
International Catholic Child Bureau
International Commission of Jurists
International Federation of Landscape Architects
International Federation of Senior Police Officers
International Federation of Women in Legal Careers
International Maritime Committee
International Organization of Employers
International Road Transport Union
International Society of Biometeorology
International Union of Producers and Distributors of Electrical Energy
International Union of Pure and Applied Chemistry
Latin American Iron and Steel Institute
Muslim World League
Mutual Assistance of the Latin American Government Oil Companies
Pan-Pacific and South-East Asia Women's Association
Union of International Associations
World Council of Management
World Federation of the Deaf
World Peace Council
World Peace through Law Centre

5 points

Agudath Israel World Organization
Amnesty International
Chamber of Commerce of the United States of America
International Association for Social Progress
International Board on Books for Young People
International Brain Research Organization
International Commission on Radiation Units and Measurements
International Council on Alcohol and Addictions
International Federation for Housing and Planning
International Federation for Parent Education
International Federation of Automatic Control
International Federation of Human Rights
International Federation of Social Workers
International League against Rheumatism
International Rural Housing Association
International Statistical Institute
International Touring Alliance
International Union against Venereal Diseases and the Treponematoses
International Union of Latin Notariat
International Union of Railways
International Union of School and University Health and Medicine
International Young Christian Workers
Latin American Shipowners Association
Lutheran World Federation
Pacific Science Association
Pax Romana/International Catholic Movement for Intellectual and
    Cultural Affairs/International Movement of Catholic Students
Salvation Army
Society for Comparative Legislation
Union of Industries of the European Community
Union of National Radio and Television Organizations of Africa
World Leisure and Recreation Association
World Medical Association
World Organization for Early Childhood Education

APPENDIX C
Territorial Units in the Global Political System, 1980

No.	Country or Territory	Status	1980 Population (000)	1980 GNP AT MARKET PRICES Amount (U.S. $ Millions)	1980 GNP AT MARKET PRICES Per Capita (U.S. $)	Date of Admission to United Nations
	AFRICA					
1	Algeria	Independent	18,594	36,410	1,960	1962
2	Angola	Independent	7,078	3,320	470	1976
3	Benin (formerly Dahomey)	Independent	3,567	1,080	300	1960
4	Botswana	Independent	821	730	890	1966
5	Burundi	Independent	4,512	830	180	1962
6	Cameroon, United Republic of	Independent	8,503	5,660	670	1960
7	Canary Islands	Spanish Territory	1,138	—	—	—
8	Cape Verde	Independent	324	100	300	1975
9	Central African Republic	Independent	2,294	680	300	1960
10	Chad	Independent	4,524	530	120	1960
11	Comoros	Independent	335	100	300	1975
12	Congo, People's Republic of	Independent	1,537	1,120	730	1960
13	Djibouti	Independent	119	170	1,430	1977
14	Egypt	Independent	41,995	23,140	550	1945
15	Equatorial Guinea	Independent	363	120	330	1968
16	Ehiopia	Independent	32,601	4,320	130	1945
17	Gabon	Independent	551	2,420	4,390	1960
18	Gambia, The	Independent	601	150	250	1965
19	Ghana	Independent	11,450	4,920	430	1957
20	Guinea	Independent	5,014	1,590	320	1958
21	Guinea-Bissau	Independent	573	130	230	1974
22	Ivory Coast	Independent	7,937	9,920	1,250	1960
23	Kenya	Independent	16,402	6,630	400	1963

APPENDIX C *Continued*
Territorial Units in the Global Political System, 1980

No.	Country or Territory	Status	1980 Population (000)	1980 GNP AT MARKET PRICES		Date of Admission to United Nations
				Amount (U.S. $ Millions)	Per Capita (U.S. $)	
24	Lesotho	Independent	1,339	520	390	1966
25	Liberia	Independent	1,863	980	530	1945
26	Libya	Independent	2,977	25,730	8,640	1955
27	Madagascar	Independent	8,742	3,030	350	1960
28	Madeira	Portuguese Territory	265	—	—	—
29	Malawi	Independent	5,968	1,390	230	1964
30	Mali	Independent	6,906	1,340	190	1960
31	Mauritania	Independent	1,634	530	320	1961
32	Mauritius	Independent	957	1,020	1,070	1968
33	Morocco	Independent	20,242	17,440	860	1956
34	Mozambique	Independent	10,473	2,810	270	1975
35	Niger	Independent	5,305	1,760	330	1960
36	Nigeria	Independent	77,082	85,510	1,100	1960
37	Reunion	French Territory	491	2,010	4,090	—
38	Rwanda	Independent	5,046	1,040	200	1962
39	São Tomé and Príncipe	Independent	85	60	710	1975
40	Senegal	Independent	5,661	2,560	450	1960
41	Seychelles Islands	Independent	65	120	1,850	1976
42	Sierra Leone	Independent	3,474	950	270	1961
43	Somalia	Independent	3,645	470	130	1960
44	South Africa	Independent	29,285	66,960	2,290	1945
45	South-West Africa (Namibia)	South African Territory	909	1,420	1,560	—
46	Spanish North Africa	Spanish Territory	153	—	—	—
47	St. Helena	United Kingdom Territory	5	—	—	—
48	Sudan	Independent	18,691	8,640	460	1956

APPENDIX C *Continued*
Territorial Units in the Global Political System, 1980

No.	Country or Territory	Status	1980 Population (000)	1980 GNP AT MARKET PRICES Amount (U.S. $ Millions)	Per Capita (U.S. $)	Date of Admission to United Nations
49	Swaziland	Independent	547	380	690	1968
50	Tanzania, United Republic of	Independent	17,934	4,780	270	1961
51	Togo	Independent	2,699	1,020	380	1960
52	Tunisia	Independent	6,363	8,340	1,310	1956
53	Uganda	Independent	13,201	3,750	280	1962
54	Upper Volta	Independent	6,908	1,110	160	1960
55	Zaire	Independent	28,291	6,340	220	1960
56	Zambia	Independent	5,645	3,220	570	1964
57	Zimbabwe	Independent	7,360	4,640	630	1980
	Totals for Africa		471,044	363,940	770	
	States in UN Totals for Africa		468,083	360,510	770	
	ASIA					
1	Afghanistan	Independent	15,488	3,720	240	1976
2	Bahrain	Independent	364	2,350	6,450	1971
3	Bangladesh	Independent	88,656	11,170	130	1974
4	Bhutan	Independent	1,298	110	80	1971
5	Brunei	Independent	191	2,620	13,720	—
6	Burma	Independent	35,289	5,910	170	1948
7	China, People's Republic of	Independent	956,848	283,250	300	1945
8	China, Republic of (Taiwan)	Independent	17,480	6,990	400	—
9	Hong Kong	United Kingdom Territory	5,068	21,500	4,240	—
10	India	Independent	663,596	159,430	240	1945
11	Indonesia	Independent	151,894	61,770	410	1950

APPENDIX C Continued
Territorial Units in the Global Political System, 1980

No.	Country or Territory	Status	1980 Population (000)	1980 GNP AT MARKET PRICES		Date of Admission to United Nations
				Amount (U.S. $ Millions)	Per Capita (U.S. $)	
12	Iran	Independent	38,082	6,090	160	1945
13	Iraq	Independent	13,084	39,500	3,020	1945
14	Israel	Independent	3,878	17,440	4,500	1949
15	Japan	Independent	116,782	1,152,910	9,880	1956
16	Jordan	Independent	3,190	3,270	1,020	1955
17	Kampuchea (formerly Cambodia)	Independent	8,872	—	—	1955
18	Korea, People's Democratic Republic of (North)	Independent	17,914	13,080	730	—
19	Korea, Republic of (South)	Independent	38,197	58,580	1,530	—
20	Kuwait	Independent	1,372	30,900	22,520	1963
21	Laos	Independent	3,721	340	90	1955
22	Lebanon	Independent	3,161	3,380	1,070	1945
23	Macão	Portuguese Territory	275	640	2,330	—
24	Malaysia	Independent	13,436	22,410	1,670	1957
25	Maldive Islands	Independent	148	40	270	1965
26	Mongolia	Independent	1,669	1,570	940	1961
27	Nepal	Independent	14,010	1,980	140	1955
28	Oman	Independent	891	3,900	4,380	1971
29	Pakistan	Independent	82,441	24,870	300	1947
30	Philippines	Independent	48,400	34,350	710	1945
31	Qatar	Independent	220	6,020	27,360	1971
32	Saudi Arabia	Independent	8,367	100,930	12,060	1945
33	Singapore	Independent	2,391	10,700	4,470	1965
34	Sri Lanka	Independent	14,738	3,990	270	1955
35	Syria	Independent	8,979	12,030	1,340	1945

APPENDIX C *Continued*
Territorial Units in the Global Political System, 1980

No.	Country or Territory	Status	1980 Population (000)	1980 GNP AT MARKET PRICES		Date of Admission to United Nations
				Amount (U.S. $ Millions)	Per Capita (U.S. $)	
36	Thailand	Independent	46,455	31,140	670	1946
37	United Arab Emirates	Independent	796	26,850	33,730	1971
38	Viet Nam, Democratic Republic of	Independent	52,299	8,890	170	1977
39	Yemen (San'a), Arab Republic of	Independent	5,926	2,680	450	1947
40	Yemen (Aden), People's Democratic Republic of	Independent	1,890	810	430	1967
	Totals for Asia		2,487,756	2,178,110	880	
	States in UN Totals for Asia		2,408,631	2,074,700	860	
	OCEANIA					
1	American Samoa	United States Territory	32	180	5,620	—
2	Australia	Independent	14,616	142,240	9,730	1945
3	Cook Islands	New Zealand Territory	18	20	1,110	—
4	Fiji	Independent	619	1,160	1,870	1970
5	French Polynesia	French Territory	155	1,004	6,480	—
6	Guam	United States Territory	120	740	6,170	—
7	Kiribati	Independent	58	50	860	—
8	Nauru	Independent	8	—	—	—
9	New Caledonia	French Territory	154	1,100	7,140	—
10	New Zealand	Independent	3,100	23,160	7,470	1945
11	Nieu	New Zealand Territory	6	3	500	—
12	Papua New Guinea	Independent	3,082	2,360	770	1975

APPENDIX C Continued
Territorial Units in the Global Political System, 1980

No.	Country or Territory	Status	1980 Population (000)	1980 GNP AT MARKET PRICES Amount (U.S. $ Millions)	Per Capita (U.S. $)	Date of Admission to United Nations
13	Solomon Islands	Independent	221	110	500	1978
14	Tonga	Independent	97	50	520	—
15	Trust Territory of the Pacific Islands (Micronesia)	United States Territory	143	120	840	—
16	Tuvalu	Independent	7	4	570	—
17	Vanuatu	Independent	109	60	550	1981
18	Wallis and Futuna Islands	French Territory	10	10	1,000	—
	Totals for Oceania		22,711	172,431	7,590	
	States in UN Totals for Oceania		21,903	169,150	7,720	
	AMERICAS					
1	Antigua	Independent	75	100	1,330	1981
2	Argentina	Independent	27,064	66,430	2,460	1945
3	Bahamas	Independent	237	800	3,380	1973
4	Barbados	Independent	253	760	3,000	1966
5	Belize	Independent	162	160	990	1981
6	Bermuda	United Kingdom Territory	60	660	11,000	—
7	Bolivia	Independent	5,600	3,190	570	1945
8	Brazil	Independent	123,032	243,240	1,980	1945
9	Canada	Independent	23,940	242,530	10,130	1945
10	Cayman Islands	United Kingdom Territory	17	—	—	—
11	Chile	Independent	11,104	23,980	2,160	1945
12	Colombia	Independent	27,520	31,570	1,150	1945
13	Costa Rica	Independent	2,213	3,820	1,730	1945

APPENDIX C *Continued*
Territorial Units in the Global Political System, 1980

No.	Country or Territory	Status	1980 Population (000)	1980 GNP AT MARKET PRICES		Date of Admission to United Nations
				Amount (U.S. $ Millions)	Per Capita (U.S. $)	
14	Cuba	Independent	9,978	7,880	790	1945
15	Dominica	Independent	80	50	620	1978
16	Dominican Republic	Independent	5,431	6,200	1,140	1945
17	Ecuador	Independent	8,354	10,230	1,230	1945
18	El Salvador	Independent	4,812	2,690	560	1945
19	French Guiana	French Territory	66	180	2,730	—
20	Grenada	Independent	98	80	820	1974
21	Guadeloupe	French Territory	330	1,270	3,850	—
22	Guatemala	Independent	7,262	7,790	1,070	1945
23	Guyana	Independent	884	550	620	1966
24	Haiti	Independent	5,008	1,340	270	1945
25	Honduras	Independent	3,691	2,070	560	1945
26	Jamaica	Independent	2,192	2,250	1,030	1962
27	Martinique	French Territory	312	1,510	4,840	—
28	Mexico	Independent	71,911	144,000	2,000	1945
29	Montserrat	United Kingdom Territory	11	20	1,820	—
30	Netherlands Antilles	Netherlands Territory	256	1,100	4,300	—
31	Nicaragua	Independent	2,737	1,930	700	1945
32	Panama	Independent	1,834	3,170	1,730	1945
33	Paraguay	Independent	3,067	4,110	1,340	1945
34	Peru	Independent	17,779	16,470	930	1945
35	Puerto Rico	United States Commonwealth	3,199	11,070	3,460	—
36	Saint Kitts-Nevis-Anguilla	United Kingdom Territory	70	50	710	—
37	Saint Lucia	Independent	120	110	920	1979
38	Saint Pierre and Miquelon	French Territory	6	—	—	—

APPENDIX C *Continued*
Territorial Units in the Global Political System, 1980

No.	Country or Territory	Status	1980 Population (000)	1980 GNP AT MARKET PRICES		Date of Admission to United Nations
				Amount (U.S. $ Millions)	Per Capita (U.S. $)	
39	Saint Vincent	Independent	122	60	490	1980
40	Suriname	Independent	389	1,000	2,570	1975
41	Trinidad and Tobago	Independent	1,139	5,110	4,490	1962
42	Turks and Caicos Islands	United Kingdom Territory	7	—	—	—
43	United States of America	Independent	227,640	2,582,460	11,340	1945
44	Uruguay	Independent	2,900	8,240	2,840	1945
45	Venezuela	Independent	13,913	54,220	3,900	1945
46	Virgin Islands	United States Territory	95	630	6,630	—
47	Virgin Islands	United Kingdom Territory	12	—	—	—
	Totals for Americas		616,892	3,495,080	5,670	
	States in UN Totals for Americas		612,451	3,478,590	5,680	
	EUROPE					
1	Albania	Independent	2,734	2,020	740	1955
2	Austria	Independent	7,507	76,530	10,190	1955
3	Azores	Portuguese Territory	289	—	—	—
4	Belgium	Independent	9,920	119,770	12,070	1945
5	Bulgaria	Independent	8,862	37,390	4,220	1955
6	Byelorussia	U.S.S.R. Republic	*	*	*	*
7	Channel Islands	United Kingdom Territory	131	900	6,870	—
8	Cyprus	Independent	628	2,210	3,520	1960
9	Czechoslovakia	Independent	15,318	89,260	5,830	1945
10	Denmark	Independent	5,123	66,350	12,950	1945
11	Faeroe Islands	Danish Territory	43	440	10,230	—

APPENDIX C Continued
Territorial Units in the Global Political System, 1980

No.	Country or Territory	Status	1980 Population (000)	1980 GNP AT MARKET PRICES		Date of Admission to United Nations
				Amount (U.S. $ Millions)	Per Capita (U.S. $)	
12	Finland	Independent	4,779	47,280	9,890	1955
13	France	Independent	53,713	627,700	11,690	1945
14	Germany, Democratic Republic of	Independent	16,737	120,940	7,230	1973
15	Germany, Federal Republic of	Independent	61,561	827,790	13,450	1973
16	Gibraltar	United Kingdom Territory	29	150	5,170	—
17	Greece	Independent	9,440	42,190	4,470	1945
18	Greenland	Danish Territory	50	430	8,600	—
19	Holy See	Independent	1	—	—	—
20	Hungary	Independent	10,713	44,990	4,200	1955
21	Iceland	Independent	228	2,620	11,490	1946
22	Ireland	Independent	3,365	16,130	4,790	1955
23	Isle of Man	United Kingdom Territory	64	300	4,690	—
24	Italy	Independent	57,042	368,860	6,470	1955
25	Liechtenstein	Independent	26	210	8,000	—
26	Luxembourg	Independent	358	5,200	14,530	1945
27	Malta	Independent	364	1,190	3,270	1964
28	Monaco	Independent	26	—	—	—
29	Netherlands	Independent	14,144	161,440	11,410	1945
30	Norway	Independent	4,086	51,610	12,630	1945
31	Poland	Independent	35,578	139,780	3,930	1945
32	Portugal	Independent	9,933	23,140	2,330	1955
33	Romania	Independent	22,268	52,010	2,340	1955
34	San Marino	Independent	21	—	—	—

APPENDIX C Continued
Territorial Units in the Global Political System, 1980

No.	Country or Territory	Status	1980 Population (000)	1980 GNP AT MARKET PRICES		Date of Admission to United Nations
				Amount (U.S. $ Millions)	Per Capita (U.S. $)	
35	Spain	Independent	37,430	199,780	5,340	1955
36	Sweden	Independent	8,310	111,900	13,470	1946
37	Switzerland	Independent	6,373	106,300	16,680	—
38	Turkey	Independent	45,356	66,080	1,460	1945
39	Ukraine	U.S.S.R. Republic	*	*	*	1945
40	Union of Soviet Socialist Republics	Independent	266,666	1,212,030	4,550	1945
41	United Kingdom	Independent	55,888	442,820	7,920	1945
42	Yugoslavia	Independent	22,344	58,570	2,620	1945
	Totals for Europe		797,448	5,126,310	6,430	
	States in UN Totals for Europe		790,395	5,017,580	6,350	
	World Totals		4,395,851	11,335,871	2,580	
	States in U.N. Totals for World		4,301,463	11,100,530	2,580	

*Included in data for U.S.S.R.

Source: For most population figures, United Nations, Map No. 3105, Rev. 1 (F), June 1981; for most GNP figures, International Bank for Reconstruction and Development: World Bank Atlas, 1981: Gross National Product, Population, and Growth Rates (Washington, D.C.: IBRD, 1982); for population and GNP for countries not included in the previous two sources, Statesmens Yearbook, 118th edition (London: MacMillan Press, 1981).

The Charter of the United Nations

We the peoples of the United Nations determined

to save succeeding generations from the scourge of war, which twice in our lifetime has brought untold sorrow to mankind, and

to reaffirm faith in fundamental human rights, in the dignity and worth of the human person, in the equal rights of men and women and of nations large and small, and

to establish conditions under which justice and respect for the obligations arising from treaties and other sources of international law can be maintained, and

to promote social progress and better standards of life in larger freedom,

and for these ends

to practice tolerance and live together in peace with one another as good neighbors, and

to unite our strength to maintain international peace and security, and

to ensure, by the acceptance of principles and the institution of methods, that armed force shall not be used, save in the common interest, and

to employ international machinery for the promotion of the economic and social advancement to combine our efforts to accomplish these aims.

Accordingly, our respective Governments, through representatives assembled in the city of San Francisco, who have exhibited their full powers found to be in good and due form, have agreed to the present Charter of the United Nations and do hereby establish an international organization to be known as the United Nations.

Chapter 1
Purposes and Principles

Article 1

The Purposes of the United Nations are:

1. To maintain international peace and security, and to that end: to take effective collective measures for the prevention and removal of threats to the peace, and for the suppression of acts of aggression or other breaches of the peace, and to bring about by peaceful means, and in conformity with the principles of justice and international law, adjustment or settlement of international disputes or situations which might lead to a breach of the peace;

2. To develop friendly relations among nations based on respect for the principle of equal rights and self-determination of peoples, and to take other appropriate measures to strengthen universal peace;

3. To achieve international cooperation in solving international problems of an economic, social, cultural, or humanitarian character, and in promoting and encouraging respect for human rights and for fundamental freedoms for all without distinction as to race, sex, language, or religion; and

4. To be a center for harmonizing the actions of nations in the attainment of these common ends.

Article 2

The Organization and its Members, in pursuit of the Purposes stated in Article 1, shall act in accordance with the following Principles.

1. The Organization is based on the principle of the sovereign equality of all its Members.

2. All Members, in order to ensure to all of them the rights and benefits resulting from membership, shall fulfill in good faith the obligations assumed by them in accordance with the present Charter.

3. All Members shall settle their international disputes by peaceful means in such a manner that international peace and security, and justice, are not endangered.

4. All Members shall refrain in their international relations from the threat or use of force against the territorial integrity or political independence of any state, or in any other manner inconsistent with the Purposes of the United Nations.

5. All Members shall give the United Nations every assistance in any action it takes in accordance with the present Charter, and shall refrain from giving assistance to any state against which the United Nations is taking preventive or enforcement action.

6. The Organization shall ensure that states which are not Members of the United Nations act in accordance with these Principles so far as may be necessary for the maintenance of international peace and security.

7. Nothing contained in the present Charter shall authorize the United Nations to intervene in matters which are essentially within the domestic jurisdiction of any state or shall require the Members to submit such matters to settlement under the present Charter; but this principle shall not prejudice the application of enforcement measures under Chapter 7.

Chapter 2
Membership

Article 3

The original Members of the United Nations shall be the states which, having participated in the United Nations Conference on International Organization at San Francisco, or having previously signed the Declaration by United Nations of January 1, 1942, sign the present Charter and ratify it in accordance with Article 110.

Article 4

1. Membership in the United Nations is open to all other peace-loving states which accept the obligations contained in the present Charter and, in the judgment of the Organization, are able and willing to carry out these obligations.

2. The admission of any such state to membership in the United Nations will be affected by a decision of the General Assembly upon the recommendation of the Security Council.

Article 5

A Member of the United Nations against which preventive or enforcement action has been taken by the Security Council may be suspended from the exercise of the rights and privileges of membership by the General Assembly upon the recommendation of the Security Council. The exercise of these rights and privileges may be restored by the Security Council.

Article 6

A Member of the United Nations which has persistently violated the Principles contained in the present Charter may be expelled from the Organization by the General Assembly upon the recommendation of the Security Council.

Chapter 3
Organs

Article 7

1. There are established as the principal organs of the United Nations: a General Assembly, a Security Council, an Economic and Social Council, a Trusteeship Council, an International Court of Justice, and a Secretariat.
2. Such subsidiary organs as may be found necessary may be established in accordance with the present Charter.

Article 8

The United Nations shall place no restrictions on the eligibility of men and women to participate in any capacity and under conditions of equality in its principal and subsidiary organs.

Chapter 4
The General Assembly

Composition

Article 9

1. The General Assembly shall consist of all the Members of the United Nations.
2. Each Member shall have not more than five representatives in the General Assembly.

Functions and Powers

Article 10

The General Assembly may discuss any questions or any matters within the scope of the present Charter or relating to the powers and functions of any organs provided for in the present Charter, and, except as provided in Article 12, may make recommendations to the Members of the United Nations or to the Security Council or to both on any such questions or matters.

Article 11

1. The General Assembly may consider the general principles of cooperation in the maintenance of international peace and security, including the principles governing disarmament and the regulation of armaments, and may make recommendations with regard to such principles to the Members or to the Security Council or to both.

2. The General Assembly may discuss any questions relating to the maintenance of international peace and security brought before it by any Member of the United Nations, or by the Security Council, or by a state which is not a Member of the United Nations in accordance with Article 35, paragraph 2, and, except as provided in Article 12, may make recommendations with regard to any such questions to the state or states concerned or to the Security Council or to both. Any such question on which action is necessary shall be referred to the Security Council by the General Assembly either before or after discussion.

3. The General Assembly may call the attention of the Security Council to situations which are likely to endanger international peace and security.

4. The powers of the General Assembly set forth in this Article shall not limit the general scope of Article 10.

Article 12

1. While the Security Council is exercising in respect of any dispute or situation the functions assigned to it in the present Charter, the General Assembly shall not make any recommendations with regard to that dispute or situation unless the Security Council so requests.

2. The Secretary-General, with the consent of the Security Council, shall notify the General Assembly at each session of any matters relative to the maintenance of international peace and security which are being dealt with by the Security Council and shall similarly notify the General Assembly, or the Members of the United Nations if the General Assembly is not in session, immediately the Security Council ceases to deal with such matters.

Article 13

1. The General Assembly shall initiate studies and make recommendations for the purpose of:

a. promoting international cooperation in the political field and encouraging the progressive development of international law and its codification;

b. promoting international cooperation in the economic, social, cultural, educational, and health fields, and assisting in the realization of human rights and fundamental freedoms for all without distinction as to race, sex, language, or religion.

2. The further responsibilities, functions, and powers of the General Assembly with respect to matters mentioned in paragraph 1 (b) above are set forth in Chapters 9 and 10.

Article 14

Subject to the provisions of Article 12, the General Assembly may recommend measures for the peaceful adjustment of any situation, regardless of origin, which it deems likely to impair the general welfare or friendly relations among nations, including situations resulting from a violation of the provisions of the present Charter setting forth the Purposes and Principles of the United Nations.

Article 15

1. The General Assembly shall receive and consider annual and special reports from the Security Council; these reports shall include an account of the measures that the Security Council has decided upon or taken to maintain international peace and security.

2. The General Assembly shall receive and consider reports from the other organs of the United Nations.

Article 16

The General Assembly shall perform such functions with respect to the international trusteeship system as are assigned to it under Chapters 12 and 13, including the approval of the trusteeship agreements for areas not designated as strategic.

Article 17

1. The General Assembly shall consider and approve the budget of the Organization.

2. The expenses of the Organization shall be borne by the Members as apportioned by the General Assembly.

3. The General Assembly shall consider and approve any financial and budgetary arrangements with specialized agencies referred to in Article 57 and shall examine the administrative budgets of such specialized agencies with a view to making recommendations to the agencies concerned.

Voting

Article 18

1. Each member of the General Assembly shall have one vote.

2. Decisions of the General Assembly on important questions shall be made by a two-thirds majority of the members present and voting. These questions shall include: recommendations with respect to the maintenance of international peace and security, the election of the non-permanent members of the Security Council, the election of the members of the Economic and Social Council, the election of members of the Trusteeship Council in accordance with paragraph 1 (c) of Article 86, the admission of new Members to the United Nations, the suspension of the rights and privileges of membership, the expulsion of Members, questions relating to the operation of the trusteeship system, and budgetary questions.

3. Decisions on other questions, including the determination of additional categories of questions to be decided by a two-thirds majority, shall be made by a majority of the members present and voting.

Article 19

A Member of the United Nations which is in arrears in the payment of its financial contributions to the Organization shall have no vote in the General Assembly if the amount of its arrears equals or exceeds the amount of the contributions due from it for the preceding two full years. The General Assembly may, nevertheless, permit such a Member to vote if it is satisfied that the failure to pay is due to conditions beyond the control of the Member.

Procedure

Article 20

The General Assembly shall meet in regular annual sessions and in such special sessions as occasion may require. Special sessions shall be convoked by the Secretary-General at the request of the Security Council or of a majority of the Members of the United Nations.

Article 21

The General Assembly shall adopt its own rules of procedure. It shall elect its President for each session.

Article 22

The General Assembly may establish such subsidiary organs as it deems necessary for the performance of its functions.

Chapter 5
The Security Council

Composition

Article 23

1. The Security Council shall consist of fifteen Members of the United Nations. The Republic of China, France, the Union of Soviet Socialist Republics, the United Kingdom of Great Britain and Northern Ireland, and the United States of America shall be permanent members of the Security Council. The General Assembly shall elect ten other Members of the United Nations to be nonpermanent members of the Security Council, due regard being specially paid, in the first instance to the contribution of Members of the United Nations to the maintenance of international peace and security and to the other purposes of the Organization, and also to equitable geographical distribution.

2. The non-permanent members of the Security Council shall be elected for a term of two years. In the first election of the non-permanent members after the increase of the membership of the Security Council from eleven to fifteen, two of the four additional members shall be chosen for a term of one year. A retiring member shall not be eligible for immediate reelection.

3. Each member of the Security Council shall have one representative.

Functions and Powers

Article 24

1. In order to ensure prompt and effective action by the United Nations, its Members confer on the Security Council primary responsibility for the maintenance of international peace and security, and agree that in carrying out its duties under this responsibility the Security Council acts on their behalf.

2. In discharging these duties the Security Council shall act in accordance with the Purposes and Principles of the United Nations. The specific powers granted to the Security Council for the discharge of these duties are laid down in Chapters 6, 7, 8, and 12.

3. The Security Council shall submit annual and, when necessary, special reports to the General Assembly for its consideration.

Article 25

The Members of the United Nations agree to accept and carry out the decisions of the Security Council in accordance with the present Charter.

Article 26

In order to promote the establishment and maintenance of international peace and security with the least diversion for armaments of the world's human and economic resources, the Security Council shall be responsible for formulating, with the assistance of the Military Staff Committee referred to in Article 47, plans to be submitted to the Members of the United Nations for the establishment of a system for the regulation of armaments.

Voting

Article 27

1. Each member of the Security Council shall have one vote.

2. Decisions of the Security Council on procedural matters shall be made by an affirmative vote of nine members.

3. Decisions of the Security Council on all other matters shall be made by an affirmative vote of nine members including the concurring votes of the permanent members; provided that, in decisions under Chapter 6, and under paragraph 3 of Article 52, a party to a dispute shall abstain from voting.

Procedure

Article 28

1. The Security Council shall be so organized as to be able to function continuously. Each member of the Security Council shall for this purpose be represented at all times at the seat of the Organization.

2. The Security Council shall hold periodic meetings at which each of its members may, if it so desires, be represented by a member of the government or by some other specially designated representative.

3. The Security Council may hold meetings at such places other than the seat of the Organization as in its judgment will best facilitate its work.

Article 29

The Security Council may establish such subsidiary organs as it deems necessary for the performance of its functions.

Article 30

The Security Council shall adopt its own rules of procedure, including the method of selecting its President.

Article 31

Any Member of the United Nations which is not a member of the Security Council may participate, without vote, in the discussion of any question brought before the Security Council whenever the latter considers that the interests of that Member are specially affected.

Article 32

Any Member of the United Nations which is not a member of the Security Council or any state which is not a Member of the United Nations, if it is a party to a dispute under consideration by the Security Council, shall be invited to participate, without vote, in the discussion relating to the dispute. The Security Council shall lay down such conditions as it deems just for the participation of a state which is not a Member of the United Nations.

Chapter 6
Pacific Settlement of Disputes

Article 33

1. The parties to any dispute, the continuance of which is likely to endanger the maintenance of international peace and security, shall, first of all, seek a solution of negotiation, enquiry, mediation, conciliation, arbitration, judicial settlement, resort to regional agencies or arrangements, or other peaceful means of their own choice.

2. The Security Council shall, when it deems necessary, call upon the parties to settle their dispute by such means.

Article 34

The Security Council may investigate any dispute, or any situation which might lead to international friction or give rise to a dispute, in order to determine whether the continuance of the dispute or situation is likely to endanger the maintenance of international peace and security.

Article 35

1. Any Member of the United Nations may bring any dispute, or any situation of the nature referred to in Article 34, to the attention of the Security Council or of the General Assembly.

2. A state which is not a Member of the United Nations may bring to the attention of the Security Council or of the General Assembly any dispute to which it is a party if it accepts in advance, for the purposes of the dispute, the obligations of pacific settlement provided in the present Charter.

3. The proceedings of the General Assembly in respect of matters brought to its attention under this Article will be subject to the provisions of Articles 11 and 12.

Article 36

1. The Security Council may, at any stage of a dispute of the nature referred to in Article 33 or of a situation of like nature, recommend appropriate procedures or methods of adjustment.

2. The Security Council should take into consideration any procedures for the settlement of the dispute which have already been adopted by the parties.

3. In making recommendations under this Article the Security Council should also take into consideration that legal disputes should as a general rule be referred by the parties to the International Court of Justice in accordance with the provisions of the Statute of the Court.

Article 37

1. Should the parties to a dispute of the nature referred to in Article 33 fail to settle it by the means indicated in that Article, they shall refer it to the Security Council.

2. If the Security Council deems that the continuance of the dispute is in fact likely to endanger the maintenance of international peace and security, it shall decide whether to take action under Article 36 or to recommend such terms of settlement as it may consider appropriate.

Article 38

Without prejudice to the provisions of Articles 33 to 37, the Security Council may, if all the parties to any dispute so request, make recommendations to the parties with a view to a pacific settlement of the dispute.

Chapter 7
Action with Respect to Threats to the Peace,
Breaches of the Peace, and Acts of Aggression

Article 39

The Security Council shall determine the existence of any threat to the peace, breach of the peace, or act of aggression and shall make recommendations, or decide what measures shall be taken in accordance with Articles 41 and 42, to maintain or restore international peace and security.

Article 40

In order to prevent an aggravation of the situation, the Security Council may, before making the recommendations or deciding upon the measures provided for in Article 39, call upon the parties concerned to comply with such provisional measures as it deems necessary or desirable. Such provisional measures shall be without prejudice to the rights, claims, or position of the parties concerned. The Security Council shall duly take account of failure to comply with such provisional measures.

Article 41

The Security Council may decide what measures not involving the use of armed force are to be employed to give effect to its decisions, and it may call upon the Members of the United Nations to apply such measures. These may include complete or partial interruption of economic relations and of rail, sea, air, postal, telegraphic, radio, and other means of communication, and the severance of diplomatic relations.

Article 42

Should the Security Council consider that measures provided for in Article 41 would be inadequate or have proved to be inadequate, it may take such action by air, sea, or land forces as may be necessary to maintain or restore international peace and security. Such action may include demonstrations, blockade, and other operations by air, sea, or land forces of Members of the United Nations.

Article 43

1. All Members of the United Nations, in order to contribute to the maintenance of international peace and security, undertake to make available to the Security Council, on its call and in accordance with a special agreement or agreements, armed forces, assistance, and facilities, including rights of passage, necessary for the purpose of maintaining international peace and security.

2. Such agreement or agreements shall govern the numbers and types of forces, their degree of readiness and general location, and the nature of the facilities and assistance to be provided.

3. The agreement or agreements shall be negotiated as soon as possible on the initiative of the Security Council. They shall be concluded between the Security Council and Members or between the Security Council and groups of Members and shall be subject to ratification by the signatory states in accordance with their respective constitutional processes.

Article 44

When the Security Council has decided to use force it shall, before calling upon a Member not represented on it to provide armed forces in fulfillment of the obligations assumed under Article 43, invite the Member, if the Member so desires, to participate in the decisions of the Security Council concerning the employment of contingents of that Member's armed forces.

Article 45

In order to enable the United Nations to take urgent military measures, Members shall hold immediately available national air-force contingents for combined international enforcement action. The strength and degree of readiness of these contingents and plans for their combined action shall be determined, within the limits laid down in the special agreement or agreements referred to in Article 43, by the Security Council with the assistance of the Military Staff Committee.

Article 46

Plans for the application of armed force shall be made by the Security Council with the assistance of the Military Staff Committee.

Article 47

1. There shall be established a Military Staff Committee to advise and assist the Security Council on all questions relating to the Security Council's military requirements for the maintenance of international peace and security, the employment and command of forces placed at its disposal, the regulation of armaments, and possible disarmament.

2. The Military Staff Committee shall consist of the Chiefs of Staff of the permanent members of the Security Council or their representatives. Any Member of the United Nations not permanently represented on the Committee shall be invited by the Committee to be associated with it when the efficient discharge of the Committee's responsibilities requires the participation of that Member in its work.

3. The Military Staff Committee shall be responsible under the Security Council for the strategic direction of any armed forces placed at the disposal of the Security Council. Questions relating to the command of such forces shall be worked out subsequently.

4. The Military Staff Committee, with the authorization of the Security Council and after consultation with appropriate regional agencies, may establish regional subcommittees.

Article 48

1. The action required to carry out the decisions of the Security Council for the maintenance of international peace and security shall be taken by all the Members of the United Nations or by some of them, as the Security Council may determine.

2. Such decisions shall be carried out by the Members of the United Nations directly and through their action in the appropriate international agencies of which they are members.

Article 49

The Members of the United Nations shall join in affording mutual assistance in carrying out the measures decided upon by the Security Council.

Article 50

If preventive or enforcement measures against any state are taken by the Security Council, any other state, whether a Member of the United Nations or not, which finds itself confronted with special economic problems arising from the carrying out of those measures shall have the right to consult the Security Council with regard to a solution of those problems.

Article 51

Nothing in the present Charter shall impair the inherent right of individual or collective self-defense if an armed attack occurs against a Member of the United Nations, until the Security Council has taken the measures necessary to maintain international peace and security. Measures taken by Members in the exercise of this right of self-defense shall be immediately reported to the Security Council and shall not in any way affect the authority and responsibility of the Security Council under the present Charter to take at any time such action as it deems necessary in order to maintain or restore international peace and security.

Chapter 8
Regional Arrangements

Article 52

1. Nothing in the present Charter precludes the existence of regional arrangements or agencies for dealing with such matters relating to the maintenance of international peace and security as are appropriate for regional action, provided that such arrangements or agencies and their activities are consistent with the Purposes and Principles of the United Nations.

2. The Members of the United Nations entering into such arrangements or constituting such agencies shall make every effort to achieve pacific settlement of local disputes through such regional arrangements or by such regional agencies before referring them to the Security Council.

3. The Security Council shall encourage the development of pacific settlement of local disputes through such regional arrangements or by such regional agencies either on the initiative of the states concerned or by reference from the Security Council.

4. This Article in no way impairs the application of Articles 34 and 35.

Article 53

1. The Security Council shall, where appropriate, utilize such regional arrangements or agencies for enforcement action under its authority. But no enforcement action shall be taken under regional arrangements or by regional agencies without the authorization of the Security Council, with the exception of measures against any enemy state, as defined in paragraph 2 of this Article, provided for pursuant to Article 107 or in regional arrangements directed against renewal of aggressive policy on the part of any such state, until such time as the Organization may, on request of the Governments concerned, be charged with the responsibility for preventing further aggression by such a state.

2. The term enemy state as used in paragraph 1 of this Article applies to any state which during the Second World War has been an enemy of any signatory of the present Charter.

Article 54

The Security Council shall at all times be kept fully informed of activities undertaken or in contemplation under regional arrangements or by regional agencies for the maintenance of international peace and security.

Chapter 9
International Economic and Social Cooperation

Article 55

With a view to the creation of conditions of stability and well-being which are necessary for peaceful and friendly relations among nations based on respect for the principle of equal rights and self-determination of peoples, the United Nations shall promote:

a. higher standards of living, full employment, and conditions of economic and social progress and development;

b. solutions of international economic, social, health, and related problems; and international cultural and educational cooperation; and

c. universal respect for, and observance of, human rights and fundamental freedoms for all without distinction as to race, sex, language, or religion.

Article 56

All Members pledge themselves to take joint and separate action in cooperation with the Organization for the achievement of the purposes set forth in Article 55.

Article 57

1. The various specialized agencies, established by intergovernmental agreement and having wide international responsibilities, as defined in their basic instruments, in economic, social, cultural, educational, health, and related fields, shall be brought into relationship with the United Nations in accordance with the provisions of Article 63.

2. Such agencies thus brought into relationship with the United Nations are hereinafter referred to as specialized agencies.

Article 58

The Organization shall make recommendations for the coordination of the policies and activities of the specialized agencies.

Article 59

The Organization shall, where appropriate, initiate negotiations among the states concerned for the creation of any new specialized agencies required for the accomplishment of the purposes set forth in Article 55.

Article 60

Responsibility for the discharge of the functions of the Organization set forth in this Chapter shall be vested in the General Assembly and, under the authority of the General Assembly, in the Economic and Social Council, which shall have for this purpose the powers set forth in Chapter 10.

Chapter 10
The Economic and Social Council

Composition

Article 61

1. The Economic and Social Council shall consist of fifty-four Members of the United Nations elected by the General Assembly.

2. Subject to the provisions of paragraph 3, eighteen members of the Economic and Social Council shall be elected each year for a term of three years. A retiring member shall be eligible for immediate re-election.

3. At the first election after the increase in the membership of the Economic and Social Council from twenty-seven to fifty-four members, in addition to the members elected in place of the nine members whose term of office expires at the end of that year, twenty-seven additional members shall be elected. Of these twenty-seven additional members, the term of office of nine members so elected shall expire at the end of one year, and of nine other members at the end of two years, in accordance with arrangements made by the General Assembly.

4. Each member of the Economic and Social Council shall have one representative.

Functions and Powers

Article 62

1. The Economic and Social Council may make or initiate studies and reports with respect to international economic, social, cultural, educational, health, and related matters and may make recommendations with respect to any such matters to the General Assembly, to the Members of the United Nations, and to the specialized agencies concerned.

2. It may make recommendations for the purpose of promoting respect for, and observance of, human rights and fundamental freedoms for all.

3. It may prepare draft conventions for submission to the General Assembly, with respect to matters falling within its competence.

4. It may call, in accordance with the rules prescribed by the United Nations, international conferences on matters falling within its competence.

Article 63

1. The Economic and Social Council may enter into agreements with any of the agencies referred to in Article 57, defining the terms on which the agency concerned shall be brought into relationship with the United Nations. Such agreements shall be subject to approval by the General Assembly.

2. It may coordinate the activities of the specialized agencies through consultation with and recommendations to such agencies and through recommendations to the General Assembly and to the Members of the United Nations.

Article 64

1. The Economic and Social Council may take appropriate steps to obtain regular reports from the specialized agencies. It may make arrangements with the Members of the United Nations and with the specialized agencies to obtain reports on the steps taken to give effect to its own recommendations and to recommendations on matters falling within its competence made by the General Assembly.

2. It may communicate its observations on these reports to the General Assembly.

Article 65

The Economic and Social Council may furnish information to the Security Council and shall assist the Security Council upon its request.

Article 66

1. The Economic and Social Council shall perform such functions as fall within its competence in connection with the carrying out of the recommendations of the General Assembly.

2. It may, with the approval of the General Assembly, perform services at the request of Members of the United Nations and at the request of specialized agencies.

3. It shall perform such other functions as are specified elsewhere in the present Charter or as may be assigned to it by the General Assembly.

Voting

Article 67

1. Each member of the Economic and Social Council shall have one vote.

2. Decisions of the Economic and Social Council shall be made by a majority of the members present and voting.

Procedure

Article 68

The Economic and Social Council shall set up commissions in economic and social fields and for the promotion of human rights, and such other commissions as may be required for the performance of its functions.

Article 69

The Economic and Social Council shall invite any Member of the United Nations to participate, without vote, in its deliberations on any matter of particular concern to that Member.

Article 70

The Economic and Social Council may make arrangements for representatives of the specialized agencies to participate, without vote, in its deliberations and in those of the commissions established by it, and for its representatives to participate in the deliberations of the specialized agencies.

Article 71

The Economic and Social Council may make suitable arrangements for consultation with non-governmental organizations which are concerned with matters within its competence. Such arrangements may be made with international organizations and, where appropriate, with national organizations after consultation with the Member of the United Nations concerned.

Article 72

1. The Economic and Social Council shall adopt its own rules of procedure, including the method of selecting its President.

2. The Economic and Social Council shall meet as required in accordance with its rules, which shall include provision for the convening of meetings on the request of a majority of its members.

Chapter 11
Declaration Regarding Non–Self-Governing Territories

Article 73

Members of the United Nations which have or assume responsibilities for the administration of territories whose peoples have not yet attained a full measure of self-government recognize the principle that the interests of the inhabitants of these territories are paramount, and accept as a sacred trust the obligation to promote to the utmost, within the system of international peace and security established by the present Charter, the well-being of the inhabitants of these territories, and, to this end:

a. to ensure, with due respect for the culture of the peoples concerned, their political, economic, social, and educational advancement, their just treatment, and their protection against abuses;

b. to develop self-government, to take due account of the political aspirations of the peoples, and to assist them in the progressive development of their free political institutions, according to the particular circumstances of each territory and its peoples and their varying stages of advancement;

c. to further international peace and security;

d. to promote constructive measures of development, to encourage research, and to co-operate with one another, and, when and where appropriate, with specialized international bodies with a view to the practical achievement of the social, economic, and scientific purposes set forth in this Article; and

e. to transmit regularly to the Secretary-General for information purposes, subject to such limitation as security and constitutional considerations may require, statistical and other information of a technical nature relating to economic, social, and educational conditions in the territories for which they are respectively responsible other than those territories to which Chapters 12 and 13 apply.

Article 74

Members of the United Nations also agree that their policy in respect of the territories to which this Chapter applies, no less than in respect of their metropolitan areas, must be based on the general principle of good-neighborliness, due account being taken of the interests and well-being of the rest of the world, in social, economic, and commercial matters.

Chapter 12
International Trusteeship System

Article 75

The United Nations shall establish under its authority an international trusteeship system for the administration and supervision of such territories as may be placed thereunder by subsequent individual agreements. These territories are hereinafter referred to as trust territories.

The basic objectives of the trusteeship system, in accordance with the Purposes of the United Nations laid down in Article 1 of the present Charter, shall be:

Article 76

a. to further international peace and security;

b. to promote the political, economic, social, and educational advancement of the inhabitants of the trust territories, and their progressive development towards self-government or independence as may be appropriate to the particular circumstances of

each territory and its peoples and the freely expressed wishes of the people concerned, and as may be provided by the terms of each trusteeship agreement;

c. to encourage respect for human rights and for fundamental freedoms for all without distinction as to race, sex, language, or religion, and to encourage recognition of the interdependence of the peoples of the world; and

d. to ensure equal treatment in social, economic, and commercial matters for all Members of the United Nations and their nationals, and also equal treatment for the latter in the administration of justice, without prejudice to the attainment of the foregoing objectives and subject to the provisions of Article 80.

Article 77

1. The trusteeship system shall apply to such territories in the following categories as may be placed thereunder by means of trusteeship agreements:

a. territories now held under mandate:

b. territories which may be detached from enemy states as a result of the Second World War; and

c. territories voluntarily placed under the system by states responsible for their administration.

2. It will be a matter for subsequent agreement as to which territories in the foregoing categories will be brought under the trusteeship system and upon what terms.

Article 78

The trusteeship system shall not apply to territories which have become Members of the United Nations, relationship among which shall be based on respect for the principle of sovereign equality.

Article 79

The terms of trusteeship for each territory to be placed under the trusteeship system, including any alteration or amendments, shall be agreed upon by the states directly concerned, including the mandatory power in the case of territories held under mandate by a Member of the United Nations, and shall be approved as provided for in Articles 83 and 85.

Article 80

1. Except as may be agreed upon in individual trusteeship agreements, made under Articles 77, 79, and 81, placing each territory under the trusteeship system, and until such agreements have been concluded, nothing in this Chapter shall be construed in or of itself to alter in any manner the rights whatsoever of any states or any peoples or the terms of existing international instruments to which Members of the United Nations may respectively be parties.

2. Paragraph 1 of this Article shall not be interpreted as giving grounds for delay or postponement of the negotiation and conclusion of agreements for placing mandated and other territories under the trusteeship system as provided for in Article 77.

Article 81

The trusteeship agreement shall in each case include the terms under which the trust territory will be administered and designate the authority which will exercise the administration of the trust territory. Such authority, hereinafter called the administering authority, may be one or more states or the Organization itself.

Article 82

There may be designated, in any trusteeship agreement, a strategic area or areas which may include part or all of the trust territory to which the agreement applies, without prejudice to any special agreement or agreements made under Article 43.

Article 83

1. All functions of the United Nations relating to strategic areas, including the approval of the terms of the trusteeship agreement and of their alteration or amendment, shall be exercised by the Security Council.

2. The basic objectives set forth in Article 76 shall be applicable to the people of each strategic area.

3. The Security Council shall, subject to the provisions of the trusteeship agreements and without prejudice to security considerations, avail itself of the assistance of the Trusteeship Council to perform those functions of the United Nations under the trusteeship system relating to political, economic, social, and educational matters in the strategic areas.

Article 84

It shall be the duty of the administering authority to ensure that the trust territory shall play its part in the maintenance of international peace and security. To this end the administering authority may make use of volunteer forces, facilities, and assistance from the trust territory in carrying out the obligations towards the Security Council undertaken in this regard by the administering authority, as well as for local defense and the maintenance of law and order within the trust territory.

Article 85

1. The functions of the United Nations with regard to trusteeship agreements for all areas not designated as strategic, including the approval of the terms of the trusteeship agreements and of their alteration or amendment, shall be exercised by the General Assembly.

2. The Trusteeship Council, operating under the authority of the General Assembly, shall assist the General Assembly in carrying out these functions.

Chapter 13
The Trusteeship Council

Composition

Article 86

1. The Trusteeship Council shall consist of the following Members of the United Nations:

a. those Members administering trust territories;

b. such of those Members mentioned by name in Article 23 as are not administering trust territories; and

c. as many other Members elected for three-year terms by the General Assembly as may be necessary to ensure that the total number of members of the Trusteeship Council is equally divided between those Members of the United Nations which administer trust territories and those which do not.

2. Each member of the Trusteeship Council shall designate one specially qualified person to represent it therein.

Functions and Powers

Article 87

The General Assembly and, under its authority, the Trusteeship Council, in carrying out their functions, may:

a. consider reports submitted by the administering authority;

b. accept petitions and examine them in consultation with the administering authority;

c. provide for periodic visits to the respective trust territories at times agreed upon with the administering authority; and

d. take these and other actions in conformity with the terms of the trusteeship agreements.

Article 88

The Trusteeship Council shall formulate a questionnaire on the political, economic, social, and educational advancement of the inhabitants of each trust territory, and the administering authority for each trust territory within the competence of the General Assembly shall make an annual report to the General Assembly upon the basis of such questionnaire.

Voting

Article 89

1. Each member of the Trusteeship Council shall have one vote.

2. Decisions of the Trusteeship Council shall be made by a majority of the members present and voting.

Procedure

Article 90

1. The Trusteeship Council shall adopt its own rules of procedure, including the method of selecting its President.

2. The Trusteeship Council shall meet as required in accordance with its rules, which shall include provision for the convening of meetings on the request of a majority of its members.

Article 91

The Trusteeship Council shall, when appropriate, avail itself of the assistance of the Economic and Social Council and of the specialized agencies in regard to matters with which they are respectively concerned.

Chapter 14
The International Court of Justice

Article 92

The International Court of Justice shall be the principal judicial organ of the United Nations. It shall function in accordance with the annexed Statute, which is based upon the statute of the Permanent Court of International Justice and forms an integral part of the present Charter.

Article 93

1. All Members of the United Nations are *ipso facto* parties to the Statute of the International Court of Justice.

2. A state which is not a Member of the United Nations may become a party to the Statute of the International Court of Justice on conditions to be determined in each case by the General Assembly upon the recommendation of the Security Council.

Article 94

1. Each member of the United Nations undertakes to comply with the decision of the International Court of Justice in any case to which it is a party.

2. If any party to a case fails to perform the obligations incumbent upon it under a judgment rendered by the Court, the other party may have recourse to the Security Council, which may, if it deems necessary, make recommendations or decide upon measures to be taken to give effect to the judgment.

Article 95

Nothing in the present Charter shall prevent Members of the United Nations from entrusting the solution of their differences to other tribunals by virtue of agreements already in existence or which may be concluded in the future.

Article 96

1. The General Assembly or the Security Council may request the International Court of Justice to give an advisory opinion on any legal question.

2. Other organs of the United Nations and specialized agencies, which may at any time be so authorized by the General Assembly, may also request advisory opinions of the Court on legal questions arising within the scope of their activities.

Chapter 15
The Secretariat

Article 97

The Secretariat shall comprise a Secretary-General and such staff as the Organization may require. The Secretary-General shall be appointed by the General Assembly upon the recommendation of the Security Council. He shall be the chief administrative officer of the Organization.

Article 98

The Secretary-General shall act in that capacity in all meetings of the General Assembly, of the Security Council, of the Economic and Social Council and of the Trusteeship Council, and shall perform such other functions as are entrusted to him by these organs. The Secretary-General shall make an annual report to the General Assembly on the work of the Organization.

Article 99

The Secretary-General may bring to the attention of the Security Council any matter which in his opinion may threaten the maintenance of international peace and security.

Article 100

1. In the performance of their duties the Secretary-General and the staff shall not seek or receive instructions from any government or from any other authority external to the Organization. They shall refrain from any action which might reflect on their position as international officials responsible only to the Organization.

2. Each Member of the United Nations undertakes to respect the exclusively international character of the responsibilities of the Secretary-General and the staff and not to seek to influence them in the discharge of their responsibilities.

Article 101

1. The staff shall be appointed by the Secretary-General under regulations established by the General Assembly.

2. Appropriate staffs shall be permanently assigned to the Economic and Social Council, the Trusteeship Council, and, as required, to other organs of the United Nations. These staffs shall form a part of the Secretariat.

3. The paramount consideration in the employment of the staff and in the determination of the conditions of service shall be the necessity of securing the highest standards of efficiency, competence, and integrity. Due regard shall be paid to the importance of recruiting the staff on as wide a geographical basis as possible.

Chapter 16
Miscellaneous Provisions

Article 102

1. Every treaty and every international agreement entered into by any Member of the United Nations after the present Charter comes into force shall as soon as possible be registered with the Secretariat and published by it.

2. No party to any such treaty or international agreement which has not been registered in accordance with the provisions of paragraph 1 of this Article may invoke that treaty or agreement before any organ of the United Nations.

Article 103

In the event of a conflict between the obligations of the Members of the United Nations under the present Charter and their obligations under any other international agreement, their obligations under the present Charter shall prevail.

Article 104

The Organization shall enjoy in the territory of each of its Members such legal capacity as may be necessary for the exercise of its functions and the fulfillment of its purposes.

Article 105

1. The Organization shall enjoy in the territory of each of its Members such privileges and immunities as are necessary for the fulfillment of its purposes.

2. Representatives of the Members of the United Nations and officials of the Organization shall similarly enjoy such privileges and immunities as are necessary for the independent exercise of their functions in connection with the Organization.

3. The General Assembly may make recommendations with a view to determining the details of the application of paragraphs 1 and 2 of this Article or may propose conventions to the Members of the United Nations for this purpose.

Chapter 17
Transitional Security Arrangements

Article 106

Pending the coming into force of such special agreements referred to in Article 43 as in the opinion of the Security Council enable it to begin the exercise of its responsibilities under Article 42, the parties to the Four-Nation Declaration, signed at Moscow, October 30, 1943, and France, shall, in accordance with the provisions of paragraph 5 of that Declaration, consult with one another and as occasion requires with other Members of the United Nations with a view to such joint action on behalf of the Organization as may be necessary for the purpose of maintaining international peace and security.

Article 107

Nothing in the present Charter shall invalidate or preclude action, in relation to any state which during the Second World War has been an enemy of any signatory to the present Charter, taken or authorized as a result of that war by the Governments having responsibility for such action.

Chapter 18
Amendments

Article 108

Amendments to the present Charter shall come into force for all Members of the United Nations when they have been adopted by a vote of two-thirds of the members of the General Assembly and ratified in accordance with their respective constitutional processes by two-thirds of the Members of the United Nations, including all the permanent members of the Security Council.

Article 109

1. A General Conference of the Members of the United Nations for the purpose of re-

viewing the present Charter may be held at a date and place to be fixed by a two-thirds vote of the members of the General Assembly and by a vote of any nine members of the Security Council. Each Member of the United Nations shall have one vote in the conference.

2. Any alteration of the present Charter recommended by a two-thirds vote of the conference shall take effect when ratified in accordance with their respective constitutional processes by two-thirds of the Members of the United Nations including all the permanent members of the Security Council

3. If such a conference has not been held before the tenth annual session of the General Assembly following the coming into force of the present Charter, the proposal to call such a conference shall be placed on the agenda of that session of the General Assembly, and the conference shall be held if so decided by a majority vote of the members of the General Assembly and by a vote of any seven members of the Security Council.

Chapter 19
Ratification and Signature

Article 110

1. The present Charter shall be ratified by the signatory states in accordance with their respective constitutional processes.

2. The ratifications shall be deposited with the Government of the United States of America, which shall notify all the signatory states of each deposit as well as the Secretary-General of the Organization when he has been appointed.

3. The present Charter shall come into force upon the deposit of ratifications by the Republic of China, France, the Union of Soviet Socialist Republics, the United Kingdom of Great Britain and Northern Ireland, and the United States of America, and by a majority of the other signatory states. A protocol of the ratifications deposited shall thereupon be drawn up by the Government of the United States of America which shall communicate copies thereof to all the signatory states.

4. The states signatory to the present Charter which ratify it after it has come into force will become original Members of the United Nations on the date of the deposit of their respective ratifications.

Article 111

The present Charter, of which the Chinese, French, Russian, English, and Spanish texts are equally authentic, shall remain deposited in the archives of the Government of the United States of America. Duly certified copies thereof shall be transmitted by that Government to the Governments of the other signatory states.

IN FAITH WHEREOF the representatives of the Governments of the United Nations have signed the present Charter.

DONE at the city of San Francisco the twenty-sixth day of June, one thousand nine hundred and forty-five.

Universal Declaration of Human Rights

Preamble

Whereas recognition of the inherent dignity and of the equal and inalienable rights of all members of the human family is the foundation of freedom, justice and peace in the world,

Whereas disregard and contempt for human rights have resulted in barbarous acts which have outraged the conscience of mankind, and the advent of a world in which human beings shall enjoy freedom of speech and belief and freedom from fear and want has been proclaimed as the highest aspiration of the common people,

Whereas it is essential, if man is not to be compelled to have recourse, as a last resort, to rebellion against tyranny and oppression, that human rights should be protected by the rule of law,

Whereas it is essential to promote the development of friendly relations between nations,

Whereas the peoples of the United Nations have in the Charter reaffirmed their faith in fundamental human rights, in the dignity and worth of the human person and in the equal rights of men and women and have determined to promote social progress and better standards of life in larger freedom,

Whereas Member States have pledged themselves to achieve, in co-operation with the United Nations, the promotion of universal respect for and observance of human rights and fundamental freedoms,

Whereas a common understanding of these rights and freedoms is of the greatest importance for the full realization of this pledge,

Now, therefore,

The General Assembly

Proclaims this Universal Declaration of Human Rights as a common standard of achievement for all peoples and all nations, to the end that every individual and every organ of society, keeping this Declaration constantly in mind, shall strive by teaching and education to promote respect for these rights and freedoms and by progressive measures, national and international, to secure their universal and effective recognition and observance, both among the peoples of Member States themselves and among the peoples of territories under their jurisdiction.

Article 1

All human beings are born free and equal in dignity and rights. They are endowed with reason and conscience and should act towards one another in a spirit of brotherhood.

Article 2

Everyone is entitled to all the rights and freedoms set forth in this Declaration, without distinction of any kind, such as race, colour, sex, language, religion, political or other opinion, national or social origin, property, birth or other status.

Furthermore, no distinction shall be made on the basis of the political, jurisdictional or international status of the country or territory to which a person belongs, whether it be independent, trust, non-self-governing or under any other limitation of sovereignty.

Article 3

Everyone has the right to life, liberty and the security of person.

Article 4

No one shall be held in slavery or servitude; slavery and the slave trade shall be prohibited in all their forms.

Article 5

No one shall be subjected to torture or to cruel, inhuman or degrading treatment or punishment.

Article 6

Everyone has the right to recognition everywhere as a person before the law.

Article 7

All are equal before the law and are entitled without any discrimination to equal protection of the law. All are entitled to equal protection against any discrimination in violation of this Declaration and against any incitement to such discrimination.

Article 8

Everyone has the right to an effective remedy by the competent national tribunals for acts violating the fundamental rights granted him by the constitution or by law.

Article 9

No one shall be subjected to arbitrary arrest, detention or exile.

Article 10

Everyone is entitled in full equality to a fair and public hearing by an independent and impartial tribunal, in the determination of his rights and obligations and of any criminal charge against him.

Article 11

1. Everyone charged with a penal offence has the right to be presumed innocent until proved guilty according to law in a public trial at which he has had all the guarantees necessary for his defence.

2. No one shall be held guilty of any penal offence on account of any act or omission which did not constitute a penal offence, under national or international law, at the time when it was committed. Nor shall a heavier penalty be imposed than the one that was applicable at the time the penal offence was committed.

Article 12

No one shall be subjected to arbitrary interference with his privacy, family, home or correspondence, nor to attacks upon his honour and reputation. Everyone has the right to the protection of the law against such interference or attacks.

Article 13

1. Everyone has the right to freedom of movement and residence within the borders of each State.

2. Everyone has the right to leave any country, including his own, and to return to his country.

Article 14

1. Everyone has the right to seek and to enjoy in other countries asylum from persecution.

2. This right may not be invoked in the case of prosecutions genuinely arising from non-political crimes or from acts contrary to the purposes and principles of the United Nations.

Article 15

1. Everyone has the right to a nationality.

2. No one shall be arbitrarily deprived of his nationality nor denied the right to change his nationality.

Article 16

1. Men and women of full age, without any limitation due to race, nationality or religion, have the right to marry and to found a family. They are entitled to equal rights as to marriage, during marriage and at its dissolution.

2. Marriage shall be entered into only with the free and full consent of the intending spouses.

3. The family is the natural and fundamental group unit of society and is entitled to protection by society and the State.

Article 17

1. Everyone has the right to own property alone as well as in association with others.

2. No one shall be arbitrarily deprived of his property.

Article 18

Everyone has the right to freedom of thought, conscience and religion; this right includes freedom to change his religion or belief, and freedom, either alone or in community with others and in public or private, to manifest his religion or belief in teaching, practice, worship and observance.

Article 19

Everyone has the right to freedom of opinion and expression; this right includes freedom to hold opinions without interference and to seek, receive and impart information and ideas through any media and regardless of frontiers.

Article 20

    1. Everyone has the right to freedom of peaceful assembly and association.

    2. No one may be compelled to belong to an association.

Article 21

    1. Everyone has the right to take part in the government of his country, directly or through freely chosen representatives.

    2. Everyone has the right of equal access to public service in his country.

    3. The will of the people shall be the basis of the authority of government; this will shall be expressed in periodic and genuine elections which shall be by universal and equal suffrage and shall be held by secret vote or by equivalent free voting procedures.

Article 22

    Everyone, as a member of society, has the right to social security and is entitled to realization, through national effort and international co-operation and in accordance with the organization and resources of each State, of the economic, social and cultural rights indispensable for his dignity and the free development of his personality.

Article 23

    1. Everyone has the right to work, to free choice of employment, to just and favourable conditions of work and to protection against unemployment.

    2. Everyone, without any discrimination, has the right to equal pay for equal work.

    3. Everyone who works has the right to just and favourable remuneration ensuring for himself and his family an existence worthy of human dignity, and supplemented, if necessary, by other means of social protection.

    4. Everyone has the right to form and to join trade unions for the protection of his interests.

Article 24

    Everyone has the right to rest and leisure, including reasonable limitation of working hours and periodic holidays with pay.

Article 25

    1. Everyone has the right to a standard of living adequate for the health and well-being of himself and of his family, including food, clothing, housing and medical care and necessary social services, and the right to security in the event of unemployment, sickness, disability, widowhood, old age or other lack of livelihood in circumstances beyond his control.

    2. Motherhood and childhood are entitled to special care and assistance. All children, whether born in or out of wedlock, shall enjoy the same social protection.

Article 26

    1. Everyone has the right to education. Education shall be free, at least in the elementary and fundamental stages. Elementary education shall be compulsory. Technical and professional education shall be made generally available and higher education shall be equally accessible to all on the basis of merit.

2. Education shall be directed to the full development of the human personality and to the strengthening of respect for human rights and fundamental freedoms. It shall promote understanding, tolerance and friendship among all nations, racial or religious groups, and shall further the activities of the United Nations for the maintenance of peace.

3. Parents have a prior right to choose the kind of education that shall be given to their children.

Article 27

1. Everyone has the right freely to participate in the cultural life of the community, to enjoy the arts and to share in scientific advancement and its benefits.

2. Everyone has the right to the protection of the moral and material interests resulting from any scientific, literary and artistic production of which he is the author.

Article 28

Everyone is entitled to a social and international order in which the rights and freedoms set forth in this Declaration can be fully realized.

Article 29

1. Everyone has duties to the community in which alone the free and full development of his personality is possible.

2. In the exercise of his rights and freedoms, everyone shall be subject only to such limitations as are determined by law solely for the purpose of securing due recognition and respect for the rights and freedoms of others and of meeting the just requirements of morality, public order and the general welfare in a democratic society.

3. These rights and freedoms may in no case be exercised contrary to the purposes and principles of the United Nations.

Article 30

Nothing in this Declaration may be interpreted as implying for any State, group or person any right to engage in any activity or to perform any act aimed at the destruction of any of the rights and freedoms set forth herein.

*Adopted and proclaimed by General Assembly
Resolution 217A (III)
of 10 December 1948.*

INDEX

ABOUT THE AUTHOR

Harold K. Jacobson was born in Detroit, Michigan, in 1929. After earning his Ph.D. at Yale University in 1955, he taught for two years at the University of Houston. He then returned to the University of Michigan, where he had received his undergraduate education, and where he has been a member of the faculty since 1957. He was chairman of the Department of Political Science from 1972 to 1977. He is now professor of Political Science and program director in the Center for Political Studies of the Institute for Social Research. On three occasions he has been a visiting professor at the Graduate Institute of International Studies of the University of Geneva. He was the World Affairs Center Fellow in 1959–1960 and the Visiting Research Scholar at the European Center of the Carnegie Endowment for International Peace in 1970–1971. Professor Jacobson has served on the editorial boards of the *American Journal of International Law*, *International Organization*, the *International Studies Quarterly*, and the *Journal of Conflict Resolution*. He is the author of *The U.S.S.R. and the UN's Economic and Social Activities* (1963) and coauthor of *Diplomats, Scientists and Politicians: The United States and the Nuclear Test Ban Negotiations* (1966), *The Anatomy of Influence: Decision Making in International Organization* (1973), *The Emerging International Economic Order: Dynamic Processes, Constraints, and Opportunities* (1982), and *Environmental Protection: The International Dimension* (1983). He has published several articles in professional journals and he edited *America's Foreign Policy* (1960, 1965). He was President of the International Studies Association during 1982–1983. He is a member of the Executive Committee of the U.S. National Commission for UNESCO and a member of the Board of Directors of the United Nations Association of the U.S.A.